Lecture Notes in Computer Science 14020

The series Lecture Notes in Computer Science (LNCS), including its subseries Lecture Notes in Artificial Intelligence (LNAI) and Lecture Notes in Bioinformatics (LNBI), has established itself as a medium for the publication of new developments in computer science and information technology research, teaching, and education.

LNCS enjoys close cooperation with the computer science R & D community, the series counts many renowned academics among its volume editors and paper authors, and collaborates with prestigious societies. Its mission is to serve this international community by providing an invaluable service, mainly focused on the publication of conference and workshop proceedings and postproceedings. LNCS commenced publication in 1973.

Margherita Antona · Constantine Stephanidis
Editors

Universal Access in Human-Computer Interaction

17th International Conference, UAHCI 2023
Held as Part of the 25th HCI International Conference, HCII 2023
Copenhagen, Denmark, July 23–28, 2023
Proceedings, Part I

Springer

Editors
Margherita Antona
Foundation for Research and Technology
Heraklion, Crete, Greece

Constantine Stephanidis
Foundation for Research and Technology
Heraklion, Crete, Greece

ISSN 0302-9743 ISSN 1611-3349 (electronic)
Lecture Notes in Computer Science
ISBN 978-3-031-35680-3 ISBN 978-3-031-35681-0 (eBook)
https://doi.org/10.1007/978-3-031-35681-0

This Springer imprint is published by the registered company Springer Nature Switzerland AG
The registered company address is: Gewerbestrasse 11, 6330 Cham, Switzerland

Foreword

Human-computer interaction (HCI) is acquiring an ever-increasing scientific and industrial importance, as well as having more impact on people's everyday lives, as an ever-growing number of human activities are progressively moving from the physical to the digital world. This process, which has been ongoing for some time now, was further accelerated during the acute period of the COVID-19 pandemic. The HCI International (HCII) conference series, held annually, aims to respond to the compelling need to advance the exchange of knowledge and research and development efforts on the human aspects of design and use of computing systems.

The 25th International Conference on Human-Computer Interaction, HCI International 2023 (HCII 2023), was held in the emerging post-pandemic era as a 'hybrid' event at the AC Bella Sky Hotel and Bella Center, Copenhagen, Denmark, during July 23–28, 2023. It incorporated the 21 thematic areas and affiliated conferences listed below.

A total of 7472 individuals from academia, research institutes, industry, and government agencies from 85 countries submitted contributions, and 1578 papers and 396 posters were included in the volumes of the proceedings that were published just before the start of the conference, these are listed below. The contributions thoroughly cover the entire field of human-computer interaction, addressing major advances in knowledge and effective use of computers in a variety of application areas. These papers provide academics, researchers, engineers, scientists, practitioners and students with state-of-the-art information on the most recent advances in HCI.

The HCI International (HCII) conference also offers the option of presenting 'Late Breaking Work', and this applies both for papers and posters, with corresponding volumes of proceedings that will be published after the conference. Full papers will be included in the 'HCII 2023 - Late Breaking Work - Papers' volumes of the proceedings to be published in the Springer LNCS series, while 'Poster Extended Abstracts' will be included as short research papers in the 'HCII 2023 - Late Breaking Work - Posters' volumes to be published in the Springer CCIS series.

I would like to thank the Program Board Chairs and the members of the Program Boards of all thematic areas and affiliated conferences for their contribution towards the high scientific quality and overall success of the HCI International 2023 conference. Their manifold support in terms of paper reviewing (single-blind review process, with a minimum of two reviews per submission), session organization and their willingness to act as goodwill ambassadors for the conference is most highly appreciated.

This conference would not have been possible without the continuous and unwavering support and advice of Gavriel Salvendy, founder, General Chair Emeritus, and Scientific Advisor. For his outstanding efforts, I would like to express my sincere appreciation to Abbas Moallem, Communications Chair and Editor of HCI International News.

July 2023 Constantine Stephanidis

HCI International 2023 Thematic Areas and Affiliated Conferences

Thematic Areas

- HCI: Human-Computer Interaction
- HIMI: Human Interface and the Management of Information

Affiliated Conferences

- EPCE: 20th International Conference on Engineering Psychology and Cognitive Ergonomics
- AC: 17th International Conference on Augmented Cognition
- UAHCI: 17th International Conference on Universal Access in Human-Computer Interaction
- CCD: 15th International Conference on Cross-Cultural Design
- SCSM: 15th International Conference on Social Computing and Social Media
- VAMR: 15th International Conference on Virtual, Augmented and Mixed Reality
- DHM: 14th International Conference on Digital Human Modeling and Applications in Health, Safety, Ergonomics and Risk Management
- DUXU: 12th International Conference on Design, User Experience and Usability
- C&C: 11th International Conference on Culture and Computing
- DAPI: 11th International Conference on Distributed, Ambient and Pervasive Interactions
- HCIBGO: 10th International Conference on HCI in Business, Government and Organizations
- LCT: 10th International Conference on Learning and Collaboration Technologies
- ITAP: 9th International Conference on Human Aspects of IT for the Aged Population
- AIS: 5th International Conference on Adaptive Instructional Systems
- HCI-CPT: 5th International Conference on HCI for Cybersecurity, Privacy and Trust
- HCI-Games: 5th International Conference on HCI in Games
- MobiTAS: 5th International Conference on HCI in Mobility, Transport and Automotive Systems
- AI-HCI: 4th International Conference on Artificial Intelligence in HCI
- MOBILE: 4th International Conference on Design, Operation and Evaluation of Mobile Communications

List of Conference Proceedings Volumes Appearing Before the Conference

1. LNCS 14011, Human-Computer Interaction: Part I, edited by Masaaki Kurosu and Ayako Hashizume
2. LNCS 14012, Human-Computer Interaction: Part II, edited by Masaaki Kurosu and Ayako Hashizume
3. LNCS 14013, Human-Computer Interaction: Part III, edited by Masaaki Kurosu and Ayako Hashizume
4. LNCS 14014, Human-Computer Interaction: Part IV, edited by Masaaki Kurosu and Ayako Hashizume
5. LNCS 14015, Human Interface and the Management of Information: Part I, edited by Hirohiko Mori and Yumi Asahi
6. LNCS 14016, Human Interface and the Management of Information: Part II, edited by Hirohiko Mori and Yumi Asahi
7. LNAI 14017, Engineering Psychology and Cognitive Ergonomics: Part I, edited by Don Harris and Wen-Chin Li
8. LNAI 14018, Engineering Psychology and Cognitive Ergonomics: Part II, edited by Don Harris and Wen-Chin Li
9. LNAI 14019, Augmented Cognition, edited by Dylan D. Schmorrow and Cali M. Fidopiastis
10. LNCS 14020, Universal Access in Human-Computer Interaction: Part I, edited by Margherita Antona and Constantine Stephanidis
11. LNCS 14021, Universal Access in Human-Computer Interaction: Part II, edited by Margherita Antona and Constantine Stephanidis
12. LNCS 14022, Cross-Cultural Design: Part I, edited by Pei-Luen Patrick Rau
13. LNCS 14023, Cross-Cultural Design: Part II, edited by Pei-Luen Patrick Rau
14. LNCS 14024, Cross-Cultural Design: Part III, edited by Pei-Luen Patrick Rau
15. LNCS 14025, Social Computing and Social Media: Part I, edited by Adela Coman and Simona Vasilache
16. LNCS 14026, Social Computing and Social Media: Part II, edited by Adela Coman and Simona Vasilache
17. LNCS 14027, Virtual, Augmented and Mixed Reality, edited by Jessie Y. C. Chen and Gino Fragomeni
18. LNCS 14028, Digital Human Modeling and Applications in Health, Safety, Ergonomics and Risk Management: Part I, edited by Vincent G. Duffy
19. LNCS 14029, Digital Human Modeling and Applications in Health, Safety, Ergonomics and Risk Management: Part II, edited by Vincent G. Duffy
20. LNCS 14030, Design, User Experience, and Usability: Part I, edited by Aaron Marcus, Elizabeth Rosenzweig and Marcelo Soares
21. LNCS 14031, Design, User Experience, and Usability: Part II, edited by Aaron Marcus, Elizabeth Rosenzweig and Marcelo Soares

22. LNCS 14032, Design, User Experience, and Usability: Part III, edited by Aaron Marcus, Elizabeth Rosenzweig and Marcelo Soares
23. LNCS 14033, Design, User Experience, and Usability: Part IV, edited by Aaron Marcus, Elizabeth Rosenzweig and Marcelo Soares
24. LNCS 14034, Design, User Experience, and Usability: Part V, edited by Aaron Marcus, Elizabeth Rosenzweig and Marcelo Soares
25. LNCS 14035, Culture and Computing, edited by Matthias Rauterberg
26. LNCS 14036, Distributed, Ambient and Pervasive Interactions: Part I, edited by Norbert Streitz and Shin'ichi Konomi
27. LNCS 14037, Distributed, Ambient and Pervasive Interactions: Part II, edited by Norbert Streitz and Shin'ichi Konomi
28. LNCS 14038, HCI in Business, Government and Organizations: Part I, edited by Fiona Fui-Hoon Nah and Keng Siau
29. LNCS 14039, HCI in Business, Government and Organizations: Part II, edited by Fiona Fui-Hoon Nah and Keng Siau
30. LNCS 14040, Learning and Collaboration Technologies: Part I, edited by Panayiotis Zaphiris and Andri Ioannou
31. LNCS 14041, Learning and Collaboration Technologies: Part II, edited by Panayiotis Zaphiris and Andri Ioannou
32. LNCS 14042, Human Aspects of IT for the Aged Population: Part I, edited by Qin Gao and Jia Zhou
33. LNCS 14043, Human Aspects of IT for the Aged Population: Part II, edited by Qin Gao and Jia Zhou
34. LNCS 14044, Adaptive Instructional Systems, edited by Robert A. Sottilare and Jessica Schwarz
35. LNCS 14045, HCI for Cybersecurity, Privacy and Trust, edited by Abbas Moallem
36. LNCS 14046, HCI in Games: Part I, edited by Xiaowen Fang
37. LNCS 14047, HCI in Games: Part II, edited by Xiaowen Fang
38. LNCS 14048, HCI in Mobility, Transport and Automotive Systems: Part I, edited by Heidi Krömker
39. LNCS 14049, HCI in Mobility, Transport and Automotive Systems: Part II, edited by Heidi Krömker
40. LNAI 14050, Artificial Intelligence in HCI: Part I, edited by Helmut Degen and Stavroula Ntoa
41. LNAI 14051, Artificial Intelligence in HCI: Part II, edited by Helmut Degen and Stavroula Ntoa
42. LNCS 14052, Design, Operation and Evaluation of Mobile Communications, edited by Gavriel Salvendy and June Wei
43. CCIS 1832, HCI International 2023 Posters - Part I, edited by Constantine Stephanidis, Margherita Antona, Stavroula Ntoa and Gavriel Salvendy
44. CCIS 1833, HCI International 2023 Posters - Part II, edited by Constantine Stephanidis, Margherita Antona, Stavroula Ntoa and Gavriel Salvendy
45. CCIS 1834, HCI International 2023 Posters - Part III, edited by Constantine Stephanidis, Margherita Antona, Stavroula Ntoa and Gavriel Salvendy
46. CCIS 1835, HCI International 2023 Posters - Part IV, edited by Constantine Stephanidis, Margherita Antona, Stavroula Ntoa and Gavriel Salvendy

47. CCIS 1836, HCI International 2023 Posters - Part V, edited by Constantine Stephanidis, Margherita Antona, Stavroula Ntoa and Gavriel Salvendy

https://2023.hci.international/proceedings

Preface

The 17th International Conference on Universal Access in Human-Computer Interaction (UAHCI 2023), an affiliated conference of the HCI International (HCII) conference, provided an established international forum for the exchange and dissemination of scientific information on theoretical, methodological, and empirical research that addresses all issues related to the attainment of universal access in the development of interactive software. It comprehensively addressed accessibility and quality of interaction in the user interface development life-cycle from a multidisciplinary perspective, taking into account dimensions of diversity, such as functional limitations, age, culture, background knowledge, etc., in the target user population, as well as various dimensions of diversity which affect the context of use and the technological platform and arise from the emergence of mobile, wearable, ubiquitous, and intelligent devices and technologies.

UAHCI 2023 aimed to help, promote, and encourage research by providing a forum for interaction and exchanges among researchers, academics, and practitioners in the field. The conference welcomed papers on the design, development, evaluation, use, and impact of user interfaces, as well as standardization, policy, and other non-technological issues that facilitate and promote universal access.

Universal access is not a new topic in the field of human-computer interaction and information technology. Yet, in the new interaction environment shaped by current technological advancements, it becomes of prominent importance to ensure that individuals have access to interactive products and services that span a wide variety of everyday life domains and are used in fundamental human activities. The papers accepted to this year's UAHCI conference present research, methods, and practices addressing universal access issues related to user experience and interaction, and approaches targeted to provide appropriate interaction means to individuals with specific disabilities, but also issues related to extended reality – a prominent technological medium presenting novel accessibility challenges, as well as advancements in learning and education.

Two volumes of the HCII 2023 proceedings are dedicated to this year's edition of the UAHCI conference. The first part focuses on topics related to Design for All methods, tools and practice, interaction techniques, platforms and metaphors for Universal Access, understanding the Universal Access User Experience, as well as designing for children with Autism Spectrum Disorders. The second part focuses on topics related to Universal Access to XR, Universal Access to learning and education, and assistive environments and quality of life technologies.

Papers of these volumes are included for publication after a minimum of two single-blind reviews from the members of the UAHCI Program Board or, in some cases, from members of the Program Boards of other affiliated conferences. We would like to thank all of them for their invaluable contribution, support and efforts.

July 2023

Margherita Antona
Constantine Stephanidis

17th International Conference on Universal Access in Human-Computer Interaction (UAHCI 2023)

Program Board Chairs: **Margherita Antona**, *Foundation for Research and Technology - Hellas (FORTH), Greece* and **Constantine Stephanidis**, *University of Crete and Foundation for Research and Technology - Hellas (FORTH), Greece*

Program Board:

- João Barroso, *INESC TEC and UTAD, Portugal*
- Ingo Bosse, *Interkantonale Hochschule für Heilpädagogik (HFH), Switzerland*
- Laura Burzagli, *CNR, Italy*
- Pedro J.S. Cardoso, *University of Algarve, Portugal*
- Silvia Ceccacci, *University of Macerata, Italy*
- Nicole Darmawaskita, *Arizona State University, USA*
- Carlos Duarte, *Universidade de Lisboa, Portugal*
- Pier Luigi Emiliani, *National Research Council, Italy*
- Andrina Granic, *University of Split, Croatia*
- Gian Maria Greco, *Università di Macerata, Italy*
- Simeon Keates, *University of Chichester, UK*
- Georgios Kouroupetroglou, *National and Kapodistrian University of Athens, Greece*
- Barbara Leporini, *CNR-ISTI, Italy*
- John Magee, *Clark University, USA*
- Daniela Marghitu, *Auburn University, USA*
- Jorge Martín-Gutiérrez, *Universidad de La Laguna, Spain*
- Maura Mengoni, *Università Politecnica delle Marche, Italy*
- Silvia Mirri, *University of Bologna, Italy*
- Federica Pallavicini, *Università degli Studi di Milano-Bicocca, Italy*
- João M.F. Rodrigues, *University of Algarve, Portugal*
- Frode Eika Sandnes, *Oslo Metropolitan University, Norway*
- J. Andrés Sandoval-Bringas, *Universidad Autónoma de Baja California Sur, Mexico*
- Volker Sorge, *University of Birmingham, UK*
- Hiroki Takada, *University of Fukui, Japan*
- Philippe Truillet, *Université de Toulouse, France*
- Kevin Tseng, *National Taipei University of Technology, Taiwan*
- Gerhard Weber, *TU Dresden, Germany*

The full list with the Program Board Chairs and the members of the Program Boards of all thematic areas and affiliated conferences of HCII2023 is available online at:

http://www.hci.international/board-members-2023.php

HCI International 2024 Conference

The 26th International Conference on Human-Computer Interaction, HCI International 2024, will be held jointly with the affiliated conferences at the Washington Hilton Hotel, Washington, DC, USA, June 29 – July 4, 2024. It will cover a broad spectrum of themes related to Human-Computer Interaction, including theoretical issues, methods, tools, processes, and case studies in HCI design, as well as novel interaction techniques, interfaces, and applications. The proceedings will be published by Springer. More information will be made available on the conference website: http://2024.hci.international/.

General Chair
Prof. Constantine Stephanidis
University of Crete and ICS-FORTH
Heraklion, Crete, Greece
Email: general_chair@hcii2024.org

https://2024.hci.international/

Contents – Part I

Understanding the Universal Access User Experience

Contents – Part II

Design for All Methods, Tools and Practice

Designing Ethics-Aware DecidArch Game to Promote Value Diversity in Software Architecture Design Decision Making

Razieh Alidoosti[1,2(✉)], Patricia Lago[1], Eltjo Poort[3], and Maryam Razavian[4]

[1] Vrije Universiteit Amsterdam, Amsterdam, The Netherlands
{r.alidoosti,p.lago}@vu.nl
[2] Gran Sasso Science Institute, L'Aquila, Italy
[3] CGI, Rotterdam, The Netherlands
eltjo.poort@cgi.com
[4] Eindhoven University of Technology, Eindhoven, The Netherlands
m.razavian@tue.nl

Abstract. Software systems are increasingly being employed in people's lives and society. They can improve, but also negatively affect the quality of life and interfere with human rights by, *e.g.,* undermining the individuals' and society's values and causing ethical issues. To prevent such issues, software architects need to take ethical considerations into account at the early stages of design, *e.g.,* when making architecture design decisions. Such considerations regard stakeholders, ethical values and their relations, ethical concerns, and ethical decisions. Addressing ethical considerations is especially difficult for software architects because of (i) the lack of training in ethics and philosophy, (ii) the existence of inherent ambiguity in ethical values, and (iii) the lack of methodological support in dealing with ethical and social implications of software systems, and eliciting and operationalizing ethical values. This study employs a design science methodology for developing a card-based game (called Ethics-Aware DecidArch), helping software architects reflect on ethical considerations, and creating an atmosphere to foster inclusivity by supporting the values of different stakeholders when making group decisions. The game was played in four sessions, each including four professional software architects from two multinational IT companies. This study presents lessons learned from playing the game through a participant survey and qualitative data analysis. The results show that the game helped software architects (i) reflect on different solutions for resolving ethical concerns, (ii) make ethical decisions along with providing reasons behind such decisions, and (iii) reflect on the operationalization of ethical values and their trade-offs.

Keywords: Software Architecture · Design Decision Making · Ethics · Inclusion · Design Science Methodology · Game

M. Antona and C. Stephanidis (Eds.): HCII 2023, LNCS 14020, pp. 3–26, 2023.
https://doi.org/10.1007/978-3-031-35681-0_1

1 Introduction

Ethics in the context of software engineering (or SE ethics) refers to *a set of principles and rules that guide software professionals to adhere to the welfare, justice, and safety of users and society* [12]. Over the last decade, SE ethics has received growing attention: software systems are increasingly pervasive in people's lives and support more and more tasks in modern society; as such, they can have important social and ethical implications on individuals and society.

Software systems can impact individuals and society by undermining their values and sometimes cause ethical issues. Such issues arise in situations where there are conflicts between right and wrong and ethical values are not respected. An example of ethical issues can be considered in the usage of web browsers and their relevant tracking and profiling technologies. Although it can play a critical role in mediating the interactions between end users and web pages, it can expand e-commerce vendors' ability to collect, process, and exploit personal data. Thus, web browsers can violate the privacy of end users by undermining the ethical values of privacy and confidentiality [25]. To address such issues and support ethical values, there is a need to take ethical considerations (presented in Sect. 2.2) into account at the early stages of system design (*e.g.*, when making architecture design decisions).

In previous work [2], we found the need in software architecture design to focus on concepts from an ethical perspective, such as stakeholders (who are directly or indirectly affected by systems), ethical values and their relations, and ethical concerns. Also, we found that software architects face difficulties in addressing ethics, due to (i) lack of training in ethics and philosophy, (ii) existence of inherent ambiguity in ethical values, and (iii) lack of methodological support in dealing with ethical and social implications of software systems, and eliciting and operationalizing ethical values [2,3]. To address the above (ethical perspective and difficulties), by adopting a design science methodology, we designed a card-based game (Ethics-Aware DecidArch) for the purpose of reflection. Drawing on the familiarity of cards as game tools, our game can be immediately effective in prompting discussion from an ethical perspective [8].

Our game is *the redesign of the DecidArch game*[1] (proposed in [9,15]) which focuses on activities such as addressing stakeholders' concerns, making design decisions and providing reasoning behind such decisions. Moreover, it helps making quality attribute trade-offs in the context of software architecture. Given the similarities in the focus of this game and our study (*e.g.*, making trade-offs), we chose it as the base of our game to help software architects reflect on such activities from an ethical point of view. This is due to the fact that software architects mainly have not been trained in these activities from an ethical perspective.

After three pilot sessions were conducted in cooperation with Vrije Universiteit Amsterdam (VU) and Eindhoven University of Technology (TU/e), the

[1] It includes changing both cards and playing rules of the DecidArch game wrt ethical concerns, *e.g.*, adding Wild Cards and carrying out the game as role-play.

game was *officially played*[2] by professional software architects from two multinational IT companies. There were four sessions, each with four players, with the majority having 10–20 years of experience in different sectors of the IT industry. Based on the results gathered from playing the game, and by (i) using a participant survey and (ii) conducting qualitative data analysis, we concluded that the game helped software architects reflect on possible solutions aimed to resolve ethical concerns, enable consideration of ethical aspects in design reasoning, and reflect on operationalizing ethical values and making trade-offs among ethical values.

This paper is an extension of our previous work [1], where we proposed a game to enable reflection on ethical considerations among software architects. There, we have reported a summarized overview of the above-mentioned results of the game. Whilst in this paper, we discuss in detail the findings revealed from both the survey and the qualitative analysis. We also focus on the impacts of the game on group decision making, and explore it from an inclusion perspective to realize how it enables including various stakeholders' values when architecting software systems. Herein, our contributions are as follows:

- Exploring the findings revealed from the qualitative analysis of the game sessions.
- Analyzing the game's effects on the group decision making around ethical considerations.
- Analyzing the game from the view of inclusion.

The rest of the paper is organized as follows. In Sect. 2, we discuss related works and background concepts used in our game (the same as in [1]). In Sect. 3, we illustrate our methodology, including problems and objectives, game design and execution, and data collection and analysis. In Sect. 4, we explain the game (the same as in [1]). In Sect. 5, we present an analysis of the data gathered from the players, and in Sect. 6 we discuss the practical impacts and potential improvements of the game and analyze the game from an inclusion perspective. In Sect. 7, we discuss the threats that may affect the validity of our results. Finally, in Sect. 8, we conclude and present our thoughts on future work.

2 Related Work and Background

In this section, we discuss the literature related to our work. We then explain the background concepts underlying our game design.

2.1 Related Work

Over the last decade, there has been significant interest in game design that supports architecture design decisions. For example, Lago *et al.* [9,15] propose the

[2] Under the supervision of researchers, the game was played, recorded, and evaluated as a basis for the analysis.

game 'DecidArch' to be played by students in the context of software architecture. This game helps create awareness about the rationale behind architecture design decisions, create an understanding of inter-dependencies between design decisions, and enable making trade-offs among quality attributes. Cervantes *et al.* [7], propose the game 'Smart Decisions' to explain important concepts associated with architecture design to students and practitioners. By simulating several software design iterations, the game helps with selecting design concepts (like requirements) during the design process, analyzing design decisions, giving feedback regarding decisions consequences, and deeper discussions about the complexities of architecture design. Schriek *et al.* [22] propose a card game to help novice designers prompt architecture design reasoning. The cards used in the game act as triggers for the designers to explore the design space and use the reasoning techniques suggested by the chosen card. Similar to our game, these works focus on aspects like making architecture design decisions, providing the reasoning behind decisions, and making trade-offs among various requirements when architecting software systems. However, it must be considered that the mentioned games do not pay any attention to ethical considerations.

Other works use card-based tools or games to target ethical considerations in building software systems which are not specific to software architecture. For example, Lachlan and Peter [8] focus on supporting the building of an ethical system. By proposing the tool 'Moral-IT Deck', they increase ethics awareness, promote thinking, prompt reflection on normative aspects, and address emerging ethical risks in the design process. In doing so, they use a deck to reflect on values and a board map for taking action. Belman *et al.* [6] focus on facilitating values-conscious design in the context of digital games. By proposing the 'Grow-A-Game' cards, they aim to explore how values can be embedded in the design features of games, help group brainstorm, and game design based on a set of prescribed values. Kheirandish *et al.* [14] propose the tool 'HuValue' that focuses on training students to address human values within the software design process and enriching design concepts wrt human values. The tool, including 45 value words and 207 picture cards, aims to increase the designer's awareness of human values, and bridge the gap between the abstract level of human values and the practical level of design. Ballard *et al.* [5] focus on building responsible artificial intelligent technologies from an ethical point of view by designing the game 'Judgement Call'. The game helps designers consider ethical concerns when developing AI-driven technologies, discuss ethical dilemmas that result from technology, and consider the broader societal impact of technology. Friedman and Hendry [10] focus on involving human values during design processes. By developing 'Envisioning' cards, the authors aim to raise awareness upon the long-term and systemic effects of technologies, and facilitate designers' humanistic and technical imaginations. Similar to these works, the key idea accomplished by our game is the enabling of reflection and increasing awareness about ethical aspects. With our game, we are interested in stimulating the following activities in the context of software architecture: discussion on affected stakeholders and their values, value conflict, and making design decisions with consideration of ethical implications. It should be noted that, however, these works do not focus on supporting ethical aspects when making architecture design decisions.

2.2 Background

Based on the ISO/IEC/IEEE 40210:2011 standard [17], relevant works in software architecture (*e.g.,* [4,15]), and in SE ethics (*e.g.,* [2,3]), we adopted the concepts shown in Fig. 1, as ethical considerations in software architecture. There, the concepts of software architecture are tailored to be used from an ethical point of view. For example, in the figure, we have 'ethical value' instead of 'quality attribute'. In the following, we explain the main concepts and their relations.

Stakeholder. Stakeholders are individuals, groups, or organisations that use the system, build the system, or are affected by the system. There are different stakeholders in relation to a system that can directly or indirectly receive harm or benefit from it. As pointed out in [3], stakeholders can be divided into three overarching roles in terms of their relations with the system, *i.e.,* system development organisation, system users, and indirect stakeholders. These roles should particularly be determined based on the system and the purpose for which it has been designed. Consider Electronic Health Record (EHR) system for use in hospitals [13]. In the context of this system, software designers, hospital personnel, and patients are examples of the system development organisation, system users, and indirect stakeholders, respectively. Each role is specifically concerned with ethical value(s) that need to be supported in relation to the system.

Ethical Value. A value is what a person or group of people consider important in life [11]. In accordance to the relation of various stakeholders with a system, stakeholders also favor different values. In the example of EHR, software designers may focus more on the ethical values related to system design and implementation (*e.g.,* accuracy), while hospital personnel, for which the system is built, may care only about the values associated with their own goal achievement (*e.g.,* accessibility). Further, values (similar to software requirements) can contradict or complement each other. When one value is addressed, another value can be undermined, *e.g.,* in the EHR system, the two values of accessibility and privacy (as a value of patients) can contradict each other. Thus, there is a need to make trade-offs among competing values [2].

Ethical Concern. In the context of software systems, ethical concern refers to an issue that can potentially undermine or corrupt ethical values. For example, consider Radio Frequency Identification (RFID) technology, which is used for the automated identification of products. The RFID systems are vulnerable to various attacks (like eavesdropping) that can cause privacy violations for people who hold an RFID tag [16]. Such an issue can create privacy concerns for system users, as it can transfer sensitive information to unauthorized parties and adversely affect the value of privacy.

Ethical Decision. A design solution results from a series of decisions in both the problem- and solution space [23]. Software architecture is a level of design at which the most important decisions (technical and non-technical) should be made. Applying an ethical lens to software architecture decision making, can bring a focus to the need for supporting ethical values among software architects. In this way, architects need to consider the impacts of ethical aspects on decisions in both problem and solution spaces. For example, decisions in the problem space, such as defining the system scope and identifying stakeholders, should be made wrt the social and ethical implications of the system on stakeholders, the values at stake, and the probability of encountering new ethical concerns. Continuing with the example of RFID, software architects may need to make a decision(s) to support the privacy of users by, *e.g.,* encrypting data before loading it into the data warehouse. Similarly, decisions in the solution space should be based on ethical aspects, *e.g.,* the selection among different options should be made according to their impacts on different ethical values. In the context of RFID systems, the selection between two options of 'symmetric encryption' and 'asymmetric encryption' depends upon their impacts on various values, *e.g.,* efficiency and privacy, and tradeoffs among them. It also should be noted that the process of ethical decision making involves ethical reasoning. By ethical reasoning, we mean providing rationales behind decisions regarding ethical concerns in order to choose suitable option(s).

A design solution is often made by the decisions of a group of practitioners [20]. *Group decision making* is a dynamic process that includes several steps: problem identification, sharing information, alternative generation, alternative evaluation, and consensus reaching. In this process, as the number of alternatives increases, the challenges that practitioners should face increase. The common challenges are conflict resolution and reaching consensus, which dealing with them is a key aspect of any group discussion [20]. Still, very little has been done to truly understand how conflicts can be managed and how architecture design decisions can be made by practitioners, especially when ethical considerations are involved.

3 Methodology

In this section, we describe the problems and study objectives, game design, game execution, data collection, and data analysis.

3.1 Problems and Objectives

According to the focus group study conducted on SE ethics in [2], we uncovered a list of problems, namely: (i) the lack of focus on stakeholders and their ethical concerns and values (especially those who could be indirectly affected by a system); (ii) the lack of attention to ethical and social implications of design decisions; (iii) difficulties in operationalizing values and making trade-offs among

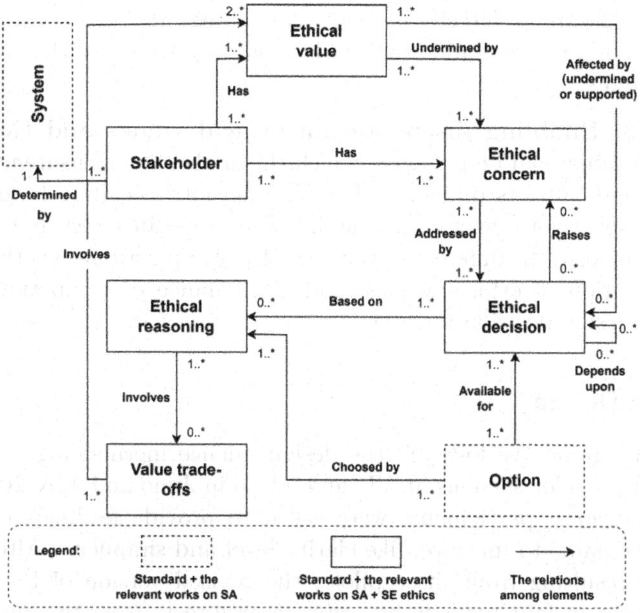

Fig. 1. Ethical considerations in software architecture, as used in game design (adopted from [1]).

them. Regarding these problems, our study focuses on the following Research Question (RQ):

RQ: How can we enable reflection on ethical considerations among software architects when architecting software systems?

By reflecting on ethical considerations, we mean challenging one's thinking about such considerations [19]. Accordingly, the design objectives for our game are:

Objective 1: Enabling discussion on stakeholders and their ethical concerns. Different stakeholders (directly or indirectly affected by the system) need to be supported by the system in terms of respecting their ethical values. Identifying all stakeholders relevant to the system and supporting their values and concerns are not an easy task as there is no specific process to recognize them during system design [2]. The proposed game aims to encourage software architects to reflect on different stakeholders and their ethical concerns, and include their values.

Objective 2: Enabling discussion on ethical decision making and ethical reasoning. Analyzing and dealing with the ethical and social implications of software systems are not easy for software architects because there is not any means of guidance in the current software development methodologies to identify the potential ethical issues. Software architects usually use their own moral judgment in decision making and reasoning about such issues [2]. The game aims to motivate software architects to think about design decisions' implications on ethical values and the reasoning that underpins such decisions when architecting software systems.

Objective 3: Enabling discussion on ethical values and their trade-offs. Ethical values can be personal, which this makes the measurement of their importance and impacts difficult. They are also intrinsically relevant and can positively or negatively affect each other [2]. The game aims to stimulate software architects to discuss the different options and their implications on ethical values, the concretization of ethical values, and the balance of competing values in architecture design decision making.

3.2 Game Design

To design the game, we followed the design science methodology in [24], and conducted three pilot sessions at VU and TU/e in June and July 2022. During these pilot sessions, participants were asked to provide feedback on different aspects of the game to improve, like clarity level and simplicity. After applying the changes resulting from these pilots, the revised version of the game was officially played in four sessions by software architects from two multinational IT companies (in September and October 2022).

The game uses a deck of cards that were designed around a real case, called *Discrimination by Design*. Details about the Ethics-Aware DecidArch game are available online[3].

3.3 Game Execution

We played the game with 4 teams of software architects in 4 separate sessions. Each session, starting with an introduction to the game, included 4 software architects and lasted for about 90 min. The majority of architects had 10–20 years of experience in architecting software systems in different sectors of the IT industry[4]. In Table 1, we show the participants' demographic data.

3.4 Data Collection

To collect the data and assess the extent to which the goals of the game are fulfilled, we created a survey including multiple-choice and open-ended questions. According to the game's goals, the survey includes statements with the three themes: (i) stakeholders and their concerns, (ii) ethical decision making and ethical reasoning, and (iii) ethical values and their trade-offs. It should be noted that the participant survey was the same in all game sessions. In addition, the game sessions were audio-recorded and then transcribed.

[3] https://github.com/S2-group/DecidArch/tree/main/DecidArch-V4%20(HCII23).

[4] Most players have worked in more than one IT sector.

Table 1. Participant demographics

Measure	Item	Percentage (%)
Gender	Male	75%
	Female	25%
IT Sector	Marketing	6.25%
	Railway engineering	6.25%
	Government	18.75%
	Finance	25%
	Manufacturing	12.5%
	Telecommunication	6.25%
	Transportation	12.5%
	Hi-Tech	6.25%
	Education	18.75%
	Police	6.25%
	Insurance	6.25%
	Utilities	6.25%
	Information Technology	31.25%
	Logistics	25%
	Other	18.75%
Experience	Less than 5	18.8%
	5-10	12.5%
	10-20	50%
	More than 20	18.8%

3.5 Data Analysis

To investigate how players reflect on ethical considerations, we analyzed the transcripts of each session[5]. We followed the suggestion of Miles and Huberman [18] to have an initial set of codes (as a start-list). We developed our start-list based on the concepts and their relations shown in Fig. 1.

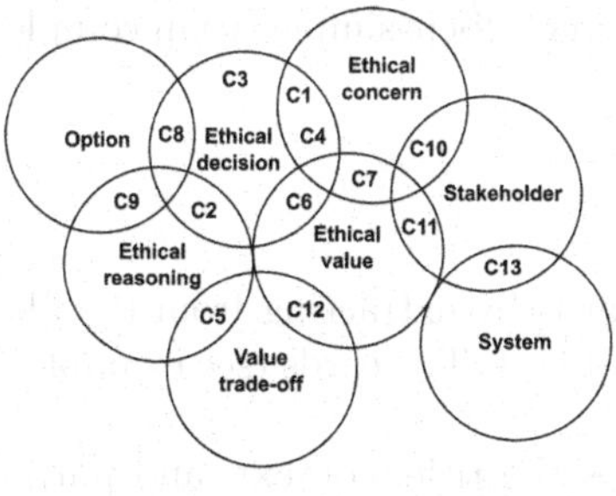

Fig. 2. Articulated codes for qualitative data analysis. These codes are: (C1): *ethical concern-addressed by-ethical decision*, (C2): *ethical decision-based on-ethical reasoning*, (C3): *ethical decision-depends on-ethical decision*, (C4): *ethical decision-raises-ethical concern*, (C5): *ethical reasoning-involves-value trade-off*, (C6): *ethical value-affected by-ethical decision*, (C7): *ethical value-undermined by-ethical concern*, (C8): *option-available for-ethical decision*, (C9): *option-choosed by-ethical reasoning*, (C10): *stakeholder-has-ethical concern*, (C11): *stakeholder-has-ethical value*, (C12): *value trade off-involves-ethical value*, and (C13): *stakeholder-determined by-system*

[5] We used ATLAS.ti as a tool to analyze the sessions' transcripts.

We represent our codes as a Venn diagram (see Fig. 2), in which circles are the concepts (*i.e.,* system, stakeholder, ethical value, ethical concern, ethical decision, ethical reasoning, value trade-off, and option). We identified 13 relations among these concepts that could lead us to articulate 13 codes (summarized in the caption of Fig. 2). According to the figure, the code placed in a conjunction area of each two circles (*i.e.,* concepts) shows the relation between those two concepts. For example, C1 depicts the relation of 'addressed by' between two concepts of 'ethical concern' and 'ethical decision'.

4 Ethics-Aware DecidArch Game

In this section, we explain the case under study, the game cards, and the game mechanism, respectively.

4.1 The Case Under Study

The case used in this study (Discrimination by Design) is about tuning a library management system by designing a new configuration parameter (named 'Modesty'). This system provides members access to the different categories of books in the library. By setting the 'Modesty' parameter, the system aims to refuse loans of some book categories (like feminism and women's movement) to the female members for respecting cultural differences. Any attempts by female members to check these categories are to be registered in the database. The reason for having such a system is the fact that the company (as a sponsor of the system) is opening up new strategic markets, and the survival of the company depends on its success in these new markets. The case was inspired by similar dilemmas in industry, albeit simpler than complex projects yet useful for learnability.

4.2 Game Cards

We designed a deck of cards by extracting from the above-mentioned case and the concepts presented in Fig. 1. The cards (see examples in Fig. 3) are as follows.

Project Card. It describes the title, context, and purpose of the system whose software architecture is the focus of the game.

Stakeholder Card. It describes the specific role of game players in terms of goal and ethical values that they may be concerned with. Each value is described by a short definition and the level of importance (*i.e.,* V-importance[6]) for that specific role, in which a higher number means higher importance. There are five stakeholder cards wrt our case: (1) product managers ('system development

[6] It is determined based on the importance of ethical values from the perspective of different stakeholders in the context of the case.

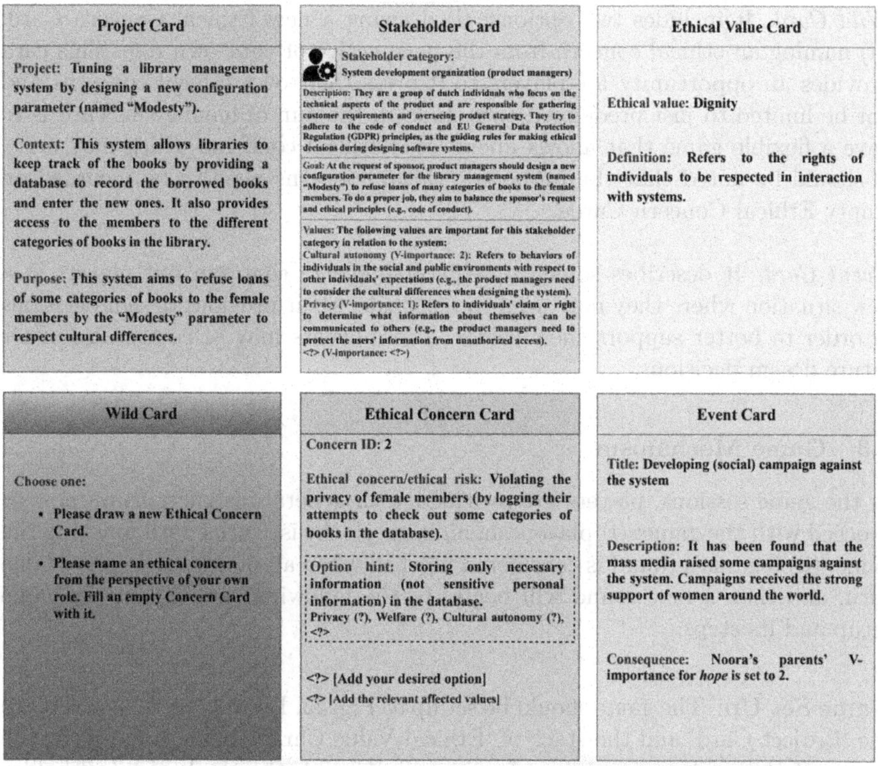

Fig. 3. Examples of the game cards

organisation' category), (2) sponsor ('system development organisation' category), (3) library's female members like Noora ('system users' category), (4) society X ('indirect stakeholders' category), and (5) Noora's parents ('indirect stakeholders' category).

Ethical Value Card. It describes a value term (*e.g.,* dignity) along with its definition. In deciding to include a proper set of ethical values in the game, this card can work as guidance for different roles to have their own values in addition to the predetermined ones. The stack of ethical value cards is non-exhaustive and mainly focuses on preliminary values relevant to the determined project in the game.

Ethical Concern Card. It describes an ethical concern caused by the system that can affect stakeholders by undermining their values. The card includes a hint for possible solutions (*i.e.,* option hint) to resolve the ethical concern, namely a pointer to the suitable options. The concern needs to be addressed by proposing an appropriate option with consideration of its implications on relevant ethical values, *i.e.,* '++', '+', '=', '−', and '−−', which stand for very positively, positively, neutral, negatively, and very negatively, respectively.

Wild Card. It includes two options: (i) drawing a new Ethical Concern Card; (ii) naming an ethical concern from the perspective of your own role. This card provides an opportunity for players to express their own ethical concerns and not be limited to just predefined ones. Indeed, the aim of having this card is to have a flexible game that allows unexpected ethical concerns which may arise. It should be noted that the proposed ethical concerns need to be recorded on empty Ethical Concern Cards.

Event Card. It describes some unpredictable events that can put players in a new situation where they may need to reconsider their previous design decisions in order to better support their values. These events may of course also affect future design decisions.

4.3 Game Mechanism

In the game sessions, players are provided with general instructions on how to proceed with the game: (i) players should take clockwise turns until finishing the game; (ii) a game's round is considered finished when all players have played one turn, and then a new round will begin. In the following, we explain the game setup and its steps.

Game Set Up: The game should be set up as Fig. 4a. First, players should place the 'Project Card' and the stack of 'Ethical Value Cards' facing upwards at the center of the table as a means of guidance. Second, the stack of 'Stakeholder Cards' should be shuffled, while each player draws one card from the top of the stack to identify their role during the game[7]. Third, the stacks of 'Ethical Concern and Wild Cards' and 'Event Cards' should be shuffled separately and placed facing downward within the players' sight. Finally, each player should be provided with a 'Decision Preparation Template'[8], and a 'Decision Taking Template'[9] should be allocated to the group.

How to Play the Game: After setting up the game, the following steps need to be taken in order to play the game (see Fig. 4b).

In step ① *(i.e., 'draw an Ethical Concern or Wild Card')*, each player needs to draw one card from the stack of 'Ethical Concern and Wild Cards'. In this step, the act depends on the drawn card, either the 'Ethical Concern Card' or 'Wild Card'.

[7] After the determination of their roles, they should read 'Ethical Value Cards' to be guided to have their own ethical value(s) wrt their role's perspective (although this is optional). It is worth noting that the player responsible for the role of indirect stakeholders has two choices, *i.e.*, society X or Noora's parents.

[8] This template is for each player to record their decisions and reasoning behind decisions.

[9] This template is to record the group decisions, the reasoning behind decisions, and the effects of the decisions on the relevant values.

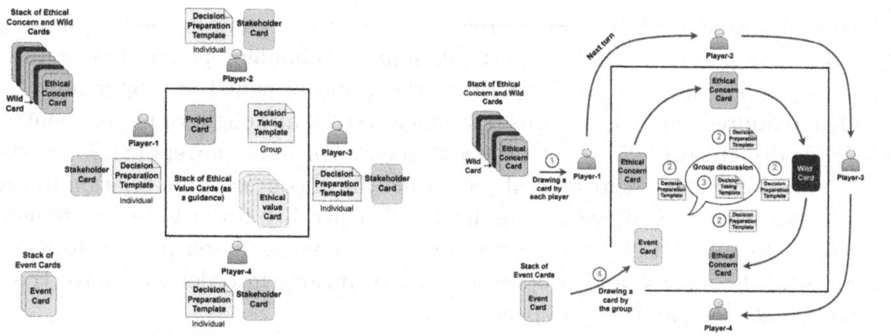

(a) (b)

Fig. 4. Game mechanism (adopted from [1]): (a) Game setup and (b) How to play the game

In step ② (*suggest an option*), all players should suggest an option to address each ethical concern. Indeed, each player should propose a suitable option for satisfying their role in terms of supporting their values. Finally, players should write down their choice and rationale/reasoning behind it on their 'Decision Preparation Template'.

Step ③ (*choose an option*) requires the group members to collaboratively decide and choose an option to address each ethical concern. Each player should tell the other players which option they suggest and their rationale for that suggestion. Once all players have shared their suggestions, a decision can collectively be made. The collective decision should be written down by players, along with the reasoning behind it, and its effects on the relevant values (*i.e.*, '++', '+', '=', '−', or '−−') on the 'Decision Taking Template'.

At the end of each round, in step ④ (*draw an Event Card*), the group should draw an Event Card and assesses the effect of the event on their previous and future design decisions. Players may need to reconsider previously taken decisions.

The game should be terminated upon reaching the designated time limit. Finally, the group must collect all filled templates and materials, put them in the designated envelope, and return them to the game organizers.

5 Results

5.1 Survey Results

The following presents the findings resulting from the analysis of the survey data.

Finding 1: The Game Prompted Reflection on Possible Solutions to Resolve Ethical Concerns from Different Stakeholders' Perspectives. The responses to statements $S1.1$-$S1.3$ (see Fig. 5) show that the game enabled players to challenge possible solutions for resolving ethical concerns. Almost all players indicated that the use of role-playing in the game helped them analyze different potential solutions wrt different stakeholders' perspectives (statement $S1.1$). For most players (68.75%), the game provided an opportunity to think and address ethical concerns (statement $S1.2$), although some were neutral (25%) or disagreed (6.25%) with the statement. For most players (81.25%), the game encouraged the expression of potential ethical concern(s) in relation to the system (statement $S1.3$), yet some displayed neutrality towards this statement (18.75%). In total, using role-playing in the game stimulated players to think about ethical concerns and propose relevant solutions in order to resolve them wrt different stakeholders' perspectives.

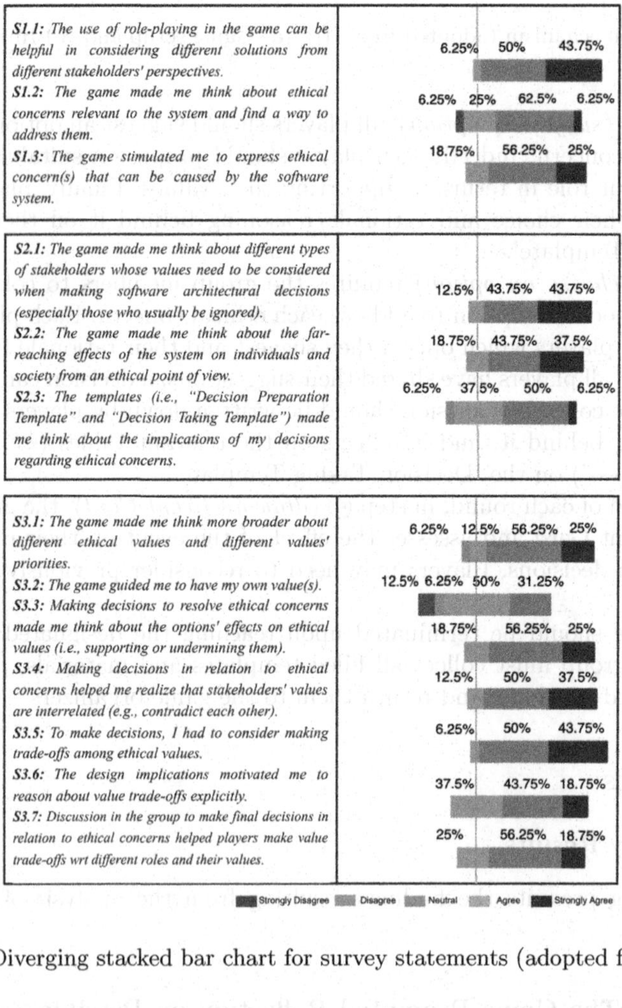

Fig. 5. Diverging stacked bar chart for survey statements (adopted from [1])

Finding 2: The Game Enabled Consideration of Ethical Aspects in Design Decisions and Design Reasoning. The responses to statements $S2.1$-$S2.3$ (see Fig. 5) demonstrate that the game prompted players to make ethical decisions and provide the reasoning behind such decisions. The majority of players (87.5%) indicated that the game helped them think about different stakeholders (statement $S2.1$) and consider the extensive effects of the system on individuals and society when making architecture design decisions (around 81.25% of players) (statement $S2.2$). For most players (56.25%), the use of templates could assist them in thinking about decisions' implications regarding ethical concerns (statement $S1.3$), although some were neutral (37.5%) or disagreed (6.25%) with this statement. By encouraging thinking about the far-reaching effects of the system on individuals and society from an ethical point of view, the game assisted players make decisions based on ethical implications and provide the explicit reasoning behind their decisions.

Finding 3: The Game Enabled Reflection on Value Operationalization and Value Trade-Offs. The responses to statements $S3.1$-$S3.7$ (see Fig. 5) show that the game helped players reflect on operationalizing values and making trade-offs among competing values. Most players agreed with these statements. The overall impression from the statements' responses were positive, despite the neutrality amongst some players. However, as an improvement point, it was suggested that the game needs to better foster the identification of the personal values of participants. By stimulating thinking about the impacts of different solutions on ethical values, the game helped players make design decisions with consideration of values and their relations.

5.2 Game Session Results

The findings relevant to the analysis of the game sessions' transcripts are presented below.

Finding 4: Issues that Were Mostly Reflected in Group Discussions Around Ethical Considerations. During brainstorming different solutions, we found that the game enabled architects to reflect on several issues mainly. This reflection could help architects put forward agreement and disagreement points at the forefront of their discussion of ethical considerations (see Table 2).

Ex-1 and *Ex-5* show the reflection of players (*i.e.*, agreement and disagreement) on *the solutions proposed for resolving ethical concerns.* In *Ex-1*, players made an agreement on the suggested option, which was offering other alternatives for female members. *Ex-5* shows *[S1-P2]*[10] disagreed with the solution suggested by *[S1-P3]*, *i.e.*, keeping the registration anonymous. These two examples indicate the reflection on selecting the suitable solution wrt concerns about different roles and the system's purpose.

[10] In the following, *[Si-Pj]* indicates the player *Pj* of the session *Si*.

Ex-2 and *Ex-6* show the reflection on *the affected values by the suggested solutions.* In *Ex-2*, players agreed that using the notification module cannot affect the value of dignity. *Ex-6* shows, taking different roles, players disagreed on whether storing only the phone number of members affects privacy. These two examples indicate the reflection of players on ethical values that can be associated with and potentially affected by the suggested solutions.

Ex-3 and *Ex-7* show the reflection on *the solutions' effects on the relevant values.* In *Ex-3*, players agreed on the effects of the suggested solution on the relevant values, which was undermining privacy while supporting fairness. *Ex-7* shows the disagreement of players *[S1-P3]* and *[S1-P1]* about the positive and negative effects of the suggested option on the value of social power. These two examples demonstrate the reflection of players on how ethical values can be influenced by the suggested solutions.

Ex-4 and *Ex-8* show the reflection on *the quantification of the solutions' effects on the relevant values.* In *Ex-4*, players agreed on the extent of the solution's effects on privacy which should be very high ('++'). *Ex-8* shows players opposed each other on the extent to which the solution can affect freedom. Players *[S4-P2]* and *[S4-P3]* (as a product manager and sponsor, respectively) indicated the effect is very high ('++') while from the perspective of *[S4-P1]* (*i.e.*, Noora) that solution could not provide that much freedom, and the effect was considered only high ('+'). These two examples indicate the reflection of players on the degree to which the relevant values can be affected by the solutions (*i.e.*, very positively, positively, neutral, negatively, and very negatively).

Finding 5: Enabling of Ethical Reasoning. The analysis of game sessions revealed three types of ethical reasoning. Table 3 represents those reasoning types.

Ex-1 shows *[S3-P4]* suggested a solution option, *i.e.*, having a system backdoor, for access of female members of the library to the forbidden books. By underlying that the solution can undermine the system reputation, *[S3-P3]* could prove the unsuitability of the solution from an ethical perspective. This conversation shows that players provided rationale for *the weaknesses of the solution from an ethical point of view* when making architecture design decisions.

Ex-2 shows *[S4-P2]* argued why the solution of 'the library registration with the phone number instead of ID number' could be helpful in balancing the relevant values. He stated that by not using the users' sensitive data while supporting the system functionalities and the company's prestige, the solution could help balance the values of privacy and reputation. This conversation shows that players provided rationale for *making trade-offs among ethical values.*

Ex-3 shows *[S1-P3]* reasoned about the certainty of the solution from an ethical perspective, by indicating the alignment of the suggested solution with GDPR and assuring data protection and privacy. This conversation shows that players provided rationale for *the certainties of the solution from an ethical point of view.*

Table 2. Data excerpts related to the reflection when challenging possible solutions

Participants' dialogue	Interpretation
Ex-1: [S1-P3]: I want the user to stay on my website or whatever the system is or the app. [S1-P2]: That should be your thing. You want to use your system. [S1-P4]: Yeah, that's correct. But I also want to moderate it because I find it important that some sources are not suitable for some audiences. [S1-P2]: Yeah. Do you think that providing other alternatives would help your audience? [S1-P3]: You can describe them? [S1-P2]: Yeah, you can actually do quite like that area. Do you get suggestions just like Netflix? [S1-P3]: Yeah. And at times, they show you just the opposite thing to what you were searching for, and you still stick. What do you think? [S1-P2]: I like the idea. [S1-P4]: A bit of censoring. [S1-P2]: Yeah, they recommend it. I still have the freedom to choose whatever book I would like to read. As long as it doesn't block my search bar	*The players reflected on the alternative options that were proposed to resolve ethical concerns. They had an agreement on the selection of options*
Ex-2: [S4-P3]: Using the notification module does not have any impact on dignity. [S4-P2]: yeah, I agree. It cannot be affected. [S4-P1]: Yeah	*The players reflected on the values that could be affected by the proposed option. They had an agreement on the affected values*
Ex-3: [S3-P3]: What is the effect of option on fairness? [S3-P4]: It is positive. [S3-P3]: Why? [S3-P2]: How can it be fair? [S3-P4]: Because you are considering females as well as males. [S3-P3]: I agree, agree	*The players reflected on the effect(s) of the proposed option on the relevant values. They had an agreement on the option's effects*
Ex-4: [S3-P3]: Privacy? [S3-P1]: It's positive because the option is giving commitment. [S3-P3]: But it is one '+', not two. [S3-P2]: Yes, agree, double '+'	*The players reflected on the extent to which values could be affected by the proposed option. They had an agreement on the quantification of the solutions' effects on the relevant values*
Ex-5: [S1-P3]: My safeguard for my role is that I want to protect the privacy of my girl. So that's why I want to keep the registration anonymous. So don't fill in anything. So stay anonymous for that part. So don't get to a name or something that can be related to her. [S1-P2]: Yeah, but again, if you borrow books from the library, you need to bring them back. It can be yours. [S1-P3]: You don't have the record. You can use anonymous things in between not related directly to how it's being borrowed	*The players reflected on the alternative options that were proposed to resolve ethical concerns. They disagreed on the selection of options*
Ex-6: [S4-P1]: I think asking only for the phone number cannot affect privacy. [S4-P3]: By the way, I think the opposite. By having the phone number, we can track them and elicit other personal data	*The players reflected on the values that could be affected by the proposed option. They disagreed on the affected values*
Ex-7: [S1-P3]: Then it's one plus sign because I agree, and also with the wealth, it helps me to gain to sell the system. [S1-P3]: Social power is a '+'. Right. [S1-P1]: Well, it's a '-' for me. [S1-P4]: You cannot see other people's concerns	*The players reflected on the effect(s) of the proposed option on the relevant values. They disagreed on the option's effects*
Ex-8: [S4-P1]: Freedom? I think it is negative. [S4-P3]: I think it is a double '+' because the solution failed in the previous steps. [S4-P1]: a little bit, but not that much. [S4-P3]: In comparison with before, you have freedom. [S4-P2]: I think it should be a double '+'. [S4-P1]: It can be fair if you say I give you a 50% discount, but if you only provide a 5% discount, It should not be a double '+', maybe one '+'	*The players reflected on the extent to which values could be affected by the proposed option. They disagreed on the quantification of the solutions' effects on the relevant values*

Table 3. Data excerpts related to different ethical reasoning when making design decisions

Participants' dialogue	Interpretation
Ex-1: [S3-P4]: My solution is to find a backdoor to access the resources, those that are available for males but not for females. [S3-P2]: You can find a male friend and ask him to bring that book. [S3-P1]: Like using another's accounts. [S3-P4]: No, I want to hack the system. [S3-P3]: I cannot entirely agree with this solution, and I, as a sponsor, would ask the development team to stop you. [S3-P4]: I don't think so because you only want to make money. [S3-P3]: Yes, but it can cause some harm to the reputation of the system, and the country may decide to use another system instead. [S3-P2]: It means that the system works weakly and can cause some scandal for the company	*The players reasoned about the weaknesses of the proposed option from an ethical perspective*
Ex-2: [S4-P2]: This option can be good because that allows the female member to register only with a phone number. Then if she wants to access the lock category, she should enter her ID number. This solution cannot damage the system's reputation and does not have an impact on privacy as well	*The players provided the reason for balancing ethical values*
Ex-3: [S1-P3]: So my role is that of product manager, so I have to balance the needs of the stakeholder, the customer, and also, like, the ethical concerns or something. And also, I'm operating within the Netherlands, so it says that you are within the Netherlands. So I think I will still store the information but with consent. If I have the consent, then I'm already, and I get the consent because, of course, I have to comply with GDPR. So I want to eliminate the possibility of paying huge fines. So that is why I still store the information but with the concern that is my way of making it	*The players reasoned about the certainty of the proposed option from an ethical perspective*

Finding 6: Ways of Reflection on Ethical Values. Using examples from the transcripts (see Table 4), we illustrate how the game stimulated players to make reflection towards ethical values.

Example *Ex-1* shows players *[S4-P3]* and *[S4-P1]* discussed the meaning of freedom from the perspective of two roles, *i.e.*, product manager and Noora. This example demonstrates that the game enabled players to discuss the meaning of ethical values from different stakeholders' perspectives. *Understanding the meaning of values* from different perspectives could help players easily concertize values and support them when making design decisions.

Ex-2 shows players *[S2-P4]* and *[S2-P2]* discussed the importance of different values. *[S2-P4]* referred to privacy as an essential value, while *[S2-P2]* considered social power as a high-priority value. This example demonstrates that the game enabled players to discuss the importance of ethical values from different roles' perspectives. *Understanding the importance and priority of ethical values* could help players support the most important ones and make necessary trade-offs among the values.

Ex-3 shows *[S2-P1]* expressed a new ethical value (*i.e.,* the value of [company's name]) that was important in relation to the project. This example demonstrates that the game stimulated players to *think about other ethical values* that could be affected by the system, in addition to the predetermined ones.

Ex-4 shows players *[S2-P4]* and *[S2-P3]* discussed the positive and negative effects of the option (*i.e.,* gender-proofing of members) on the value of welfare. This example demonstrates that the game stimulated players to discuss the solutions' effects on the relevant values. *Understanding the ethical implications of the solutions on values* could lead players to make the right decisions from an ethical perspective.

Ex-5 shows players discussed the extent of the effects of 'gender proofing' on privacy, whether it is only one or two minus signs. This example demonstrates that the game enabled players to discuss the extent to which the solutions affected the relevant values. *Understanding the quantification of the solutions' effects* could help players balance ethical values.

Ex-6 shows players discussed the reconsideration of the made decision, which was the members' authorization based on their pictures, in order to safeguard privacy. They finally decided to ask members only for their phone numbers to protect privacy. This example demonstrates that the game enabled players to support important ethical values and resolve value conflicts, by *reconsidering previously made decisions.*

6 Discussion

In the following, we discuss the game's practical impacts and its possible improvements and analyze the game from the perspective of inclusivity.

Table 4. Data excerpts related to the reflection on ethical values

Participants' dialogue	Interpretation
Ex-1: [S4-P3]: In total, what does freedom mean? Let's specify our definition. [S4-P1]: It implies that a girl should have access to everything when she is thirty. But, she should not have when she is seventeen. [S4-P3]: Age is not a matter. Let me bring you an example. Consider a specific society that does not allow people to have access to books with criminal subjects because it believes that these kinds of books can negatively affect their way of thinking. That is not related to age	*The players discussed the different meanings of a value (using examples) in order to conceptualize it*
Ex-2: [S2-P4]: ... So I am worried about privacy. So for me, the hint of actually requiring ID to check out, which is a bad one, because then. [S2-P1]: That's not. [S2-P4]: A violation of privacy. Right? [S2-P3]: And I care about welfare and protection of well being of all people. And this could potentially also impact welfare because if someone moves the data that you are renting all these feminine groups, you may be in danger. Now I'm worried about your welfare for privacy state, but for you, you might be in danger by then. [S2-P2]: So, for me, it's the other way around because I want to achieve social power and attain dominance	*The players discussed the importance of different values from the perspective of different stakeholder roles*
Ex-3: [S2-P1]: Also, the younger one, because you also have the [company's name] values as one of your concerns. [S2-P3]: values of [company's name]? [S2-P4]: The [company's name]'s mission statement is to have a company where we all enjoy working together	*The players expressed their own values that seemed relevant to the system, in addition to the predetermined ones*
Ex-4: [S2-P4]: Okay, so what I wrote down is required proof of gender when registering as a member only, and then only you have to show your library pass, and the system knows ... What would you score it on? Welfare? [S2-P3]: Welfare refers to the well-being of all people. So I don't know necessarily think this is good for the well-being of all people. [S2-P4]: So you think it's a '-'? [S2-P3]: It is one minus sign, yeah	*The players discussed the different effects of the suggested option on values*
Ex-5: ... [S2-P1]: But is it one or two '-' for privacy? [S2-P3]: One, because two '-' would be too much. [S2-P1]: Can't go too long. [S2-P3]: You can't go, right? [S2-P4]: Yeah. [S2-P3]: Every time you have to give your ID to pick up books. That is more than two '-', I think. [S2-P4]: That is two	*The players discussed the extent to which the proposed option could affect values*
Ex-6: [S3-P4]: What about authenticating using third-party tools? Is it possible not to authorize it? [S3-P3]: We can moderate the decision related to it. [S3-P2]: For example, we can do it without asking for pictures, only the phone number. [S3-P1]: Yeah, only with the phone number. [S3-P3]: What about the effect of the changed decision on values right now? For example, on informed consent? [S3-P2]: It's like before. [S3-P1]: No, it changes. [S3-P3]: But privacy would become better	*In order of supporting the important values, the players discussed reconsidering the decisions that were previously made*

6.1 Reflections on the Game's Practical Impacts

By motivating software architects to think about potential ethical concerns, enabling them to brainstorm possible options for resolving such concerns, and motivating them to propose and evaluate alternative options from the perspectives of different stakeholders, the game provided an opportunity to make group decisions around ethical considerations.

The findings described in Sect. 5.2 serve as a basis to explore how the game could be effective in dealing with the common challenges in group decision making (like conflict resolution and reaching consensus).

Conflict Resolution and Making Trade-offs. During the group decision making process in game sessions, we observed that conflicts occurred among ethical values within and/or among decisions. To deal with such conflicts, two game features were helpful for architects: (i) the V-importance determined for stakeholders' values and (ii) the need to provide the rationale for decisions. As an indicator to show the priority of values for different stakeholders, the V-importance helped architects decide on which values they need to focus on in the context of the system. In the decision making process, architects also had to justify their proposed options by providing reasoning from an ethical perspective. As revealed in finding 5, the most frequent reasoning was about (i) the weaknesses (or strengths) of the solution from an ethical point of view, (ii) making trade-offs among ethical values, and (iii) the certainties (or uncertainties) of the solution from an ethical point of view. Expressing this reasoning in an explicit way enabled architects easily explore the decisions' effects on ethical values. This further helped them to compare the decisions' effects on each value with the corresponding

V-importance, determine where to balance values, and how to satisfy different stakeholders in terms of supporting their values.

Although reasoning around alternative options can help better manage value conflicts, future research needs to elicit different reasoning types when making design decisions around ethical considerations.

Reaching Consensus and Making Decisions. During the group decision making process in game sessions, we observed that the game enabled architects to bring the agreement and disagreement points to the forefront. These points were issues that needed to be discussed more among players to arrive at an agreement (as presented in finding 4), namely: (i) the solutions proposed for resolving ethical concerns, (ii) the affected values by the suggested solutions, (iii) the solutions' effects on the relevant values, and (iv) the quantification of the solutions' effects on the relevant values. It should be noted that although these issues were frequently raised in the group discussion of all game sessions, we observed other cases in which players needed to arrive at a consensus, *e.g.,* value conceptualization. By bringing the challenging issues to the forefront, the game provided insights for architects on where there is a need to arrive at a consensus in order to make decisions, and helped them proceed with the discussion around ethical considerations.

In the light of improving the consensus process and the group decision making around ethical considerations, we suggest determining the most occurring issues in the group discussion. This can lead to an increase in the familiarity of software architects with challenging problems and, consequently, conducting efficient and effective decision making over such considerations.

6.2 The Inclusion Aspect of the Game

By inclusion in this study, we mean involving different stakeholders as equal partners in the design decision making process, having their voices heard on ethical issues, and considering their diverse ethical values. Infusing value diversity and inclusion is an important part of system design because doing so can help develop systems that are ethically responsible against a wide variety of stakeholders.

In the software engineering field, architects are well accustomed to thinking about the direct stakeholders of systems. However, there is no systematic way for them to expand the scope of stakeholders to include indirect stakeholders (*e.g.,* society at large). Considering this, our game was designed in such a way as to take a wide range of stakeholders into account, both directly and indirectly affected by the system. As different stakeholders were supposed to be involved in the game (using role-playing), architects had to be mindful of divergent preferences and values that needed to be supported in relation to the system. Taking on the role of various stakeholders allowed architects to see through others' eyes, empathize, and highlight the potential harm that might happen to stakeholders.

By involving different stakeholder roles and providing an equal opportunity for them to discuss the ethical issues at hand (in both the problem and solution space), the game fostered a sense of inclusion to support value diversity. Motivated by this, we conjecture that the game can be used by software architects as a part of their program in the software design process to orient discussion around ethical considerations and combat systemic biases that can adversely affect inclusion, diversity, and equity within the design field.

6.3 Possible Game Improvements

The following potential improvements can help enriching the game in future versions:

Generalizing the Game to be Applicable for any Case in Different Companies. The game can be designed so as not to be specific to any particular case. This makes it possible to use the game to deal with various ethical situations in different companies.

The Possibility of Determining the Potential Consequences of Events by Players. Including the possibility of determining the potential consequences of events by stakeholder roles. With this revision, the players would be able to explore the possible effects of events on different stakeholders and their values in the design decision making process and accordingly reconsider the decisions already made, to support the affected values.

The Complete Determination of Values and Their Importance by Players. Allowing different roles to completely identify the list of values that they are mostly concerned with and specify their importance, instead of having a pre-determined set of values (though open to adding). This revision can help include more opinions and experiences regarding ethical decision-making situations.

7 Threats to Validity

In this section, we discuss the main threats to validity and the related mitigation actions. We organize them according to the classification by Runeson and Höst [21].

Construct Validity. It refers to what extent the operational measures can represent what the researcher has in mind wrt research questions. One potential threat to this validity is related to the environment in which the game was carried out. This threat was mitigated by having instructors in the game sessions who presented the game and interfered only when clarifications were asked. This could potentially lead to a different interaction style amongst players compared to interactions conducted without interference.

Internal Validity. It refers to the ability to draw correct conclusions from the collected data. One threat to this validity is relevant to the quality of the survey answers due to the usage of the Likert scale. To mitigate this threat, we used open-ended questions at the end of the survey's statements where players could add their remarks and opinions.

External Validity. It refers to the ability to generalize the experiment results. One potential threat to this validity is related to the experience and background of participants. Players from two multinational IT companies who mitigate this threat conducted the game. Players hold different background knowledge, experience in various IT projects, and of course, varied interests.

Reliability. It refers to whether the process of study and analysis are consistent over time across researchers and methods. One threat to this validity can be related to the reliability of qualitative data analysis. This threat was mitigated by coding the data based on the presented concepts and their relations (in Fig. 1). Additionally, two researchers were asked to interpret and evaluate the data independently. When required, a joint discussion was conducted to provide an objective analysis.

8 Conclusions

This paper presents the Ethics-Aware DecidArch game that aims to enable software architects to reflect upon ethical considerations when making architecture design decisions. The game also wants to open the floor to incorporate a wider variety of divergent perspectives and give equal opportunities to different stakeholders to express their values for influencing the system design from an ethical perspective.

By analyzing the survey data and the transcripts of the game sessions, we observed that the game helped achieve the study objectives, *i.e.*, enabling discussion on stakeholders, their ethical values and concerns, ethical decision making and reasoning, and value trade-offs.

Our study resulted in a number of future research directions. These include: (i) conducting a larger data collection to generalize the experiment results, (ii) finding a way to orient the discussion around ethical considerations when making architecture design decisions, (iii) providing a comprehensive list of different types of ethical reasoning, (iv) proposing a systematic way to make ethical values concrete and bring them from an abstract level to a concrete level, and (v) providing a list of value conflicts that occur most frequently in software architecture design.

Further, we plan to run experiments where game sessions are used in the early phases of IT projects and evaluate their effectiveness in including ethical aspects in architecture design. We plan to use the game with novice architects, too, this time for training purposes. By giving insights into ethical considerations in software architecture design and by providing promising future research directions in this area, we hope software architects be able to build ethically responsible systems.

Acknowledgments. We would like to acknowledge our gratitude to the S2 group at VU and BE cluster members at TU/e, and the software architects from two multinational IT companies who have helped develop the game and provided valuable feedback. Also, we thank Antony Tang for his feedback on earlier versions of this work.

References

1. Alidoosti, R., Lago, P., Poort, E., Razavian, M.: Ethics-aware DecidArch game: designing a game to reflect on ethical considerations in software architecture design decision making. In: 20th International Conference on Software Architecture Companion (ICSA-C). IEEE (2023)
2. Alidoosti, R., Lago, P., Poort, E., Razavian, M., Tang, A.: Incorporating ethical values into software architecture design practices. In: 19th International Conference on Software Architecture Companion (ICSA-C), pp. 124–127. IEEE (2022)
3. Alidoosti, R., Lago, P., Razavian, M., Tang, A.: Ethics in software engineering: a systematic literature review. Tech. rep., Vrije Universiteit Amsterdam (2022). https://tinyurl.com/39crpyn2
4. Babar, M.A., Dingsøyr, T., Lago, P., Van Vliet, H.: Software architecture knowledge management. Springer, Heidelberg (2009). https://doi.org/10.1007/978-3-642-02374-3
5. Ballard, S., Chappell, K.M., Kennedy, K.: Judgment call the game: Using value sensitive design and design fiction to surface ethical concerns related to technology. In: Proceedings of the 2019 on Designing Interactive Systems Conference (2019)
6. Belman, J., Nissenbaum, H., Flanagan, M., Diamond, J.: Grow-A-Game: a tool for values conscious design and analysis of digital games. In: DiGRA Conference, vol. 6, pp. 1–15 (2011)
7. Cervantes, H., Haziyev, S., Hrytsay, O., Kazman, R.: Smart decisions: an architectural design game. In: Proceedings of the 38th International Conference on Software Engineering Companion, pp. 327–335 (2016)
8. D. Urquhart, L., J. Craigon, P.: The Moral-IT Deck: a tool for ethics by design. J. Respons. Innov. **8**(1), 94–126 (2021)
9. De Boer, R.C., Lago, P., Verdecchia, R., Kruchten, P.: Decidarch v2: An improved game to teach architecture design decision making. In: International Conference on Software Architecture Companion (ICSA-C). IEEE (2019)
10. Friedman, B., Hendry, D.: The envisioning cards: a toolkit for catalyzing humanistic and technical imaginations. In: Proceedings of the SIGCHI Conference on Human Factors in Computing Systems, pp. 1145–1148 (2012)
11. Friedman, B., Kahn, P.H., Borning, A., Huldtgren, A.: Value sensitive design and information systems. In: Doorn, N., Schuurbiers, D., van de Poel, I., Gorman, M.E. (eds.) Early engagement and new technologies: Opening up the laboratory. PET, vol. 16, pp. 55–95. Springer, Dordrecht (2013). https://doi.org/10.1007/978-94-007-7844-3_4
12. Gotterbarn, D.: Software engineering ethics. Encyclopedia of Software Engineering (2002)
13. Grünloh, C.: Using technological frames as an analytic tool in value sensitive design. Ethics Inf. Technol. **23**(1), 53–57 (2021)

14. Kheirandish, S., Funk, M., Wensveen, S., Verkerk, M., Rauterberg, M.: HuValue: a tool to support design students in considering human values in their design. Int. J. Technol. Des. Educ. **30**(5), 1015–1041 (2020)
15. Lago, P., Cai, J.F., de Boer, R.C., Kruchten, P., Verdecchia, R.: Decidarch: Playing cards as software architects. In: Proceedings of the 52nd Hawaii International Conference on System Sciences (2019)
16. Lee, S.M., Hwang, Y.J., Lee, D.H., Lim, J.I.: Efficient authentication for low-cost RFID systems. In: Gervasi, O., et al. (eds.) ICCSA 2005. LNCS, vol. 3480, pp. 619–627. Springer, Heidelberg (2005). https://doi.org/10.1007/11424758_65
17. May, I.: Systems and software engineering-architecture description. Technical report, ISO/IEC/IEEE 42010 (2011)
18. Miles, M.B., Huberman, A.M.: Qualitative data analysis: an expanded sourcebook. SAGE (1994)
19. Razavian, M., Tang, A., Capilla, R., Lago, P.: In two minds: how reflections influence software design thinking. J. Softw. Evol. Process **28**(6), 394–426 (2016)
20. Rekhav, V.S., Muccini, H.: A study on group decision-making in software architecture. In: International Conference on Software Architecture, pp. 185–194. IEEE/IFIP (2014)
21. Runeson, P., Höst, M.: Guidelines for conducting and reporting case study research in software engineering. Empir. Softw. Eng. **14**(2), 131–164 (2009)
22. Schriek, C., van der Werf, J.M.E.M., Tang, A., Bex, F.: Software architecture design reasoning: a card game to help novice designers. In: Tekinerdogan, B., Zdun, U., Babar, A. (eds.) ECSA 2016. LNCS, vol. 9839, pp. 22–38. Springer, Cham (2016). https://doi.org/10.1007/978-3-319-48992-6_2
23. Tang, A., Aleti, A., Burge, J., van Vliet, H.: What makes software design effective? Des. Stud. **31**(6), 614–640 (2010)
24. Wieringa, R.J.: Design science methodology for information systems and software engineering. Springer, Heidelberg (2014). https://doi.org/10.1007/978-3-662-43839-8
25. Xu, H., Crossler, R.E., BéLanger, F.: A value sensitive design investigation of privacy enhancing tools in web browsers. Decis. Support Syst. **54**(1), 424–433 (2012)

A Multimodal Installation Exploring Gender Bias in Artificial Intelligence

Mihaela Dobreva[1], Tea Rukavina[2], Vivian Stamou[3](✉), Anastasia Nefeli Vidaki[4,5], and Lida Zacharopoulou[6]

[1] National Academy of Arts, Shipka 1 Street, Sofia, Bulgaria
[2] AI & DATA, 17 Rue Ledion, 75014 Paris, France
[3] NKUA, University of Athens, ILSP/Athena R.C., 15784, Athens, Greece
vivianstamou@gmail.com
[4] NKUA, University of Athens, 15772 Athens, Greece
[5] European Commission, Rue Luxemburg 40, 1000 Brussels, Belgium
[6] Athens School of Fine Arts, Pireos 256, 18233 Athens, Greece

Abstract. The "Blackbox AI" installation, developed as part of the EthicAI = LABS project, seeks to raise awareness about the social impact and ethical dimension of artificial intelligence (AI). This interdisciplinary installation explores various domains to bring to light the underrepresentation of women in STEM fields and the biases present in AI applications. The gender-swapped stories of women's experiences of discrimination in the workplace, collected by survey, showcase common patterns and explore the effect of flipping the gender. The text-to-image generation experiment highlights a preference for men in STEM professions and the prevalence of social and racial biases. The facial recognition examples demonstrate the discriminatory effects of such technologies on women, while the image generation investigation poses questions about the influence of AI technology on beauty, with the aim to empower women by pointing out bias in AI tools. The ultimate goal of the project is to challenge visitors to rethink their role in creating our digital future and address the issue of gender bias in artificial intelligence.

Keywords: artificial intelligence (AI) · gender bias · discrimination · technology · social impact

1 Introduction

Blackbox AI is a multidisciplinary art installation in the form of a labyrinth, inspired by Bruno Latour's characterization of new technologies as "black boxes" [1], where the input and the output are only known to the user, while the process remains untransparent. The project aims to raise awareness of gender bias in artificial intelligence (AI) applications that can lead to the (self-)exclusion of women from technology. Different aspects of this phenomenon are explored, namely natural language processing and algorithmic facial recognition biases, beauty standards, gender stereotypes in the collected testimonials, and women's access to the STEM work field. Through our exhibition and

M. Antona and C. Stephanidis (Eds.): HCII 2023, LNCS 14020, pp. 27–46, 2023.
https://doi.org/10.1007/978-3-031-35681-0_2

the interaction with the audience, we wanted to empower women to have more agency by pointing out the biases in artificial intelligence, tackle discrimination issues, and challenge all visitors to rethink their role in the creation of our common digital future, as consumers, as developers, and as human beings.

The paper is organized as follows: in the first part, the concept of the installation is described and illustrated with several examples, together with the context and the motivation for the project. Then, each of the five parts of the exhibition is explained in detail, showing the relevant research and describing the experiment methodology, followed by a short commentary on the results. Also, the challenges of combining scientific and artistic approaches in creating the exhibits are outlined, with a conclusion focusing on the scientific contribution of the paper, and the implications its findings could have on the development and design of new AI applications.

2 Multimodal Installation Concept

2.1 Project Genesis

Our team was formed during the EthicAI = Labs 2022 project organized by Goethe Institut. During our preliminary research on ethical issues in AI, we realized that, despite our diverse backgrounds, we all shared similar gender discrimination experiences regarding technology in our academic and working environments. To address this topic, we came up with the idea of an art installation in the form of a maze with several separate parts displaying the bias women encounter either in their AI-related field of work, or because of various applications of AI embodying and enhancing already existing discriminatory practices. We elaborated five parts depicting our own professional expertise into which the installation could be split, focusing on women's careers in STEM, the analysis of testimonials of gender bias in the workplace, NLP applications, facial recognition biases, and beauty standards. At the end of the first event in Sofia, we presented our project proposal with a performance incorporating our personal gender bias stories, and six months later, the final project presentation and installation at the EthicAI = Forum event in Athens.

2.2 Description of the Installation

The work was exhibited in Goethe Institut Athens during the EthicAI = Forum event in November 2022. It consisted of informative posters on AI about women's access to STEM fields and proposals for their integration, a display of the stories collected via a survey on discrimination and self-exclusion in the workplace who have undergone gender swap, a text-to-image display showing discriminatory elements in the natural language processing software Dall-E, a display of magazine covers produced with StyleGAN2 with adaptive discriminator augmentation (ADA) challenging beauty standards, and of a booklet on algorithmic facial recognition biases. All those parts were separated by black fabric hanging on the ceiling and thus creating the atmosphere of a labyrinth. The interaction with the audience was a crucial part of the exhibition and a source of inspiration for our further work. The visitors could either guide themselves or engage with the five presenters. A 3D model of the installation, together with a photograph taken during the exhibition opening in Athens are shown on Fig. 1.

(a) (b)

Fig. 1. (a) Graphical representation of the Blackbox AI installation; (b) Photograph taken during the exhibition opening in Athens in November 2022

3 The Biased Workplace Through an AI Lens

3.1 Gender Bias in Artificial Intelligence Applications

Although developed by specialists, Artificial Intelligence (AI) is not confined to specialized usage, on the contrary; an ever-larger number of users interact with it on a daily basis through applications on digital devices, especially smartphones, without being necessarily aware of it. AI technology is what powers vocal assistants and face unlocking features on our phones, not to mention applications and services such as social media, search engines, and recommender systems used in retail or in entertainment apps. Taking into account that approximately 8 billion people have a mobile subscription, and that more than 60% of the world's population uses the internet [1], the spectrum of people having access to AI widens. In this context, the question of who creates the different applications that construct our digital environment, and that, in consequence, give shape to our daily life, becomes more and more relevant.

AI, A Biased Decision Maker. Companies and organizations that develop AI have to be aware of the implications that their products have on shaping and controlling user experiences, tastes, and behavior, and set the tone to how people perceive AI and human-machine interaction in general. For instance, the legitimacy of AI-decision making in public affairs as perceived by the general public increases when the tools become more transparent, and when they provide clear justifications for their decisions [3]. With a rising number of AI applications influencing important decisions affecting human lives (judicial system, bank and insurance, warfare, medicine, recruitment), questions about the ethical and responsible way of using artificial intelligence are becoming increasingly important. AI is not inherently biased, but since it is learning from historical data, it can reproduce or even amplify many of the biases and discrimination present in our society. They can be related to a different number of factors (often combined), including race, origin, gender, age, religion, disability, or sexual orientation.

Since one of the objectives of our research is to evaluate the influence artificial intelligence can have on women's careers, we focus here on the use of AI tools in recruitment. Based on technologies such as NLP, and facial and vocal recognition, AI applications can intervene in different stages of the process, from finding promising candidates, performing assessment and profiling, to facilitating communication. As noted by [4], the use of AI in the recruitment process comes with several ethical ambiguities, especially in what concerns its effect on workforce diversity. On the positive side, the use of AI could reduce human bias and thus lead to diversification of a company's workforce, opening up the job market for people from a wider range of socioeconomic backgrounds. This could benefit women and other minority candidates when applying for roles that are traditionally male-dominated. But, the ethical risks could outweigh the benefits if algorithmic bias becomes systemic, and if AI tools learn to select candidates based on certain profiles and traits that are issued from imbalance datasets. This could disadvantage specific minority groups, and thus lead to a decrease in workforce diversity.

For example, one well-covered media story of a gender-biased AI application is the Amazon recruiting tool that showed bias against women. According to [5], the company's experimental hiring tool used artificial intelligence to give job candidates scores ranging from one to five stars, and thus help recruiters find the ideal candidate by automating part of the process. The company realized its new system was not rating candidates for software developer jobs and other technical posts in a gender-neutral way, and was penalizing women's profiles. That is because Amazon's computer models were trained to assess applicants by observing patterns in resumes submitted to the company for over ten years. Most came from men, a reflection of male dominance across the tech industry.

Another, even broader implication of AI usage on women in the workplace, could be related to job automation. The replacement of humans by artificial intelligence in the workplace is likely to happen first for the disposable and easily-automatable jobs, and this could affect lower classes and women disproportionately, since they are more often found in precarious situations. People who develop AI tools are likely to "survive" this shift towards a new paradigm and, in addition, reap the benefits of taking the leadership role in creating and deciding how our digital future will look like.

Inequality in the Tech Workplace. Diverse teams are more successful and more likely to outperform, and the companies in the tech sector should strive for more equal and gender-balanced teams. However, the present data paints a bleak picture: women account for barely 25% of employees in the STEM (Science, Technology, Engineering, Mathematics) field, and only 15% of data scientists are female [6]. Regarding salary distribution, in the European Union the gender pay gap is still 13%, when we take into account average hourly earnings of full time employees in all work sectors [7]. These differences are due to a large number of inequalities such as sectoral segregation, women's unequal share of unpaid work at home, the glass ceiling, and pay discrimination.

So, why do women still *choose* not to go into tech? Is this a real, conscious choice based on true preferences and available information, or a consequence of how society shapes our tastes and behavior? In [8], authors highlight the powerful social, economic, political and technical structures and conditions that shape people's choices. "While there are few gender differences in IT skills, there are differences in attitudes, interest and self-confidence in computer use." and "Girls' lack of interest in IT links to the image of the field as a male-gendered, boring, asocial, unfriendly, difficult and intimidating subject." [8] The exacerbation of differences is not only related to exclusion perpetrated by others (dominant group), but women and girls often exhibit self-exclusion behavior, where they withdraw from a situation or potentially uncomfortable social context to avoid the perceived negative consequences it could bring. This is especially true in male-dominated environments where women feel unwelcome, and thus helps reinforce the stereotype that "engineering is not for girls", widening the already large gap between genders in software development, AI engineering, and data science teams.

How to Make AI More Inclusive. Can gender bias related to the development and use of artificial intelligence applications be completely eliminated? The short answer is: no. But, there are mitigation strategies and approaches that can help minimize the negative impacts such as discrimination and unfairness. They can be divided into two broad categories: technical and non-technical actions. Technical actions deal with data and algorithms used in the creation of the machine learning model, and its supervision. In pre-processing this means paying attention to the way data are collected and prepared, and checking if the training dataset is balanced. Then, an adequate model has to be chosen for each type of analysis, while selecting the appropriate target / objective function. In post-processing, the model performance has to be checked on a global level, but also for specific groups to prevent discrimination.

Non-technical actions are related to governance and the regulatory framework, and they include questioning oneself (whether in a leadership/management or a development role) about data usage and protection, and detect potential sources of problems before starting a new AI project. Commitment on the part of companies and organizations is crucial to work towards diversity in the tech sector by implementing a targeted HR policy, and adhering to one of the different AI charters and labels available to ensure compliance from design. Also, professionals in the tech sector, especially in data science, are encouraged to organize and attend presentations and ethical AI events, and communicate about the subject in the media with the goal to familiarize the general public with AI and initiate discussion about its influence on society as a whole.

The ensemble of these approaches can be regrouped under the concept of responsible AI that includes the following broad areas: data governance, privacy and security, transparent and explainable AI, equality and fairness, accountability, and environmental impact.

3.2 Explaining Gender Bias Through Infographics

Translating the ideas and findings presented in this section into a format that could be suitable for showcasing as part of our exhibition was a challenging task. Instead of choosing a digital format (as was the case for the other four parts of the installation), we opted here for a physical exhibit, creating five infographics that were printed as large-format posters. Following the best practices of data visualization, our goal was to have a clear and user-friendly information layout, so the posters were designed using Canva software that allows for a large variety of choice in what concerns graphical elements. The data was taken from the multiple sources cited above. The posters cover the following topics, as shown on Fig. 2: (i) Gender equality in the workplace; (ii) How do we choose our career?; (iii) Artificial Intelligence: how does it work?; (iv) AI tools in recruitment; and (v) Can we eliminate gender bias in AI apps?

This hybrid way of presenting the five distinct parts of our project allowed us to interact with the audience in different manners. The printed posters attached to pieces of black cloth hanging from the ceiling created the impression of a labyrinth, and visitors could walk and move between them at their own pace.

Fig. 2. Infographics used in the multimodal installation to showcase gender (in)equality in the workplace with an emphasis on gender bias in AI applications

The goal of this exhibit was to raise awareness on the pressing topics of gender bias in AI, and the lack of women in development roles in the tech sector. The visitors of the exhibition, coming from different backgrounds and having varying levels of familiarity with the presented topics, reacted to the posters in a different manner. Some people were more into extensive and solitary reading of the material presented, and others were more open to discussion, readily seeking out to start a conversation with one of the hosts. We have observed a high level of audience engagement: on the one hand, the visitors already familiar and/or specialized in the subject of gender bias in AI through their own research or studies were more prone to discuss specific details of algorithmic implementation or the regulatory framework, while on the other hand, the visitors who were new to the topic had a tendency to focus on long-term societal implications of potentially biased AI applications they interact with on a daily basis, including social media. The "eye-opening" effect they shared as feedback reassured us in our conviction of the value of science communication through art installations.

4 Survey and Gender-Swapped Stories

4.1 Survey Motivation

For the purposes of our multimodal installation, we decided to collect testimonials about gender bias in the workplace. The aim of the survey was twofold, to gather qualitative data on the experiences of women in the STEM fields in order to understand the patterns that emerge, and to use the gender-swapped version of the stories as part of the installation in order to explore its impact.

There has been a growing body of literature on the underrepresentation of women in the STEM fields, but few focus on the gendered experiences of studying or working in the STEM fields, and how the engineering culture affects women's occupational decision-making. Often described as "Dude-Culture" or "Bro-Culture", it is traditionally male-dominated and hence male-oriented [9, 10].

The goal of this survey is to enrich that latter body of literature, illuminating the subtler aspects of gender bias, and using those stories as part of an artistic installation. We were interested not only in illustrating different experiences of gender bias in the workplace, but also in understanding more about how these biases have shaped women's behavior in the professional world, and more specifically exploring the phenomena of impostor syndrome and self-exclusion. Impostor phenomenon or "impostorism" refers to the experience of high-achieving individuals (particularly women) who, despite being successful, attribute their accomplishments to luck, and fear being exposed as frauds [11]. By the term self-exclusion, we are referring to the behavior of women opting out of certain fields or situations because they feel as if they don't "*fit in*". Considering that both self-efficacy and a sense of belonging are crucial factors in retaining women in STEM careers, relating to career confidence and higher levels of persistence and optimism [12], our theorizing is that if impostor syndrome is experienced as low self-efficacy, self-exclusion can be observed when the sense of belonging is undermined.

4.2 Research Methodology

The data collection consisted of an online questionnaire. The analysis of the questions as well as the gender-swapping of the testimonials was performed using Python 3.9 in JupyterLab.

Data Collection. The questionnaire was shared online in October 2022, asking for women working in the STEM fields to recount their experiences. It consisted of three demographic questions (q1: *Age Range*, q2: *Area of Work/Research*, q3: *Country of Residence*), followed by two open-text questions. The first open-text question (q4) was about gender bias and professional life and was phrased as follows:

> "*Have you ever experienced or witnessed discrimination in your professional life related to the fact that you are a woman? Can you please give at least one example? It can include inappropriate comments or gestures, sexual harassment, employment policies (regarding hiring, salary, promotions, training), etc.*"

The second open-text question (q5) was related to Impostor Syndrome and Self-exclusion, and was asking:

> "*As a woman, have you ever felt like an impostor and/or self-excluded yourself from a situation because you thought you didn't belong to the group, you weren't competent enough, or you just wanted to avoid discrimination or problems in the future? Can you please give at least one example?*"

Survey Data Analysis. We received 142 responses in total from 13 countries in Europe. The age range distribution of the respondents was as follows: 18–24 (26.6%), 25–34 (55.2%), 35–44 (14%), and 45–64 (4.2%). Responses were analyzed according to the qualitative content analysis [13]. The areas of work and research were grouped into the following categories: STEM (N = 68), Non-STEM (N = 48), Non-STEM-male-dominated (N = 11), and Uncategorized (N = 15). We decided to create the Non-STEM-male-dominated category as it offered valuable qualitative data regarding the experiences in those fields that were very similar to the STEM ones. Those stories, although presented in the final exhibition, can be omitted for the purposes of the current study in order to focus on STEM experiences. STEM included respondents from the fields of Engineering (N = 17), Science (N = 22), Technology (N = 8), Finance (N = 17), and Maritime (N = 4). Non-STEM-male-dominated categories included respondents from Law (N = 7) and Culinary Industry (N = 4). Respondents who didn't provide enough information (e.g. responded as "*Student*" or "*Private Sector*") and their field could not be inferred from their open-text questions were coded in the Uncategorized class.

Responses were further labeled depending on their answers regarding bias. Out of the 142 respondents, 124 had experienced some form of gender bias in their professional life, amounting to 87% of the total sample. When Non-STEM and Uncategorized respondents were removed from the study, this percentage rose to 92%. Respondents who answered they hadn't experienced gender bias in the workplace or did not provide any further information regarding their experience were subsequently dropped from the sample, resulting in a final sample of 71 respondents. The results of the analysis of their answers are described in the section below.

4.3 Survey Findings

Examining the stories about gender bias and professional life, we have discovered a lot of common patterns between the experiences shared by the respondents. These patterns are also relevant and seem to echo the findings of previous research on the subject [14]. Data were segmented and patterned by a category scheme deductively determined [15].

At least 12 respondents describe "*being stuck*" with the easy or administrative tasks at work, being expected to run the office errands, and being bypassed for promotions. Also, 12 respondents mentioned having heard the phrases "*You are too sweet/beautiful for* X" or "X *is not for young girls*", in a professional setting, where X was their field of study or work. At least 10 respondents reported being discouraged by their own professors ("*it's not for women*", "*you don't belong here*", "*don't try*", "*girls stop gossiping to let the men concentrate*", "*you are not technical enough*", "*you don't need to know the subject, as you are studying engineering only to find husbands*"). Respondents also mentioned having to tolerate inappropriate conversations and a "Bro-culture" environment (11 respondents), comments on appearance (8 respondents), and being called with diminutive names (5 respondents).

Another two very popular scenarios of discriminatory behavior that the testimonials showcased can be described as the following: In the first one, male line managers or colleagues avoid addressing speech to the respondent and their proposals are ignored, but when the same proposals are made by other male colleagues they are being praised (7 respondents). In the second scenario, clients or other stakeholders outside the team are doubting the skills or the seniority of the person and are asking for the male colleague or the manager, even after being told that they are the manager or that the male colleague is someone unrelated to the field of expertise needed for the project (7 respondents). Some of the respondents had received inappropriate gestures or touch (7 respondents) or had experienced sexual harassment (2 respondents).

Finally, some other patterns that emerge were related to being asked about marital status or future pregnancy plans at interviews (6 respondents), people implying a sexual relationship with a professor or manager if high grades or promotions were achieved (4 respondents), being underpaid with regards to male colleagues of the same level (3 respondents), and being perceived by people outside the organization as assistants instead of equal stakeholders (3 respondents).

Regarding Impostor Syndrome and self-exclusion, the analysis also revealed some indicative trends, with almost 1 in 3 respondents having experienced one of the two.

Stories of self-exclusion provide us with a very insightful understanding of gender discrimination in male-dominated fields and its effect. First of all, respondents described family and school discouraging them from pursuing a career in those fields and *'making them feel that it's not for them and that they would never fit in or be good enough.'* Some of the respondents persisted and followed their aspirations while others report that this affected their choice of career. In the workplace, a common pattern of behavior observed was avoiding speaking in meetings or leaving the lead to male colleagues as they would be taken more seriously by external stakeholders. A very characteristic testimonial was the following:

> *"Sometimes I know I am right about something and I know my field, but male clients and male colleagues don't take me seriously, question my proposals and think they know better. So, sometimes I stop trying to impress or convince them and just quietly step out of the situation or let them proceed as they want ".*

In addition, some of the respondents answered that they chose not to participate in specific projects or groups because there was a sexist culture, they felt left out of conversations as the male colleagues appeared to "*bond better*" with male supervisors, were extra reserved in conferences not to come across as flirty, or they avoided publishing and going to conferences because their supervisor had expressed sexual interest in them.

Finally, testimonials of impostor syndrome describe feeling not good enough, thinking that male colleagues are smarter and more efficient, having to work harder than their male colleagues in order to prove their worth and be considered as equal members of the team, and hesitating to apply for promotions.

4.4 Gender Swapping and the Installation

Gender in the testimonials was swapped algorithmically and the gender-swapped version of the stories was projected on a plain black background as part of the installation (Fig. 3). We argue that this change, although very simple, had a powerful effect on the visitor. During the exhibition, people reading these stories commented feeling surprised and wondering if the stories were real. If there is no gender bias in the workplace and people have the same opportunities, why did these stories suddenly sound fictional and absurd, and why are we so used to expecting a woman to narrate these kinds of incidents? Gender swapping can be transgressive by emphasizing social conventions that shape gender construction [16]. Examples of gender-swapped stories included the following:

> *"A supervising physician had told me that Greece is still behind in accepting men as surgeons and that I am a handsome boy, and it would be such a pity if no patients came to me for surgery and I won't have the money to buy new bags."*

"I'm an environmental engineer and although I want to participate in the progress meetings of projects, just to get informed, I never ask because I believe I'm a young man who doesn't belong there."

"My boss expects me to organize all the shopping for the office because I am a man so I am better at it."

"The appointed professor chose me to work with a specific patient. However, the female practitioners commented that I have been chosen because I am handsome and blonde. And kind of started spreading around to other colleagues that I might have slept with the professor."

"A lot of times I find myself giving the lead in meetings to women since I consider that they would be accepted more by the stakeholders."

Similar approaches have been followed in gender-swapped fairy tales [17] and gender-swapped movie reboots [18]. However, these attempts are mostly focused on having women relive men's stories [19], while what we wanted to achieve is the opposite: make the male visitors empathize with the women's experiences in the workplace, understand the subtle aspects of everyday sexism and all the discouragement women in the STEM fields have to fight against, starting from school and family to university and the workplace.

Fig. 3. Gender-swapped stories exhibit, Athens, November 2022

4.5 Discussion and Future Research

While things have changed significantly for young professional women, societal perceptions of engineering as masculine deter women from entering the profession and as a result, the stereotype is reinforced [14]. With respect to equal opportunities for women in non-traditional fields, the discourse says both "*engineering is man's work*" and "*women can be engineers, too*". In order to understand the experiences of these women, we need to understand more about how the dominant discourse constructs this relationship and the subject positions available to women within it [20]. Currently, the partnership of men and women in engineering as lived in the experiences of many women engineering students continues to be asymmetrical and hierarchical [10].

The findings from this small study are offered as a contribution to the body of literature focusing on women's experiences in male-dominated fields, opening a discussion around the topic of self-exclusion of women in STEM fields, and exploring the effect of gender-swapped stories as part of an art installation.

In the future, we would like to continue and expand our survey, gather responses from more countries, and restructure the questionnaire to help the exploratory analysis of the data. An idea for expansion would be to ask respondents who answered they haven't experienced bias or impostor syndrome to elaborate on the reasons why. This could provide helpful information about the different strategies women apply when adjusting to the male-dominated educational and professional fields [15]. Finally, regarding the presentation of the gender-swapped stories as part of an installation, we would like to experiment with using a gender-neutral AI voice to narrate the stories in conjunction with the text.

5 Text-To-Image Generation

5.1 Bias in Text-To-Image Generation

Text to image generators are multimodal transformer or diffusion models which rely on language-text data pairs acquired from world wide web for the purposes of generating realistic images of high quality. The input to these models consists of textual prompts which are fed into the model in order to produce images. These models can perform tasks such as image editing, 3D visualization, adding contextual details, combining concepts (compositionality), and mimicking specific art styles. Evaluation can be applied by assessing the accuracy of text-to-image alignment or by judging the quality of the generated images. However, this only provides a limited perspective on the functionality of these models. Text-to-image models have a tendency to replicate biases present in their training data. Recent studies have explored biases in multimodal models by examining the relationship between professions, gender, and race [21] and further try to encapsulate this aspect into the evaluation process [22].

Bias are attributed either to (i) language models which have been found to propagate gender bias via investigating their static [23, 24], or contextualized word embeddings such as BERT [25], and also to ii) image captioning [26]. Recent efforts have aimed to address the challenges coming from bias in the data, and by adopting techniques for "debiasing" [27]. These methods involve learning new word/embedding representations for specific biased concepts. However, the root of the cause still remains unclear, while it is uncertain whether it arises from the training data, the model architecture or its parameters. Moreover, the introduction of new metrics for measuring the diversity of generated images has been crucial for both reducing the bias and promoting fairness in the system's outputs [28].

5.2 Gender Targeted Prompts

The linguistic stimuli are designed to highlight careers in STEM or high-status occupations (e.g. doctor, lawyer). Additionally, we have considered gender representation statistics for the selected occupations, drawing information from Eurostat statistics [29]. Our experiment involves two steps: (i) text generation and (ii) text-to-image generation. In the first step, we used "natural language instruction" via the OPENAI model *text-davinci-edit-001* to semi-automatically generate 40 sentences which contain the selected professions. We used an example sentence, such as **"The [profession]** examined the patient. Then **[pronoun]**.." as input for the model, and asked it to generate similar sentences by replacing the [profession] and the [location] and also by completing the sentence. The purpose of this sentence structure was to highlight gender marking by establishing a coreference relation between the noun in the first clause and the pronoun in the second. Most English nouns do not inherently denote gender, such as the word "doctor". Therefore, by using this specific sentence structure, we aimed to "force" the gender marking in our prompts.

Fig. 4. Example of generated images with DALLE-2 for the conditions: (1) gender-neutral, (2) gender-marked.

In the next step, namely for the text-to-image generation we used two types of prompts: (i) the profession itself (i.e., doctor), (ii) the combination of two clauses which are connected via coreference. The different types of prompts represent two conditions, namely "gender-neutral" and "gender-marked". Therefore, the result consists of a prompt pair: (1a) "Doctor" and (1b) "The doctor examined the patient. Then she wrote a prescription". We utilized DALLE-2 for text-to-image generation, which is a 12-billion parameter version of GPT-3. The model is capable of generating images based on text descriptions [30]. For each prompt, we generated four sample images, as shown in Fig. 4.

In conclusion, the documentation of DALLE-2 [31] highlights a bias in the model towards individuals who appear white or male, and our findings support this observation. Our study found that even a "gender-neutral" prompt generated images that were biased towards men. In addition, in the "gendered-marked" condition, the model frequently produced images depicting male as the main subjects (see Fig. 4. 2a). Furthermore, in cases where the system correctly identified a female person, she was mostly represented as Asian (see Fig. 4. 2b). These results align with previous studies, such as the one conducted in [24], which looked at contextual embeddings models and found evidence of gender bias towards certain professions in the context of coreference resolution.

Language models play a critical role in many AI applications and it is important to address the issue of bias propagation in these systems. By considering additional factors such as demographic information and measurements of underrepresentation, we can contribute towards creating fairer and more accurate language models. However, it's important to remember that language is a social phenomenon that carries the views of its speakers, making it imperative to take a holistic approach to address these issues.

6 Image Generation

6.1 Technology and Cultural Impact

In his essay "AI aesthetics" [32], Lev Manovich tries to describe the connection between AI technology and aesthetics and the huge impact technology has on our perception.

While algorithms have been employed in artistic creation by artists since the 1960s, today industrial-scale "cultural AI" is built into devices and services used by billions of people. Instead of being an instrument of a single artistic imagination, AI has become a mechanism for influencing the imaginations of billions. Gathered and aggregated data about the cultural behaviors of multitudes is used to model our "aesthetic self," predicting our future aesthetic decisions and likes – and potentially guiding us towards choices preferred by the majority [32].

One of the most intriguing problems that machine learning is dealing with is the generation of photorealistic portrait images of humans or animals with high precision. While trying to solve this problem, mathematicians and programmers have developed and refined several machine-learning models. From the early 2000s until now the evolution of the quality in terms of both resolution and the realistic outcome has been widely progressing. These models are used in different aspects of HCI in correlation with aesthetics, such as to enhance beauty in face filters, in software for photo and video editing, or to suggest similar content.

The fascination with this technological process of generating images with machine learning and neural networks comes from the fact that behind the realistic photo portrait that is generated (that nowadays cannot be distinguished from a "real" photography of a person neither by a human being or a computer), lays an enormous amount of computational power, equations and model training, but also a brilliant concept developed by large groups of people. The problem of the simulacrum as formulated by Baudriard [33] is becoming even more popular and valid nowadays. But where the "black box" problem appears is that the majority of people who are influenced by generated or enhanced images, use them or even produce them without knowing how the process works and of what are the hidden sides of model training - like scraping images from the internet that are personal or have rights.

6.2 Representation of the Topic

The image generation section of the multimodal installation consists of a four-minute-long animation. Instead of trying to produce perfect and realistic images, the results shown in the animation are from an undertrained model. In this manner, we are trying to "open the black box" in front of the audience, showing the process of image generation and how the algorithm is trying to produce the "correct" output. The output images were produced with the StyleGAN2 with adaptive discriminator augmentation (ADA) model [34] trained on a data set consisting of more than 500 free magazine covers and mockups. Surprisingly, the output created had more than interesting aesthetical qualities resembling that of abstract and expressionist art (Fig. 5). The creativity of "the mistake" was meant to provoke a better resemblance to the "human" artistic process, and in this manner, make the computational process more comprehensible to the audience. It exposes the beautiful idea that the computer also walks through thousands of "failed" attempts in order to create the "perfect image".

Fig. 5. Example of generated images with StyleGAN 2 - ADA Pytorch, trained on a set of free images of magazine covers.

7 Facial Recognition

7.1 Algorithmic Facial Recognition

The notion of facial recognition describes the scientific field that investigates how biological systems capture the face and how computational systems imitate them. For this purpose, biological systems deploy optical sensors of different kinds, designed by nature to fit to the environment in which the carrier lives. Similarly, computational systems use various mechanically manufactured optical devices or sensors to capture and process persons in the best possible way [35]. A specific kind of facial recognition is the biometric or algorithmic one, which by applying AI-generated tools aims to automate extraction, digitalization, and analysis through a comparison of the spatial and geometric distribution of the facial characteristics, mainly for identification purposes [36].

Algorithmic facial recognition systems have vastly expanded, by escaping the narrow premises of law enforcement and impregnating every part and parcel of everyday life – from economy, to health, education, and entertainment. Irrespective of the position taken by someone with regard to the deployment and extensive use of new technologies (whether it would be a more deterministic or a more conservative one), the issues that arise, first and foremost in terms of ethics and, secondarily, at a societal level need to be studied and addressed in detail. The threat to certain fundamental rights caused by biases integrated into AI coexists along with the threath to human integrity, diversity and, in the very end, democracy.

7.2 Relevant Research and Problem Statement

While conducting research in the field of biases in AI, one would get in touch with the work of Joy Buolamwini, a MIT researcher and the founder of the Algorithmic Justice League, an organisation that combines art and research to raise awareness of the social implications and possible risks of AI applications. Together with Timnit Gebru, they tested three AI facial recognition algorithms that classified each face according to gender; namely the ones offered by Microsoft, IBM and Face++ in order to check whether those algorithms would be able to attribute the correct gender to the inserted face images. For this purpose, they tried to create a reliable and balanced dataset input, which unfortunately proved not to be enough. Those systems appeared to be more successful in recognizing white males, whereas the highest error rate in recognition was observed in women with black skin colour [37]. It is worth mentioning that the applications deployed for the experiment constituted a part of the commercial use of AI, accessible to the general public and developed by big tech companies.

The difficulty of AI facial recognition algorithms to recognize female faces is, from a technological perspective, undoubtedly, the outcome of the use of less representative training data in what concerns gender. However, the sociological one should be also taken into consideration, since those systems are developed by humans and aim to serve their needs. The misrepresentation of women in the public sphere, from which data are often data extracted, or the misconceptions and prejudice that still exist in our societies are transferred and incorporated in the technological products and, in many cases, further reproduced by them. This process creates a vicious circle, menacing gender equality and the promise of a trustworthy, impartial and ethical AI.

7.3 Methodology

One of the goals of our art installation was to point out existing biases in AI applications, especially ones used by big audiences that are available on a translational level and easily accessible. This would allow us to raise awareness by highlighting how AI-generated products that appear harmless can entail dangers that we, as consumers, have not noticed or even considered. The concept of a tangible booklet as one stop in the labyrinth route was gradually developed. Thus, this would not be an ordinary book, rather a story about faces, female ones. Each and every face in it belongs to a woman who has been active in her professional life in the IT and AI sector; pioneers, entrepreneurs, leaders, aspiring figures in their field of expertise, to whom AI facial recognition algorithms seem to attribute specific characteristics and overlook their bright professional background. For them, they are either good or bad looking human beings and in most of the cases sensitive, vulnerable ones with low self-esteem (Fig. 6).

Fig. 6. Booklet content.

In order to demonstrate how AI can become prejudicial towards women, two applications were used: Face reader scanner-analyser and Golden Ratio Face - Face Shape. The first one claims to be able to reveal some elements of one's personality by reading their facial characteristics, and is used by more than 50k users. The second one scores their face according to its own (and unclear) beauty standards, and characterizes them either as ugly or as beautiful, and has been downloaded by more that 1M users. The results of this experiment were showcased in the contents of the book. The visitors of the exhibition had the chance to test the applications themselves, become part of this experiment, elaborate upon their results, their feelings and thoughts, and leave their feedback at the end of the book, continuing and reviving the already-existing narrative.

7.4 Conclusions and Thoughts

The purpose of the book was irrelevant to physical appearance, beauty, or personality traits. The experiment carried out was not subject to further statistical analysis, but solely targeted at raising awareness, bringing up the issue of facial recognition and generally the stance of AI towards gender issues, being part of the larger image and message that our exhibition tried to convey. Nevertheless, some conclusions could be drawn that would in the long run assist relevant research or art generation, but also raise multidisciplinary debates on the topic of AI gender biases.

Male faces were more easily detected and tended to receive a better beauty score compared to the female ones, where the score gaps would be bigger. In addition, more women compared to men were characterized as sensitive and with low self-esteem, while men appeared more sportive and determined. Sensitivity as a personality trait has been historically related to women, and leadership was seen as a male feature. After numerous tests using women's and men's facial images while drafting the booklet and during the exhibition, it has become clear to us that some stereotypes that humans have been carrying for centuries are transferred into the algorithms they themselves create. Unfortunately, no matter how far women have come, AI facial recognition tends to be biased against them.

Is there a way out? Regarding facial recognition, many suggestions have made their appearance. Lately, efforts have taken place with GDPR [38] or the proposed AI Act [39] to set up a strict, prohibitive framework; at least within Europe, accompanied by ethical guidance. A number of further preventive and repressive measures have been proposed, such as the establishment of oversight and monitoring, judicial review and accountability mechanisms, with emphasis given to public debate and the principle of proportionality, along with the imposition of safeguards and good practices, giving priority to educative and art initiatives, through which messages can be conveyed more easily and to a larger number of people. Facial recognition could be a valuable tool if used with prudence and free from biases and misconceptions.

8 Conclusion

Gender bias in technology and especially AI is seen as a burning issue. Furthermore, it is one without a concrete answer, since it constitutes an ethical matter that will continue to appear and escalate following different technological developments. The way we choose to deal with it and the methods we apply to empower larger groups of users to gain more knowledge and make decisions regarding this topic is crucial for the future of our society. Addressing it with "Blacbox AI", our interactive multimodal art installation, aimed to put visitors in a situation where, by receiving information on the topic of gender bias, they discover that the navigation through the maze starts to get easier and that it gradually becomes more transparent, accessible to all, as AI and technology should be in the first place.

After gathering feedback and impressions from the exhibition, we aim to develop our installation further. Our main goal is to present it again to the public as part of an art exhibition or a specialized event. We plan to continue exploring the topic with more interventions in different venues, in order to raise the voices of women in the AI field, creating a space for dialogue among experts, artists, decision makers, and the general public, as well as having an impact on our local communities.

The multiple artistic and scientific outcomes of this work can be a basis for rethinking how we approach the design of novel artificial intelligence applications. Our goal with this installation was to change the paradigm when developing AI tools, to start with inclusivity by design, and not just as mitigating the consequences of already biased applications. Each exhibit and the underlying research bring to life one facet of this subject of gender bias in AI, and we hope that it could be perceived as a starting point for questioning hard-wired notions and stereotypes about the appropriate place of women as users, but also as creators and developers of new technologies.

Acknowledgments. The authors gratefully acknowledge Goethe Institut for funding the BlackboxAI installation developed as part of the 2022 edition of the EthicAI=LAB project. In particular, we would like to express our thanks to our mentors Mihaela Constantinescu, Marinos Koutsomichalis, and Fatih Sinan Esen for their expert guidance and encouragement during the development of this work.

References

1. Latour, B.: Science in Action – How to Follow Scientists & Engineers Through Society, Harvard University Press (1988)
2. Mobile cellular subscriptions and Individuals using the internet. World Bank. https://data.worldbank.org/indicator/IT.CEL.SETS. Accessed 2 May 2023
3. de Fine Licht, K., de Fine Licht, J.: Artificial intelligence, transparency, and public decision-making. AI Soc. **35**(4), 917–926 (2020). https://doi.org/10.1007/s00146-020-00960-w
4. Hunkenschroer, A.L., Luetge, C.: Ethics of AI-enabled recruiting and selection: a review and research agenda. J. Bus. Ethics **178**, 977–1007 (2022)
5. Dastin, J.: Amazon scraps secret AI recruiting tool that showed bias against women. Reuters, San Francisco (2018). https://www.reuters.com/article/us-amazon-com-jobs- automation-insight-idUSKCN1MK08G. Accessed 2 Sept 2023
6. The Global Gender Gap Report. World Economic Forum, Switzerland (2018). https://www3.weforum.org/docs/WEF_GGGR_2018.pdf. Accessed 2 Sept 2023
7. The gender pay gap situation in the EU. https://ec.europa.eu/info/policies/justice-and-fundamental-rights/gender-equality/equal-pay/gender-pay-gap-situation-eu_en. Accessed 2 Sept 2023
8. Vainionppa, F., Kinnula, M., Iivari, N., Molin-Juustila, T.: Girls in IT: intentionally self-excluded or products of high school as a site of exclusion? Internet Res. **31**(3), 846–870 (2021)
9. Miller, R.A., Vaccaro, A., Kimball, E.W., Forester, R.: "It's dude culture": Students with minoritized identities of sexuality and/or gender navigating STEM majors. J. Diver. High. Educ. **14**(3), 340–352 (2021)
10. Stonyer, H.: Making engineering students - making women: the discursive context of engineering education. Int. J. Eng. Educ. **18**(4), 392–399 (2002)
11. Tao, K.W., Gloria, A.M.: Should I Stay or Should I Go? The role of Impostorism in STEM persistence. Psychol. Women Q. **43**(2), 151–216 (2019)
12. Clark, S.L., Dyar, C., Inman, E.M., et al.: Women's career confidence in a fixed, sexist STEM environment. Int. J. STEM Educ. **8**, 56 (2021)
13. Mayring, P.: Qualitative content analysis. forum qualitative sozialforschung/forum: Qual. Soc. Res. **1**(2) (2000)
14. Phipps, A.: Engineering women: the 'gendering' of professional identities. Int. J. Eng. Educ. **18**(4), 409–414 (2002)
15. Makarova, E., Aeschlimann, B., Herzog, W.: Why is the pipeline leaking? Experiences of young women in STEM vocational education and training and their adjustment strategies. Empir. Res. Vocation. Educ. Train. **8**(1), 1–18 (2016). https://doi.org/10.1186/s40461-016-0027-y

16. Lam, C.: Female friendships on film: understanding homosocial interaction in gender swapped films. In: The International Encyclopedia of Gender, Media, and Communication, pp. 1–5 (2020)
17. Williams, Z.: Gender Swapped Fairy Tales review – 'Handsome and the Beast' and the ugly brothers. The Guardian (2020). https://www.theguardian.com/books/2020/oct/28/gender-swapped-fairy-tales-review-handsome-and-the-beast-and-the-ugly-brothers. Accessed 2 Oct 2023
18. Kiffe, J.J.: Gender-Swapped Remakes: Writing a Screenplay to Promote Realistic and Diverse Representation in Female-Centric Films. Portland State University (2020)
19. Hess, A.: The trouble with Hollywood's gender flips, New York Times. https://www.nytimes.com/2018/06/12/movies/oceans-8-gender-swap.html. Accessed 2 Oct 2023
20. Henwood, F.: Engineering difference: discourses on gender, sexuality and work in a college of technology. Gend. Educ. **10**(1), 35–49 (1998)
21. Ross, C., Katz, B., Barbu, A.: Measuring social biases in grounded vision and language embeddings. In: Proceedings of the 2021 Conference of the North American Chapter of the Association for Computational Linguistics: Human Language Technologies, pp. 998–1008 (2021)
22. Cho, J., Zala, A., Bansal, M.: Dall-eval: Probing the reasoning skills and social biases of text-to-image generative transformers. arXiv preprint arXiv:2202.04053 (2022)
23. Caliskan, A., Bryson, J.J., Narayanan, A.: Semantics derived automatically from language corpora contain human-like biases. Science **356**(6334), 183–186 (2017)
24. Zhao, J., Wang, T., Yatskar, M., Ordonez, V., Chang, K.-W.: Gender bias in coreference resolution: Evaluation and debiasing methods. In: Proceedings of the 2018 Conference of the North American Chapter of the Association for Computational Linguistics: Human Language Technologies, vol. 2, pp.15–20. New Orleans, Louisiana (2018)
25. Zhao, J., et al.: Gender bias in contextualized word embeddings. NAACL (2019)
26. Hirota, Y., Nakashima, Y., Garcia, N.: Quantifying societal bias amplification in image captioning. In: 2022 IEEE/CVF Conference on Computer Vision and Pattern Recognition (CVPR), pp. 13440–13449. New Orleans, LA, USA (2022)
27. Gal, R., et al.: An Image is Worth One Word: Personalizing Text-to-Image Generation using Textual Inversion (2022)
28. Bansal, H., Yin, D., Monajatipoor, M., Chang, K-W: how well can text-to-image generative models understand ethical natural language interventions?. In: Proceedings of the 2022 Conference on Empirical Methods in Natural Language Processing, pp. 1358–1370. Abu Dhabi, United Arab Emirates (2022)
29. Human resources in science and technology. Eurostat. https://ec.europa.eu/eurostat/statistics-explained/index.php?title=Human_resources_in_science_and_technology& oldid=395960. Accessed 10 Feb2023
30. Ramesh, A., et al.: Zero-shot text-to-image generation. In: International Conference on Machine Learning, pp. 8821–8831. PMLR (2021)
31. Mishkin, P., Ahmad, L., Brundage, M., Krueger, G., Sastry, G.: DALL· E 2 Preview - Risks and Limitations (2022) https://github.com/openai/dalle-2preview/blob/main/system-card.md. Accessed 9 Feb 2023
32. Manovich, L.: AI Aesthetics. Strelka press (2018)
33. Baudrillard, J.: Simulacra and simulations (1981). In: Crime and Media, pp. 69–85. Routledge (2019)
34. Karras, T., Laine, S., Aittala, M., Hellsten, J., Lehtinen, J., Aila, T.: Analyzing and improving the image quality of stylegan. In: Proceedings of the IEEE/CVF Conference on Computer Vision and Pattern Recognition, pp. 8110–8119 (2020)
35. Martinez, A.M.: Face recognition, Overview. In: Jain, S. L. (ed) Encyclopedia of Biometrics. Springer, Boston, MA (2009)

36. Smith, M., Miller, S.: The ethical application of biometric facial recognition technology. AI Soc. , 1–9 (2021). https://doi.org/10.1007/s00146-021-01199-9
37. Buolamwini, J., Gebru, T.: Gender shades: intersectional accuracy disparities in commercial gender classification. In: Proceedings of the 1st Conference on Fairness, Accountability and Transparency, PMLR 81, pp. 77–91 (2018)
38. Regulation (EU) 2016/679 of the European Parliament and of the Council of 27 April 2016 on the protection of natural persons with regard to the processing of personal data and on the free movement of such data, and repealing Directive 95/46/EC (General Data Protection Regulation) (Text with EEA relevance). OJ L 119, 4.5.2016, pp. 1–88
39. Proposal for a regulation of the European Parliament and of the Council laying down harmonized rules on artificial intelligence (artificial intelligence act) and amending certain union legislative acts. COM/2021/206 final

Overcoming the Fragmentation: A Proposal of Model Ontology, Architecture System and Web-Based Implementation for Planning the Persons with Disability's Life Project

Mabel Giraldo(✉), Fabio Sacchi, and Serenella Besio

University of Bergamo, Bergamo, Italy
mabel.giraldo@unibg.it

Abstract. In recent decades important changes in the disability area occurred, both at regulatory-political and socio-cultural level, urging to rethink the Life Project of persons with disabilities (PwD) from a lifelong and life wide perspective. From the Nineties, in Italy this change has been introduced by a policy agenda introducing the construct of individual Life Project as a crucial mean to guarantee rights and quality of life aimed at fully implementing the principle of social inclusion. However, this evolution continues to clash with standard and fragmented solutions that does not respond to the need of an individualized, emancipatory, rights-based planning. The paper presents a model of PwD' Life Project developed by the researchers in Special Education of University of Bergamo (UNIBG) as a result of the "Training Program on Life Project related to the *Dopo di Noi*" promoted in collaboration with Agenzia Tutela Salute (ATS) of Bergamo. Adopting a participatory design approach, UNIBG researchers follow a three steps model: 1) defining the conceptual framework (ontology) with respect to disability, the rights of the PwD and the load-bearing features and steps characterizing the individual Life Project planning; 2) organizing the overall architecture of the system; 3) designing a low-fidelity prototype. The current state of the art of the UNIBG research contributes to inform PwD's Life Project design process and preliminary results highlight the overall validity of the model ontology and the proposed architecture. As next research step, the prototype will be discussed with some selected stakeholders participating in ATS-UNIBG "Training Program" to collect their feedback and proceed with the re-design phase.

Keywords: Life Project · Disability · Low-fidelity Prototyping

The contribution was conceived, designed, and realized by all authors. Mabel Giraldo wrote §1, Fabio Sacchi wrote §3 and both authors wrote §2 and §4. Serenella Besio participated in the research design framework and in the conception of UNIBG Life Project model ontology and related architecture and first prototype.

M. Antona and C. Stephanidis (Eds.): HCII 2023, LNCS 14020, pp. 47–60, 2023.
https://doi.org/10.1007/978-3-031-35681-0_3

1 Background

1.1 A Life Project for Persons with Disabilities: Criticalities and Benefits of Its Web-Based Implementation

In recent decades a change in considering disability has happened, at regulatory-political and socio-cultural level urging to rethink the Life Project of persons with disabilities (PwD) from a lifelong [1] and life wide perspective [2].

In Italy this evolution was launched by Law n. 104/1992 which established the right to education, instruction, and professional training of the PwD (art. 3) and, for the first time, give to the school and social inclusion process a unitary global legislative framework. Responding to this mandate, further dedicated policies were approved to support the Life Project of the persons with disabilities. To this regard, Law n. 328/2000, *Legge quadro per la realizzazione del sistema integrato di interventi e servizi sociali*, introduced in the Italian regulatory system the "Individual Project": a document prepared for each person with disabilities to create personalized paths in which the different interventions are coordinated in order to respond adequately to the needs and aspirations of the beneficiary. Over the years, the construct of Life Project became even more crucial to guarantee rights and quality of life aimed at fully implementing the principle of social inclusion. According to the development of new cultural and epistemological perspectives promoting person-centered empowering approaches (e.g., *United Nations Convention on the Rights of Persons with Disabilities*), Life Project represents the core of the Law n. 112/2016, n. 112, *Disposizioni in materia di assistenza in favore delle persone con disabilità grave prive del sostegno familiar*. Among its principles, the law recognized the importance and the role of individualized paths to promote the well-being, full social inclusion and autonomy of PwD.

However, the value of this regulatory framework continues to clash with standard and fragmented solutions not responding to the need of an individualized, emancipatory, rights-based planning. Precisely in relation to this, the literature highlighted several shortcomings.

- The lack of a unique and shared life-long planning model, approach and tools used at all institutional levels to consider the different PwD's contexts/activities and to coordinate them coherently within the individual's Life Project [3].
- The need to promote individualized planning that looks at the PwD within his/her contexts and across different life stages: i) considering the specific needs, ii) coherently optimizing the activities/interventions by the different stakeholders involved and iii) ensuring continuity in terms of transferring knowledge/experience [4], especially at the crossroad of life transition moments.
- Poor connection between stakeholders/institutions/caregivers involved to support PwD's inclusion across the different life stages and contexts [5], especially in the transition to adulthood [6] which implies a reconfiguration of support systems/services and welfare protections [7].
- Family members/caregiver and PwD are often left alone at the mercy of complex decisions and choices taken by the different social, education, school and healthcare stakeholders leading to risk of undesirable outcomes, uncertainty [8], instead of

mutual respecting for their skills and knowledge, and shared planning and decision making [9].

- A general inconsiderateness of the right of the PwD to actively contribute and participate in all the different Life Project design phases by gathering his/her aspirations, desires, needs, strengths and limitations [10]: in fact, in most cases Life Project design occurs about the individual and not with the individual [11] recognizing his/her formal right to participate, but not making him/her protagonists and co-agents of the overall process.

Addressing these challenges implies to:

- promote individualized Life Project planning considering the PwD within the plurality of contexts and across the different life stages in order to optimize and integrate multidisciplinary interventions and ensure continuity [3, 4];
- create a local support network including all the different stakeholders involved, over time, in the Pwd's Life Project design process and hypothesize a new tool allowing them sharing/communicating data/documents and make information easily and quickly accessible, updated in real time and usable not only by technicians, but families and PwD themselves (e.g., web-based platform, database, etc.) [12];
- enhance family members/caregivers' perspectives and, in particular, guarantee the protagonism of the PwD in his/her own Life Project design phases [6, 13];
- adopt a unique, longitudinal, participatory, and global methodological and theoretical model in order to recognize the multidimensional aspects characterizing PwD's life stages/contexts [4].

Several studies try to address these shortcomings and challenges and, given the current availability of technology, the future of web-based Life Project development is very promising and its benefits are evident in the literature [14]. First, such a solution gives the opportunity to organize and display several pieces of information in a unique folder/database for presenting, archiving, and transferring. This allows to: i) share data, in synchronized/asynchronized mode, across institutions/stakeholders using more compact and flexible storage and portability options [15]; ii) make information easily/quickly accessible, updated in real time by all the stakeholders involved in the life planning process [16]; iii) increase the opportunities to directly involve PwD and family members/caregivers [17].

According to this latter point, PwD' involvement might support them to develop and fully display their self-determination and have an active role throughout the design process [18], and, at the same time, it calls the developers to put careful attention to the issues of accessibility/usability [19] for different types of users (with and without disabilities) with various levels of digital skills [17].

The theoretical, methodological, and operational complexity intrinsic to PwD's Life Project and the plurality of actors and contexts involved, requires a web-based design process grabbing the different and specific issues, facets, knowledge, information, skills of all the stakeholders and collecting their perspectives. In this sense, as above mentioned, prototyping (and especially low-fidelity type) represents a key step for our study purpose.

1.2 Prototyping: Methodologies and Evidence from the Literature

Prototyping is a process designed to simulate or perform some functions of the final system to preliminary evaluate its main features, functional modalities and its usability and responsiveness to the requests/needs of the various users involved [20]. It leads to a draft design (prototype) preceding the development of the final design layout. Prototype fidelity is crucial and refers to the different degree to which a model of the system resembles the target/final solutions [21–23].

For this reason, prototypes can be referred to as low (LF) or high fidelity (HF). HF means the prototype is substantially similar to the final product, highly functional and with most of the components developed and integrated [23, 24]. High fidelity prototyping can be used to deliver prototypes to users that are as similar as possible to the finished product or to pinpoint components to test [25].

Conversely, LF provides for limited functions and interactions prototyping efforts. These prototypes are not intended to show in detail how the application operates, but they are constructed to depict concepts, design options, and screen layouts, rather than to model the user interaction with a system. Storyboard presentations and proof-of-concept prototypes fall into this category. In general, LF prototypes demonstrate the general look/interface and provide limited or no functionality [23, 26]. Due to these characteristics, LF prototyping allows developers/users to focus more on design/concepts and make the design process highly accessible to all and, independently of their design skills, they can participate by contributing with their own inputs/insights. According to this, this kind of prototype is most suitable to participatory design approach or codesign research and in the case of different types of end users [27].

Building from this foundation, this paper presents the model ontology of the PwD' Life Project, its related system architecture and the LF prototype developed by the researchers in Special Education of University of Bergamo (UNIBG) as a result of the "Training Program on Life Project related to the After Us" promoted in collaboration with Agenzia Tutela Salute (ATS). UNIBG Life Project model and its prototype are useful for easily and quickly collecting, editing, consulting, organizing, and sharing information by the stakeholders involved in the PwD's design process, at all institutional levels/contexts across the different age groups.

2 The UNIBG Model of Life Project and Its Prototype

2.1 Research Introduction and Objectives

Agenzia Tutela Salute (ATS) of Bergamo, in compliance with the decree n. XI/3404/2020 of the Lombardy Region (Italy), promotes in 2022 a "Training Program on Life Project related to the *Dopo di Noi*" in collaboration with the researchers in Special Education of the University of Bergamo. The program, carried out from January to June 2022, involved 163 participants, representatives of different institutions of the Bergamo area, involved in promoting and implementing socio-educational, healthcare and welfare services and interventions in the field of inclusion of PwD's; more precisely, there were educators, representatives of family associations and officers of private-public administration in healthcare and social service sectors. By collecting the voices of all the participants, the training course aimed at developing a theoretical and operational model of PwD's Life Project that could be used, over time, at all institutional levels by all the stakeholders engaged across the different age groups and related contexts.

2.2 Methods

Adopting a participatory design approach [28], UNIBG researchers follow a three steps model [12]: 1) defining the conceptual framework (ontology) with respect to disability, the rights of the PwD and the load-bearing features and steps characterizing the individual Life Project planning; 2) organizing the overall architecture of the system; 3) according to AGID Guidelines[1] and Web Content Accessibility Guidelines 2.0[2], designing a prototype in order to setting-up, at a later time, prototype workflow/wireframe and, after co-design sessions, the final web-based implementation.

For the latter prototyping phase, a participatory approach was adopted involving all participants according to an iterative design process (several cycles of conception, prototyping, evaluation, redesign) [23]. Moreover, as the web-based UNIBG Life Project model has a complex ontology and architecture including many features (used at different times to enter different data) and engaging different users (who need ad hoc functions and display options for each kind of user), researchers implement a LF prototype in order to "materialize ideas", make them evident, and, if necessary, to redesign them quickly.

3 Results

The following results have been achieved according to the three steps model and end with the prototyping phase. Workflow and wireframe and the following web-based implementation represent the next research steps to be achieved.

3.1 Model Ontology

Addressing the shortcomings/challenges acknowledged by the literature, the model ontology is based on the following aspects.

1. The adoption of the *International Classification of Functioning, Disability and Health* (ICF) (WHO, 2020[3]) as a descriptive, operative and planning model for disability as it guarantees to: i) account the complexity of the person in his/her life systems and throughout lifespan; ii) consider personal and environmental factors (life contexts, their components, roles, etc.), describing the latter as barriers and facilitators; iii) focus on activity and participation used to describe the person as an active and social being, within the communities to which he/she belongs.

[1] See: https://docs.italia.it/italia/designers-italia/design-linee-guidadocs/it/stabile/doc/prototyping/prototipare-un-servizio.html (retrieved: January 29th, 2023).

[2] See: https://www.w3.org/TR/WCAG20/ (retrieved: January 29th, 2023).

[3] UNIBG researchers decide to adopt ICF 2020 edition as it includes the revision of most of the codes related to ICF-CY (WHO, 2007), covers the entire lifespan.

2. The engagement of PwD, family members and stakeholders involved in the different life contexts/stages/transitions and related Life Project planning.
3. The identification of the different load-bearing features characterizing the individual Life Project across the lifespan and the definition of the "priority domains"[4] and "autonomy goals"[5], specific to different age groups[6].
4. The establishment of a professional figure (case manager) who, in the light of his/her professional skills in the educational/social/disability fields: i) creates and coordinates the stakeholders network; ii) guides and integrates all the Life Project data and planning process; iii) identifies the strategies to guarantee stakeholders participation, especially PwD.

3.2 Architecture

The UNIBG model of Life Project architecture is composed by four distinct and interconnected components.

1. *Initial Analysis Framework*: collecting PwD's priorities in activity/participation by each stakeholder in his/her life contexts, specifying needs, criticality/strength, barriers/facilitators.
2. *Synthesis Framework*: summarizing the priorities in activity/participation comparing the information collected in the previous framework to reach PwD's maximum possible autonomy.
3. *Design Framework*: planning features and steps for the realization of the individual Life Project (objectives, any barriers/facilitators, actions/tasks, stakeholders involved, timing, resources and tools for monitoring/evaluation).
4. *Transition Profile*: at the crossroad of the different age stages, mapping the PwD's developmental profile with reference to the outcomes and autonomy goals (fully/partially) achieved, suggestions for the project planning of the further age stage.

3.3 Prototyping UNIBG Model of Life Project

The model ontology and architecture of the UNIBG Life Project led to design a first LF prototype in order to setting-up, at a later time, prototype workflow/wireframe and, after co-design workshops, the final web-based implementation.

The application (accessible through users' browsers) uses a dynamic server-side development language code and relational database for data storage, with a specific

[4] Adopting ICF terminology, a "domain" is «a practical and meaningful set of related physiological functions, anatomical structures, actions, tasks, or areas of life» (WHO, 2001:33). In the UNIBG model, "priority domain" is a practical and meaningful set of related actions, tasks, or life areas identified as a need or strength. It has been selected within the chapters in which the ICF "Activity and Participation component" is divided according to the concept of priority.

[5] It represents the adaptive behaviors expected for the age group considered. It is not a clinical construct, but an adaptive reference to support Life Project design process aimed at promoting the autonomy of the person with disability. The "autonomy goals" and their intrinsic evolutionary development are extremely important for the construction of the person's life project and are reported, in relation to the "domains" and chronological age group considered.

[6] Age groups have been identified based on the main life steps of the person with disability.

user interface for editing, surfing and filling the four components. The system uses Adobe's ColdFusion technology, while the database is Microsoft's SQL Server. The application is developed in accordance with the HTML 5 standard and according to the W3C recommendations on Cascading Style Sheets (CSS3), uses jquery, bootstrap and jquery plugins. Given the project characteristics and its target population, accessibility issues have been addressed considering the Web Content Accessibility Guidelines 2.0 to provide improved access to multimodal content to users with a variety of functioning.

The UNIBG Life Project prototype is composed by: i) admin area (UNIBG researchers); ii) work area providing differentiated screens and related features according to the three group of users (UG) (UG1: case manager; UG2: PwD and family members/caregiver/guardian; UG3: social, educational, school and healthcare stakeholders). These 3 UGs correspond to different user interfaces and account profiles allowing them to interact through graphical icons and audio indicators with the screens/tabs related to the four components of the system architecture. Each homepage/screen includes contextual instruction adapted to the specific UGs and related competency area/level. All elements/options of the user interface will be further validated using a participatory approach [28] by user experience and through next co-design workshops.

Initial Analysis Framework. In total, there are 9 *Initial Analysis Frameworks*, one for each ICF chapter of the "Activity and Participation Component", such as: Learning and application of knowledge, General tasks and demands, Communication, Mobility, Personal care, Domestic life, Interaction and interpersonal relationships, Basic areas of life, Social, civic and community life. Specific "domains" are associated with each of these chapters. The purpose of this document is to analytically gather together the priorities in PwD's activity and participation (top right) identified by each stakeholder involved (first column) – including PwD and family members/caregivers – coherently to his/her specific project perspective and in the age range considered. Each user selects two different "priority domains" for each ICF chapter and related needs, criticality/strength, barriers/facilitators (Fig. 1).

Synthesis Framework. Starting from the "priority domains" identified in the *Initial Analysis Frameworks* by all the stakeholders, this tab collects, in a unique web page, two main "priority domains" for each of the 9 ICF chapters of the "Activity and Participation Component". For each of them, expected "autonomy goals" are selected in relation to the domain/age group considered and related barriers/facilitators are reported (Fig. 2). This document is drafted by the case manager during a meeting with all the stakeholders and consequently represents a fundamental tool-guide to: i) foster dialogue; ii) orient the decision-making process; iii) focus on PwD's self-determination/autonomy; iv) lay the basis for the next planning step (*Design Framework*).

Design Framework. The *Design Framework* represents the planning tool for the achievement of the PwD's "autonomy goals" across his/her life contexts in the age range considered. The case manager coordinates this phase. The *Design Framework* includes two sections: *A1 - Objectives, Barriers and Facilitators* (Fig. 3); *A2 - Actions, Subjects, Resources and Timeframes* (Fig. 4). For each of the 2 "priority domains" identified in the *Synthesis framework* relating to the different chapters of the ICF "Activity and Participation Component", the *Design Framework* aims at analytically presenting and organizing

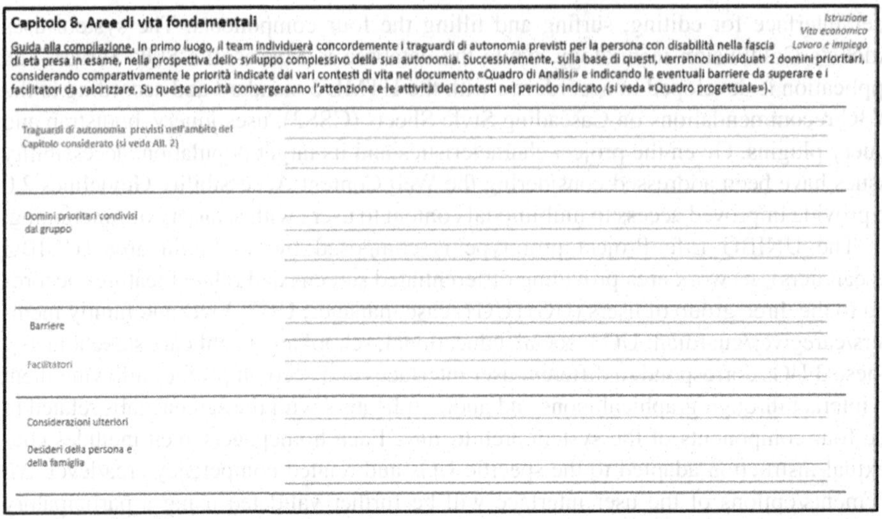

Capitolo 8. Aree di vita fondamentali

Istruzione
Vita economico
Lavoro e impiego

Guida alla compilazione. In primo luogo, il team individuerà concordemente i traguardi di autonomia previsti per la persona con disabilità nella fascia di età presa in esame, nella prospettiva dello sviluppo complessivo della sua autonomia. Successivamente, sulla base di questi, verranno individuati 2 domini prioritari, considerando comparativamente le priorità indicate dai vari contesti di vita nel documento «Quadro di Analisi» e indicando le eventuali barriere da superare e i facilitatori da valorizzare. Su queste priorità convergeranno l'attenzione e le attività dei contesti nel periodo indicato (si veda «Quadro progettuale»).

Traguardi di autonomia previsti nell'ambito del Capitolo considerato (si veda All. 2)

Domini prioritari condivisi dal gruppo

Barriere

Facilitatori

Considerazioni ulteriori

Desideri della persona e della famiglia

Fig. 1. Example of *Initial analysis framework* related to ICF chapter n. 8.

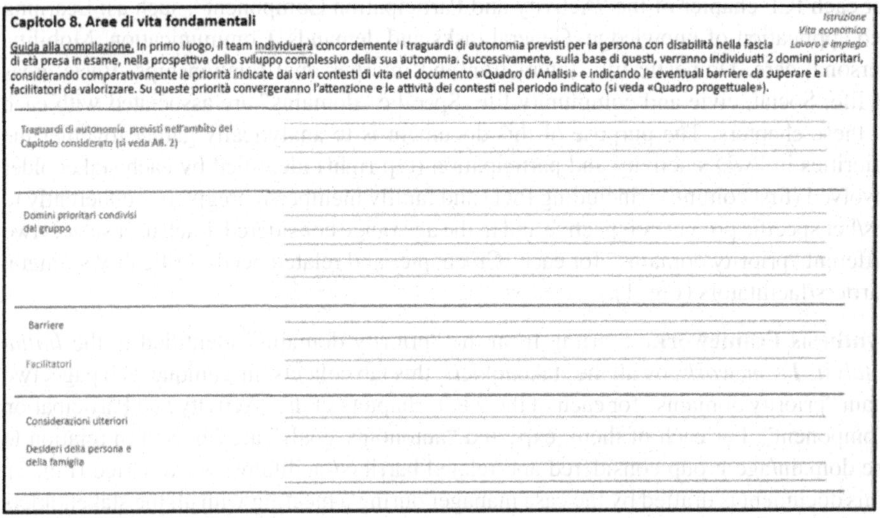

Capitolo 8. Aree di vita fondamentali

Istruzione
Vita economico
Lavoro e impiego

Guida alla compilazione. In primo luogo, il team individuerà concordemente i traguardi di autonomia previsti per la persona con disabilità nella fascia di età presa in esame, nella prospettiva dello sviluppo complessivo della sua autonomia. Successivamente, sulla base di questi, verranno individuati 2 domini prioritari, considerando comparativamente le priorità indicate dai vari contesti di vita nel documento «Quadro di Analisi» e indicando le eventuali barriere da superare e i facilitatori da valorizzare. Su queste priorità convergeranno l'attenzione e le attività dei contesti nel periodo indicato (si veda «Quadro progettuale»).

Traguardi di autonomia previsti nell'ambito del Capitolo considerato (si veda All. 2)

Domini prioritari condivisi dal gruppo

Barriere

Facilitatori

Considerazioni ulteriori

Desideri della persona e della famiglia

Fig. 2. Example of *Synthesis Framework* related to ICF chapter n. 1.

the different "goals" (indicating possible barriers/facilitators) (A1) and related activities realized by the various stakeholders according to their professional/personal competence (A2).

Transition Profile. The Transition Profile is composed of three sections: *B1 - Assessment of previous three-year outcomes* (Fig. 5); *B2 - Autonomy goals sheet (*Fig. 6*); B3 - Summary sheet* (Fig. 7). Drafted by the case manager, this document aims at: i) after the outcome assessment at the *Design Framework* activities, reporting the state of

Capitolo 1. Apprendimento e applicazione delle conoscenze – Sezione A1: Obiettivi, barriere e facilitatori

Guida alla compilazione. In primo luogo, il team declinerà gli obiettivi di autonomia per ciascuno dei domini prioritari individuati nella Quadro di sintesi relativo al presente capitolo. Successivamente identificherà per ciascun obiettivo le eventuali barriere da eliminare e i facilitatori da valorizzare.

Es: Apprendimento di base

Domini prioritari (DP) (riportare, se presenti, i domini prioritari indicati nella «Scheda di sintesi»)	DP 1: DP 2:
Obiettivi (OB) (declinare, per ciascuno dei domini prioritari un obiettivo di autonomia)	Ob 1: Ob 2:
Barriere e Azioni (riportare le barriere al conseguimento per ogni obiettivo e le azioni per la loro riduzione/eliminazione . Per ogni barriera indicare tra parentesi la sigla (BPe) se la barriera è già presente, (BPo) se la barriera potrebbe emergere durante le attività previste per il conseguimento dell'obiettivo)	Barriere e Azioni obiettivo 1: Barriere e Azioni obiettivo 2:
Facilitatori e Azioni (riportare i facilitatori al conseguimento di ogni obiettivo. Per ogni facilitatore indicare tra parentesi la sigla (FPe) se il facilitatore è già presente, (FPo) se il facilitatore potrebbe emergere durante le attività previste per il conseguimento dell'obiettivo)	Facilitatori e azioni obiettivo 1: Facilitatori e azioni obiettivo 2:

Fig. 3. Example of *Synthesis Framework* (section A1) related to ICF chapter n. 1.

Capitolo 1. Apprendimento e applicazione delle conoscenze - Sezione A2: Azioni, soggetti, risorse e tempi

Guida alla compilazione. Per ogni dominio individuato nella sezione A1, il team compilerà la seguente tabella progettuale.

Es: Apprendimento di base

Sezione A2 – Dominio 1								
	Contesti di vita	**Dettaglio attività**	**Soggetti coinvolti**	**Risorse necessarie**	**Azioni per rimuovere barriere**	**Azioni per potenziare i facilitatori**	**Tempi di realizzazione**	**Modalità e tempi di valutazione**
Obiettivo 1	Casa/famiglia							
	Riabilitazione							
	Educazione / formazione							
	Ricreazione e tempo libero							
	....							
	Contesti di vita	**Dettaglio attività**	**Soggetti coinvolti**	**Risorse necessarie**	**Azioni per rimuovere barriere**	**Azioni per potenziare i facilitatori**	**Tempi di realizzazione**	**Modalità e tempi di valutazione**
Obiettivo 2	Casa/famiglia							
	Riabilitazione							
	Educazione / formazione							
	Ricreazione e tempo libero							
	....							

Fig. 4. Example of Synthesis Framework (section A2) related to ICF chapter n. 1.

achievement of each "autonomy goals" (complete, partial or not); ii) summarizing for each "autonomy goal" the arrival point and any indications to support planning for the next age group; iii) presenting and organizing, in a coherent and analytical manner, the development profile of the person with disabilities in relation to the autonomy goals identified for the age group considered (Fig. 8). The *Transition Profile* represents both the end of the planning work carried out for a given age group and the starting point for the drawing up of the *Initial Analysis Framework* for the following age stage.

Capitolo 1. Apprendimento e applicazione delle conoscenze –
Valutazione esiti progettazione triennio precedente

Esperienze sensoriali intenzionali
Apprendimento di base
Applicazione delle conoscenze

Data della valutazione:
La persona con disabilità partecipa alla fase valutativa?
□ Sì □ No
Se "no", perché?

Altri soggetti che partecipano alla fase valutativa

Cognome	Nome	Ruolo	Contatti	Annotazioni

Fig. 5. Example of *Transition Profile* (section B1) related to ICF chapter n. 1.

Capitolo 1. Apprendimento e applicazione delle conoscenze

Esperienze sensoriali intenzionali
Apprendimento di base

Sez. B2: Scheda dei traguardi di autonomia

Guida alla compilazione. Sulla base degli esiti della valutazione relativa al presente capitolo e contenuta nel Documento Progettuale indicare se gli i traguardi di autonomia previsti sono stati raggiunti, parzialmente raggiunti o non raggiunti. Per i traguardi di autonomia raggiunti o non raggiunti compilare le voci della tabella.

(Esperienze sensoriali intenzionali): riportare qui il traguardo di autonomia prefissato per la fase conclusa

Stato	Specificazioni (motivazioni, modalità, tempi di realizzazione)	Raccomandazioni per la fase successiva (barriere e facilitatori)
Raggiunto		
Non raggiunto		
Parzialmente raggiunto		

(Apprendimento di base): riportare qui il traguardo di autonomia prefissato per la fase conclusa

Stato	Specificazioni (motivazioni, modalità, tempi di realizzazione)	Raccomandazioni per la fase successiva (barriere e facilitatori)
Raggiunto		
Non raggiunto		
Parzialmente raggiunto		

Fig. 6. Example of *Transition Profile* (section B2) related to ICF chapter n. 1.

4 Final Considerations and Next Steps

The UNIBG model and prototype of the Life Project differs from other similar experiences recently developed in the disability studies which, although interesting and innovative, are often experimental, localized to single municipalities or to a specific PwD's life context/stage. In this regard, at international and national level, some research have been conducted, such as web-based individualized educational plan [29–32] or transition plan to adulthood and related life contexts [33–36], patient folders/electronic health records used in the healthcare or even welfare worker dossiers [37, 38]. To our knowledge,

- Schede riassuntiva cia di età 0-3anni					
Capitoli	Domini	Traguardo di autonomia raggiunti	Fattori ambientali		Indicazioni a supporto della successiva fascia di età
			Prodotti e tecnologia, atteggiamenti, relazioni e sostegno sociale	Servizi, sistemi e politiche	
rendimento e applicazione delle oscenze	Esperienze sensoriali intenzionali Apprendimento di base				
npiti e richieste generali	Intraprendere un compito singolo				
unicazione	Comunicare - ricevere Comunicare - produrre Conversazione e altre tecniche di comunicazione				
bilità	Cambiare e mantenere una posizione corporea Trasportare, spostare e maneggiare oggetti Camminare e spostarsi				
a delle propria persona	Lavarsi Cura di singole parti Bisogni corporali Vestirsi Mangiare Bere				
domestica					
razioni e relazioni interpersonali	Interazioni interpersonali generali Relazioni interpersonali particolari				
e di vita fondamentali	Istruzione				
sociale, civile e di comunità	Vita nella comunità Ricreazione e tempo libero Diritti umani				

Fig. 7. Example of *Transition Profile* (section B3) related to ICF chapter n. 1.

A scopo esemplificativo - 14-16 anni					
Capitoli	Domini	Traguardi di autonomia raggiunti	Fattori ambientali		Indicazioni a supporto della successiva fascia di età
			Prodotti e tecnologia, atteggiamenti, relazioni e sostegno sociale	Servizi, sistemi e politiche	
Apprendimento e applicazione delle conoscenze	Esperienze sensoriali intenzionali Apprendimento di base Applicazione delle conoscenze				
Compiti e richieste generali	Intraprendere un compito singolo Intraprendere un compito singolo Intraprendere compiti articolati				
Comunicazione	Comunicare - ricevere Comunicare - produrre Conversazione e altre tecniche di comunicazione	Utilizza la CAA per comunicare e conversare con gli altri	Utilizza un comunicatore dinamico personalizzato	Ha fruito nel xxx dei sostegni regionali per l'acquisto di tecnologie	Incrementare l'utilizzo del comunicatore in contesti esterni a quelli consueti Migliorare la conoscenza e l'utilizzo delle regole di conversazione
Mobilità	Cambiare e mantenere una posizione corporea Camminare e spostarsi Muoversi usando mezzi di trasporto				
Cura della propria persona	Lavarsi Prendersi cura di singole parti del corpo Bisogni corporali Vestirsi Mangiare Bere Prendersi cura della propria salute	Sa farsi la doccia con l'aiuto di una persona	Persone: necessità di supporto per alcune attività	Percepisce indennità di accompagnamento	Con il necessario allenamento sistematico, può raggiungere un grado maggiore di autonomia nel farsi la doccia
Vita domestica	Procurarsi un posto in cui vivere Procurarsi beni e servizi				
Interazioni e relazioni interpersonali	Interazioni interpersonali generali Relazioni interpersonali particolari				
Aree di vita fondamentali	Istruzione Lavoro Vita economica				

Fig. 8. Example of *Development profile* related to 14–16 age group.

in Italy, a preliminary web-based implementation initiative considering the different PwD' contexts in a lifespan perspective is *Matrici Ecologiche*[7] software used for drafting and planning the support systems in terms of economics and human resources and epidemiological information related to the individual Life Project.

The current state of the art of the UNIBG research contributes to inform PwD's Life Project by proposing a new model for collecting, editing, consulting, organizing, and sharing information by the stakeholders involved in the design process. It is conceived to be usable, over time, at all institutional levels by all the stakeholders (including PwD)

[7] See: https://www.matriciecologiche.net/ (retrieved: January 29th, 2023).

engaged across the different age groups and related contexts. Preliminary results confirm the relevance of adopting a participatory approach for the definition of the UNIBG Life Project model ontology/architecture and its prototype and main research outcomes are shown below.

Model Ontology. Adopting the ICF framework, the model ontology considers personal and environmental factors that influenced PwD's across different contexts and life stages and prevents the loss of information thanks to the participation of all the stakeholders involved in the design process, including PwD and his/her family members/caregivers.

Architecture. The four interrelated components ensure collective and collegial participation in the PwD's Life Project design and facilitates the decision-making process (person's description, intervention area and goals selection, activities/tasks planning, monitoring and evaluation procedures identification, results/skills achievement).

Prototype. The first prototype of UNIBG model of Life Project presented here will be discussed with some selected stakeholders participating in ATS-UNIBG "Training Pro-gram on Life Project related to the *Dopo di Noi*" (ensuring equal representation of different final users, institutional levels, Bergamo areas, professional area) in order to collect their feedback and proceed with the re-design phase and related medium-high fidelity prototype release (workflow/wireframe, errors correction, implementation of existing features; introduction and integration of new features/functions compatibility with a more evolved web-based environment) up to the final web-based implementation.

References

1. Field, J., Leicester, M.: Lifelong Learning: Education Across the Lifespan, 2nd edn. Routledge, London (2003)
2. Jackson, N. J.: Learning for a complex world: A lifewide concept of learning, education and personal development. Authorhouse (2011)
3. Ianes, D., Cramerotti, S.: Il piano educativo individualizzato. Progetto di vita, vol. 1. Edizioni Erickson, Trento (2009)
4. Bianquin, N.: L'ICF a supporto di percorsi personalizzati lungo l'arco della vita. Pensa Multimedia, Lecce (2020)
5. Bindels-de Heus, K.G., van Staa, A., van Vliet, I., Ewals, F.V., Hilberink, S.R.: Transferring young people with profound intellectual and multiple disabilities from pediatric to adult medical care: parents' experiences and recommendations. Intellect. Dev. Disabil. **51**(3), 176–189 (2013)
6. Giraldo, M., Bianquin, N., Sacchi, F.: Step into adulthood: exploring transition experiences of young adults with disabilities through a narrative inquiry. Giornale Italiano di Educazione alla Salute, Sport e Didattica Inclusiva **5**(4), 1–14 (2021)
7. McDonnell, J., Hardman, M.L.: Successful Transition Programs: Pathways for Students with Intellectual and Developmental Disabilities. Sage Publications, London (2009)
8. Shurr, J. C., Minuk, A.: Parent perspectives and beliefs on inclusive education for students with intellectual disability. In: Shurr, J.C., Minuk, A. (eds.) The Routledge Handbook of Inclusive Education for Teacher Educators, pp. 58–71. Routledge, India (2023)
9. Kurth, J.A., Love, H., Pirtle, J.: Parent perspectives of their involvement in IEP development for children with autism. Focus Autism Other Develop. Disabil. **35**(1), 36–46 (2020)

10. Hammel, J., Magasi, S., Heinemann, A., Whiteneck, G., Bogner, J., Rodriguez, E.: What does participation mean? An insider perspective from people with disabilities. Disabil. Rehabil. **30**(19), 1445–1460 (2008)
11. Butterworth, J., Steere, D.E., Whitney-Thomas, J.: Using person-centered planning to address personal quality of life. Qual. Life Appl. Persons Disabil. **2**, 5–23 (1997)
12. Cramerotti, S., et al.: Un sistema esperto per la stesura di PEI e PDP. Erickson, Trento (2015)
13. Bellacicco, R., Dell'Anna, S., Micalizzi, E., Parisi, T.: Nulla su di noi senza di noi: Una ricerca empirica sull'abilismo in Italia. FrancoAngeli, Milano (2022)
14. McGee, P., Diaz, V.: Wikis and podcasts and blogs! Oh, My! what is a faculty member supposed to do? Educause Rev. **42**(5), 28–41 (2007)
15. Clark, J.E.: E-portfolios at 2.0: Surveying the field. Association of American Colleges and Universities Peer Rev. **11**(1), 1–4 (2009)
16. Xuesong, S., Olfman, L., Ractham, P.: Designing e-portfolio 2.0: Integrating and coordinating web 2.0 services with e-portfolio systems for enhancing users' learning. J. Inform. Syst. Educ. **18**(2), 203–215 (2007)
17. Black, J.: Digital transition portfolios for secondary students with disabilities. Interv. Sch. Clin. **46**(2), 118–124 (2010)
18. Test, D.W., Fowler, C.H., Wood, W.M., Brewer, D.M., Eddy, S.: A conceptual framework of self-advocacy for students with disabilities. Remed. Spec. Educ. **26**(1), 43–54 (2005)
19. Cooper, M., Heath, A.: Access for all to eLearning. Res. Reflect. Innov. Integrat. ICT Educ. **2**, 1139–1143 (2009)
20. Real, R. M., Snider, C., Goudswaard, M., Hicks, B.: Dimensions of prototyping knowledge: characterising prototype evaluation methods and their contributions to design knowledge. In: Real, R.M. (eds.) Design Computing and Cognition 2022, pp. 643–660. Springer, Cham (2023). https://doi.org/10.1007/978-3-031-20418-0_38
21. Wensveen, S., Matthews, B.: Prototypes and prototyping in design research. In: Rodgers, P.A., Yee, J. (eds.) Routledge Companion to Design Research, pp. 262–276. Routledge, London (2014)
22. Lim, Y.K., Stolterman, E., Tenenberg, J.: The anatomy of prototypes: prototypes as filters, prototypes as manifestations of design ideas. ACM Trans. Comput. Hum. Interact. **15**(2), 1–27 (2008)
23. Pernice, K.: UX prototypes: low fidelity vs. high fidelity. Nielsen Norman Group. https://www.nngroup.com/articles/ia-view-prototype/. Accessed 21 Jan 2023
24. Sauer, J., Franke, H., Ruettinger, B.: Designing interactive consumer products: utility of paper prototypes and effectiveness of enhanced control labeling. Appl. Ergon. **39**(1), 71–85 (2008)
25. Hawthorn, D.: Interface design and engagement with older people. Behav. Inform. Technol. **26**(4), 333–341 (2007)
26. Mathias, D., Hicks, B., Snider, C., Ranscombe, C.: Characterising the affordances and limitations of common prototyping techniques to support the early stages of product development. Proc. Int. Des. Conf. Des. **3**, 1257–1268 (2018)
27. Kang, B., Crilly, N., Ning, W., Kristensson, P.O.: Prototyping to elicit user requirements for product development: using head-mounted augmented reality when designing interactive devices. Des. Stud. **84**, 101–147 (2023)
28. Simonsen, J., Robertson, T.: Routledge International Handbook of Participatory Design. Routledge, New York (2013)
29. Bianquin, N.: ICF, Profilo di funzionamento e Buona Scuola. Un nuovo modello di progettazione per l'alunno con disabilità. L'Integrazione Scolastica e Sociale **18**(3), 269–285 (2019)
30. Zhu, L., Huang, R., Wang, X., Wang, Y.: Research on personalized teaching model for individual user in isi: a web-based learning systems platforms. In: 2008 International Conference on Computer Science and Software Engineering, pp. 789–792. IEEE (2008)

31. Cramerotti, S., Ianes, D.: An ontology-based system for building individualized education plans for students with special educational needs. Procedia Soc. Behav. Sci. **217**(32), 192–200 (2016)
32. Chen, C.M.: Intelligent web-based learning system with personalized learning path guidance. Comput. Educ. **51**(2), 787–814 (2008)
33. Traina, I., Mannion, A., Leader, G.: Curriculum di preparazione al lavoro: come supportare i giovani adulti con disabilità intellettiva nel passaggio dalla scuola al lavoro. Giornale Italiano dei Disturbi del Neurosviluppo, 2, 0, **7**(2), 77–81 (2016)
34. Wills, K.V., Rice, R.: ePortfolio Performance Support Systems: Constructing, Presenting, and Assessing Portfolios. Parlor Press LLC, New York (2013)
35. Giorgini, F.: An interoperable ePortfolio tool for all. In: Sustaining TEL: From Innovation to Learning and Practice. In: 5th European Conference on Technology Enhanced Learning, EC-TEL 2010, Barcelona, Spain, September 28-October 1(5), 2010, pp. 500–505. Springer, Berlin Heidelberg (2010)
36. Clancy, M., Gardner, J.: Using digital portfolios to develop non-traditional domains in special education settings. Int. J. ePortfolio **7**(1), 93–100 (2017)
37. Maritz, R., Aronsky, D., Prodinger, B.: The international classification of functioning, disability and health (ICF) in electronic health records. Appl. Clin. Inform. **8**(03), 964–980 (2017)
38. Tyler, C.V., Jr., Schramm, S., Karafa, M., Tang, A.S., Jain, A.: Electronic health record analysis of the primary care of adults with intellectual and other developmental disabilities. J. Policy Pract. Intellect. Disabil. **7**(3), 204–210 (2010)

Best Practice for Inclusive Journey Mapping and Diversity in User Participation

Till Halbach(✉), Kristin Skeide Fuglerud, and Trenton W. Schulz

Norsk Regnesentral, Oslo, Norway
till.halbach@nr.no

Abstract. This work investigates how co-creation workshops, in which user journeys and personas are developed jointly with workshop participants, can be made as inclusive as possible for a wide range of participants and thus personas and journeys. The discussion is based on five recent research projects with 28 workshops in total and more than 78 participants, resulting in 31 user journeys and 25 personas. The lessons learned have been summarized as best-practice recommendations for the implementation of inclusive persona work and journey mapping. It is shown that both physical and virtual journey mapping workshops may result in a great diversity of personas and variety of journeys, provided that the participants are highly diverse, that universally designed tools and aids are used, and that inclusive techniques and protocols are followed.

Keywords: Digital inclusion · universal design · accessibility · diversity · design thinking · participatory design · customer journey · persona · scenarios

1 Introduction

User journeys, also referred to as customer journeys, is a well known concept in user experience research and service design to tell the narrative of the connection between an organization and a user/customer from the user's point of view [1]. User journeys help organizations understand the experienced circumstances of a series of events by a user regarding the organization, including channels, touch points and key interactions, as well as the users' emotions, needs, preferences, etc. In this work, we refer to a user journey as the combination of a persona/user profile with a particular scenario and a user flow towards the goal in the given scenario. Journey mapping denotes the process of developing user journeys. Here, this is also referred to as workshop.

Since its first introduction in 1998, the concept of user journeys has evolved further and nowadays comes in various flavors and is practiced differently. Journey mapping in a physical setting usually involves tangible tools like wall-mounted paper, sticky notes, stickers and similar. The use of digital tools, such as Mural, Miro, Adobe Illustrator and similar [2], has experienced a considerable boost in recent years for virtual settings, mainly due to the Covid-19 pandemic, which often meant that any user participation could only be done remotely.

M. Antona and C. Stephanidis (Eds.): HCII 2023, LNCS 14020, pp. 61–73, 2023.
https://doi.org/10.1007/978-3-031-35681-0_4

However, user participation is often limited by considering an average user, as many tools and associated methods, regardless of being physical or virtual, do not take accessibility for people with impairments into account, such as reduced sensory, motor, or cognitive abilities. As a consequence, users with varying abilities and disabilities are typically not well represented in user journeys either.

The work investigates how journey mapping can be made as inclusive as possible in practice by considering a wide range of users, in particular users with impairments and chronic conditions. The overall objective is a greater user journey diversity and user participation throughout an entire development or research project.

The article is structured as follows. After the discussion of selected related work, we present recent research projects in which personas and journey mapping activities took place and their results in terms of proper methodology. Then, the lessons learned and resulting recommendations are discussed before the conclusion is drawn.

2 Related Work

In this section, selected related literature is discussed.

Thinking about and including users in the design of the system tends to lead to a system that is easier to use for the people using the system. Methods of such participatory design have been shown to help include users and democratize the design of systems [3]. Yet, there may be issues that are missed when people with disabilities are only consulted during the evaluation of a solution instead of through the entire process [4].

Research has shown that people with impairments are often not considered in the design of digital solutions, leading to solutions that are inaccessible, or at best challenging to use for people with impairments [5]. Others have noted that activities for generating ideas for a design are often not accessible to people with disabilities, and facilitators should consider adapting activities to include a larger audience [6].

How personas with disabilities can be generated and exploited has been investigated [7, 8]. The authors recommend combining personas with stories and using them both actively together with stakeholders in research and industry projects to help finding accessibility issues and improve solutions' extent of universal design.

The use of inclusive personas has been suggested [9], calling for the participation of a wide set of users with multiple perspectives and a wide spectrum of human experiences. While the author explicitly mentions the benefits of involving people from vulnerable groups and minorities, the concept of permanent, temporary, and situational difficulties would apply to basically anybody and as such can enrich the personal traits of every persona.

The development of personas and scenarios for the representation of the needs of marginalized user groups has been discussed [8]. The authors found that inclusive and participatory persona scenario creation can be a feasible and effective method to supplement other qualitative and quantitative methods to uncover user needs for universal and inclusive design purposes.

The authors from a recent literature review recommend to involve diverse users in inclusive co-creation processes like user groups and workshops [10]. Special attention should herein be given to accessible tools and methods in both physical and virtual sessions.

3 Persona and Journey Mapping Workshops

Here, we present five recent research projects in which persona and journey mapping activities were conducted.

3.1 Project 1: Accessible Feedback

In this project, which lasted from 2020 to 2022, 15 workshops were carried out with in total 30 participants. Due to the Covid-19 pandemic, all of these activities were performed remotely by means of video conferencing tools. The work resulted in 13 personas and 14 user journeys, and we also conducted a pilot workshop to test the equipment and methodology.

The context for the journeys were the online services of the Norwegian Labour and Welfare Administration (NAV) who deliver a wide range of public services and social benefits in Norway with regard to work and unemployment, job seeking, illness, workplace facilitation, and many more. User representatives were recruited through the interest organizations participating in the project.

The following scenarios were developed:

- A younger male with mental-health issues and depression tendencies applies for unemployment benefits
- A middle-aged female cancer survivor with long-term issues reports on her employment situation
- A middle-aged female cancer patient with various side effects of the treatment, fatigue and chronic pain applies for social security benefits
- An immigrant worker in his early 30ies needs help to find a job
- A young student applies for assistive technology
- A highschool dropout with a heart failure needs basic advice for his work life
- A newly retired pensioner needs help to sort out an additional tax payment
- An elderly pensioner asks for assistance regarding his pension
- A younger woman with reduced hearing places a registration for an sign language interpreter
- A newly immigrated and separated woman applies for an advance for social security benefits
- A father applies for financial support as a caregiver for his intellectually disabled son
- A male in his early 30ies with ADHD and his mother report on his employment situation
- A male in his early 30ies with ADHD and his mother apply for social-security benefits
- A younger female with limited vision applies for reading and writing assistance

The main target group of the personas and user journeys were the development and design teams at NAV, and the intention was that both should be put up on the office walls. As NAV was not interested in a pleasing graphical design but rather to get as many scenarios as possible, a plain text document was chosen for a persona, and a spreadsheet for a user journey. Please see the description of the "Video for all" project for illustrations and specification of content.

Several of the user journeys also detail the experiences of caregivers, including relatives, guardians, friends, as well as staff and volunteers of interest organizations.

3.2 Project 2: Video for All

"Video for All" was active from 2022 to 2023 and dealt with e-consultations in the health sector, for consultations, treatment of illness, rehabilitation, and such.

Three patient journeys and corresponding personas were written in 1 digital and 2 physical workshops with 10 participants in total, 3 to 4 per workshop. The participants were recruited by making contact with relevant health undertakings and interest organizations. Each meeting was carried out by 2 facilitators. The following scenarios were developed:

- A vision-impaired father (in his 30ies) needs a doctor's eyes on the rash of his daughter through a smartphone
- Treatment of a middle-aged woman with bipolar disorder over a longer time period by means of video communication tools
- An elderly aphasia patient needs a virtual appointment as part of a polyclinic rehabilitation after stroke

The target groups of the personas and patient journeys were mainly health personnel and executives, in particular those with procurement responsibility. Here, personas and patient journeys were the building blocks for guidelines and an e-learning tutorial on inclusive video consultation in the health sector. Therefore, each persona was formulated in a plain list-structured text document with short and keyword-like descriptions, while the patient journey was organized in a spreadsheet. The persona description contains all important personality traits, such as gender, age, health, etc. Each patient journey was put into a tabular format, with the chronological order of events and a detailed description of each event in terms of channel, perceived experience, etc.

3.3 Project 3: Capable

The Capable project was funded by the Research Council of Norway and lasted from 2018 to 2021. The aim of this project was to create a digital tool that enables citizens to actively use their clinical and personal health information. The tool concentrated on three areas: medication, nutrition, and coordination of health service information. Persona descriptions together with health history and future scenarios constituted what we call person scenarios. The persona scenarios represented users with various health challenges and impairments with an age range of 23–75 years.

Participants were recruited from three non-governmental disability and health advocacy organizations (NGOs), which were also partners in the project. We conducted five physical workshops at the premises of the NGOs. The participants represented people with rheumatism, people with Chronic obstructive pulmonary disease (COPD), people with cardiovascular diseases (CVD), people with low vision, and people who are blind. There were three user participants in each workshop, fifteen in total. Each workshop lasted around 2–3 h, including a break with some food, and the participants got a gift card as a compensation for their contribution.

There was one researcher leading the discussion, and the discussion's audio recording was used as support when writing the persona scenarios. This resulted in five personas descriptions with associated health journeys. These journeys contained the details of how the persona would access, manage and handle information related to medication, coordination, and nutrition. The descriptions were based on the participants' experiences and put into a realistic narrative. The workshop participants were challenged to create scenarios for the use of a tool to help the persona to overcome some of the previously identified challenges.

The following persona scenarios were developed:

- A 43-year old female with arthritis and fibromyalgia, who is forced to handle a large number of different medications, and combined with outdated information at various healthcare actors
- A 69-year old male with tablet- and diet-regulated diabetes II and elevated cholesterol, going through rehabilitation after a heart attack and a coronary artery bypass (PCI) surgery, where the medicines after PCI cause potency problems
- A 23-year old male from a minority group, with retinitis pigmentosa (RP) and reduced vision and acuity and a progressive eye condition
- A 63-year old female with diabetes I and glaucoma, who lost her vision gradually until it was diminished completely
- A 75-year old female with gene-triggered COPD grade 3, which started with asthma and bronchitis when she was a child

The persona scenario descriptions target mainly the R&D development team. They were analyzed together with results from other user-centered design activities to create the requirements for prototype solutions [11]. Each patient story was based on a template with headings or prompts to describe various aspects of the persona and health journey, including personality traits, gender, age, education, work, ICT experience, values, health challenges connected to medication, coordination and nutrition, as well as suggestions for new tools. The persona scenario was summarized as a mixture between free text and bullet points.

3.4 Project 4: iStøtet (IT Support for Visually Impaired Elderly)

The aim of this project, lasting from 2019 to 2022, was to explore barriers and seek to find solutions to achieve increased mastery and use of smartphones by elderly people with a visual impairment [12].

Among the methods used in the project were persona and user journey workshop. We conducted two workshops with participants recruited from local county groups of the Norwegian Association for the Blind and Partially Sighted. There were six participants in each workshop, and each was organized as two groups with three participants. Each group created one persona and user journey with focus on the challenges of being part of the information society, including motivation, access to teaching resources and support. In each group there were one researcher who led the discussion and one participant from the project group who assisted with note taking. Although the discussion was quite free, the researcher tried to ensure that the group covered all aspects of a template that was prepared in advance. The template contained the attributes gender, name, age, place of residence, life situation, personality traits, values, disability or disease, education, work, ICT usage, assistive technology, ICT skills, interest in and motivation for learning technology, training in technology and technical barriers.

The following four persona scenarios were developed:

- A 75-year old female with low ICT literacy and reduced residual vision due to age-related macular degeneration (AMD), facing more and more information barriers, further affecting her psychological and physiological well-being
- A 77-year old male with a technical education and ample experience and interest in the use of ICT, who is affected by AMD and a gradual deterioration of eyesight, and who experiences various challenges when using a smartphone without sight, and under educational training
- A 51-year old well educated female physiotherapist with deteriorated eyesight, who had learned and mastered technology and assistive technology well, both at work and privately, and who feels forced to apply for social benefits after a longer struggle against a variety of ICT barriers, in particular the one caused by the upgrade of a domain-specific software system, which made work impossible for her
- A 63-year old woman who lost her sight completely in one eye and almost in the other due to blood infection, who encounters various challenges with finding public information, and who needs to turn to a number of public actors and undergo different types of training

The persona journeys were summarized in free text as a coherent four- to five-page story. The target group of the persona journeys are mainly politicians, the public sector, municipal authorities and other visually impaired people. As it is challenging to convey such long stories in presentations, short versions of the stories have been made. One of the persona journeys will also be published as part of a podcast series by the Norwegian Association for the Blind and Partially Sighted.

3.5 Project 5: Close the Gap

"Close the Gap" is a Norwegian public innovation project that started in 2021 and is still running. The goal of the project is to develop simulation training that can prepare healthcare workers to share and communicate information with each other in the context of patient home visits. Some care workers may not have received the necessary training before they are out in patients' homes. The project's objective, though, was not to map a patient's journey, but to find vignettes or small, repeatable sets of events which occur in a home visit, and which can be used in multiple simulation scenarios [13].

One in-person workshop was carried out with nine participants and five researchers. The participants were general practitioners, nurses, and advisors in three municipality development centers for nursing homes and home health care. Before the workshop, we had created two example journeys that were elicited with the help of a healthcare consultant involved in training in this area. The example journeys depict a patient at home with a deteriorating condition. We presented these journeys to the participants and pointed out examples of situations of a possible repeating pattern, but we also stressed that there could be other variations to the journey.

We then split the participants into three groups for working on creating possible vignettes based on concrete examples. There was no recording of the workshop to avoid accidental capture of personal information of other people not participating (e.g., anecdotes of a patient visit), but researchers took notes to capture any issues that were raised.

For capturing the vignettes, we used a spreadsheet for each group. Each group, however, used the spreadsheet a little differently. For example, one group worked jointly on the worksheet after some initial discussion, another group talked and worked on the whiteboard before they transferred the information to the worksheet.

The groups had only an hour and 45 min to create the vignettes. But by the end of the workshop, we had five vignettes, covering different ways of how a patient's condition could worsen and how the tools could be used to discover this and to communicate this with other healthcare workers [14]. The vignettes have been used for further development in the simulation scenarios.

4 Results

This section summarizes the persona and journey mapping activities and methodological results across all aforementioned projects.

All projects have in common that personas and journeys were developed in a co-creation process between researchers/facilitators and user/patient/client representatives. This is in accordance with practitioners' view that involving users is the most important factor during the mapping process [15]. One project consisted solely of virtual/remote activities, three projects had carried out in-person meetings only, and one project had both virtual and physical meetings. In total, 28 workshops with more than 78 participants in total were carried out, and 31 user journeys were developed along with 25 personas and scenarios.

The workshop participants were recruited with the help of the civil-society organizations involved in each project. A great share of participants had sensory and cognitive challenges including reduced or no vision, reduced hearing or deafness, anxiety and/or traumas, dyslexia, and various mental degradations common among elderly. Another share had chronic conditions, such as aphasia and conditions common among cancer survivors. A third group of participants were immigrants and people with a foreign culture, meaning foreign-language speakers. In some instances, we also invited helpers from the aforementioned organizations, as well as close relatives, such as parents and other caregivers, to the workshops. Project 5, however, was the exception as none of the participants had known disabilities.

While all of the pre-Covid-19 projects held physical workshops, such activities became entirely virtual during the pandemic, and since 2022 we use both depending on the circumstances. However, none of the workshops has been hybrid yet. In virtual settings, we typically make use of video conferencing software such as Microsoft Teams and Zoom for direct communication, and plain text documents and spreadsheets (Google Docs and Sheets) for joint collaboration. Both are reported to have good accessibility for virtual meetings [16, 17]. In physical settings, a workshop is carried out quite similar to a focus group, relying solely on oral information, that is, without the use of tangible tools.

Our experiences with both physical and virtual user journey mapping show first of all that it is possible to conduct virtual workshops in an inclusive manner for a diverse population. That is, we were able to write detailed descriptions of personas and their experiences in the form of user journeys, all of which were quality assured and finally accepted by the participants. With virtual workshops, it was not only possible to continue the research and development during the pandemic at all, but virtual journey mapping offers also multiple advantages: It can be argued that virtual meetings allow for a wider geographical spread, that they require a reduced investment of the participants' time, and it is reportedly easier for the participation of certain user groups, in particular those who experience more challenges with travel than the average. As such, virtually conducted workshops contribute to more diversity in the population. On the other hand, virtual workshops are likely to exclude individuals with low IT and ICT literacy, or who lack such skills entirely. Some participants were also attracted by the social aspects of physical workshops in particular, where they could mingle with "peers" and exchange experiences, which is an important factor that is often missing in virtual settings.

During the journey mapping, it was crucial to accommodate for the needs and preferences of each participant. For instance, while we relied on screen sharing and the conveyance of visual information for those with a hearing impairment, as well as sign language interpreters, the strategy followed for individuals with a vision impairment was oral communication, such as read aloud strategies. For people with anxiety, we offered one-to-one sessions, whereas for those with low IT literacy, we asked technically savvy helpers to join a (virtual) workshop. Ideally, physical workshops would be the preferred workshop format for reaching those target groups.

5 Discussion of Results, Lessons Learned and Recommendations for Inclusive Journey Mapping

In the following, the lessons learned from conducting personas and user journey workshops are discussed, together with our recommendations for developing user journeys with a high degree of diversity. The recommendations are structured in groups of recommendations related to each other, and they have been derived based on the discussion of experiences with inclusive workshops by the researchers involved in each project.

5.1 Participants

We got good results in the form of a wide spread of stories about user experiences when both participants with their individual-level experience, i.e. end users, and representatives from civil-society organizations participated in the workshops. In most cases, these representatives not only know the wide range of user needs but also challenges and core issues across the entire organization, and often they may act as stand-ins for multiple users and thus increase a workshop's level of diversity. Regarding personal users, the recommendation is to prioritize people with reduced functional abilities (sensory, motor, cognition or compound issues), people with a migration or other cultural background, as well as the elderly, who often have low ICT skills and multiple impairments. The goal of this is to increase the diversity of the final product, i.e., user journeys, and to be able to quickly and efficiently uncover so-called pain points, or problematic areas, as compared to average users.

When it comes to the recruitment of users and user representatives, we recommend contacting non-governmental organizations and national interest organizations such as the Association of the Blind and Partially Sighted, the Association of the Deaf, the CP Association, etc.

It can be beneficial not only to include personal users, but also related roles such as relatives, helpers, assistants, guardians, etc. to highlight any challenges from their point of view as well. It would be wise to hold separate workshops where personal users and other roles are not mixed.

We recommend 1 to 3 user representatives with roughly the same background and similar experiences. For individuals with psychological challenges (e.g. social anxiety), there should not be more than one. Otherwise, one should aim for 2 to 3 participants to avoid having to cancel in the case of no shows. In case of more participants, one runs the risk of the situation becoming too chaotic, or that someone will not speak up. A similar background is important so that the participants can agree on a common story that everyone can identify with. This will also make it easier for everyone to participate in the discussion and to contribute.

The recruitment itself and the background of the participants can in practice not be controlled entirely, and thus there will always be an element of uncertainty. We have had participants both with and without assistive technology, and with a PC, tablet or smartphone, i.e. large, medium and small screens. Many of those with small screens have had difficulty reading any shared screen content and can hence be categorized as being visually impaired. When there are too different backgrounds, it could be beneficial to divide the group into several workshops with smaller groups using break-out rooms.

Other than that, it has been shown to be advantageous to gather users who need a particular interpreter, say a sign language interpreter, in the same group.

5.2 Methodology

Conducting workshops as virtual/digital video meetings has multiple advantages as compared to physical meetings. Typically, this makes it possible to recruit participants with a greater geographical spread and thus greater variety in background. Many participants also said that they were glad that they did not have to travel to a venue to take part in a workshop. Sometimes, for instance during the Covid-19 shutdowns, virtuality was the one thing that made it possible to hold workshops at all. This is contrasted by another share of participants who underlined the advantage of gathering in a physical and thus social setting, and who pointed out the importance of a paid lunch. The type of the meeting (virtual/in person) should therefore be carefully considered with regard to circumstances such as travel restrictions, distance, possible impairments among individuals in the target group, etc.

Our projects showed the importance of pointing out to the participants that a persona is an artificial person, and that a user journey – though rooted in reality and the participants' own experiences – partially may be made up and condensed from multiple experiences. As such, events, names and other circumstances are anonymized, and participants can think and speak freely without having to state whether they are telling their own, a friend's or fictitious experiences. It also enables them to reflect on each other's experiences, compare their own experiences to those of other participants, etc. This is in contrast to focus groups, where participants may hesitate to disclose their experiences [8]. In such cases, it might be crucial that the service owner not be present, such that the participants utter their opinion more freely. For participants with almost traumatizing experiences with owners of digital services in the past, a persona's third view may almost have a therapeutic effect, as this adds a certain distance to their memories. One should nevertheless be ready to handle strong emotional reactions from the participants, and a listening, understanding, and empathic way of being is essential.

In principle, the duration of a workshop and any breaks should be agreed upon individually with the participants. In virtual workshops, we have had good experiences with sessions of two hours and a 10-min break after approximately one hour for participants with "average" cognitive capacity. In case of fatigue, for example, it would be appropriate to have shorter meetings and more frequent breaks.

A workshop duration of 2 h means little time to develop an entire persona and the accompanying user journey. We therefore recommend to either start with the user journey and ask the participants to find a common experience they could build on first, and fill in gaps in the persona in the last 20 min or so of the workshop, or to switch forth and back between persona work and journey mapping. Usually, many details of the persona fall into place during the development of the user journey anyhow. Our experience is also that most informants quickly understand the task after the initial explanation, in particular when they are shown/told about the respective templates for collaboration.

The number of workshop facilitators will depend on the number of participants and their background. We have used 1 to 3 facilitators with good results. One facilitator may be enough if the person in question is experienced enough, and if the groups are homogeneous. However, then one will not be able to divide the participants into several breakout groups if necessary. Multiple facilitators also provide the opportunity for a debrief afterwards to reconcile impressions. It is an advantage to have several facilitators in the case of many elderly people, people with psychological or cognitive challenges and people with multiple assistive technologies.

Particularly in virtual meetings, it has been very important to make audio recordings in order to be able to go through the recording afterwards and extract more information for the persona and the user journey. However, in physical meetings and with multiple facilitators, taking notes has in general been sufficient. The transcription of any audio recordings has been deemed as not necessary.

The facilitators may type directly into the digital documents / templates as the participants speak, so that both persona and user journey are being developed continuously. In virtual workshops, the documents were shared with the participants by screen sharing, as well as reading aloud what was written. Visual sharing of the screen is particularly important for those with reduced hearing, and reading aloud works well in most cases for blind participants. Sometimes, we also shared document links, so that the participants could write directly into the templates, but almost no one made use of this, and therefore we dropped this in later workshops.

Both the persona and the user journey will typically need to be complemented and partly rewritten after the workshop, as the facilitators won't have time to fill in all the information in the right places immediately, and because the "temperature may rise" when participants talk at a high pace and simultaneously. In addition, some narratives are very complex and might have many elements. As a result, both the persona and the user journey should be reviewed and quality assured by the participants. It is therefore recommended to come to an agreement with the participants to send over both documents for approval afterwards. In our projects, the participants have always accepted this request. Typically, there have been few proposals for changes afterwards.

During the last 5 to 10 min of a workshop, it is beneficial to ask the participants regarding their opinion about the workshop and how the journey mapping could be improved. This gives the opportunity for a continuous improvement of the methodology.

It is important to find out about any personal requirements and needs before a workshop, so that it is easier to plan the appropriate number of facilitators. An introductory round at the start of the workshop to clarify challenges, equipment, experiences and expectations is beneficial.

Next, it is advantageous to attach an information letter about privacy, the workshop and the journey mapping process in the meeting announcement, so that the participants have time to read it in advance. This to save time during the workshop.

5.3 Tools and Digital Environments

For the persona work, we have used a slightly modified text document template from previous research projects. This template has been shown to work very well for creating a fictitious but believable person. It contains the descriptions of the following traits: Gender, age, municipality, situation in life, possible illness, impairments, and chronic conditions, personality, education and/or work, ICT literacy, as well as important life events. It is complemented by a name and a facial picture.

In Norway's public sector, the Norwegian Association of Local and Regional Authorities (KS) offers a user journey template for journey mapping [18], but the spreadsheet turned out to be far too large and also had to be adapted to some extent. Among other things, we have made the sheet smaller so that it can easier be screen-shared, removed redundant fields, improved the evaluation scale, etc. But even the simplified sheet had several fields that were rarely used in our research projects. The user journey sheet has therefore been further simplified and contains now only the following fields: Columns mirror the chronological order of events (steps), and each step is a compound of the most important event descriptors: Action, contact point, channel, equipment, and personal experience, as well as feedback in terms of criticism and praise and improvement suggestions.

We used text-based, i.e. not graphical, tools to avoid making it difficult for visually impaired to participate, especially since many of the graphic tools are said not to be universally designed. In practice, the workshop participants did not write much themselves, but rather they liked to read what was written in the templates by the facilitator. It is also important that the participants are able to review the completed text afterwards in an accessible format. Our approach was to give the participants access to the documents directly in the cloud (Google Drive/Docs/Sheets), and this has worked well, also for screenreader users.

We have used Teams as a meeting tool, which has proven to be fine for that purpose. The challenges some participants had (and sometimes also facilitators) were related to problems with logging in, sharing the screen, especially with a screenreader, that the chat area sometimes did not update, etc. Navigating inside Teams using only the keyboard was also challenging for some. Most participants had the microphone on all the time, so that they could speak at any time. With such small groups as we had this was not a problem. The chat channel was, among others, used to share URLs, but when that didn't work, we used email as a backup. Generally speaking, it is wise to take into account some start-up delays related to the technical setup right before / in the beginning of meetings, that is, for checking that the sound is OK, that everyone can see, has access to the documents, can use the chat area, etc.

When sharing the screen, it has proven to be an advantage with multiple computer screens (or application windows); one for the common document (text or spreadsheet), and one for the participants, their facial expressions and their body language.

Among some elderly people and people with low ICT skills, it has been challenging to handle digital meeting invitations and calendar entries. We have therefore made good experience with sending out reminders by email no later than the day before the meeting, where the use of digital meeting tools was also explained. In addition, it was useful to provide the meeting leader's telephone number as an alternative communication channel. Several participants have made use of this in the event of technical difficulties, delays and other unforeseen events. Also finding the right time using tools such as Doodle has been challenging for some participants and therefore needs to be explained / helped with.

6 Conclusion

We have presented five projects where personas were developed and journey mapping activities were carried out in a joint manner in workshops with user (patient) involvement. The implications of how the workshops were conducted in detail in terms of modality, tools and aids, participant background, recruitment, etc. have been discussed for the entirety of projects. The lessons learned in the process have further been summarized as concrete best-practice recommendations for the implementation of inclusive persona work and journey mapping.

Our experiences show that it is feasible to conduct both physical and virtual journey mapping workshops with valid and good results, resulting in convincing personas with a high degree of diversity and realistic journeys that describe a great variation of experiences. It is crucial to involve participants with a wide range of backgrounds and traits, in particular users with impairments/disabilities and chronic conditions, to make use of universally designed tools, aids and other means, and – more importantly – to adhere to inclusive methods, techniques, and protocols.

The recommendations of this work may contribute to a greater variety of personas and journeys with a high degree of diversity in the future.

Acknowledgements. This research is partially supported by the Norwegian Research Council under project number 321059 *Close the Gap – Simulation-based training for collaboration within and between healthcare services.*

References

1. Schneider, J., Stickdorn, M.: This is Service Design Thinking: Basics, Tools, Cases. Wiley (2011)

2. Durga, A.K., Kanaka Durga, A.: Tools for Design Thinking. Design Thinking, pp. 3–13 (2022). https://doi.org/10.1201/9781003189923-2
3. Bjerknes, G., Bratteteig, T.: User participation and democracy: a discussion of scandinavian research on system development. Scand. J. Inf. Syst. **7**, 1 (1995)
4. Ladner, R.E.: Design for user empowerment. Interactions **22**, 24–29 (2015)
5. Henni, S.H., Maurud, S., Fuglerud, K.S., Moen, A.: The experiences, needs and barriers of people with impairments related to usability and accessibility of digital health solutions, levels of involvement in the design process and strategies for participatory and universal design: a scoping review. BMC Public Health **22**, 35 (2022)
6. Bennett, C.L., Shinohara, K., Blaser, B., Davidson, A., Steele, K.M.: Using a Design Workshop To Explore Accessible Ideation. Association for Computing Machinery (2016)
7. Schulz, T., Skeide Fuglerud K.: Creating personas with disabilities. In: Miesenberger, K., Karshmer, A., Penaz, P., Zagler, W. (eds.) Computers Helping People with Special Needs. ICCHP 2012. LNCS, vol. 7383. Springer, Berlin, Heidelberg (2022). https://doi.org/10.1007/978-3-642-31534-3_22
8. uglerud, K.S., Schulz, T., Janson, A.L., Moen, A.: Co-creating persona scenarios with diverse users enriching inclusive design. In: Antona, M., Stephanidis, C. (eds.) Universal Access in Human-Computer Interaction. Design Approaches and Supporting Technologies. HCII 2020. LNCS, vol. 12188. Springer, Cham (2020). https://doi.org/10.1007/978-3-030-49282-3_4
9. Francioni, F.: The Upfront Guide to Designing Inclusive Personas. In: Usability Geek [Internet]. 9 Apr 2020 [cited 27 Jan 2023]. https://usabilitygeek.com/the-upfront-guide-to-design-inclusive-personas/
10. Fuglerud, K.S., Halbach, T., Snaprud, M.: involving diverse users for inclusive technology development. In: IADIS International Conference on Interfaces and Human Computer Interaction 2021 (part of MCCSIS). IADIS Press (2021). http://www.iadisportal.org/digital-library/iadis-international-conference-interfaces-and-human-computer-interaction-ihci
11. Janson, A.L., Moen, A., Fuglerud, K.S.: Design of the capable health empowerment tool: citizens' needs and expectations. Stud Health Technol. Inform. **270**, 926–930 (2020)
12. Fuglerud, K.S., Tunold, S., Kjæret, K.: Social contact for older people with visual impairment through mastery of smartphones: barriers and suggested solutions. In: Verma, I. (ed.) Universal Design 2021: From Special to Mainstream Solutions, pp. 415–428. IOS Press (2021)
13. Simulation Interoperability Standards Organization. SISO-GUIDE-006–2018 – Guideline on Scenario Development for Simulation Environments (2018)
14. Hannay, J.E., Fuglerud, K.S., Leister, W., Schulz, T.: Scenario design for healthcare collaboration training under suboptimal conditions. In: Duffy, V.G. (ed.) Digital Human Modeling and Applications in Health, Safety, Ergonomics and Risk Management Health, Operations Management, and Design, pp. 197–214. Springer International Publishing, Cham (2022)
15. Joyce A. Journey-Mapping Impact: Research Findings. In: Nielsen Norman Group [Internet]. 19 Dec 2021 [cited 28 Sep 2022]. Available: https://www.nngroup.com/articles/journey-mapping-impact/
16. OsloEconomics. Kunnskapsstatus – konsekvenser av fjernundervisning og universell utforming av digitale møteplattformer. 2022 Jan. Report No.: 2021–68
17. Tollefsen, M., Lunde, M., Sandnes, F.E., Herstad, J., Olaussen, E., Knarlag, K.: Universell utforming av webinarer – Universell utforming av webinarer Tips for å få med alle i digital læring og samarbeid. Media LT (2020)
18. Kommunesektorens interesseorganisasjon. Ny tjenestereise. In: KS [Internet]. 2019 [cited 31 Jan 2023]. https://www.ks.no/fagomrader/innovasjon/innovasjonsledelse/veikart-for-tjenesteinnovasjon/alle-verktoy/ny-tjenestereise/

How to Ensure Web Accessibility in Digital Services to Improve the Competitive Advantage of an Organization

Terhi Kärpänen[1,2,3](✉)

[1] Laurea University of Applied Sciences, Ratatie 22, 01300 Vantaa, Finland
terhi.karpanen@laurea.fi
[2] The University of Helsinki, Yliopistonkatu 4, 00100 Helsinki, Finland
[3] Estonian Business School, A. Lauteri 3, 10114 Tallinn, Estonia

Abstract. Digitalization and digital services have brought new challenges to organizations. Digital services need to be designed for all, and services need to be accessible to all people. Because of the prevalence of digital services, they should be available and accessible to all people regardless of any limitations that they may have. Web accessibility enhances and improves the usage of digital services for all people by considering technical requirements and cognitive accessibility features such as usability, and understandable content in digital services. This literature review was conducted through meta-synthesis. The purpose of this study was to review the qualitative literature and studies on web accessibility features increasing competitive advantages in digital services and to identify areas of inquiry for future qualitative research in this context. Based on the literature review analyses, the author defined three themes: how web accessibility in digital services can increase competitive advantage. These themes included different competitive advantage features which were categorized under each theme. Based on the literature review results, an understanding of the existing qualitative research and suggestions for possible competitive advantages of web accessibility for the organization was obtained.

Keywords: Web Accessibility · Cognitive Accessibility · Competitive Advantage

1 Introduction

Digital services need to design to serve all people by ensuring good quality, content, structure, and usability. Digital services may change rapidly, new digital services can appear, and people need to adapt to be able to effectively use digital services and participate in society. Digitization influences businesses and operations, not only in the public sector but also in the private sector. Entrepreneurs and companies are struggling; how should they compete in a digital environment with an attractive and understandable product offering and content? Digitalization has brought changes, e.g. changes to service offerings for markets, customers, and the business itself. Consumers' behavior has

M. Antona and C. Stephanidis (Eds.): HCII 2023, LNCS 14020, pp. 74–87, 2023.
https://doi.org/10.1007/978-3-031-35681-0_5

changed i.e. physical locations to the digital environment, and therefore, the development of digital services is very important for business. Increased digital solutions can bring and enable different economic acts and provide a better customer and service experience (Saunila, Rantala & Ukko 2017; Rantala, Ukko, Saunila, Puolakoski & Rantanen 2019). According to Rantala et al. (2019), digital technologies affect all aspects of people's lives, to drive innovation and increase customer value. Digital services, content, and offerings should be available and accessible to all people regardless of any limitations that they may have. People who have limitations to using digital services benefit the most when digital services are accessible and designed for assistive technology.

Web Accessibility in digital services means that people with a diverse range of hearing, movement, sight, and cognitive abilities can operate and use digital services (W3C 2018a, b). Digital solutions and services should be designed to work for all people – whatever their hardware, software, language, location, or ability – and the products and services should be accessible to all people (Serhat 2019; W3C 2018a, b). Digital services should be designed by the defined technical accessibility criteria but understandable content, language, and usability should also be considered in the design process. Thus, accessibility is essential for developers and organizations that want to create high-quality websites and web tools, and not exclude people from using their products and services (W3C 2018a, b).

It is important to study this field to understand the importance of web accessibility in digital services as a competitive advantage for the providers of digital services. There is no clear understanding of the competitive advantages of implementing accessible digital services, and not enough qualitative research helps to provide a deeper understanding of the web accessibility point of view. Despite much empirical research being based on web accessibility, much of it has focused on the limitations itself of assistive technology, not on accessibility in digital services or accessibility as a competitive advantage. Most of the accessibility studies focus on web accessibility literature reviews (e.g. the studies by Borg, Lantz & Gulliksen 2015); Manzoor & Vimarlund 2017; Kärpänen 2021). Competitive advantage or value creation through digital services studies have been published (Jeansson, Nikou, Lundqvist, Marcusson, Sell & Walden 2017; Rantala et al. 2019; Saunila et al. 2017), but these studies do not include web accessibility point of view. In business administration or management science, the research has focused on theoretical models (Heerdt & Strauss 2004), and the issue of web accessibility or empirical research has gained little attention. One interesting quantitative research publication (Schmutz, Sonderegger & Sauer 2017) showed that implementing Web Content Accessibility Guidelines (WCAG) criteria for a website improves user performance and users' subjective experience for both non-disabled users and users with visual impairments, which was unexpected because the main objective of accessibility guidelines is to support users with disabilities. Web Content Accessibility Guidelines (WCAG) cover a wide range of recommendations for making Web content more accessible. The author argues that the term web accessibility and its meaning in the digital context, as well as its benefits and advantages to businesses and organizations, can be difficult to understand by only using quantitative research evidence.

Although a large body of research has been conducted in the area of web accessibility, there is still a lack of qualitative research and a lack of understanding of the web accessibility benefits and competitive advantages of an organization. This field has been studied from a user point of view but not enough from an organizational point of view. This literature review aimed to fill these gaps and review the qualitative research in this context and identify areas of inquiry for future qualitative research. The research question is the following: How to ensure web accessibility in digital services to improve the competitive advantage of an organization? Following this introduction, the paper outlines the methodological section and findings. Finally, the results, limitations, and future research suggestions are discussed.

2 The Research Methodology

The literature review was carried out to identify all the qualitative studies whose focus was on demonstrating the benefits of accessible digital services. Based on the nature of the research, a meta-synthesis is a more suitable approach to conducting a literature review. This format is suitable for summarising the qualitative studies, drawing conclusions about the topic, and identifying the possible gaps.

This literature review followed the meta-synthesis's principles and process. A meta-synthesis is very close to a systematic literature review, and its purpose is to provide a more comprehensive description of a phenomenon. The idea behind meta-synthesis is to study different studies on the same subject so that their nuances, assumptions, and textual environments can be 'revealed'. The synthesizer thus seeks to interpret the original research results of other researchers (Walsh & Downe 2005; Zimmer 2006: 312). Meta-synthesis enables insights that no other method can provide. The meta-synthesis approach follows a six-step structure: define the research question and the inclusion criteria, select the studies, assess their quality, extract and present the formal data, analyze the data and express the synthesis (Lachal, Revah-Levy, Orri & Moro 2017).

The process of meta-synthesis is depicted (see Fig. 1). Meta-synthesis requires a formulated research question. Defining the research question was an important step for this research.

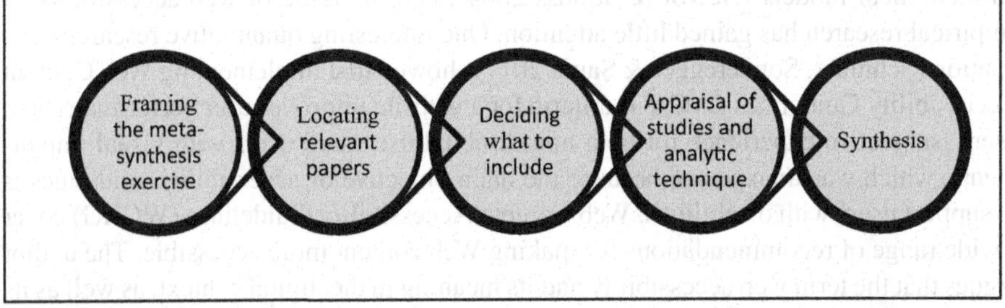

Fig. 1. The meta-synthesis process according to Walsh and Downe (2005).

2.1 Inclusion Criteria

Due to fast changes in digital services and digitalization, one inclusion criterion was that the articles must have been written in the last five years. The review covers the years from 2016 until the end of 2021. The focus was on conducting a meta-synthesis reviewing qualitative research papers and articles.

This review consisted of an overall understanding of the keywords 'accessibility in digital services' and studies related to a digital service's competitive advantage and benefits in this field. The review sought to identify all the qualitative studies related to accessibility in a digital environment and its business benefits. Purely quantitative research and literature reviews were excluded. The exceptions were mixed-method research from which the qualitative research parts were included. All the articles in the search scope, excluding the Association for Computing Machinery (ACM) search, were peer-reviewed in the above-mentioned period (2016–2021) and were qualitative research studies written in English.

2.2 The Search Strategy

The author conducted the keyword searches by using the keywords in the accessibility, digital, and business advantage fields by using "OR and "AND" relations. The accessibility-related search words were a mandatory part of the search process. The searches included variations of accessibility terms, such as cognitive accessibility, accessibility in digital services, web accessibility, digital inclusion, and digital accessibility. Accessibility itself can mean a physical environment, and due to that, it was not included in the search. Since this review was focused on searching for the advantages of web accessibility, the author used variations of the words to include, such as business advantage, business benefit, customer benefit, consumer benefit, competitive advantage, customer value, business value, advantage, and strategic advantage. The criteria for the search words are shown in Fig. 2.

("web accessibility") OR ("cognitive accessibility") OR ("digital accessibility") OR ("accessibility in digital service*") OR ("digital inclusion*") OR ("e-inclusion*") AND
("benefit*") OR ("satisfaction*")" OR ("competitive* advantage*") OR ("value*") OR ("advantage*") OR ("strategic advantage*") OR ("advantage*") OR ("market value*") OR ("business*value*") OR ("revenue*") OR ("profit*") OR ("gain*") OR ("enabler*")

Fig. 2. Search criteria.

The author searched for publications in various databases – such as EBSCO Information Services, ACM (Association for Computing Machinery), ProQuest, Web of Science, and Google Scholar – with the help of a professional librarian. ACM was selected due to the digital aspect of this literature review. In the ACM search, the author was not able to identify whether the articles were peer-reviewed. Based on the text field, abstracts were obtained from articles that dealt with accessibility, web accessibility, digital accessibility, or cognitive accessibility in a digital environment, and the advantages of web accessibility.

The author identified the articles by screening the full texts, keywords, and abstracts with a combination of search words. Before the screening, 3500 articles were related to the search words about the full text. The selection criteria were refined to the selection of abstracts as the abstracts allowed for more detailed restrictions on the target group, the content of the article, and the methodological choices when compared with the title and full-text information. The author identified 127 articles in total that were related to the advantages of web accessibility services at the abstract level. Then the author excluded the literature reviews, quantitative research, duplicates, and other articles that did not meet the criteria based on the findings of the research. The result was 11 articles which the author included in the literature review. The search strategy and the selection and exclusion criteria for titles, abstracts, and the full text are shown in Fig. 3.

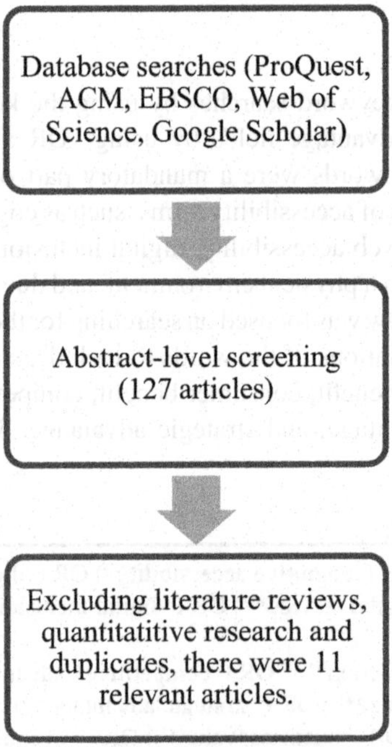

Fig. 3. A search strategy flow diagram.

2.3 Critical Appraisal and Data Analysis

The literature review focused on a search for qualitative studies in the body of articles. The author of the synthesis sought to make an interpretation based on the original interpretations (i.e. based on the research results of other researchers). The approach is interpretive (Walsh & Downe 2005). One of the elements of qualitative and interpretive research is the use of a critical appraisal checklist. The Critical Appraisal Skills Programme (CASP) tool and its checklist were used to appraise the quality of the studies included in the review (CASP 2018). The technique has an interpretive, rather than aggregating, intent, in contrast to a meta-analysis of quantitative studies. The data analysis process started by reading the titles and abstracts of each article. The process was manual and followed the principles of meta-synthesis and CASP. The findings were coded and grouped by categories and, finally, in themes. The results of the analyses consist of the themes that were developed in the analyses. The authors, year, country, data collection method, participants, and possible benefits were identified from the articles.

3 Results

This section presents the results by themes and the characteristics of the research. Most of the articles were published in the years 2017 and 2020. One study was from the year 2018 and one study was from the year 2020. There were no recent studies from the year 2021. The common methods used in the articles were semi-structured interviews and mixed-method studies that included different kinds of evaluations. The studies were from different countries.

Overall, most of the studies revealed accessibility challenges and barriers when using digital services. Some of the studies were case studies or mixed-method studies that included a qualitative part (Almasoud & Mathkour 2019; Calvo, Seyedarabi & Savva 2016; Gonçalves, Rocha, Martins & Branco 2018; Williams, Clarke, Gardiner, Zimmerman & Tomasic 2019; Kous & Polančič 2019; Palani, Fourney, Williams, Larson, Spiridonova & Morris, 2020). Five studies were purely qualitative, either semi-structured interviews or focus-group interviews (Velleman, Nahuis & Van der Geest 2017; Leitner, Strauss & Stummer 2016; Okonji & Ogwezzy 2018; Newman, Browne-Yung, Raghavendra, Wood & Grace 2017; Abad-Alcalá, L., Llorente-Barroso, C., Sánchez-Valle, M., Viñarás-Abad, M., Pretel-Jiménez, M. 2017).

The study participants varied in each study. In most of the studies, the participants were people with some kind of limitations (e.g. people with visual impairments or people with cognitive challenges) who were using digital services (Goncalves et al. 2018; Williams et al. 2019; Kous & Polančič, 2019; Palani et al. 2020; Okonji & Ogwezzy 2018; Newman et al. 2017; Abad-Alcalá et al. 2017). An almost equal number of studies had been conducted with experts or people without disabilities or limitations (Velleman et al. 2017; Leitner et al. 2016; Almasoud & Mathkour 2019; Calvo et al. 2016; Gonçalves et al., 2018; Palani et al. 2020). The studies related to technical implementations, technical requirements (e.g. WCAG 2.1. Standards), transcoding, or solutions were usually mixed-method studies, including expert evaluation or user testing. These studies were mostly found in the ACM database search (Almasoud & Mathkour 2019; Calvo et al. 2016; Williams et al. 2019; Palani et al. 2020). The characteristics of the research and the themes are summarised in Table 1.

Table 1. The characteristics of the studies and the themes included in this.

Author (year)	Country	Data collection	Participants	Themes
Abad-Alcalá et al (2017)	Spain	Focus groups (n = 4 focus groups, n = 28 participants)	Elderly people	User experience Responsibility Differentiation
Almasoud & Mathkour (2019)	Global	Expert evaluation and tool implementation (n = 2)	Expert evaluations (5 websites)	Responsibility
Calvo et al. (2016)	Global	Expert evaluation and qualitative recommendations based on evaluations (n = 7)	Expert evaluations (62 reviews)	User experience Responsibility Differentiation
Gonçalves et al. (2018)	Portugal	Case study and mixed method: evaluations (n = 3 experts), blind people for testing site (n = 20)	Expert evaluation of e-commerce platforms Blind people testing e-commerce sites	User experience Responsibility Differentiation
Kous & Polančič (2019)	Slovenia	Mixed method: usability testing, log analyses, interviews (n = 6), questionnaires	People with dyslexia	User experience Responsibility Differentiation
Leitner et al. (2016)	Austria, Germany, Switzerland	Case study: website evaluations and semi-structured interviews (n = 12)	Business manager interviews in separate business fields	User experience Responsibility Differentiation
Newman et al. (2017)	Australia	Interviews (n = 18)	Young people with disabilities	Responsibility Differentiation
Okonji & Ogwezzy (2018)	Nigeria	Interviews (n = 30)	Visual impairments (people 60 or over)	Responsibility Differentiation
Palani et al. (2020)	United States	Eye-tracking, eye-tracking, search log, and self-report (n = 27)	People with and without dyslexia	User experience Responsibility Differentiation
Velleman et al. (2017)	Netherlands	Semi-structured interviews with experts (n = 18)	Experts in the field of accessibility and municipal stakeholders	User experience Responsibility Differentiation
Williams et al. (2019)	United States	Case study and mixed methods: screen reader evaluation (n = 21)	Screen reader users	User experience Responsibility Differentiation

The majority of the studies that were examined were related to seeking benefits derived from implementing accessible digital services in either the public or private sector. After coding and grouping the studies by category, the author defined three themes based on the analyses. Each theme contained different features. The themes were: (1) user experience, (2) responsibility, and (3) differentiation (with technical requirements and content). The author grouped different benefit features under different themes. Each theme contained different features, but under some themes, there were similar features. The themes and different features are shown in Table 2.

Table 2. Themes and features.

Themes	Features
User experience	Customer loyalty Customer satisfaction Better usability A better user experience
Differentiation (with technical requirements and content)	Better digital service quality Better SEO ranking Access to all devices Cost efficiency (e.g. lower maintenance costs) Better digital service quality Understandable content and structure
Responsibility	Design for old people Design for dyslexic people Design for the young and old who have limitations Design for blind people Design for people with visual impairments A better corporate image Social responsibility Social commitment Prioritizing legislation

3.1 User Experience

The 'user experience' theme included features such as a better user experience, customer loyalty, customer satisfaction, and better usability. Based on the study findings all the studies revealed that users or organizations benefit when digital services are easy to use. Providing easy-to-use digital services increased better usability and the user experience for customers and consumers. The study by Velleman et al. (2017) on public sector services showed that one benefit of providing accessible digital services is that citizens are more satisfied with the municipality. The study by Leitner et al. (2016) investigated business managers' motivations and business impacts on private sector accessible digital services. In this study, based on the study participants' opinions, customer satisfaction and customer loyalty were seen as economic motivation factors, and an accessible website mainly increased customer loyalty, turnover, and customer base. Customer loyalty was seen to be heavily related to a firm's profitability. In particular, elderly people were mentioned as forming a rapidly growing segment with significant purchasing power but with limitations related to using digital services (Leitner et al.2016). One important factor related to customer experience was the possibility to do, for example, online tasks independently (Abad-Alcalá et al. 2017). This study by Abad-Alcalá et al. (2017) focused on senior citizens' online tasks, and one conclusion was that senior citizens would be satisfied and motivated if they could carry out tasks without any help from others.

In studies that focused on better and understandable content, the participants stated that better and personalized, accessible content and using common design patterns and elements all provide a better experience for users (Kous & Polančič 2019; Calvo et al. 2016; Abad-Alcalá et al. 2017). In particular, senior citizens will benefit from clear content presented in large fonts and contrasting colors. The high contrast was good for them as well as the minimalist design and simple content (Abad-Alcalá et al. 2017). The study by Leitner et al. (2016) highlighted the important fact that an excessive focus on the aesthetic design of an online service may limit usability and cause frustration for the customer.

The studies related to accessible technical implementations or solutions (Williams et al. 2019; Palani et al. 2020) showed that technology enhancements for different digital tools or applications provided better usability and a better user experience when using digital services, and it positively influenced performance. One study was related to individual website adjustments and their benefits for people with dyslexia (Kous & Polančič 2019). The study participants of the study by Kous and Polančič (2019) agreed that there was a better user experience when website contrast and font size were appropriate. Studies concerning expert evaluations and usability testing showed that implementing WCAG requirements or assistive tools in digital services enabled better usability and a better user experience for customers (Goncalves et al. 2018; Calvo et al. 2016). By following the WCAG requirements and having a simple design, users will be able to complete tasks easily and this leads to a better user experience.

3.2 Differentiation by Technical and Content Implementation

The 'differentiation' theme included features from technical and content implementation in digital services, considering web accessibility requirements. The benefit features identified in the studies which fit under this theme were better website quality, a better search engine optimization (SEO) ranking, the possibility to access services with all devices, cost efficiency by implementing WCAG requirements, efficient website management, better digital service quality, and understandable content. The study by Leitner et al. (2016) revealed accessible websites' higher ranking in search engine results and higher website traffic from accessible web presences. An accessible web presence increased website traffic, and website quality and provided better visibility in SEO.

The most common finding from studies was that by following WCAG criteria and requirements in digital service implementations, organizations provide a good basis for digital-service quality and other benefits. The study by Velleman et al. (2017) pointed out that the WCAG standards can be used as a tool to convince other departments or management to develop digital services. Participants from the study by Velleman et al. (2017) stressed that there are many benefits when digital services are accessible (e.g. the management of the website is less expensive when the quality of the technical code is good). Other benefits were a faster website, responsive digital services, and a better ranking in search engines. The study by Velleman et al. (2017) revealed that digital-service quality assurance, implemented with help of external experts, helped municipalities in many ways (e.g. by saving costs on external inspections or preventing implementation problems in an early stage of the process, thus saving expensive repairs at a later stage). Based on the findings of the study by Leitner et al. (2016), accessible websites usually have a higher quality than inaccessible ones and accessible websites can reduce costs in the long run (e.g. a long-term investment can lead to cost efficiencies in the end).

By providing assistive technology for digital-service users, organizations improve digital service quality. The studies by Newman et al. (2017) and Okonji and Ogwezzy (2018) showed that voice recognition software was a good addition for people who had disabilities (e.g. people with dyslexia or visual impairments). Based on the findings of the study by Almasoud and Mathkour (2019), assistive technologies may help to deliver webpage content in a form that is comprehensible to these users. The study by Leitner et al. (2016) showed that websites with numerous design elements tend to be more voluminous, and thus require longer download times. A longer download time can be a crucial issue for many customers, and thus decisive for the success of the firm.

The results of the study by Leitner et al. (2016) revealed that web accessibility implementation may provide a competitive advantage if competitors do not have accessible digital services. In the study, interviewees pointed out that technical requirements were among the major motivations for web accessibility implementation in some sectors. The improvement of website quality correlated with the value of the web presence for the organization, and it was noted as being more important in those organizations where there were more content fluctuations on the website. Accessibility included several measures that increased simplicity, clarity, usability, download speed, and website quality among organizations (Leitner et al. 2016).

3.3 Responsibility

The 'responsibility' theme contained features from the studies, such as Design for All principles, a better corporate image, social responsibility, social commitment, and prioritizing legislation. Most of the studies pointed out the importance of designing services for all people, that is, for people with or without limitations and disabilities. The 'Design for All' feature included studies where the participants had a limitation in using digital services (e.g. people with visual impairments, young people with disabilities, and people with cognitive limitations) (Goncalves et al. 2018; Williams et al. 2019; Kous & Polančič 2019; Palani et al. 2020; Okonji & Ogwezzy 2018; Newman et al. 2017; Abad-Alcalá et al. 2017). One study showed an important aspect: if all people can use a website, they do not have to call customer services or visit in person in a physical location (Velleman et al. 2017). This can save costs and show citizens that the organization takes responsibility only if necessary. The study by Leitner et al. (2016) explained Design for All as a design that involves social aspects, such as equality, ethical behavior, social commitment, and having a responsible attitude toward society. These features should be seen as the drivers for an organization in web-accessibility implementation.

Studies on visual impairment, blind people, and screen reader users were the most common studies. One study done by expert evaluations evaluated better accessibility for blind people with an accessibility tool extension and following WCAG requirements for digital services (Almasoud & Mathkour, 2019). The study by Okonji and Ogwezzy (2018) was related to financial inclusion, and it showed the importance of accessibility when visually impaired older adults use financial services. The participants of this study mentioned that some companies were giving people opportunities to make payments for services ordered online and that such facilities helped many users to take better control of their finances and afforded them more advantages due to their convenience. However, such benefits eluded many people with vision impairment due to a lack of equal access when compared with sighted users (Okonji & Ogwezzy 2018). The study by Williams et al. (2019) concerned screen-reader users and how they benefit from accessible services and assistive technology. The study by Gonçalves et al. (2018) focused on blind people's e-commerce website usage. When companies are following the WCAG requirements in their digital services, blind people can use and make purchases from the e-commerce website. For blind people and people with visual impairments, websites and e-commerce sites must be developed following guidelines that allow the good functioning of the screen-reader functions.

The legislation was part of the 'responsibility' theme. Organizational responsibility and legislation were mentioned in the study of Velleman et al. (2017). The legislation, especially in EU countries, includes accessibility standards that need to be followed in the public sector (European Commission 2019). The stakeholders of companies or organizations which need to follow legislation indicated that legislation influences the perceived importance among people and its priority in the design process. In the study by Velleman et al. (2017), the study participants mentioned accessibility standards as an instrument with which to convince other departments and management to develop a new website. Some municipalities in the study hired experts to support them in this process (Velleman et al. 2017). Corporate culture's role and improving the corporate image through web accessibility were seen as the motivation factors for organizations' social responsibility implementation (Leitner et al. 2016).

4 Discussion

This literature review aimed to obtain an understanding of existing qualitative research on how web accessibility in digital services can increase competitive advantage for an organization. The author defined three main categories of competitive advantage themes based on the literature review and added different competitive advantage features under these themes. It is possible that some of the features would have fitted under other themes as well. The web accessibility field is wide containing technical requirements of digital services, the usability of digital services, and understandable content. It means that people can understand, navigate, and interact with the web (W3C 2018a, b). In this light and based on this literature review results, web accessibility can be seen as one source of competitive advantage for organizations.

All the studies focused in some way on web accessibility or cognitive accessibility in digital services and its different elements, such as technical implementation, understandable content, or user-centered design. An interesting observation was that web accessibility could offer many benefits to organizations. Web accessibility could improve the customer experience and usability of digital services and provide cost efficiency. The web-accessible design of websites or digital services can improve usability, user experience, customer loyalty, and customer satisfaction for both people who have limitations to using digital services and for users who do not. All users benefit from digital services which follow web content accessibility guidelines (WCAG). Web accessibility features in digital services can reduce costs e.g. the costs of digital service maintenance. When digital services e.g. website works properly, users do not need to contact the organization by phone or visit, if they find all the needed information from digital services.

Responsibility themes included social responsibility and legislation. The author highlighted in this theme that designing services for all people is part of the responsibility. Currently, the Web Accessibility Directive in 2016 requires all public sector websites and applications in EU member states to implement, enforce, and maintain a uniform set of accessibility standards. The rules laid down in the Directive reflect the Commission's ongoing work to build a social and inclusive European "Union of equality", where all Europeans can take a full and active part in the digital economy and society (European Commission 2019). In several countries, especially in the EU, various efforts are being made to promote the best accessibility practices due to existing and upcoming country legislation. In addition to this directive, there is a newer directive, the European Accessibility Act 2019 (EAA), which requires that both the public and private sector actors guarantee the accessibility of certain products and services.

Although the author used different databases to search for relevant articles, it is possible that some related articles do not appear in this review, e.g., articles in languages other than English or using different terminology. The author identified the articles with exact search words (e.g. "web accessibility"). Future research should be more concentrated on the web accessibility benefits for companies or organizations that result from cognitive accessibility implementation (e.g. from implementing understandable content or easy-to-use digital services). Most of the cognitive accessibility features are not part of WCAG criteria.

Considering the limited studies included in this review, it is recommended that more studies and literature reviews are conducted. Overall the number of studies that met the search criteria was small. The results of this literature review may not represent the full breadth of understanding of qualitative studies in this field.

5 Conclusion

This literature review pointed out different competitive advantage features for organizations, such as differentiation in technical requirements and content, user experience, and responsibility. Based on the literature review results, an understanding of the existing qualitative research was obtained and web accessibility competitive advantages for the organization.

There is a need for a deeper understanding of how web accessibility in digital services increases competitive advantages for organizations. Technical implementation (e.g. following WCAG standards) will increase the competitive advantage of organizations because by using the same technical requirements in website design, organizations' Search Engine Optimization improves. Providing understandable content and easy-to-use structures in digital services may bring even more competitive advantage or cost benefits to organizations.

There are not enough qualitative studies in this field, and more qualitative research is needed. With the results of this literature review, it was possible to understand the benefits of web-accessible digital services and the competitive advantages resulting from them, although the number of research studies was small. More research is needed to understand the importance and benefits of web-accessible digital services for public and private sector organizations. Digital services are changing continuously, and new web accessibility requirements updates come regularly. Organizations may not understand all of the benefits that accessible digital services can bring them. Thus, it is important to raise awareness of the web accessibility benefits and competitive advantages for an organization.

References

Abad-Alcalá, L., Llorente-Barroso, C., Sánchez-Valle, M., Viñarás-Abad, M., Pretel-Jiménez, M.: Electronic government, and online tasks: towards the autonomy and empowerment of senior citizens. Profesional De La información **26**(1), 34–42 (2017). https://doi.org/10.3145/epi.2017.ene.04

Almasoud, S.K., Mathkour, H.I.: Instant adaptation enrichment technique to improve web accessibility for blind users. In: Proceedings of the 2019 3rd International Conference on Information System and Data Mining (ICISDM 2019), pp.159–164. Association for Computing Machinery, New York, NY, USA (2019). https://doi.org/10.1145/3325917.3325931

Borg, J., Lantz, A., Gulliksen, J.: Accessibility to electronic communication for people with cognitive disabilities: a systematic search and review of empirical evidence. Univ. Access Inf. Soc. **14**(4), 547–562 (2014). https://doi.org/10.1007/s10209-014-0351-6

Calvo, R., Seyedarabi, F., Savva, A.: Beyond web content accessibility guidelines: expert accessibility reviews. In Proceedings of the 7th International Conference on Software Development and Technologies for Enhancing Accessibility and Fighting Info-exclusion (DSAI 2016) pp. 77–84. Association for Computing Machinery, New York, NY, USA (2016). https://doi.org/10.1145/3019943.3019955

European commission. https://ec.europa.eu/digital-single-market/en/web-accessibility. Accessed 13 Feb 2022

Critical Appraisal Skills Programme, CASP. https://casp/uk.net/wp-content/uploads/2018/01/CASP-Qualitative-Checklist-2018.pdf. Accessed 13 Feb 2022

Gonçalves, R., Rocha, T., Martins, J., et al.: Evaluation of e-commerce websites accessibility and usability: an e-commerce platform analysis with the inclusion of blind users. Univ. Access Inf. Soc. **17**(3), 567–583 (2018). https://doi.org/10.1007/s10209-017-0557-5

Heerdt, V., Strauss, C.: A cost-benefit approach for accessible web presence. In: Miesenberger, K., Klaus, J., Zagler, W.L., Burger, D. (eds.) ICCHP 2004. LNCS, vol. 3118, pp. 323–330. Springer, Heidelberg (2004). https://doi.org/10.1007/978-3-540-27817-7_49

Jeansson, J., Nikou, S., Lundqvist, S., Marcusson, L., Sell, A., Walden, P.: SMEs' online channel expansion: value creating activities. Electron. Mark. **27**(1), 49–66 (2016). https://doi.org/10.1007/s12525-016-0234-1

Kous, K., Polančič, G.: Empirical insights of individual website adjustments for people with dyslexia. Sensors **19**(10), 2235 (2019). https://doi.org/10.3390/s19102235

Kärpänen, T.: A literature review on cognitive accessibility. Stud. Health Technol. Inform. **282**, 259–270 (2021). https://doi.org/10.3233/SHTI210402

Lachal, J., Revah-Levy, A., Orri, M., Moro, M.R.: Meta-synthesis: an original method to synthesize qualitative literature in psychiatry. Front. Psych. **8**, 269 (2017). https://doi.org/10.3389/fpsyt.2017.00269

Leitner, M.-L., Strauss, C., Stummer, C.: Web accessibility implementation in private sector organizations: motivations and business impact. Univ. Access Inf. Soc. **15**(2), 249–260 (2014). https://doi.org/10.1007/s10209-014-0380-1

Manzoor, M, Vimarlund, V.: E-services for the social inclusion of people with disabilities: a literature review. Technol. Disabil. **29**(1–2), 15–33 (2017)

Newman, L., Browne-Yung, K., Raghavendra, P., Wood, D., Grace, E.: Applying a critical approach to investigate barriers to digital inclusion and online social networking among young people with disabilities. Info Syst. J **27**, 559–588 (2017). https://doi.org/10.1111/isj.12106

Okonji, P.E., Ogwezzy, D.C.: Financial inclusion: perceptions of visually impaired older Nigerians. J. Enabl. Technol. **12**(1), 10–21 (2018). https://doi.org/10.1108/JET-08-2017-0033

Palani, S., Fourney, A., Williams, S., Larson, K., Spiridonova, I., Morris, M.R.: An eye tracking study of web search by people with and without dyslexia. In: Proceedings of the 43rd International ACM SIGIR Conference on Research and Development in Information Retrieval, pp. 729–738. Association for Computing Machinery, New York, NY, USA, (2020). https://doi.org/10.1145/3397271.3401103

Rantala, T., Ukko, J., Saunila, M., Puolakoski, H., Rantanen, H.: Creating sustainable customer value through digitality. World J. Entrepren. Manage. Sustain. Develop. **15**(4), 325–340 (2019). https://doi.org/10.1108/WJEMSD-08-2018-0077

Saunila, M., Rantala, T., Ukko, J.: Characteristics of customer value creation in digital services. J. Serv. Sci. Res. **9**(2), 239–258 (2017). https://doi.org/10.1007/s12927-017-0012-4

Serhat, K.: Moving toward a universally accessible web: Web accessibility and education. Assist. Technol. **31**(4), 199–208 (2019). https://doi.org/10.1080/10400435.2017.1414086

Schmutz, S., Sonderegger, A., Sauer, J.: Implementing recommendations from web accessibility guidelines: a comparative study of nondisabled users and users with visual impairment. Hum. Factors **59**(6), 956–972 (2017). https://doi.org/10.1177/0018720817708

Walsh, D., Downe, S.: Meta-synthesis method for qualitative research: a literature review. J. Adv. Nurs. **50**(2), 204–211 (2005). https://doi.org/10.1111/j.1365-2648.2005.03380.x

Williams, K., Clarke, T., Gardiner, S., Zimmerman, J., Tomasic, A.: Find and seek: assessing the impact of table navigation on information look-up with a screen reader. ACM Trans. Access. Comput. **12**, 1–23 (2019). https://doi.org/10.1145/3342282

Velleman, E.M., Nahuis, I., van der Geest, T.: Factors explaining adoption and implementation processes for web accessibility standards within eGovernment systems and organizations. Univ. Access Inf. Soc. **16**(1), 173–190 (2015). https://doi.org/10.1007/s10209-015-0449-5

W3C: Web Content Accessibility Guidelines. https://www.w3.org/standards/webdesign/accessibility. Accessed 24 Sept 2022

W3C: The Business Case for Digital Accessibility. https://www.w3.org/WAI/business-case/. Accessed 24 Oct 2022

Zimmer, L.: Qualitative meta-synthesis: a question of dialoguing with texts. J. Adv. Nurs. **53**(3), 311–318 (2006). https://doi.org/10.1111/j.1365-2648.2006.03721.x

Inclusiveness of Citizen Science. How People with Disabilities Can Participate in Citizen Science Approaches

Daniel Krüger[1], Sarah Krümpelmann[2], Bastian Pelka[1], and Ann Christin Schulz[1](✉)

[1] Sozialforschungsstelle Dortmund, Department of Social Sciences, TU Dortmund University, Dortmund, Germany
{daniel2.krueger,bastian.pelka, annchristin.schulz}@tu-dortmund.de
[2] Sozialheld*innen e.V., Berlin, Germany
sarah@sozialhelden.de

Abstract. The article starts by stating that "citizen science" holds great potential for the participation of people with disabilities in research and development, but also for research on disability-relevant topics. But how can citizen science be designed in an inclusive way? For this purpose, the paper describes a methodological framework in which citizens with disabilities as well as their representatives and stakeholders are involved in a concrete research and development process - following a high level on Arnstein's [1] ladder of participation. In this, people with disabilities not only take on a supplier function for scientists, but also co-determine research topics, instruments and outcomes. The paper describes a five-stage research process in which the "Wheelmap" - an online road map that shows wheelchair barriers - is jointly expanded by researchers from the project team and people from the target group. As a result, the Wheelmap is expanded through a citizen science approach and insights into the development of inclusive research methods are derived through the analysis of this process.

Keywords: Citizen Science · Methodology · Inclusive Research

1 Introduction: Citizen Science for Inclusion

1.1 Citizen Science

The very term 'Citizen Science' makes it clear what its conceptual idea is about: the science system and citizens coming together. However, the concept of citizen science is also accompanied by a terminological development. Citizen Science has long been associated with natural science research, for example with the annual Christmas Bird Count, which was first conducted in the year 1900 without reference to the term "science". Despite these associations, the term Citizen Science was already taken up by other disciplines in the 1990s [5]. With the Horizon 2020 research framework programme, the European

M. Antona and C. Stephanidis (Eds.): HCII 2023, LNCS 14020, pp. 88–98, 2023.
https://doi.org/10.1007/978-3-031-35681-0_6

Commission made a paramount contribution to opening up the concept of Citizen Science to other scientific disciplines and to its dissemination in the European Union in the work programme 'Science with and for Society' [4]. The increasing prevalence of Citizen Science brings to the fore the question of how and why citizens are involved in research and what the actual opportunities for participation are in practice [2]. Are citizens included as low-cost or no-cost data providers? Do they determine research questions or even develop their own research projects?

When asking about different forms and degrees of participation in Citizen Science, the reference can be made to the established stages of the ladder of citizen participation by Arnstein [1]. The eight levels of participation in this classification range from pure manipulation of citizens to citizens actively taking control. Arnstein [1] summarizes those eight steps in three categories: "nonparticipation", "degrees of tokenism" and "degrees of citizen control". At least these three categories can be applied to citizen science: non-participation corresponds to approaches in which citizens are not involved in scientific work at all, they may not even get informed about the research. Tokenism as symbolic involvement in scientific processes corresponds to pseudo-participation in citizen science. Citizens may be interviewed as knowledge carriers or may be informed about research results without the possibility to give feedback. The goal of participatory citizen science in the sense of Arnstein's gradations, however, would be citizen control. Citizens are then partners and share responsibility in a citizen science research context. They also shape the planning and take over tasks of the management. With Arnstein, this level of participation also meant sole control of citizens over collaborations as the maximum level of empowerment. Participation would therefore basically be overcome and power relations reversed between citizens and professional scientists. In the IncluScience project described below, a setting was established in which professional scientists and citizen scientists with disabilities share responsibility and decision-making power on an equal footing.

1.2 The Need for Inclusive Research Methods

The question of the degree of participation in Citizen Science depends on how accessible the actual research is. On the one hand, barriers to participation can be artificially and intentionally created by not giving citizens a say in research design or the development of the research questions. On the other hand, even such citizen science research can contain barriers that rely on full citizen participation from the very beginning. Barriers in this regard go back to the research practice and pose the question of its inclusive design. With the ratification of the UNCRPD [6], the signatory states committed themselves to ensuring that people with disabilities can participate fully in society. For the science system as a whole as part of society, this results in the demand for an inclusive transformation. For the opening of the science system to society with Citizen Science, this means that an opening for people with disabilities must also be part of it. The decision to shape a research in the sense of Citizen Science has different reasons, which for example concern field access, are intended to strengthen trust in science or the relevance of results [3]. Moreover, Citizen Science must not only be a decision of professional scientists to open their research for participation. It can also be citizens that decide to conduct research on a topic they are interested in - sometimes together with professional scientists, sometimes without their involvement. What these motives have in common is on the one hand the improvement of research by drawing on the expertise and resources of citizens and on the other hand to move control over research topics and outcomes to citizens, especially those that would profit from that very research. While citizens with disabilities must always have the opportunity to participate in Citizen Science, in some projects their participation is specifically needed to ensure the quality of the research and to enhance the relevance of results. This refers to projects that conduct research on the living environment of people with disabilities or - in the sense of research and development - are intended to make concrete contributions to a more inclusive society. With the maxim "nothing about us without us", the necessity of the participation of citizens with disabilities in such Citizen Science is mandatory.

1.3 The Project "IncluScience"

The German NGO *Sozialheld*innen* ("social heroes") has been involved in the process towards an inclusive society in the form of various projects since 2004. The overarching goal of the organisation's work is to ensure that persons with disabilities can make equal use of products and services and are considered as a consumer group from the outset. This also means that persons with disabilities are actively included and involved right from the development stage. For over 15 years, institutions and companies have been supported in adopting new perspectives and developing innovative solutions. This approach is what the *Sozialhelden*innen* call "disability mainstreaming". This means that disability is represented in all areas of society. Disability should be considered in all processes from the very beginning, e.g. in urban development, in product design, in digitalization and even in science. The accessibility created in the process should ultimately lead to an inclusive society.

In this sense, the best-known project is Wheelmap.org, an online map for wheelchair-accessible places. Wheelmap.org is an app on which users themselves can describe the wheelchair accessibility of places such as restaurants, museums or toilets. Through the app, these ratings are visible to all other users.

The Wheelmap is currently being further developed in the Citizen Science project IncluScience in cooperation with the Sozialforschungsstelle (Social Research Center) at the TU Dortmund University and funded by the German Federal Ministry of Education and Research. Based on two to three so-called "verticals" or types of places (e.g. cafés, doctors' offices, bus stops), accessibility criteria beyond wheelchair accessibility are developed and integrated into the Wheelmap. This process is co-created from the beginning with researchers with and without disabilities, citizens (also with and without disabilities) and disabled persons' representatives. The process was designed to represent Arnstein's level of "degrees of citizen control". It started with the selection of the verticals, included the definition of the criteria and encompassed the implementation of this research in the actual public online version of the Wheelmap.

2 The IncluScience Research Framework

2.1 Research Question

As explained above, Citizen Science aims at bringing the science system and citizens together in order to jointly solve societal problems. This issues two directions of research, aiming at how the science system moves towards citizens – and aiming at citizens moving in the direction of the science system. People with disabilities are at the intersection of both directions, as they are part of the groups addressed to as "citizens" and "researchers", but also "experts" in many research fields connected to participation, health or barriers. In the project described above, we used this as a background for our research framework: It becomes clear that participation and barriers are major levers for the emergence and further development of Citizen Science.

Therefore, we developed a research question encompassing both "directions":

RQ1: How can people with disabilities participate in Citizen Science approaches?

RQ1 includes people with disabilities in roles as "citizens" as well as "occupational researchers" and as well as "experts" in specific domains. The verb "can" refers both to competences and capabilities that people with disabilities bring in, but also to fostering and hindering factors that influence participation opportunities. Finally, our notion of "participation" is aware of different steps on a "ladder of participation" [1] that start from pure instrumentalisation, but should reach a state where people with disabilities are participating in setting up research topics, goals, methods, instruments and budgets.

2.2 Methodological Framework

The research framework consists of three iteration loops, each of which integrates a new prototype for a place description (e.g. "indoor swimming pool", "public authority" or "pub") on the Wheelmap. At the time of writing, the first place type ("vertical") has been determined: The first vertical is to display more barrier information on the Wheelmap for the place type "doctor's surgery". Two further verticals will be determined in 2023 and 2024. Each iteration loop - and thus each new "vertical" - should methodologically build on the experiences of the previous one, with the aim of improving the research and development process of the verticals through each iteration. To this end, the methods are documented in what we call "methods toolbox" with suggestions for other Citizen Science projects and are discussed in appropriate arenas to gather feedback for improvement. Each iteration loop again consists of five steps:

1. In the first step, a list of possible place types is developed ("needs assessment"). A shortlist is first drawn up in qualitatively oriented workshops with a smaller group of people, who should, however, bring in as many different perspectives as possible. The challenge of this step is to involve people from different target groups who can inform about different barriers and requirements. For this purpose, the first step was implemented through several workshops. In two online workshops with each five participants, people with different disabilities, their stakeholders, and representatives were invited to name possible types of places. In order to include people who could not participate in one of the online workshops, an additional workshop was held in a residential group for people with disabilities in Dortmund with four participants.

In all workshops, the facilitation aimed to start from the lifeworld of the participants and to ask about situations and places where barriers were experienced and where information about places could lead to improved participation. The results of all workshops were compiled into a list; this list contained concrete types of places such as hotels, rail stations, restaurants and doctors, but also rather rough descriptions of situations such as "parking" or "shopping".

2. In a second step, the list was prioritized ("selection"). An online survey was used for this purpose, in which the location types of the list were offered for voting. Over 500 people took part in this vote. The result of the first iteration was "doctors' surgeries". Since this was a quantitative survey and was conducted during the pandemic, the data could only be collected online. The perspective of people who could not participate in online surveys was only partially taken into account by asking personal assistants to offer their assistance.
3. In a third step, information that is relevant for this type of place ("accessibility criteria") is determined. For example, a pub has very different barriers than a cinema. This step was also implemented through online workshops to which experts for this type of place and target groups of Wheelmap were invited. The following barriers were identified: Non-MRI-ready transfer chairs, X-ray units that are not accessible from below for wheelchair-users, height-adjustable couches etc.
4. In the fourth step, a testable prototype is installed on the Wheelmap ("prototyping"). This step serves to test the input of information for the new place type and to collect feedback from users in order to further improve the prototype.
5. Only after this improvement step is the new vertical made publicly available on the Wheelmap and advertised in suitable channels. Users are asked to fill in data ("co-sustainability").

The following chapter will describe the actual research and development activities within this framework.

3 Discussion: The IncluScience Methodology

3.1 First Vertical

The first vertical was co-designed between May 2021 and November 2022 and was heavily influenced by the pandemic. No face-to-face meetings were possible and ICT equipment was scarce and difficult to buy. The methodology had to consider the changing demands of this situation.

Needs Assessment. As a first step, two two-hour needs assessment workshops (May 20th, 2021; May 26th, 2021) were conducted, each with five stakeholders from the group of people with disabilities. Thereby, perspectives and needs of the Wheelmap target groups were asked and an exchange among each other was encouraged. The project team agreed to conduct the needs assessment workshops online on the Zoom video conferencing platform due to the ongoing coronavirus pandemic. As the invited guests were recruited through networks of the Wheelmap community, they were experienced in using online technology. There were no obstacles or problems during the workshop. It should only be noted that due to the digital implementation of the workshop, not all people could be reached equally, among other things due to a lack of digital infrastructures (no internet access), insufficient digital skills or inhibition thresholds (fear, complexity). On the other hand, it could also reach people who could not have been reached in a face-to-face workshop. For example, people with mobility restrictions or from other regions. The digital orientation therefore creates new opportunities for participation, but also a risk of exclusion.

Stakeholders were actively recruited for the two workshops by invitations from the social heroes to self-advocacy organizations and individuals with expertise. Furthermore, the German Association for the Blind and Visually Impaired (DBSV), the German Disabled Sports Association (DBSV) and the German Federation of the Deaf (DGB) willingly provided experts in their own right to participate in the workshops as well as their networks such as newsletters and email lists. In terms of quality, the broad invitation and the targeted approach to the target group ensured that people with a wide range of expertise as well as different types of disabilities were represented in the workshops. Nevertheless, it can be assumed that especially the digital communication channels do not reach all persons from the target group. In addition, a bias can arise through the selection of networks, organizations and associations. If, for example, those are selected in which people with hearing impairments are predominantly represented, these will logically also be predominantly reached. A broad network that includes different groups of people with different types/forms of disability as well as experts in their own right is therefore just as essential as addressing them through different channels (digital and analogue).

The need for information on accessibility in specific places was raised in open discussion rounds. In addition, the open structure of the workshop allowed for the identification of further needs and questions of the participants.

Selection. Through the two needs assessment workshops, it was possible to draw up a list of criteria according to which the first vertical had to be searched for. These are the following criteria:

- Addressing the community at eye level
- Addressing the community in their language, e.g. in simple/easy language, sign language
- Accessibility of the methods to involve people with disabilities

In the next step, a place type survey was designed based on the results of the needs assessment workshops. The survey included questions about tools and technologies used to provide information about accessibility on site or to find and reach places. Furthermore, the specific question was asked for which type of places accessibility information is considered most important.

The survey was implemented digitally (in Google Forms) and then sent to over 400 stakeholders - primarily to disability representatives and advisory councils as well as to disability representatives and advisory boards of German cities and municipalities - in order to get as many participants as possible. In addition, 10 associations representing diverse people with disabilities were also asked to participate in the survey. Additionally, the survey was distributed through the Sozialhelden Newsletter with over 20,000 subscribers. For the participation of people with disabilities, the survey was deliberately designed to be short and in simple language. In terms of content, the question on requirements for the accessibility of places was used to determine how diverse the group of participants is and whether people with different disabilities took part in the survey. In the end, over 500 persons participated in the survey, with most of them favoring "doctors' surgeries" (22.8%) as the first vertical. The second most voted for was "public transport" (14.3%), followed by "toilets" (12.7%), "restaurants, cafés and pubs" (10.1%). But it turned out that especially the group of people with cognitive impairments is still underrepresented, whereas wheelchair users, on the other hand, are in a clear majority. This is a result of using social heroes' networks that have a focus on people with mobility restrictions, as the Wheelmap started with this domain of barriers.

Accessibility Criteria. In an online workshop with experts and target groups of the Wheelmap, the first vertical ("doctors' surgeries") was discussed in order to understand which barriers in this specific type of place might be of interest. Here, a discussion spun around the question which type of doctors' surgery might issue which barriers: Are there different barriers one might be interested to have on the Wheelmap for a general practitioner (GP), a dentist or a gynecologist? The original idea of the research team referred to general practitioners and dentists, but not to any specialist practices, because there is a wide differentiation of specialists that could not be represented in depth on the Wheelmap. However, in the course of the workshop, it became clear that this original view should be reconsidered - even given the fact that one wheelchair user was part of the research team and several more took part in the needs assessment workshops. The reason is that for the most part the same barriers apply to GPs, specialists or dentists - which the research team did not foresee. The requirements for accessibility identified by the accessibility criteria workshop attendants are the same for all medical spaces: barrier-free access to registration, registration options in simple/easy language, height-adjustable couches etc. The same applies to other levels, such as the waiting room, access to the treatment rooms, etc. Only specialist services such as X-ray, dentist chair, ultrasound or gynecological examination in the gynecology chair require specific requirements. This level of consideration was not perceived before the workshop and led to a fundamental expansion of the level of consideration of the first vertical from general to specific practices. To give some examples, especially the aspect of adaptability was often mentioned as an important criterion for an accessible medical practice. This means that there are height-adjustable couches and chairs, but also removable armrests or mobile treatment devices. Furthermore, access to the doctor's office was discussed during the workshop. The participants also specifically criticized this term, as it is very comprehensive for them. Access is about different aspects, such as access to the building, to the practice, but also to the treatment room. The same applies to the criteria for accessibility of the door. The workshop showed that a barrier-free door is much more than just an automatic opening. Rather, it requires additional information, such as "Does the door open inwards or outwards?", "Does the door swing?", "How cumbersome is the door?", "Does the door have a handle, a bell or an electric door opener?". These examples show that the criteria of accessibility defined by the IncluScience team must be presented in a more differentiated way by the target group. The target group thus led to an adaptation and expansion of the list of criteria. The affected person's perspective was particularly fruitful in this step, as non-affected persons were not able to identify such a large number of barriers as affected persons do.

Prototyping. The process for the implementation of the first vertical ("doctors' surgery") into Wheelmap.org ("prototyping") proceeded in a collaborative approach with the developers of Wheelmap as well as citizen scientists with disabilities who had been participating within the IncluScience project at various stages. Based on a desktop research on existing barrier checklists, the Wheelmap team proposed a list of criteria measuring the accessibility of medical practices which included structural properties such as elevators, steps, ramps, door widths, etc. as well as communication features such as translators, information in easy language and sign language. This list was then presented to stakeholders and Wheelmap users who discussed the criteria and edited the list. A particular point of discussion was whether to include subjective criteria to the list such as the capacity and experience of medical staff in the treatment of patients with disabilities. In order to guarantee the reliability and validity of the data, it was decided to exclusively use descriptive indicators to describe the accessibility of doctors' offices.

The next step of the process is the creation of a so-called "white label" on Wheelmap.org in order for users to test the criteria created. This means that the vertical is not yet present on the public Wheelmap app but can be tested by users who have access to the whitelabel. Together with the Incluscience researchers, users tested the criteria in a mapping scenario.

To test whether the new vertical prototype can be implemented on the main Wheelmap app, selected users were testing how well they can fill in the list of accessibility criteria for medical practices. The objective of this step was to test whether users are able to understand the questions in the form and whether they are able to provide the data reliably.

The indicators for success are: if the data is measurable, comprehensible and uniquely answerable (i.e. would every user give the same answer).

One aim of the project is to expand the user base of Wheelmap.org to persons with various disabilities, including persons with visual and auditory impairments as well as cognitive and developmental disabilities. Therefore, the new prototype was also tested to see how accessible it is. Once these findings are evaluated and implemented where possible, Wheelmap.org as a whole will become more accessible for more users as a result.

Mapping. Once the prototype was tested in the field, it was shared with regular Wheelmap users to start the mapping process. "Mapping" describes the act of users collecting accessibility data on a specific place and integrating it into Wheelmap.org. This was done through a survey. Once the data was inserted, it could be accessed on the Wheelmap app by any user.

There are two types of mapping processes. On the one hand, individual users map one or multiple places according to their accessibility. On the other hand, Wheelmap community managers set up so-called "mapping events", in which multiple users are instructed on the mapping process and then go outside to begin the mapping. Mapping campaigns are often initiated with volunteer organizations, local governments as well as companies. Mapping campaigns can also be organized for a specific type of place, for example schools, cafes or government buildings. The mapping process for the first vertical "doctors' surgeries" will be held both individually as well as coordinated through mapping campaigns starting in spring 2023. In this case one target group for an organized mapping campaign will be doctors who are able to map their own practices. While doctors are experts on the features of their own practice, they may be unfamiliar with the standards of accessibility. Therefore, it is necessary to train this group in order to receive quality data.

3.2 Second Vertical

The ambition of the research design with three iterations was to improve the methodology after each round and come to a tested methodology applicable to other citizen science projects. Based on the analysis of the first vertical creation process, the research team decided to apply the following changes to the second iteration:

- More workshops should be held in presence instead of online meetings in order to better include persons that do not use digital media.
- A wider invitation of stakeholders should assure a better representation of types of disabilities and overcome the overrepresentation of people with mobility impairments.
- A better announcement of the offered assistance (written interpreter, sign language interpreter) should invite persons that rely on these forms of assistance.
- An offer of an allowance for expenses should mitigate economic participation barriers.

Needs Assessment. According to these changes, but still under the restrictions of the pandemic, the needs assessment workshop of the second vertical was planned to take place at a presence scientific conference (INSIST conference in Berlin, October 6th 2022). The research team invited both academic researchers and persons possibly using the Wheelmap to that conference. The conference was aiming at the intersection of academic research and citizens, was at no charge and held in a barrier free venue that was easily accessible via public transport within Berlin. Our communication towards the target group offered different forms of assistance. However, no persons from the target group registered for this - a result the research team ascribed to the pandemic situation and the physical distance people with disabilities seeked to other people in this phase.

Against the planned improvements described above, the needs assessment workshop finally took place digitally on 10th November 2022. The stakeholders were actively invited to the workshop by the Social Heroes at an early stage. Assistance was already announced in the invitation. Furthermore, it was checked to what extent financial support from the project budget was possible. The latter was made possible so that all participants could be offered an allowance. In addition, compared to the first vertical, digital breakout rooms were used to encourage discussion at eye level. The number of participants in each breakout room should not exceed five.

The broad invitation as well as the targeted approach to the target group meant that not only more people with great expertise but also with different types of disabilities took part. However, there is also the problem for the second vertical that more people with mobility impairments tend to be reached than those with other types of disabilities.

Only the participation of persons with visual impairments improved, but not those with hearing or cognitive impairments.

Selection. Based on the needs assessment workshops and the resulting padlet, it was possible to list different types of places that are of particular interest to the participants in terms of accessibility criteria. Depending on the location type, sub-location types were also formed and any barriers that arise there were listed. For example, the location type "traffic space" with its sub-location types "kerbs, zebra crossings, traffic lights, car parks, petrol stations and bus stops" was addressed and barriers such as cobblestones, no pedestrian zone and too short green phases at traffic lights were highlighted. In addition to this, a survey with questions about types of places, its barriers and the needed accessibility information was designed and given to the community. However, it is not possible at the moment to make any statements on selection due to the ongoing activity of the survey.

4 Conclusion

The data collection for the first vertical took place in the pandemic and had to be conducted online. The exclusion of people who do not participate in online formats ("offliners") was only partially addressed by including their representatives, stakeholders or assistants and by facilitating workshops in a residential group for people with disabilities in Dortmund. An analysis of the composition of the participants revealed not only the disadvantage of offliners but also other lines of exclusion. One runs between residents of large cities or rural areas. In rural areas, significantly less information is available on the Wheelmap and significantly fewer people participate in data collection. In order to do justice to their claim of inclusion, the two following iterations must also show participation conditions for people from rural areas in order to be able to collect data there as well. A similar gap can be assumed - probably due to the online form - for older people. They were also underrepresented in the workshops; a finding that corresponds with the socio-demographics of "offliners". The following verticals should also better address this target group.

Overall, it can be stated that the recruitment of participants and thus the representation of their needs on the Wheelmap strongly depends on the access to these target groups. While the project had excellent contacts to the (digitally active) target group of wheelchair users and good contacts to the associations of blind, visually impaired and hearing-impaired people, there is a lack of approach concepts and contacts to people with cognitive disabilities, people in rural areas and elderly people. We suppose a link to the fact that Sozialhelden is an activist group that strongly builds on digital media and therefore predominantly establishes contacts to people using digital media, while "offliners" feel less involved. Steps for improvement must be taken by building up a network of contacts to the underrepresented target groups and their representatives.

References

1. Arnstein, S.R.: A ladder of citizen participation. J. Am. Inst. Plann. **35**(4), 216–224 (1969)
2. Eckhardt, J., Krüger, D.: Teilhabe durch co-creation. In: Schröer, A., Blättel-Mink, B., Schröder, A., Späte, K. (eds.) Innovation in und von Organisationen. Springer Nature, Wiesbaden (2023)
3. European Commission.: Citizen Science: elevating research an innovation through societal engagement. Publications Office of the European Union (2020a). https://data.europa.eu/doi/10.2777/624713. Accessed 9 Feb 2023
4. European Commission.: Science with and for society in Horizon 2020. Achievements and recommendations for Horizon Europe (2020b). https://op.europa.eu/en/publication-detail/-/publication/770d9270-cbc7-11ea-adf7-01aa75ed71a1. Accessed 9 Feb 2023
5. Kullenberg, C., Kasperowski, D.: What is citizen science? - a scientometric meta-analysis. PLoS ONE **11**(1), 1–16 (2016). https://doi.org/10.1371/journal.pone.0147152
6. UN General Assembly: Convention on the Rights of Persons with Disabilities: resolution/adopted by the General Assembly, 24 January 2007, A/RES/61/106. https://www.un.org/en/development/desa/population/migration/generalassembly/docs/globalcompact/A_RES_61_106.pdf. Accessed 9 Feb 2023

CognitiveNet: Enriching Foundation Models with Emotions and Awareness

Riccardo Emanuele Landi[1(✉)], Marta Chinnici[2], and Gerardo Iovane[3]

[1] Rigenera S.r.l., Via Aventina 7, Rome 00153, Italy
riccardo.landi@rigenera2020.it
[2] ENEA-R.C. Casaccia, Via Anguillarese 301, Rome 00123, Italy
marta.chinnici@enea.it
[3] Department of Computer Science, University of Salerno, Via Giovanni Paolo II, Fisciano 84084, Italy
giovane@unisa.it

Abstract. Foundation models are gaining considerable interest for their capacity of solving many downstream tasks without fine-tuning parameters on specific datasets. The same solutions can connect visual and linguistic representations through image-text contrastive learning. These abilities allow an artificial agent to act similarly to a human, but significant cognitive processes still need to be introduced in the learning process. The present study proposes an advancement to more human-like artificial intelligence by introducing CognitiveNet, a learnable architecture integrating foundation models. Starting from the latest studies in the field of Artificial Consciousness, a hierarchy of cognitive layers has been modeled and pre-trained for estimating the emotional content of images. By employing CLIP as the backbone model, significant concordant emotional activity was produced. Furthermore, the proposed model overcomes the accuracy of CLIP in classifying CIFAR-10 and -100 datasets through supervised optimization, suggesting CognitiveNet as a promising solution for solving classification tasks through online meta-learning.

Keywords: artificial emotion · awareness · computational consciousness · foundation models · computer vision · online learning · meta-learning

1 Introduction

Investigations on foundation models [1] are significantly advancing Artificial Intelligence toward human-like intelligence. These solutions employ self-supervised learning to pre-train a model which can solve extensive downstream tasks. Solutions based on the alignment of image and text representations [2–4,7] can provide language semantics to visual instances, as well as images to language sentences, without fine-tuning parameters on a dataset specifically collected to solve a task. These characteristics translate at least two human abilities in the artificial agent: i) the learning of an object without experiencing the object itself more than once, i.e., *zero-shot* capacity [5]; ii) the semantic connection

M. Antona and C. Stephanidis (Eds.): HCII 2023, LNCS 14020, pp. 99–118, 2023.
https://doi.org/10.1007/978-3-031-35681-0_7

of visual and linguistic content [2,6]. These two aspects provide a considerable advancement of deep learning models toward artificial general intelligence. Before foundation models, the agent was required to process a lot of data to learn the instances which associate an object to its semantics; furthermore, the learning of new objects required performing new training phases. The above results enhance the effectiveness of a single general model for solving problems of various kinds. Some of the most successful models in Natural Language Processing [8,9] and Computer Vision [2,10] seem to converge towards the identification of a single general model useful for solving many (hypothetically all) tasks of interest, i.e., a model which guarantees the *homogenization* [1]. A transformer-based architecture [11] could be fundamental for an agent as the mind is essential for a human to learn. This hypothesis is motivated by the fact that many transformer-based solutions are being compared with human performances [9] and all these models are characterized by similar architectures. Therefore, the study of human cognition seems significant for improving existing deep learning models, as well as designing new architectures for achieving superior performances in solving downstream tasks [12]. The present study proposes an advancement of foundation models towards human like-intelligence by introducing CognitiveNet, an architecture that integrates foundation models with artificial emotional activity and awareness. In particular, the solution integrates an encoder with cognitive layers inspired by the concepts of human sensation, perception, emotion, affection, attention, awareness, and consciousness. For conducting experiments, the CLIP model (Contrastive Language-Image Pre-Training) [2] was employed for processing images. In particular, the model was pre-trained emotionally and tested on two benchmarking datasets (CIFAR-10 and -100) to evaluate our awareness model in performing classification. The emotional activity, instead, was tested on videos showing emotional scenes to prove the consistency of the model's reactions. The results show that CognitiveNet improves the accuracy of CLIP in classifying CIFAR-10 and -100 datasets by employing our model of awareness through supervised optimization. Furthermore, the proposed solution consistently estimates the emotional content of visual stimuli sequences. The proposed model was revealed to be a suitable solution for optimizing zero-shot transfer in performing supervised classification through online meta-learning.

Providing artificial emotional activity and awareness to foundation models allows the investigation of new architectures that take into account important factors of human cognition, as well as advance deep learning towards artificial general intelligence. In Sect. 2, a background related to the research in foundation models is presented, while in Sect. 3 the proposed solution is described. Finally, Sects. 4 and 5 are dedicated to the conducted experiments and conclusions, respectively.

2 Background

Some of the most influential foundation models are BERT [8], GPT-3 [9], and CLIP [2]. The first, BERT, was designed by introducing bi-directional self-attention to the original Transformer architecture [11]. The model learns representations for both single and pair of sentences through self-supervised pre-training. Then, the model successfully transfers to a wide range of natural language tasks through fine-tuning. BERT improves the Transformer architecture [11] by introducing bidirectionality in the text processing. In their study, Brown et al. [9] proposed GPT-3, an autoregressive large language model based on a classical transformer-based architecture composed of 175 billion parameters trained on a wide set of corpora. The authors tested the model's transfer learning abilities on language modeling, cloze, completion, question answering, and translation tasks. The results show that GPT-3 achieves strong zero-shot performances when compared with state-of-the-art solutions. The model still suffers from decoherence, useless repetitions, and contradictions, which, as suggested by the authors, could be faced by learning an objective function from humans or by employing reinforcement learning. They also suggested introducing images for learning better multi-modal representations. With CLIP, Radford et al. [2] provided evidence of the robustness of zero-shot learners based on contrastive learning of image and text representations. The authors achieved comparable accuracy to supervised ImageNet models by learning aligned representations of images and texts. Their approach consists of employing two separate image and text encoders for generating two temporary embeddings; these representations are then projected in a new learnable space in which their cosine similarity is maximized through the cross-entropy loss function. The training was performed on a dataset consisting of 400 million image-text pairs. This form of self-supervised learning allows aligning image and text representations in a new learnable multi-modal space. The zero-shot capacity of CLIP in image processing is reached through the learning of image representations that are similar to text embeddings in their related semantic space. In this context, contrastive learning permits learning a multi-modal hypothesis for image and text processing, as well as a flexible solution for zero-shot transfer. The model was evaluated on tasks of image classification, optical character recognition, action recognition, geo-localization, and object detection, achieving competitive results with respect to the related supervised backbones.

Foundation models are flexible in solving many multi-modal tasks, but they still lack important human cognitive processes. Apart from BERT, which requires parameter tuning for solving downstream tasks, GPT-3 and CLIP can learn representations of the world through zero-shot transfer, a capacity that makes an artificial agent comparable to human-like intelligence. However, these models do not possess emotions and awareness, which are distinguishable factors of human cognition [13]. Foundation models do not possess the ability to evaluate their inputs and outputs for dynamically conditioning the responses. The process of estimating the emotional content of world instances could be beneficial for a model to filter eventual responses characterized by inequity and fairness. Under the above premises, the present study proposes CognitiveNet for providing foundation models with artificial emotional activity and awareness.

3 CognitiveNet

CognitiveNet is inspired by the studies of Iovane et al. [14] and Iovane and Landi [15]. As shown in Fig. 1, it consists of an encoder, seven cognitive layers, and an emotion classifier. For classification tasks, the architecture can be integrated with a classifier evaluating the output of the cognitive layers. In the latest advancements, the authors of the prodromal study focused on the scientific coherency of the proposed architecture of cognitive layers; instead, in the present work it was intended to optimize the model for being executed through a GPU and evaluated as a model for providing artificial emotions and awareness to a foundation model. The proposed solution is shown in Fig. 1, in which all the components of the architecture, together with the related interactions, are considered.

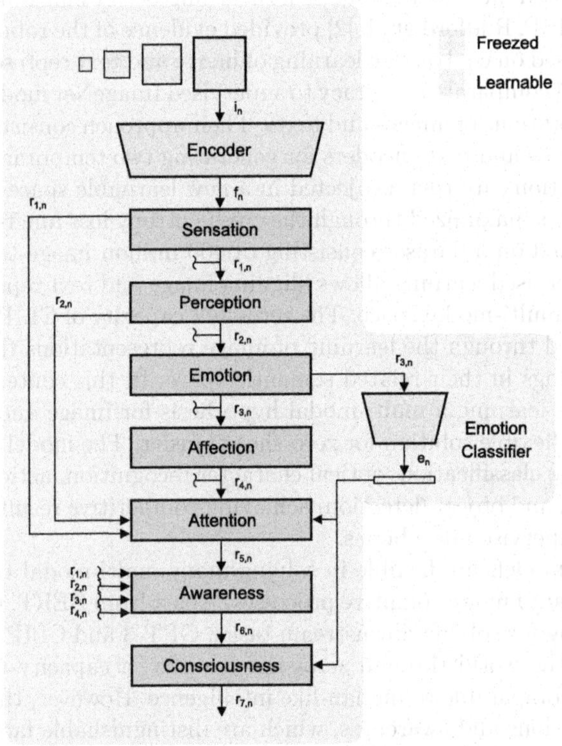

Fig. 1. CognitiveNet in the emotional pre-training phase.

Each image that arrives at the agent at the time instant n is processed by an encoder to produce an embedding representing the most significant features of the input. The obtained representation is subsequently acquired by the Sensation cognitive layer, which computes a new representation, i.e., a cognitive instance (in the present work, the output of cognitive layers is called *cognitive instance*). After passing the first cognitive layer, the data enter the Perception, Emotion, Affection, Attention, Awareness, and Consciousness cognitive layers, sequentially. The Emotion cognitive instance is also evaluated by an emotion classifier, which associates the given embedding to an instance of the emotional spectrum, i.e., a softmax output providing the probabilities related to anger, disgust, fear, happiness, sadness, surprise, and neutral state. The Attention cognitive layer evaluates the emotional spectrum and acquires the Sensation, Perception, Emotion, and Affection representations for computing a weight of attention.

The first layer, i.e., the Sensation, imposes a threshold to the input and enriches the learned representation with a memory whose elements decay exponentially according to a removal period. The Perception, Emotion, and Affection cognitive layers enrich the learned representation of the input with a memory whose elements decay with polynomial low according to the related removal periods. The Attention cognitive layer is not learnable and extracts an attention weight by evaluating the Sensation, Perception, and Affection cognitive instances, together with the emotional spectrum estimated by the emotion classifier coupled with the Emotion cognitive layer. Awareness produces a weight by evaluating the learned representations of the first four cognitive layers (i.e., Sensation, Perception, Emotion, and Affection) by projecting them into hyperspheres. Finally, the Consciousness cognitive layer computes a weight by associating each of the Awareness hyperspheres to a moral semantic depending on the output of the emotion classifier; then, the layer connects the hyperspheres into an interconnected graph characterized by energy and entropy. In the subsequent Sections, a formal definition of each cognitive layer is provided.

The training and inference of CognitiveNet are composed of the following phases:

1. ***Emotional pre-training***: initializes the model with an emotional history (i.e., with the emotional cognitive biases); this phase allows a foundation model to acquire artificial emotion.
2. ***Awareness training***: in case it is intended to apply the model for learning a classifier on a given dataset, the Awareness cognitive layer can be employed for doing so by selecting the cognitive layer from which consider the representations for generating the hyperspheres; this phase allows an agent to acquire artificial awareness, as well as perform online meta-learning.
3. ***Emotional inference***: the model is employed for inferring the emotional reaction to a visual stimulus, the related Awareness' hypersphere, and the Consciousness' graph; this phase allows a foundation model to produce artificial emotion.
4. ***Awareness inference***: in case the model is applied for classification, the Awareness cognitive layer is employed for inferring the label associated with a visual stimulus; this phase allows a foundation model to produce artificial awareness, as well as perform classification based on the knowledge acquired through online meta-learning.

The model is end-to-end learnable, but the present study considers freezing the encoder and the last four cognitive layers, i.e., Affection, Attention, Awareness, and Consciousness.

3.1 Sensation, Perception, Emotion and Affection

The Sensation acquires a sequence of S embeddings of size F and learns a new representation by modulating the input with an exponential decay function. The output of the cognitive layer is defined as

$$\mathbf{r}_{1,n} = Sum_2(Expand_{S,0}(Thr_{H,2}(\mathbf{x}_n)) \cdot Expand_{F,3}(\mathbf{D}_1)) \cdot \mathbf{W}_1, \tag{1}$$

with

$$\mathbf{D}_1 = UpTri(\mathbf{J}) \cdot ExpDecay(\mathbf{L}), \tag{2}$$

$$ExpDecay(\mathbf{L}) = \frac{1}{1-e}(e^{-\frac{\mathbf{L}}{T_1}} - e), \tag{3}$$

where $\mathbf{x}_n \in \mathbb{R}^{F \times 1}$ is the input vector provided at the time instant n, $\mathbf{D}_1 \in \mathbb{R}^{S \times S}$ is the decay matrix, $\mathbf{J} \in \mathbb{R}^{S \times S}$ is a unit matrix, $\mathbf{W}_1 \in \mathbb{R}^{S \times F}$ is the vector of weights, $\mathbf{L} \in \mathbb{Z}^{S \times 1}$ is a linear vector of integers defined in the range $[0, S]$, where S is the size of the time window and F is the size of the input vector, while $T_1 > 0$ is the removal period of the cognitive layer. The *ExpDecay* function computes the exponential decay vector, while *UpTri* provides an upper triangular matrix. The function Sum_2 computes the matrix sum along the second dimension, while $Expand_{F,3}$ provides the expansion of F along the third dimension, where F is the size of the input vector $\mathbf{x}_n$. Similarly, $Expand_{S,0}$ adds a new dimension and provides the expansion of S elements along that dimension, where S is the size of the time window. Finally, the $Thr_{H,2}$ function sets to zero all the elements with a magnitude lower than a threshold H. Figure 2 shows the architecture of the Sensation cognitive layer.

This layer models the human sensation by considering the threshold under which a stimulus is not perceived [16] and a short-term memory [17] through which past processed stimuli are weighted.

The Perception, Emotion, and Affection acquire a sequence of S embeddings of size F and learn a new representation by modulating the input with a polynomial decay function. The output of the cognitive layers is defined as

$$\mathbf{r}_{i,n} = Sum_2(Expand_{S,0}(\mathbf{x}_n) \cdot Expand_{F,3}(\mathbf{D}_i)) \cdot \mathbf{W}_i, \tag{4}$$

with

$$\mathbf{D}_i = UpTri(\mathbf{J}) \cdot PolyDecay(\mathbf{L}), \tag{5}$$

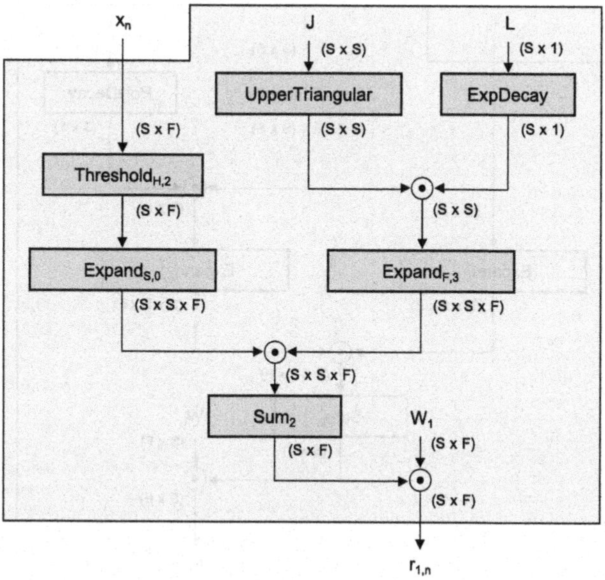

Fig. 2. The Sensation cognitive layer.

$$PolyDecay(\mathbf{L}) = \frac{T_i + 1}{T_i}\left(\frac{1}{\mathbf{L}+1} - \frac{1}{T_i + 1}\right), \tag{6}$$

where $i \in \{2, 3, 4\}$ is the index identifying the Perception, Emotion, and Affection cognitive layers, $\mathbf{x}_n \in \mathbb{R}^{S \times F}$ is the input vector provided at the time instant n, $\mathbf{D}_i \in \mathbb{R}^{S \times S}$ is the decay matrix of the i-th cognitive layer, $\mathbf{J} \in \mathbb{R}^{S \times S}$ is the unit matrix, $\mathbf{W}_i \in \mathbb{R}^{S \times F}$ is the vector of weights of the i-th cognitive layer, $\mathbf{L} \in \mathbb{Z}^{S \times 1}$ is a linear vector of integers defined in the range $[0, S]$, where S is the size of the time window and F is the size of the input vector, while $T_i > 0$ is the removal period of the i-th cognitive layer. The *PolyDecay* function computes the polynomial decay vector, while *UpTri* provides an upper triangular matrix. The function Sum_2 computes the matrix sum along the second dimension, while $Expand_{F,3}$ provides the expansion of F along the third dimension, where F is the size of the feature vector. Similarly, $Expand_{S,0}$ adds a new dimension and provides the expansion of S elements along that dimension, where S is the size of the time window. Figure 3 shows the architecture of the Perception, Emotion, and Affection cognitive layers.

The Perception was considered as a filter of the Sensation cognitive instances, while the Emotion associates the Perception's cognitive instance with the emotions of anger, disgust, fear, happiness, sadness, surprise, and the neutral state. The Affection was considered as a filter of the Emotion cognitive instances. The emotional classes were chosen according to the essential categorization provided by Ekman [18].

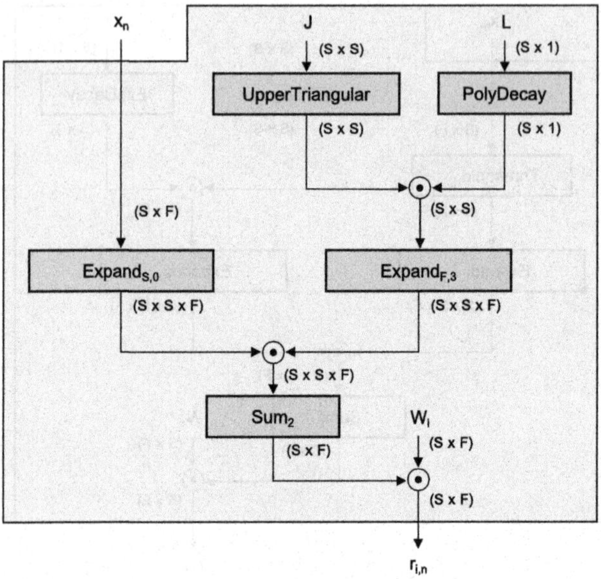

Fig. 3. The architecture adopted for the Perception, Emotion, and Affection cognitive layers.

3.2 Attention, Awareness and Consciousness

The Attention evaluates the emotional spectrum and acquires the Sensation, Perception, Emotion, and Affection cognitive instances to provide a weight of attention. The output of the cognitive layer is defined as

$$\mathbf{r}_{5,n} = Max(Stack_1(\mathbf{A}_1, \mathbf{A}_2, Pad_{F-7,2}(\mathbf{e}_n^T), \mathbf{A}_4)), \tag{7}$$

with

$$\mathbf{A}_i = \frac{Sum_1(\mathbf{r}_{i,n})}{Max_1(\mathbf{B}_i, Max_2(Sum_1(\mathbf{r}_{i,n}) - Min_2(Sum_1(\mathbf{r}_{i,n}))))}, \tag{8}$$

where $i \in \{1, 2, 4\}$ is the index identifying the Sensation, Perception, and Affection cognitive layers, $\mathbf{e}_n \in [0, 1]^{7\times1}$ is the emotional spectrum, $\mathbf{A}_i \in \mathbb{R}^{1\times F}$ is the local attention associated with the i-th cognitive layer, where $\mathbf{B}_i \in \mathbb{R}^{1\times1}$ is the historical upper bound reached by the local attention before normalization. Functions Max_1 and Max_2 compute the maximum of the input along the first and second dimensions, respectively, while Sum_1 provides the sum along the first dimension. Figure 4 shows the architecture of the Attention cognitive layer.

Attention depends on Sensation and Perception since human attention involves the perception of a stimulus. The cognitive layer depends also on Emotion and Affection, as human attention depends significantly on the emotion the subject feels as a consequence of a stimulus [19,20]. This layer models visual bottom-up attention, i.e., attention affected by external factors only.

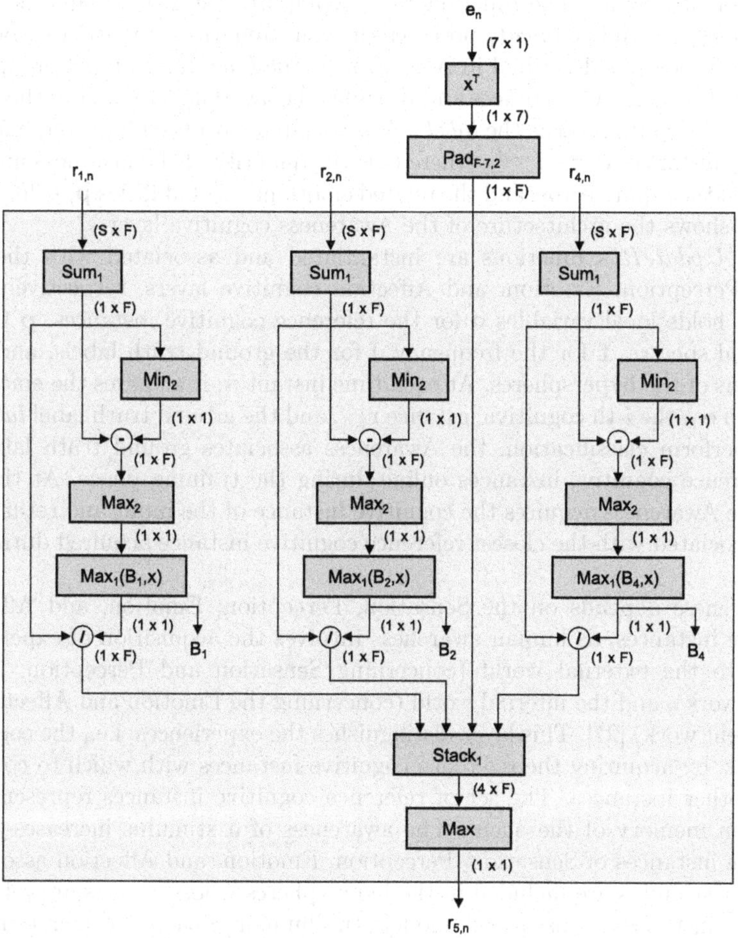

Fig. 4. The Attention cognitive layer.

The Awareness acquires the Sensation, Perception, Emotion, and Affection cognitive instances, produces the related hyperspheres, and learns four weights associated with the above cognitive layers. The result is a weight of awareness, which is defined as

$$\mathbf{r}_{6,n} = \mathbf{r}_{5,n} \cdot Sum_1(Concat_1(\mathbf{a}_1, \mathbf{a}_2, \mathbf{a}_3, \mathbf{a}_4) \cdot \mathbf{W}_6), \tag{9}$$

with

$$(\mathbf{a}_i, label, \mathbf{o}_i, \mathbf{p}_i) = UpdateRIs(\mathbf{e}_n^T, Sum_1(\mathbf{r}_{i,n}), label_{GT}), \tag{10}$$

where $i \in \{1, 2, 3, 4\}$ is the index identifying the Sensation, Perception, Emotion, and Affection cognitive layers, $\mathbf{e}_n \in [0, 1]^{7\times1}$ is the emotional spectrum, $\mathbf{a}_i \in [0, 1]^{1\times1}$ is the awareness related to the i-th cognitive layer, and $\mathbf{W}_6 \in \mathbb{R}^{4\times1}$ is the vector of weights. The function Sum_1 computes the matrix sum along the first dimension, while $Concat_1$ provides the concatenation of matrices along the same dimension. As described in Algorithm 1, the $UpdateRIs$ function updates the reference cognitive instances and provides the awareness related to the input. The procedure also returns the $label \in \mathbb{Z}$ associated with the input, the reference cognitive instances $\mathbf{o}_i \in \mathbb{R}^{C\times F}$, where C is the quantity of the instances and F is the size of the input vector, and the related emotional probabilities $\mathbf{p}_i \in [0, 1]^{C\times7}$. Figure 5 shows the architecture of the Awareness cognitive layer.

Four $UpdateRIs$ functions are instantiated and associated with the Sensation, Perception, Emotion, and Affection cognitive layers, respectively. The function holds local variables $\mathbf{o}$ for the reference cognitive instances, $\mathbf{p}$ for the emotional spectra, $\mathbf{f}$ for the frequency, $\mathbf{l}$ for the ground truth labels, and R as the radius of the hyperspheres. At each time instant n, it acquires the emotional spectrum $\mathbf{e}_n$, the i-th cognitive instance $\mathbf{r}_{i,n}$, and the ground truth label $label_{GT}$.

To perform classification, the Awareness associates ground truth labels to the reference cognitive instances online during the training phase. At the test time, the Awareness acquires the cognitive instance of the input and returns the label associated with the closest reference cognitive instance acquired during the training.

Awareness depends on the Sensation, Perception, Emotion, and Affection cognitive instances, as human awareness involves the acquisition of experiences related to the external world (concerning Sensation and Perception, in the present work), and the internal world (concerning the Emotion and Affection, in the present work) [21]. This layer distinguishes the experiences, i.e., the cognitive instances, by acquiring the reference cognitive instances with which to compare all the other instances. The set of reference cognitive instances represents the long-term memory of the agent. The awareness of a stimulus increases as the cognitive instances of Sensation, Perception, Emotion, and Affection associated with that stimulus are included in the hyperspheres whose centers are reference cognitive instances. This aspect models the human capacity of increasing the awareness of a stimulus by incrementally acquiring experiences related to the stimulus itself [22].

Consciousness connects the Awareness' hyperspheres locally to the Sensation, Perception, Emotion, and Affection spaces, associates the hyperspheres with moral semantics, and learns four weights of consciousness associated with the above cognitive layers. The result is a weight of consciousness. The output of the cognitive layer is defined as

$$\mathbf{r}_{7,n} = \mathbf{r}_{6,n} \cdot Sum_1(Concat_1(\mathbf{Y}_1, \mathbf{Y}_2, \mathbf{Y}_3, \mathbf{Y}_4) \cdot \mathbf{W}_7), \tag{11}$$

with

$$(\mathbf{Y}_i, \mathbf{Q}_i) = UpdateGraph(\mathbf{o}_i, \mathbf{p}_i), \tag{12}$$

Algorithm 1: Procedure for updating the reference cognitive instances.

Procedure: *UpdateRIs*
Data: $\mathbf{o} \in \mathbb{R}^{C\times F}$, $\mathbf{d} \in \mathbb{Z}^{C\times 1}$, $\mathbf{p} \in [0,1]^{C\times 7}$, $\mathbf{f} \in \mathbb{R}^{C\times 1}$, $\mathbf{l} \in \mathbb{Z}^{C\times 1}$, $R > 0$
Require: $\mathbf{e} \in [0,1]^{1\times 7}$, $\mathbf{x} \in \mathbb{R}^{1\times F}$, $label_{GT} \in \mathbb{Z}$
Result: $\mathbf{a} \in [0,1]^{1\times 1}$, $label \in \mathbb{Z}$, $\mathbf{o} \in \mathbb{R}^{C\times F}$, $\mathbf{p} \in [0,1]^{C\times 7}$

```
c ← Size_1(o)
if c = 1 then
    o ← x
    l ← [label_GT]
    f ← [1]
    p ← e
    a ← [1]
    label ← label_GT
    return a, label, o, p
else
    dists ← Dist_1(o, x)
    dists_logic ← dists > R
    NewInstance ← not 0 in dists_logic
    if NewInstance then
        if Training then
            o ← Stack_1(o, x)
            l ← Stack_1(l, [label_GT])
            f ← Stack_1(f, [1])
            p ← Stack_1(p, e)
            a ← [1]
            label ← label_GT
            return a, label, o, p
        else
            index ← ArgMin_2(dists_logic)
            f[index] ← f[index] + 1
            a ← [f[index]/Max(f)]
            label ← l[index]
            return a, label, o, p
        end
    else
        index ← ArgMin_2(dists_logic)
        f[index] ← f[index] + 1
        a ← [f[index]/Max(f)]
        label ← l[index]
        return a, label, o, p
    end
end
```

where $i \in \{1, 2, 3, 4\}$ is the index identifying the Sensation, Perception, Emotion, and Affection cognitive layers, $\mathbf{Y}_i \in [0,1]^{1\times 1}$ is the consciousness intensity of the i-th cognitive layer, $\mathbf{Q}_i \in \mathbb{R}^{C\times C}$ is the adjacency matrix, $\mathbf{W}_7 \in \mathbb{R}^{4\times 1}$ the vector of weights, $\mathbf{o}_i \in \mathbb{R}^{C\times F}$ are the reference cognitive instances, and $\mathbf{p}_i \in \mathbb{R}^{C\times F}$ the related emotional probabilities, where C is the quantity of reference cognitive

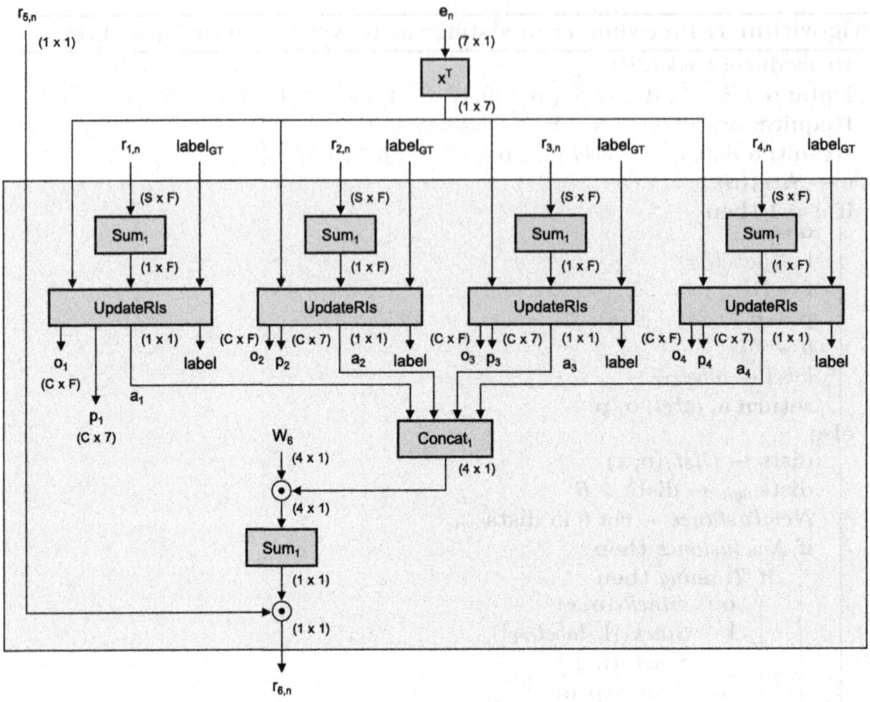

Fig. 5. The Awareness cognitive layer.

instances and F is the size of the input vector. The function Sum_1 computes the sum, while $Concat_1$ concatenates the matrices along the first dimension. As described in Algorithm 2, the *UpdateGraph* function updates the Consciousness Graph and provides an intensity of consciousness intensity related to the input. The procedure also returns the adjacency matrix $\mathbf{Q} \in \mathbb{R}^{C \times C}$ of the graph.

The layer computes the index of the most intense emotion in the emotional spectra and associates that index with a moral semantic. A moral semantic consists of one element in the set $\{-1, 0, 1\}$, in which -1, 0, and 1 indicate a negative, neutral, and positive semantic, respectively. The indices associated with the emotions of anger, disgust, fear, and sadness are connected to a negative semantic (-1); the index of the neutral state is connected to a neutral semantic (0); finally, the indices representing the emotions of happiness and surprise are connected to a positive semantic (1).

Consciousness is represented as a graph in which each edge between two nodes is associated with the mean of the semantics of the nodes multiplied by the distance between the nodes themselves. The Consciousness Graph is represented by the adjacency matrix $\mathbf{Q}$. The final Consciousness cognitive instance is given

Algorithm 2: Procedure for updating the graph of Consciousness.

Procedure: *UpdateGraph*
Data: $E_b > 0$, $H_b > 0$
Require: $\mathbf{o} \in \mathbb{R}^{C \times F}$, $\mathbf{p} \in [0, 1]^{C \times 7}$
Result: $\mathbf{Y} \in [0, 1]^{1 \times 1}$, $\mathbf{Q} \in \mathbb{R}^{C \times C}$
$c \leftarrow Size_1(\mathbf{o})$
if $c = 1$ **then**
  $\mathbf{Y} \leftarrow [1]$
  $\mathbf{Q} \leftarrow [0]$
  return $\mathbf{Y}, \mathbf{Q}$
else
  $\mathbf{args} = ArgMax_2(p)$
  $\mathbf{args}[\mathbf{args} = 0] = -1$
  $\mathbf{args}[\mathbf{args} = 1] = -1$
  $\mathbf{args}[\mathbf{args} = 2] = -1$
  $\mathbf{args}[\mathbf{args} = 3] = 1$
  $\mathbf{args}[\mathbf{args} = 4] = 0$
  $\mathbf{args}[\mathbf{args} = 5] = -1$
  $\mathbf{args}[\mathbf{args} = 6] = 1$
  $\mathbf{Q}_{args} = Expand_{C,2}(\mathbf{args})$
  $\mathbf{Q}_{sems} = (\mathbf{Q}_{args}^T + \mathbf{Q}_{args})/2$
  $\mathbf{Q}_{dists} = Dist_1(\mathbf{o}, \mathbf{o})$
  $\mathbf{Q} = \mathbf{Q}_{dists} \cdot \mathbf{Q}_{sems}$
  $E = Energy(\mathbf{Q})$
  $H = Entropy(\mathbf{Q})$
  $E_b = Max(E_b, E)$
  $H_b = Max(H_b, H)$
  $\mathbf{Y} = [E/E_b + H/H_b]$
  return $\mathbf{Y}, \mathbf{Q}$
end

by the sum of the normalized energy and entropy contributions in the above graph.

In Algorithm 2, the energy and entropy of a matrix $\mathbf{X}$ are defined as

$$Energy(\mathbf{X}) = Sum(Abs_{1,2}(\mathbf{X})), \tag{13}$$

$$Entropy(\mathbf{X}) = Abs(-Mean(Log_{1,2}(Softmax_{1,2}(\mathbf{X})))), \tag{14}$$

where $Log_{1,2}$ and $Softmax_{1,2}$ compute the logarithm and the softmax functions along the first and second dimensions of a matrix, respectively. The *Abs* function provides the absolute value of a scalar, while $Abs_{1,2}$ is the absolute value of all matrix elements. The functions *Sum* and *Mean* compute the sum and mean of the whole matrix. Figure 6 shows the architecture of the Consciousness cognitive layer.

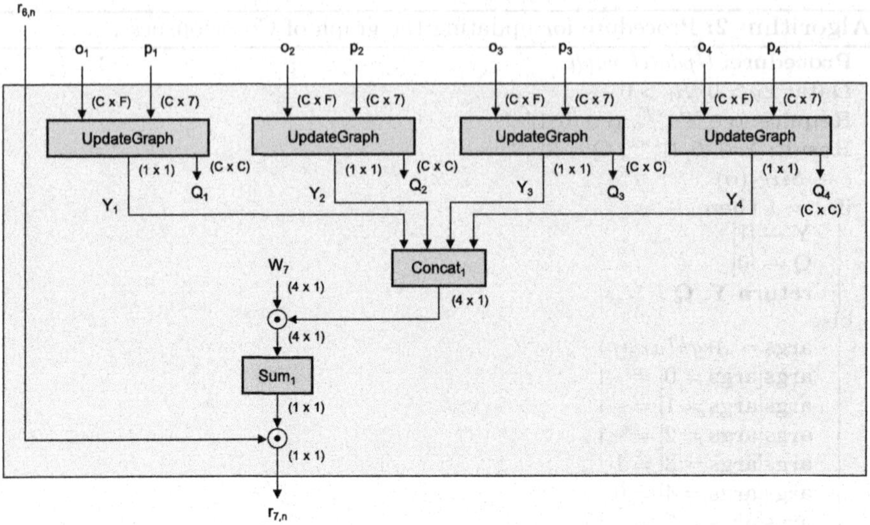

Fig. 6. The Consciousness cognitive layer.

This layer models consciousness as the capacity of an artificial agent to connect experiences and give them moral attributes. The content of consciousness, therefore, can be described by the energetic and entropic contributions of the above connections.

4 Experiments

The emotional pre-training phase was performed by learning the Sensation, Perception, and Emotion cognitive layers for classifying the EMOd dataset [23]. The database provides 1019 images eliciting emotional reactions. In the present study, as shown in Fig. 7, it was decided to associate the visual stimuli to the considered emotional classes of anger, disgust, fear, happiness, sadness, surprise, and the neutral state. In particular, 48, 31, 87, 65, 303, 97, and 68 samples were associated with the above classes, respectively, of which 80% of the samples were collected for the training set. For the emotional pre-training a window size $S = 1$, batch size of 32, and learning rate of 0.001 were chosen. The radius R_i of the hyperspheres associated with the i-th cognitive layer were initialized as unitary and optimized during the training by computing the third of the minimum distance among the collected reference cognitive instances. The threshold $H = -\infty$ was chosen for filtering the Sensation's input, while the removal period T_i of the i-th cognitive layer was fixed as unitary.

To employ the model for classification, the datasets CIFAR-10 and -100 [24] were considered. Testing the model on a generic classification task allows getting proof of whether CognitiveNet's cognitive layers improve the performances of the backbone. Given that CognitiveNet performs the classification of cognitive

Fig. 7. Examples of EMOd images associated with the considered emotional sets of anger (a), disgust (b), fear (c), happiness (d), neutral (e), sadness (f), and surprise (g).

instances by comparing them with the acquired reference cognitive instances, the task of classifying is characterized by an online meta-learning approach. In fact, the ability to learn a classifier online is guaranteed by the continuous acquisition of reference cognitive instances, as well as their association with ground truth labels. Instead, meta-learning is characterized by the evaluation of previous predictions when producing inference. The Awareness training is online and incremental; therefore, for learning a classifier for CIFAR-10 and -100, an initialization of CognitiveNet was imposed at the beginning of each epoch. Therefore, the model acquires hyperspheres characterized by different reference cognitive instances at each epoch. The training stops when the optimal set of reference cognitive instances is found.

In the present work, it was decided to experiment CognitiveNet with a zero-shot encoder for generating features, which can consistently project inputs into a semantic space. It was decided to employ the original pre-trained CLIP encoder [2], with a size of the input vector $F = 512$, for conducting our experiments; in particular, a vision transformer [10] and the encoder of a text-based transformer [11] were employed for producing aligned representations of images and texts, respectively. CognitiveNet was employed for classifying CIFAR-10 and -100 by applying the Awareness cognitive layer in the spaces of the Sensation (S-Awareness), Perception (P-Awareness), Emotion (E-Awareness), and Affection (A-Awareness) cognitive layers, as well as in the original feature space, i.e., the space of the embeddings directly provided by CLIP. Furthermore, a comparison with the original zero-shot transfer was also provided. The machine employed for the experiments was equipped with an Intel Core i9 processor, 62 GB of RAM, 610 GB of SSD HDD, and GPU NVIDIA RTX A5000. Given that CognitiveNet employs an incremental form of meta-learning, the GPU memory usage

Table 1. CognitiveNet results on CIFAR-10 by employing the Awareness for classification.

Results on CIFAR-10				
Model	**RIs**	**Accuracy**	**GPU Mem. Usage (GB)**	**Inference Time (ms)**
CLIP (zero-shot transfer)	No	0.8737	1.64	9.13 ± 20.57
CognitiveNet (CLIP) (Awareness) (ours)	6250	0.8777	1.65	9.18 ± 20.75
	9053	0.8813	1.66	9.24 ± 20.68
	10745	0.8904	1.68	9.34 ± 20.79
CognitiveNet (CLIP) (S-Awareness) (ours)	8743	0.8777	1.77	15.89 ± 20.41
	11941	0.8962	1.72	16.34 ± 20.36
	16499	**0.8992**	1.77	16.73 ± 26.2
CognitiveNet (CLIP) (P-Awareness) (ours)	10361	0.8777	1.73	16.17 ± 20.29
	13973	0.8831	1.76	16.55 ± 20.32
	14327	0.8833	1.77	16.4 ± 20.12
CognitiveNet (CLIP) (E-Awareness) (ours)	5687	0.8654	1.73	16.58 ± 25.95
	7470	0.8733	1.78	16.65 ± 20.13
	9088	0.8738	1.79	16.9 ± 20.3
CognitiveNet (CLIP) (A-Awareness) (ours)	2442	0.8349	1.72	15.79 ± 20.44
	2756	0.8365	1.72	16.21 ± 20.36
	3037	0.8368	1.73	16.15 ± 20.34

Table 2. CognitiveNet results on CIFAR-100 by employing the Awareness for classification.

Results on CIFAR-100				
Model	**RIs**	**Accuracy**	**GPU Mem. Usage (GB)**	**Inference Time (ms)**
CLIP (zero-shot transfer)	No	0.5518	1.82	8.99 ± 20.53
CognitiveNet (CLIP) (Awareness) (ours)	14989	0.6044	1.7	9.37 ± 20.85
	25324	0.6383	1.74	9.42 ± 20.9
	28263	**0.6458**	1.75	9.63 ± 20.88
CognitiveNet (CLIP) (S-Awareness) (ours)	17282	0.6055	1.75	16.09 ± 20.28
	21069	0.6225	1.99	19.03 ± 20.48
	28398	0.6378	2.41	20.65 ± 20.13
CognitiveNet (CLIP) (P-Awareness) (ours)	16830	0.6007	2.2	19.94 ± 20.23
	20540	0.6085	2.17	20.45 ± 20.25
	22804	0.6129	2.19	21.04 ± 20.48
CognitiveNet (CLIP) (E-Awareness) (ours)	11998	0.564	1.83	16.41 ± 20.33
	14480	0.5784	2.32	23.16 ± 20.13
	17310	0.5748	1.78	16.9 ± 20.23
CognitiveNet (CLIP) (A-Awareness) (ours)	12514	0.5493	1.82	17.73 ± 20.44
	13717	0.5518	1.83	17.86 ± 20.14
	14671	0.5538	1.84	17.94 ± 20.45

and inference time were evaluated in addition to the accuracy. Tables 1 and 2 show the results concerning the training of classifiers based on the CLIP encoder and the Sensation, Perception, Emotion, and Affection Awareness.

The emotional pre-training achieved 72.23% accuracy on the EMOd test set consisting of 138 samples. Apart from the classifier trained on CIFAR-10 and based on Affection Awareness, all the trained models overcame the original zero-shot transfer in terms of accuracy. On CIFAR-10, it was found that the most accurate model is CognitiveNet employing the S-Awareness, while on

CIFAR-100 the most promising model was CognitiveNet employing Awareness directly on the output of CLIP. In classifying CIFAR-10, the highest amount of reference cognitive instances was acquired by the most accurate model, i.e., the S-Awareness, which uses 12% more GPU and takes 45% more inference time than the original zero-shot transfer. On the same dataset, the model overcoming the accuracy of the zero-shot transfer by keeping memory usage and inference time limited is the Awareness applied directly to the embeddings produced by CLIP, with 6250 reference instances. In classifying CIFAR-100, the highest amount of reference instances was acquired by S-Awareness with 28390 instances; the model uses 24.48% more GPU and takes 56.46% more inference time than the zero-shot transfer. On the same dataset, the model overcoming the accuracy of the backbone by keeping limited the memory usage is the E-Awareness, with 11998 reference cognitive instances.

In all the experiments, each model employing the Awareness for classification increases its performances as the acquired reference cognitive instances increase. However, it is interesting to notice that while all the classifiers trained on CIFAR-10 through the Awareness employ more memory than the original CLIP encoder, the best classifier trained on CIFAR-10 is more spatially efficient than the same original backbone even though it collected much more reference cognitive instances. Furthermore, the classifiers trained on CIFAR-100 provided much more improvement than the same classifiers learned on CIFAR-10 when compared to the original zero-shot transfer. The most accurate model trained on CIFAR-100 achieves 14% more accuracy, 3.84% less GPU usage, and 6.65% more inference time than the backbone.

To test the behavior of CognitiveNet in producing artificial emotional activity it was decided to let the model process 25 videos eliciting the considered emotional classes. Table 3 shows the considered types of scenes employed as the ground truth.

Each test consists of providing video frames to the model and computing the weight distributions associated with the produced emotions. The videos are heterogeneous in duration, varying from 4 to 20 minutes, and the weight distributions are computed by dividing the number of reference instances associated with the emotional classes by the total amount of reference cognitive instances.

Table 3. Topics of the episodes provided as a test for analyzing the emotional activity.

Topics of the test episodes	
GT Class	**Topics**
Anger	Intensive farming, pollution
Disgust	Disgusting compilation
Fear	Explosions, war, dangerous roads, burnings
Happiness	Sport celebration, wedding party
Neutral	Walking in the city, daily life scene
Sadness	Funeral, emergency room scene, injuries
Surprise	Art gallery, animals scene, extreme sports scene, surfing

Table 4. Emotional weight distributions extracted from the episodes provided as a test.

Emotional distributions extracted from the test episodes (95% confidence intervals)								
GT Class	Episodes (N)	Anger ($p = 0.1383$)	Disgust ($p < 0.001$)	Fear ($p < 0.001$)	Happiness ($p < 0.001$)	Neutral ($p = 0.0105$)	Sadness ($p < 0.001$)	Surprise ($p = 0.0046$)
Anger	4	0.14 ± 0.07	0.05 ± 0.05	0.08 ± 0.07	0.01 ± 0.01	0.46 ± 0.12	0.03 ± 0.02	0.23 ± 0.08
Disgust	2	0.1 ± 0.01	0.58 ± 0.13	0.04 ± 0.05	0.03 ± 0.01	0.05 ± 0.04	0.06 ± 0.02	0.14 ± 0.08
Fear	4	0.02 ± 0.02	0.01 ± 0.01	0.47 ± 0.21	0.0 ± 0.0	0.36 ± 0.28	0.05 ± 0.06	0.09 ± 0.06
Happiness	3	0.03 ± 0.02	0.0 ± 0.0	0.03 ± 0.01	0.39 ± 0.06	0.21 ± 0.06	0.04 ± 0.01	0.3 ± 0.13
Neutral	3	0.0 ± 0.0	0.0 ± 0.0	0.01 ± 0.01	0.0 ± 0.0	0.91 ± 0.12	0.03 ± 0.04	0.05 ± 0.08
Sadness	4	0.12 ± 0.15	0.06 ± 0.05	0.09 ± 0.06	0.11 ± 0.08	0.3 ± 0.1	0.25 ± 0.07	0.07 ± 0.04
Surprise	5	0.02 ± 0.01	0.01 ± 0.01	0.08 ± 0.05	0.02 ± 0.01	0.36 ± 0.26	0.02 ± 0.01	0.51 ± 0.22

For each ground truth set, a one-way ANOVA test was performed by specifying the related p-value, adopting 0.05 as the salient threshold for significance. Table 4 shows the results obtained from the test.

As can be seen from the results, apart from the anger-related episodes, which do not cause significant differences in the production of anger, CognitiveNet significantly produces the emotion concordant with the ground truth of the group episodes. Therefore, except for the anger-related episodes, the model correctly elicits artificial emotional activity as a consequence of the processed visual stimuli. However, regarding the production of anger, it is noticeable that the model acquires a significant quantity of reference cognitive instances associated with anger for both the anger- and sadness-related groups of episodes. It is possible that, based on the cognitive biases provided to the model, the model tends to react angrily to sadness-related stimuli.

5 Conclusions

In the present study, a solution was proposed for integrating foundation models with emotions and awareness. Starting from the latest research on Artificial Consciousness, a hierarchy of cognitive layers inspired by the human cognitive processes of sensation, perception, emotion, affection, attention, awareness, and consciousness was defined and employed for producing artificial emotional activity and awareness. The proposed model, called CognitiveNet, was pre-trained on the EMOd dataset of images eliciting emotional reactions by employing CLIP as the backbone foundation model. The solution was tested on 25 videos for estimating the emotional distributions of cognitive instances for each group of episodes associated with the classes of anger, disgust, fear, happiness, sadness, surprise, and the neutral state. The results show that, apart from the anger- and sadness-related groups of episodes, for which CognitiveNet does not provide significant differences in the production of anger, the same model produces an emotional activity that is coherent with the content of videos. Furthermore, the solution was employed for learning a classifier on the CIFAR-10 and -100 datasets. The results show that CognitiveNet overcomes the zero-shot performances of the original CLIP encoder by employing the Awareness cognitive layer. In particular, superior accuracy was found on CIFAR-10 by applying the Awareness on the

Sensation features, while the Awareness directly applied on the original CLIP embeddings provided better accuracy on CIFAR-100.

CognitiveNet represents a solution for integrating foundation models with emotional activity and awareness. The emotions produced by the model as a consequence of the acquisition of world instances could be significant for verifying the moral content in both model's input and output. For instance, in the case of GPT-3, given that the corpus on which that model was trained is enormous, the estimation of the emotional content in the acquired input and output texts would allow the model to autonomously filter or module its responses. This process could be significant for facing the issues of inequity and fairness that can affect foundation models. CognitiveNet can also learn an emotional activity directly from humans online through our model of awareness, but this experimentation is intended to be deferred to a future study. By considering CLIP for image processing only, the proposed model could be employed on a social robot for improving the interaction with a user by supporting the estimation of the emotional context. Finally, the proposed model represents a valuable solution for performing online meta-learning. A more in-depth investigation of the effectiveness of CognitiveNet in solving classification tasks could generalize the results achieved in the present study.

References

1. Bommasani, R., et al.: On the opportunities and risks of foundation models. arXiv preprint arXiv:2108.07258 (2021)
2. Radford, A., et al.: Learning transferable visual models from natural language supervision, In: International Conference on Machine Learning, pp. 8748–8763 (2021)
3. Yuan, L., et al.: Florence: a new foundation model for computer vision. arXiv preprint arXiv:2111.11432 (2021)
4. Pham, H., et al.: Combined scaling for open-vocabulary image classification. arXiv e-prints (2021)
5. Pourpanah, F., et al.: A review of generalized zero-shot learning methods. IEEE Transactions on Pattern Analysis and Machine Intelligence (2022)
6. Ramesh, A., et al.: Zero-shot text-to-image generation. In: International Conference on Machine Learning. PMLR (2021)
7. Yu, J., et al.: Coca: Contrastive captioners are image-text foundation models. arXiv preprint arXiv:2205.01917 (2022)
8. Jacob, D., Ming-Wei, C., Kenton, L., Kristina, T.: BERT: pre-training of deep bidirectional transformers for language understanding. In: Association for Computational Linguistics (ACL), pp. 4171–4186 (2019)
9. Tom, B. B., et al.: Language models are few-shot learners. arXiv preprint arXiv:2005.14165 (2020)
10. Dosovitskiy, A., et al.: An image is worth 16x16 words: transformers for image recognition at scale. arXiv preprint arXiv:2010.11929 (2020)
11. Vaswani, A., et al.: Attention is all you need. In: Advances in Neural Information Processing Systems 30 (2017)

12. Roy, A., Ghosal, D., Cambria, E., Majumder, N., Mihalcea, R., Poria, S.: Improving zero-shot learning baselines with commonsense knowledge. Cogn. Comput. **14**(6), 2212–2222 (2022)
13. Tyng, C.M., Amin, H.U., Saad, M.N., Malik, A.S.: The influences of emotion on learning and memory. Front. Psychol. **8**, 1454 (2017)
14. Iovane, G., Fominska, I., Landi, R.E., Terrone, F.: Smart sensing: an info-structural model of cognition for non-interacting agents. Electronics **9**(10), 1692 (2020)
15. Iovane, G., Landi, R.E.: From smart sensing to consciousness: an info-structural model of computational consciousness for non-interacting agents. arXiv preprint arXiv:2209.02414 (2022)
16. Libet, B., Alberts, W.W., Wright, E.J., Feinstein, B.: Responses of human somatosensory cortex to stimuli below threshold for conscious sensation. Science **158**, 1597–1600 (1967)
17. Kim, K.H., Bang, S.W., Kim, S.R.: Emotion recognition system using short-term monitoring of physiological signals. Med. Biol. Eng. Comput. **42**(3), 419–427 (2004)
18. Ekman, P., Friesen, W.V.: Constants across cultures in the face and emotion. J. Pers. Soc. Psychol. **17**(2), 124 (1971)
19. Van Hooff, J.C., Devue, C., Vieweg, P.E., Theeuwes, J.: Disgust- and not fear-evoking images hold our attention. Acta Physiol. (Oxf) **143**(1), 1–6 (2013)
20. Van Hooff, J.C., van Buuringen, M., El M'rabet, I., de Gier, M., van Zalingen, L.: Disgust-specific modulation of early attention processes. Acta Physiol. (Oxf) **152**, 149–157 (2014)
21. Hussain, A., Aleksander, I., Smith, L.S., Barros, A.K., Chrisley, R., Cutsuridis V.: Brain inspired cognitive systems, Springer Science & Business Media, vol. 657 (2009). Springer, NY (2009). https://doi.org/10.1007/978-0-387-79100-5
22. Atas, A., Vermeiren, A., Cleeremans, A.: Repeating a strongly masked stimulus increases priming and awareness. Conscious. Cogn. **22**(4), 1422–1430 (2013)
23. Fan, S., et al.: Emotional attention: a study of image sentiment and visual attention. In: Proceedings of the IEEE Conference on Computer Vision and Pattern Recognition, pp. 7521–7531 (2018)
24. Krizhevsky, A., Hinton, G.: Learning multiple layers of features from tiny images (2009)

ICT Accessibility Requirements Tool – Version 1.2 – Implementing Experts' Contributions, Improvements, and Suggestions

Márcio Martins[1(✉)], Francisco Godinho[2], Pedro Gonçalves[2], and Ramiro Gonçalves[1]

[1] INESC TEC and University of Trás-os-Montes and Alto Douro, Vila Real, Portugal
{marciom,ramiro}@utad.pt

[2] University of Trás-os-Montes and Alto Douro, Vila Real, Portugal
{godinho,pgoncalves}@utad.pt

Abstract. The Accessibility Requirements Tool for Information and Communication Technologies (FRATIC) was developed within the work of a doctoral project, at the University of Trás-os-Montes and Alto Douro, and may be used at various stages of public procurement processes as well as projects and developments that include ICT products and services. This tool helps to consult, determine and assess the accessibility requirements for ICT products and services in European Standard EN 301 549 supporting the legislation in the field of public procurement for the countries of the European Union – Directive 2014/24/EU. This paper focuses on the implementation of contributions, improvements, and suggestions from 25 experts in the fields of accessibility, assistive technologies and public procurement, gathered from usability tests and semi-structured interviews, which were conducted on FRATIC version 1.1. The implementation of these has resulted in an improved version of the tool: FRATIC 1.2.

Keywords: Accessibility Requirements Tool for ICT · European Standard EN 301 549 · Public procurement · Accessibility · Usability

1 Introduction

In the European Union (EU), and particularly in Portugal, a high percentage of the population lives with some kind of disability or impairment [1, 2]. In the Portuguese scenario, as in other countries, there is an unequal distribution of opportunities between people with disabilities and the general population. Throughout history, not enough practices and policies have been observed to overcome inequalities, social injustices, and the exclusion of this population from many sectors of society. The Information and Communication Technologies (ICT) are one of the areas where this problem is present from the very beginning, first in terms of access to these technologies, and later regarding the conditions of use and interaction.

Implementing accessibility in different areas, in particular in the digital and ICT areas, as they are available to and used by many people, and as they have a major

M. Antona and C. Stephanidis (Eds.): HCII 2023, LNCS 14020, pp. 119–136, 2023.
https://doi.org/10.1007/978-3-031-35681-0_8

relevance and influence in today's society, is an effective and efficient way to promote and achieve the general principles of the Convention on the Rights of Persons with Disabilities, endorsed on December 13, 2006, at the United Nations General Assembly in New York [3].

Accessibility is improving and it is likely to continue this way thanks to a recent strong EU legal framework, namely with Directive 2014/24/EU [4], on public procurement, Directive 2016/2102/EU [5], on the accessibility of the websites and mobile applications of public sector bodies, and Directive 2019/882/EU of the European Accessibility Act [6], on accessibility requirements for products and services – all three of which have already been incorporated into national law in Portugal. All member states that have not yet done so should also incorporate the same directives into their national legal systems.

In the EU, with strong influence on national, European, and global industries, we are on the verge of a comprehensive approach to ICT with the implementation of EN 301 549 specifying accessibility requirements for ICT products and services [7]. At issue are the accessibility criteria that must be considered in the member states' public procurement decisions regarding hardware, software, Web applications and content, telecommunications, emergency services, and other ICT products and services. Portugal – and the national public administration in particular – has little experience in such a broad area of e-accessibility. Nevertheless, Portugal was the first European country to enact legislation on Web accessibility and should be prepared for the expansion of this topic to other products and services within the information society, to which this work intends to make an important contribution.

Currently, regarding ICT, there are no tools at national or European level with the potential to assist in complying with the European standard on accessibility requirements for public procurement procedures relating to ICT products and services, and in providing designers with techniques to make accessibility an inherent part of ICTs. The development of such tools is crucial insofar as the EN 301 549 standard by itself is not sufficient, mainly because it is a very long document – containing about 300 accessibility requirements – complex, heavy and time consuming to use, very technical, difficult to cross-reference information, and not intuitive [8].

This paper focuses on the implementation of contributions, improvements, and suggestions from 25 experts in the fields of accessibility, assistive technologies, and public procurement, gathered from usability tests and semi-structured interviews, carried out in order to achieve a standardized usability and accessibility evaluation, as well as the validation of FRATIC version 1.1. The implementation of these has resulted in an improved version: FRATIC 1.2.

2 State of the Art

In a society where more and more ICTs are being used, it is both a priority and essential to guarantee full accessibility for everyone in order to ensure the social and digital inclusion of people with special needs or even people in general [9–12]. People with disabilities have proven throughout multiple technological resources that when these include accessibility features, they are early adopters of new technologies [13, 14]. Thus, the technology potential and political will must be used to the full and no effort should be spared to meet the goal of universal access to ICT products and services.

In the US, public procurement has effectively been used as a very effective tool to promote accessibility and it is this approach that lies at the heart of Directive 2014/24/EU and the EU's European Accessibility Act [15], where there is a growing awareness of the need for widely usable ICTs.

The US developed a web-based tool, the Accessibility Requirements Tool (ART)[1], to determine and incorporate relevant Sect. 508 accessibility requirements into both procurement documentation and internal developments for ICT products and services. The ART tool is all-inclusive, offers interactive, step-by-step guidance on how to determine the accessibility requirements applicable to an ICT, and provides an exportable, easy-to-follow list of Sect. 508 requirements to be included as part of the procurement package so that suppliers understand the requirements they need to meet. Similarly, the EU has created the Accessible ICT Procurement Toolkit[2] to assist on enforcing EN 301 549, and to provide information on how accessibility applies to the different stages of the public procurement process [16]. However, this toolkit is no longer available.

The ICT Accessibility Requirements Tool (FRATIC) was developed under a PhD research project at the University of Trás-os-Montes and Alto Douro. This Excel-based tool may be used at various stages of public procurement processes, as well as in ICT-related development projects [17]. It helps consulting, determining and assessing EN 301 549 accessibility requirements for ICT products and services [7, 18–21] supporting the legislation on public procurement for the EU countries – Directive 2014/24/EU [4] – and can provide comprehensive and detailed reports.

This paper focuses on the implementation of contributions, improvements and suggestions from 25 experts in the areas of accessibility, assistive technologies and public procurement, gathered from usability tests and semi-structured interviews on FRATIC version 1.1, thus resulting in an improved version: FRATIC 1.2.

3 Methodology

Design-Science Research (DSR) was the research method chosen to guide the work plan developed for the doctoral project of which this work is a part. The origins of this research method date back to 1992, under the name of "Design Experiment", having been introduced by Brown [22] and Collins [23, 24]. Several representations of the DSR method have been proposed to date [25–29]. In 2007, Hevner [30] suggests a new representation of its framework, in which there is an overlap of the research focus into three cycles: the relevance cycle, the design cycle, and the rigor cycle.

This study focuses on the gathering and implementation of improvements, contributions, and suggestions from 25 experts in the areas of accessibility, assistive technologies, and public procurement. The improvements, contributions, and suggestions were included in FRATIC version 1.1 through usability tests [31] and semi-structured interviews [8], and were collected in the first rigor cycle, while their implementation, which resulted in FRATIC version 1.2, is part of the second design cycle of the DSR method adopted in the PhD project.

[1] Accessibility Requirements Tool, available at https://www.section508.gov/art.

[2] Accessible ICT Procurement Toolkit, available from December 2014 to February 2021 at http://mandate376.standards.eu/

For each of the participants' suggestions and contributions, as well as for some improvements to be made found in the usability tests, their implementation priority was identified – divided into three levels (priority 1, priority 2 and priority 3) – considering the number of participants suggesting the improvements, the amount of errors (mistakes and wrong clicks detected) that each one can prevent, and the interaction and design improvements. It should be noted that to calculate the occurrence of errors that each suggestion/improvement can prevent, the errors were categorized and classified considering the level of relevance and severity, and that notwithstanding identifying the priority for implementation, all improvements, contributions, and suggestions from the experts were implemented.

4 Study Elements

4.1 Participants

Participants in the usability tests and semi-structured interviews were required to meet certain inclusion criteria: 1) being an expert and/or a person interested in the areas of accessibility, assistive technologies, and public procurement; 2) having at least three years of experience in one of these areas; 3) having a computer with ZOOM® software, a sound system with speakers and microphone, a webcam, and strong Internet access.

4.2 Study Background

The restrictions imposed by the COVID-19 pandemic dictated that data collection was carried out remotely, that is, through video calls using the ZOOM® tool, between the researcher and the participants, using several features of this platform, namely: video and audio of host and participant, audio and video recording of the session, screen sharing of the host, and remote control provided by the host.

4.3 Data Collection Techniques and Instruments

Based on the objectives defined for this study, supported by the defining characteristics of the paradigms and the research methods applied, several data collection techniques and instruments were used. Notably, we employed the observation technique and document collection, and the instruments for usability tests and semi-structured interviews [8, 31].

It is important to mention that this study, including the instruments and the supporting materials used in the interviews and in the usability tests previously carried out, were previously examined and received a unanimous Ethical Favorable Opinion, with process reference Doc14-CE-UTAD-2021, by the Ethics Committee of the University of Trás-os-Montes and Alto Douro in Vila Real, Portugal.

Usability Tests

Usability tests – during which the tasks and subtasks shown in Appendix I were performed – were followed by a structured interview [32] using standardized instruments – post-task questionnaires of the Single Ease Question (SEQ) type [33, 34] and post-test of the System Usability Scale (SUS) type [34–36] –, and by a subjective evaluation of seven accessibility features (Ease of use; Readability; Button size; Memorability; User friendliness; Language adequacy; Overall level of satisfaction), considering the basic principles of Universal Design [37], the existing content type and the platform where FRATIC was implemented.

Semi-structured Interviews

A semi-structured interview, consisting of 19 open and closed questions present in Appendix II, was also designed to gather objective answers to specific questions. A thematic analysis was used for the interviews qualitative analysis, which aimed at identifying, analyzing, and reporting patterns (themes) in the data, enhancing the understanding of the explicit and implicit meanings associated with textual data [38, 39]. The goal was to obtain the participants' perceptions on the topics: "EN 301 549", "other tools", "FRATIC usability", "FRATIC functionalities" and "FRATIC target audience" [8].

5 Results

Monitoring and following up on how the experts felt about the user experience and their evaluation of FRATIC with systematic usability methods, and using expert tests and interviews, was essential to gain information about the performance, the participants' subjective satisfaction with FRATIC and the qualitative components of the tool's usability and accessibility features, thus achieving very positive results, and showing great acceptance and satisfaction from experts and potential users. Notwithstanding the accomplished results, some objective data, the identification of participants' suggestions and contributions during the interviews, as well as some improvements to be made identified in the usability tests have demonstrated the need to perform some corrections [8, 31].

5.1 Collecting Contributions, Improvements, and Suggestions

To collect and analyze the data obtained in the usability tests and in the post-test semi-structured interviews, several standardized techniques and instruments were used, thus allowing the identification of the contributions, improvements and suggestions of the 25 experts in the areas of accessibility, assistive technologies and public procurement [8, 31].

The instruments used to collect and analyze the data obtained in the usability tests [31], namely the observation guide, and the post-test interview were essential to identify suggestions and contributions from the participants to improve the FRATIC functionalities.

In the observation guide it was possible to identify these suggestions and contributions through the number and type of mistakes, the type of questions, comments, and behaviors of the participants while performing the tasks. During the semi-structured interviews [8], conducted post-test, a qualitative analysis and some of the questions in particular allowed to collect that information, mainly for the following six questions:

- 5. 5. Did you have any difficulties adapting when you started using FRATIC? Regarding organization or amount of information, for example.
- 6. As you were using the tool, did the features seem intuitive to you?

- 7. Did you experience any difficulties when using or creating content on FRATIC? In any of the tasks in this usability test or others.
- 8. If so, what do you think could be done to overcome these difficulties?
- 9. When filtering the accessibility requirements, do you find it pertinent to pre-view the notes for each requirement along with its description? Or do you think that the description of each requirement would suffice, since in case of need you would consult more information in the Consultation section?
- 18. Given your knowledge in the area of assistive technologies/accessibility and the experience with FRATIC, do you have any remarks or suggestions to improve the features of the tool?

5.2 Prioritizing the Execution of Contributions, Improvements, and Suggestions

For each of the participants' suggestions and contributions, as well as for some improvements to be made found in the usability tests, their implementation priority was identified – divided into three levels (priority 1, priority 2 and priority 3) – considering the number of participants suggesting the improvements, the amount of errors (mistakes and wrong clicks detected) that each one can prevent, and the interaction and design improvements, as shown in Table 1. In order to calculate the occurrence of errors that each suggestion/improvement can prevent, the errors were categorized and classified considering the level of relevance and severity of the errors that occurred when performing the tasks in FRATIC, considering the following two categories and their respective classifications: (1) mistake: the participant made a mistake in a way that could jeopardize the task – one mistake was worth 1 error; (2) wrong click: the participant made a wrong click, not jeopardizing, but unnecessary for the task – one wrong click was worth 0.5 errors. It is important to note that when a suggestion/contribution had different priority levels in the two variables considered, the higher priority of the two prevailed.

Table 1. Implementation priority (occurrence of errors and number of participants).

Implementation priority	Occurrence of errors (mistakes + wrong clicks)			Number of participants suggesting		
	≤ 2	$3 \leq 4$	≥ 5	≤ 2	$3 \leq 4$	≥ 5
Priority 1	X			X		
Priority 2		X			X	
Priority 3			X			X

5.3 Contributions, Improvements, and Suggestions from the Experts

Table 2 briefly identifies the suggestions and contributions from the participants, as well as some improvements to be made, detected during the usability tests, that may decrease the number and type of mistakes, the number of wrong clicks, and increase the effectiveness, efficiency, and overall user satisfaction with FRATIC's functionalities.

Table 2. Participants' contributions and suggestions implemented.

Suggestion/Contribution No	Participants	Suggestions and contributions	Implementation priority		
			1	2	3
1	4, 7, 14	Inserting help, explanation or associated additional information in all text fields and options for the filtering mechanisms	X		
2	1, 2, 12, 13, 14, 15, 17, 19, 23, 25	Increasing the size of some content, notably the buttons, the arrows in the drop-down lists, and the elements that allow selecting options. At the bottom, arranging the interactive elements with a minimum CSS dimension of 44px height and width	X		
3	4, 5, 11	Adding help on the sections (tabs), as well as on all mandatory (text and selection) fields, with information about the requirement	X		
4	4, 7, 10, 13, 22	Separating the content of the four FRATIC sections (tabs) by steps, to guide the user through the ordering of the content	X		
5	9, 10, 13, 22	Using a consistent color palette to associate colors with the different areas, steps and functions, with consistency between FRATIC sections (tabs) to easily identify, locate and remember information. To ensure full integration of color-blind people, using graphic symbols from the ColorADD[a] code as a color identification system for the different sections and steps. Also using different colors or alternating tones in the FRATIC section names (tabs)		X	
6	7	Setting equal identification in the drop-down lists that have the same options, to increase consistency and decrease some possible confusion		X	

(continued)

Table 2. (*continued*)

Suggestion/Contribution No	Participants	Suggestions and contributions	Implementation priority		
			1	2	3
7	13, 19, 25	Increasing the area to select/unselect options available in the filtering mechanisms, by assigning the designation of each option associated to the corresponding selectable element (label associated to the field)		X	
8	7, 13, 21	Highlighting the identification of reports by increasing the size of the titles and headings and changing the color of the titles and headings and the background to allow for easier identification and location of each report	X		
9	4, 7, 9, 13, 15, 18, 21, 25	Reorganizing the information regarding evaluation and reports: firstly place the accessibility evaluation buttons before the tables with information about the results, and then add an area just for reports, so that the information sequence makes more sense and it is easier to locate it	X		
10	18	Adding numbering or acronyms in the applicable conditions of the second FRATIC section (tab)			X
11	3, 22	Changing the header of the "Compliance" column to "Complies with Standard", modifying all the information that such a change implies			X
12	10	Inserting help and additional information in the " Complies with Standard" column regarding the need for the user to evaluate all accessibility requirements to get the evaluation results			X
13	4, 16, 20, 23	Differentiating the text and color between the buttons to generate reports, save data, and open folders		X	

(*continued*)

Table 2. (*continued*)

Suggestion/Contribution No	Participants	Suggestions and contributions	Implementation priority		
			1	2	3
14	1, 2, 3, 6, 8, 10, 12, 14, 15, 18, 22	Showing more clearly the dependence/independence or the hierarchical level of filters (drop-down lists/tables with options)	X		
15	10	Improving and simplifying the help for the filtering mechanism of the Consult section (tab), making it clearer, particularly about the types of filters available and the many combinations between them for more refined consultations			X
16	17	Adding a placeholder in the text field (search) of the Consult section (tab)			X
17	5, 6, 8, 12, 13, 17, 21	Adding a functionality to search/locate content in the Information section (tab)	X		
18	25	Making the links in the Information section (tab) look more like clickable elements			X
19	2, 25	Checking if there is any "X" in column B when the user clicks on the exclude requirements feature. If not, the alert message "No requirement with X in column B. Please check." should appear		X	
20	8, 12	Checking if there is any "X" in column B when the user clicks on the exclude requirements feature. If so, the alert message "Do you really want to exclude the accessibility requirement(s) with X in column B?" should appear	X		
21	2, 6, 10	Adding in the accessibility assessment information the value range [0, 10], as well as what the minimum and maximum values represent, namely that 0 means not at all complying with the standard, and 10 means fully complying with the standard		X	

(*continued*)

Table 2. (*continued*)

Suggestion/Contribution No	Participants	Suggestions and contributions	Implementation priority		
			1	2	3
22	10	Aligning the content (text) of the first column of the tables to the left, for a more optimal display of the information			X
23	14	When creating or saving files in FRATIC the date information placed in their name must contain the following format yyyy/mm/dd, and not the format dd/mm/yyyy, because this format will facilitate the search, mechanization of the file system			X
24	17	Fixing the spelling error that exists in some alert messages by replacing "friltrar" (friltering) with "filtrar" (filtering)			X
25	13, 18	Uniformizing the size and identification (color and location) of the buttons, setting all of them to the same height, placing the main action buttons on the left side, relative to the secondary action buttons, and with a different color (light blue)		X	
26	14	Adding, in the columns' explanation table, the clarification about the purpose and target (reports for internal and external use) of the information completed in the Notes column of the sections (tabs) "Common ICTs and Other ICTs" and "Directive (Web and Mobile Applications)			X
27	1, 4, 7, 23	Writing the meaning of existing acronyms in full, as well as in the help elements of the different fields		X	
28	7	Adding instructions in the different category types in the Information section (tab)			X

(*continued*)

Table 2. (*continued*)

Suggestion/Contribution No	Participants	Suggestions and contributions	Implementation priority		
			1	2	3
29	7	Changing the name of the four FRATIC sections (tabs) by deleting the text "FRATIC -" from those sections and adding "(Web and Mobile Applications)" in the second section (tab)			X
30	10	Sorting alphabetically the lists of existing links in the categories of the Information section (tab)	X		
31	13	Reorganizing the content in the four FRATIC sections (tabs) so as to remove as much as possible the need for users, especially those with visual limitations and using a screen reader or magnifying system, to perform horizontal scanning	X		
32	13	Using one color (green) for all the fields that are used for interaction, ultimately being more of a reference and increasing consistency		X	
33	13	Setting the label of the text field of the Consult section (tab) clickable, rerouting the cursor to the writing field		X	
34	13	After using the buttons, positioning the cursor consistently			X
35	15	Adding a feature to directly open FRATIC's folder (location) and the files created/saved when using the tool			X
36	15	Adding contact information, for questions, contributions, and suggestions, and for updates at the end of each FRATIC section (tab)			X

(*continued*)

Table 2. (*continued*)

Suggestion/Contribution No	Participants	Suggestions and contributions	Implementation priority		
			1	2	3
37	18	Adding to the tables with the evaluation results the row "Total ICT Accessibility", both for functional performances and for groups of people with special needs, with bold text and with a background in a different color than the other rows in the tables		X	
38	17, 25	In the drop-down list options "Web Content/Mobile Application (Directive 2016/2102/EU)", in the section (tab) Directive (Web and Mobile Apps), removing the part of the text "(Directive 2016/2102)" as it may be confusing		X	
39	13	Creating VPAT®-like outputs, a document as exists in the US under Sect. 508, for aggregation to ICTs with information about their accessibility and to help manufacturers, distributors, and/or importers complying with the legislation	X		
40	22	Adding a field with CPV (Common Procurement Vocabulary) code information for the selected ICT in the filtering mechanism, from Sections (tabs) EN 301 549 and Directive (Web and Mobile App), thus helping the public body to find this information for the preparation of the tender specifications and the tender notice, as well as in other process management tasks		X	
41	9, 16, 21	Enabling grouping/ungrouping the results of the filtering mechanisms of each section (tab), in order to avoid unnecessary scrolling		X	

(*continued*)

Table 2. (*continued*)

Suggestion/Contribution No	Participants	Suggestions and contributions	Implementation priority		
			1	2	3
42	13, 25	Facilitating or adding a more interactive, click-only alternative to the Exclude requirements method with an X in column B		X	
43	7, 11, 21	The text field (search) in the Consult section (tab) filtering mechanism should allow you to search in different parts of the requirements: All Information; ID and Title; Description; Notes	X		
44	13, 15	When FRATIC provides informational or alert messages (windows) the location of these should match that of the mouse cursor, so that all users can see them	X		

[a]ColorADD® – The ColorADD code is a unique, universal, inclusive, and non-discriminatory color identification system, based on graphic symbols, which allows color-blind people to identify colors, developed by a Portuguese graphic designer and professor at the University of Minho.

In total 44 suggestions and contributions from the participants were implemented, i.e. all those identified in the table above, 14 of priority level 1 execution, 15 of priority level 2 and 15 of priority level 3, thus resulting in version 1.2 of the tool. Because the testers are experts in the fields of accessibility, usability, assistive technologies, and public procurement, these suggestions and contributions will enable users in general to have a better experience when using FRATIC version 1.2, including and particularly users with special needs.

6 Final Considerations

FRATIC's prototype intends to simplify the lives of a growing number of users, by creating and purchasing more accessible and usable products, at a competitive price and without additional costs. In conclusion, the international market will grow and society will be able to benefit from ICT products and services designed with appropriate responses for people of all ages and with any kind of disability or impairment. We hope that FRATIC can simplify the implementation of EN 301 549 accessibility requirements in public procurement procedures for ICT products and services, as well as the work of designers and developers to make ICT products and services more accessible and usable by all.

The usability tests and interviews with experts in the areas of accessibility, assistive technologies, and public procurement allowed us to understand the level of complexity and usefulness of FRATIC, as well as to identify the main capabilities, limitations and their suggestions and contributions to improve the existing functionalities of the tool and to add others. The experience of the experts in those areas was crucial for the suggestion of improvements in some aspects, in order to overcome some difficulties felt, mainly related to the location and size of some contents, navigation, amount of information presented, division, and instructions in the different tasks and graphical aspects of the interface, and we believe that the respective implementations will allow users in general to have a better experience with the use of the new FRATIC version, including and particularly users with special needs.

The usability tests and post-test semi-structured interviews with experts, as well as the collection and analysis of their data, allowed us to both gather feedback from the participants – assembling a total of 44 contributions, improvements, and suggestions – and implement it, resulting in FRATIC version 1.2, thus suppressing the occurrence of errors and, above all, significantly improving accessibility and the level of interaction and design.

From this study's results, it is expected that the FRATIC development may simplify the management and use of the information in EN 301 549 in public procurement procedures for ICT products and services, as well as the work of ICT designers and developers.

Acknowledgments. This work is financed by FCT, Fundação para a Ciência e a Tecnologia (Portuguese Foundation for Science and Technology), supported by funding from POPH/FSE.

This article reflects the views only of the author, and FCT cannot be held responsible for any use which may be made of the information contained therein.

Appendix I – Tasks and Subtasks for the Usability Tests

Task	Objective	Subtask	Section
1	Determining the accessibility requirements for a common ICT	1.1 Naming the ICT	EN 301 549
		1.2 Determining the requirements for the common ICT and functional performance declarations	
		1.3 Excluding accessibility requirements	
2	Generating the report "Request Text" with information about technical criteria for a cell phone	2.1 Creating the "Request Text" report	EN 301 549

(*continued*)

(*continued*)

Task	Objective	Subtask	Section
		2.2 Saving filtered data and requirements	
3	Determining the accessibility requirements for a mobile application, with given conditions	3.1 Naming the ICT	Directive (Web and Mobile Applications)
		3.2 Determining the requirements for a mobile application by selecting the respective applicable conditions	
4	Creating the "Accessibility Evaluation" report with information about technical criteria for a mobile application, with its respective evaluation	4.1 Assessing accessibility	Directive (Web and Mobile Applications)
		4.2 Creating the "Accessibility Evaluation" report	
5	Querying to the accessibility requirements and the corresponding types of compliance check	5.1 Querying by type of technologies - European standard requirements	Querying
		5.2 Querying by common ICT type+text	
6	Finding a particular content in the Information section	6.1 a) Finding the link to Directive (EU) 2019/882 on accessibility requirements for products and services	Information
		6.1 b) Finding the link to download the Color Contrast Analyzer tool	

Appendix II – Semi-structured Interview (Post-test) Script

1. Have you ever participated, or are you participating in any way in public procurement procedures for ICT products and services?
2. In order to determine accessibility requirements and their means of verifying compliance for a specific ICT, do you think that the official EN 301 549 document (PDF) alone is intuitive, easy to understand, and quick to use, to be considered as sufficient for possible interested parties to perform such tasks? Why?
3. Do you know of any tools that can help to globally evaluate the technical accessibility criteria specified in EN 301 549?
4. If so, how often have you used them or how often do you use them?
5. Did you have any difficulties adapting when you started using FRATIC? Regarding organization or amount of information, for example.
6. As you were using the tool, did the features seem intuitive to you?

7. Did you experience any difficulties when using or creating content on FRATIC? In any of the tasks in this usability test or others.
8. If so, what do you think could be done to overcome these difficulties?
9. When filtering the accessibility requirements, do you find it pertinent to preview the notes for each requirement along with its description? Or do you think that the description of each requirement would suffice, since in case of need you would consult more information in the Consultation section?
10. Do you think that using FRATIC can bring some benefits to those who need to determine and evaluate the technical criteria, covered by EN 301 549, for a specific ICT?
11. Among the people you know, to whom would the FRATIC tool be useful? Describe this person professionally.
12. Considering the scope of EN 301 549, do you think the fact that the tool brings together the ability to determine and evaluate the requirements of many different ICTs could be a determining factor in its utility and success?
13. Do you think the FRATIC tool could contribute to the compliance with the Directive 2016/2102/EU rules, on accessibility of websites and mobile applications of public bodies, and the Decree Law No. 83/2018, of October 19, which transposes the aforementioned Directive into the national legal framework? Justify.
14. Do you think this tool could contribute to the introduction and compliance with technical accessibility criteria in public procurement of ICT products and services?
15. Do you think FRATIC can contribute to the creation and purchase of technology accessible to all?
16. Aiming at achieving a more inclusive society, do you think that the potential of this tool could be useful for you or for other people?
17. Do you think it is relevant to have FRATIC functionalities available on the Web, or simultaneously available both on the Web and in Microsoft Excel?
18. Given your knowledge in the area of assistive technologies/accessibility and the experience with FRATIC, do you have any remarks or suggestions to improve the features of the tool?
19. Finally, do you have any further comments, or thoughts?

References

1. European Commission: People with disabilities have equal rights - The European Disability Strategy 2010–2020, European Commission. European Commission, Brussels (2010)
2. INE: Health and disabilities in Portugal: 2011. Instituto Nacional de Estatística, IP, Lisbon (2012)
3. United Nations: Convention on the Rights of Persons with Disabilities. United Nations, New York (2006)
4. European Parliament: Directive 2014/24/EU of the European Parliament and of the Council of 26 February 2014 on public procurement and repealing Directive 2004/18/CE, Official Journal of the European Union, pp. 65–242. Strasbourg (2014)
5. European Parliament: Directive (EU) 2016/2102 of the European Parliament and of the Council of 26 October 2016 on the accessibility of websites and mobile applications of public sector bodies, Official Journal of the European Union, pp. 1–15. Strasbourg (2016)

6. European Parliament: Directive (EU) 2019/882 of the European Parliament and of the Council of 17 April 2019 on the accessibility requirements for products and services, Official Journal of the European Union (2019). https://eur-lex.europa.eu/legal-content/PT/TXT/HTML/?uri=CELEX:32019L0882&from=EN. Accessed 30 May 2022
7. ETSI, CEN, and CENELEC: EN 301 549 V3.2.1 - Accessibility requirements for ICT products and services, European Telecommunications Standards Institute (2021)
8. Martins, M., Godinho, F., Gonçalves, P., Gonçalves, R.: Expert validation of the ICT Accessibility Requirements Tool prototype. In: HCI International 2022 - 24th international conference on Human-Computer Interaction (2022)
9. Emiliani, P.L., Stephanidis, C.: Universal access to ambient intelligence environments: opportunities and challenges for people with disabilities. IBM Syst. J. **44**(3), 605–619 (2005)
10. McKinney, S., Horspool, A., Willers, R., Safie, O., Richlin, L.: Using Second Life with learning-disabled students in higher education. Innov. J. Online Educ. **5**(2) (2008)
11. Magnusson, L., Hanson, E., Borg, M.: A literature review study of information and communication technology as a support for frail older people living at home and their family carers. Technol. Disabil. **16**(4), 223–235 (2004)
12. Foley, A., Ferri, B.A.: Technology for people, not disabilities: ensuring access and inclusion. J. Res. Spec. Educ. Needs **12**(4), 192–200 (2012)
13. Bares, R., Vickers, S., Istance, H.O.: Gaze interaction with virtual on-line communities: levelling the playing field for disabled users. Univers. Access Inf. Soc. **9**(3), 261–272 (2010)
14. Martins, M., Cunha, A., Oliveira, I., Morgado, L.: Usability test of 3Dconnexion 3D mice versus keyboard+ mouse in Second Life undertaken by people with motor disabilities due to medullary lesions. Univers. Access Inf. Soc. **14**(1), 5–16 (2015)
15. Easton, C.: Website accessibility and the European Union: citizenship, procurement and the proposed Accessibility Act. Int. Rev. Law Comput. Technol. **27**(1–2), 187–199 (2013)
16. ITU: Accessible Europe 2019 Background Paper, Standards in the Procurement of Accessible ICT Products and Services. International Telecommunication Union, Geneva, Switzerland (2019)
17. Martins, M., Gonçalves, R., Godinho, F., Novais, J.: Benefits of EN 301 549 for each group of people with special needs. In: Proceedings of the 8th International Conference on Software Development and Technologies for Enhancing Accessibility and Fighting Info-exclusion, pp. 123–128 (2018)
18. ETSI, CEN, and CENELEC: EN 301 549 V1.1.1 - Accessibility requirements suitable for public procurement of ICT products and services in Europe," European Telecommunications Standards Institute. France (2014)
19. ETSI, CEN, and CENELEC: EN 301 549 V1.1.2 - Accessibility requirements suitable for public procurement of ICT products and services in Europe, European Telecommunications Standards Institute. France (2015)
20. CEN and CENELEC: EN 17161:2019 - Design for All - Accessibility following a Design for All approach in products, goods and services - Extending the range of users, Eur. Comm. Stand. (2019)
21. ETSI, CEN, and CENELEC: EN 301 549 V2.1.2 - Accessibility requirements for ICT products and services, European Telecommunications Standards Institute (2018)
22. Brown, A.L.: Design experiments: theoretical and methodological challenges in creating complex interventions in classroom settings. J. Learn. Sci. **2**(2), 141–178 (1992)
23. Collins, A.: Toward a design science of education. In: Scanlon, E., O'Shea, T. (eds.) New Directions in Educational Technology, pp. 15–22. Springer Berlin Heidelberg, Berlin, Heidelberg (1992). https://doi.org/10.1007/978-3-642-77750-9_2
24. Bayazit, N.: Investigating design: a review of forty years of design research. Des. Issues **20**(1), 16–29 (2004)

25. Peffers, K., Tuunanen, T., Rothenberger, M.A., Chatterjee, S.: A design science research methodology for information systems research. J. Manag. Inf. Syst. **24**(3), 45–77 (2007)
26. Wang, F., Hannafin, M.J.: Design-based research and technology-enhanced learning environments. Educ. Technol. Res. Dev. **53**(4), 5–23 (2005)
27. Vaishnavi, V., Kuechler, W.: Design research in information systems. Design Science Research in Information Systems and Technology (2004). http://desrist.org/desrist/content/design-science-research-in-information-systems.pdf. Accessed 20 May 2022
28. Gregg, D.G., Kulkarni, U.R., Vinzé, A.S.: Understanding the philosophical underpinnings of software engineering research in information systems. Inf. Syst. Front. **3**(2), 169–183 (2001)
29. March, S.T., Smith, G.F.: Design and natural science research on information technology. Decis. Support Syst. **15**(4), 251–266 (1995)
30. Hevner, A.R.: A three cycle view of design science research. Scand. J. Inf. Syst. **19**(2), 4 (2007)
31. Martins, M., Godinho, F., Gonçalves, P., Gonçalves, R.: Usability and accessibility evaluation of the ICT accessibility requirements tool prototype. In: HCI International 2022 - 24th international conference on Human-Computer Interaction (2022)
32. Cohen, L., Manion, L., Morrison, K.: Research Methods in Education, 8th Ed. Routledge, London (2017)
33. Sauro, J.: If you could only ask one question, use this one. MeasuringU (2010). https://measuringu.com/single-question/. Accessed 22 Apr 2022
34. Sauro, J., Lewis, J.R.: Quantifying the User Experience: Practical Statistics for User Research. Morgan Kaufmann (2016)
35. Lewis, J.R., Utesch, B.S., Maher, D.E.: UMUX-LITE - When There's No Time for the SUS. Proc. CHI **2013**, 2099–2102 (2013)
36. Padrini-Andrade, L., et al.: Evaluation of usability of a nEonatal hEalth information systEm according to thE usEr's pErcEption. Rev. Paul. Pediatr. **37**(1), 90–96 (2019)
37. Story, M., Mueller, J.L., Mace, R.L.: The universal design file: designing for people of all ages and abilities. Revised Edition (1998)
38. Braun, V., Clarke, V.: Using thematic analysis in psychology. Qual. Res. Psychol. **3**(2), 77–101 (2006)
39. Braun, V., Clarke, V.: Successful Qualitative Research: A Practical Guide for Beginners. Sage (2013)

Empowering Creativity Through Children's Assistive Design Workshops with Orthorigami

Jessica Reese(✉) and Jinsil Hwaryoung Seo

Texas A&M University, College Station, TX 77843, USA
jlb70@tamu.edu, hwaryoung@exchange.tamu.edu

Abstract. The tactile nature of smart materials, coupled with a maker approach and fabrication technology, is considered to empower children in creative design. We describe how children's creativity was fostered through designing customized assistive devices using Orthorigami, made out of Shape Memory Polymer (SMP) using folding techniques [24]. Three day participatory making workshops are conducted with children ages 9-12 with a set of activities including: idea brainstorming, sketching, sculpting, laser-cutting, and making e-textiles. The study outlines what types of fabrication and crafting technology make the hands-on nature of SMP accessible to children for design of DIY Assistive Technology (AT). It also outlines, how using SMP fosters creativity and collaboration, and enables children to feel confident in their design capabilities.

Keywords: smart materials · interactive design · participatory making · assistive technology · shape memory polymer · e-textiles · crafting · creativity

1 Introduction

Smart materials, such as SMPs and shape memory alloys (SMAs), have been used in interactive art installations, smart textiles, smart crafts, wearable, and medical technologies. The behavior of these materials provides a unique leveraging tool for interactive design. Previous researchers have explored interactive design with smart materials [4,6,7,10,15,21]. These researchers have described how to harness the input/output nature of certain smart materials to provide a truly distinctive design. To date, much of this research focuses on the fabrication, engineering, and structural components involved in the creation of interactive design with smart materials. However, a gap remains. Giles *et al.*, when speaking of "smart" e-textiles, points out that this gap in research excludes the tactile potential of the material to create interactive experiences, especially from the perspective of maker culture. Giles *et al.* seeks to fill this gap through workshops that explore how the visually impaired use e-textiles to create objects that are meaningful to them. These researchers explore how crafting and making with

M. Antona and C. Stephanidis (Eds.): HCII 2023, LNCS 14020, pp. 137–153, 2023.
https://doi.org/10.1007/978-3-031-35681-0_9

e-textiles can be made more accessible to create an empowering experience for makers [9]. Our work similarly addresses the gap between smart materials and maker culture. However, this work also wishes to explore an additional hole within the current research, namely how children create and design with smart materials, specifically SMP. We use participatory design workshops to examine this gap. Also, the workshops explore how making with SMP affects the children's confidence in their design capabilities and provides them with a positive, enabling experience.

Another area of interest in the intersection of maker culture and smart materials is how the tactile nature of SMPs can be coupled with maker culture to create customized Assistive Technology (AT). AT generally requires adjustment and customization to meet the changing needs of the users. Commercially available devices do not offer this type of adaptability, and large percentages of these devices end up unused or abandoned [12,22,25]. These devices focus predominately on physical needs but overlook environment, user preferences and expectations, and psychological and social aspects related to using AT [25]. A maker approach can address these issues by allowing the tailor-making of AT to meet various needs [3]. Therefore, we examine how children create and design with SMP to make DIY AT. Additionally, we seek to identify what types of fabrication or crafting technology aid children in the process of making DIY AT.

In summary, our research will address three questions: How children make and design AT with SMP? What types of tools or fabrication or crafting technology aid children in design with SMP? How using SMP in design can affect children's creativity and confidence?

2 Background

2.1 Smart Material with Children

Smart materials provide an active role with sensory feedback that can influence how makers create and design. A few previous researchers, have engaged children with these materials and assessed how children learn through this active/sensory design experience or how they design and create with these active materials. Qi and Buechley combined SMAs with paper origami techniques to create dynamic craft and art installation projects. In their workshop, 9-15 year olds created a SMA flapping crane. The activity fostered an increased interest in electronics and provided an exceptional method for teaching circuitry design [23]. Jacoby and Buechley explored how children can use capacitive touch with conductive ink, paper, and controllers for narrative storytelling and for stimulating creative interactive design. Their work showed that working with conductive ink was intuitive and comfortable for children. Children were able to use conductive ink in a versatile manner as a story-boarding tool, and some children able to combine function and aesthetics to fit a specific purpose within their design [14]. Takegawa *et al.* asked children to design, discuss, and test the function a musical instrument by drawing different shapes on paper with conductive ink. Their system creates a musical instrument prototype that can be flexibly and intuitively customized by conductive ink [26]. Minuto focused on introducing smart material and building interfaces with these materials with children age 9. Workshops to guided the children in the creation of automated puppet plays by combining SMAs, origami, thermochromic paint, visual programming with a modified type of Scratch programming, and a cardboard theater to display their work. Their results showed that children learned new skills related and methods of expression. Also, the use of smart materials fostered greater interest in storytelling [20]. Beuchley *et al.* examined how children work with computationally enriched e-textiles. They presented an electronic sewing kit, termed Sewing Circuits, in preliminary workshops with children and young adults ranging from ages 8-18. Almost every participant was able to construct a working circuit, and children expressed interest in integrating customized, fabric-based artifacts in their lives [2]. Kuznetsov *et al.* developed workshops for junior high youth and local adult artists that introduced DIY screen-printing fabrication with thermochromic, UV sensitive, and conductive ink. The researchers introduced a readily available medium for interactive art creation and storytelling. The youth viewed their work as "art and science" and they transitioned easily between screen-printing, traditional crafting, circuit prototyping, and use collaboration among their fellow participants create storylines. This work showed that screen-printing with smart inks is easy to access, reproducible, and naturally supports collaborative making [16]. These previous researchers show that the introduction of smart materials as a tool can provide an accessible medium with an "active" role in inspiring children toward innovative and collaborative thinking.

2.2 DIY Assistive Technology

Previous works in AT show the promise of DIY techniques for addressing the deficiencies of current AT. However, significant barriers exist for individuals with disabilities or their caregivers. Many lack confidence in their design ability, proper tools for designing AT, and communication among users and designers of DIY AT. Hook *et al.* defined these barriers through interviews with occupational therapists, a medical physics practitioner, teachers at an additional needs school, and a person who makes DIY assistive technology as a hobby. These interviews highlight obstacles to designing DIY assistive technology: lack of confidence in ability to build a device, time requirements to build a device outside of the normal care for a child, and uncertainty that the end product will suitable in strength, function, and aesthetics as a medical device [11]. Buehler *et al.* surveyed makers (including both users and friends or loved ones, most without prior expertise) of 3D printed DIY AT on Thingverse. They identified the current trend in which designers of AT do not have disabilities or training in AT and suggest that DIY AT could benefit from creating more exposure to end-users and more communication between designers and users. The paper points out again that users with disabilities may not feel confident making their own DIY AT [3]. In case studies making DIY AT with adoptees and adoptive parents, Hurst and Tobias discovered that users of AT often have specific ideas for alteration of design and a willingness to learn how to create DIY technology [13]. McDonald *et al.* introduced 3D printing to physical therapists (PTs) for augmentation or making of AT. Their work demonstrated that PTs have unique knowledge of end users' medical needs and are accustomed to modifying existing AT for comfort. There were also certain limitations, specifically PTs' lack of background in 3D modeling, making the creation and design process of high fidelity customized devices more difficult, and that 3D printing materials also provide certain limitations in regards to comfort [18]. Lin *et al.* looked at a single study that coupled designers with a quadriplegic patient to create a game controller and a mouse. The research implies that prototyping and digital fabrication techniques can help to create an accessible device that meets specific needs and may be a preferable alternative when optimal fit and particular design details are necessary. However, additional training may be required to obtain the skills necessary to create a DIY AT [17]. Meissner *et al.* tries to address how people with disabilities experience DIY AT. Their results demonstrate that AT designers with disabilities feel empowered through making and see the benefit of learning maker skills for creating DIY AT for self-directed accessibility hacks [19]. Although, the work of creating a tailor-made device through DIY AT is encouraging there are still questions about what tools aid in making DIY AT, how to instill confidence (even if there is interest) in the makers of AT, and how to increase communication among makers and users of AT.

3 Orthorigami Workshops

3.1 Preparation of Workshop Materials

Our workshop program is based on the Orthorigami (orthotics made using folding techniques) technique developed Reese *et al.*. The previous work describes the how the SMP was fabricated into 2D sheets used for this study [24]. The structure of the Orthorigami workshop was based on several preliminary workshops to determine which activities supported students thinking about the novel material and the task at hand. Design materials and activities were carefully chosen based on the observation from these preliminary workshops.

An overview of the Orthorigami workshop activities and concepts is given in Table 1. The final workshop chose to use play-dough sculpting, because preliminary workshops showed participants found 3D design difficult on their own hand. A life cast of a hand for sculpting was prepared with Alja-Safe alginate by Smooth On. Thermochromic painting was introduced as an added aesthetic component for design. To make thermochromic paint, a generous amount of Solar Color Dust thermochromic powder was mixed with paint using a paintbrush. For example, blue thermochromic powder was mixed with red paint to create purple when cold and red when heated. Example scenes with 1-2 color changing components were made for demonstration. For the final workshop, more time was allotted to explaining this activity to go through more examples of color mixing and what the resulting color would be when heated to give participants a greater understanding of color theory. The researchers also made examples of paper prototypes, including a thumb brace and wrist brace designs with varying attachment points, to depict how to paper was representative of a wrist brace. These paper prototypes examples were made into fabric brace design examples to show how attachment was accomplished with velcro or other means, and how seams are created to hold the SMP. For the e-textile, a sheet of SMP with holes on each side was created by same casting method in Reese *et al.* [24]. An example e-textile was created by sanding the surface of the SMP and drawing a leopard face on the sanded surface. Fabric backing was added containing conductive thread and a coin cell battery connecting two green LEDs aligned behind the leopard eyes. This example to demonstrated how to connect electronic sewing and thinking through placement of LEDs to enhance aesthetic design.

Table 1. Orthorigami Workshop Activities

Day	Activities	Design Concepts
1	Demo commercial wrist brace, Video demo of SMP Material Experimentation with SMP, Design with Play-dough Sculpting on Hand, Laser-Cutting a Paper-Prototype, Iterative Adjustments of Paper Prototypes, Final Wrist Brace Design Sketch, CNC Machining of SMP Supports	Brainstorming, Material Experimentation, Crafting (Sculpting), Iterative Design, Fabrication Technology, Smart Material Design (SMP)
2	Laser-Cutting Fabric Design, Sewing Final Design, Reflection on Wrist Brace Design, Thermochromic Painting Demo, Color Mixing Introduction, Thermochromic Painting	Brainstorming, Fabrication Technology, Material Experimentation, Crafting (Painting, Sewing) Aesthetic Design Smart Material Design (Thermochromic)
3	E-textile Introduction and Demo, Simple Circuitry Introduction, Creation, Extrapolating New Designs of E-textile Bracelet from Workshop Activities	Brainstorming, Fabrication Technology, Material Experimentation, Crafting (Sewing), Smart Materials Design (E-textile, Conductive Thread), Integrative Thinking

3.2 Orthorigami Workshop

Participants. For the Orthorigami workshops, participants were recruited through university mailing lists to participate in a creative assistive design workshop. The age range for the workshop was ages 9-12 with interest in arts and crafts and creating assistive devices for medical applications. The design of the Orthorigami workshop took place over three days with each day consisting of a 2.5 h session. The composition of the participants is given in Table 2. Upon entering the workshop, the parents and participants were given the chance to ask questions and parental consent and minor assent forms were obtained. At the beginning of the workshop, a pre-study survey was administered to understand the participants background in with different artistic forms and assistive devices. Participants' prior art experiences from the pre-study survey are given in Fig. 1.

Table 2. Participant Background Information

Participant ID	Age	Gender	Participant ID	Age	Gender
ID17	11	F	ID21	10	M
ID18	11	M	ID22	11	M
ID19	12	F	ID23	10	F
ID20	9	M	ID24	9	F

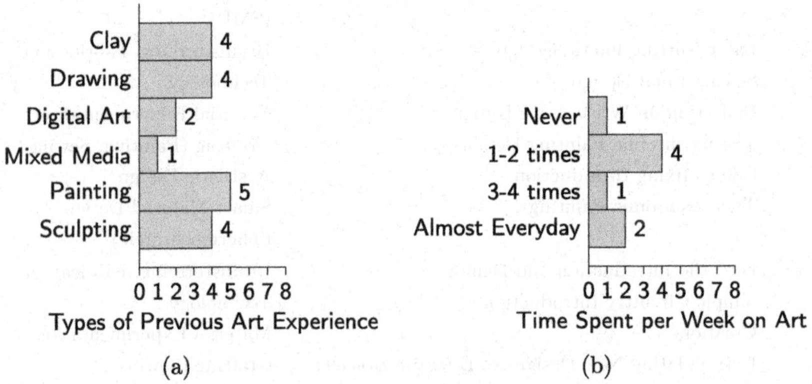

Fig. 1. Description of Previous Participant Art Experiences

Workshop Structure and Materials

Day 1. Participants were introduced to the concepts of assistive technology, wearable device and SMP. They started designing a wrist brace using play-dough, paper and 2D SMP sheets, custom-made by the research team. In order to demonstrate the structure and function of a wrist, participants were given the opportunity to wear a commercially available wrist brace for approximately 30 min. The participants were allowed to reflect on how different available commercial braces had differing placement and types of metal support components and attachment. Next, participants were introduced to the concept of shape change within a SMP through a video demonstration that depicts the shape memory cycle of folding and unfolding through placing SMP in cups filled with different temperature water. Then participants were given pieces of the SMP material created by the researchers for a hands-on demo. These pieces heated with a warm hair dryer to become malleable, and participants were then allowed to bend the material and freeze the bent shape by holding the SMP under cold water or sticking it in the fridge. The material was again heated with a hair dryer in which it returned to its original shape.

The participants were asked to design a wrist brace that incorporates the SMP material. As a part of the design, participants were required to provide support for the wrist area, but free to choose whether to implement additional support for the fingers or not. Participants were given a cement cast hand asked to create a 3D design of the brace by sculpting with play-dough on the hand. Once the design was done, the play-dough was removed from the hands carefully and laid out flat on paper and traced. The Glowforge laser-cutter took a picture of the traced design and then laser-cut a paper prototype. The paper prototypes were attached to the participants' hands using tape. After having the prototype on their hand, participants were asked to think about the fit of the paper on their hand and given the opportunity to cut and assess new prototypes based on iterative adjustments. Through this iterative process a final design was sketched out on paper. Participants were asked to include the specific details (aesthetic components, where the SMP will be positioned, how the device will attach, ect.) in the sketch of the final design. A depiction of the method of this design process is given in Fig. 2a-d. The shapes of the SMP in these final designs were scanned and converted into a drawing file to be used on a CNC machine. The CNC machine was used to cut the 2D SMP sheets in the shape of the final design of the support pieces.

Day 2. The second day children were given their machined SMP and the Glowforge was used with their final design sketches to cut the fabric components of the wrist brace. The participants, with help of the research team, sewed fabric for the design using sewing machines and the SMP was placed in the sewn brace. Participants were then introduced to the concept of thermochromic painting by showing videos of thermochromic materials, powder and paint, changing color with temperature. The participants were also given scenes painted by the research team and allowed to use the warm hair dryer to see how the thermochromic paint in the scene changed. Some of these example scenes included: a field of bluebonnets and Indian paintbrushes where the bluebonnets disappeared when heated, a cat caught in a rain cloud where the went away when

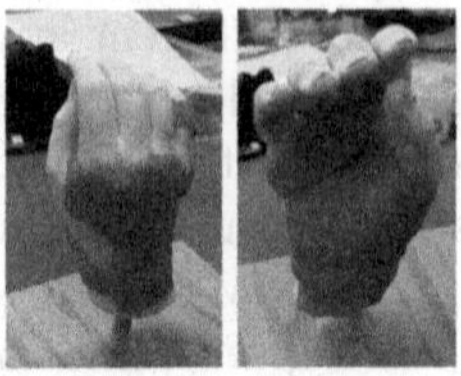

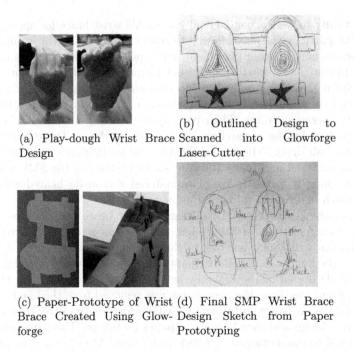

(a) Play-dough Wrist Brace Design

(b) Outlined Design to Scanned into Glowforge Laser-Cutter

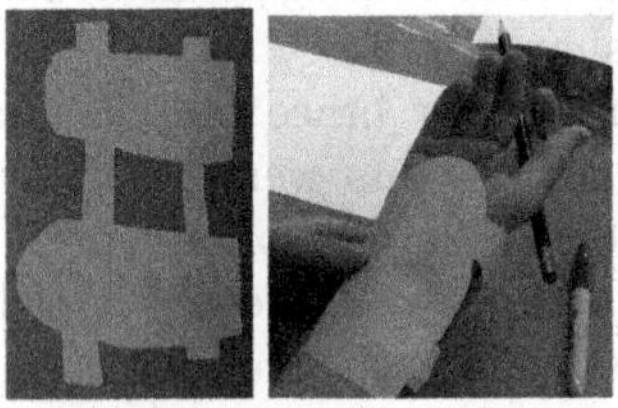

(c) Paper-Prototype of Wrist Brace Created Using Glowforge

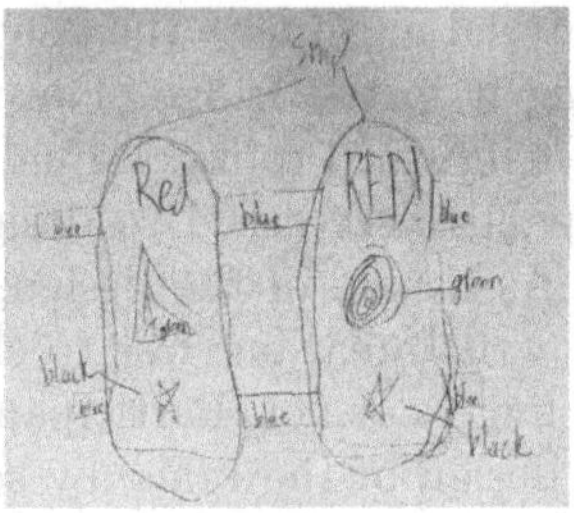

(d) Final SMP Wrist Brace Design Sketch from Paper Prototyping

Fig. 2. Design Process for the Wrist Brace

heated, and a scene where the grass in a field turns from brown to green. Color mixing with regards to primary, secondary, and tertiary colors was explained in the context of thermochromic painting. The participants were asked to predict what colors would appear when the thermochromic paint mixture was cool or heated. For example, if blue thermochromic powder (that changes to white when heated) is mixed with red paint, then the mixture will appear purple when cool and red when heated. After this introduction, participants were then asked to paint a scene containing 1-2 color changing components and to plan how the color will change within these components. Thermochromic powders of blue, yellow, magenta, green, and red were given to mix with various colors of paint. Participants were then given the choice of adding a color changing component to their final wrist brace design. After completion of the design, participants were allotted some time to discuss durability, practicality, fit, and aesthetics of their design with the group. Pictures of the participants final design is given in Fig. 3.

Day 3. The final day of the workshop participants were given the opportunity to expand their creation with a different smart material, e-textiles. Participants were introduced to what an e-textile was by being shown videos of interactive

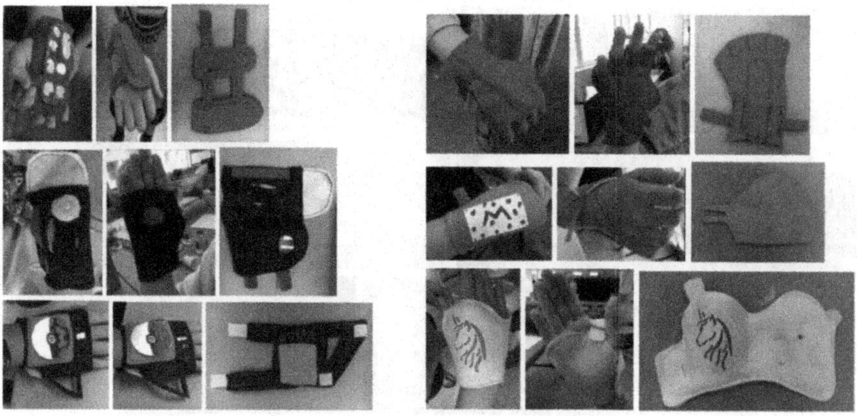

Fig. 3. Examples of Participants Final Brace SMP Designs: (Top Left) Breathable Design with Thermochromic Clouds, (Middle Left) Space-Themed Design with a Rocket Ship, Galaxy, and Moon, (Bottom Left) Fashionable Ninja Blade Design with Thermochromic Pokémon Masterball, (Top Right) Glove Design from the Design Process in Figs. 2a-d, (Middle Right) SMP Brace Design with Thermochromic Initials, (Bottom Right) Design with Layered Laser-cut Fabric Depicting Unicorn

wearables, such as clothing and shoes with LEDs incorporated and a phone operated LED necklace. The participants were also given an explanation of simple circuit design including how to connect a battery, switch, and LED. Participants were given a rectangular shaped fabric, rectangular shaped SMP, conductive thread, LEDs, and a coin-cell battery and asked to use soft-circuitry to design a shape-changing wearable bracelet. Pink, green, blue, yellow, or white Lilypad LEDs were available to be used in their design. Participants were given the choice to either draw on the surface of the SMP and integrate the LED into the fabric underneath the drawing or to leave the surface of the SMP clear and design a scene on the fabric with LEDs. Examples of the final design are given in Fig. 4. Afterwards, participants were asked to discuss their design with the group. At the end of the workshop, a post-survey was given that asked about their experience in the workshop and asked them to extrapolate their design experience to the creation of new assistive devices or designs for themselves or others. The parent's of the participants were also given a survey to complete.

4 Data Collection and Analysis Methods

The data collected for the study consisted of video interviews taken during the workshop, a pre-workshop survey, a post-workshop survey for participants and parents, and photos of the participants work. The video interviews were transcribed and placed into a spreadsheet. From the transcribed videos, the phrasing was coded to identify themes from the data. The coding for the elements attributed to the design process were derived from the categories described by

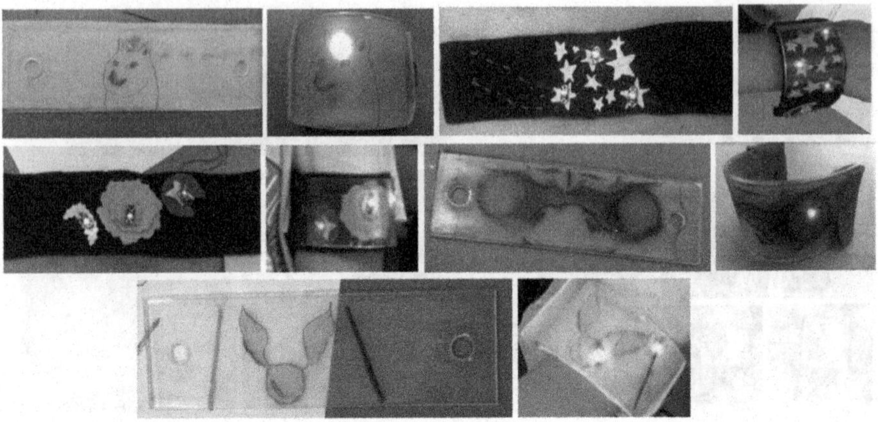

Fig. 4. Examples of Participants E-textiles: (Top Left) Doge internet meme with a halo on top, (Top Right) Clear SMP Surface with Fabric Design of Stars and Threaded Constellations, (Middle Left) Clear SMP Surface with Fabric Design of Rippling Water and Flower Lilypad, (Middle Right) Sanded SMP Surface Design of King Crimson from JoJo's Bizarre Adventure, (Bottom) Sanded SMP Surface Design of wand and Golden Snitch from Harry Potter

Brown. Brown described as passing through three phases in design: inspiration (circumstances that motivate a search for solutions), ideation (the process of generating, developing, and testing ideas that lead to solutions), and implementation (charting a path to marketing) [1].

The final designs themselves were considered artefacts. Coding was also used to describe the designs having to do with the aesthetics of the design such as color, texture, structural support, and images. The analysis of these final designs and the participants' drawings also used questions given by Clarke and Freeman and Mathison to analyze visual discourses [5,8].

Further coding was also done to describe the experience of the participants which included codes derived from conversation about their work and related answers in the surveys. These codes help encompass themes related to the participant's process and emotion regarding their end work, their ability to create, and how they felt about the tools used during the creation process.

5 Results and Discussion

The participatory workshop was a success. All participants were able to create a customized wrist brace and e-textile of their own design using DIY concepts and SMP. Participants reporting an average (on a scale of 1-5) of 4.5 on how they felt about the workshop, of 4.1 on how they felt about the wrist brace they designed, and of 4.5 on how they felt about the e-textile they designed. Participants felt engaged in making process, felt aided by the use of fabrication technology, felt inspired to create new AT, and were able to bridge various crafting concepts presented in the workshop. Through our analysis we identified the following themes to discuss: (1) Participatory Making of DIY AT and (2) Creativity, Inspiration, and Integrative Thinking.

5.1 Participatory Making of DIY AT: Experience and Accessibility

The process of making is a complex process involving problem consideration, brainstorming, creation, iteration, evaluation, and integration of concepts. Even for highly motivated designers, there are still barriers due to lack of experience when creating a new functional product. Fabrication tools and techniques are needed that make unfamiliar design accessible to the average user. A major component of designing Orthorigami, is the ability to imagine a 2D to 3D origami shape change. Children and users of AT do not necessarily have experience with 3D spatial design or modeling software. Therefore, the introduction of sculpting with play-dough aided the participants in design of their AT. ID19 states that the play-dough aided in the design process, because it would have been tough to start with 2D first. McDonald *et al.*'s research also pointed out the preference to sculpting in aiding in design. The study found that 76.3% physical therapists who were taught how to use 3D modeling software, still preferred design with play-dough and 3D scanning of the design over 3D modeling of DIY AT. The Glowforge laser cutter also provided a valuable tool for iterating multiple intricate prototypes to test against the participant's hand. Participant's were able to place the designs on their hands using tape and discuss with the researchers where the fit of the design was too lose or cutting into the skin too much. ID17 pointed out to the research team that the fit of the straps of the original paper prototype was too big on her hand and that the attachment point where the velcro goes was too tiny. Based on this type of feedback new designs were able to be re-cut quickly with the laser-cutter or modified with scissors. The ease of use of the laser cutter also foster how future designs were created or modified. For example, ID18 chose to use the laser-cutter in the e-textile design, Fig. 4 (Middle Right), to cut the stars in the design, due to the fact they were small and intricate.

Children and users of AT do not necessarily possess medical knowledge or training to design AT. Designing AT with smart materials presented two main challenges to participants. The first challenge was to address how to provide adequate structural support with flexibility, wearability, and breathability. Second participants were challenged by designing with new and unfamiliar smart materials. Wearing the various commercial prototypes aided children in thinking through how typical devices addressed the first challenge. Also, children were able to consider, for their own design, how modifications could be made to create a better device. ID17 when reflecting on the final design stated, *"I feel like it could maybe like wider SMP because when you do this (places wrist in flexion), you can still move your wrist this way."* ID21 compares the SMP brace to design to one of the commercial braces, *"My brace is kind of like this (pointing out one of the commercial braces) except it has holes for each finger, so that it gives you more flexibility."* ID17 describes the SMP brace as, *"I think that mine is very durable. Like it's very wearable. Because like it's very simple and doesn't take a genius to understand how to function the whole thing. That's what I don't really like about some straps (pointing to the ones on the commercial braces) is that sometimes you have to weave them through the little loops. And then the loops rub against your arm and then all of that. So this is just felt and Velcro and a strip of plastic."*

The workshop and materials engaged participants and generated excitement in design. ID17 described her experience as *"all of it being fun"*. ID23 when asked what their perception of the material was said *"I like it. It's a really fun material."*. At the beginning of the workshop, ID20 seemed disinterested in participating in the workshop, stating they couldn't make a brace, and felt compelled to be there because their parent signed them up. By the end of the workshop, ID20 was able to share how they designed their brace, felt the skill level was not as difficult as originally perceived, and was motivated to integrate a favorite D&D concept, a bag of holding, into a new design. The workshop also encouraged them to co-design and collaborate with the researchers, as well as, their peers participating in the workshop. Few of the participants had experience with sewing, the researchers helped in sewing co-design with regards to advising participants on stitching space requirements for placement of aesthetic or electronic components and for seams. The researchers also taught techniques and assisted participants in thinking through how to make mixes for their thermochromic color changing choices and using the appropriate amount of thermochromic powder to create a significant change. For example, ID19 stated they wanted to do a Pokéball on their SMP brace design. The researchers encouraged the participant to think color change options that like red to white, through a collaborative discussion ID19 decided to use a Pokémon masterball changing from purple to red. The workshop motivated participants to consult the research team and each other on how to take their designs from an idea phase to a product phase. During the brace design, ID20 asked to see ID22's SMP brace design because it gave him an idea. ID22 proceeded to explain how they created the sculpted the face component to aid in execution of ID20's idea. ID24 created a galaxy (swirl) on the play-dough model of the SMP brace design. Through co-design with the research team a fabric equivalent of the galaxy was created to add texture.

5.2 Creativity, Inspiration, and Integrative Thinking

Each participant's work represented a unique, tailor-made wearable AT or e-textile. Participants chose personal preferences to integrate into their final designs such as nature; favorite animals, characters, or themes; colors; and textures. In Fig. 3 (Middle Left) ID24's design is an inspired favorite space theme: *"And I'm doing mine like space theme...like that's a rocket ship, that's supposed to be a shark and then that's a [inaudible]."* In Fig. 4 (Middle Left) ID19's design is a favorite anime character, King Crimson, from the series Jojo's Bizarres Adventures. Figure 3 (Bottom Right) ID23 incorporated a character, a unicorn, by textured layering of laser-cut felt materials in the SMP wrist brace design. In Fig. 4 (Middle Left), ID17's design uses texture to depict a lily pad and rippling water. ID17 describes the work as *"So, this was a lily pad cut out like a little lily. This was something a lot of people thought was a flower. Well some people also thought it...but it's just the ripples in the water that you see when you drop something in there and you just touch the water when you just see the wave and reflection."*.

Their designs also represented creative integration of between smart materials, such as thermochromic components or SMP, electronics, and design. In Fig. 3 (Bottom Left) ID19's design incorporates a ninja blade and thermochromic Pokémon ball that changes from a purple Masterball to a standard red Poké ball. In Fig. 3 (Middle Right) ID17's final design uses favorite colors and thermochromic paint that changes from purple to pink to place an initial on the SMP brace design. In Fig. 3 (Top Left) ID18's SMP brace design uses thermochromic clouds changing from pink to white. In Fig. 4 (Bottom), ID23's design incorporates a Harry Potter wand and golden snitch as a favorite theme, but accentuates the wand and snitch using LEDs. ID18's e-textile design, in the same figure (top right), integrates LEDs to light up the stars and conductive thread as a representation of constellations. ID22's design is a favorite internet character, Doge, with a halo above it's head illuminated by a white LED. These final designs of the SMP brace and e-textile represent a merging of purpose, functionality, and fashion.

Participants were inspired to share their work with friends and family, discussing what they had created, how the device was created, and how the material worked. Parents were asked if their children were interested in discussing the workshop with themselves or peers. ID23's parent stated, *"Yes, she showed her friend how her design worked and how it was made (polymer, play-dough, laser-cutter)."* ID17's parent stated the participant discussed, *"more the experience and the thermo-sensitive nature of the polymer. She talked about designing the brace and also painting with heat sensitive paint."* ID20's parent responded, *Yes, ID20 is so excited about this workshop. He discussed with me and his dad, and his brother. He kept saying, "We learned cool stuff like cutter with laser and polymer smart shape."*

Participants were motivated to an increased interest in art or exploration of design. ID17's parent stated when asked if there were any changes in their art creativity or activity post-workshop, *"She has already been very interested in home made "goo", playing substances like 'play-dough', 'oobleck' types and this will certainly keep that interest active."*. ID19's parent said *"He tried to use light bulb and sun light to see the color painted shift from purple to red."* ID24's parent said *"Already interested in slime, and now really wants to make devices."*

At the end of the workshop, all the participants expressed they felt confident to design and make things. On the post-survey participants were asked to brainstorm by bridging the materials they have used in the workshop to design new innovative creations. Examples of their brainstorming based creations with LEDs are given in Fig. 5. The designs represent the integration of LEDs into wearables, AT, and personalized dishware to enhance fashion or functionality.

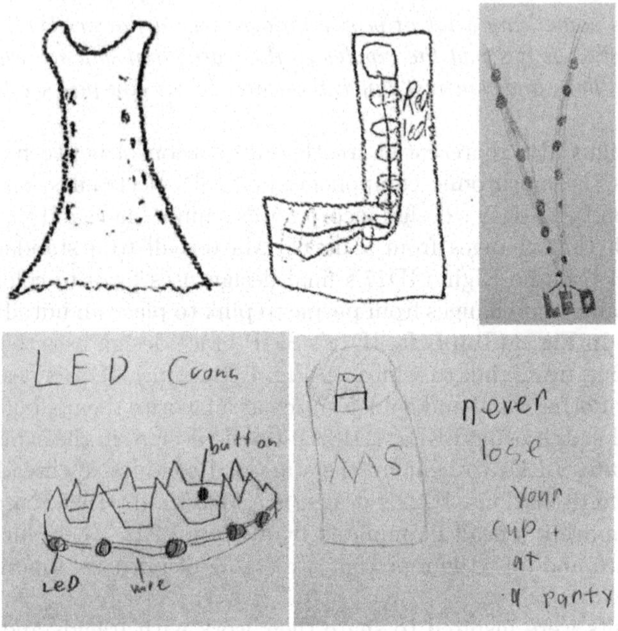

Fig. 5. Examples of Participants Brainstorming Design with LEDs: (Top Left) LED Dress, (Top Middle) Ankle Brace with Red LEDs, (Top Right) LED necklace, (Bottom Left) LED crown, and (Bottom Right) LED koozie (Color figure online)

Participants were also asked if they could think of other uses for SMP outside of AT or wearable design. Their responses demonstrated integrative critical thinking with regards to the material functionality. ID19 said, *"We could make something out of this and then you compress it and then heat it up again and it turns back again. Like you can make stuff portable, because like if you make a uh bowl and you take the bowl and you turn it into a ball and then if you heat it up again. Then you've got your bowl."* ID17 suggested making a small water bottle that can be stretched out. ID17 describes the device as, *"Like if we had the same bottle or if we had a bottle this size, like we just thought I don't want this big a bottle because I don't want to carry it around just squish it together. Or you just want to carry a small little emergency water bottle, because you don't have water carrier you can, because I've seen these people who carry something like that and then they make their own little filter and they just attach it on like if they are tired or something."*

6 Conclusion and Future Work

The research addressed these questions: How children make and design with smart materials, specifically SMP? How children create and design with SMP to make DIY AT? How using SMP in design can affect children's creativity and confidence and provide a positive, enabling experience? What types of tools or fabrication or crafting technology aid children in design of DIY AT? The workshop showed participants felt confident to create designs with SMP. Specifically, the participants were able to brainstorm new designs that incorporated the concepts introduced in the workshop. Participants were innovative in their choices regarding implementation of smart materials into the design. They created unique artefacts of intricate personalized designs, and they were excited to share their work and experience with friends and family members. The workshop stimulated an increased interest in art. The materials and activities in the workshop helped participants to have a positive outlook with regards to their ability to design DIY AT. Smart materials proved to be an accessible medium and an "active" participant in aiding in design with children. The experience cultivated bringing together different aspects of design and encouraged further inspiration of art and design.

The tools used in the workshop, showed that low-tech DIY design through crafting helped participants feel confident and understand how to design. Observing commercial braces and learning about the materials assisted participants in thinking through designing with smart materials and a device that was functional. The activities in the workshop engaged the participants fostering creativity and excitement in the design process. Participants actively discussed with others how to execute their ideas in a final design.

Although, over half the participants had worn a brace or had a close family member with a disability, this preliminary work was not able to include individuals with extensive experience with AT. Future participatory workshops would involve users of AT in co-design with children or involve children who use AT in design. Future work would build on this workshop to assess if involving users of AT might require different fabrication technology or techniques to aid in co-design. Also, to assess how children's perception about user's of AT may change through the co-design process. Do children show an increased awareness of challenges or needs of those with disabilities? Do children understand what questions are appropriate to ask users of AT to help aid in the design of AT? How will children's design change when considering input from those with disabilities?

References

1. Brown, T., et al.: Design thinking. Harv. Bus. Rev. **86**(6), 84 (2008)
2. Buechley, L., Elumeze, N., Eisenberg, M.: Electronic/computational textiles and children's crafts. In: Proceedings of the 2006 Conference on Interaction Design and Children, pp. 49–56. IDC 2006, Association for Computing Machinery, New York, NY, USA (2006). https://doi.org/10.1145/1139073.1139091

3. Buehler, E., et al.: Sharing is caring: assistive technology designs on Thingiverse, pp. 525–534. Association for Computing Machinery, New York, NY, USA (2015). https://doi.org/10.1145/2702123.2702525
4. Chan Vili, Y.Y.: Investigating smart textiles based on shape memory materials. Textile Res. J. **77**(5), 290–300 (2007)
5. Clarke, A.E.: Situational analysis: grounded theory after the postmodern turn. SAGE (2005)
6. Coelho, M.: Programming the material world a proposition for the application and design of transitive materials (2007)
7. Du, J., Markopoulos, P., Wang, Q., Toeters, M., Gong, T.: Shapetex: Implementing shape-changing structures in fabric for wearable actuation. In: Proceedings of the Twelfth International Conference on Tangible, Embedded, and Embodied Interaction, pp. 166–176. TEI 2018, Association for Computing Machinery, New York, NY, USA (2018). https://doi.org/10.1145/3173225.3173245
8. Freeman, M., Mathison, S.: Researching children's experiences. Sandra Mathison. Guilford Press, Melissa Freeman (2009)
9. Giles, E., van der Linden, J., Petre, M.: Weaving lighthouses and stitching stories: blind and visually impaired people designing e-textiles. In: Proceedings of the 2018 CHI Conference on Human Factors in Computing Systems, p. 1–12. CHI 2018, Association for Computing Machinery, New York, NY, USA (2018). https://doi.org/10.1145/3173574.3174044
10. Groeger, D., Chong Loo, E., Steimle, J.: Hotflex: Post-print customization of 3D prints using embedded state change. In: Proceedings of the 2016 CHI Conference on Human Factors in Computing Systems, pp. 420–432. CHI 2016, Association for Computing Machinery, New York, NY, USA (2016). https://doi.org/10.1145/2858036.2858191
11. Hook, J., Verbaan, S., Durrant, A., Olivier, P., Wright, P.: A study of the challenges related to DIY assistive technology in the context of children with disabilities. In: Proceedings of the 2014 Conference on Designing Interactive Systems. p. 597–606. DIS 2014, Association for Computing Machinery, New York, NY, USA (2014). https://doi.org/10.1145/2598510.2598530
12. Hurst, A., Kane, S.: Making "making" accessible. In: Proceedings of the 12th International Conference on Interaction Design and Children, pp. 635–638. IDC 2013, Association for Computing Machinery, New York, NY, USA (2013). https://doi.org/10.1145/2485760.2485883
13. Hurst, A., Tobias, J.: Empowering individuals with do-it-yourself assistive technology. In: The Proceedings of the 13th International ACM SIGACCESS Conference on Computers and Accessibility, pp. 11–18. ASSETS 2011, Association for Computing Machinery, New York, NY, USA (2011). https://doi.org/10.1145/2049536.2049541
14. Jacoby, S., Buechley, L.: Drawing the electric: Storytelling with conductive ink. In: Proceedings of the 12th International Conference on Interaction Design and Children, pp. 265–268. IDC 2013, Association for Computing Machinery, New York, NY, USA (2013). https://doi.org/10.1145/2485760.2485790
15. Kaihou, T., Wakita, A.: Electronic origami with the color-changing function. In: Proceedings of the Second International Workshop on Smart Material Interfaces: Another Step to a Material Future, pp. 7–12. SMI 2013, Association for Computing Machinery, New York, NY, USA (2013). https://doi.org/10.1145/2534688.2534690

16. Kuznetsov, S., Fernando, P., Ritter, E., Barrett, C., Weiler, J., Rohr, M.: Screen-printing and tei: Supporting engagement with steam through DIY fabrication of smart materials. In: Proceedings of the Twelfth International Conference on Tangible, Embedded, and Embodied Interaction, pp. 211–220. TEI 2018, Association for Computing Machinery, New York, NY, USA (2018). https://doi.org/10.1145/3173225.3173253
17. Lin, H.W., Aflatoony, L., Wakkary, R.: Design for one: a game controller for a quadriplegic gamer. In: CHI '14 Extended Abstracts on Human Factors in Computing Systems, pp. 1243–1248. CHI EA 2014, Association for Computing Machinery, New York, NY, USA (2014). https://doi.org/10.1145/2559206.2581334
18. McDonald, S., et al.: Uncovering challenges and opportunities for 3D printing assistive technology with physical therapists. In: Proceedings of the 18th International ACM SIGACCESS Conference on Computers and Accessibility, pp. 131–139. ASSETS 2016, Association for Computing Machinery, New York, NY, USA (2016). https://doi.org/10.1145/2982142.2982162
19. Meissner, J.L., Vines, J., McLaughlin, J., Nappey, T., Maksimova, J., Wright, P.: Do-it-yourself empowerment as experienced by novice makers with disabilities. In: Proceedings of the 2017 Conference on Designing Interactive Systems, pp. 1053–1065. DIS 2017, Association for Computing Machinery, New York, NY, USA (2017). https://doi.org/10.1145/3064663.3064674
20. Minuto, A.: Materials that matter: Smart materials meet art & interaction design, Ph. D. thesis, University of Twente, Netherlands (2016). https://doi.org/10.3990/1.9789036541695. sIKS dissertation series no. 2016-38
21. Ou, J., Yao, L., Tauber, D., Steimle, J., Niiyama, R., Ishii, H.: JamSheets: thin interfaces with tunable stiffness enabled by layer jamming. In: Proceedings of the 8th International Conference on Tangible, Embedded and Embodied Interaction, pp. 65–72. TEI 2014, Association for Computing Machinery, New York, NY, USA (2014). https://doi.org/10.1145/2540930.2540971
22. Phillips, B., Zhao, H.: Predictors of assistive technology abandonment. Assist. Technol. **5**(1), 36–45 (1993). https://doi.org/10.1080/10400435.1993.10132205. pMID: 10171664
23. Qi, J., Buechley, L.: Animating paper using shape memory alloys. In: Proceedings of the SIGCHI Conference on Human Factors in Computing Systems, pp. 749–752. CHI 2012, Association for Computing Machinery, New York, NY, USA (2012). https://doi.org/10.1145/2207676.2207783
24. Reese, J., Seo, J.H., Srinavasa, A.: Orthorigami: Implementing shape-memory polymers for customizing orthotic applications. In: Proceedings of the Fourteenth International Conference on Tangible, Embedded, and Embodied Interaction, pp. 123–130. TEI 2020, Association for Computing Machinery, New York, NY, USA (2020). https://doi.org/10.1145/3374920.3374957
25. Scherer, M.J.: Outcomes of assistive technology use on quality of life. Disabil. Rehabil. **18**(9), 439–448 (1996). https://doi.org/10.3109/09638289609165907. pMID: 8877302
26. Takegawa, Y., Fukushi, K., Machover, T., Terada, T., Tsukamoto, M.: Construction of a prototyping support system for painted musical instruments. In: Nijholt, A., Romão, T., Reidsma, D. (eds.) ACE 2012. LNCS, vol. 7624, pp. 384–397. Springer, Heidelberg (2012). https://doi.org/10.1007/978-3-642-34292-9_27

Bridging Values: The Inclusion of Young Generations in Computing

Anna Szlavi[1(✉)], Serena Versino[2], Irene Zanardi[3], Karolina Bolesta[4], and Letizia Jaccheri[1]

[1] Norwegian University of Science and Technology, Trondheim, Norway
{anna.szlavi,letizia.jaccheri}@ntnu.no
[2] University of Pisa, Pisa, Italy
serena.versino@phd.unipi.it
[3] Università della Svizzera Italiana, Lugano, Switzerland
irene.zanardi@usi.ch
[4] Warsaw School of Economics, Warsaw, Poland
kboles@sgh.waw.pl

Abstract. There is a constantly growing need for skilled professionals in the computing field, which poses challenges for finding the right people for the job. According to the 2022 Digital Economy and Society Index, 55% of companies have problems filling their tech positions. At the same time, the computing sector is going through a diversity crisis, as the majority of its players are Global Northern, heterosexual, white, able-bodied men. Technology permeates our lives, so a lack of diversity in the tech industry, especially when designing software, can lead to bias and exclusionary user experiences. As a consequence, we need to attract young people - for instance, Generation Z (GenZ), born between the mid-1990s and the 2010s - to computing majors. Moreover, there is a need for actions with a retention plan and a strategy to guide a more diverse group toward leadership roles both in academia and industry. Even though the awareness about Diversity, Equity, and Inclusion (DEI) is continually being raised, interventions that focus on inclusiveness are still necessary. With the present paper, we aim to contribute to a better alignment of how to design interventions for including younger people in computing. According to research, GenZ cares about social values and a meaningful contribution to society, that is, DEI, as part of their work. In this paper we are presenting an intervention project, designed to increase DEI in computing, as part of which we collected testimonials by stakeholders working in computing. As a quality check, we performed content analysis after the completion of the project, to investigate to what extent the experiences listed by CS professionals and the interests of GenZ align with one another. Applying multiple methods of cross-checking, we confirmed the presence of social aspects in the lived experiences of CS professionals. Findings show that professionals in the field recognize computing's social embeddedness, which aligns with younger students' values and expectations and confirms that computing is a valid choice to achieve their goals of making a positive change in society. This study is part of a larger effort proposed and realized by EUGAIN, a Horizon Europe-sponsored COST Action, whose purpose is to create a European network that enhances gender balance and diversity in the field of computing.

M. Antona and C. Stephanidis (Eds.): HCII 2023, LNCS 14020, pp. 154–170, 2023.
https://doi.org/10.1007/978-3-031-35681-0_10

Keywords: gender balance · DEI · computing · intervention · generation Z

1 Introduction

Technology has become so widespread nowadays that it penetrates people's daily lives. This, on the one hand, results in a constantly growing need for skilled professionals in the computing field[1]. According to the 2022 Digital Economy and Society Index, 55% of companies have problems filling their tech positions [2]. On the other hand, due to technology's ubiquitous role, it is essential to create software which is useful and usable for a wide range of people. This requires diverse development teams so team members can check each other's blind spots and avoid bias [3]. Studies show that diversity also leads to greater creativity and success [4]. Despite this, computing is a homogeneous field: the workforce predominantly constitutes white, cis-gendered, heterosexual, Global Northern, young, middle-class men [5]. Women constitute only 19% of the computing job market within Europe [6].

Even though the awareness about Diversity, Equity, and Inclusion (DEI) in computing is continually being raised, interventions that focus on inclusiveness are still necessary. In order to tackle the growing demand for computing professionals and to achieve DEI, we need to reach young people - for instance, GenZ, born between the mid-1990s and the 2010s [7] - to join computing majors.

In this paper we are presenting an intervention project, proposed and realized by EUGAIN [8], a Horizon Europe-sponsored COST Action, whose purpose is to create a European network that enhances gender balance, and broadly DEI, in the field of computing. Within the frames of this project, we have designed an initiative that focuses specifically on the better involvement of young people in computing, through short interviews with role models, posted on social media. The project proved to be one of the most successful interventions of the Action, achieving promising results in terms of total views. Therefore, the authors decided to build a content analysis-focused research study on it, in order to understand which key features of this novel intervention intended for GenZ have been successful.

In this study, we are analyzing the testimonials collected for the intervention project, which were produced by stakeholders working in computing, in order to identify the key features describing their experiences in the field. We extracted 31 keywords and grouped them in five macro themes: *Computing*, *Academia*, *Skills*, *Society* and *Gender*. Then, we checked the robustness of our findings with

[1] "The word computing refers to a goal-oriented activity requiring, benefiting from, or associated with the creation and use of computers. [...] computing includes a variety of interpretations such as designing and constructing hardware and software systems for a wide range of purposes: processing, structuring, and managing various kinds of information; problem solving by finding solutions to problems or by proving a solution does not exist; making computer systems behave intelligently; creating and using communications and entertainment media; and finding and gathering information relevant to any particular purpose." [1]

different methods, and confirmed them. The purpose of our examination, which marries data mining and feature extraction methods, is to check the content of the testimonials, more precisely to see how much the perception of computing and the interest of GenZ are consistent with each other. Our goal is to contribute to a better understanding of how to design interventions that target younger generations, with the purpose of achieving DEI in computing.

2 Background

2.1 Inclusion in Computing

Gender balance is one of the main challenges of the 21stcentury. According to the UN, one of the Sustainable Development Goals (UN SDG5) is to achieve gender equality [9]. Women are at a disadvantage in a number of areas compared to men. For example, girls are forced to leave education earlier than boys [10], growing up they are less likely to get well-paid jobs [11] or be in leadership roles [10], and they are more often victims of domestic violence [12]. When it comes to the digital world, women are underrepresented in both technical and decision-making roles, which leads to software that excludes the female perspective and reinforces binary gender hierarchies [13]. Being a complex and deeply entrenched problem, gender equality requires concerted efforts in multiple areas of life, including technology.

There is an increasing awareness of the need for inclusion in computing. In fact, tech companies often join the DEI conversation because they realized it is beneficial for their image as an employer. As a consequence, there are a number of initiatives whose purpose is to channel a more diverse crowd into computing education, as well as actions that focus on retention and strategies that guide a more diverse group toward leadership roles in both academia and industry. Role models, networking, and mentoring are among the key strategies to involve non-stereotypical players into the field. In the following, we will present one example for each of the above approaches to increase DEI through the gender perspective.

Firstly, Girls' Day is an international program and campaign, running annually from the early 2000s, with the aim of promoting STEM fields to girls in primary and secondary education mainly through role models (see: in Germany, in Hungary, and in Australia for example[2]). Every year a high number of universities, research institutes, and corporations in the STEM field offer to host and organize programs for girls within the frames of this one-day event. The goal is to give girls a first-hand experience about studying and/or working in the field, not just regarding the environment and the types of activities the different jobs involve, but also through meeting relatable role models in the field [14]. Studies show that role models, especially non-stereotypical role models, have a crucial impact on making computing accessible for women [15–18].

[2] Germany: https://www.girls-day.de/ueber-den-girls-day/was-ist-der-girls-day2/english; Hungary: https://lanyoknapja.hu; Australia: https://www.gdostem.com.au.

Secondly, to raise awareness about bias within higher education, Girl Project Ada[3] aims to contribute to the effort of helping more women to graduate in the computing field. Ada, operating at the Norwegian University of Science and Technology, organizes social and career events for women, so it puts a lot of attention to networking as its tool. Networking and the visibility of female peers have shown to enhance retention [19].

Thirdly, Women STEM UP[4], a European collaboration project with five partner institutions, aims to increase DEI in STEM – and mainly computing – education through a mentorship scheme. By acknowledging the positive effect of female mentors on the success of female students in computing [20], the initiative wishes to facilitate retention and contribute to a growing awareness of DEI in computing education through its mentorship and inspiration academy.

2.2 EUGAIN

To achieve DEI goals in computing, in 2020 Horizon Europe sponsored EUGAIN[5], a 4-year COST Action, whose goal is to improve gender balance in the field of computing through creating and strengthening a multi-cultural European community of academics. By doing so, it aims to use the tools of role models, networking, and mentoring, as described in the previous section, to enhance DEI. Based primarily in academia, the initiative has five working groups, focusing on multiple aspects of DEI in computing. EUGAIN wishes not only to map and invigorate the different areas of computing education, it also wishes to connect the findings to the industry, as well as to design interventions for inclusion. Starting in November 2020, EUGAIN has over 150 members from 39 European countries as of November 2022, at the half-time of the project.

Inclusiveness necessitates the acknowledgement that gender is only one dimension of an individual's identity, and as such, exclusion and bias cannot be eradicated with a single focus on binary gender. As the Theory of Intersectionality points out, the overlapping dimensions of identity, such as gender, sexuality, socio-economic status, ethnicity, religion, nationality, dis/ability, and education, affect one's experiences as a whole [21]. The combination of these factors can account for the individual's unique disadvantages and challenges; thus, inclusiveness can only be achieved with a shift in approach.

In fact, the need for more workforce and more DEI in computing underscores the urgency of finding better ways to attract young people to the computing field. GenZ, also called as digital natives [22], has a pronouncedly different view on the digital world, as well as on social values, than previous generations [23]. Due to their early exposure to the internet and digital technologies, they are much more aware of social issues and global problems than other generations [24], appreciating and expecting the values of DEI from their work environments [25]. They cherish career paths that allow them to realize themselves and meaningfully contribute to social issues according to their values [26].

[3] see link https://www.ntnu.edu/ada.

[4] see link: https://www.women-stem-up.eu.

[5] The fifth author is the Chair of the present Action.

In line with this, the Action puts great emphasis on supporting younger generations within the field. Early career academics receive support through grants, joint projects, networking, and mentorship within the Action. This way, EUGAIN aims to serve as an intervention that helps the retention of young people in computing and contribute to a more diverse leadership within academia and industry. In the summer of 2022 a new role was created within the Core Group to better fit with this specific goal. Even if it is not a tradition in COST projects, this Action decided to appoint a Young Researcher and Innovator Coordinator, in order to more efficiently manage the group of about 50 PhDs and postdocs within the community called Young Researchers and Innovators (YRIs). Thanks to the dedicated efforts, the Action now has an active early career group, even with people from GenZ.

2.3 Project GenZ

One of the recent projects carried out by early career researchers within EUGAIN[6] has the aim to design an intervention that attracts and includes young people in the field. Acknowledging the importance of role models for thriving in computing [16–18], this group of young researchers wanted to reach out to GenZ by creating short visual content: interviews about primarily young role models and mentor figures. Over 30 testimonials were collected from diverse stakeholders from the field, both from industry and academia, all over Europe.

We designed a library of brief videos, shortening each of the testimonials, in order to share them on social media, such as YouTube[7] and TikTok[8], the main channels for GenZ [27]. By this, the project had the intention of boosting both the visibility and the desirability of the field for younger people, portraying it as an inclusive field.

The videos were posted on EUGAIN's YouTube channel between December 2022 and February 2023. Parallel to this, a TikTok account was also created, so that the videos could be posted there too between January 2023 and February 2023. Figure 1 shows the examples which were created for the YouTube channel (i.e., horizontal longer videos) and the TikTok social platform (i.e., vertical shorter videos). The latter example can be used for the YouTube channel in the "shorts" section as well.

An example of a shorter video for the TikTok channel or YouTube Shorts is shown in Fig. 1b. One of the videos posted on YouTube's Shorts section, featuring specifically GenZ stakeholders (master students of CS), reached over 300 views over a weekend. Within three days of being posted, our first TikTok video had about 255 views (i.e., it collected about 85 views on average per day). According to statistics, in 2022 young women between the ages of 18 and 24 made up 24% of TikTok's global audience (i.e., three billion app downloads globally), while male users in that same age group make up roughly 18% of the app's users [28].

[6] The first four authors consisted of this team.
[7] see link https://www.youtube.com/@eugain7063.
[8] see account @eugaincost.

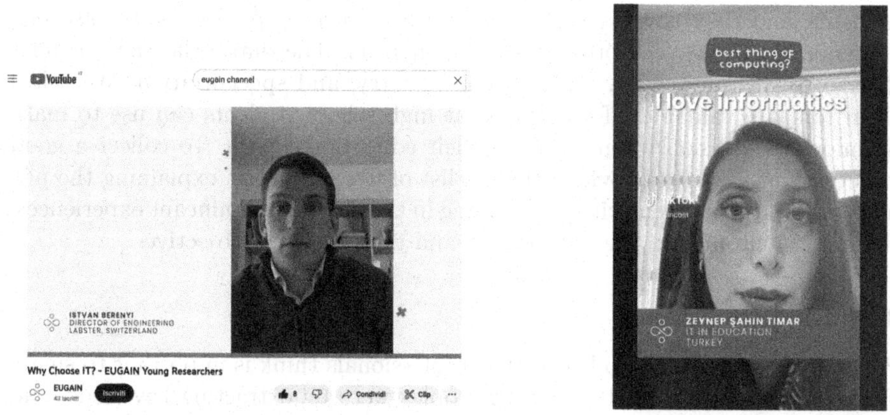

(a) YouTube: longer video (b) TikTok: shorter video

Fig. 1. Video examples

These statistics shed light on the possible visibility we may reach by using this social network.

Due to the popularity of the intervention, the authors saw an opportunity in analyzing the testimonials and their potential to motivate young generations in choosing computing. With the present paper, we aim to contribute to a better alignment of how to design interventions for including younger people in computing.

3 Methodology

According to research, GenZ is concerned with social values and making a significant contribution to society [29], specifically DEI, as part of their profession. In order to identify and classify the main characteristics that best describe experiences in the sector, we created a data collection of testimonies gathered by the YRIs of EUGAIN during the Project GenZ. In this study, we want to investigate to what extent the recognized themes and interests of GenZ align with one another. For the analysis of transcripts, we applied text mining approaches that enable to analyze textual data for the extraction of meaningful information and patterns present in natural language text originally organized as unstructured data [30].

3.1 Data Collection Process

During the Project GenZ, YRIs of EUGAIN collected 31 testimonials between October and December 2022. Stakeholders were asked to describe their professional path and what role DEI play in their perception of it in brief, 1–2 minute videos. The participants work in the computing field, both in academia and industry, and they cover a variety of positions such as professors, researchers, students, managers, UX professionals, and so on. The data collection includes diverse profiles in gender, job position, country, and specialization. We asked them to share valuable information that high school students can use to make an informed decision when choosing their educational path. To collect a good variety of answers, we provided them a list of five questions, explaining the primary motivations for entering and staying in the field, the significant experiences, the work environment, the advantages, and the long-term objectives.

3.2 Data Processing

We analyzed their texts to learn what professionals think is important to share. We wanted to see what the recurring topics were by extracting keywords, and if the keywords were social-related, to see if professional perceptions of computing aligned with the values sought by GenZ. To accomplish this, we used term frequency count and feature extraction after cleaning and pre-processing the texts.

Data Cleaning and Lexical Analysis. From the video recordings, we generated the transcripts[9] and manually fixed any misspelling we discovered. We calculated the length of each transcript as the count of characters in the strings. They are 741 characters length on average (Mdn=625). We normalized the distribution of transcript lengths by number of transcripts, and the bimodal distribution revealed two peaks, the highest ranged between 250 and 750 characters. Then, in the lexical analysis, we pre-processed the data. We standardized the corpus appearance, reduced data sparseness and applied data cleaning approaches (e.g., converting the text into lower case characters, removing punctuation, unnecessary symbols and stop words[10]). In the Tokenization process[11], the lexical analyzer reads the source program's stream of characters from left to right, chop them into tokens and retrieve the terms used in the corpus which then, have been tagged using the Part-of-speech (POS) technique[12]. At this stage, the root form of the word called lemma[13], is altered by the presence of prefixes or suffixes that define its grammatical purpose. Therefore, in order to reduce the dimensionality of the description of documents within the collection (i.e., the vocabulary), we applied the Lemmatization approach[14]. Once we removed

[9] Python library SpeechRecognition 3.9.0.

[10] Stop words are frequent terms that don't offer meaningful information for the task [30].

[11] The Tokenization is the process of dividing the input text into collections of characters that have a collective meaning (called tokens) [30].

[12] Part-of-speech tagging (POS) determines the part of speech tag, e.g. noun, verb, adjective, etc. for each term [30].

[13] A lemma or lexeme or canonical form is a single dictionary entry with a single meaning [30].

[14] Lemmatization methods map verb forms to the infinite tense and nouns to the singular form [30].

the inflectional morphology, we built the vocabulary with lemmas [30]. We analyzed the frequencies of the nouns [31] in the vocabulary and thus, we identified the primary keywords of the domain. As follows, we grouped them into five themes. *Computing* theme contains keywords that are concerned with technical aspects of computing field, such as the development of cutting-edge technologies. *Academia* theme groups keywords related to the educational background and research activities in the field. *Skills* theme refers to the use of problem-solving techniques, the pooling of ideas and the creativity aimed at facing technological challenges. *Society* theme includes keywords about the main driver that led participants to get into the field, that is the desire to make an impact on the global community and the enhancement of the people's quality of life. Finally, *Gender* theme concerns women and includes narratives about the gender-based barriers perceived by stakeholders in choosing a career in computing.

Feature Extraction. Separately, we adopted different natural language processing (NLP) approaches for both the processing of data and the clustering analysis, in order to compare the results with the frequency count. In this procedure, we transformed input sentences by using Count Vectorizer[15] and we represented each document in a numeric matrix using the Bag-of-words technique[16]. Therefore, we created a vector representation per document and a weight has been assigned to each lemma based on its frequency in the document. We adopted the TF-IDF[17] as weighting factor. In the last stage, we applied the Principal Component Analysis (PCA)[18] for reducing the dimensionality of data and noise in the K-means cluster analysis [32]. The optimal number of clusters (K) has been defined by calculating and comparing the Silhouette Index, the Calinski-Harabasz Index and the Elbow method [33], the latter provided the optimal K. We calculated the Sum Square Error (SSE)[19] of each cluster and in correspondence of the fifth one, the curve formed an angle ("elbow") where the distortion value had the largest decrease (at 0.43 score) reporting the optimal K equal to 5. Finally, in order to confirm our results, we used the keywords search to find relationships between the five themes and the K-means clusters.

---

[15] Scikit learn Python package.

[16] In the Bag-of-words (BOW) representation, text (such as a sentence or a document) is treated as an unordered collection of words by using a fixed length sparse vector containing word occurrence counts [30].

[17] TF-IDF (Term Frequency-Inverse Document Frequency) is a numerical statistic which reveals that a word is how important to a document in a collection [30].

[18] The Principal Component Analysis (PCA) is used to project the original feature space onto a lower dimensional subspace including a subset of variables from a larger set, based on which original variables have the highest correlations with what is called principal components [32].

[19] The Sum Square Error is the sum of the average Euclidean Distance of each point against the centroid [33].

4 Findings

In this section we summarize results from the frequency and feature extraction analysis. At first, we examined the vocabulary of the whole corpus, we identified its key features by frequency count and grouped them in themes by manually evaluating examples from the corpus. Apart, we applied different techniques for data clustering (i.e., PCA and K-means). Finally, we analyzed the vocabulary of each cluster and the keywords search allowed us to confirm the frequency count results.

Frequency Analysis. After the corpus normalization, we built a word cloud[20] from the vocabulary in order to visualize the most frequent terms. As shown in Fig. 2, where the frequency of each lemma is displayed with font size and color, the most recurring words were informatics, computer, and person. We sorted the frequencies in decreasing order and established a threshold a priori (N=5): lemmas that occurred more than five times have been considered as representative, otherwise they have been excluded.

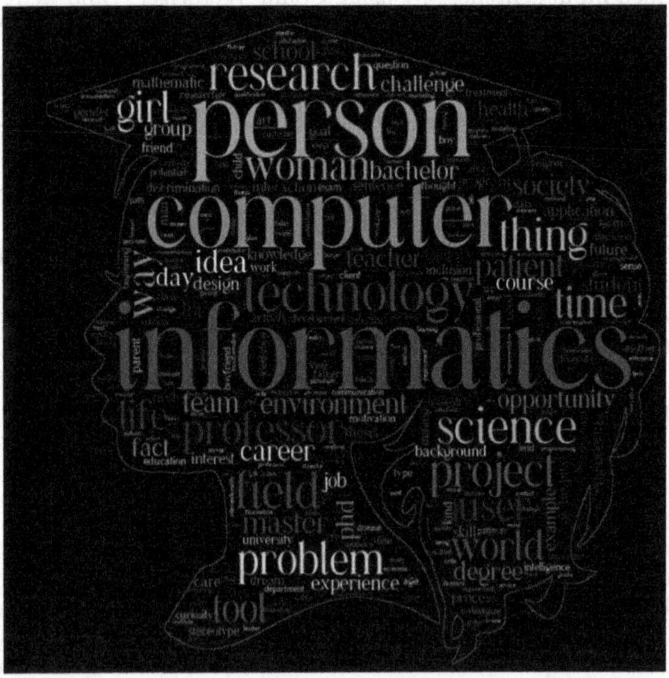

Fig. 2. Vocabulary

[20] In text analytics, word clouds provide an overview by distilling text down to words that appear with highest frequency [34].

Table 1. Themes, keywords and examples from the corpus.

Theme	Keywords	Examples
Computing	informatics, computer, technology, science, field, project, user, tool, career, job	*"I work in health informatics and mainly I am focused on a subject that is called process mining that is a subdiscipline of data mining and our goal is finding workflow activity from data....", "..very powerful tool that can be used to create user-friendly.."*
Academia	research, professor, master, bachelor, degree, teacher, phd, school, student, course	*"..my work is doing research in the area of artificial intelligence..", "My professors helped me to find the right PhD program.."*
Skills	problem, idea, team, challenge, group	*"I really enjoy working in IT because you can really solve complex problems..", "At the same time, we can work together sharing ideas.."*
Society	person, world, life, society	*"How to develop solutions that improve the life of people..", "I wanted to make a change in the world.."*
Gender	woman, girl	*"In high school I was in a class of 15 girls with non-scientific orientation..", "I believe girls/women are discouraged from studying Informatics at a very early age.."*

Table 2. Frequency distribution by theme

Theme	Keywords	Occurrences	Lemmas
Computing	10	33%	24%
Academia	10	20%	24%
Skills	5	9%	12%
Society	4	12%	10%
Gender	2	5%	5%
not relevant	(-)	21%	25%
Total	**31**	**100%**	**100%**

Therefore, we analyzed 45% of the 729 total occurrences of lemmas present in the vocabulary and 13% of the 326 total lemmas. From the frequency analysis we detected 31 keywords. After that, we conducted a corpus search and categorized them into five major themes. Table 1 reports some examples extracted from the corpus. Table 2 shows the frequency distribution of keywords, and the percentage distribution of occurrences and lemmas over the threshold by theme.

As we can see, *Computing* includes 10 keywords representing about 33% of total occurrences and 24% of total lemmas. This theme is the most representative in terms of occurrences. *Academia* groups 10 keywords representing about 20% of total occurrences and 24% of total lemmas. *Skills* and *Society* show similar frequencies, 9% and 12% of total occurrences and 12% and 10% of total lemmas respectively. Overall, *Gender* is the less frequent (i.e., 2 keywords representing about 5% of total occurrences and 5% of total lemmas). Finally, *Not relevant* groups conversational terms - that are not meaningful for the task - and cross-theme lemmas such as "opportunity" (e.g., *Computing-Skills* in *"..the opportunity of creating through technology attracted my interest.."*).

Table 3. Percentage distribution of keywords by theme and most frequent keywords

Theme	Keyword	Occurrences
Computing	informatics	20%
	computer	14%
	technology	13%
	science	10%
	field	10%
	project	9%
	user	8%
	tool	7%
	career	5%
	job	4%
	Total	**100%**

(a) Tot. Occurrences=118

Theme	Keyword	Occurrences
Academia	research	17%
	professor	14%
	master	10%
	bachelor	9%
	degree	9%
	teacher	9%
	phd	9%
	school	9%
	student	7%
	course	7%
	Total	**100%**

(b) Tot. Occurrences=69

Theme	Keyword	Occurrences
Society	person	48%
	world	19%
	life	19%
	society	14%
	Total	**100%**

(c) Tot. Occurrences=42

Theme	Keyword	Occurrences
Skills	problem	30%
	idea	21%
	team	18%
	challenge	15%
	group	15%
	Total	**100%**

(d) Tot. Occurrences=33

Theme	Keyword	Occurrences
Gender	woman	50%
	girl	50%
	Total	**100%**

(e) Tot. Occurrences=18

Keyword	Nr. Occurrences
informatics	24
person	20
research	12
problem	10
woman	9

(f) Most frequent keywords per theme

Table 3(a,b,c,d,e) show the distribution of keywords' occurrences by theme in percentage. According to Table 3(a), "informatics" is the most representative over 10 keywords in *Computing* (i.e., 20% of the 118 total occurrences). *Academia* in Table 3(b) shows that "research" is the most representative over 10 keywords (i.e., 17% of the 69 total occurrences). Table 3(c) refers to *Society* and shows that "person" is the most representative over 4 keywords (i.e., 48% of the 42 total occurrences). However, "person" was used in opposite cases referring to both encouraging or discouraging situations. In *Skills*, Table 3(d), "problem" is the most representative keyword over 5 (i.e., 30% of the 33 total occurrences). Finally, in Table 3(e), *Gender*'s keywords are equally distributed over 18 total occurrences. Additionally, scrolling through the absolute frequencies of the vocabulary in decreasing order, we built Table 3(f) that reports the most frequent keywords by theme, in the follow-

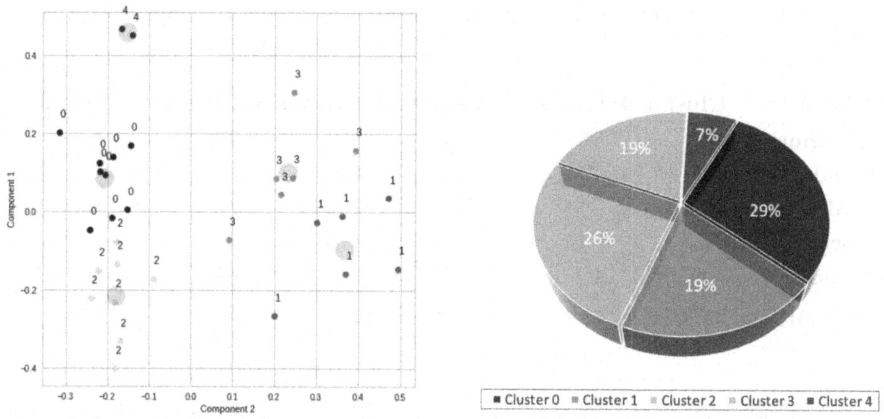

(a) K-means clustering (b) % Distribution of transcripts by cluster

Fig. 3. Clusters (K=5)

Table 4. Distribution of occurrences and lemmas by cluster

Cluster	Tot. Occurrences	Occurrences (>N)	Tot. Lemmas	Lemmas(>N)
0	260	62%	143	31%
1	105	53%	65	25%
2	253	56%	158	30%
3	124	58%	79	34%
4	42	36%	33	18%

ing order: "informatics" in *Computing*, "person" in *Society*, "research" in *Academia*, "problem" in *Skills* and "woman" in *Gender.*

Feature Extraction. As shown in Fig. 3a, the y-axis and x-axis represents, respectively, the first and second component we identified with the PCA. The plot shows the results of the K-means clustering; data points are grouped by clusters with different colors and the grey circles are the centers[21]. As we can see, the clustering analysis identified five classes as the analysis of frequencies.

As shown by Fig. 3b, the largest clusters are 0 and 2, representing about 55% of the corpus overall. At this stage, we used the same approach as before to assess the frequencies of lemmas by cluster. We built a vocabulary per each cluster, we sorted the frequencies in decreasing order and fixed the threshold a priori ($N = 2$): lemmas that appeared at least two times were considered indicative of the cluster; otherwise, they were excluded. Table 4 shows the percentages of occurrences and

[21] Centers or centroids correspond to the arithmetic mean of data points assigned to the cluster [30].

Table 5. Bivariate frequency distribution of lemmas by theme and cluster (Tot. lemmas=56)

Theme	Cluster 0	Cluster 1	Cluster 2	Cluster 3	Cluster 4	%Total
Computing	16%	5%	11%	5%	2%	39%
Academia	7%	4%	11%	9%	(-)	30%
Skills	7%	(-)	4%	(-)	2%	13%
Society	4%	(-)	4%	4%	2%	13%
Gender	(-)	4%	(-)	2%	(-)	5%
%Total	33%	13%	29%	20%	5%	100%

lemmas that we have analyzed by cluster, for instance, we analyzed 62% of 260 total occurrences and 31% of 143 total lemmas for Cluster 0.

We found a match between the set of 31 keywords and the vocabularies of the clusters for a total of 56 lemmas. Table 5 shows the bivariate frequency distribution of matching lemmas by cluster and theme. It reports also the conditional distributions by theme and cluster (% Total).

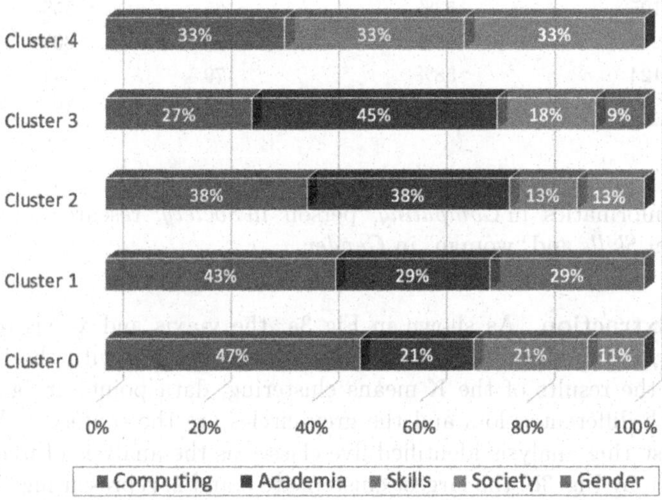

Fig. 4. % Distribution of themes per cluster

About 33% of total lemmas matched with the set of keywords in Cluster 0, in particular about 16% with the ones of *Computing* theme. About 29% of total lemmas matched with the set of keywords in Cluster 2, in particular about 11% respectively with the ones of *Computing* and *Academia*. About 20% of total lemmas matched with the set of keywords in Cluster 3, in particular about

9% with the ones of *Academia*. Cluster 1 and 4 showed the lowest matching rates. Overall, the conditional distributions by theme show that about 69% of total lemmas matched with *Computing* and *Academia* (i.e., respectively 39% and 30%).

Figure 4 shows the percentage distribution of themes calculated over the total matching lemmas per cluster. *Computing* is dominant in Cluster 0 (47%) and Cluster 1 (43%), and it is present in each cluster. *Academia* is dominant in Cluster 3 (45%). *Computing*, *Skills* and *Society* are equally distributed in the smallest cluster (i.e., Cluster 4). *Gender* is present in Cluster 1 (29%) and Cluster 3 (9%). In Cluster 2, *Computing* and *Academia* are equally distributed (38% respectively) as *Society* and *Gender* (13% respectively).

5 Discussion

According to Leslie et al. (2021) [29], GenZ cares about social values and a meaningful contribution to society, that is, DEI, as part of their work. In this paper we collected testimonials by stakeholders working in computing in order to extract and group the key features in macro themes when describing experiences in the field. We wanted to check to what extent the identified themes and the interest of GenZ are consistent with each other.

In the analysis of frequencies, 31 keywords were extracted. In the qualitative follow-up, we detected and analyzed samples from the corpus according to keywords. Similarly to the analysis of frequencies, the feature extraction technique produced five classes, and we used the keywords to uncover a correspondence between the themes and the clusters. The clusters turned out to be cross-thematic with some of them having dominant themes.

In line with the analysis of frequencies, *Computing* was significantly represented in all clusters (especially, in Cluster 0, the biggest one). This can be due to the domain of analysis. In addition, the *Academia* theme is present in four out of five clusters, particularly Cluster 3. These two themes tend to co-occur, most likely as a result of how actively scientific research participates in the advancement of modern technology. The *Skills* theme is present in three over five clusters and co-occur with *Society* but not with *Gender*. The co-occurrence with *Society* can be due to the tendency of participants of linking specific *Skills* with the development of technologies that can have an impact on society. The *Society* theme represents the main driver for participants to enter the field, and indeed, it is present in four out of five clusters. *Gender* is the less represented theme over the clusters and it is mainly concentrated in Cluster 1.

The *Society* theme, which is cited in four out of five clusters, and the *Gender* theme, which is mentioned in two out of five clusters, both revealed the presence of social features overall. From the viewpoint of DEI, we can group them into a macro-theme involving social issues and refer to it as the *DEI* theme. We observed that the *DEI* theme includes narratives about women and gender-based barriers in the computing industry as both mentioned in the *Gender* theme. However, the main motivator of *Society*, which is important to potential GenZ students, was perceived as being stronger, encouraging the participants to pursue a career in computing.

6 Conclusion

Nowadays, despite efforts to ensure inclusiveness, only a tiny portion of students select computing. Diversity in education and industry is also far from being realized [35–37], notwithstanding the calls for its enhancement [3,38]. The misalignment between GenZ and the values associated with computing is one potential factor [29]. In order for younger people to see computing as a viable career option, it is essential to demonstrate how it can help them realize their goal of having a positive impact on the environment and society through their work.

According to the findings of this study, while GenZ perceives computing as a career that is misaligned with their values, professionals in the field recognize the social embeddedness of their work contributions. As a result, in order to diversify the field by engaging and attracting younger people to computing, we should continue to promote and share the positive impact of the field on society.

In this study, we presented an intervention effort by EUGAIN. We chose to assess the information we were publishing on a social media platform to discover what professionals consider important to share with younger generations, and if the content was naturally connected with the beliefs of GenZ. In future work, we hope to collect additional testimonials while tackling intersectionality more fully, such as by engaging more non-binary and LGBTQ+ stakeholders to share their experiences and serve as role models. To accomplish DEI in computing, we must promote a varied set of role models who represent an inclusive atmosphere.

Acknowledgements. This project was partially supported by COST Action CA19122 - EUGAIN (European Network for Gender Balance in Informatics).

References

1. Clear, A., Parrish, A.: Computing Curricula 2020 CC2020, Paradigms for Global Computing Education encompassing undergraduate programs in Computer Engineering, Computer Science, Cybersecurity, Information Systems, Information Technology, Software Engineering with data science. Association for Computing Machinery (ACM) IEEE Computer Society (IEEE-CS), p. 23 (2020)
2. European Commission. Digital Economy and Society Index (DESI) (2022)
3. Landoni, M., Szlávi, A.: Human computer interaction-gender in user experience. In International Conference on Human-Computer Interaction, pp. 132–137. Springer, Cham (2022). https://doi.org/10.1007/978-3-031-06417-3_18
4. Diversity in Tech. The benefits of diversity in tech (2022)
5. Peters, A., et al.: Gender-inclusive HCI research and design: a conceptual review. Found. Trends Hum.-Comput. Interact. **13**(1), 1–69 (2020)
6. European Commission. Women in digital scoreboard (2021)

7. Dimock, M.: Defining generations: where millennials end and generation z begins. Pew Res. Center **17**(1), 1–7 (2019)
8. COST. Action website (2023)
9. United Nations. Goal 5: Achieve gender equality and empower all women and girls (2022)
10. Winthrop, R., Sperling, G.B.: What works in girls' education: evidence for the world's best investment. Brooking Institution (2016)
11. Kirkup, G.: ICT as a tool for enhancing women's education opportunities, and new educational and professional opportunities for women in new technologies. United Nations Division for the Advancement of Women (UNDAW) (2002)
12. European Union Agency for Fundamental Rights (FRA). Violence against women: an eu-wide survey (2014)
13. Buolamwini, J., Gebru, T.: Gender shades: intersectional accuracy disparities in commercial gender classification. In: Proceedings of Machine Learning Research, vol. 81, pp. 1–15 (2018)
14. Szlávi, A., Bernat, P.: Young women's barriers to choose IT and methods to overcome them - a case study from Hungary. Teaching Mathematics and Computer Science (2020)
15. Happe, L., et al.: Effective measures to foster girls' interest in secondary computer science education. Educ. Inf. Technol. **26**, 2811–2829 (2021)
16. Szlávi, A.: Barriers, role models, and diversity: women in IT. Central-European J. New Technol. Res. Educ. Pract. **3**(3), Dec (2021)
17. González-Pérez, S., Mateos de Cabo, R., Sáinz, M.: Girls in stem: is it a female role-model thing? (2020)
18. Oyserman, D., Terry, K., Bybee, D.I.: A possible selves intervention to enhance school involvement. J. Adolescence **25**(3), 313–26 (2002)
19. Convertino, C.: Nuancing the discourse of underrepresentation: a feminist post-structural analysis of gender inequality in computer science education in the us. Gender Educ. **32**(5), 594–607 (2020)
20. Lyon, L.A., Green, E.: Coding boot camps: enabling women to enter computing professions. ACM Trans. Comput. Educ. **21**(2), (2021)
21. Crenshaw, K.: Demarginalizing the intersection of race and sex: a black feminist critique of antidiscrimination doctrine, feminist theory and antiracist policies. Univ. Chic. Leg. Forum **1989**(1), 139–167 (1989)
22. Prensky, M.: Digital natives, digital immigrants part 2: do they really think differently? On the horizon (2001)
23. Fodor, M., Jaeckel, K.: What does it take to have a successful career through the eyes of generation z-based on the results of a primary qualitative research. Int. J. Lifelong Educ. Leadership **4**(1), 1–7 (2018)
24. Lanier, K.: 5 Things HR professionals need to know about generation Z: thought leaders share their views on the HR profession and its direction for the future. Strategic HR review (2017)
25. Nguyen Ngoc, T., et al.: Generation Z job seekers' expectations and their job pursuit intention: evidence from transition and emerging economy. Int. J. Eng. Bus. Manage. **14**, 18479790221112548 (2022)
26. Bohdziewicz, P.: Career anchors of representatives of generation Z: some conclusions for managing the younger generation of employees. Zarządzanie Zasobami Ludzkimi, (6 (113)-" Managing Diversity in the Context of International HRM"), 57–74 (2016)
27. Media Insight Project. The news consumption habits of 16- to 40-year-olds (2022)

28. Jiang, Y.: Social media platforms and public relations for brand promotion. BCP Business Manage. **34**, 769–775 (2022)
29. Leslie, B., et al.: Generation Z perceptions of a positive workplace environment. Employee Responsibilities Rights J. **33**(3), 171–187 (2021)
30. Hotho, A., Nürnberger, A., Paaß, G.: A brief survey of text mining. J. Language Technol. Comput. Linguist. **20**(1), 19–62 (2005)
31. Hulth, A.: Improved automatic keyword extraction given more linguistic knowledge. In: Proceedings of the 2003 Conference on Empirical Methods in Natural Language Processing, pp. 216–223 (2003)
32. Ding, C., He, X.: Cluster structure of K-means clustering via principal component analysis. In: Dai, H., Srikant, R., Zhang, C. (eds.) PAKDD 2004. LNCS (LNAI), vol. 3056, pp. 414–418. Springer, Heidelberg (2004). https://doi.org/10.1007/978-3-540-24775-3_50
33. Gustriansyah, R., Suhandi, N., Fery, A.: Clustering optimization in RFM analysis based on k-means. Indones. J. Electr. Eng. Comput. Sci **18**(1), 470–477 (2020)
34. Heimerl, F., et al.: Word cloud explorer: text analytics based on word clouds. In: 2014 47th Hawaii International Conference on System Sciences, pp. 1833–1842 (2014)
35. Dias Canedo, E., et al.: Barriers faced by women in software development projects. Information **10**(10), 309 (2019)
36. Statista. Software developer gender distribution worldwide as of 2022 (2022)
37. Barr, V.: Gender diversity in computing: are we making any progress? (2017)
38. Serebrenik, A.: Social software engineering. Technische Universiteit Eindhoven, November 2022. Intreerede, gehouden op 4 november 2022, aan de Technische Universiteit Eindhoven

Design with and for Children: The Challenge of Inclusivity

Sveva Valguarnera and Monica Landoni(✉)

Università della Svizzera Italiana, Lugano, Switzerland
monica.landoni@usi.ch

Abstract. In this position paper we will discuss the challenges of inclusivity when involving children in collaborative design. The HCI community is strongly committed to promoting inclusive user studies as the way to foster a better understanding of users and their needs. Similarly, researchers in Child Computer Interaction (CCI) are actively promoting the direct engagement of young users. However, inclusivity still proves to be a challenge, with the involvement of parents and guardians being the first step to take. Discussion will be driven by literature in CCI as well as by our experience running a project involving very young children in the co-design of technology to support the development of pre-reading skills. We will present the concept of child as protagonist as championed by recent literature and explore whether and how the community has embraced it over time. We will look at different domains, context and age groups as starting point for a systematic analysis of the available approaches to reach out and be inclusive when running user studies involving children. Our experience with the recruitment of young children and the struggle to make our study inclusive will provide an insight into a dimension seldomly discussed in literature and will enable us to elaborate on open issues for the CCI as well as the HCI communities to reflect on.

Keywords: children · codesign · collaborative design · inclusivity

1 Introduction

In recent years, children have started using technology earlier and earlier, with children as young as 3 or 4 already using tablets and computers, both for education and for entertainment. However, children are not independent in their use of technology, which strongly depends on the opinions of their parents, caregivers and teachers. Therefore, researchers should aim to involve both children and adults as stakeholders in the design of technology for children, as well as experts in the fields of education and child psychology.

Nevertheless, children's involvement should not be seen as subordinate to the adults, and instead they should be at the center of the design process, taking a protagonist role as championed by Iversen et al. [19].

In this paper, we will first outline the most relevant research on how to involve children, parents and other adult stakeholders in the design of new technology;

M. Antona and C. Stephanidis (Eds.): HCII 2023, LNCS 14020, pp. 171–184, 2023.
https://doi.org/10.1007/978-3-031-35681-0_11

then we will write about our own experience in involving children in co-design sessions, both at school and in an extra-curricular setting, detailing our insights and observations, but also the struggles and challenges that we faced in our work. Finally, we will draw our conclusions and provide points of reflections for the community.

2 Related Work

In this section, we will discuss the most relevant research on involving users in design, then specifically on involving children, parents and guardians, outlining both the theory and the methods used in the research.

2.1 Involving Users in Design

Participatory design originated in Scandinavia in the 1970s, and it was originally meant as a way to involve factory workers in the research and design of new software for their workplace [22]; as such, it concerned the idea of democratising work [3]. However, it quickly grew and now its concepts are used throughout the world, as it has shown to have many benefits: for example, involving users in the design process has a positive effect on both the success of the system and the satisfaction of its users [20]. The process of co-design also has inherent ethical qualities, as users can express and share their experiences [35]. It can be seen as an empowering process, in which users are involved in the design of products that will raise their quality of life [17].

2.2 Designing with and for Children

While in the past co-designing was mainly performed with adult users, in the last decades children have also started being involved in the design of new technology, first as testers, then as informants and finally, as design partners in their own right [9]. According to Read et al. (2002) [27], the ideal age for collaborative design is between 7 and 10 years old, as children of that age have a good capacity of abstraction and reflection, but they are still very imaginative, and they lack prejudices and preconceptions. In this age range, both brainstorming and prototyping work well as design methods: while children uncover a higher number of design ideas when prototyping, they provide more detailed criteria when brainstorming [31]. Many methods to evaluate technology with children, such as the Fun Toolkit, have also been developed for older children, at least 7 years old [28].

Some techniques developed for older children, such as the Cooperative Inquiry [8], have been successfully adapted for younger children with some changes, such as allowing the children to draw their ideas instead of writing them down and working in smaller groups [10]. Both Superti et al. (2020) [37] and Farber et al. (2002) [10] emphasize that children work better in smaller groups. This is also supported by [2], who goes beyond that to present evidence that younger children, aged 4 to 5 years old, have the most difficulty in working collaboratively, and work better in pairs.

Other techniques have been proven to be useful with older preschoolers, but still present challenges with children on the younger side of this age range: for example, Barendregt & Bekker (2013) [1] used the drawing intervention method to elicit design ideas with children aged 4 to 7 years old, and found that the younger children found it hard to collaborate, and had difficulty using drawings to communicate design ideas. This was also true for Hiniker et al. (2017) [14], who used *Fictional Inquiry* and *Comicboarding*, techniques developed to elicit insights from adults users, with children aged 4 to 6 years old; while 5 and 6 years old were able to successfully generate design ideas, 4 years old children had more difficulties in doing so. However, younger children still participated enthusiastically, suggesting that with more adult facilitation, they could participate fully in the design process. This is also confirmed by Farber et al. (2002) [10], who note "More adult facilitation" as one of the changes to design methods needed to involve younger children. However, Marco et al. (2013) [21] report that less structured sessions, that required a small amount of instructions to be given to children, tended to elicit more reliable and valuable data for researchers.

There are also many design methods developed specifically for younger children. For instance, as envisioned by Iversen et al. [19] and following an approach centred on constructive play practice, aimed at creating a story-line and establishing a cooperative process, children can become protagonists in the design process [33]. Another example is *Mixing Ideas* [12] that has been used to foster collaboration among young children. A technique called *Play-based design* has also been developed for younger children, involving make-believe play activities with an adult facilitator [37].

Even though collaborative design has made progress toward inclusivity by involving kids of a wider age range than before, it is still difficult to successfully involve younger kids, and there is still much research to be done in this area. This research is crucial because kids are starting to use technology at a younger age than ever, and as a result, they should be involved in the design of the technology they use.

2.3 The Role of Parents

Parents' perspectives and insights are important in the design of technology for children, as they are not yet independent users. As a consequence, many studies have explicitly looked for parental feedback into their own needs and perspectives, concerning for example the safety and suitability aspect and the use of technology for learning. Some studies have also compared parents' and children's perspectives, or considered activities shared by parents and children.

Parents' Perspective on the Safety and Suitability of Technology. Sobel et al. (2017) [32] involved 87 adult guardians (parents and other family members, 70% female) with surveys and interviews to gather insight on their perception of location-based mobile games and specifically *Pokemon GO*. While adults valued how playing with *Pokemon GO* led to an increase in exercise and outdoor time, they had concerns about safety in the real-world environment.

Quayumm et al. (2021) [26] conducted semi-structured interviews with 25 parents (8 fathers and 17 mothers) of children aged 10 to 15 on the topic of children's cybersecurity risks, with parents believing that children should both know about security risks and be able to think critically and be skeptical of what they find on the internet.

Sun et al. (2021) [36] who interviewed 23 parents of children aged 1 to 11 years old to gather insight on their perception of physical and digital safety risks that smart home technology pose for their children, finding that parents encountered unanticipated risks when introducing smart home technology into their homes, and that as children grow up, the perceived risks shift from physical to digital safety.

However, the perspectives on technology can vary even within a family, with set of parents having different ideas and perspectives. Derix and Leong (2020) [7] used the probes method to gather insight from 17 participants from 8 families with at least one children under the age of 12. The 8 family sets were composed of 6 families with a mother and father, one family with two mothers, and one family where a mother, an aunt and a grandmother shared parenting responsibilities. In most families, one parents engaged with the probes in a most comprehensive way than the other(s), and when collective responses to the probes were compared with individual ones, in many cases the collective response coincided with the response from the parent who had engaged more with the probes, who was also the parents with more domestic and childcare responsibilities.

Parents' Perspectives on Technology for Learning. Hightower et al. (2019) [13] conducted semi-structured interviews with 12 mothers of children aged 3 to 5.5 years old to examine their beliefs about the role of media in their children's STEM learning, with the aim of identifying areas where parents need the help of technology in supporting their children's learning. Parents reporting using media as a support tool for STEM learning, with the belief that media should be used as a reinforcement of concepts that had already been introduced to the children, while also expressing concern about finding appropriate media for their children's age and educational level.

Yu et al. (2020) [39] interviewed parents who had obtained coding kits for their children to use at home, to understand what they expected from their children's use of the kits, what roles would the parents play, and if they had any concerns about the activity. The participants were 18 parents - 13 mothers and 5 fathers - of children aged 3 to 9 years old. While parents perceived the benefits of coding kits, they also had concerns such as having limited programming knowledge to help their children.

Solyst et al. (2022) [34] ran a survey involving 133 parents - 105 mothers and 21 fathers - of children in middle and high school. The survey asked about parents' perception of computer science, and how important they felt it was for their children to learn computer science. The results of the survey shows that parents' first perception of computer science includes using devices and apps, instead of designing and developing them, and when this misconception is corrected, parents feel that the importance of computer science declines. While only few participants expressed skepticism about computer science, and most believed that their children are capable of learning it, a limited number of parents actively encourage children to learn computer science, with parents more familiar with computer science more likely to encourage children to follow the same path.

Involving Both Parents and Children in Design. Several studies have involved both parents and children, on various levels, in the design of technology. Horton and Read (2012) [16] surveyed 12 parents and their children aged 6 to 10 years old, with parents being asked what technology they had in their home, who owned or whether it was shared, and whether the child was allowed to use it. Children were only asked what technology they had at home. According to the results of the survey, children can accurately report on what technology they have at home, however they do not always associate the items they have at home with the ones their parents report they have access to.

Oygür et al. (2021) [23] also compared children's and parents' perspectives, interviewing 17 families with children aged between 7 and 12 years old, who regularly used wearable devices to track their physical activities. The interviews involved 18 parents, of which 15 were mothers and 3 were fathers. This study showed that children and parents value different aspects and have different motivations in using wearables: while parents' motivation primarily involve their children's health and well-being, children are more concerned with entertainment and accomplishment in reaching their goals.

Sadka and Zuckerman (2017) [29] involved both parents and children in a co-making activity at home, showing their results in a two dimensional scale with two metrics: parent initiative - with low initiative corresponding to the "mentor" role and parent as peer and high initiative corresponding to the "peer" role - and attention, a prerequisite for a successful co-making activity and for both peer and mentor role, with the latter being preferable as more focused on the child's learning process than on the completion of the activity.

Hoffman et al. (2013) [15] performed a 6-weeks long study to evaluate an in-car game with six families with children aged 10 to 12 years old, finding that adults and children have different expectations and desires, while parents were also concerned that introducing a game during car journeys might shift their children's focus towards the screen, detaching them from the family and the environment.

Yip et al. (2016) [38] involved 16 families - parents and children - recruited through a local middle school in a series of 9 co-design sessions over 10 months, using the Cooperative Enquiry method. They noted the different ways in which parents engaged with the co-design activity: both passively and supportively, acting as advocates for their children, and as parental managers. They also noted the concerns that the parents had with the co-design activity, such as the fear that they would take time away from their children's school work and the sacrifices that they met to come to the sessions.

Garg and Sengupta (2020) [11] conducted three collaborative design sessions with children, with the third and final session including parents as design companions. During this sessions, the parents elaborated on their children's designs by adding features related to social engagement, parental controls and privacy.

Overall, it is clear that the majority of studies involving parents are relatively recent and that mothers make up the majority of the parents in these studies. However, there is a significant bias because participation in these studies is always voluntary and because the parents who take part are also the parents who are willing to use technology with their children. Nevertheless, parental worries about privacy, digital safety, and control are recurring themes that we can find throughout the literature.

2.4 The Role of Teachers

Involving teachers in the design of technology can have a positive effect on learning outcomes [6]and in them taking ownership and agency not only in the design, but also in the dissemination of the innovation [25].

Teachers can also be involved as facilitators in evaluation activities, showing that they are able to identify similar usability problems as the researchers with very little training [24], even if they are seen as authority figures by students - while researchers are not.

Moreover, teachers expect and experience different user gains when participating in co-design activities in the classroom, both for themselves and for the children [4]. For example, they expect that both they and their students will learn more about technology, and that the children will have fun. However, as teachers often have little time for these activities, Börjesson et al. [4] also suggests to organise design activities as part of teachers' professional development curriculum, to make it easier for them to participate.

This was in fact Celeptoku et al. (2020)'s approach [5], as they organised a professional development workshop in which 22 teachers learned about computer science and created lessons plans to integrate it in the classroom. The workshop allowed teachers to see computer science's potential to teach critical thinking and to prepare students for their future, while at the same time allowing researchers to delve into teachers' perceptions and expectations of the role computer science can play in the classroom.

Teachers' needs and preferences for digital activities to be used in schools are crucial to ensure that the activities are carried out in the classrooms, as when teachers have a positive attitude towards an innovation, they tend to use it more in their class [30]: for example, teachers prefer games that promote learning and align well with the school curriculum, while at the same time improving soft skills and increasing engagement with computers [18].

3 Our Experience

During the course of our project, we conducted several different user studies, ranging from semi-structured interviews with teachers, parents and experts to evaluations and collaborative design sessions with children, held both in schools and in extracurricular settings.

In this section, we will outline the methods we used to recruit participants, organise the studies and analyse the data, the challenges we encountered and the insight that we were able to gather.

3.1 Working with Schools

We started working with preschools in 2019, partnering with a private preschool in Lugano to conduct an user study with children aged 3 to 6 years old, who would be evaluating a reading app on a tablet. In Switzerland, preschool is a form of non-compulsory education, however it still has a country-mandated curriculum to follow. Because of this, we decided to partner with a private school that offered extended hours for working parents, and as such had the time for activities that went beyond the school curriculum.

While the headmistress of the school was enthusiastic about our project, the teachers were hesitant, as most of them were reluctant to use technology in the classroom - for example, while every classroom was equipped with an interactive whiteboard, only the English teacher used it. Other teachers commented that children already got significant screen time at home, and did not see the need to also introduce technology at school.

We prepared consent forms for the parents, which included a presentation of our project, a brief survey on their children's reading habits, and an informed consent that the parent would have to sign. We also included our contact numbers so that parents who had questions could be able to call us.

While the majority of parents signed the consent form, some parents did not want their children to participate in the activity, while others called us with concerns and questions.

Performing our user study in a school had several tangible advantages: for example, we were able to have individual time with each child, while the other children went on with their activities with the teacher; furthermore, teachers were able to choose the best times in the day for us to perform our study - when the children were neither too tired or too excited - and they also advised us on each child's individual personality and mood.

On the other hand, we had to schedule our study in the days when teachers had time for us, since the activity we offered was considered optional and as such should not interfere with school activities.

After the 2020 COVID-19 pandemic, we tried to resume our work with schools, and we were able to conduct semi-structured interviews with preschool teachers as a way to understand how their perspective on technology in school had shifted.

However, both during and after the closures teachers had a considerably increased workload, and as such we were not able to conduct any more co-design sessions or user studies within the school.

It should be noted that we also tried to partner with the public schools in the city area, as we believed that this would have allowed us to interact with a more diverse population of children. However, as mentioned before public school in Switzerland have significant oversight by the cantonal authorities, and as such it is more difficult for them to find the time to perform activities that are not in the curriculum. While we were able to secure a semi-structured interview with a teacher who had been in charge of online learning during the school closures, we were unable to follow up with any school visits.

3.2 Designing in a Non-school Context

During our project, we also conducted user studies in non-school settings, mainly the university and a local children's library.

Since our university offers a week-long summer camp for children of employees, we decided to run a co-design session during the camp, using drawings as a method to elicit children's design ideas.

However, this choice posed many logistical challenges. First, it was necessary to obtain permission from the Ethics Committee together with approval of the legal office of the university, and then parents had to sign an informed consent. Since the camp schedule was tightly packed, and the camp participants were of mixed age - with several children older than the age range in which we were interested - we had to negotiate with the camp entertainers to find a time and a place that were suitable for everyone, as well on relying on them to provide an alternative activity for older children during the same time frame. While in the end we were able to run the activity, since we only had one session with children with whom we were not familiar, we only obtained limited insight.

We also partnered with a local children's library to involve children in a series of collaborative design sessions to inform the design of technology to help children foster pre-reading skills.

The library staff was enthusiastic to help, and circulated the information about our project and the consent form through the library's mailing list, composed of parents who are regular users of the library.

We were able to conduct two separate sets of sessions, involving more than 15 children in total, using a separate space that was also provided to us by the library.

Partnering with the library had many advantages for us: it was a known entity with which many parents were already familiar, and we could rely on the mailing list to circulate information about the project. By running a study over several weeks, we were able to build a relationship with the children, which allowed us to gain significant insight and generate interesting design ideas. When we ran our second set of co-design sessions, several children who had participated in the first set also signed up.

However, there were also some disadvantages: first, as the children were recruited through the library's mailing list, there was a selection bias in the children who participated in the study, as they were already familiar and interested in books and reading, and came from families who also valued reading.

Since we ran the activity at the end of the school day, children were often tired or excited, and it was difficult for them to focus on activities such as reading. While we did not want to be seen as authority figures, we strove to build a relationship with each child, which allowed us to run the activity more smoothly. We valued communication with the parents - some of whom were curious about our project and asked many questions - but we also felt that most parents did not really care about the specifics of the project, thinking of our user study as "another activity organised by the library", which meant that they had a hour in which they could run errands while someone else minded their children. This led to problems such as parents not telling us when their children would be absent due to illness, or when they wanted to completely withdraw from the study, and parents often being late bringing their children to the library, which cut into our already scarce time with them.

Overall, the support of the library was crucial to the success of the study, as they supplied us with projectors, pillows for the children and facilities that allowed us to run our study as smoothly as possible.

3.3 Ethical Considerations

As mentioned in the description of our studies we engaged with the necessary procedures to obtain ethical approval from our university as well as dealt with specific requirements as issued by the institutions hosting the studies. Therefore, we carefully described our study so that parents, guardians, as well as educators could get a clear picture of the type of involvement required from participants. We made sure the scope and objectives of our research were explicitly stated, and the same was for details on how and where gathered data was going to be stored and whether these would be shared with other members of the research community. We then paid particular care in explaining children the purpose of our visits and the kind of activity we would like to engage them with while also clarifying how participation was on voluntary base. It was also important for us that children felt at all times safe and comfortable, and never excluded from any of the proposed activities which we adapted to different needs and skills, as these vary greatly in such a young age group.

4 Conclusions

Here we will outline what we learned from the challenges that we encountered during the course of our project, and how we want to address them in the future.

4.1 The Challenge of Recruitment

One of the main challenges was recruiting children for our study. In this respect, working with schools has a big advantage over trying to recruit children for after school activities, as most children in the class will be able to participate - provided that their parents sign the consent form.

However, schools usually have very little flexibility when organising activities outside the curriculum, so it is necessary to compromise with teachers and with the administration to find time for user studies.

Working with a library combines the best of both worlds: on one hand, we were able to recruit children through an established institution that already had a community of parents and children readers, but since the activity was organised after school we had much more flexibility in when and how we organised our study.

However, it is worth mentioning that the turn out to the sessions was not great, with many children attending only a limited number of sessions and some signing up but never attending. Since we had anticipated this issue, we accepted more children that we had estimated we would need, as we - correctly - assumed that not all of them would attend every session.

We also had to compromise on the age range of the children who enrolled in the activity, as some parents would only bring their child if their younger sibling was allowed to attend - even if they were younger than the cutoff age of 4 years old. In the end, this was a blessing in disguise, as those younger children also attended the second set of sessions, allowing us to follow their development over a period of months.

Overall, we believe that partnering with established institutions with ties to the community, such as libraries, code clubs or summer camps can be a valuable alternative for those researchers who do not have the possibility to conduct research within a school, or who need more flexibility than a school can offer.

4.2 Ensuring Diversity

While collaborative design sessions usually involve a small number of children, it is important to avoid selection bias as much as possible, and try to have a wide range of diverse children in terms of gender, nationality and socio-economic factors.

Of course, this is not always possible in every individual study; for this reason, we strongly advocate for the usefulness of replication studies, conducted for example in different countries or with different populations.

Working with schools can help provide a diverse group of children, although that is very dependent on the school. When we worked with a private preschool, for example, most of the parents were well-off professionals, but they also came from several different countries as the university nearby attracts foreign skilled workers. In a public school, we would a find a wider socio-economic range of students, but depending on the school we could have had a majority of local students or a significant refugee and migrant population.

On the other hand, when participants voluntarily apply to take part in a study - as it was the case with our co-design session in the library - it is much harder to have a diverse group of participants, as we have little control on who decides to take part. While, given enough volunteers, it is possible to use screening surveys to select participants, in our experience finding willing participants was already an issue in itself, even without performing any kind of selection.

4.3 Running the Sessions

When working with children, it is important to put them at ease and build a relationship with them. Because of this, we believe that it is important to run multi-session studies, with the aim of getting to know children and getting the children to know one another, if they do not already.

For the same reason, each session should begin with a short ice-breaking activity and eventually a snack, to help children get into the right mindset for collaborative design.

According to our personal experience, it is ideal to have at least three researchers present for each session, with one of them taking notes and recording the session. Having multiple researchers present enabled us to give individual attention to each child, allowed even shy or younger children, who were reluctant to participate, to be fully involved with the activity.

In fact, one of the most significant challenges that we encountered was running the sessions in such a way to keep all children engaged and in a state of flow, even if they were not only of different ages - between 4 and 6 years old - but they also had very different personalities, with some very outgoing children who always spoke and some shy children who were reluctant to express themselves.

We believe that each child should be empowered to create and share design ideas during a collaborative design session; this meant that we had to find a balance between giving space to younger, shy children to express themselves and allowing older, extroverted children to participate in the activities without dominating the conversation.

4.4 Mediating Needs

As mentioned in the description of our studies, parents play an important role in enabling and facilitating children's participation. They often had a conservative approach towards technology; while acknowledging its importance for their children's future, they were very cautious about introducing it yet as they are generally afraid of exposing children to the risks of becoming addicted to screen time.

Similarly, teachers were remarking on the importance of non-digital skills and competences to develop before exposing children to the distractions of the digital world. Children instead were captivated by technology, and in particular by screens and toy robots interacting with them via speech, colors and music.

We decided to be very upfront and describe in details the kind of content and technology we would present to children in the various sessions and this transparency was well received by the involved adults, that in exchange gave us their trust. Needless to say, mediating between the need for control and protection as advocated by parents and that for engaging children with examples of the current technology in order to get their early feedback proved one of the complex challenges in this research. We managed to find a common ground by listening to educators and being respectful towards all stakeholders.

Overall our lesson learned is that inclusivity does not come easily; instead it requires careful planning and effort, but being open and ready to listen is already a good step towards it.

References

1. Barendregt, W., Bekker, T.: Exploring the potential of the drawing intervention method for design and evaluation by young children. In: CHI'13 Extended Abstracts on Human Factors in Computing Systems, pp. 193–198 (2013)
2. Benford, S., et al.: Designing storytelling technologies to encouraging collaboration between young children. In: Proceedings of the SIGCHI Conference on Human Factors in Computing Systems, pp. 556–563 (2000)
3. Björgvinsson, E., Ehn, P., Hillgren, P.A.: Participatory design and "democratizing innovation". In: Proceedings of the 11th Biennial Participatory Design Conference. PDC '10, pp. 41–50. Association for Computing Machinery, New York, NY, USA (2010). https://doi.org/10.1145/1900441.1900448
4. Börjesson, P., Barendregt, W., Eriksson, E., Torgersson, O., Bekker, T.: Teachers' expected and perceived gains of participation in classroom based design activities. In: Proceedings of the 2019 CHI Conference on Human Factors in Computing Systems, pp. 1–9 (2019)
5. Celepkolu, M., O'Halloran, E., Boyer, K.E.: Upper elementary and middle grade teachers' perceptions, concerns, and goals for integrating CS into classrooms. In: Proceedings of the 51st ACM Technical Symposium on Computer Science Education, pp. 965–970 (2020)
6. Cviko, A., McKenney, S., Voogt, J.: Teachers as co-designers of technology-rich learning activities for early literacy. Technol. Pedagog. Educ. **24**(4), 443–459 (2015)
7. Derix, E.C., Leong, T.W.: Probes to explore the individual perspectives on technology use that exist within sets of parents. In: Proceedings of the 2020 ACM Designing Interactive Systems Conference, pp. 519–531 (2020)
8. Druin, A.: Cooperative inquiry: developing new technologies for children with children. In: Proceedings of the SIGCHI Conference on Human Factors in Computing Systems, pp. 592–599 (1999)
9. Druin, A.: The role of children in the design of new technology. Behav. Inf. Technol. **21**(1), 1–25 (2002)
10. Farber, A., Druin, A., Chipman, G., Julian, D., Somashekhar, S.: How young can our design partners be? Technical report (2002)
11. Garg, R., Sengupta, S.: Conversational technologies for in-home learning: using co-design to understand children's and parents' perspectives. In: Proceedings of the 2020 CHI Conference on Human Factors in Computing Systems, pp. 1–13 (2020)
12. Guha, M.L., Druin, A., Chipman, G., Fails, J.A., Simms, S., Farber, A.: Mixing ideas: a new technique for working with young children as design partners. In: Proceedings of the 2004 Conference on Interaction Design and Children: Building a Community, pp. 35–42 (2004)

13. Hightower, B., Sheehan, K., Lauricella, A., Wartella, E.: Exploring parent use of early stem media to inform design for children. In: Proceedings of the 18th ACM International Conference on Interaction Design and Children, pp. 102–108 (2019)
14. Hiniker, A., Sobel, K., Lee, B.: Co-designing with preschoolers using fictional inquiry and comicboarding. In: Proceedings of the 2017 CHI Conference on Human Factors in Computing Systems, pp. 5767–5772 (2017)
15. Hoffman, G., Gal-Oz, A., David, S., Zuckerman, O.: In-car game design for children: child vs. parent perspective. In: Proceedings of the 12th International Conference on Interaction Design and Children, pp. 112–119 (2013)
16. Horton, M., Read, J.C.: Parents and children having and using technology: what should we ask? In: Proceedings of the 11th International Conference on Interaction Design and Children, pp. 252–255 (2012)
17. Hussain, S.: Empowering marginalised children in developing countries through participatory design processes. CoDesign **6**, 99–117 (2010). https://doi.org/10.1080/15710882.2010.499467
18. India, G., O, A., Diwakar, N., Jain, M., Vashistha, A., Swaminathan, M.: Teachers' perceptions around digital games for children in low-resource schools for the blind. In: Proceedings of the 2021 CHI Conference on Human Factors in Computing Systems, pp. 1–17 (2021)
19. Iversen, O.S., Smith, R.C., Dindler, C.: Child as Protagonist: Expanding the Role of Children in Participatory Design, pp. 27–37. Association for Computing Machinery, New York, NY, USA (2017). https://doi.org/10.1145/3078072.3079725
20. Kujala, S.: User involvement: a review of the benefits and challenges. Behav. Inf. Technol. **22**(1), 1–16 (2003)
21. Marco, J., Baldassarri, S., Cerezo, E.: Nikvision: developing a tangible application for and with children. J. Univers. Comput. Sci. **19**(15), 2266–2291 (2013)
22. Nygaard, K., Bergo, O.T.: Planlegging, styring og databehandling: grunnbok for fagbevegelsen: Datamaskiner, systemer og språk. Del 2 (1974)
23. Oygür, I., Su, Z., Epstein, D.A., Chen, Y.: The lived experience of child-owned wearables: comparing children's and parents' perspectives on activity tracking. In: Proceedings of the 2021 CHI Conference on Human Factors in Computing Systems, pp. 1–12 (2021)
24. Pardo, S., Vetere, F., Howard, S.: Teachers' involvement in usability testing with children. In: Proceedings of the 2006 Conference on Interaction Design and Children, pp. 89–92 (2006)
25. Penuel, W.R., Roschelle, J., Shechtman, N.: Designing formative assessment software with teachers: an analysis of the co-design process. Res. Pract. Technol. Enhanc. Learn. **2**(01), 51–74 (2007)
26. Quayyum, F., Bueie, J., Cruzes, D.S., Jaccheri, L., Vidal, J.C.T.: Understanding parents' perceptions of children's cybersecurity awareness in Norway. In: Proceedings of the Conference on Information Technology for Social Good, pp. 236–241 (2021)
27. Read, J.C., Gregory, P., MacFarlane, S., McManus, B., Gray, P., Patel, R.: An investigation of participatory design with children-informant, balanced and facilitated design. In: Interaction Design and Children, pp. 53–64. Eindhoven (2002)
28. Read, J.C., MacFarlane, S.: Using the fun toolkit and other survey methods to gather opinions in child computer interaction. In: Proceedings of the 2006 Conference on Interaction Design and Children, pp. 81–88 (2006)
29. Sadka, O., Zuckerman, O.: From parents to mentors: parent-child interaction in co-making activities. In: Proceedings of the 2017 Conference on Interaction Design and Children, pp. 609–615 (2017)

30. Santos, M.L., Prudente, M.: Perceptions of public-school teachers on the use of virtual laboratories in teaching science. In: 2022 13th International Conference on E-Education, E-Business, E-Management, and E-Learning (IC4E), pp. 35–39 (2022)
31. Sluis-Thiescheffer, W., Bekker, T., Eggen, B.: Comparing early design methods for children. In: Proceedings of the 6th International Conference on Interaction Design and Children, pp. 17–24 (2007)
32. Sobel, K., Bhattacharya, A., Hiniker, A., Lee, J.H., Kientz, J.A., Yip, J.C.: It wasn't really about the pokémon: parents' perspectives on a location-based mobile game. In: Proceedings of the 2017 CHI Conference on Human Factors in Computing Systems, pp. 1483–1496 (2017)
33. Södergren, A.C., Van Mechelen, M.: Towards a child-led design process a pilot study: when pre-schoolers' play becomes designing. In: Proceedings of the 18th ACM International Conference on Interaction Design and Children, pp. 629–634 (2019)
34. Solyst, J., Yao, L., Axon, A., Ogan, A.: "it is the future": Exploring parent perspectives of CS education. In: Proceedings of the 53rd ACM Technical Symposium on Computer Science Education, vol. 1, pp. 258–264 (2022)
35. Steen, M.: Co-design as a process of joint inquiry and imagination. Des. Issues **29**(2), 16–28 (2013)
36. Sun, K., Zou, Y., Radesky, J., Brooks, C., Schaub, F.: Child safety in the smart home: parents' perceptions, needs, and mitigation strategies. Proc. ACM Hum.-Comput. Interact. **5**(CSCW2), 1–41 (2021)
37. Superti Pantoja, L., et al.: Play-based design: giving 3-to 4-year-old children a voice in the design process. In: Proceedings of the 2020 CHI Conference on Human Factors in Computing Systems, pp. 1–14 (2020)
38. Yip, J.C., et al.: The evolution of engagements and social bonds during child-parent co-design. In: Proceedings of the 2016 CHI Conference on Human Factors in Computing Systems, pp. 3607–3619 (2016)
39. Yu, J., Bai, C., Roque, R.: Considering parents in coding kit design: understanding parents' perspectives and roles. In: Proceedings of the 2020 CHI Conference on Human Factors in Computing Systems, pp. 1–14 (2020)

Validation of the PTPI Scale for Technology Products Among Users with Disabilities

Carmen Van Ommen[1], Barbara S. Chaparro[1](✉), Joseph R. Keebler[1], Sanjay Batra[2], and Mei Lu[2]

[1] Department of Human Factors and Behavioral Neurobiology, Embry-Riddle Aeronautical University, Daytona Beach, FL 32114, USA
rescoc@my.erau.edu, barbara.chaparro@erau.edu

[2] Google LLC., User Research, Devices and Services, Mountain View, CA 94043, USA

Abstract. The Perceptions of Technology Product Inclusivity (PTPI) Scale was previously validated to assess perceptions of inclusivity with a wide variety of technology products and users. This study explores the use of the PTPI with a specific population, technology product users with disabilities, to determine if the scale appropriately assesses their perceptions of technology product inclusivity. The PTPI was administered via Qualtrics to 201 participants who self-reported having a disability. The technology products evaluated in this study covered 23 categories and contained a variety of products within those categories. A confirmatory factor analysis (CFA) was conducted to assess model fit. The CFA results indicated that the PTPI has acceptable model fit for all five subscales: Personal Connection, Product Challenges, Confidence in Usage, Meets Expectations, and Company Empathy. Thus, the PTPI is appropriate to use with technology product users with disabilities. Future research can be done to show how the validated 5-factor PTPI varies across technology products targeted to disabled users to identify design characteristics contributing to perceptions of inclusivity.

Keywords: Technology Product Design · Inclusivity · Scale Validation

1 Introduction

Customers often wish to have products and services customized to their preferences or needs [1]. Customization could range in complexity from changing the color of the product, to how the product performs and operates. Customized products and services are more personal to the customer, which creates a stronger emotional bond, and offering personalization correlates with higher levels of customer loyalty and satisfaction [1–4]. Customers are more likely to purchase products that allow for self-expression or a positive self-presentation. Studies with Gen Z consumers demonstrate that they often purchase products to demonstrate "who they are" to others and facilitate a sense of belonging [5, 6].

M. Antona and C. Stephanidis (Eds.): HCII 2023, LNCS 14020, pp. 185–196, 2023.
https://doi.org/10.1007/978-3-031-35681-0_12

The term "inclusive design" has been defined by designer Susan Goltsman as "designing a diversity of ways for users to participate so that everyone has a sense of belonging" [7]. Because self-expression and inclusivity is important to consumers, it can be a source of disappointment when they cannot purchase or use products that align with their self-identity or are restricted from being able to interact with their preferred social group. For example, a hearing aid manufacturer in Australia advertised hearing aids that were less visible, suggesting that they were less "ugly" than large hearing aids. By framing the advertisement in this way, users of the larger and more visible hearing aids may experience feelings of shame or embarrassment [8].

The Perceptions of Technology Product Inclusivity (PTPI) scale is a new, validated instrument to assess user perceptions of inclusivity [9]. The 25-item scale includes five factors: Personal Connection, Product Challenges, Confidence in Usage, Meets Expectations, and Company Empathy (see Appendix for items within each factor). Table 1 [9] provides a brief description of each subscale.

Table 1. Description of Each Subscale

Subscale	Description
Personal Connection	Having a sense of belonging or personal connection to the product.
Product Challenges	Challenges or demands experienced when using a product.
Confidence in Usage	Perceptions of confidence and self-efficacy when using the product.
Meets Expectations	Perceptions of how well the product works to meet users' needs.
Company Empathy	Perceptions of the company in terms of trust and their intentions to design for diverse audiences.

1.1 Inclusive Design Interactions with People with Disabilities

While having a sense of inclusion with technology products is important to all consumers, one segment of the population that may feel excluded more often are people with disabilities. A 2018 survey reports 12.6% of people in the United States stated having a disability [10]. Additionally, a study by Yin et al. at the American Institutes for Research [11] indicates that the market segment of people with disabilities who were working-aged had an after-tax disposable income of approximately $490 billion. A Nielsen [12] study also found that households with people with disabilities made more shopping trips, spent more money, and tended to have more brand loyalty.

People with disabilities may often face challenges in purchasing that people without disabilities do not face. A study on technology buying habits of people with disabilities in the UK revealed that "90% of these consumers were affected at the decision-making stage of purchases by either; limitations of design (products, services or venues not being inclusive or accessible), limitations in available information, and/or how information was presented" [13]. Overall, 31% of respondents were impacted by all three of the aforementioned aspects [13]. Not only were their decisions impacted by how technology products interacted with their disability, 65% of respondents indicated they feel limited in their choices of what to buy due to accessibility or inclusion barriers [13]. When looking at customization of products, “26% did not feel able to request adjustments or identify their preferences or needs when they tried to buy a product or services” [13]. People with disabilities may have specific needs that are not considered when developing products, such as requiring the product to be lightweight, or have dimmed screens. Due to these needs, people with disabilities may seek out recommendations or reviews by other people with disabilities [13]. Because of these unique needs or barriers, people with disabilities may feel excluded more often, and the areas of potential exclusion may not be intuitive to product designers who are not experienced with access barriers presented when having a disability. Therefore, having a tool that allows measurement of perceptions of technology product inclusivity may be helpful in assessing overall feelings of inclusivity, as well as pinpoint specific areas that may require improvement.

1.2 Purpose

The purpose of this study is to determine if the PTPI factors are valid for technology product users with disabilities. While the PTPI was validated with a large sample, only 13.44% percent of the population of the participants in the final CFA, or 79 participants, reported a disability [9]. A larger sample size is required in order to statistically validate the scale with this population. This will help ensure that the scale items are appropriate in measuring the perception of technology product inclusion with this population, as their needs or experiences with inclusion may differ.

2 Method

2.1 Participants

The study was approved by the author’s university Institutional Review Board. The study sample consisted of 201 participants recruited from within the United States. Participants were either recruited from Prolific, an online survey distribution platform, or from email solicitation to a database of technology consumers with a self-reported disability. Participants ranged in age from 18–75. 10.95% of participants were older adults (60 years of age or older) and 54.23% were people of color. Table 2 provides a summary of participant demographics and category of self-reported disability.

Table 2. Demographics of Participants (N = 201)

Variable	EFA Value
Age in Years (M ∓ SD)	39.87 ∓ 13.48
Age Range in Years	18–75
Gender (%)	
Male	46.77%
Female	47.76%
Transgender	0.50%
Nonbinary	4.48%
Prefer to self-describe	0.50%
I prefer not to answer	0.00%
Ethnicity (%)	
American Indian/Alaskan Native	5.47%
Asian/Pacific Islander	13.43%
Black/African American	12.44%
Hispanic/Latino	14.43%
White (not of Hispanic origin)	43.78%
Biracial/multiracial/mixed	8.46%
I prefer not to answer	1.00%
Education Level (%)	
High school	10.95%
Some college	21.89%
Associates Degree	10.95%
Vocational/Technical College	2.99%
Bachelor's Degree	26.87%
Master's Degree	17.41%
Doctorate or Professional Degree	8.46%
I prefer not to answer	0.50%
Self-identify as having a disability[a]	
Physical	44.28%
Visual	28.36%
Auditory	23.88%
Cognitive/Mental	29.35%
Emotional	15.92%
Other	1.49%

[a]Participants could select more than one disability type, so percentages of disability type may sum to more than total percentage of disability.

2.2 Materials

Qualtrics Online Survey Software was used to create the survey which included the following sections:

1. Consent form
2. Make and model of the technology product under evaluation (participants entered the name in a text field)
3. Basic questions about familiarity and frequency of use of the product
4. Product evaluation statements
   a. These statements were randomized and five statements per screen were displayed to minimize scrolling
   b. Each statement was evaluated on a 7-point rating scale (1 = strongly disagree, 7 = strongly agree; N/A option at the end of the scale)
5. Overall satisfaction rating (1 = extremely dissatisfied, 7 = extremely satisfied)
6. Overall inclusion rating ("Overall, I feel included as a user of this product."; 1 = strongly disagree, 7 = strongly agree)
7. Net Promoter Score (NPS)
8. System Usability Score (SUS; [14])
9. Basic demographic questions (e.g. age, gender, disability)

Other than entering text into the text field describing the make and model of the technology product, no questions required a response from participants.

2.3 Procedure

Information about the study and the survey link were shared via email or on the survey distribution platform Prolific. The survey links were open for 13 days for the Prolific survey and 15 days for the surveys distributed via email list. Participants who completed the survey were compensated for their time. On average, participants took approximately 12 min to complete the survey (M = 719 s, SD = 1019 s; 3 outliers removed).

3 Results

3.1 Technology Products

The majority of the technology products participants chose to evaluate were used daily and had been purchased 6 months or longer prior to taking the survey. Since the survey instructions asked participants to choose a technology product that they use frequently, it was expected that many of these products would be products that participants liked. The mean ratings for overall satisfaction (1 = extremely dissatisfied, 7 = extremely satisfied), confirmed these expectations (M = 5.75, SD = 1.187). Table 3 provides a summary of the technology products evaluated in the study. Overall, the technology products evaluated in this study covered 23 categories and contained a variety of products within those categories.

Table 3. Overview of the Technology Product Categories Represented

Technology Product Category	Percentage
Smartphone	28.36%
Smart Speaker	10.45%
Computer	9.45%
Smart Watch	8.46%
Gaming Device	6.97%
Headphones	3.98%
Home Products	3.98%
Smart TV	3.48%
Fitness Tracker	3.48%
Other	2.99%
Tablet	2.49%
Smart Doorbell	1.99%
Speaker/Sound System	1.99%
Vehicle	1.99%
eReader	1.99%
Audio Equipment	1.99%
Security System	1.49%
Software	1.00%
Smart Thermostat	1.00%
Digital Camera	1.00%
Computer Accessories	0.50%
TV Accessories	0.50%
Smart Display	0.50%

3.2 CFA Results

To determine if the PTPI is appropriate to use to measure perceptions of technology product inclusivity with people with disabilities, a confirmatory factor analysis (CFA) was conducted to assess model fit for the 5-factor model proposed in previous work [9].

Normality
Inspection of the histograms and results of the Shapiro-Wilk test revealed that most of the items deviated significantly from a normal distribution. Most items were considered moderately negatively skewed (i.e., skewness <|2| and kurtosis <7; [15]). Since this analysis is intended to be exploratory in nature, the data was not transformed.

Missing Data
N/A responses were treated as missing data during both studies. In total, 4.14% of

the data was missing. Little's MCAR test results ($\chi^2 = 428.275$, df = 411, p = .268) indicated that the data was missing completely at random. All variables or scale items (n = 25) and 14.9% of cases, or participants (n = 30) contained at least one missing value. The percentage of missing values for each variable ranged from 0.14% to 4.17%.

The expectation maximization method was used to replace missing data. Since there was less than 10% of data missing overall and for each variable, the difference in end result between methods for replacing data is not as great. Therefore expectation maximization was used as it is consistent with how missing data was replaced during the original validation study [9].

Model Fit Assessment

To evaluate model fit, the model (displayed in Fig. 1) and the three fit indices used in the original validation process for the PTPI were evaluated, alongside the chi-square test statistic [9]. These three fit indices were the Comparative Fit Index (CFI; [16]), root mean square error of approximation (RMSEA; [17]), and the Tucker Lewis Index (TLI; [18]). The results of the model fit assessment are displayed in Table 4, along with the recommended cutoff values for acceptable fit for each indice.

Table 4. Model Fit Statistics (N = 201)

Fit Index	Value	Recommended Cutoff Values for Acceptable Fit	References
$\chi 2$	$\chi 2 = 434.68$, df = 265, p = .000	N/A	N/A
CFI	.934	0.90–0.95, >0.95 indicates good fit	[16, 19]
RMSEA	0.054 [0.044, 0.064]	0.06–0.08, <.06 indicates excellent fit	[20, 21]
TLI	.918	0.90–0.95, >0.95 indicates good fit	[19]

Scale Reliability and Validity Assessment

After the assessment of model fit, the reliability, convergent, and discriminant validity of the scale was assessed [22]. For reliability, we report values in Table 4. Reliability values for all factors or subscales were above the suggested threshold of .7, indicating the individual scale factors are all consistent in their measurement. To test construct validity, we utilized an assessment of average variance extracted (AVE) values and maximum shared variance (MSV). For AVE, which helps to ascertain convergent validity, two factors were slightly below the suggested threshold of .5, indicating convergent validity concerns [23]. These two factors were Personal Connection and Confidence in Usage. For MSV, which allows us to test for discriminant validity, values should be less than AVE values. The results showed that the factors of Company Empathy, Meets Expectations, and Confidence in Usage had MSV values greater than AVE values. The results of the validity values are shown in Table 5.

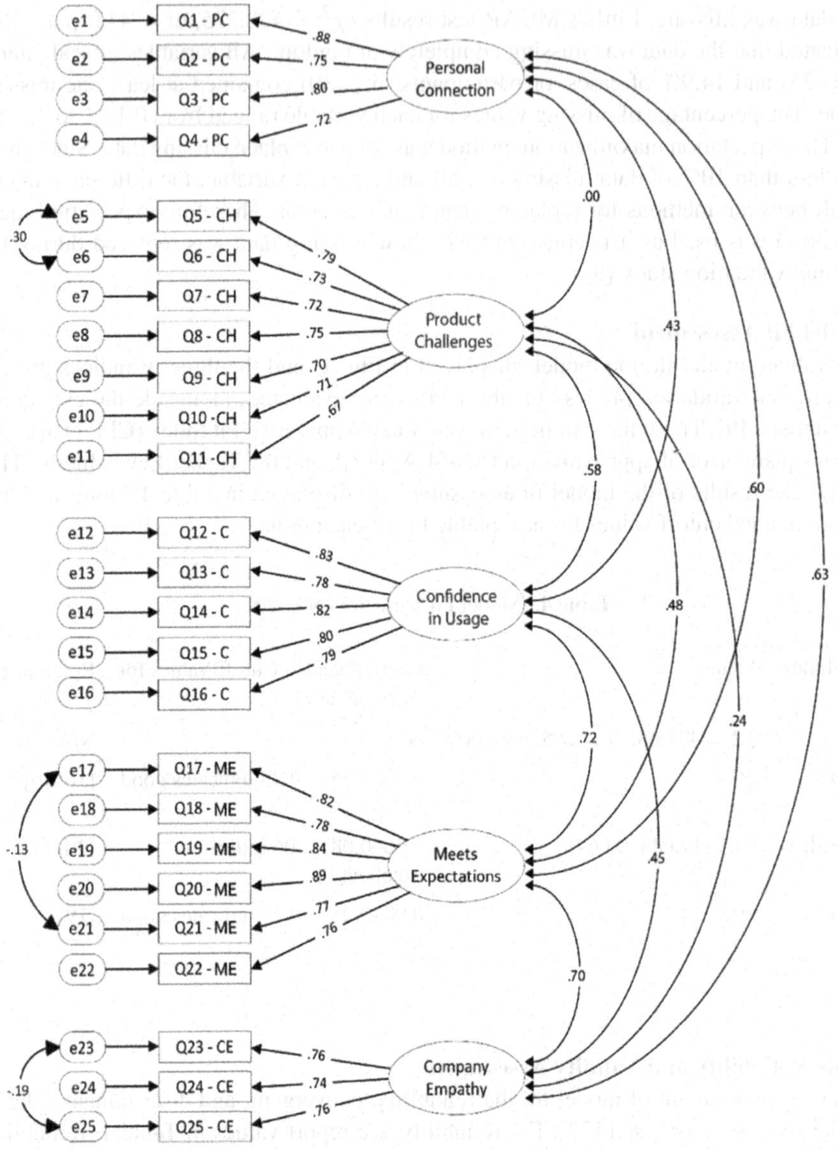

Fig. 1. PTPI Scale Model [9]

4 Discussion

Experiences that people with disabilities have with technology products may differ from those who do not have a disability. People with disabilities may experience barriers when purchasing or using products, which may include not being able to access information about products and not being able to purchase products that fit their needs [13]. This study validated the PTPI as an appropriate scale to measure perceptions of technology product

Table 5. Reliability, Convergent, and Discriminant Validity Results

	CR	AVE	MSV
Factor 1: Personal Connection	0.775	0.462	0.327
Factor 2: Product Challenges	0.913	0.600	0.557
Factor 3: Confidence in Usage	0.800	0.448	0.557
Factor 4: Meets Expectations	0.862	0.510	0.566
Factor 5: Company Empathy	0.755	0.507	0.566

inclusivity among users with disabilities. When using a scale to measure a construct, past research has shown that there may be areas where the scale needs to be modified in order to be understood by people with disabilities [24]. This may include presenting the scale in different formats, such as being read aloud or presented in Braille, or could include modifying scale items, such as simplifying the wording or response options of those items. In the current study, participants did not indicate issues with the presentation or wording of the scale items, thus we do not currently recommend modifications to the scale in this area. It is important to note that accessibility needs of people with disabilities vary, and modifications may be required if presenting the scale to people who have more accessibility needs.

4.1 Future Research

Results of the original validation of the PTPI, as well as results of the current study suggests that the PTPI is appropriate for use with a diverse audience. While participants from specific audiences such as people of color or older adults are represented in both studies, future research should continue to statistically validate the PTPI with a larger sample size of these more specific populations in order to ensure that it is appropriate for use.

Additionally, the PTPI is intended to inform design decisions of technology products. Future research should explore the PTPI with specific products as well as specific design features to explore which aspects contribute to perceptions of inclusivity. Future research could also explore products that were purchased for different use cases, such as for enjoyment versus out of necessity. Finally, products evaluated in this study and the original validation study have generally been products with which participants are satisfied. Future research should include validation of the PTPI with unsatisfying technology products.

Funding. This work was supported by a fellowship awarded to Embry-Riddle Aeronautical University by Google to study factors contributing to perceptions of inclusive design of technology. The fellowship provided stipend and tuition to CVO. Participant compensation was provided through funding by Google.

Appendix

PTPI

Instructions: Please rate the following statements on a scale from "Strongly Disagree" to "Strongly Agree". If a statement does not apply, select "N/A" (see Fig. 2).

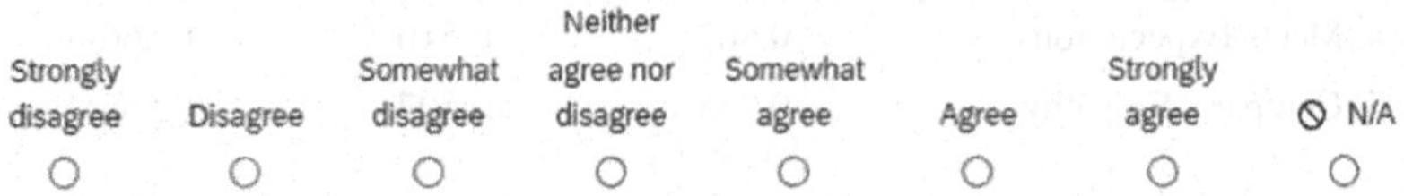

Fig. 2. Rating Scale

Personal Connection

1. I have a sense of belonging when I use this product.
2. The look of this product allows me to feel like I belong.
3. I feel a personal connection to this product.
4. When using this product, I feel my choices express my "true self".

Product Challenges

5. This product is emotionally demanding to use.
6. This product is mentally demanding to use.
7. This product is physically demanding to use.
8. For this product to work, I had to make changes to it beyond my expectations.
9. It's hard for me to use this product on my own.
10. When using this product, I struggle to do things I should be good at.
11. When using this product, I feel like my actions had unintended consequences.

Confidence in Usage

12. I am confident that I know how to use this product.
13. It is easy for me to learn how to use this product.
14. I am good at using this product.
15. I feel very capable using this product.
16. It's easy for me to remember how to use this product.

Meets Expectations

17. This product meets my expectations.
18. This product is reliable.
19. I consider my product usage experience a success.
20. This product works well for me.
21. I feel in control of my product experience.
22. There is a good fit between what this product offers me and what I am looking for in this product.

Company Empathy

23. Overall, the company that made this product is trustworthy.

24. The company that made this product makes good-faith efforts to address the concerns of customers like me.
25. I feel like the company considered the needs of customers like me when designing this product.

References

1. Coelho, P.S., Henseler, J.: Creating customer loyalty through service customization. Eur. J. Mark. (2012)
2. Sashi, C.M.: Customer engagement, buyer-seller relationships, and social media. Manage. Decision (2012)
3. Ball, D., Coelho, P.S., Vilares, M.J.: Service personalization and loyalty. J. Serv. Mark. (2006)
4. Bock, D.E., Mangus, S.M., Folse, J.A.G.: The road to customer loyalty is paved with service customization. J. Bus. Res. **69**(10), 3923–3932 (2016)
5. Shin, S.-A., Jang, J.-O., Kim, J.-K., Cho, E.-H.: Relations of conspicuous consumption tendency, self-expression satisfaction, and SNS use satisfaction of Gen Z through SNS activities. Int. J. Environ. Res. Public Health **18**(22), 11979 (2021)
6. Lee, Y.: A study on the effects of the SNS use focused on the social relationships on the self-expression in SNS, off-line activity, and the life satisfaction. J. Convergen. Culture Technol. **6**(1), 301–312 (2020)
7. Holmes, K.: Mismatch: How Inclusion Shapes Design. The MIT Press (2018)
8. Rowlands, L.: 'Ugly' hearing aid ad leaves parents fuming. Stuff (2015). https://www.stuff.co.nz/life-style/parenting/baby/caring-for-baby/68919793/ugly-hearing-aid-ad-leaves-parents-fuming. Accessed 12 Sept 2022
9. Van Ommen, C., Chaparro, B.S., Keebler, J.R., Batra, S., Lu, M.: Development and validation of a scale to assess consumer perceptions of technology product inclusivity (PTPI). Manuscript submitted for publication (2022)
10. Erickson, W., Lee, C., von Schrader, S.: Disability Statistics from the American Community Survey (ACS). Ithaca, NY: Cornell University Yang-Tan Institute (YTI). Retrieved from Cornell University Disability Statistics (2022). www.disabilitystatistics.org
11. Yin, M., Shaewitz, D., Overton, C., Smith, D.-M.: A hidden market: the purchasing power of working-age adults with disabilities. American Institutes for Research (2018). Retrieved January 18, 2023, from https://www.air.org/sites/default/files/2022-03/Hidden-Market-Spending-Power-of-People-with-Disabilities-April-2018.pdf. Accessed 18 Jan 2023
12. The Nielsen Company. Reaching prevalent, diverse consumers with disabilities (2016). http://www.nielsen.com/content/dam/corporate/us/en/reportsdownloads/2016-reports/reaching-prevalent-diverse-consumers-with-disabilities.pdf
13. Business Disability Forum. (Technology and entertainment media: What disabled consumers choose to buy and why (2022). https://businessdisabilityforum.org.uk/knowledge-hub/resources/technology-what-disabled-consumers-choose-to-buy-and-why/. Accessed 18 Jan 2023
14. Brooke, J.: SUS-A quick and dirty usability scale. Usabil. Evalu. Indust. **189**(194), 4–7 (1996)
15. Finney, S.J., DiStefano, C.: Nonnormal and categorical data in structural equation modeling. In: Hancock, G.R., Mueller, R.O. (eds.) Structural Equation Modeling: A Second Course, 2nd edn, pp. 269–314. IAP, Charlotte, NC (2013)
16. Bentler, P.M.: Comparative fit indexes in structural models. Psychol. Bull. **107**(2), 238 (1990)
17. Steiger, J.H.: Statistically based tests for the number of common factors. Paper presented at the annual meeting of the Psychometric Society, Iowa City, IA (1980)
18. Tucker, L., Lewis, C.: A reliability coefficient for maximum likelihood factor analysis. Psychometrika **38**, 1–10 (1973)

19. Hu, L., Bentler, P.M.: Cutoff criteria for fit indexes in covariance structure analysis: conventional criteria versus new alternatives. SEM. **6**(1), 1–55 (1999)
20. Browne, M.W., Cudeck, R.: Alternative ways of assessing model fit. Sage focus editions, vol. 154, pp. 136–136 (1993)
21. Fabrigar, L.R., Wegener, D.T., MacCallum, R.C., Strahan, E.J.: Evaluating the use of exploratory factor analysis in psychological research. Psychol. Methods **4**, 272–299 (1999)
22. Gaskin, J.: ValidityMaster, Stats Tools Package (2016). http://statwiki.gaskination.com. Accessed 7 Feb 2023
23. Hair, J., Black, W., Babin, B., Anderson, R.: Multivariate data analysis 7th edn.
24. Van Ommen, C., & Chaparro, B. S.: Assessing video game satisfaction of gamers with disabilities. In: Proceedings of the Human Factors and Ergonomics Society Annual Meeting, vol. 65, no. 1, pp. 822–826. Los Angeles, CA: SAGE Publications, Sage CA (2021)

Design Recommendations Based on Speech Analysis for Disability-Friendly Interfaces for the Control of a Home Automation Environment

Nadine Vigouroux[1(✉)], Frédéric Vella[1], Gaëlle Lepage[2,3], and Éric Campo[4]

[1] IRIT, UNRS 5505, Université Paul Sabatier, 118 Route de Narbonne, 31062 Toulouse, France
{nadine.vigouroux,frederic.vella}@irit.fr
[2] GIHP, 10 Rue Jean Gilles, 31100 Toulouse, France
[3] UT2J, Campus Mirail, 5 allée Antonio Machado, 31058 Toulouse, France
[4] LAAS, CNRS, UT2J, 7 Avenue du Colonel Roche, 31400 Toulouse, France
eric.campo@laas.fr

Abstract. The objective of this paper is to describe the study on speech interaction mode for home automation control of equipment by impaired people for an inclusive housing. The study is related to the HIP HOPE project concerning a building of 19 inclusive housing units. 7 participants with different types of disabilities were invited to carry out use cases using voice and touch control. Only the results obtained on the voice interaction mode through the Amazon voice assistant are reported here. The results show, according to the type of handicap, the success rates in the speech recognition of the command emitted on the equipment and highlight the errors related to the formulation, the noisy environment, the intelligible speech, the speech segmentation and the bad synchronization of the audio channel opening.

Keywords: spoken interaction · speech disorder · motor impairment · visually impaired and hearing impairment · smart home

1 Introduction

In France, the ELAN law of November 23, 2018 introduces the concept of inclusive housing and defines it as a mode of housing (excerpt from Article L.281-1 of the CASF): "*intended for people with disabilities and the elderly who have the choice, as their main residence, of a grouped mode of living, among themselves or with other people (…) and accompanied by a social and shared life project*". Due to the changes and obstacles of this new type of housing, it seems interesting to study the technological needs of people with disabilities, taking into account their physical and material environment, allowing them to live in an inclusive habitat with the greatest possible autonomy.

Varriale et al. [1] have identified the role and function of home automation, for people with disability through a deep review, specifically they aim to outline if and how the

M. Antona and C. Stephanidis (Eds.): HCII 2023, LNCS 14020, pp. 197–211, 2023.
https://doi.org/10.1007/978-3-031-35681-0_13

home automation solutions can support people with disability improving their social inclusion. Vacher et al. [2] described an audio-based interaction technology that allows the user to have full control over their home environment and detect distress situations for the elderly and visually impaired people. These two research works show the need to study home automation technologies for the autonomy of people with disabilities.

The study presented in this paper is related to the HIP HOPE project concerning a building on the Montaudran site in Toulouse (France) in which 19 inclusive housing units will be built. This inclusive housing project is a participatory housing project characterized by economic, generational, social and cultural diversity. It will welcome students, as well as and disabled people, families with young children and seniors. This project aims at social inclusion through culture, popular education and solidarity. It concerns people with all types of disabilities, including a majority of residents with motor or neurological disabilities, or with neurodegenerative diseases (multiple sclerosis, Charcot's disease, Huntington's disease, Parkinson's disease).

These homes are part of an architectural and environmental project based on the principles of sustainable development and energy savings, in a warm, friendly, open, bright and secure housing approach. The project will include up to twenty apartments within a larger residence (100 to 120 units) in order to allow for a mix of publics and social inclusion. The cultural component will promote this social inclusion. Each apartment of the project will be designed to be accessible and will be equipped with home automation with simple and adapted control functionalities such as voice and touch interaction, and not only by push button type. Vigouroux et al. [3] reported the experiment design carried out in a living Lab to identify the most accessible interaction modes for home automation controls.

In this context, the objective of this article is to describe an experiment conducted in this living lab to focus on the voice interaction mode for home automation control of equipment by impaired people in order to provide recommendations for its implementation in HIP HOPE housing.

Section 2 addresses the various researches in the field of speech recognition for the elderly and people with motor and speech impairments. Section 3 describes the experimental framework with emphasis on the infrastructure of the Smart Home of Blagnac (MIB)[1], the study population and the scenarios. Section 4 analyses the interaction logs and proposes a typology of speech recognition errors. The last section discusses the results and proposes research perspectives for a better usability and acceptability of speech recognition and voice assistants in the context of smart homes.

2 Related Works

Advances in voice recognition and natural language processing have reached a level of maturity and performance that their deployment in smart houses, on smartphones etc. is becoming widespread. Today, people are using this technology to perform a lot of everyday tasks in their homes like home automation (turn off/on lights, turn off/on TV, etc.).

[1] http://mi.iut-blagnac.fr.

The literature review shows that recent studies explore the usability and the usefulness of automatic speech recognition and voice assistants for elderly people [4] and for people with motor and speech impairment [5]. Recently Brewer et al. [6] reported a work focused on perceptions of voice assistant use by elderly people. The authors showed how conversational and human-like expectations with voice assistants lead to information breakdowns between the older adult and voice assistant. They also discussed how voice interfaces could better support older adults' health information seeking behaviours and expectations.

Kowalski et al. [7] explored the possible benefits and barriers to the use of Google Home voice assistants in the context of smart home technology by older adults. They found that older adults could naturally identify various already available applications of voice assistants such information hand-free, translator or memory aid, etc. However, the group of older adults reported that with little training and encouragement older participants could start using voice assistants to their satisfaction and empowerment.

We can observe many designs of voice applications for the elderly and people with motor disabilities integrating voice assistants [8–10] and [11]. Some applications use voice components such as Google Home [7], Google Assistant [12] and Amazon's Alexa [13].

Alexakis et al. [8] described an IoT Agent, a Web application for monitoring and controlling a smart home remotely. This IoT Agent integrates a chat bot that can understand text or voice commands using natural language processing. This current implementation is totally based on third party APIs and open source technologies. Their implementation exploits the typical IoT infrastructures by providing an enhanced user experience and usability of the underlying IoT system with the integration of natural language processing and voice recognition, MQTT and many other technologies. Although the article describes the implementation in depth, the authors make no mention of performance measurements on the language processing tools.

Ismail et al. [9] proposed low cost framework on smartphone and Raspberry Pi boards which uses a hybrid Support Vector Machine (SVM) with a Dynamic Time Warping (DTW) algorithm to enhance the speech recognition process. The results show 97% accuracy and that patients and elderly people are accessing and controlling IoT devices in smart homes and hospitals. The system's limitation is the difficulty of speech recognition if the user's voice is affected by illness or is not clear enough to be detected.

Lokitha et al. [10] proposed a comparative study of two algorithms: the first is the Support Vector Machine (SVM) and the second is Convolutional Neural network (CNN) for command identification of Speech disabled and Paralyzed People. The CNN model yields an accuracy of 90.62%, whereas the SVM algorithm gives a very low accuracy (58.42%). The authors suggest increasing the learning database with real speech signals collected from patients to improve the performance of the system future and of the model for continuous speech.

Netinant et al. [11] have designed a speech recognition system on raspberry Pi using the Google Speech Recognition API with a special emphasis on disabled and elderly individuals. However, the authors reported that their system's accuracy in recognizing speech for four command words in Thai and English language for disabled and elderly users should be weighed against the country's national language. While this study is interesting, it is limited in the number of speakers and orders.

Isyanto et al. [12] implemented IoT-based smart home voice commands for disabled people using Google Assistant to control TV, lights, etc. However, the authors reported that, the Google Assistant application accepts voice commands when the pronunciation is correct.

Mtshali and Khubisa [14] presented a system smart objects and a voice assistant such as Amazon Alexa, Google Home, Google Assistant, Apple Siri, etc. to recognize voice commands, from a person with physical disabilities through three use cases. However, the authors do not mention any evaluation of the accuracy obtained.

Malavasi et al. [15] have developed low-cost voice systems for environmental control through simplified and accessible user interfaces by adapting to dysarthric speech, or to more general language disorders through adaptation processes.

This related background shows that many research and innovation approaches are underway in terms of recognition methods and tools, in the use of OpenHAB interoperability tools [15], MQTT[2] (Message Queuing Telemetry Transport) communication protocols [8], https (HyperText Transfer Protocol), and some studies on the acceptability of voice assistants, mainly by the elderly.

We also note that these systems are becoming widespread on smartphones and embedded boards such as Raspberry Pi. Although all the studies agree on the benefits of this mode of interaction for autonomy of elderly and disabled people, several authors highlight the need to acquire speech disorder databases in order to build acoustic models adapted to these disorders and the need to conduct experiments on larger populations with speech disorders.

3 Experiment

3.1 Material

Living Lab Description

The experimentation was carried out in MIB which served as a Living Lab. Its objective is to provide researchers with a study and research platform to observe people in situation using the different prototypes. It has an apartment (see Fig. 1) of 70 m^2 allowing making experiments with impaired people. It is composed of different rooms: living room, kitchen, corridor, bedroom, bathroom and toilet. It is equipped with various connected objects and motorized furniture that can be controlled by speech interaction, touch on tablets/phones or by wall switches such as a removable sink and washbasin in the kitchen and toilet, television, a medical bed, shutters, lighting and automatic alert devices. It also has an infrastructure for experiments with microphones, cameras and motion sensors.

Infrastructure Description

The MIB infrastructure is composed of an MQTT Broker server, an OpenHAB interoperability server, a touch device, a Fire TV Cube voice assistant from Amazon and several connected objects that are connected to a Wifi box (see Fig. 2) which allows to assign an IP address to each connected object.

[2] Https://mqtt.org/.

Fig. 1. Smart Home at the University Institute of Technology in Blagnac.

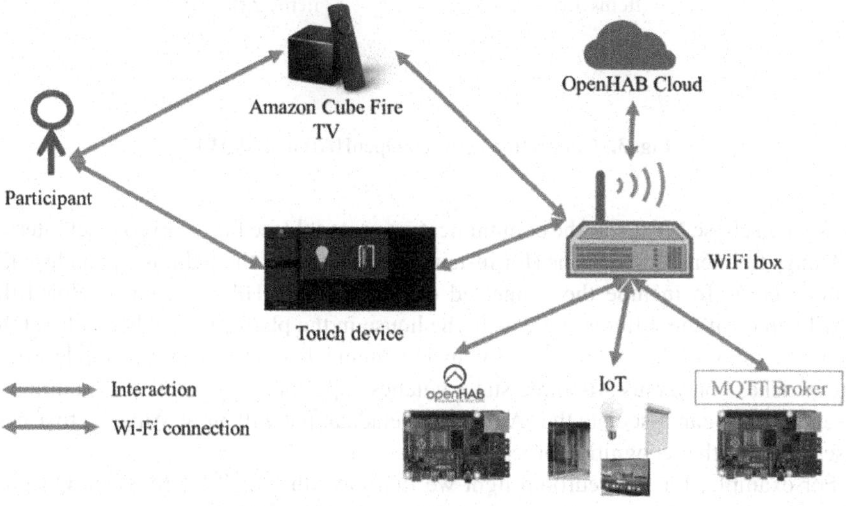

Fig. 2. Overall system architecture.

We selected the interoperability platform because it allows the interconnection of connected objects using communication protocols (MQTT, https, etc.). It also enables the design of interfaces by means of tools that it supports (for example, the HABPanel application for the design of graphic interfaces). It includes some skills to connect the voice assistants such as Amazon Echo, Google Home, etc.

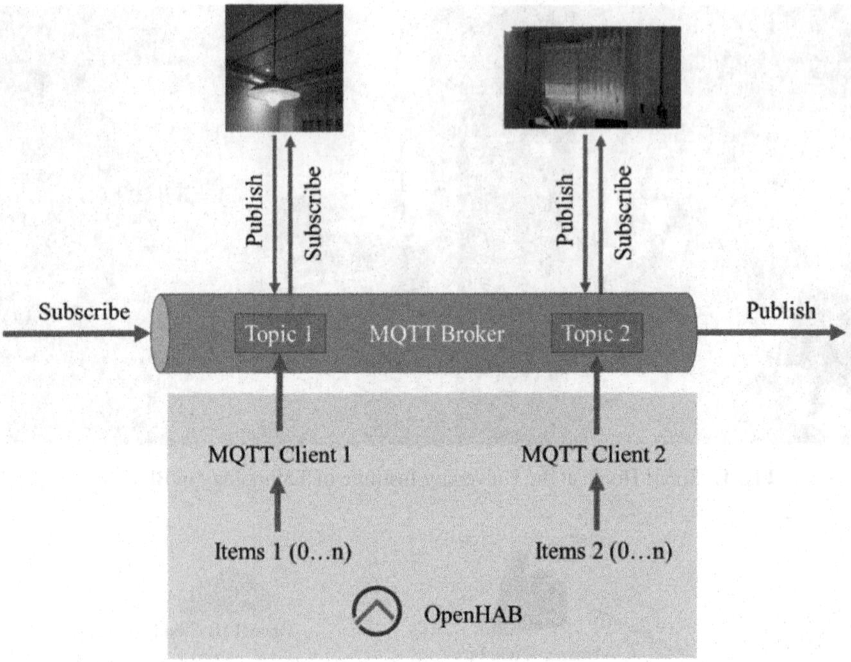

Fig. 3. Connection between OpenHAB and MQTT.

We then chose MQTT as the communication protocol (see Fig. 3) to connect Internet Of Things to interaction buttons (for instance, to turn on/off the light, to open/close the shutters, etc.). To include the connected objects on OpenHAB, we first defined the MQTT topics of the different objects in the house in the platform. We then defined the OpenHAB items of these objects by giving them item labels and interaction modes (two-state switches –on versus off– three-state switches –up, stop, down –, etc.). In addition to these items, we can associate the "Amazon" metadata that will allow Amazon to access these items for the recognition process.

For example, for the bedroom light we first have the MQTT ((Message Queuing Telemetry Transport) topics described in a hierarchical way [16] to:

- request the light status: api/1/room/bedroom/lamp/ceiling/id/1/indication (*publish*)
- turn the light on and off: api/1/room/bedroom/lamp/ceiling/id/1/request followed by on or off (*subscribe*).

The OpenHAB platform also allows two items to be distinguished for the same MQTT topics. This functionality allows the design of several interaction modes, for example:

- one for the touch tablet called "touch room light"

- and another for the voice assistant called "voice room light" by adding the "Amazon" metadata.

This metadata allows the Amazon Cube Fire TV device to access item labels stored on the OpenHAB Cloud to connect Internet Of Things with the voice recognition (see Fig. 2). Indeed, the OpenHAB platform secures the access of items through the Cloud by means of credentials. To configure Amazon's Fire TV Cube, it is necessary to download the Alexa application on a smartphone and then integrate the OpenHAB skill from the Alexa application.

We can then associate the action "open the shutters" in Fire TV Cube with several language utterances such as "*open the shutters of the living room*", "*open living room shutters*", "*open the roller shutters in the living room*", etc. All these utterances should be associated with the "living room shutter" item in OpenHAB.

OpenHAB also allows the design of more advanced use cases consisting of elementary actions as described above. We use deterministic rules with respect to the item states and the item order to design use cases. Based on this principle, we have developed the call "for help" which consists of the following elementary actions: I open the front door; I turn on the hall light; I turn on the bedroom light and a spoken message "help is on the way" is broadcast throughout the house.

Voice Assistant

For the speech interface, we chose the Fire TV Cube from Amazon because it allowed controlling by voice the television with a Molotov account and the home automation.

The list of items defined in OpenHab illustrates how the light in the bedroom is switched on.

```
- Item 'GF_Bedroom_Light' received command ON
- Item 'GF_Bedroom_Light' predicted to become ON
- Item 'GF_Bedroom_Light' changed from OFF to ON
```

3.2 Population

The participants were recruited through an association for the integration of physically disabled people (GIHP). This set of participants of all ages and with different impairments represents the population that will live in the HIP HOPE home automation flats. They are representative of the residents' profile who will occupy these inclusive habitats: 7 persons with impairments (1 intellectual impairment, 4 motor disabled people including 2 with speech disorders, 1 visual and 1 hearing impairments) participated in this study. Table 1 also lists the home automation and assistive technologies desired by these individuals, collected from interviews.

Table 1. Table of participants extracted from [3].

Participant	Age/ Gender	Impairment	Activities	Technology needs for smart home
101	63/M	Hearing impairment	Pharmacist, now retired	Adapted intercom with high quality visuals to see the person and read their lips; connected objects with visual feedback; flashing lights; app on phone to detect someone's presence or an abnormal noise.
102	72/M	Visual impairment	Computer science now retired	Easy to implement; efficient and responsive technology, limit the number of steps, preference for voice control with voice feedback on actions performed; home automation control (shutters, light, alarm) but with reliability and ease of use.
104	39/F	Cerebral Palsy	Employee in an association and volunteer	Interfaces for home automation control (shutters, front door); voice control difficult in case of fatigue, so have the touch mode; connected intercom without the need to pick up the phone.
202	18/M	Trisomy syndrome	Student	Smartphone application to help organise activities, to encourage initiatives (coaching application).
204	19/M	Cerebral palsy	Student	Smartphone control system for gates, garages and front doors to be autonomous; smartphone remote control for TV, robotic arm.
300	38/F	Myopathy	Volunteer	Home automation to control the environment (with voice command); robotic arm (help for cutting, grabbing objects, grooming), adapted intercom (easy to open and to communicate).
302	70/F	Polio	Secretary, retired and volunteer	Opening of the gate from your home; automated bay window; automation control of equipment for individual and mobile homes; fall detector or easy emergency call.

3.3 Scenarios

We defined the scenarios (see Table 2 and Table 3) based on the environmental control needs expressed during the interviews. We invited the participants to use the speech interaction modality described (Sect. 3.1) to control the equipment of the Smart Home in two use cases (a controlled and a free scenario).

Table 2. Controlled scenario: "Controlling your environment".

Instruction:	Use the touch tablet and/or the voice command to control the house
Initial conditions of the MIB:	Shutters closed, all lights on, motorized furniture is in down position. The person can be with their caregiver in the house but they must not interact with the voice and touch controls
Example of a control: You go into the kitchen	Open the shutter, Turn off the light, Raise the kitchen furniture, etc.

Table 3. Free scenario: "Activities of daily living when getting out of bed"

Instruction:	Use the touch tablet and/or the voice command to control the house
Initial conditions of the MIB	The participant is sitting on the bed or in the wheelchair with the lights off. When the scenario is started, the participant is asked to perform a number of tasks in the order he/she wishes
Example of tasks	You go and have breakfast; You turn on the TV in the living room to watch a news channel, sitting on the sofa or in your armchair; You feel unwell and call for help (panic button, medallion or voice command) "*Alexa, help*"

We have invited the participants to perform both the free and the controlled scenario. However, they were free to choose the order of using the tactile modality or the spoken modality. Then, we gave the scenario either in paper or in digital form for ease of understanding, depending on the participant's impairment. The visual impaired participant had the scripts printed in Braille.

Figure 4 shows on the bottom left screen the visualization of the participant's speech signal, on the top right screen the view of the four rooms of the house and the status of the connected objects in the house. These screens enabled the experimenter to observe the participant's behavior.

Fig. 4. Experimenter's observation workstation.

3.4 Appropriation Phase

The experimenter proceeded to demonstrate the two interaction modes for the same command. He then explained the need to open the recognition audio channel of the Amazon Fire TV system. The experimenter drew the participant's attention to the need for feedback from the Amazon Fire TV system (voice feedback "okay") and visually (blue light display). Given the language difficulties of some participants, we selected the channel opening word that was easiest for the participant to pronounce, from these three words (Amazon, Alexa, Echo). The experimenter then invited the participant to carry out three types of command in each mode to ensure that the instructions were correctly understood. The duration of this task varied greatly depending on the participants, mainly for participants with speech disorders.

3.5 Speech Interaction Data

All dialogues between the participant and the Amazon Fire TV were transcribed in order to match the channel corresponding to the utterance produced by the participant with the one recognized by the recognition system. We also transcribed the sentence corresponding to the channel openings (See Table 4).

The aim of this transcription is to measure the recognition performance but also the difficulties of opening the communication channel of this type of voice assistant for our study population. We have added a comment field in which the transcriber can notify, for example, the bad synchronisation of the production of the utterance with the opening of the channel, syllable or word accentuations according to the participants, pauses between the entities of a syntactic structure, etc.

4 Results

The results are deduced from the analysis of the transcribed data in the format described in Table 4.

Table 4. Transcription format.

Type of speech act	Spoken utterance	Recognized utterance	Comments

4.1 Spoken Interaction Rate

Participants produced 146 utterances with a very variable number of utterances depending on the participant (4 utterances for participant 204 including 3 reformulations and 47 utterances for participant 104). The overall correct recognition rate was 76.03% and the recognition error rate was 23.97%. The Fig. 5 shows that participant 104 had a recognition error rate of 53.2% and a reformulation rate of 10.6%. The experimenter always opened the communication channel for this participant. Participant 204 had a recognition error rate of 100%. This participant did not wish to continue with this mode of interaction. For participant 300, the recognition rate is 100%. Participants 101, 202, 302 and 102 had an average recognition error of 12.13% and a standard deviation of ± 2.96. With the exception of participants 104 and 204, no other participant had a problem opening the communication channel.

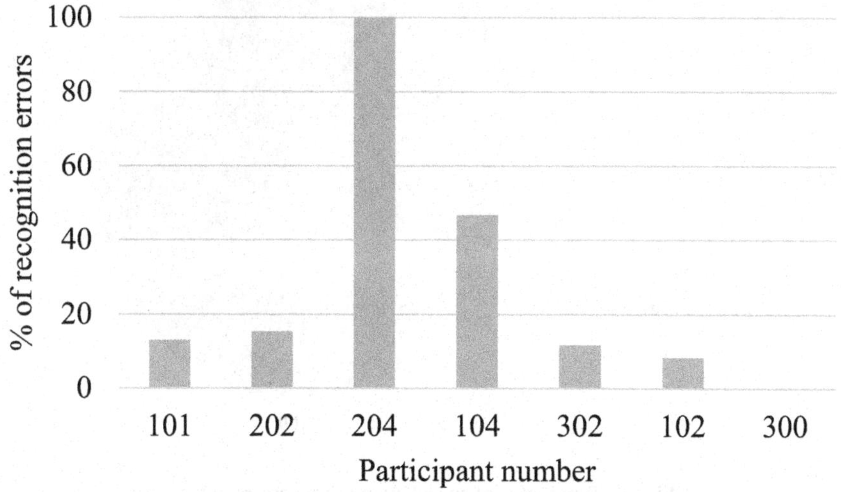

Fig. 5. Percentage of speech recognition errors per participant.

4.2 Typology of Recognition Errors

We have carried out a typology of recognition errors in order to propose recommendations for the design of voice assistants and voice interaction systems for people impairments. The Fig. 6 illustrates the percentage according to the causes of errors.

- Communication channel opening problem

We identified two reasons: 1) The speaker did not speak the trigger keyword (Alexa, Amazon, Echo) or did not speak loud enough so the communication channel was not opened but the speaker continued to speak. In this case, the oral utterance was not subject to the recognition process; 2) A synchronization problem between the recognition process and the speaker. We have identified two situations: either the person started speaking immediately before the feedback from the Fire Cube TV was obtained, or he/she spoke too late after the feedback. In both cases, the utterance was not subjected to the recognition process.

- Noisy environment

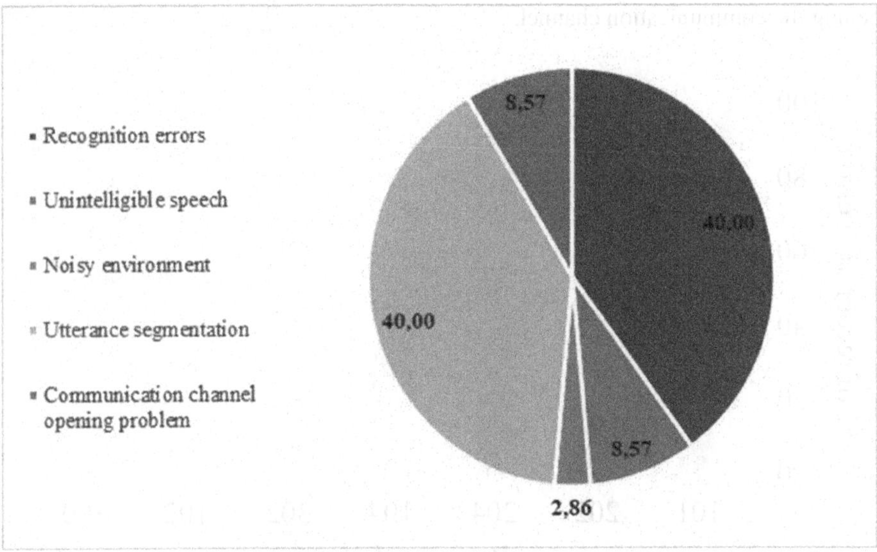

Fig. 6. Typologies of speech recognition errors in %.

The environment was noisy (loud TV) and the system did not recognize the utterance.

- Utterance segmentation

These errors corresponded to pauses made between words in an utterance (participant 202 and 204) and or the accentuation of syllables at the end of a word. This mode of speech corresponded to speech in isolated words.

- Unintelligible speech

This speech was also unintelligible to a human being. The speech reading and the interaction context (location of the person in the room) did not enable the experimenter to understand the communication intention of the participant. Participant 204 wished to abandon voice interaction despite efforts to rephrase in favor of tactile interaction.

- Recognition errors

Errors that could not be classified in the previous categories are considered as recognition errors without classification. They generally corresponded to phonetic confusions (mispronunciation of the word "living room" in the statement "open the shutter of the living room") by the recognition system due to the participant's speech difficulties.

5 Discussion

This pre-study shows that recognition accuracy is variable depending on the speakers' communication abilities. We have identified two difficulties that speech technologies will have to take into account, namely:

- Articulatory difficulties in the production of oral utterances due to speech disorders. Analyzes of the participants' oral utterances (204 and 104) identified the following difficulties: the production of words in syllables, the accentuation of some phonetic units, pauses between words, repetitions, and a slower speech rate. Thus, the acoustic representation of the speech signal of speakers with speech disorders is different from those without speech disorders. We propose some recommendations to adapt recognition systems to speech disorders:

  – Record databases with various speech disorders to adapt the acoustic models of recognition units like Lokitha et al. [10];
  – Adapt the language models to take into account syntactic structures (pause, repetitions, syllabification of words, etc.);
  – Link simplified utterances to the same command to avoid production errors as much as possible (e.g., instead of the utterance "open the living room roller shutters", accept also the utterance "open living room shutter"); This simplification of grammar was proposed by Malavasi et al. [15];
  – Use other multiple information such as lip movement to increase the likelihood of the recognition system as done by the hearing impaired.

- Their ability to pronounce in the right tempo (the opening word of the communication channel and the oral statement corresponding to the command). The bad management of the communication channel (not waiting for the feedback of Amazon, forgetting to open the channel) is a blocking point. The results of this pre-study suggest that the appropriation phases of the vocal interaction are more important, especially for subjects with attentional difficulties (participant 202), to adjust the intervals of maintaining the opening channel according to the participants. For participant 104, the experimenter opened the communication channel. To remedy this situation, we propose a push button or a button on an interface (tablet, smartphone) where the validation of a click would emit a pre-recorded vocal message that would allow the opening of the communication channel.

5 of the 7 participants preferred speech interaction to tactile interaction. Participant 204 would prefer to use voice if the speech recognition worked for him "because with fatigue it would be more efficient". People with speech disorders do not want to be excluded from voice interaction.

6 Conclusion

The development of the smart home facilitates human activities. However, the problem is the limited activities for disabled people. This paper describes an experiment with seven different disabled people interacting with smart home equipment with the Amazon Alexa assistant.

The related work shows that many technological innovations on speech recognition for smart homes are being carried out. This maturity of speech recognition technology has enabled usability and acceptability studies for elderly and disabled people. Secondly, the infrastructure based on OpenHAB and MQTT is described. Then, we report the speech accuracy for each participant with an average accuracy of 76.03%. We note very poor performance (100% and 46.8% of false recognition rate) for the two speech impaired participants. This suggests two research axis to be pursued: the development of acoustic and language models for people with speech impairments, the development of more intelligent voice assistants integrating more developed natural language and dialogue components, the proposal of alternative modalities such as interactive interaction or multimodal combination (voice, tactile, lip movement, eye movement, gesture). In terms of perspective, we propose to extend our study population to non-technophile people and to analyze tactile interactions.

Acknowledgment. The study is partially funded by the Occitanie Region (France). The authors thank the participants and the GIHP association.

References

1. Varriale, L., Briganti, P., Mele, S.: Disability and home automation: insights and challenges within organizational settings. In: Lazazzara, A., Ricciardi, F., Za, S. (eds.) Exploring Digital Ecosystems. LNISO, vol. 33, pp. 47–66. Springer, Cham (2020). https://doi.org/10.1007/978-3-030-23665-6_5

2. Vacher, M., et al.: Experimental evaluation of speech recognition technologies for voice-based home automation control in a smart home. In: 4th workshop on Speech and Language Processing for Assistive Technologies, 99–105 (2013). https://hal.archives-ouvertes.fr/hal-00953244
3. Vigouroux, N., Vella, F., Lepage, G., Campo, E.: Usability study of tactile and voice interaction modes by people with disabilities for home automation controls. In: Miesenberger, K., Kouroupetroglou, G., Mavrou, K., Manduchi, R., Covarrubias Rodriguez, M., Penáz, P. (eds.) Computers Helping People with Special Needs. ICCHP-AAATE 2022. LNCS, vol. 13342. Springer, Cham(2022). https://doi.org/10.1007/978-3-031-08645-8_17
4. Vacher, M., et al.: Evaluation of a context-aware voice interface for ambient assisted living: qualitative user study vs. quantitative system evaluation. ACM Trans. Access. Comput. **7**, 2, Article 5, 36 p (2015). https://doi.org/10.1145/2738047
5. Jefferson, M.: Usability of automatic speech recognition systems for individuals with speech disorders: Past, present, future, and a proposed model (2019)
6. Brewer, R., Pierce, C., Upadhyay, P., Park, L.: An empirical study of older adult's voice assistant use for health information seeking. ACM Trans. Interact. Intell. Syst. **12**(2), 1–32 (2022)
7. Kowalski, J., et al.: Older adults and voice interaction: a pilot study with google home. In: Extended Abstracts of the 2019 CHI Conference on Human Factors in Computing Systems, pp. 1–6 (2019)
8. Alexakis, G., Panagiotakis, S., Fragkakis, A., Markakis, E., Vassilakis, K.: Control of smart home operations using natural language processing, voice recognition and IoT technologies in a multitier architecture. Designs **3**(3), 32 (2019)
9. Ismail, A., Abdlerazek, S., El-Henawy, I.M.: Development of smart healthcare system based on speech recognition using support vector machine and dynamic time warping. Sustainability **12**(6), 2403 (2020)
10. Lokitha, T., Iswarya, R., Archana, A., Kumar, A., Sasikala, S.: Smart voice assistance for speech disabled and paralyzed people. In: 2022 International Conference on Computer Communication and Informatics (ICCCI), pp. 1–5. IEEE (2022)
11. Netinant, P., Arpabusayapan, K., Rukhiran, M.: Speech recognition for light control on raspberry pi using python programming. In: 2022 The 5th International Conference on Software Engineering and Information Management (ICSIM), pp. 33–37. IEEE (2022)
12. Isyanto, H., Arifin, A.S., Suryanegara, M.: Design and implementation of IoT-based smart home voice commands for disabled people using Google Assistant. In: 2020 International Conference on Smart Technology and Applications (ICoSTA), 1–6. IEEE (2020)
13. Yue, C.Z., Ping, S.: Voice activated smart home design and implementation. In: 2017 2nd International Conference on Frontiers of Sensors Technologies (ICFST), pp. 489–492 (2017)
14. Mtshali, P., Khubisa, F.: A smart home appliance control system for physically disabled people. In: 2019 Conference on Information Communications Technology and Society (ICTAS), pp. 1–5. IEEE (2019)
15. Malavasi, M., et al.: An innovative speech-based interface to control AAL and IoT solutions to help people with speech and motor disability. In: Cavallo, F., Marletta, V., Monteriù, A., Siciliano, P. (eds.) ForItAAL 2016. LNEE, vol. 426, pp. 269–278. Springer, Cham (2016). https://doi.org/10.1007/978-3-319-54283-6_20
16. van den Bossche, A., et al.: Specifying an MQTT tree for a connected smart home. In: Mokhtari, M., Abdulrazak, B., Aloulou, H. (eds.) ICOST 2018. LNCS, vol. 10898, pp. 236–246. Springer, Cham (2018). https://doi.org/10.1007/978-3-319-94523-1_21

Interaction Techniques, Platforms and Metaphors for Universal Access

Haptic Feedback to Support the Conceptualization of the Shape of Virtual Objects: An Exploratory Study

S. Ceccacci[1](✉), C. Gentilozzi[2], A. Marfoglia[1], T. Santilli[1], M. Mengoni[3], S. A. Capellini[4], and C. Giaconi[1]

[1] Department of Education, Cultural Heritage and Tourism, University of Macerata, Macerata, Italy
{silvia.ceccacci,alessandra.marfoglia,t.santilli1, catia.giaconi}@unimc.it

[2] Department of Science of Education, University Niccolò Cusano, Roma, Italy
chiara.gentilozzi@unicusano.it

[3] Department of Industrial Engineering and Mathematical Science, Università Politecnica delle Marche, Ancona, Italy
m.mengoni@univpm.it

[4] Departamento de Fonoaudiologia, São Paulo State University "Júlio de Mesquita Filho", UNESP, São Paulo, Brazil
sacap@uol.com.br

Abstract. Virtual museum systems have been shown to play a key role in enhancing visitor's experience and increasing the accessibility of cultural artifacts. In this context, the use of haptic interfaces based on force feedback could increase the level of immersivity of these systems and the quality of the interaction between visitors and cultural artifacts, introducing tactile information that could enrich the experience of all people, also in the case of visitors with disability. However, HD present limits concerning the ease of use of the device. This paper provides the results of an exploratory research carried out within the Research center of Teaching and learning, Disability and Educational Technology of the University of Macerata (TIncTec), consisting in two studies. Study 1 aims to analyze the learning performance of people with and without disabilities concerning this device. Study 2 aims to assess whether HD can provide useful support for conceptualizing the shape of virtual objects. To this end, we considered the 6 DoF high fidelity force feedback Geomagic Touch X by 3D system. A total of 30 people has been involved, including both children and adults with and without disabilities. The considered VR applications were developed in Unity 3D, using the 3D Systems Openhaptics Unity Plugin. The results provide useful insights for the design of future HD-based applications, showing how haptic technology can properly support visitors with disability in virtual museum environments in an inclusive perspective.

Keywords: Haptic Interfaces · Force Feedback · XR Technologies · Cultural Heritage · Accessibility · Inclusive Museum · Virtual Museum · Special Education

M. Antona and C. Stephanidis (Eds.): HCII 2023, LNCS 14020, pp. 215–228, 2023.
https://doi.org/10.1007/978-3-031-35681-0_14

1 Introduction

In the last thirty years, the relationship between museums, societies and communities has been evolving and leaning towards an increasing centrality of visitors' experience, enhancing immersive dimensions that can engage visitors, especially through the use of virtual reality technologies [1]. Scientific literature [1–9] has shown that the application of such tools in the field of cultural heritage plays a key role in attracting visitors, enhancing their experience and increasing the accessibility of cultural artifacts and artworks. On the other hand, these technologies might not represent the best solution to all people: they could result as cumbersome, distracting, or ineffective to visitors who are not familiar with technology [10]. The aforementioned issues could lead to situations in which technology is an obstacle to the cultural heritage accessibility. In this context, the use of force feedback devices (such as haptic tools) can increase the level of immersivity in virtual environments and the quality of the interaction between the visitor and the virtual artifact. Indeed, force feedback devices introduce tactile information that enriches the exploration of virtual objects, as well as the level of visitors' engagement and virtual reality (VR) system's accessibility [11]. Therefore, haptic device technology can also increase the level of cultural inclusion, since the level of inclusivity that people with disability can experience is connected to the number of participation occasions in cultural and social contexts [9], enhancing visitors' experience.

In this context, this study aims at the evaluation of haptic instrumentation focusing on the educational relationship and inclusion.

2 Research Background

Haptic technology can simulate the sense of touch in a virtual environment by applying a force or vibration to the user that simulates a tactile sensation when virtually coming into contact with a virtual object [12]. The virtual object is often a polygonal mesh with a texture which can be manipulated and explored through movements in different degrees of freedom (DoF) [13]. Concerning the domain of cultural heritage, tactile information (such as weight, roughness, etc.) could integrate visual perception [14] as discussed in several studies [12, 15–17]. Therefore, haptic devices can potentially widen the accessibility of cultural artifacts and artworks, allowing a greater level of interaction and inclusion [12, 18]. In fact, if the combination of audio and visual information paved the way for overcoming verbal communication barriers [19], haptic technology can provide a medium for learning by doing, enriching the environment presented through visual and auditory modalities [19].

Though haptic devices can be an asset for a broader cultural heritage fruition [11], scientific literature [20–27] has mostly focused on its use in the military, medical and industrial fields. This situation leads to a very limited number of studies that analyse their potential application in formal and informal educational contexts, such as museums and cultural spaces [14, 15, 18, 28–31].

To the best of our knowledge, no study has focused on studying the impact of such technologies on the experience of people with disabilities. Yet, some studies [32] dogmatically presume an unquestionable benefit to people with disabilities, though they do not support their statements with references or scientific proof. Concerning formal education, no study has explored the possibility of applying HD to support the conceptualisation of objects' shape yet. While a few studies [11, 33, 34] have explored the use of HD to enhance the interaction of visitors with archaeological finds and digitally reproduced artifacts, one might need to consider that, in order to ensure an authentic and inclusive interaction with the digital object (also in the case of cultural artifacts), the haptic feedback needs to adequately support the perception and conceptualization of shapes, also in the case of people with disabilities.

As stated in [35], no study has analysed the technological solutions developed in tactile museums yet, where real and virtual dimensions coexist, engaging the visitors to test their perception. This gap is also motivated by the scarcity of applications on a vast scale [14]. To this end, it is possible to acknowledge studies and applications that have combined visualisation technologies with tactile technologies, such as the Museum of Pure Form [36, 37] or the Museum of Gold in Bogota [38]. Other studies and applications aim at reducing the distance between the visitor and the artwork, as "The interactive Art Museum" application created by the University of Southern California [39], or the 2D mouse created by the University of Glasgow [14], and, lastly, the "Probos™ Console Touch & Discover Systems" developed by the Manchester Museum [40].

The current limits of haptic technology in the exploration of shapes are two. The first one concerns the necessity of training the device, which one might find excessively time consuming. The second one is related to the risk of losing contact with the object while navigating the areas that present discontinuities in surface curving (for instance, sharp edges or small curving radiuses). It seems reasonable to question to which degree such limits influence the level of accessibility in the cultural experience of people with disabilities and investigate their independence and autonomy in the use of haptic devices.

In this context, this study focuses on force feedback haptic devices, with two major research objectives. The first one consists in assessing the ease of learning of this technology by people with disabilities. Secondly, this research aims at assessing the capability of this technology to support the conceptualisation of objects' shapes.

3 Exploratory Research Protocol

Two exploratory studies have been carried out within the Research center of Teaching and learning, Inclusion, Disability, and Educational Technology (TIncTec) of the University of Macerata, respectively with the aims to determine whether:

- Learning to use a commercially available force feedback haptic device based on stilus to interact with virtual objects is easy for people with disabilities;
- Haptic feedback can provide useful support for conceptualizing the shape of virtual objects.

To this end, we considered the 6 DoF high fidelity force feedback Geomagic Touch X by 3D system [41]. A total of 30 people has been involved, including both children and adults with and without disabilities. In both studies, people were asked to interact with the haptic device to navigate/manipulate virtual objects displayed on a Philips Led 24" full HD pc monitor while seated at a height-adjustable desk to ensure maximum comfort during interaction.

The considered VR applications were developed in Unity 3D [42], using the 3D Systems Openhaptics Unity Plugin [43]. They enable users to interact with virtual objects by means of a virtual probe: a virtual stylus that moves solid with the haptic device handpiece. Once the point of the stylus comes into contact with the virtual object, the Touch X returns force feedback to the user who is holding the pen through the mechanical actuators of the device, thus simulating the "collision" of the stylus with the surface of the virtual object and the resistance that the virtual material itself opposes, based on the action-reaction principle. Moreover, by pushing the button situated on the device handpiece, it is possible to "attach" the virtual probe to the virtual object at the point of contact. In this way, it is possible to move the virtual object inside the virtual scene, by simply moving the handpiece along the three axes (x, y, z) or through pitch, roll and yaw angles. All of the experiments have been audio and video recorded.

3.1 Study 1

The first study concerns training and aims at comparing the learning performance observed in the case of people with and without disabilities. Users were explained how to interact with the virtual object through the haptic device and were asked to interact with it in order to become familiar with two basic operations: navigation and object manipulation. As aesthetic experience can positively affect learning outcome, improving learning engagement and motivation [44, 45], to foster people's learning motivation, the considered virtual objects were high-fidelity digital copies of archaeological artifacts (Fig. 1), realized based on the method described in [46].

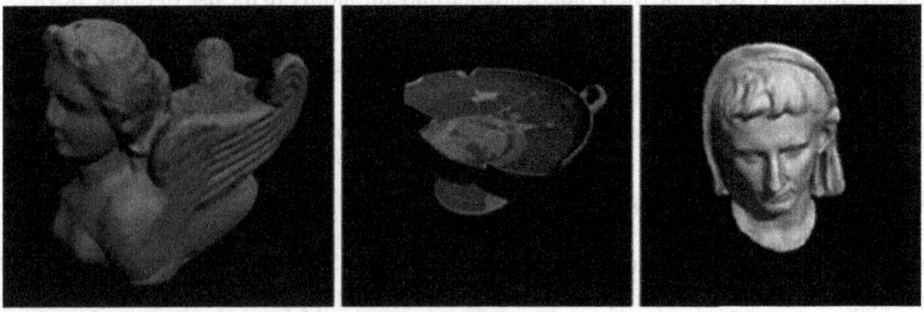

Fig. 1. Digital copies of archeological finds, part of the collection of the "Museo Archeologico Nazionale delle Marche", used during the training.

The ease of learning of the tool has been qualitatively analyzed through a Video Interaction Analysis (VIA) [47] conducted by three independent experts in human-computer interaction, considering the evaluation items reported in Table 1.

Table 1. Evaluation Criteria considered for VIA

Evaluation Criteria	Evaluation Items
Learning Effectiveness	Number of repetitions of the explanation % time spent navigating independently/unsupported Number of requests for support
Learning Efficiency	Total time of explanation Time to learn how to navigate the object Time to learn how to manipulate the object
Satisfaction	Results provided by Emotion Recognition system User's comments

3.2 Study 2

The second study aims at investigating whether the interaction with virtual objects via the haptic device, compared to the interaction with physical objects, can support the conceptualization of objects' shapes. Both simple (i.e., circle, triangle, square) and complex (i.e., five-pointed star) plane shapes have been considered.

The study was conducted according to a repeated-measure design. Each person interacted with all five shapes related materials. The order through which the shapes were proposed was counterbalanced across subjects. For each shape, involved people were asked to interact with:

- Traditional typhlo-didactic materials, reproducing shapes in relief, commonly used to support the conceptualization of the considered plane geometric forms (Fig. 2);
- Digital copies of the typhlo-didactic materials (Fig. 3, A e B) and virtual objects that reproduce the typhlo-didactic materials "in negative", by means of concavities instead of reliefs (Fig. 3, a e b).

Fig. 2. Example of typhlo-didactic materials of "Federazione Nazionale delle Istituzioni Pro Ciechi" used to support the conceptualization of the shape of a five-pointed star.

For each shape, people were asked at first to freehand draw it. Then, they were asked to:

- interact with the three considered typhlo-didactic materials (Fig. 2);
- assess for each typhlo-didactic material which degree the sensation originating from the interaction would recall the idea of the considered shape by using a 1–5 Likert Scale (1 corresponding to a complete absence of recall sensation and 5 corresponding to the greatest recall sensation);
- determine, among the proposed materials, which one would provide the greatest recall sensation;
- interact with the virtual objects reproducing each considered typhlo-didactic materials both in relief and in negative;
- assess for each digital typhlo-didactic materials (in relief and in negative) to which degree the sensation originating from the interaction would recall the idea of the considered shape by using a 1–5 Likert Scale (1 corresponding to a complete absence of recall sensation and 5 corresponding to the greatest recall sensation);
- asses which among the considering relief-negative couple of digital typhlo-didactic materials would provide the greatest recall sensation;
- determine, among all the considering digital typhlo-didactic materials, which one would provide the greatest recall sensation;
- determine, among the preferred physical and digital typhlo-didactic materials, which one would provide the greatest recall sensation.

Finally, the subjects were asked to handsfree draw again the considered shape.

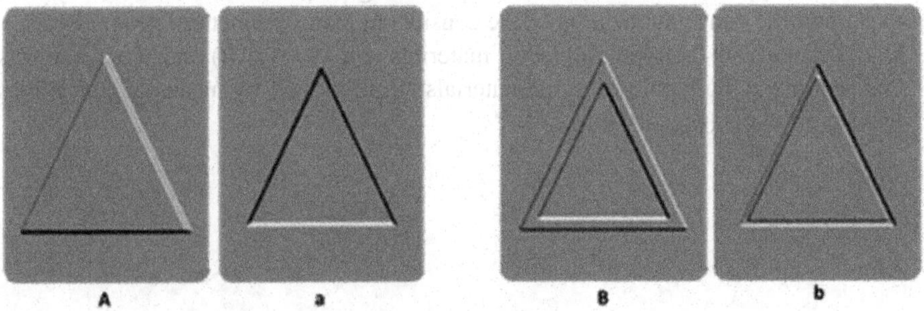

Fig. 3. Example of digital copies of typhlo-didactic materials used to support the conceptualization of the shape of a triangle (images A and B), and virtual objects that reproduce the same typhlo-didactics materials "in negative" (images a and b).

3.3 Participants

Recruitment activities took place during the first edition of InclusionL@b, a week-long workshop open to students with dsa and disabilities, families, managers and personal services coordinators, organized at the initiative of the TIncTec Center of the University of Macerata. A total of 32 subjects have been recruited as participants to the experiment, with 24 of them completing the training. Specifically, three age ranges were considered: 11 children from 10 to 14 years, (1 with a mild intellectual disability and 2 with Specific Learning Disorders), 12 adolescents from 14 to 17 (2 with a mild intellectual disability and 2 with Specific Learning Disorders) and 9 adults from 18 to 46 years (1 with a physical disability).

4 Results and Discussion

4.1 Study 1

Repeated-measure ANOVA was performed on the data to test the learning performances observed in the case of people with and without disabilities, taking into consideration respectively the age and the presence of disability in the test subjects.

In general, no statistically significant differences were observed between the three groups in relation to the efficacy of the learning process (duration of instruction-giving, amount of time needed to get familiar with the navigation and manipulation controls). Instead, concerning the efficiency of the learning process, a statistically significant difference emerged in relation to the number of adaptations of the instruction-giving, $F(2, 21) = 3.790$, $p = .039$.

Tukey HSD test for multiple comparisons has highlighted how the mean value of instruction-giving adaptations requested by children is different from the one requested by adolescents ($p = .021$, 95% C.I. = [0.39, 4.22]) and the one requested by adults ($p = .030$, 95% C.I. = [0.23, 3.96]). Indeed, as Table 2 reports, children and adolescents needed a higher number of adaptations of the instruction-giving compared to adults.

On the other hand, concerning the level of autonomy and need of support, no significant differences were noticed among the groups.

The comparison of performance data of participants with and without disabilities highlights statistically significant differences both in terms of efficacy and efficiency of the learning process.

Table 2. Comparison of children, adolescents and adults performance.

	Children		Adolescents		Adults	
Evaluation Criteria	M	SD	M	SD	M	SD
Learning efficacy						
Number of adaptations	4	1,55	4	2,29	2	1,13
% autonomy time	0,51	0,29	0,63	0,21	0,57	0,3
Number of support requests	4	1,31	3	1,74	2	1,41
Learning efficiency						
Amount of instruction-giving time	226	89,56	164	89,59	186	91,82
Amount of navigation time	164	75,59	162	82,77	129	60,99
Amount of manipulation time	150	73,07	124	57,53	127	36,36

Specifically, results show a statistically significant difference concerning:

- the number of instruction-giving adaptations, $F(1, 31) = 3.583$, $p = .038$;
- the number of support requests, $F(1, 31) = 8.040$, $p = .008$;
- the amount of time required to learn the navigation control, $F(1, 31) = 4.721$, $p < 0.038$;
- the amount of time required to learn the manipulation control, $F(1, 31) = 3.583$, $p = .033$.

As one might notice by examining data reported in Table 3, people with disability needed a deeper instruction-giving adaptation, a higher number of support interventions during navigation, and a higher amount of time to learn how to navigate and manipulate the objects using the haptic device, on average.

No statistically significant differences have emerged in relation to the overall duration of the instruction-giving and the percentage of time during which the device was utilised independently.

The qualitative analysis underlines how experts focused on interaction and communication, observing a strong interest and active engagement of all participants in general.

Table 3. Comparison of people with and without disability performances

	People without disability		People with disability	
Evaluation Criteria	M	SD	M	SD
Learning efficacy				
Number of adaptations	3	1,98	5	3,5
% autonomy time	0,57	0	0,53	0,17
Number of support requests	3	1,6	6	4,95
Learning efficiency				
Amount of instruction-giving time	191	90,27	277	235,79
Amount of navigation time	153	73,13	243	162,16
Amount of manipulation time	127	58,94	192	124,38

Concerning children without disability, a simple and clear language was used, with a colloquial and friendly communication style. The instruction-giving was adapted to highlight the playful aspect of the interaction with the device and create a positive environment, in order to support their attention holding. However, data shows how children required more support from researchers conducting the experiment.

Concerning adolescents and adults, a more specific language was used. With the group of adolescents, a historical explanation and references to the objects' peculiarities (such as the sphynx's grooved wings) enriched the instruction-giving to stimulate their motivation and interest. Such support was not needed by adults, leading to a shorter duration of the instruction-giving phase, as well as a smaller amount of learning time compared to the other groups. Adults showed more homogeneous results in the attention holding and engagement levels.

Concerning people with disability, a colloquial style and specific language was used based on the needs of the person. Results show a good level of participation, a significantly higher amount of time required to learn how to use the device and number of support requests compared to the other groups.

Posture and grasping of the handle of the device was also analysed: people with disability generally presented more cases of incorrect grasping of the handle.

4.2 Study 2

A two-factors Repeated-measure ANOVA was performed to analyse the impact of the factor "typhlo-didactic material" (i.e., Material 1: physical objects; Material 2: virtual copies; Material 3: virtual copies "in negative") and of the factor "shape" (i.e., circle, triangle, square and five-pointed star) on the conceptualisation of objects' shapes. Since no statistically significant differences were detected taking into consideration the age and the presence of disability in the test subjects, the data are analyzed and presented as a whole. Results revealed that there was a statistically significant interaction between the effects of typhlo-didactic material and shape, $F(6, 138) = 2.277$, $p < .040$. (Fig. 4).

Simple main effects analysis showed that typhlo-didactic material did have a statistically significant effect on the conceptualisation of the objects' shapes, $F(2, 46) = 5.946$, $p = 0.005$. Post hoc analysis with a Bonferroni adjustment revealed that Material 3 ($M = 4.104$, $SD = 0.096$) supported the conceptualization significantly better than Material 1, (Mean diff = 0.453, 95% C.I. [0.055, 0.852], $p = .022$), while there is no significant difference between Material 3 and Material 1. However, post hoc analysis with a Bonferroni adjustment does not reveal statistically significant difference between shapes.

These results suggest the participants have favoured the virtual object over the real object (or vice versa) depending on the shape they were interacting with. As the diagram reported in Fig. 1 shows, the virtual objects that reproduce the typhlo-didactic materials "in negative" provided the greatest recall sensation for shape 1, 2 and 3 (respectively circle, triangle and square). Indeed, one might explain these results by considering that the negative digital reproduction, by presenting concavities, makes it easier for the participant to navigate the object following its shape: the edge of the virtual probe remains "stuck" in the digital groove, "sliding" along its lengths. The only case in which the physical material was preferred by the participants is in the conceptualization of the five-pointed star shape. One might explain this exception by considering that the star, being a more complex and discontinuous shape, presents higher chances for the participant of losing contact with the virtual object, impeding a fluid navigation of the shape.

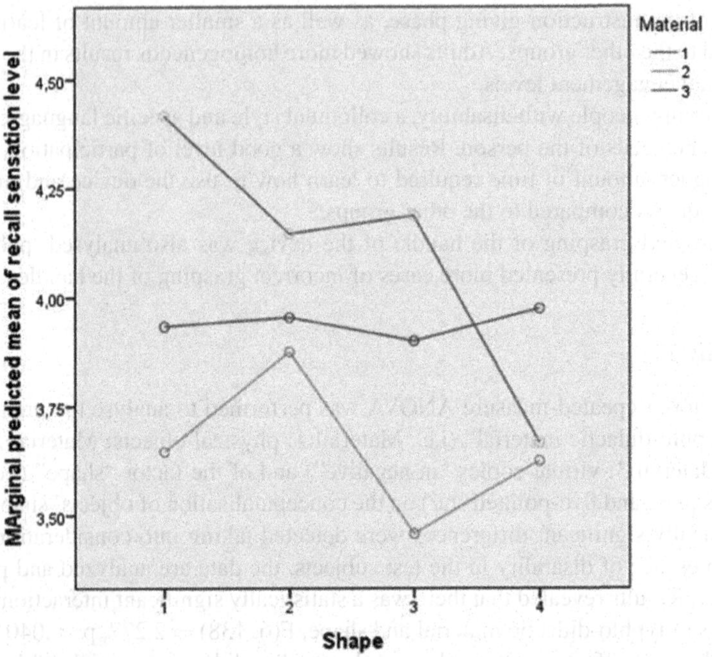

Fig. 4. Marginal predicted mean of recall sensation level of the three materials (i.e., Material 1: traditional typhlo-didactic materials reproducing shapes in relief; Material 2: digital copies of typhlo-didactic materials; Material 3: virtual reproduction "in negative" by means of concavities instead of reliefs) based on the four shapes.

5 Conclusion and Perspectives

The presented explorative research highlights how virtual environments can create original forms of interaction, fostering active participation and broader cultural fruition. Therefore, museum experience can respond to an increasingly heterogeneous audience when it aims at increasing cultural accessibility, thanks to the utilisation of new languages, never seen interaction forms and personalised solutions [8, 9, 34, 48–52]. Concerning the technological aspects, the thoughtful and not invasive integration of technological devices in museum paths poses the necessity of exploiting their potential through the creation of quality content that can be implemented in strategies that aim at fulfilling the visitors' needs and enhance cultural heritage [8, 49, 53].

In order to be credible, a museum that implements digital tools must acknowledge the premise that technology can never represent an end, but rather a means through which contents can be vehiculated and culture can be spread in innovative ways. Being aware that digital environments could never replace the real visit of a museum, such environments can contribute to increasing cultural accessibility and communicate cultural information to a broader audience. Therefore, the physical fruition of cultural heritage, favouring technology-mediated approaches, is not replaced, but rather vehiculated in a different way to stimulate the audience's interest and curiosity [7, 9, 54]. In conclusion, virtual museums can have a real impact in terms of promotion of social inclusion if the accessibility requirements meet potential forms of personalisation, also through the use of haptic devices and tactile information.

Concerning future perspectives, results highlight how haptic technology could properly support the conceptualisation of objects' shape, opening up the possibility of using haptic devices to increase accessibility for people with low vision or blindness. Nevertheless, our exploratory research shows the current limits of this technology, consisting in the risk of losing contact with the virtual object. Such limits could be overcome by appropriately designing the virtual objects to facilitate their navigation and manipulation. In terms of practical use of this technology, our study underlines that the application of haptic devices in museum contexts requires the presence of qualified operators who are able to guide visitors and teach them how to interact with the device. This need comes from the evident difference between the interaction modalities of haptic devices and the other interfaces that people are generally used to come to contact with ordinarily. Therefore, further research is needed to identify possible guidelines for the design of usable software applications. One possible way to achieve this goal may be through the implementation processes of co-design with people with disabilities. In fact, as suggested by [9], this would contribute to a diffusion of sensitivity and thus accessibility of the contexts themselves, as well as to the implementation of inclusive processes.

References

1. Neuburger, L., Egger, R.: An afternoon at the museum: through the lens of augmented reality. Information and communication technologies in tourism. In: Proceedings of the International Conference in Rome, Italy, 24–26 January 2017, pp. 241–254 (2017)
2. Noh, Z., Sunar, M.S., Pan, Z.: A review on augmented reality for virtual heritage system. In: International Conference on Technologies for E-Learning and Digital Entertainment (2009)
3. Carrozzino, M., Bergamasco, M.: Beyond virtual museums: Experiencing immersive virtual reality in real museums. J. Cult. Herit. **11**(4), 452–458 (2010)
4. Rua, H., Alvito, P.: Living the past: 3D models, virtual reality and game engines as tools for supporting archaeology and the reconstruction of cultural heritage–the case-study of the Roman villa of Casal de Freiria. J. Archaeol. Sci. **38**(12), 3296–3308 (2011)
5. McCall, V., Gray, C.: Museums and the 'new museology': theory, practice and organisational change. Museum Manage. Curatorship **29**(1), 19–35 (2014)
6. He, Z., Wu, L., Li, X.R.: When art meets tech: the role of augmented reality in enhancing museum experiences and purchase intentions. Tour. Manage. **68**, 127–139 (2018)
7. Leopardi, A., et al.: X-reality technologies for museums: a comparative evaluation based on presence and visitors experience through user studies. J. Cult. Herit. **47**, 188–198 (2020)
8. Giaconi, C., Ascenzi, A., Del Bianco, N., D'Angelo, I., Capellini, S.A.: Virtual and augmented reality for the cultural accessibility of people with autism spectrum disorders: a pilot study. Int. J. Inclusive Museum **14**(1), 95–106 (2021)
9. Shogren, K.A., Caldarelli, A., Del Bianco, N., D'Angelo, I., Giaconi, C.: Co designing inclusive museum itineraries with people with disabilities: a case study from self-determination. Educ. Sci. Soc. **2**, 214–226 (2022)
10. Leopardi, A., Ceccacci, S., Mengoni, M.: A New paradigm for the enjoyment and exploitation of cultural heritage based on spatial augmented reality: the case of the ducal palace of Urbino. In: Proceedings of the ASME 2021 International Design Engineering Technical Conferences and Computers and Information in Engineering Conference, vol. 2, pp. 1–8 (2021)

11. Ceccacci, S., Generosi, A., Leopardi, A., Mengoni, M., Mandorli, A.F.: The role of haptic feedback and gamification in virtual museum systems. J. Comput. Cultural Heritage (JOCCH) **14**(3), 1–14 (2021)
12. Butler, M., Neave, P.: Object appreciation through haptic interaction. In: Hello! Where are you in the landscape of educational technology? Proceedings Ascilite Melbourne 2008 (Melbourne, VIC), pp. 133–141 (2008)
13. Bergamasco, M., Frisoli, A., Barbagli, F.: Haptics technologies and cultural heritage applications. In: Proceedings of Computer Animation 2002 (CA 2002), pp. 25–32. IEEE (2002)
14. Brewster, S.A.: The impact of haptic 'touching' technology on cultural applications. In: Hemsley, J., Cappellini, V., Stanke, G. (eds.) Digital Applications for Cultural Heritage Institutions. Routledge, London (2005)
15. Brogni, B.A., Avizzano, C.A., Evangelista, C., Bergamasco, M.: Technological approach for cultural heritage: augmented reality. In: 8th IEEE International Workshop on Robot and Human Interaction. RO-MAN 1999 (Cat. No. 99TH8483), pp. 206–212. IEEE (1999)
16. Dettori, A., et al.: Art Touch with CREATE haptic interface. In: ICAR Proceedings, International Conference on Advanced Robotics, p. 269 (2003)
17. Reuter, P., Riviere, G., Couture, N., Mahut, S., Espinasse, L.: ArcheoTUI—driving virtual reassemblies with tangible 3D interaction. J. Comput. Cultural Heritage (JOCCH) **3**(2), 1–13 (2010)
18. Comes, R.: Haptic devices and tactile experiences in museum exhibitions. J. Ancient History Archaeol. **3**(4) (2016)
19. Hamza-Lup, F.G., Stanescu, I.A.: The haptic paradigm in education: challenges and case studies. Internet High. Educ. **13**(1–2), 78–81 (2010)
20. Okamura, A.M.: Methods for haptic feedback in teleoperated robot-assisted surgery. Ind. Robot. **31**(6), 499–508 (2004)
21. Bethea, B.T., et al.: Application of haptic feedback to robotic surgery. J. Laparoendosc. Adv. Surg. Tech. **14**(3), 191–195 (2004)
22. Okamura, A.M.: Haptic feedback in robot-assisted minimally invasive surgery. Curr. Opin. Urol. **19**(1), 102–107 (2009)
23. Panait, L., Akkary, E., Bell, R.L., Roberts, K.E., Dudrick, S.J., Duffy, A.J.: The role of haptic feedback in laparoscopic simulation training. J. Surg. Res. **156**(2), 312–316 (2009)
24. Aziz, F.A., Mousavi, M.: A review of haptic feedback in virtual reality for manufacturing industry. J. Mech. Eng. **40**(1), 68–71 (2009)
25. Bolopion, A., Régnier, S.: A review of haptic feedback teleoperation systems for micromanipulation and microassembly. IEEE Trans. Autom. Sci. Eng. **10**(3), 496–502 (2013)
26. Overtoom, E.M., Horeman, T., Jansen, F.W., Dankelman, J., Schreuder, H.W.R.: Haptic feedback, force feedback, and force-sensing in simulation training for laparoscopy: a systematic overview. J. Surg. Educ. **76**(1), 242–261 (2019)
27. El Rassi, I., El Rassi, J.M.: A review of haptic feedback in tele-operated robotic surgery. J. Med. Eng. Technol. **44**(5), 247–254 (2020)
28. Bergamasco, M., Brogni, A., Frisoli, A., Salvini, F., Vignoni, M., Anna, S.S.S.: Tactual exploration in cultural heritage. XIV Round Table Computer-Aided Egyptology, Pisa (IE2002) (2002)
29. Petrelli, D., Ciolfi, L., Van Dijk, D., Hornecker, E., Not, E., Schmidt, A.: Integrating material and digital: a new way for cultural heritage. Interactions **20**(4), 58–63 (2013)
30. Vignoni, M.: Tactual Exploration in Cultural Heritage. XIV Round Table Computer-Aided Egyptology (2002)
31. Marto, A., Gonçalves, A., Melo, M., Bessa, M.: A survey of multisensory VR and AR applications for cultural heritage. Comput. Graph. **102**, 426–440 (2022)

32. Sreeni, K.G., Priyadarshini, K., Praseedha, A.K., Chaudhuri, S. (2012). Haptic rendering of cultural heritage objects at different scales. In: Isokoski, P., Springare, J. (eds.) Haptics: Perception, Devices, Mobility, and Communication. EuroHaptics 2012. LNCS, vol. 7282. Springer, Berlin, Heidelberg. https://doi.org/10.1007/978-3-642-31401-8_45
33. Krumpen, S., Klein, R., Weinmann, M.: Towards tangible cultural heritage experiences—enriching VR-based object inspection with haptic feedback. J. Comput. Cultural Heritage **15**(1), 1–17 (2021)
34. Vi, C.T., Ablart, D., Gatti, E., Velasco, C., Obrist, M.: Not just seeing, but also feeling art: Mid-air haptic experiences integrated in a multisensory art exhibition. Int. J. Hum. Comput. Stud. **108**, 1–14 (2017)
35. Asano, T., Ishibashi, Y., Minezawa, S., Fujimoto, M.: Surveys of exhibition planners and visitors about a distributed haptic museum. In: Proceedings of the 2005 ACM SIGCHI International Conference on Advances in Computer Entertainment Technology, pp. 246–249 (2005)
36. Grow, D.I., Verner, L.N., Okamura, A.M.: Educational Haptics. In: AAAI Spring Symposium: Semantic Scientific Knowledge Integration (2007)
37. Tecchia F., Ruffaldi E., Frisoli A., Bergamasco M., Carrozzino M.: Multimodal interaction for the Web. In: Trant, J., Bearman, D. (eds.) Museums and the Web 2007: Proceedings, Toronto: Archives & Museum Informatics (2007)
38. Figueroa P., et al.: Multi-modal exploration of small artifacts: an exhibition at the Gold Museum in Bogota. In: Proceedings of the 16th ACM Symposium on Virtual Reality Software and Technology, pp. 67–74 (2009)
39. Brewster S.A.: The impact of haptic 'Touching' technology on cultural applications. In: Proceedings of EVA 2001, pp. 1–14 (2001)
40. Reichinger, A., Svenja Schröder, S., Löw, C.: Spaghetti, sink and sarcophagus: design explorations of tactile artworks for visually impaired people. In: Proceedings of the 9th Nordic Conference on Human-Computer Interaction, pp. 1–6 (2016)
41. 3D System, Touch X. https://www.3dsystems.com/haptics-devices/touch-x/specifications. Accessed 7 Nov 2022
42. Unity 3D. https://unity.com/. Accessed 07 Nov 2022
43. 3D Systems Openhaptics Unity Plugin. https://assetstore.unity.com/packages/tools/integration/3d-systems-openhaptics-unity-plugin-134024. Accessed 07 Nov 2022
44. Alexiou, A., Schippers, M.C.: Digital game elements, user experience and learning: a conceptual framework. Educ. Inf. Technol. **23**(6), 2545–2567 (2018). https://doi.org/10.1007/s10639-018-9730-6
45. Alexiou, A., Schippers, M.C., Oshri, I., Angelopoulos, S.: Narrative and aesthetics as antecedents of perceived learning in serious games. Information Technology & People (2020)
46. Mengoni, M., Leopardi, A.: An exploratory study on the application of reverse engineering in the field of small archaeological artifacts. Comput. Aided Design Appl. **16**(6), 1209–1226 (2019)
47. Jordan, B., Henderson, A.: Interaction analysis: foundations and practice. J. Learn. Sci. **4**, 39–103 (1995)
48. Sandell, R.: Museums, Society, Inequality. Routledge, London (2003)
49. Giaconi, C., Del Bianco, N., D'Angelo, I., Halwany, S., Aparecida, S.A.: Cultural accessibility of people with Intellectual disabilities: a pilot study in Italy. JESET **7**(1), 17–26 (2021)
50. Bortolotti, E., Paoletti, G.: Disabilità intellettiva e accessibilità culturale. Una proposta per facilitare l'accesso alle informazioni in ambito museale. Italian J. Spec. Educ. Inclusion **9**(2), 94–104 (2021)
51. Capomagi, G., Santoro, A., D'Angelo, I., Del Bianco, N., Capellini, S.A., Giaconi, C.: L'arte a occhi chiusi. Percezione tattile ed educazione artistica, in La formazione dell'insegnante

specializzato nella scuola dell'infanzia e primaria. Esperienze e progetti a confronto, Edizioni Accademiche Italiane, Baubassin, pp. 132–144 (2021)
52. Ciccolungo B., et al.: Arte e Inclusione: un connubio possibile. In: Didattica Inclusiva nella scuola secondaria di primo e secondo grado. Esperienze e progetti in rete, Edizioni Accademiche Italiane, Baubassin, pp. 61–79 (2023)
53. Ibem, E.O., Oni, O.O., Umoren, E., Ejiga, J.: An appraisal of universal design compliance of museum buildings in Southwest Nigeria. Int. J. Appl. Eng. Res. **12**(23), 13731–13741 (2017)
54. Lisney, E., Bowen, J.P., Hearn, K., Zedda, M.: Museums and technology: being inclusive helps accessibility for all. Museum J. **56**(3), 353–361 (2013)

Moving Towards and Reaching a 3-D Target by Embodied Guidance: Parsimonious Vs Explicit Sound Metaphors

Coline Fons[1,2](✉), Sylvain Huet[2], Denis Pellerin[2], Silvain Gerber[2], and Christian Graff[1]

[1] Univ. Grenoble Alpes, Univ. Savoie Mont-Blanc, CNRS, LPNC, 38000 Grenoble, France
{coline.fons,christian.graff}@univ-grenoble-alpes.fr

[2] Univ. Grenoble Alpes, CNRS, Grenoble INP, GIPSA-lab, 38000 Grenoble, France
{coline.fons,sylvain.huet,denis.pellerin,silvain.gerber}@gipsa-lab.grenoble-inp.fr

Abstract. Sensory Substitution Devices (SSDs) assist Visually Impaired People (VIP) by providing information usually acquired by vision through another functional sensory modality. Here, we evaluate a SSD that aims to guide visually impaired people to a target by converting spatial information into sound. A balance must be struck between parsimonious and explicit guidance, so that it is precise but not imposing an excessive cognitive load. Here, we express the deviation from the target to the participant's hand. We compared three sound metaphors: 1) Binary (BI) gives only the right direction by white noise, 2) Angle-to-Pitch (AP) converts the 3-D angular deviation between a pointed direction and the right direction into sound pitch according to a continuous function, 3) Dissociated Vertical-Horizontal (DVH) dissociates the 3-D deviation into two dimensions, using pitch to provide the angular deviation projected on the horizontal plane (a continuous metaphor) and a superimposed white noise to indicate the right height (a binary metaphor). We conducted "hot and cold game" type tests in a 3-D environment. Participants, with eyes closed, moved to search and reach virtual spheres with their index finger. Each metaphor was evaluated by the time taken to reach the target, and by a questionnaire. The results show the advantage of AP over BI: it allowed a faster target hit and was considered easier to use, more efficient, and more comfortable than BI. They also show an advantage of the DVH metaphor over AP: the times to target hit were shorter, and it was considered easier to use than AP. The DVH metaphor is a good trade-off between parsimonious (use of binary information) and explicit (dissociation of the two axes) guidance. It is a first step towards smartphone SSDs applications to help find objects in a situation of visual impairment.

Keywords: Sensory Substitution · Blindness · 3-D Target Reaching · Sound Metaphor · Virtual Prototyping · Spatial Cognition · Hand Guidance

M. Antona and C. Stephanidis (Eds.): HCII 2023, LNCS 14020, pp. 229–243, 2023.
https://doi.org/10.1007/978-3-031-35681-0_15

1 Introduction

Visually Impaired People (VIP) interact with their spatial environment through their other senses, such as hearing or touch. But some tasks, including navigation or finding and reaching an object, are challenging without assistance. There is a need to develop accessible assistive technologies for VIP. Various Sensory Substitution Devices (SSDs) have been created to address this need. They provide through another functional sensory modality information captured by an artificial sensor. SSDs can be implemented within navigation applications for smartphones using GPS or synthesizing texts vocally. Navigation tasks are the main focus of most SSDs and often include obstacle avoidance [1,8,9,15,20]. Here we focus on helping people reach a targeted object with their hand without vision, a task less explored in the literature. The target can be, for example, a door handle, a doorbell button, or an object on a shelf. We aim to create the most efficient and ergonomic sound guidance in 3-D space. Most guidance systems convert the deviation from the target to the manipulated sensor in either sound [4,9,10,26] or vibration [19,28]. Below, we present arguments for the choice of an egocentric frame of reference, and we will then examine how spatial information can be conveyed through sound guidance.

1.1 Frame of Reference

When designing a Sensory Substitution Device (SSD) for guidance, there is a choice of several reference frames in which the target is positioned. The frame of reference for the choice of spatial metrics to be encoded cannot ignore the body-specific logic of the motor and cognitive systems. For example, providing the whole pixel matrix of a depth scene [14] is useless for reaching a single point, and this data's overflow is difficult to interpret. Alternatively, providing only the absolute position of the target also leads to interpretation errors [2], even if the amount of data is reduced to the essential.

Most of the time, the spatial data to be transmitted to the VIPs is collected by one or more cameras. The captured images are used to extract the deviations from the target. The camera's position determines the frame of reference in which the spatial data is captured. Thus, some devices have a camera placed on the participant's head [5,9,22], while others position the camera on the hand or forearm of the participant [4,11,19]. Some combine the two approaches by using two cameras, one on the head and one on the hand [13,28], and use one or the other depending on the participant's progression through the task (distal guidance to navigate to the target, then proximal guidance to reach the target with the hand).

When the frame of reference is a camera, it is both the sensor (which collects the data) and the pointer (reference frame in which the deviations from the target are calculated). It is an allocentric frame of reference: the spatial data are encoded in relation to an object, the camera. In contrast, an egocentric frame of reference allows data to be encoded in reference to a coordinate system that places the user's body as the origin and defines the axes of the coordinates in relation to the user's body orientation [18]. For VIPs, an egocentric frame of reference is more effective [18]: due to the visual feedback deficit, it is indeed difficult for VIPs to match their smartphone's coordinates to their egocentric coordinate system.

An egocentric frame of reference would therefore seem more suitable for a SSD guiding a visually deprived person to a target. The best frame of reference could be the finger because the hand is central in an object reaching task. Here we express the deviations with respect to the hand that has to reach the object and not with respect to the sensor that provides the raw spatial data.

1.2 Sonic Guidance

Among the spatial information that can be sent to the user, the challenge is to provide the most useful and simple elements. Two categories of sounds can be used to convey spatial information: verbal description or sonification. Verbal description in a guidance task may correspond to instructions such as "turn right", "turn left", etc. [4,5,11,19,22,23,28]. However, verbal instructions are considered slow and cumbersome [13] since they disrupt the perception/action loop. Indeed, if the user moves the sensor too quickly, at the end of the verbal instruction, it may no longer be valid. Sonification, on the other hand, is the use of nonverbal sounds to convey information or perceptual data [16]. There are two kinds of sonification [16]. Spatial sonification consists in using the natural capacities of the auditory system to locate the position of a target by virtually rendering its position. This is a technique used in [5,9,10,13] to localize the target on the horizontal plane. Some [5,9–11,13,23] also rely on non-spatial sonification, which uses the physical characteristics of sounds, such as pitch, intensity, tempo, brightness, etc., to convey guidance information. The link between the input visual data and the output sounds is therefore metaphorical.

In their research on the process of sonification design for guidance tasks, Parseihian et al. [17] found an improvement in distance perception with non-spatial sonification compared to spatial sonification. They also advise to adapt the sonification strategy to the goal of the guidance task. Indeed, they found that participants in a target reaching task were more accurate with "strategies with reference" (adding a sound reference corresponding to the target) than with "basic strategies" (based on varying the basic perceptual attributes of the sound), whereas they were slower with "strategies with reference."

In their work on sonification in three-dimensional space, Ziemer et al. [24–27] identified several requisites for creating an accurate guidance system. One of them is to integrate the three spatial dimensions into a single auditory stream; another one is to allow them to be perceived orthogonally. Perceptual orthogonality means that if two information variables are sonified simultaneously, both can be interpreted, and if one variable changes, the change in sound can be attributed to its corresponding continuum and unambiguously interpreted. It should be taken into account that physically independent sound parameters are not necessarily orthogonal in perception (e.g., pitch and intensity). They also recommend using continuous dimensions and having a high perceptual resolution (which can be measured by the just-noticeable difference).

While considering these criteria, the user's cognitive load must also be taken into account. The criteria cited by Ziemer et al. [24–27] allow for the creation of a very precise sound guidance, but a balance must be struck between precision and ease of use for the user. Indeed, Ziemer et al. [24–27], taking these criteria into account, created a sonification with a single auditory stream but five psychoacoustic quantities varying continuously along the three dimensions. Having a single stream allows one to hear all the information at once, which allows precise guidance but could also be overwhelming and produce cognitive overload.

To obtain an efficient 3-D guidance but also to decrease the cognitive load and have a comfortable device, choices between parsimonious and explicit information have to be weighed:

- Encoding the three spatial dimensions explicitly (which requires to use several auditory metrics) OR reducing the number of encoded dimension to minimize the amount of information to be processed. In the latter case, the user must infer the implicit information from the information provided.
- Using a single auditory stream for the three dimensions to have all the information at once (no need to switch attention) OR using several separate streams to reduce the amount of information on each stream. In the latter case, the user needs to switch attention between streams.
- Using continuous OR using discrete scales.

Taking into account these different choices and the literature on the subject, we created three sound metaphors, which we compared in pairs:

- Comparison 1: Angle-to-Pitch (AP) VS Binary (BI). BI gives only binary information: sound when pointing in the right direction VS no sound. Studies have shown that simple binary sound cues are enough to create a guidance system [12]. AP gives a directional deviation in angle from the target, expressed by the pitch of the sound, in continuous scales. A single sound parameter is used to express a single global 3-D spatial metric. Each dimension can be inferred by the action-perception loop. AP has several qualities highlighted by Ziemer et al. [24–27]: dimensions integrated into a single stream, high perceptual resolution (pitch), and continuous scales. But the dimensions are not orthogonal: a single sound parameter is used to encode direction on both vertical and horizontal axes. It could imply more efforts to interpret the sonification, and thus a higher cognitive load. To avoid this, the directional deviations on the two axes can be separated into two parameters on a single sound stream, as suggested by Ziemer et al. [24–27]. But integrating several sound parameters on the same stream can lead to interpretation errors and cognitive overload.
- Comparison 2: AP VS Dissociated Vertical-Horizontal (DVH). With DVH, the deviation on the horizontal axis are coded on a continuous scale, by the

pitch of the sound. The deviation on the vertical axis is coded binary by the presence of a white noise of good height. Thus the two dimensions are orthogonal, the user can interpret them separately, which should simplify the sonification and make the guidance more accurate. The use of binary information should further facilitate the sonification and decrease the amount of data to integrate and therefore the cognitive load.

To compare these three metaphors we conducted "hot and cold game" type tests in a 3-D environment. Participants, with eyes closed, moved to search and reach virtual spheres with their index finger. Each metaphor was evaluated by the time taken to reach the target and by a questionnaire.

In the following, we will present the material and method used to conduct this experiment, along with the results, which we will discuss.

2 Methods

2.1 Participants

We conducted two comparisons. For Comparison 1, fourteen sighted participants and one VIP performed the target-reaching task with the first two metaphors: BI and AP. For Comparison 2, eight other sighted participants and one other VIP participant compared the AP metaphor and the DVH metaphor. Most participants were students participating for course credit, others were volunteers (other students, friends, and relatives). All gave informed consent before participating in the study.

2.2 Engineering

Tests take the form of a virtual game consisting in reaching spheres in a 3-D space with one's index finger (see Fig. 1). A Qualisys optical motion capture system locates reflectors fixed on the participant's body. Coordinates relative to the finger and elbow positions are transmitted from the acquisition computer running Qualisys Track Manager (QTM) to the pilot computer through the Virtual Reality Peripheral Network (VRPN) protocol. In the pilot computer, our C++ control software: 1) immerses the participant into the virtual environment together with the target, using the OpenScene Graph (OSG) 3-D toolkit; 2) computes spatial metrics used in sound conversions; 3) transmits them to the PureData sound system, running on the same computer, which synthesizes the sounds accordingly and sends them to the participant; 4) drives the experimental protocol.

The target is a sphere of 30 cm diameter that can be positioned at 27 different locations on a 3*3*3 grid of 82 cm steps in x, 1.35 cm in y and at three different heights in z: 70 cm; 110 cm; 150 cm. A test block consists of a series of 6 consecutive targets to reach, positioned semi-randomly to ensure that the participant always travels a minimum distance between targets. The sequence ensures that the three x; y; z coordinates of the spheres vary between each trial.

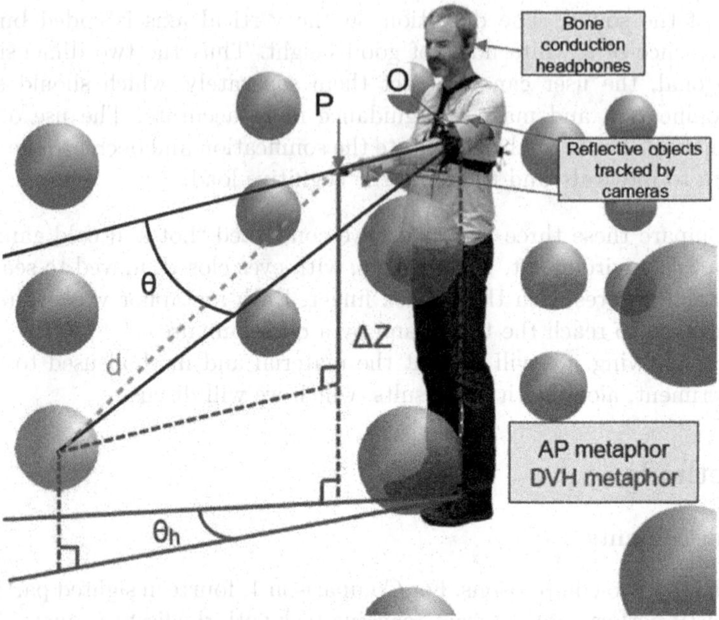

Fig. 1. Photomontage showing the reflectors used to capture the position of the participant's limbs, the virtual spheres' position (the red sphere being the target), and BI, AP and DVH metaphors' metrics. The target sphere is located at one out of 27 possible locations. The points O (elbow) and P (index finger tip) determine the direction pointed by the participant. With BI, a white noise is triggered when the line OP intersects the target (θ null). With AP, the sound's pitch additionally varies according to θ not null. With DVH, the sound's pitch varies according to θ_h, and a white noise is triggered when P is at the same height as the target.

2.3 Participant's Equipment

During the experiment, the participant was equipped with (see Fig. 1):

- Objects with reflectors mounted on them, located by the Qualisys system. They are positioned on anatomical segments corresponding to points O and P located in the frame of reference. A wrap around the finger places point P at the tip of the index finger. An armband places the point O at the elbow. The $\overrightarrow{OP}$ vector defines the direction of the participant's pointing.
- A bone conduction headset (Aftershokz Sportz3) connected to a receiver box (Mipro MI909R) to receive the sound feedback.
- A miniature keyboard (iclever Rii 2.4 GHz L * l * h = 151 * 59 * 12.5 mm) to start the next trial once the target has been reached.

2.4 Spatial Metrics

Several features are extracted from the scene to be transcoded into sounds (see Fig. 1). To compare different sound metaphors, we need to compute different geometric quantities.

For the BI metaphor and the AP metaphor, the extracted geometric features are as follows:

- The angle $\theta = \widehat{POT}$ which corresponds to the angle formed by the lines OP and OT (angular deviation).
- The distance d = [PT] (distance deviation).

For the DVH metaphor, we used two additional features:

- The angle $\theta_h = \widehat{POT_h}$, which corresponds to the projection of the angle θ on the horizontal plane parallel to the ground (angular deviation)
- The height difference $\Delta Z = |z_P - z_T|$, which corresponds to the projection of the distance [PT] on the vertical axis Z (distance deviation).

These features allow us to dissociate the deviations on the horizontal and vertical axes for the DVH metaphor.

O and P define the direction of the participant's pointing and their distance to the target. For the AP metaphor, we used a polar coordinate system. However, in classical polar coordinates, the angle between the pointed direction and target direction is considered from the same origin O. It is the case in most studies in which the camera is used to estimate both the angle and the distance to the target [4,11,19,23]. Here, we dissociated O and P. O is used to estimate the orientation of the angle θ, while P is used to estimate the distance to the target (see Fig. 2). We could have used O to estimate the distance, but in this target-reaching task with the hand, the distance is intuitively considered null when the finger touches the target.

2.5 Sound Metaphors

We transcoded the deviations in angle and distance from the target into sound parameters. The metaphors tested were as follows:

- BI (Table 1): When the participant points in the direction of the target (if the OP line intersects the target), white noise is generated. Otherwise, no sound is generated.

For the AP and DVH metaphors, the extracted spatial information is encoded by generating a sinusoid that varies in pitch. When the angle θ exceeds 90°, the sinusoid is no longer generated, allowing the participant to know that the target is behind them.

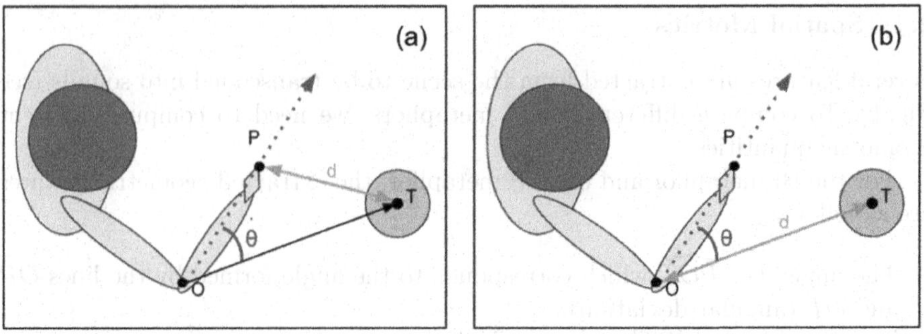

Fig. 2. Representation of classical polar coordinates versus natural pointing. (a) Natural pointing: angle θ has for origin O, and distance d has for origin P. (b) Classical polar coordinates: angle θ and distance d have the same origin O.

- AP (Table 2): The sinusoid's pitch f varies on a continuum from $fmin = 110$ Hz for $\theta max = 90°$ to $fmax = 440$ Hz for $\theta min = 5°$ so that (1) no sound is delivered from the rear (2) f is in the audible spectrum while avoiding higher pitches that are harsh in a constant stimulus. The angle-to-pitch conversion follows Steven's psychophysical law [21], a power law function:

$$log(f) = A * log(\theta) + B$$

with :

$$A = [log(fmax) - log(fmin)]/[(log(\theta min) - log(\theta max)] = 0.48$$

$$B = log(fmin) - A * log(\theta max) = 6.86$$

The intensity is constant. White noise is superimposed on the sinusoid when the OP line intersects the target (as for BI).
- DVH (Table 3): This metaphor dissociates the horizontal and vertical axes. The sinusoid's pitch varies according to the same conversion function as for AP, but according to angle θ_h which is the projected angle θ on the horizontal plane. The horizontal dimension is thus coded by the pitch, while the vertical dimension is coded by the activation of white noise when the participant points at the same height as the target position, i.e. when $\Delta Z < 15cm$ (i.e. the radius of the sphere). The intensity is constant.

2.6 Protocol

The experiment takes place in the motion capture space described above. Participants must find several targets presented in succession. Each participant makes one of two comparisons (BI VS AP or AP VS DHV). The experiment begins with a training phase, consisting of a block of six trials per metaphor. During this phase, the participant receives explanations from the experimenter on the difficulties that may arise and how to overcome them. The session continues

Table 1. Sound parameters of the metaphor BI

	Pitch	White noise
Horizontal		*OP* intersects the target
Vertical		

Table 2. Sound parameters of the metaphor AP

	Pitch	White noise
Horizontal	$\theta min = 5°, \theta max = 90°$ $fmin = 110$ Hz, $fmax = 440$ Hz	*OP* intersects the target
Vertical		

Table 3. Sound parameters of the metaphor DVH

	Pitch	White noise
Horizontal	$\theta_h min = 5°$, $\theta_h max = 90°$ $fmin = 110$ Hz, $fmax = 440$ Hz	
Vertical		$\Delta Z <$ target's radius

with the completion of four experimental blocks alternating the two metaphors. The order of passage of the metaphors is counterbalanced between the participants. Each experimental block is preceded by a refreshment block of the next metaphor. Each participant takes as many trials as necessary, and indicates when ready to start the test block.

Each block takes place as follows: the participant stands in the center of the room and closes their eyes. The participant starts the first trial as soon as they are ready by pressing the marked N key on the mini-keyboard. A start-up sound indicates the beginning of the trial. The sound feedback is triggered and changes according to the participant's movements, depending on the sound metaphor used. For the three metaphors, a buzzer (square signal) is triggered when the participant's finger passes the target ([OP] > [OT]). When the pointer P enters the target ($d < 15$ cm), only white noise is triggered, which intensity is stronger than the white noise of good direction or good height. When P stays inside the target for 400 ms, a sound indicates the victory and the end of the trial, and the sound feedback is switched off. The trial is interrupted if the participant does not reach the target within the 180-second limit, and a bell sound indicating defeat is triggered. After each trial, the participant stays on the spot and starts the next trial with the keyboard. It continues until all six trials in the experimental block are completed.

At the end of the experiment, the participants filled out a questionnaire. They were asked their general opinion about the experiment, the challenges they encountered and to rate on a Likert scale each of the two metaphors on three aspects: ease, comfort and efficiency.

3 Results

3.1 Quantitative Assessment

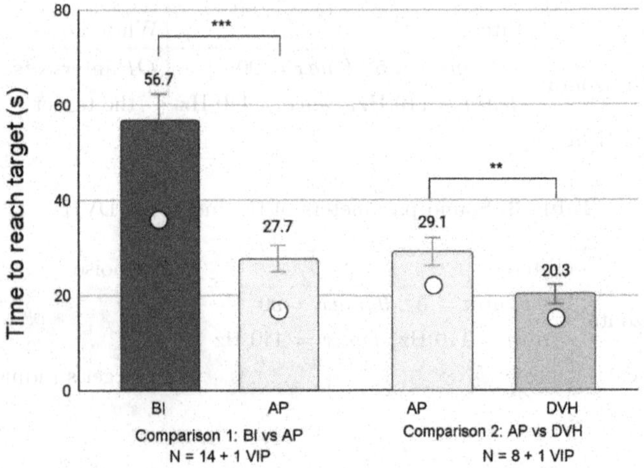

Fig. 3. Mean target-reaching times for each metaphor comparison. The white disks represent the average times obtained by visually impaired participants (VIP, one for each comparison). The bars represent the 90% confidence interval.

To compare metaphors, we measured our participants' objective performance by the time taken to reach the target. Since our response variable (time to target) is a duration with a skewed distribution, the Cox model appeared the most appropriate [7]. It allows us to analyze repeated measures without averaging the data for each participant, so it accounts for intra- and inter-participant variability. To perform our analyses, we used the *coxph* function in the *Survival* package of R software.

Comparison 1 (BI vs. AP): As shown in Fig. 3 (left) participants were 29 s faster on average with AP (M = 27.70 s; SD = 12.27 s) than with BI (M = 56.68 s; SD = 33.78 s) (z = -10.41; $p < 0.001$).

Comparison 2 (AP vs. DVH): As shown in Fig. 3 (right) participants were 10 s faster on average in the DVH condition (M = 19.70s ; SD = 10.77s) than in the AP condition (M = 29.85s ; SD = 17.70s) (z = 4.80 ; $p < 0.01$).

As we only had one visually impaired participant per metaphor comparison, their results are not included in the analyses. However, we can observe that the pattern of their results is similar to those of the sighted participants, with shorter reaching times for AP than for BI, and for DVH than for AP. Their results are represented by white circles in Figs. 3 and 4.

3.2 Subjective Rating

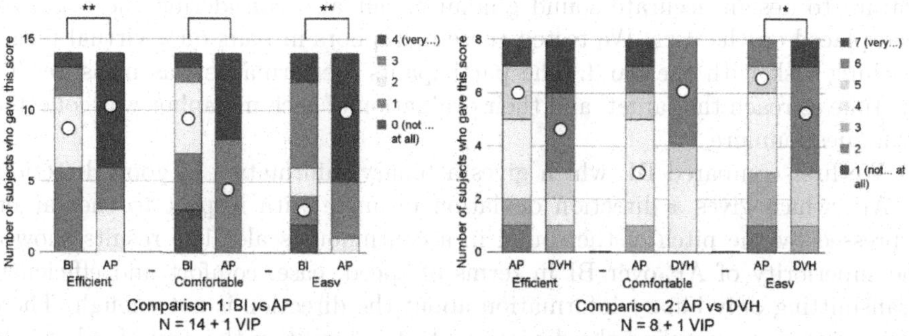

Fig. 4. Distribution of scores about efficiency, comfort, and ease-of-use for each metaphor comparison. The white circles represent the scores made by visually impaired participants (VIP one for each experiment).

Participants also gave a score to each metaphor on three criteria: efficiency, comfort, and ease. For each of the three criteria, we want to explain the form and intensity of the relationship between the score and the metaphor. The score takes as value an integer. We chose to look at the probability distribution for the values taken, and thus consider the score as an ordinal categorical variable. We performed an ordinal regression, using the *clm()* function of the ordinal package of the R software.

Comparison 1 (BI vs. AP): According to the scores given to each metaphor (see Fig. 4, left), AP is considered to be more comfortable than BI (z = -56.62, $p < 0.001$), more efficient ($z = 2.74$, $p < 0.01$) and easier to use ($z = 3.02$, $p < 0.01$).

Comparison 2 (AP vs. DVH): The task was considered easier with DVH than with AP (see Fig. 4, right) (z = -2.29; $p = 0.02$).

The scores given by the visually impaired participants are similar to those given by the sighted participants, with better scores for AP than for BI and better scores for DVH than for AP.

4 Discussion

Our goal was to create the most efficient and ergonomic sound guidance device possible to assist VIPs in target-reaching tasks. Most of the time, distance between the user and the target is calculated from the sensor, often a hand-held or head-mounted camera. Here, the frame of reference is the participant's own body, a more natural egocentric frame of reference that is appropriate for the task and the user.

We created three sound metaphors taking into account advice from the literature to design accurate sound guidance, but also considering the cognitive load placed on the user. We tested these metaphors in pairs on a virtual target reaching task with the hand. The participants' performance was measured by the time to reach the target, and their evaluation of each metaphor was collected by a questionnaire.

We first compared BI, which gives a binary information of good direction, to AP, which gives a direction deviation in angle with respect to the target, expressed by the pitch of the sound in a continuous scale. The results showed the superiority of AP over BI in terms of speed, ease, comfort and efficiency. Transmitting only binary information about the direction is not enough. There is an advantage in giving the deviations to the target in the way of a hot-cold game. With BI, the participant has to scan the space for audio information and has to make a lot of unnecessary movements to effectively scan the area. AP quickly and effortlessly provides information on a 3-D spatial metric that separates the participant from the target. AP has several qualities identified by Ziemer et al. [24–27], but its dimensions are not orthogonal. Indeed, a single sound parameter is used to encode direction on both vertical and horizontal axes. We observed that the subjects wandered around a target when they were close to it when using AP. This problem could be due to the lack of orthogonality of the dimensions. At a distance, 3-D angle variations originated essentially from movements on a horizontal plane, while vertical components could be neglected; at proximity, both azimuth and elevation deviations contributed to the same sound continuum. A confound of the gravity axis and the horizontal plane is not consistent with the embodied representation of space [3,6]. Action-perception loops allow inferring components along either axis with AP, but at the cost of an additional cognitive load. Such cost was alleviated using the DVH metaphor.

Indeed, in a second step, we compared AP to DVH, a metaphor whose deviations on the horizontal axis are coded on a continuous scale by the pitch of the sound, while the deviations on the vertical axis are coded in a binary way, by the triggering of white noise of good height. The results showed the advantage of DVH: participants were faster and found this metaphor easier than AP. With DVH, the two dimensions are orthogonal: the participant can interpret them separately. They are separated into two streams, which overlap only when the correct height is reached. The white noise of right height is an additional flow containing binary information, it does not require one to divert one's attention from the other flow to interpret it. Using binary information simplifies the sonification, reduces the amount of information to be integrated, and decreases the cognitive load.

The results of this second comparison with a metaphor that dissociates horizontal and vertical axes are consistent with those of [10], a study in which target-reaching times were shorter with a sound indicating the elevation of the target (added to spatialized sound). However, this experiment was conducted by moving an avatar in a virtual world, making it impossible to compare the latencies with our study. On the contrary, in [13], the participants were physically moving in a 3*3 m room while being immersed in a virtual environment thanks to a Virtual Reality (VR) headset. The target position on the horizontal axis was coded by spatialized sound and on the vertical axis by sound frequency. The average latency to reach the target was 25 s. We obtained comparable latencies, with 19.70 s for DVH and 29.85 s for AP.

5 Conclusion

Sightless participants reached a target faster and preferred to be guided acoustically by directional deviations from the target than by the right direction only. These advantages are enhanced when the vertical and horizontal dimensions are given by two distinct sound streams. Visually impaired participants behaved similarly to blindfolded ones. Effective sonification of target guidance requires a balance between overly detailed - or strictly necessary - information to achieve sufficient accuracy without creating cognitive overload. The first comparison AP VS BI shows the benefit of additional information over a more parsimonious metaphor. The benefits of DVH that explicitly dissociates the two axes, alleviates the participant from the cognitive load to do it oneself; the load is further reduced by converting verticality into binary information [2], which has shown sufficient to guide someone to a target [12]. The DVH metaphor is a good trade-off between parsimonious (use of binary information) and explicit (dissociation of the two axes) guidance. It is a first step towards smartphone SSDs applications to help find objects in a situation of visual impairment.

Acknowledgements. This work was supported by the Agence Nationale de la Recherche (ANR-21CE33-0011-01). It was authorized by the ethical committee CER Grenoble Alpes (Avis-2018-06-19-1).

This work has been partially supported by ROBOTEX 2.0 (Grants ROBOTEX ANR-10-EQPX-44-01 and TIRREX ANR-21-ESRE-0015) funded by the French program Investissements d'avenir.

The authors acknowledge the BIOMECA facility (GIPSA-lab UMR5216) for the experiments.

We would also like to thank Charles Fricaud, Laurent Bourque and Juliette Suslian for their contribution to this project during their internship.

References

1. Chang, W.J., Chen, L.B., Sie, C.Y., Yang, C.H.: An artificial intelligence edge computing-based assistive system for visually impaired pedestrian safety at zebra crossings. IEEE Trans. Consum. Electron. **67**(1), 3–11 (2020). https://doi.org/10.1109/TCE.2020.3037065
2. Gao, Z., Wang, H., Feng, G., Lv, H.: Exploring sonification mapping strategies for spatial auditory guidance in immersive virtual environments. ACM Trans. Appl. Percept. (TAP) (2022). https://doi.org/10.1145/3528171
3. Graf, W., Klam, F.: Le système vestibulaire: anatomie fonctionnelle et comparée, évolution et développement. C.R. Palevol **5**(3–4), 637–655 (2006). https://doi.org/10.1016/j.crpv.2005.12.009
4. Hild, M., Cheng, F.: Grasping guidance for visually impaired persons based on computed visual-auditory feedback. In: 2014 International Conference on Computer Vision Theory and Applications (VISAPP), vol. 3, pp. 75–82. IEEE (2014). https://doi.org/10.5220/0004653200750082
5. Katz, B.F., et al.: NAVIG: augmented reality guidance system for the visually impaired. Virtual Real. **16**(4), 253–269 (2012). https://doi.org/10.1007/s10055-012-0213-6
6. Lamy, J.C.: Bases neurophysiologiques de la proprioception. Kinésithérapie scientifique **472**, 15–23 (2006)
7. Letué, F., Martinez, M.J., Samson, A., Vilain, A., Vilain, C.: Statistical methodology for the analysis of repeated duration data in behavioral studies. J. Speech Lang. Hear. Res. **61**(3), 561–582 (2018). https://doi.org/10.1044/2017_JSLHR-S-17-0135
8. Lin, Y., Wang, K., Yi, W., Lian, S.: Deep learning based wearable assistive system for visually impaired people. In: Proceedings of the IEEE/CVF International Conference on Computer Vision Workshops (2019)
9. Liu, Y., Stiles, N.R., Meister, M.: Augmented reality powers a cognitive assistant for the blind. ELife **7**, e37841 (2018). https://doi.org/10.7554/eLife.37841.001
10. Lokki, T., Grohn, M.: Navigation with auditory cues in a virtual environment. IEEE Multimedia **12**(2), 80–86 (2005). https://doi.org/10.1109/MMUL.2005.33
11. Manduchi, R., Coughlan, J.M.: The last meter: blind visual guidance to a target. In: Proceedings of the SIGCHI Conference on Human Factors in Computing Systems, pp. 3113–3122 (2014). https://doi.org/10.1145/2556288.2557328
12. Marston, J.R., Loomis, J.M., Klatzky, R.L., Golledge, R.G.: Nonvisual route following with guidance from a simple haptic or auditory display. J. Vis. Impairment Blindness **101**(4), 203–211 (2007). https://doi.org/10.1177/0145482X0710100403
13. May, K.R., Sobel, B., Wilson, J., Walker, B.N.: Auditory displays to facilitate object targeting in 3D space. In: The 25th International Conference on Auditory Display (ICAD 2019). Georgia Institute of Technology (2019). https://doi.org/10.21785/icad2019.008
14. Meijer, P.B.: An experimental system for auditory image representations. IEEE Trans. Biomed. Eng. **39**(2), 112–121 (1992). https://doi.org/10.1109/10.121642
15. Neugebauer, A., Rifai, K., Getzlaff, M., Wahl, S.: Navigation aid for blind persons by visual-to-auditory sensory substitution: a pilot study. PLoS ONE **15**(8), e0237344 (2020). https://doi.org/10.1371/journal.pone.0237344
16. Parseihian, G., Gondre, C., Aramaki, M., Ystad, S., Kronland-Martinet, R.: Comparison and evaluation of sonification strategies for guidance tasks. IEEE Trans. Multimedia **18**(4), 674–686 (2016). https://doi.org/10.1109/TMM.2016.2531978

17. Parseihian, G., Ystad, S., Aramaki, M., Kronland-Martinet, R.: The process of sonification design for guidance tasks. J. Mob. Med. **9**(2), 25 (2015)
18. Ruvolo, P.: Considering spatial cognition of blind travelers in utilizing augmented reality for navigation. In: 2021 IEEE International Conference on Pervasive Computing and Communications Workshops and other Affiliated Events (PerCom Workshops), pp. 99–104. IEEE (2021). https://doi.org/10.1109/PerComWorkshops51409.2021.9430997
19. Shih, M.L., et al.: DLWV2: a deep learning-based wearable vision-system with vibrotactile-feedback for visually impaired people to reach objects. In: 2018 IEEE/RSJ International Conference on Intelligent Robots and Systems (IROS), pp. 1–9. IEEE (2018). https://doi.org/10.1109/IROS.2018.8593711
20. Spagnol, S., Hoffmann, R., Martínez, M.H., Unnthorsson, R.: Blind wayfinding with physically-based liquid sounds. Int. J. Hum Comput Stud. **115**, 9–19 (2018). https://doi.org/10.1016/j.ijhcs.2018.02.002
21. Stevens, S.: On the physiological law. Psychol. Rev. **64**, 153–181 (1957). https://doi.org/10.1037/h0046162
22. Thakoor, K., et al.: A system for assisting the visually impaired in localization and grasp of desired objects. In: Agapito, L., Bronstein, M.M., Rother, C. (eds.) ECCV 2014. LNCS, vol. 8927, pp. 643–657. Springer, Cham (2015). https://doi.org/10.1007/978-3-319-16199-0_45
23. Troncoso Aldas, N.D., Lee, S., Lee, C., Rosson, M.B., Carroll, J.M., Narayanan, V.: AIGuide: an augmented reality hand guidance application for people with visual impairments. In: The 22nd International ACM SIGACCESS Conference on Computers and Accessibility, pp. 1–13 (2020). https://doi.org/10.1145/3373625.3417028
24. Ziemer, T., Nuchprayoon, N., Schultheis, H.: Psychoacoustic sonification as user interface for human-machine interaction. arXiv preprint arXiv:1912.08609 (2019). https://doi.org/10.48550/arXiv.1912.08609
25. Ziemer, T., Schultheis, H.: A psychoacoustic auditory display for navigation. In: The 24th International Conference on Auditory Display (ICAD 2018). Georgia Institute of Technology (2018). https://doi.org/10.21785/icad2018.007
26. Ziemer, T., Schultheis, H.: Psychoacoustical signal processing for three-dimensional sonification. In: The 25th International Conference on Auditory Display (ICAD 2019). Georgia Institute of Technology (2019). https://doi.org/10.21785/icad2019.018
27. Ziemer, T., Schultheis, H.: Three orthogonal dimensions for psychoacoustic sonification. arXiv preprint arXiv:1912.00766 (2019). https://doi.org/10.48550/arXiv.1912.00766
28. Zientara, P.A., et al.: Third eye: a shopping assistant for the visually impaired. Computer **50**(2), 16–24 (2017). https://doi.org/10.1109/MC.2017.36

SpeechBalloon: A New Approach of Providing User Interface for Real-Time Generation of Meeting Notes

Donghyeon Kim[1], Suyeon Yoon[2], Jiyoung Seo[2], SeungHoon Jeong[1], and Bowon Lee[1,2](✉)

[1] Department of Electronic Engineering, Inha University, Incheon, South Korea
[2] Department of Electrical and Computer Engineering, Inha University, Incheon, South Korea
bowon.lee@inha.ac.kr

Abstract. This paper proposes SpeechBalloon, a solution for real-time generation of meeting notes for the purpose of facilitating effective communications among participants. This is especially important when some of the participants have hearing problems. To provide an assistive technology for the hearing-impaired, the proposed solution, consisting of a device application running speech-to-text and a server collecting the information from each device, provides users with meeting notes. The advantage of our proposed system is that it does not require any specific hardware for note taking as long as each meeting participant brings his/her own device such as a smartphone or a tablet. We expect our proposed SpeechBalloon can help hearing-impaired people to actively participate in real meetings and overcome any inconveniences that they have due to their disabilities.

Keywords: Meeting Notes · Speech-to-Text · UI for Hearing-Impaired · Mobile Applications

1 Introduction

Speech is one of the most important elements of communication, even for participants with hearing problems. Although many hearing-impaired people have communication difficulties due to their disability, many of those who have not completely lost their hearing still prefer verbal communication [3]. However, in a situation where multiple participants speak at a meeting, a majority of hearing-impaired people have difficulty identifying active speakers. Therefore, it is important to develop an application UI that can intuitively identify the active speaker and the content being spoken at any given time.

Various solutions have been proposed to help hearing-impaired people participate in meetings. Daham Note provides a solution for interaction between lecturer and listener in lectures involving hearing-impaired members [5]. Its *lecturer* application records the lecturer's speech and transmits it to the *listener* application, and the *listener* application records the listener's questions and

M. Antona and C. Stephanidis (Eds.): HCII 2023, LNCS 14020, pp. 244–255, 2023.
https://doi.org/10.1007/978-3-031-35681-0_16

transmits them to the *lecturer* application. Clova Note provides a meeting note-taking function for the general public or the hearing impaired [6]. Stimme provides keyword-based morse vibration for hearing impaired [2]. The application can perform speaker discrimination and deliver the recorded meeting minutes to the user after the meeting ends. However, these existing works have limitations in that they are not suitable for interactions among participants in a meeting because they do not provide recognition results in real time.

The proposed SpeechBalloon is a UI that provides location information for a meeting note generation application for hearing-impaired people. The proposed SpeechBalloon displays the location information of the speaker along with the content of the utterance in a specific area so that the user can easily identify the speaker along with the content of the utterance. Users can select seating arrangements that fit the meeting situation for easier location identification, and can share seating arrangements with other users. An application implementing the proposed SpeechBalloon is also proposed.

As a result, it is expected that hearing-impared people will be able to participate in meetings more easily through verbal communications using SpeechBallon solution proposed in our work.

2 Proposed Solution

The proposed SpeechBalloon is an intuitive note taking application with the speaker identification for hearing-impaired people that also provides the speaker's location along with the spoken text. The proposed solution provides automated meeting note taking for the hearing-impaired through speech-to-text (STT) and the UI in terms of speech balloon that also indicates the locations of active speakers for easy identification. In order to perform speaker recognition, speakers participating in the conference are required to bring their own devices. The application recognizes the utterance of a speaker closest to the device. The speech contents recognized by the individual devices through STT are transmitted to the server, and the server transmits the collected speech to all devices belonging to the same meeting. Each device receives the content of speech from the server and provides it through the SpeechBalloon UI. SpeechBalloon includes an area displaying a speaker's position and an area displaying the speaker's utterance. If the speaker inputs the location of the speaker participating in the conference in advance, then the application displays the content of the speech along with the speaker's location through the SpeechBalloon UI.

In order to easily distinguish two speakers when they are located at an adjacent distance, the SpeechBalloon UI includes a function to designate different balloon colors for each speaker. The application randomly selects the color of the speech balloon from the number of speakers through its own implemented hash function. Also, the speaker's location information provided by the user for the SpeechBalloon UI is saved even when the application is closed. In addition, users can easily share the entered location of individual participants with other users in the same chat room. In general, meetings are held in a fixed seat and seat change does not occur in the middle of the meeting, so this function is still useful even though current applications do not include the ability to recognize the actual location of a speaker.

2.1 SpeechBalloon UI

Proposed SpeechBalloon is an automatic meeting note taking application for the hearing-impaired people. Therefore, it is important to reflect the opinions of potential application users in the UI design process.

Interview with Potential Users. In order to directly reflect the opinions of the hearing-impaired people for the application UI, we conducted interviews with four hearing-impaired interviewees. The interviewees commonly preferred communication through speech and insisted on referring to the shape of the mouth as needed. In many cases, the interviewees maintained a certain level of hearing rather than complete hearing loss, and claimed that the use of hearing aids made verbal communication partially possible. Contrary to the general perception, sign language was considered as only an auxiliary means of communication in general. And there are a significant number of cases where people do not know the sign language. The interviewees claimed that they frequently use chatting applications or written conversations to communicate with others, and insisted that convenience of use and accuracy of the STT are important in the applications that they use. Regarding the SpeechBalloon UI, the interviewees requested support for various seating configurations, a function to save/load meeting notes, and the use of large font size. In addition, regarding the proposed application, the interviewees requested speaker identification support, dark mode implementation, a guide for non-disabled people, and additional functions that can be used in situations other than conference situations.

Most of the interviewees' requests were reflected in the proposed SpeechBalloon UI and application. However, speaker identification independent of the device is still under development, and guides for non-disabled people were excluded in order to pursue universal design.

Layout of the SpeechBalloon UI. Fig. 1 shows the layout of SpeechBalloon. Each SpeechBalloon includes an area (left) for displaying the speaker's position and an area (right) for displaying the contents of the speech.

The speaker's position is shown in the figure in terms of the slices on the round-shaped pie, The content of the utterance is displayed along with the speaker's nickname and utterance date and time. The balloon area containing the utterance content along with the color representing the speaker's position is automatically generated from the speaker's identification. Multiple colors allow multiple speakers in similar locations to be distinguished. The speech area also includes a tail of speech balloon indicating the speaker's position, which makes it easy to find the speaker's position even when the focus of the user's view is on the content of speech.

Fig. 1. Layout of SpeechBalloon

Figure 2 shows the UI for setting the position of the pie slice included in the SpeechBalloon corresponding to the speaker's position. The user can set the location of the speaker by touching the location of the pie slice. The location of the speaker set through the UI is stored and maintained even after restarting the application. Figure 3 shows multiple options that users can select for various seating situations.

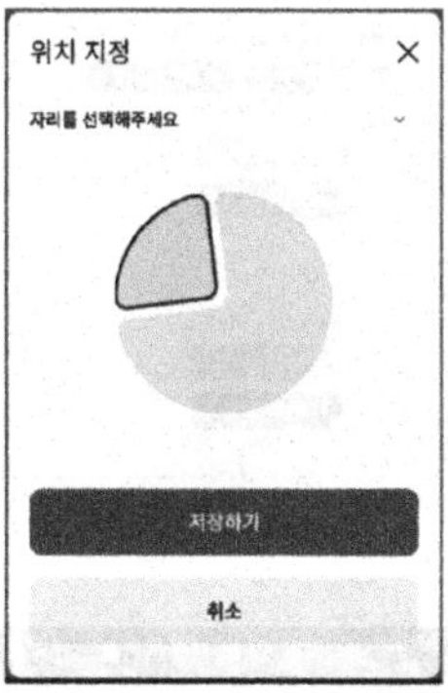

Fig. 2. Layout of the UI for setting the position

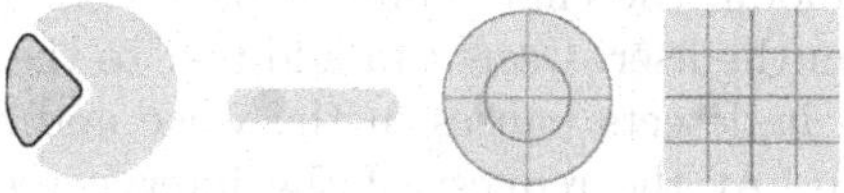

Fig. 3. Layout of the various seating situations

Figure 4 shows the seating position sharing function. When a user shares a seating position, it is transmitted through SpeechBalloon. Other users receiving this can decide whether to use the location information transmitted by the user as it is or to use it based on their own location. Users can set a specific SpeechBalloon as a notification if necessary. The contents of the notified SpeechBalloon are posted at the top of the chat room. Users can also delete notifications.

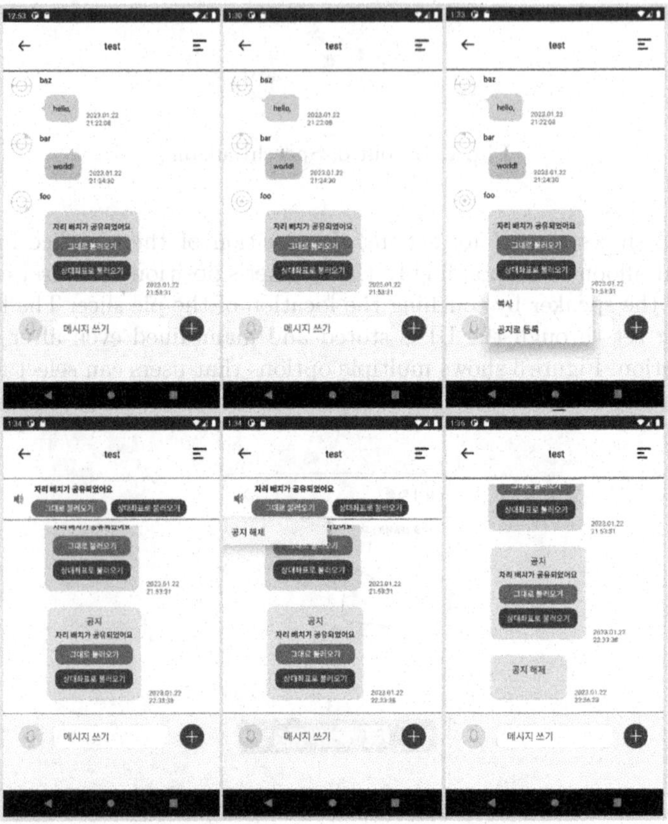

Fig. 4. Function of sharing seating position

Figure 5 shows the chat room UI composed of multiple SpeechBalloons. In addition to SpeechBalloon, the chat room UI includes a title bar and a UI to receive text input from the user. Users can add text to the chat room by typing if desired. Otherwise, it detects pauses in the voice and automatically adds a tokenized STT output. At the request of the interviewee, a function to save meeting notes as a file is implemented. The user can do that through 'Save as file' in the top-right menu bar. In addition, users can share their seating positions with other participants through 'Sharing the seating position' in the right menu bar.

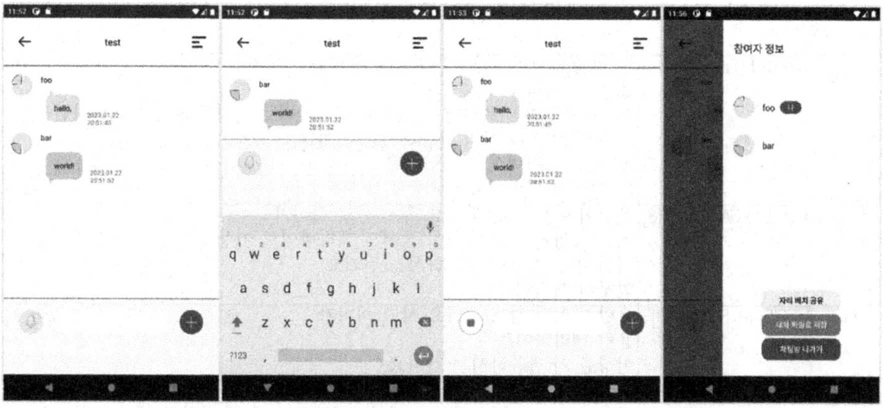

Fig. 5. Layout of chat room UI

2.2 SpeechBalloon Application

In addition to meeting note generation utilizing SpeechBalloon UI, the proposed application also provides lecture note generation and STT as well as text-to-speech (TTS) for one-on-one conversation. The proposed applications include JAVA-based native applications running on user devices and JSP-based server applications running on a server, and uses the TTS function provided by the Android operating system. Proposed application was developed for Korean speakers. For the STT function, in order to satisfy interviewees' demand for voice recognition accuracy, we compared the accuracy of multiple STT service providers. Table 1 shows the STT results of multiple STT services for a short Korean conversation, and Fig. 6 shows the error rates of multiple STT services for Korean speech. For Korean speech, the CLOVA CSR [8] and ETRI API.DATA [9] engine showed the best performance. However, it has been reported that the ETRI API.DATA engine often shows poor performance in special situations such as people with autism [1]. To secure stable performance in a general-purpose environment, the proposed application used the CLOVA CSR engine.

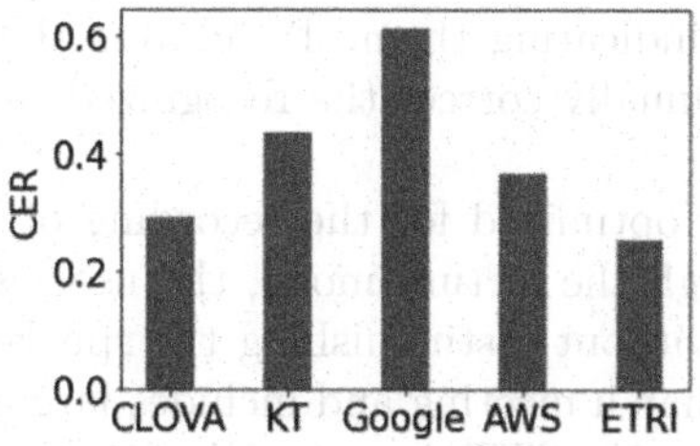

Fig. 6. Comparison of CERs of multiple STT APIs for conversations in Korean

Table 1. Output of STT engine for short Korean conversations

Ground Truth	A: 용량이 어느 정도 되나요 혹시 학교 서버가 B: 학교 서버요 A: 네 저장장치 용량이요 적어도 테라바이트 이상은 돼야죠 왜냐하면은 B: 저희 연구실 서버 말씀하시는 건가요 혹시 A: 연구실 서버요 B: 연구실 서버에서
NAVER CLOVA CSR [8]	용량이 어느 정도 되나요 혹시 학교 서버가 네 저장장치 오장 용량이 적어도 테라바이트 이상은 돼야죠 저희 연구실 서서 말슴하시는 건가요 연구실 서버에서도
Google Cloud STT [10]	용량이 어느 정도 되나요 샤크 서버가 용량 테라바이트 이상한 거 말씀하시는 건가요
AWS Transcribe [11]	용량이 어느 정도 되나요 혹시 학교 서버가 저장당지호 장용량 적어도 테러바이트 이상은 돼야 하죠 왜냐하면 저희 연구실말씀하시는 혹시 연구실
KT Cloud AI API [12]	네 목련이 어느 정도 되나요 혹시 학교 서버가 저장장치 오장 용량 적어도 테라바이트 이상하죠 왜냐하면 저희 연구실 상호 말씀하시는 거예요
ETRI API.DATA [9]	용량이 어느 정도 되나요 혹시 학교 서버가 저장장 지우장 용량 적어도 테라바이트 이상은 돼야죠 왜냐하면 저희 연구실 서버 말씀하시는 게 혹시 연구실 서버예요

2.3 Layout of SpeechBalloon Application

The proposed application includes a chat mode for generating meeting notes, a lecture mode for writing lecture notes, and a conversation mode for providing STT/TTS for one-on-one conversations. The chat mode provides speech recognition including speaker recognition. To achieve this, all meeting participants need to install and run the application on their own devices, each of which recognizes the voice of the speaker sitting closest to it. Each device runs STT for the individual speakers and shares the STT results with other devices through the server. All communications with the server are encrypted through the https protocol, so it is difficult for any intruders to intercept the communications [7]. Through this UI, the user can intuitively identify the positions of the speakers during the meeting by indicating them. To address the case of incorrect STT results, the user can manually correct the recognized texts by manually typing them.

The lecture mode is optimized for the recording of utterances provided by a single speaker. Through the lecture mode, the user can record the speaker's utterance in real time without distinguishing the speaker. In general, a lecture is in a longer duration than a meeting and includes jargons, so many recognition errors occur when performing STT, but the UI of the lecture mode allows users

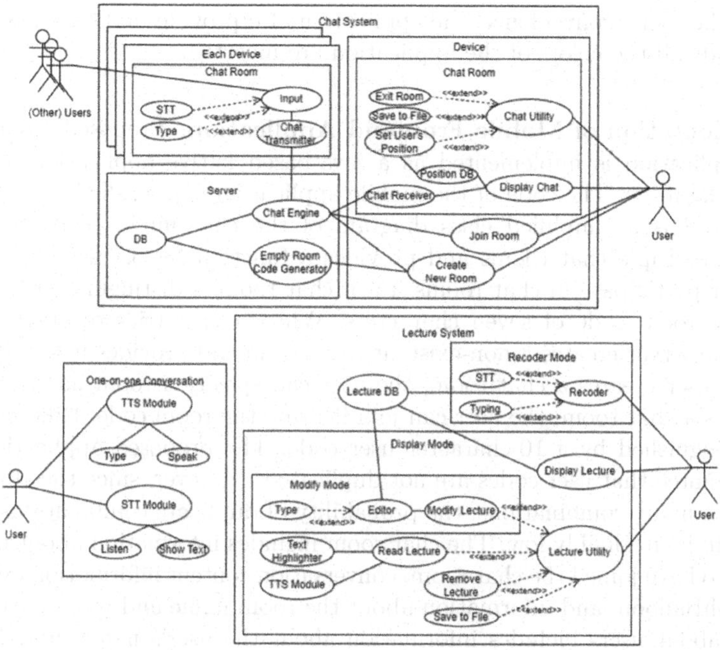

Fig. 7. UML diagram of proposed application

to correct misspelled words during STT. The lecture mode also detects pauses in speech and records the period during which speech is paused along with the content of the speech. Recorded lectures can still be modified after being saved. For the purpose of universal design, the lecture mode of the proposed application includes a function to read recorded lectures through TTS. When an utterance is recorded, the recorded pause is reflected in the TTS, providing a more realistic experience to the user. In addition, the read area is highlighted in gray and the reading area in red so that the user can easily identify the location of the current reading area. In general, reading long texts gives a lot of strain to the eyes, so it can be useful for most of the users [4].

Since the STT function can be used in more general situations along with TTS function, we designed an additional UI for the case when the user is in one-on-one conversation. For this, the screen is divided into two with different orientations. From one side, the user can enter his/her intention by typing, and when the typing is completed, the text will be played as a voice through TTS. From the other side, the other user's speech is recognized and the STT output is displayed on the screen. The two sides operate independently, so users can use both sides or only one side as needed. For example, the hearing-impaired person can be on the side to type texts to be played as a voice through TTS for the other person and to read the texts recognized by the STT of the other person on the other side who is not hearing impaired.

For the user's convenience, the application also provides a dark mode. In the dark mode all the colors of the application are inverted.

Implementation of Mobile Frontend Application. Proposed mobile frontend application is implemented as a java-based native application and uses SQLite database. The code of the mobile application is published on Github[1].

Figure 8 is a simplified class diagram of the chat mode. The chat mode includes multiple chat rooms and provides a function for users to create chat rooms or participate in chat rooms. Each chat room is distinguished by a non-duplicate room code of seven characters. When a user tries to create a chat room, the server creates a non-existent room code and provides it to the client. When a user creates a chat room, the user can specify a room name. When a user joins a chat room, the user can join it using the room code. Different users are distinguished by a 10-character user code. The proposed application does not guarantee that user codes are not duplicated. However, since the 10 characters make many combinations, the probability of duplicate combinations of user codes will be negligibly low. The chat room includes information about multiple users who have joined the chat room, conversation content information expressed in SpeechBalloon, and information about the room name and room code. Information about users includes information about the user's name, user ID, and position. The chat room provides a UI that allows users to enter positions and utterances.

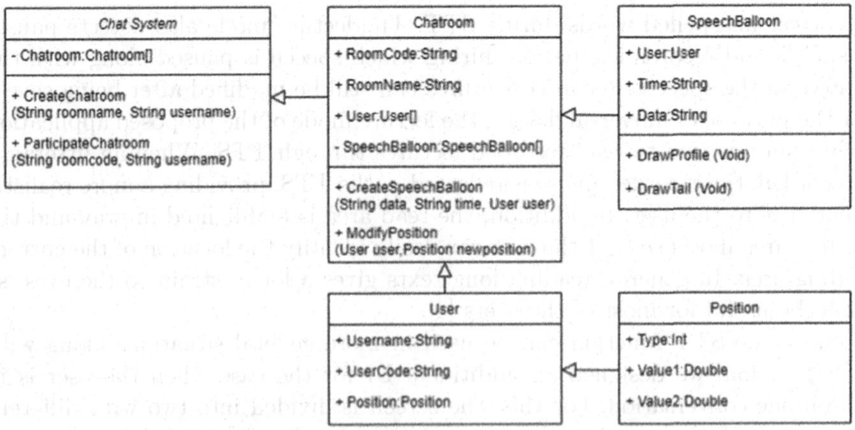

Fig. 8. Simplified UML diagram of the chat mode

Figure 9 shows the title screen of the proposed application, from the left: main title, title of chat mode, title of lecture mode, one-on-one conversation (single page). In the chat mode and lecture mode's title, users can add chat

[1] https://github.com/abc351/3fds2_app.

rooms and lectures. The one-on-one conversation page can be useful when a user with hearing difficulties needs an auxiliary function of STT/TTS in a one-on-one conversation with the general public.

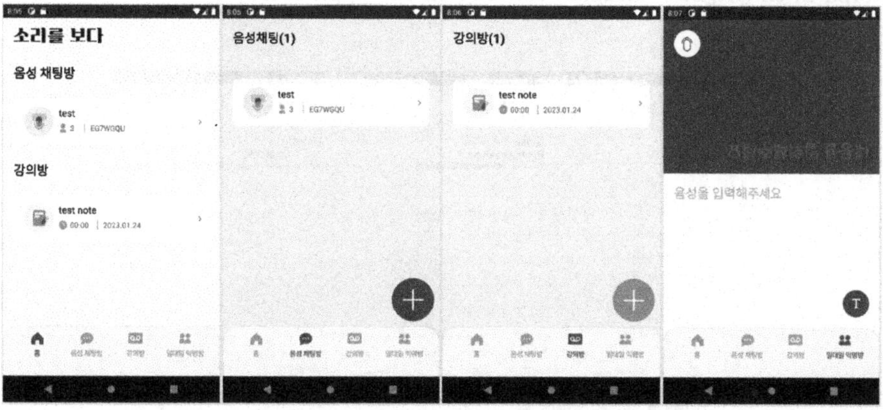

Fig. 9. Layout of Proposed Application

Figure 10 shows the UI for users to create or join a chat room. When a user tries to create a chat room, the application receives a non-duplicate room code from the server. User can create a chat room by entering a room name and user name. The user can join the chat room by entering the room code and user name.

Fig. 10. Layout of chat room adder UI

Figure 11 shows the UI of the lecture mode. In a situation where there is only one speaker, the user may record and store utterances regardless of the speaker. If necessary, the user can modify or delete the saved content and listen through TTS. The data of the lecture mode are not transmitted to the server, but are stored in the SQLite database running on the application.

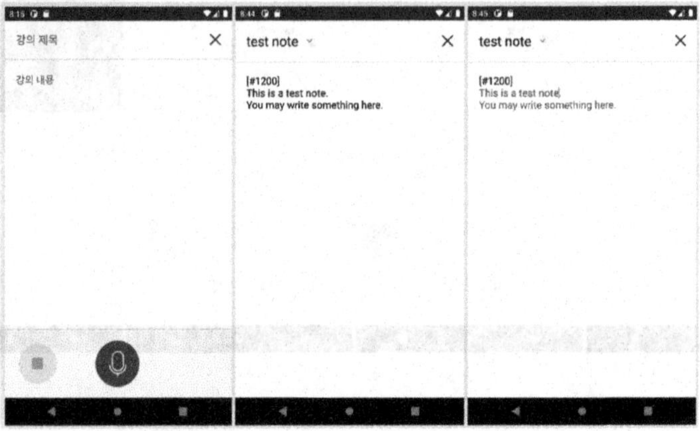

Fig. 11. Layout of lecture room UI

Implementation of Server Backend Application. Except for STT for speech recognition, the server exists only for chat mode, because lecture mode and one to one conversation do not require communication between devices. The server application is written in JSP and provided through Tomcat. User information transmitted to the server is stored in mariaDB. In addition to storing chat data, the server plays a role in generating and providing non-duplicate room codes. The code of the server application is published on Github[2].

User Feedback. We presented the SpeechBalloon application for a graduate-level class of the Department of Special Education at a university and received some feedback. Many of them were security concerns. Regarding chat records being stored on the server, a large number of people expressed concerns about the management and leakage of personal information stored on the server. In addition, there were some concerns about the method of anonymizing personal information regarding the plan to create our own STT and speaker separation engine through the collected speech data. In addition, there was a feedback that the user wants to be able to add a seat arrangement of the meeting place in response to the seat arrangement situation of various meeting places. Also, there was a feedback that it would be nice to be able to separate the speakers of users who do not bring a mobile device.

[2] https://github.com/abc351/3fds2_serv.

The collection and management of personal information by the server is one of the very sensitive topics, and it is necessary to be properly addressed. Separation of speakers who do not carry a device is the main drawback of this application.

3 Conclusion

This paper proposed SpeechBalloon, a communication aid solution for people with hearing impairment in a meeting situation. It is expected that a large number of hearing impaired people will be able to receive help at the meeting through the proposed application. Identifying a new speaker who does not have a personal device or joins during a meeting is a task that will be addressed in our future work.

Acknowledgments. This work was supported by the Ministry of Education of the Republic of Korea and the National Research Foundation of Korea (NRF-2021S1A5A2A03062440) and by the Institute of Information & Communications Technology Planning & Evaluation (IITP) grant funded by the Korea government (MSIT) (RS-2022-00155915, Artificial Intelligence Convergence Innovation Human Resources Development (Inha University)).

References

1. Suyeon, Y., Bowon, L.: Comparison of Speech-To-Text APIs of Korean of People With Autism. In: 2022 International Conference on Digital Contents (DigiCon-22), pp. 13–15 (2022)
2. Akarshani, A., Wijesuriya, V.B.: Stimme: a chat application for communicating with hearing impaired persons. In: 2019 IEEE 14th International Conference on Industrial and Information Systems (ICIIS), pp. 458–463 (2019)
3. Dammeyer, J., Lehane, C., Marschark, M.: Use of technological aids and interpretation services among children and adults with hearing loss. Int. J. Audiol. **56**(10), 740–748 (2017)
4. Wilkins, A.J., Nimmo-Smith, I.: On the reduction of eye-strain when reading. Ophthalmic Phys. Optics. **4**(1), 53–59 (1984)
5. Daham Note, https://dahamnote.honglab.org/. Accessed 30 Jan 2023
6. CLOVA Note, https://clovanote.naver.com/home. Accessed 30 Jan 2023
7. HTTP Over TLS, https://www.ietf.org/rfc/rfc2818.txt. Accessed 30 Jan 2023
8. CLOVA Speech Recognition(CSR), https://www.ncloud.com/product/aiService/csr. Accessed 02 Feb 2023
9. AI API/DATA, https://aiopen.etri.re.kr. Accessed 02 Feb 2023
10. Speech-To-Text | Google Cloud, https://cloud.google.com/speech-to-text. Accessed 02 Feb 2023
11. Amazon Transcribe, https://aws.amazon.com/ko/transcribe. Accessed 02 Feb 2023
12. AI API | KT, https://gigagenie.kt.com/business/genieAiAPI.do. Accessed 02 Feb 2023

Put Your Hands Up - or Better Down? Towards Intuitive Gesture Interaction for Diverse Users of an Assistive Robot

Franziska Legler(✉), Dorothea Langer, Lisa-Marie Lottermoser, André Dettmann, and Angelika C. Bullinger

Technische Universität Chemnitz, Straße der Nationen 62, 09111 Chemnitz, Germany
franziska.legler@mb.tu-chemnitz.de

Abstract. With the growing number of robots in public, gesture control will be increasingly common. However, there is no gesture set for robot control which is equally usable for blind and visually impaired (BVI) as well as sighted users. Hence, this study applies a three-staged process for the design of an accessible gesture set for human-robot interaction. In Step 1, 141 intuitive gestures for three different universal robot commands were elicited by BVI as well as sighted users. The gestures were categorized based on body parts usage and associated movements. Occurrence of gesture categories was compared between the subsamples and a preliminary gesture set was selected based on frequencies and calculated agreement indices. In Step 2, those gestures were analyzed according to the fulfilment of user and technical requirements for gesture interaction derived from previous literature. Gestures fitting those requirements were selected for a final gesture set of 6 gestures covering the three robot commands. Finally, Step 3 evaluated the intuitiveness of the final gesture set with BVI users. Results are discussed regarding accessible human robot interaction and future research in gesture control of BVI users.

Keywords: gesture interaction · blind and visually impaired users · human-robot interaction

1 Introduction

With the growing number of robots in public, gesture control will be increasingly common. Gestures as an important part of nonverbal communication carry specific messages for interactions [8]. It is possible to either perform gestures on a surface [e.g., 25] or in mid-air [5]. Gesture interfaces have many plausible advantages: they can complement other interaction modes in complex systems [19] or enable human-robot interaction (HRI) independent of background noises [8], and in case of mid-air gestures, without physical contact [11]. However, despite increasing research on gesture control over the last years [22, 23] impaired users are seldom included [23]. To make robot benefits in public accessible to all users, research also needs to focus on vulnerable user groups [4].

M. Antona and C. Stephanidis (Eds.): HCII 2023, LNCS 14020, pp. 256–276, 2023.
https://doi.org/10.1007/978-3-031-35681-0_17

Blind and visually impaired (BVI) users are a special case in this context. Although gestures can only be visually perceived, even congenitally blind people are using gestures as nonverbal body language [6]. But research on mid-air gestures with BVI users is rare [10]. This study is the first to explore mid-air gestures for robot control with BVI users and provides a gesture set for three basic commands by applying a participatory approach.

1.1 Midair Gesture Interface Design

Gestures are "a form of non-verbal or non-vocal communication in which visible bodily actions communicate specific messages" [8, p. 847]. They can be static or dynamic including movements of fingers, hands and arms [14]. In particular, mid-air gestures are described to be a natural and intuitive way of interaction [10].

Today, there are no standards for gesture interface development [23] but some general design requirements for gestures can be worked out from general gesture interaction literature as well as specific literature in HRI. With the aim of reducing cognitive workload and training costs, gesture design in HRI should take ergonomic factors into account [14]. To reduce cognitive workload, gestures should be compatible with every-day body language [14], but at the same time sufficiently distinct from movements performed in everyday work tasks or personal interactions to avoid false alarms of the system. Further, when designing a gesture set in comparison to only single gesture, each gesture in a predefined set should be unique and highly distinctive from the others [14] even without any further verbal commands or sounds. With increasing number of commands supported by gesture control, this becomes increasingly difficult [10]. Hence, when designing gestures in participatory approaches the number of commands needs to be restricted to ensure that users are able to propose distinguishable gestures. User-defined gestures are superior to designer- or system-defined gestures because users remember them easier, prefer them, and believe they can learn them faster [17].

Gesture elicitation is a very successful participatory approach for gesture interface development [22]. Gesture elicitation was introduced by Wobbrock and colleagues [25] as 'referent-to-symbol' approach in a study that identified intuitive gestures for a surface-computing application. They use the term 'symbolic input' [24] for a gesture and denote the intended command of that gesture as 'referent' which is followed by the related system action [25]. They specified the 'referent' of a gesture for users and then, users performed intuitive gestures ('symbolic input') [24] that could induce this 'referent' without further explanation. For example, participants could be asked to propose a gesture (=symbolic input) commanding 'safety stop' (=referent), which immediately causes the robot to stop moving (=related system action). This approach has also been successfully applied to develop a mid-air gesture set for BVI users of a smart TV [10].

Identification studies go the opposite way and can be used to validate gesture sets. Applying this 'symbol-to-referent' approach [25], designed gestures (symbolic input) are presented to users who are asked to guess their meaning or function (referent) for a given interactive system [22]. It is seldom applied in gesture elicitation studies but can help validating elicited gesture sets [22]. This is especially important because despite extensive research regarding gesture control of robots in recent years, there is no standard use of gestures for human-machine interaction in general or any specific technology application [23]. Probably, it will take some time until mid-air gesture interface standards will be established [19], as the broad range of applications differs in requirements, and large sample sizes are necessary to establish standards for a spectrum of similar applications [23].

Beyond the field of human-machine interaction, there are already standardized mid-air gesture sets, but they cannot readily be applied in HRI. Gesture sets like military signs [14], or safety signs at work, stated in European Council Directive 92/58/EEC, include many gestures that are executed with both hands, including fast and expansive movements, and use stretched arms requiring a high freedom of movement [5]. These are characteristics of gestures that can rise technical issues in context of HRI leading to reduced recognition rates, which is why technical requirements for hand gesture recognition need to be noted when designing gestures for HRI.

1.2 Technical Hand Gesture Recognition (HGR)

Hand gesture recognition (HGR) is a growing research interest but still suffers from several technical restrictions in practice. Cho and Jeong [8] even summarize that "methods are still far from satisfactory for real-life applications" (p. 847). One important point is real-time capability of the gesture recognition system [14]. To support real-time capability, it is necessary to deduce implications for gesture design that result from current technical restrictions in HGR.

Hand recognition, and in case of dynamic gestures hand tracking, build the basis of HGR. Vision-based technologies are most frequently used for mid-air gesture recognition. Vision-based HGR is unobtrusive, allows natural movement and does not require physical contact with the user, which is why it is most commonly used and likely to gain even more importance in the future [23]. However, accuracy capabilities of current technologies are limited [23]. Vision-based HGR is mostly realized in three stages: at first image acquisition, subsequently hand and finger segmentation, and finally feature extraction and integration [14]. In every stage, current technical restrictions in vision-based recognition entail specific requirements for the type of gesture producing best recognition accuracies.

Within the first stage, image acquisition, usually hands are detected by comparing color surfaces, which makes it dependent on lighting and perspective. The Microsoft Kinect Sensor is mostly applied in practice and research [e.g., 2, 8]. It enables color detection that can be used to extract hand regions by comparing hand and face color [e.g., 10]. Therefore, lighting conditions and perspective need to be considered [14]. For example, from a side view, the detectable color surface of a palm oriented horizontal to the floor is much smaller than from a frontal view. Overlapping hands in case of two-handed gestures is another difficulty [28] as the color segmentation of hands fails. The same is true if one points directly in the direction of the vision sensor and fingertips are overlapped by the palm [21].

Within the second stage, segmentation of fingers from each other and from the palm is aimed at. Combining these information generates the shape of the hand. This is done by identifying concavities within a calculated convex hull. Concavities show finger segmentations and the number of fingers [1, 14] and fingertips are identified by anchor points between fingers [21]. Hence, it should be easy to detect one or five spread fingers but all other combinations of fingers, especially grouped fingers, could be hard to identify.

The same is true for reversed hand orientation displaying equal fingers. Additionally, hand shape is mostly ignored for gesture identification of dynamic gestures [15].

Within the last stage, features of complex gestures are extracted and integrated to recognize the gesture. This stage is mainly relevant for dynamic gestures, as static gestures consist of fewer features. Hence, recognition of static gestures is comparatively less challenging [15]. The execution of dynamic gestures is characterized by inter- and intrapersonal variations in speed [5] and trajectory [21]. Further, trajectories of dynamic gestures need clear start and end positions of hands for identification [15, 29] and, to segment waypoints between start and end position, pausing positions of the palm need to be detected [15]. An additional feature used for gesture recognition is the relative position of hands and arms in comparison to body levels. Hence, both static and dynamic gestures are analyzed regarding relative position compared to head level [5, 15].

1.3 Design for Special Needs of Impaired Users

Gestures are used by BVI people and accordingly, gesture interfaces should be designed in an accessible way. BVI users' nonverbal communication contains gestures [e.g., 6, 10] and they prefer interfaces designed as closely as possible to customary products, feeling uncomfortable if they are dependent on special solutions [9]. Consequently, design activities should always target smooth interactions for all users while paying attention to inclusive approaches rather than developing special solutions for BVI users [9]. Otherwise, special user groups are excluded from experiencing the benefits provided by improving technologies [10].

Few studies investigating the use of mid-air gestures included BVI people [10]. Still, some requirements for gesture sets for BVI users can be derived from previous literature. A study by [13] investigated different target-aiming strategies with BVI users interacting with a large wall-mounted display. But rather than natural gesture interaction, the goal of this study was to find an efficient movement strategy for BVI users for pointing at a certain object on the screen. In the context of smart TV control, [10] developed a mid-air gesture set, covering 15 commonly used TV commands (e.g., Play, Pause, Next/Previous Channel) and commands that are specifically used by blind people (e.g., Open Voice Guide). Additionally, they derived some guidelines for mid-air gesture sets design for BVI users.

While commands from [10] are not transferrable to HRI due to the differing context, guidelines for designing accessible mid-air gestures for BVI users can be derived from previous literature. People with impaired vision are often less experienced with the use of gestures as a part of communication and have little prior knowledge using gestures to interact with automation devices [10]. As assistive technology is often used by elderly users, conditions that frequently occur in combination with visual impairment (e.g. motor impairments) should also be considered in order to maximize inclusion. By taking motor impairments into account, gestures should reduce physical effort [14]. Further, as proprioception is the only source for BVI people to estimate lengths and directions, all movements should be referenced to the users' body [7, 10]. Furthermore, interface designers are less familiar with the living environments of BVI users [16]. Hence, they often develop gestures based on symbols or visual references that are unknown to BVI people [10]. Therefore, instead of designing gestures according to symbols and visual references like letters they should mimic everyday actions or interaction with familiar devices like smartphones [10]. Studies with BVI users on surface gestures observed a lack of consistency and accuracy in gesture execution regarding position, line stability and form closure. Gestures from BVI users therefore generally suffer from low recognition rates [12]. Additionally, one specific feature of BVI users is carrying a white stick [3]. One-hand gestures are in line with general design recommendations [5, 14] to make them practicable in everyday life.

1.4 Research Approach and Contribution

To conclude, mid-air gesture interfaces are of rising importance regarding public robot services. They can be designed accessible for BVI users and should be as close as possible to customary interfaces for sighted users. There is no standard for robot gesture interfaces and barely research on mid-air gestures including BVI users. Moreover, accessible gesture sets from other applications cannot be transferred to HRI. Hence, in this study an accessible gesture set for HRI is designed.

It was shown that a participatory approach combining gesture elicitation and gesture identification ensures intuitiveness and usability. Requirements for selecting appropriate candidates from user-elicited gestures can be derived from general gesture interaction literature, specific literature in HRI and previous studies on gestures with BVI users. As the number of different commands needs to be restricted in gesture elicitation studies, gestures for only three commands of HRI are included in this study. START and END of an interaction are universal commands needed in every HRI application [18]. Additionally, for safety reasons a SAFETY STOP command is usually implemented in HRI, which immediately stops robot actions or movements [e.g., 20, 26, 27].

Even though user needs should be highest priority in designing gestures, disregarding technical or environmental restrictions lowers hand gesture recognition accuracy. Hence, besides general and BVI specific user requirements on robot gesture interfaces, requirements from literature on current gesture recognition technology are used for selecting appropriate user-elicited gestures for the final gesture set.

We therefore apply a three-staged process for the design of an accessible gesture set for HRI which is equally usable by BVI and sighted users:

- Step 1: Gathering intuitive gestures for three universal robot commands of BVI and sighted users, gesture categorization and selection of a preliminary gesture set
- Step 2: Comparing preselected gestures to deduced design guidelines based on user and technical requirements to extract a final gesture set
- Step 3: Evaluation of the final gesture set regarding intuitiveness

Each of the three design steps is described in Sects. 2 to 4 reporting method and results separately for each step. Section 5 gives an overall discussion of results regarding accessible HRI and future research in gesture control of BVI users.

2 Step 1: Quasi-Experiment for Gesture Collection

2.1 Method

Sample. 43 (28 female) participants were recruited for the experiment. The group of sighted users consisted of university staff, students, partners of BVI users and staff of the assistive federations. Subsample statistics are given in Table 1. BVI users were acquired from a local assistive federation for the blind and a local association for visually impaired people. The group of BVI users is heterogeneous - there is no perfect linear relationship between visual test results and remaining capabilities of an individual. Referring to legal definitions of Germany, the group of BVI participants in this research either involved 'strongly visually impaired people' with up to 5% remaining sight in the less impaired eye or 'blind people with less than 2% remaining sight'. Eyesight of 12 participants was below 5% and 8 participants were congenitally blind.

Table 1. Sample statistics of total sample and two subsamples.

Parameter	all	sighted	BVI
N	43	27	16
age (mean, [SD])	34 [13.7]	32 [15.3]	38 [9.4]
Age (range)	16 to 71	19 to 71	16 to 55

Procedure. The quasi-experiment was conducted in a laboratory setting. After signing an informed consent and a privacy declaration, participants received an oral description of a robot designed to hand over objects to BVI users and which should support an interaction by gestures. According to this robotic application, participants sat in front of the experimenter. Three cameras on tripods recorded the experiment. Participants were asked to mentally put themselves to the situation of interacting with the robot. Subsequently, they were asked to spontaneously perform a gesture to (A) START, (B) END and (C) STOP (safety stop) an imaginary interaction with that robot. To distinguish the last two commands, 'END' was further described as ending an interaction after the task of the robot was completed and 'STOP' as immediately interrupting the interaction for example in case of emergency. Participants were free to use one or two hands, or to accompany gestures by sounds or oral commands if necessary. After gesture execution, following questions were asked: How did you experience interacting through gestures? Were there any difficulties performing one or more specific gestures? Do you want to comment on anything else (positive/negative)?

Data Analysis. The analysis of the video recordings yielded detailed written descriptions of the gestures performed, allowing for the specification of gesture types along pre-defined dimensions. These contained: Number of fingers and hands used, dynamics defined as uniformity of movements and total gesture execution time, trajectories operationalized as changes of arm and hand positions relative to body parts, and use of acoustics. Within each command (START, END, SAFETY STOP), gestures were grouped into categories according to their specification along the dimensions listed above. If necessary, categories were further divided into subcategories. Although gestures were never performed in the same way by different users, subcategories represented a subset of gestures that could not be further distinguished based on the predefined dimensions. Therefore, subcategories formed the smallest unit of analysis in this study. Equal gestures performed as one-handed or two-handed gesture were assigned to the same category. In case of conflicts occurring from equal gesture categories for different robot commands, conflicts were resolved in accordance with [24]: If one gesture X was performed for different robot commands Y and Z, this gesture X was assigned to the command where it is significantly more often applied. For each category found, an agreement index A was calculated separately for each robot command according to [25]. For more information on calculation, please refer to ibid. This agreement index was also used by [10] who labeled the gestures with the highest agreement indices the "set of suitable gestures" (p. 205). The value of A is approaching 1 in case of complete agreement and approaching 0 (limited by the lower boundary of $|P_r|^{-1}$) in case of complete disagreement. Resulting, the smaller the sample included, the higher the influence of $|P_r|^{-1}$ on A. Therefore, a sample size adjusted A_{adj} is reported by calculating the lower boundary $|P_r|^{-1}$ for each category and command and subtracted from raw A (see Eq. 1).

$$A_{adj} = \frac{\sum_{r \in R} \sum_{P_i \subseteq P_r} \left(\frac{|P_i|}{|P_r|} \right)^2}{|R|} - |P_r|^{-1} \tag{1}$$

Agreement index A was also calculated across all occurring categories for one intended command to determine the overall agreement of users regarding gestures for one specific robot command.

2.2 Results

Overview of Derived Gesture Categories. Table 2 presents all categories for the three robot commands captured within Step 1 of the research approach. Overall, 18 gesture categories based on 141 performed gestures (52 gestures for command START, 44 gestures for END and 45 gestures for SAFETY STOP) were created, labeled and verbally described. For illustration, Table 10 in Appendix describes a prototypical gesture for each category. Within each category, agreement index A_{adj} (see Sect. 2.1 data analysis) was calculated to check homogeneity of the categories based on the number of subcategories and their distribution. Figure 1 shows the occurrence of each gesture category dependent on command and subsample. Following, with the aim of finding suitable gesture sets for each robotic command, results are reported separately for each command. Only gestures performed at least twice were further analyzed.

Gesture Set START. For command START, overall agreement was relatively low. Sighted users showed higher homogeneity in comparison to BVI users (see Table 3). Absolute values of A are comparable to [25] who found a range of $.100 < A < .400$ for complex gestures in a homogenous sample. Figure 1 shows the distribution of different gesture categories used by sighted and blind BVI users, indicating that the two subsamples performed different categories of gestures. Consequently, absolute frequency alone is not a suitable decision criterion. For example, the most frequent category *Beckon* was only applied by sighted users while pure *Voice command* without any gesture was only used by BVI users. *Handover-request, Waving, Raise one's hand* and *Clapping* were selected to further analyze subsample agreement.

Table 2. Adjusted agreement index A_{adj} for all gesture categories, calculated separately for each of the three robot commands. [a] bold A_{adj} shows the command to which a category was assigned in case of conflict (in accordance with [24]). [b] X = 1 incident and excluded for further analysis

Category	Adjusted agreement index A_{adj}		
	START	END	STOP
Beckon (single-arm gesture, dynamic)	281		
Waving (single-arm gesture, dynamic)	**.612**[a]	.000	
Handover request (single-arm gesture, static)	.395		
Raise one's hand (single-arm gesture, static)	.556		
Clapping (two-armed gesture, dynamic)	**.320**[a]	.222	.125
Flick one's fingers (single-arm gesture, dynamic)	.833		
Voice command (no gesture)	**.389**[a]	.111	.667
Thumbs-up sign (single-arm gesture, static)	X[b]		
Imaginary button push (single-arm g., dynamic)	X[b]	X[b]	
Sound (oral) (no gesture)	X[b]		
Sending away (single-arm gesture, dynamic)		**.225**[a]	X[b]
Stop-sign (single-arm gesture, static)		.446	**.430**[a]
Crossing (two-armed gesture, static)		.438	**.242**[a]
Nod one's head (no hand gesture, dynamic)		.500	
Boxing (single-arm gesture, static)		X[b]	
Time-out sign (two-armed gesture, static)			.500
Clenched fist (single-arm gesture, static)			X[b]
Head-shaking (no hand gesture, dynamic)			X[b]

Adjusted agreement index for category *Handover-request* was higher for sighted (A_{adj} = .375) than for BVI users (A_{adj} = .240). For category *Waving* also sighted (A_{adj} = .800) showed a higher agreement than BVI users (A_{adj} = .000). Conversely, for category *Raise one's hand* sighted (A_{adj} = .222) showed less agreement than BVI users (A_{adj} = .666). Since only one sighted user used *Clapping*, agreement could only be computed for BVI users and was A_{adj} = .250. *Waving* and *Clapping* were also performed for commands END and SAFETY STOP. Category *Waving* was excluded because it was not often applied in the BVI subsample and did not show sufficient agreement. *Handover-request, Raise one's hand* and *Clapping* were used as preliminary gesture set for further analysis.

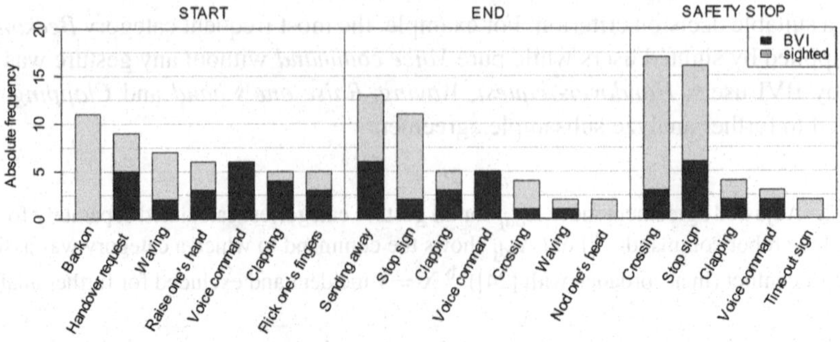

Fig. 1. Absolute frequencies of performed gestures for all commands in two subsamples.

Table 3. Agreement index for gesture categories for command START. Note: Smaller n_{cat} in subsamples resulting from categories exclusion with incident < 2 (also applies to Table 4 and 5)

Parameter	all	BVI	sighted
Overall number of performed gestures N	49	23	25
Number of different gesture categories n_{cat}	7	6	5
Agreement index A	.155	.187	.280

Gesture Set END. For command END, overall agreement was relatively low. BVI users showed a higher homogeneity in produced gestures than sighted users (see Table 4). Figure 1 shows the distribution of gesture categories between subsamples. Category *Stop-sign* was often performed. Still, this category was excluded for further analysis as users mentioned that they pre-empted this category for the later requested command SAFETY STOP. Category *Crossing* was significantly more often used for command SAFETY STOP and was therefore also excluded here. Category *Clapping* was already assigned to command START due to higher agreement (see Table 2). Accordingly, only category *Sending away* was used for comparison of sighted and BVI users. Agreement was equal for sighted (A_{adj} = .286) and BVI users (A_{adj} = .222). The category consisted of two homogeneous subcategories called *Assigning a place* and *Pushing away*, representing 4 and 5 out of 13 gestures, respectively. Both subcategories of category *Sending away* were used as preliminary gesture set for further analysis.

Table 4. Agreement index for gesture categories for command END

Parameter	all	BVI	sighted
Overall number of performed gestures N	42	16	23
Number of different gesture categories n_{cat}	7	4	5
Agreement index A	.206	.289	.278

Gesture set SAFETY STOP. Figure 1 shows the distribution of gesture categories between subsamples. For command SAFETY STOP, overall agreement was $A = .326$. Sighted users showed higher homogeneity in produced gestures than BVI users (see Table 5). Overall, homogeneity of categories was higher for command SAFETY STOP than the other two commands (see Tables 3, 4 and 5). Category *Crossing* showed high agreement in sighted ($A_{adj} = .265$) but not in BVI users ($A_{adj} = .000$). For category *Stop-sign* agreement was high for both sighted ($A_{adj} = .440$) and BVI ($A_{adj} = .333$) users. Both categories consisted of two homogeneous subcategories describable as static and dynamic, which were retained in the preliminary gesture set.

Table 5. Agreement index for gesture categories for command SAFETY STOP

Parameter	all	BVI	sighted
Overall number of performed gestures N	42	13	28
Number of different gesture categories n_{cat}	5	4	4
Agreement index A	.326	.314	.388

Preliminary Gesture Set. Step 1 of our research approach resulted in a preliminary gesture set for all three robot commands based on frequency, agreement indices and conflict freeness (see Sect. 2.1). The most prototypical gesture within each gesture category was selected. Following, the term 'gesture' is used instead of 'gesture category' as all further research steps refer to these prototypical gestures. Nine prototypical gestures were included in Step 2. The 3 START gestures included were: *Handover-request* (request to place something in the hand), *Raise one's hand* (pointing upwards to get attention) and *Clapping* (two/three times on chest height; dynamic gesture). The 2 END gestures included were: *Pushing away* (of an imaginary object from oneself; dynamic gesture) and *Assigning a place* (pointing to an imaginary distant place). The 4 SAFETY STOP gestures included were: *Crossing* (arms crossed with hands contralateral against shoulders), *Crossing dynamic* (levelly moving arms to and from each other with palms facing down; dynamic gesture), *Stop-sign* (symbolic stop-sign with stretched palm presented towards the receiver), and *Stop-sign dynamic* (symbolic stop-sign with stretched palm and quick for-/backward motion of palm; dynamic gesture).

3 Step 2: Comparison to User Needs and Technical Requirements

3.1 Method

Based on technical and user requirements in gesture interaction, 18 guidelines were deduced for gesture design (Table 6, referenced to literature introduced in Sect. 1). We rated each of the nine gestures of our preliminary gesture set on the 18 guidelines as fulfilled (= 1) or not fulfilled (= 0). As an additional evaluation criterion, we calculated the relative frequency of a gesture in relation to all gestures performed in the respective

Table 6. Overview of deduced guidelines for gesture recognition based on technical (T) and user (U) requirements

Guideline for gesture (set) design	type	based on references
(1) easy to perform and avoid cumbersome motions	T, U	2; 14; 21
(2) maximize fit with familiar situations	U	10; 14
(3) easy to remember	U	14
(4) different from motions performed in everyday work tasks or personal interactions	T, U	14
(5) different gesture in a set should be highly distinctive	T, U	14
(6) present the whole palm for recognition accuracy	T	14
(7) avoid an overlapping of hands	T	12; 28
(8) avoid an overlapping of fingers with the palm	T	21
(9) use different number of fingers for different gestures in a set	T	1; 12; 14; 21
(10) avoid differentiating dynamic gestures by hand shapes	T	15
(11) prefer static gestures over dynamic gestures	T	15
(12) use highly diverse for trajectories and speed for different dynamic gestures in a set	T	5; 21
(13) use trajectories with clear or even equal start and end positions of hands and clear pausing positions	T	5; 15; 29
(14) use different positions in comparison to head level for different gestures in a set	T	5; 15
(15) small gestures without arm/body spread	U	7
(16) prefer gestures that require only one hand	U	3; 5; 14
(17) avoid symbolic gestures/needs for visual references	U	10
(18) use body-centric gestures	U	10

gesture category, resp. subcategory. Good representativeness of the prototypical gesture for a specific command should be reflected in a high relative frequency (guideline 19). The sum of the dichotomous ratings divided by the number of applied guidelines was used as goodness rating (GR) for the comparison of gestures. For dynamic gestures, all 19 guidelines can be applied. To static gestures guidelines (10), (12) and (13) do not apply, resulting in 16 remaining guidelines for static gestures. Guideline 11 resulted in one extra point for all static gestures according to technical easiness.

Additionally, we applied "a measure of guessability" in accordance with [24] to determine which proportion of performed gestures within one command could be represented by the final gesture set for each of the three robot commands (see Eq. 2, for further information on calculation please refer to [24, p. 1871]).

$$G = \frac{\sum_{s \in S} |P_s|}{|P|} \times 100\% \tag{2}$$

3.2 Results

Table 7 shows fulfillment of gesture design guidelines of all 9 preliminary gestures. Goodness ratings (GR) showed an underperformance of the gestures *Clapping (d)* and *Crossing (d)* leading to exclusion from the final gesture set. Static and dynamic *Stop-sign* were only separated by motion while all other characteristics, including hand shape and position were equal. As the static *Stop-sign* showed slightly higher GR, it was finally selected.

Table 7. Goodness Rating and failed guidelines of the preliminary gesture set. (d) = dynamic gesture, [a] guideline partly failed

gesture	command	Goodness rating in %	numbers of failed guidelines
Handover-request	START	71	4;5;6;19
Raise one's hand	START	92	4
Clapping (d)	START	38	2;4;5[a];6;7;9;11;12;14;16[a];19
Pushing away (d)	END	79	4;11;15;19[a]
Assigning a place	END	75	4;5;6;19[a]
Crossing	STOP	86	9;19
Crossing (d)	STOP	35	4;5;6;7;11;12;13;14;16;15;19
Stop-sign	STOP	79	5;9;14
Stop-sign (d)	STOP	71	5[a];9;11;13;14;19[a]

The final gesture set for three robot commands contained six gestures which are described in Table 8. All robot commands were represented by two distinct gestures. The "measure of guessability G" [24] was used to access representativeness of selected gesture categories for all performed gesture categories within one special robot command. The resulting user-defined gesture set (see Table 8) covers 30% of all START gesture categories, 30% of all END gesture categories and 75% of all SAFETY STOP gesture categories.

4 Step 3: Evaluation-Study of Final Gesture Set

4.1 Method

Sample. Through local associations of the blind, 7 (4 female) BVI users with a mean age of 49 years (SD = 10.2) were recruited for the evaluation study. According to the legal definitions described in Sect. 2.1, six users were congenitally blind, one user had a remaining sight of 8% and lost sight at the age of one year.

Procedure. The whole study was audio- and video-recorded. The study started with a brief description of an assistive robot for handover tasks, including its purpose and the possibility for gesture interaction. After that, users were asked to mentally put themselves into the situation of interacting with the robot. A step-by-step verbal description for each of the gestures of the final gesture set (2 gestures for each of the 3 robot commands, see Table 8) was presented to the users who should perform each gesture accordingly, because it is important for users to perform gestures while purely listening to a verbal description of gestures is not sufficient to estimate gesture suitability [10]. At this point, users did not know the intended robot command. Verbal descriptions contained positions and angles of body parts as well as motions, intentionally avoiding the usage of describing words/phrases (e.g., "pointing" for gesture *Assigning a place*, to avoid associations with commands biasing subsequent command naming). Correctness of gesture performance was observed by the examiner. For the first gesture of each command, users were asked which action a robot detecting this gesture would perform.

After both gestures of one command were performed, users made a preference choice (choice-based approach, also applied in [10]). Additionally, users gave qualitative feedback concerning easiness of performance, general perception and plausibility of gestures but also commented during the study without formal request.

Data Analysis. Correctness of performance was coded dichotomously on a three-point scale as correct (= 1), slightly incorrect (= 0.5) or incorrect (= 0). The examiner was given examples on slightly correct performances, e.g., the gesture matched the intended gesture due to number of fingers and shape of palm, ensuring a correct recognition, but direction of palm was backwards instead of forwards. In case of coding insecurity, the video material was spotted and a consensus of examiners was reached. For preference choice, participants rated both gestures on a three-point scale as preferred (=1), even (= 0.5) or rejected (= 0). For both, performance correctness and preference choice of each gesture, percentage of fulfillment across all users was calculated. Correctness of the interpreted command was qualitatively analyzed. Finally, qualitative feedback for gestures and unspecific comments were summarized.

4.2 Results

Quantitative Results. Table 9 presents the results for correctness of performance and preference choice for the final gesture set (see Table 8). Overall correctness of performance was high but showed considerable variance between gestures. Verbal descriptions seemed sufficient to perform the START and END gestures while gesture *Stop-sign* caused problems for the participants. Agreement regarding preference choice was lowest within the gesture set for the command SAFETY STOP.

Qualitative Results. Preliminary interview: All BVI users were skeptical about the gesture interaction. They feared making mistakes when executing gestures and emphasized a need for training as well as additional interaction channels, more precisely voice commands. BVI users described gesture interaction as a suitable interaction modality for simple commands (confirmations/rejections, interruption of interactions or sending the robot away), particularly advantageous in noisy environments as well as for the older and hearing-impaired people. Mentioned barriers of usage were correctness of robotic gesture recognition, hidden sight between robot and user, occupied hands due to holding objects and missing feedback if the robot starts the correct action.

Table 8. Final gesture set for three robot commands; features of gesture: (d) dynamic, (s) static, \o/ two-arm,.o/ single-arm

Name, features [COMMAND]	Verbal description	Picture
Handover request (s) .o/ [START]	1. elbow resting loosely to the side of your body 2. forearm levelly angled to the front 3. palm opened towards the ceiling and forming a hollow	
Raise one's hand (s) .o/ [START]	4. make a fist side next to your head 5. elbow resting loosely to the side of your body, elbow points downwards 6. index finger extended upwards	
Pushing away (d) .o/ [END]	7. place your hand in front of chest with opened palm 8. release elbows from body slightly upward 9. turn palm away from your body, still resting on your chest 10. move the arm with outstretched palm to the side until your arm is stretched	 
Assigning a place (s) .o/ [END]	11. make a fist and extend your index finger 12. extend your arm completely 13. adjust your extended arm to an imaginary spot on the floor sideways in front of you	
Stop-sign (s) .o/ [SAFETY STOP]	14. hold your hand comfortably sideways next to the shoulder belonging to the hand 15. elbow relaxed and pointing downwards 16. outstretch your palm and aligned to the front	
Crossing (s) \o/ [SAFETY STOP]	17. make a fist with both hands 18. both elbows resting loosely to the side of your body 19. place your right fist loosely below the left shoulder and leave it there 20. place your left fist loosely below the right shoulder	

Table 9. Quantitative results of evaluation study; (d) = dynamic gesture; [a] percentage of both gestures within one command sums up to 100%

Gesture	command	correct performances	Preferred choice[a]
Handover request	START	64%	64%
Raise one's hand	START	71%	36%
Pushing away (d)	END	93%	71%
Assigning a place	END	86%	29%
Stop-sign	STOP	43%	57%
Crossing	STOP	71%	43%

Gesture set START: Six out of seven users correctly identified the intended robot command. Gesture *Handover Request* was interpreted as signaling the users' intention to ask for or to receive an object from the robot. This interpretation was in line with the use case of this study - an assistive robot designed to hand over objects to BVI users. Users imagined the robot reacting to the gesture by asking 'How may I help you', which could be interpreted as the start of an interaction. However, due to the strong association with handover situations, all users felt that the gesture *Handover Request* was unsuitable to represent a general, cross-platform START gesture. Gesture *Raise one's hand* was interpreted as a request (for attention) of the robot. Accordingly, users imagined the robot to react with system activation, waiting for an order or explicitly asking for their wishes. All users perceived this gesture as suitable to start a robotic interaction.

Gesture set END: Four out of seven users correctly identified the intended robot command. Gesture *Pushing away* was interpreted as completion of task and sending the robot away when no longer needed. Accordingly, users correctly imagined the robot to react by system inaction or moving away from the user. Gesture *Assigning a Place* was incorrectly identified as a pointing gesture. Associations were 'searching for an object' or 'guide the robot's attention towards something/somewhere'. Only one user interpreted the robot command correctly by saying that the robot would move away. This result is in line with the preference choice for gesture *Pushing away.* However, some users mentioned that performing this gesture requires moving the arm far away from the body, causing a loss of control for BVI users.

Gesture set SAFETY STOP: Two out of seven users correctly identified the intended robot command. For both gestures, *Stop-sign* and *Crossing*, the command SAFETY STOP was identified correctly by only one user each. Most users did not mention any association of command, especially for gesture *Crossing*. Interpretations of gesture *Stop-sign* varied between 'immediate deactivation of the robot', 'ending the interaction' and 'confirming robots' action'. Consequently, users could not clearly distinguish between robot commands END and SAFETY STOP. Even after the intended command was announced, users did not show a clear preference for one of the gestures, although gesture *Crossing* was criticized for requiring the use of both hands.

Overall, users expressed few problems with gesture execution during the study. The final gesture set was described as easy and feasible – even for users with motor impairments - but still unfamiliar. The users felt that controlling a robot using gestures was generally useful, but particularly important in situations where voice commands are not applicable, for example in noisy environments. Users mentioned few alternative gestures and none of them was new in comparison to results of Step 1.

5 Discussion

By applying a three-staged participatory research process, the aim of this study was to design an intuitive gesture set for HRI accessible for sighted as well as BVI users.

Step 1 identified a preliminary set of nine gestures for the three universal robot functions START, END and SAFETY STOP. Most categories were represented by both user groups. Also, contrary to former gesture elicitation studies with BVI users [10], agreement indices were comparable to gesture elicitation studies with sighted users and did not differ much between BVI and sighted users. The existence of common gestures generalizable for both user groups indicates that accessible gesture interaction in HRI can be designed for all users fulfilling the respective claim of Costa and Duarte [9]. Some gestures were proposed for several commands, but by differing participants. This result is unlike previous gesture elicitation studies, were BVI users proposed identical gestures for several commands due to the high number of examined commands [10]. Therefore, restricting the number of commands for gesture control in elicitation studies can be recommended.

Several limitations apply to Step 1 of the research. First, no randomization in robot functions was applied. This resulted in pre-empting of specific gestures for the later requested functions. A randomization could have led to different results, especially for robot functions END and SAFETY STOP. Still, we counteracted this limitation by including qualitative feedback regarding pre-empting for gesture selection. Second, the representativeness of the collected in comparison to all possible gesture categories cannot be assessed. Still, within Step 3 of our research, no new alternative gestures were performed. Finally, gestures were assigned qualitatively to categories, allowing a scope of interpretation.

The preliminary gesture set was compared to technical and user requirements within research Step 2. Goodness ratings for the fulfillment of requirements showed the practicality of six gestures forming the final gesture set for three robot commands. Absolute levels of goodness ratings of the final gesture set show that freely produced gestures met technical restrictions of HGR quite well. Still, some limitations apply to step 2. Objective weightings of different technical requirements could not be deducted from literature and were therefore not applied for the goodness ratings. Further, the applied technical requirements are expected to be beneficial for vision-based gesture recognition but could be opposed in case of gesture recognition based on motion sensors [e.g., 29]. Further research should therefore review the fit of deduced technical requirements for recognition by motion sensors.

In Step 3, we evaluated the final gesture set. Although participants expressed concerns regarding gesture control during the preliminary interview, they expressed few problems with gesture execution during the study and correctness of performance was high. Only verbal description of gesture *Stop-sign* seemed insufficient to perform the gesture correctly. In line with [10] this shows that during gesture learning, BVI users need to actually perform the gestures along a verbal description. Additionally, our study showed that a step-by-step description containing positions and angles of body parts as well as motions in a body-centered way is recommendable. Participants also emphasized a need for training which is supported by the result that they could only guess the intended robot command on occasion. However, after telling participants the associated commands, the final gesture set was described as easy and feasible, even for users with motor impairments. Within command START, gesture *Handover Request* was evaluated as only suitable for the application of a handover robot while *Raise one's hand* was preferred and evaluated as suitable for general usage. Within command END, gesture *Pushing away* was preferred, but users would need feedback that there are no potential obstacles they could bump in when executing the gesture. Gesture *Assigning a place* might be better suitable for a command like starting a search. Therefore, applicability of some of the gestures in HRI depends on context. Within command SAFETY STOP, users did not show a clear preference for one of the gestures, so both could be applied.

Despite high correctness of performance and subjective easiness and feasibility, gesture control still felt unfamiliar to BVI users and they expressed the need for additional interaction channels, more precisely voice commands. Moreover, in Step 1 some BVI users proposed pure voice commands instead of gestures. These results are in accordance with previous research indicating an unfamiliarity with gestures for BVI people resulting in a preference for speech input [3, 16]. Consequently, an accessible HRI interface should offer more than one input channels to let users choose their preferred one. Still, not preferred channels should be accessible for all users at least as a fallback interface. A redundant channel combination enhances system robustness which is especially important for safety stop functions.

Results of Step 3 are limited by restricting gesture evaluation on BVI users only. However, due to high correctness of performance with BVI users, similar or better guessability of the final gesture set by sighted users can be expected. Besides, further research should investigate technical gesture recognition of the final gesture set.

6 Conclusion

The study applied a three-staged process for designing gestures for HRI with an assistive robot accessible for BVI and sighted users. The final gesture set of six gestures for three robot commands showed good fulfillment of user and technical requirements and could be correctly performed on the basis of verbal, body-centered descriptions. The usage of static gestures can be recommended due to easiness of performance on the side of the end users as well as technical requirements for optical HGR on the other side. Contrary to high correctness of performance, BVI users were not feeling confident regarding pure gesture interaction with an assistive robot. End users should therefore be able to individualize their preferred interaction modality. Nevertheless, it is recommended to design interaction concepts for different modalities to ensure robustness of recognition. Particularly for important robot commands, like an immediate safety stop, end users should be aware of and trained for all possible input modalities to counteract potential channel malfunction. All in all, this suggests that controlling a robot using gestures is generally useful and also applicable for BVI users if special needs of this group are taken into account. For this group, gestures are particularly important in situations where voice commands are not feasible, for example in noisy environments.

Acknowledgments. This research took place within the scope of project "MIRobO" (project number 16SV7969K) supported by German Federal Ministry of Education and Research. The authors acknowledge this financial support. Federal Ministry did not have an impact on study design, data acquisition, analysis and interpretation of data as well as authoring and submission of this paper. We especially acknowledge the support of Weißer Stock e.V., SFZ Förderzentrum gGmbH as well as local associations for visually impaired people BSV Sachsen e.V. and thank our participants.

Appendix

Table 10. Description of a prototypical gesture for each category, (d) dynamic gesture, (s) static gesture, \o/ two-arm gesture, .o/ single-arm gesture, .o. no-hand gesture

Category	Description of prototypical gesture
Beckon *(d)* .o/	(1) one arm angled, elbow tight to the body side, forearm stretched levelly towards the robot, open palm directed to the ceiling, (2) partial or complete closing of palm while pulling forearm closer to the body, (3) step 1 and 2 repeated
Waving *(d)* .o/	(1) one arm angled to the side, palm directed to the front on chin level, (2) hand waving repeatedly (left to right movement)
Handover request *(s)* .o/	(1) elbow resting to the side of the body, forearm levelly angled to the front, palm opened to the ceiling forming a hollow
Raise one's hand *(s)* .o/	(1) hand clenched into a fist on head level, index finger extended upwards, elbow resting at body side
Clapping *(d)* \o/	(1) hands hitting against each other (variations: speed, frequency, chest/waist level)
Flick one's fingers *(d)* .o/	(1) flicking thumb and middle finger on chest or waist height
Voice command *(oral)* .o	e.g., "Give it to me!", "Come here!", "Hello robot", "Start!"
Thumbs-up sign *(s)* .o/	(1) arm angled, palm clenched into a fist, thumb abducted and thumb pointing upwards on chest level (variations: in front/to the side of the body)
Imaginary Button Push *(d)* .o/	(1) palm clenched into a fist, index finger abducted, arm almost completely stretched, (2) full extension of the arm, (3) followed by opposing movement until position of (1)

(continued)

Table 10. *(continued)*

Category	Description of prototypical gesture
Sound *(oral)* .o	clicking the tongue
Sending away *(d)* .o/	(1) hand placed in front of chest, palm opened and facing away from the body, elbows slightly away from the body, (2) arm movement with outstretched palm to full extension
Stop-sign *(s)* .o/	(1) hand hold sideways next to the ipsilateral shoulder, elbow pointing downwards, palm outstretched and aligned to the front
Crossing *(s)* \o/	(1) both elbows resting at the body side, both hands clenched into fists and placed on the contralateral shoulder forming a cross in front of the body
Nod one's head *(d)* .o	(1) repeated nodding of head (up and down movement)
Boxing *(d)* .o/	(1) hand clenched into a fist, (2) pushing fist quickly forwards and opening fist when arm is completely stretched
Time-out sign *(s)* \o/	(1) first arm angled in front of the body with palm stretched upwards, second forearm levelly and rectangular placed on the fingers of the first palm
Clenched fist *(s)* .o/	(1) arm angled and hand clenched into a fist
Head-shaking *(d)* .o	(1) repeated shaking of head (left to right movement)

References

1. Ananthakumar, A.: Efficient face and gesture recognition for time sensitive application. In: Proceedings of the IEEE Southwest Symposium on Image Analysis and Interpretation, pp. 117–120. IEEE, New York (2018). https://doi.org/10.1109/SSIAI.2018.8470351
2. Auquilla, A.R., Salamea, H.T., Alvarado-Cando, O., Molina, J.K., Cedillo, P.A.S.: Implementation of a telerobotic system based on the kinect sensor for the inclusion of people with physical disabilities in the industrial sector. In: Proceedings of the 4th IEEE Colombian Conference on Automatic Control, pp. 1–6. IEEE, New York (2019). https://doi.org/10.1109/CCAC.2019.8921359
3. Azenkot, S., Lee, N.B.: Exploring the use of speech input by blind people on mobile devices. In: Proceedings of the 15th International Conference on Computers and Accessibility, pp. 1–8. ACM, New York (2013). https://doi.org/10.1145/2513383.2513440
4. Babel, F., Kraus, J., Baumann, M.: Findings from a qualitative field study with an autonomous robot in public: exploration of user reactions and conflicts. Int. J. Soc. Robot. **14**(7), 1625–1655 (2022). https://doi.org/10.1007/s12369-022-00894-x
5. Barattini, P., Morand, C., Robertson, N.M.: A proposed gesture set for the control of industrial collaborative robots. In: IEEE RO-MAN: The 21st IEEE International Symposium on Robot and Human Interactive Communication, pp. 132–137. IEEE, New York (2012). https://doi.org/10.1109/ROMAN.2012.6343743
6. Bruce, S.M., Mann, A., Jones, C., Gavin, M.: Gestures expressed by children who are congenitally deaf-blind: topography, rate, and function. J. Visual Impair. Blind. **101**(10), 637–652 (2007). https://doi.org/10.1177/0145482X0710101010

7. Buzzi, M.C., Buzzi, M., Leporini, B., Trujillo, A.: Analyzing visually impaired people's touch gestures on smartphones. Multimedia Tools Appl. **76**(4), 5141–5169 (2016). https://doi.org/10.1007/s11042-016-3594-9
8. Cho, M.-Y., Jeong, Y.S.: Human gesture recognition performance evaluation for service robots. In: Proceedings of the 19th International Conference on Advanced Communication Technology, pp. 847–851. IEEE, New York (2017). https://doi.org/10.23919/ICACT.2017.7890213
9. Costa, D., Duarte, C.: Alternative modalities for visually impaired users to control smart TVs. Multimedia Tools Appl. **79**(43–44), 31931–31955 (2020). https://doi.org/10.1007/s11042-020-09656-1
10. Dim, N.K., Silpasuwanchai, C., Sarcar, S., Ren, X.: Designing mid-air TV gestures for blind people using user- and choice-based elicitation approaches. In: Proceedings of the 2016 ACM Conference on Designing Interactive Systems, pp. 204–214. ACM, New York (2016). https://doi.org/10.1145/2901790.2901834
11. Jalab, H.A., Omer, H.K.: Human computer interface using hand gesture recognition based on neural network. In: Proceedings of 5th National Symposium on Information Technology, pp. 1–6. IEEE, New York (2015). https://doi.org/10.1109/NSITNSW.2015.7176405
12. Kane, S.K., Wobbrock, J.O., Ladner, R.E.: Usable gestures for blind people: understanding preference and performance. In: Proceedings of the SIGCHI Conference on Human Factors in Computing Systems, pp. 413–422. ACM, New York (2011). https://doi.org/10.1145/1978942.1979001
13. Kim, K., Ren, X., Choi, S., Tan, H.Z.: Assisting people with visual impairments in aiming at a target on a large wall-mounted display. Int. J. Hum Comput Stud. **86**, 109–120 (2016). https://doi.org/10.1016/j.ijhcs.2015.10.002
14. Lei, Q., Zhang, H., Yang, Y., He, Y., Bai, Y., Liu, S.: An investigation of applications of hand gestures recognition in industrial robots. Int. J. Mech. Eng. Robot. Res. **8**(5), 729–741 (2019). https://doi.org/10.18178/ijmerr.8.5.729-741
15. Li, X.: Human–robot interaction based on gesture and movement recognition. Signal Process. Image Commun. **81**, 700–709. https://doi.org/10.1016/j.image.2019.115686
16. Miao, M., Pham, H.A., Friebe, J., Weber, G.: Contrasting usability evaluation methods with blind users. Univ. Access Inf. Soc. **15**(1), 63–76 (2014). https://doi.org/10.1007/s10209-014-0378-8
17. Nacenta, M.A., Kamber, Y., Qiang, Y., Kristensson, P.O.: Memorability of pre-designed and user-defined gesture sets. In: Proceedings of the SIGCHI Conference on Human Factors in Computing Systems, pp. 1099–1108. ACM, New York (2013). https://doi.org/10.1145/2470654.2466142
18. Nguyen, T.T.M., Pham, N.H., Dong, V.T., Nguyen, V.S., Tran, T.T.H.: A fully automatic hand gesture recognition system for human-robot interaction. In: Proceedings of the Second Symposium on Information and Communication Technology, pp. 112–119. ACM, New York (2011). https://doi.org/10.1145/2069216.2069241
19. Norman, D.A.: Natural user interfaces are not natural. Interactions **17**(3), 6–10 (2010). http://doi.acm.org/10.1145/1744161.1744163
20. Obaid, M., Kistler, F., Häring, M., Bühling, R., André, E.: A framework for user-defined body gestures to control a humanoid robot. Int. J. Soc. Robot. **6**(3), 383–396 (2014). https://doi.org/10.1007/s12369-014-0233-3
21. Rahim, M.A., Shin, J., Islam, M.R.: Hand gesture recognition-based non-touch character writing system on a virtual keyboard. Multimedia Tools Appl. **79**(17–18), 11813–11836 (2020). https://doi.org/10.1007/s11042-019-08448-6
22. Villarreal-Narvaez, S., Vanderdonckt, J., Vatavu, R.-D., Wobbrock, J.O.: A systematic review of gesture elicitation studies. In: Proceedings of the 2020 ACM Designing Interactive Systems Conference, pp. 855–872. ACM, New York (2020). https://doi.org/10.1145/3357236.3395511

23. Vuletic, T., Duffy, A., Hay, L., McTeague, C., Campbell, G., Grealy, M.: Systematic literature review of hand gestures used in human computer interaction interfaces. Int. J. Hum. Comput. Stud. **129**, 74–94 (2019). https://doi.org/10.1016/j.ijhcs.2019.03.011
24. Wobbrock, J.O., Aung, H.H., Rothrock, B., Myers, B.A.: Maximizing the guessability of symbolic input. In: CHI 2005 Extended Abstracts on Human Factors in Computing Systems, pp. 1869–1872. ACM, New York (2005). https://doi.org/10.1145/1056808.1057043
25. Wobbrock, J.O., Morris, M.R., Wilson, A.D.: User-defined gestures for surface computing. In: Proceedings of the SIGCHI Conference on Human Factors in Computing Systems, pp. 1083–1092. ACM, New York (2009). https://doi.org/10.1145/1518701.1518866
26. Yeasin, M., Chaudhuri, S.: Visual understanding of dynamic hand gestures. Pattern Recogn. **33**(11), 1805–1817 (2000). https://doi.org/10.1016/S0031-3203(99)00175-2
27. Zabulis, X., Baltzakis, H., Argyros, A.A.: Vision-based hand gesture recognition for human-computer interaction. In: Stephanidis, C. (ed.) The universal access handbook, pp. 1–59. CRC Press, Boca Raton (2009)
28. Zhang, B., Du, G., Shen, W., Li, F.: Gesture-based human-robot interface for dual-robot with hybrid sensors. Ind. Robot. **46**(6), 800–811 (2019). https://doi.org/10.1108/IR-11-2018-0245
29. Zhu, C., Sheng, W.: Wearable sensor-based hand gesture and daily activity recognition for robot-assisted living. IEEE Trans. Syst. Man Cybern. Part A Syst. Hum. **41**(3), 569–573 (2011). https://doi.org/10.1109/TSMCA.2010.2093883

Nonlinear Analyses of Electrogastrogram Measurements Taken During Olfactory Stimulation Altering Autonomic Nerve Activity

Eiji Takai[1,2](✉), Kohki Nakane[2], and Hiroki Takada[2]

[1] Soda Aromatic Co., Ltd., Chiba 270-0233, Japan
eiji.takai.p6@soda.co.jp
[2] Graduate School of Engineering, University of Fukui, Fukui 910-8507, Japan

Abstract. To investigate the effect of odors on the electrogastrogram (EGG) results, the EGGs were measured during olfactory stimulation with different concentrations of lavender and grapefruit odorants. Because the EGGs have been proven to be nonlinear stochastic processes, nonlinear analyses were used to analyze the EGGs. There was no difference in the translation error estimated by Wayland algorithm for all experimental groups. Moreover, it was shown that the minimum embedding dimensions estimated by the false nearest neighbors (FNN) method varied with respect to the note and concentration of odorants. Because the FNN method adopts an arbitrary threshold setting, we estimated the minimum embedding dimension using our method without the threshold. As a result, the minimum embedding dimension was estimated and determined as 2 for all experimental groups, which is different from that of the FNN method. This is likely because the proposed method is less affected by noise compared to the FNN method. These results suggest that the nonlinear analyses of EGGs are suitable for evaluating the effects of olfactory stimulation.

Keywords: Electrogastrogram · Nonlinear analysis · Olfactory stimulation

1 Introduction

1.1 Physiological Responses to Olfactory Stimulation

Various physiological responses can be triggered by the smell of odors. In experiments with rats, it has been reported that lavender oil suppresses sympathetic nerves in the adrenal gland and adipose tissue and stimulates the gastric vagal nerve [1], while grapefruit oil stimulates sympathetic nerves in the adrenal gland and adipose tissue and suppresses the gastric vagal nerve [2]. Physiological responses to olfactory stimuli can be triggered via olfactory receptors or by direct action on the brain after certain absorption in the nasal cavity. Because the physiological response in the above example was abolished by zinc sulfate treatment causing anosmia [1, 2], it is thought that the autonomic nervous system activity is affected by olfactory receptors.

M. Antona and C. Stephanidis (Eds.): HCII 2023, LNCS 14020, pp. 277–287, 2023.
https://doi.org/10.1007/978-3-031-35681-0_18

In human experiments, it has been reported that lavender oil causes a decrease in blood pressure, heart rate, and body surface temperature, which are physiological responses that occur when the parasympathetic nervous system is dominant [3], while grapefruit oil causes an increase in blood pressure, which is a physiological response that occurs when the sympathetic nervous system is dominant [4]. However, there have been no reports on human studies of changes in the gastric vagal nerve. Therefore, we examined the effects of lavender and grapefruit odorants on the stomach. Because directly measuring the gastric vagal activity is invasive, we focused on transcutaneous electrogastrography, which noninvasively measures gastric electrical activity.

1.2 Electrogastrogram (EGG)

EGGs show approximately three cycles per minute originating in the pacemaker region of the upper stomach [5]. Gastric electrical activity is controlled by the autonomic nervous system, which is stimulated by parasympathetic activity and inhibited by sympathetic activity [6]. Because the potential of the EGG is lower than that of the electrocardiogram, and it tends to be affected by noise, the electrogastrography has not been studied extensively. However, recent advances in equipment have made it possible to easily conduct measurements.

It has been reported that the mathematical model of the EGG generation mechanism in a healthy subject has nonlinearities and is described by a stochastic resonance model [7]. Specifically, it is represented by a stochastic differential equation, in which electrical signals originating from other organs are added as white noise to the electrical activity of the stomach modeled by the van der Pol equation. Therefore, to reflect these features of the EGG, we attempted to incorporate it with nonlinear analyses in this study.

1.3 Nonlinear Analyses

In nonlinear time series analysis, the state space is reconstructed using a time-delay coordinate system [8], where delay time and embedding dimension into the state space are important parameters. However, methods for obtaining these parameters have not been established. Generally, the delay time can be obtained from the autocorrelation function [9] or mutual information [10], and the embedding dimension can be estimated using the false nearest neighbors (FNN) method [11].

Because the Wayland algorithm has been previously applied as a nonlinear analysis of EGGs [12], we attempted to apply it in this study. We also performed the FNN method to estimate the minimum embedding dimension of the attractor. Furthermore, because setting the threshold for the FNN method is set arbitrarily, we also studied a recently proposed method that uses the change rate of the nearest neighbor distance as a method without the threshold [13].

This paper was written based on the papers cited [14].

2 Methods

2.1 Participants

Thirteen healthy males (mean age ± standard deviation: 22.92 ± 0.82 years) who did not suffer from gastrointestinal diseases, hypertension, chronic respiratory diseases, metabolic diseases, such as diabetes, or neurological diseases, such as Parkinson's disease participated in the experiment. The participants were fully informed of the details of the experiment in advance, and their written consent was obtained. The experiment was approved by the Ethics Committee of the Graduate School of Engineering, University of Fukui (H2019001).

2.2 Procedure

EGGs were measured with the participant in a supine position in a soundproofed laboratory. Measurements were taken for a total of 40 min: 20 min at rest and 20 min during olfactory stimulation. To avoid the influence of food, measurements were taken at least 2 h after a meal. To account for circadian rhythms, each participant underwent the measurements at the same time of day.

2.3 EGG Measurement

EGG measurements were performed using a disposable electrode for electrocardiography (Vitrode Bs: Nihon Kohden, Tokyo, Japan) with bipolar induction; one of the two electrodes was affixed to the intersection of the left midclavicular line with the second horizontal line dividing the xiphoid process and umbilicus into four equal parts. The other electrode was affixed to the left of the umbilical region (Fig. 1). The reference electrode was affixed directly above the umbilical region. Data was captured using a Biotop mini (East Medic, Ishikawa, Japan) with A/D conversion at a sampling frequency of 1 kHz. The time constant was set to 8 s and high-frequency cutoff to 0.5 Hz.

2.4 Olfactory Stimulation

A cotton ball impregnated with 1 g of odorant was placed in a 30 mL glass bottle; the glass bottle was fixed with a hand arm 5 cm above the participant's nose for olfactory stimulation. Odorants (Soda Aromatic, Tokyo, Japan) with a grapefruit or lavender note in different concentrations were used as the sample for olfactory stimulation. The details are as follows: 1) a grapefruit odorant (HG), 2) a medium-concentration grapefruit odorant (MG) prepared by diluting HG 10-fold with a solvent (triethyl citrate), 3) a low-concentration grapefruit odorant (LG) prepared by diluting GF 100-fold with the solvent, 4) a lavender odorant (HL), 5) a medium-concentration lavender odorant (ML) prepared by diluting HL 10-fold with the solvent, 6) a low-concentration lavender odorant (LL) prepared by diluting HL 100-fold with the solvent, and 7) an odorless sample (OL) of the solvent only. The samples were presented to the participants randomly considering order effects.

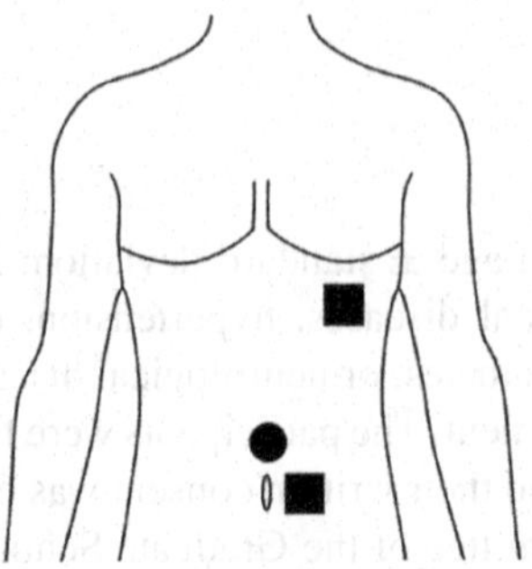

Fig. 1. Electrode attachment positions.

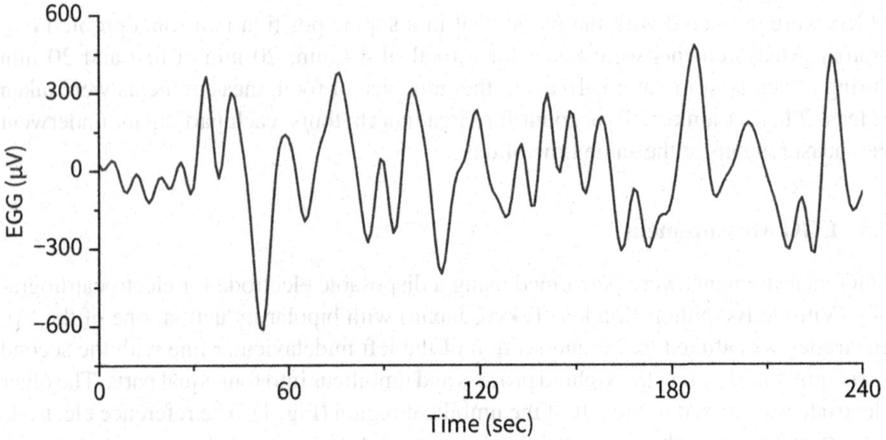

Fig. 2. Typical example of an EGG recording.

2.5 Data Preprocessing

EGGs were analyzed for approximately 17 min, processing data from 3rd to 20th min of the 20 min data log collected during olfactory stimulation. EGGs obtained at a sampling frequency of 1 kHz were resampled to 1 Hz; subsequently, a bandpass filter with a cutoff frequency of 0.015–0.15 Hz was applied to eliminate noise originating from electromyograms and surrounding electronic equipment. An example of a typical EGG is shown in Fig. 2.

2.6 Wayland Algorithm

The Wayland algorithm is a method for quantifying the determinism of the mathematical model generating a time series by estimating the smoothness of the reconstructed attractor obtained from the time series data as the translation error [15]. The translation error takes non-negative values. The closer its value is to 0, the more deterministic the mathematical model is, while the closer its value is to 1, the more random the mathematical model is. The delay time τ was determined as the minimum time when the autocorrelation function of the time series is less than $1/e$. The translation errors between the experiments were statistically compared using the Wilcoxon signed rank test (Bonferroni correction). The significance level was set at 0.05.

2.7 FNN Method

The FNN method was proposed by Kennel *et al.* to estimate the minimum embedding dimension for reconstructing attractors from time series data [11]. Based on Takens' embedding theorem [8], let $y_d(t)$ be a vector of d-dimensional attractors reconstructed from a time series. Let its nearest neighbor vector $y_d^n(t)$ and its time be t', the distance is $D_d(t, t') = \left|y_d(t) - y_d(t')\right|$ $(y_d^n(t) = y_d(t'))$. When the embedding dimension is increased to $d + 1$, the distance between $y_{d+1}(t)$ and $y_{d+1}^n(t)$ is $D_{d+1}(t, t') = \left|y_{d+1}(t) - y_{d+1}^n(t)\right|$. The number of vectors for which the change rate of the nearest neighbor distance, $D_{d+1}(t, t')/D_d(t, t')$, exceeds the set threshold R_{tol} is calculated as a percentage of all vectors in the reconstructed attractor, namely, FNN Percentage. The dimension for which the FNN Percentage first becomes zero is estimated as the minimum embedding dimension. In this study, the minimum embedding dimension was estimated by calculating the FNN Percentage for embedding dimensions 1 through 21 at several thresholds of $R_{tol} = 1, 2, 4, 8, 10$, and 15.

2.8 Estimation of the Minimum Embedding Dimension Based on the Change Rate of Nearest Neighbor Distance

Estimation of the minimum embedding dimension using the FNN method requires appropriately setting a threshold R_{tol}; however, this is done arbitrarily. Therefore, a method using the median of the change rate of nearest neighbor distance M_{tol} was proposed as a new criterion to replace the threshold R_{tol} [13]. In the proposed method, the change rate of nearest neighbor distance with increasing embedding dimension is calculated; then, the median of these values after applying the ordinary logarithm is used as M_{tol},

$$M_{tol} = Med\left(\log_{10} \frac{D_{d+1}(t, t')}{D_d(t, t')}\right) \tag{1}$$

To prevent noise from causing a true neighbor to be assessed as a false neighbor, the dimension for which M_{tol} was first less than 1 was estimated as the minimum embedding dimension. M_{tol} was calculated for embedding dimensions 1 through 21.

The criterion value for M_{tol} has been set to 1 in previous studies. In phase space, the neighbor distances involved in at least half of the delay embedding vectors have changed by a factor of 10 or more because M_{tol} is the median. By our tolerance for this value change in the neighbor distances, true neighbors were prevented from identifying as FNNs due to noise. As the side notes, it might be possible to apply a more rigorous reference value for time series where noise is reduced by a bandpass filter. In case of M_{tol} = 0, it means that there is little change in the neighbor distances involved in half of the delay embedding vectors or the vectors in the neighborhoods is closer in phase space.

Therefore, it was thought that the minimum embedding dimension could be estimated more accurately because the change rate of the neighbor distances would be smaller than that in case of $M_{tol} = 1$. In other words, the incident probability for the FNNs would be lower in case of $M_{tol} = 1$ than that in $M_{tol} = 0$. In this study, we also estimated the minimum embedding dimension in case of the rigorous criterion value $M_{tol} = 0$.

3 Results

3.1 Estimation of Translation Error Using the Wayland Algorithm

The Wayland algorithm was used to estimate the translation error in the mathematical model that generates the EGGs during olfactory stimulation. As shown in Fig. 3, there was no difference in the translation errors between the presentation of lavender and grapefruit odorants in any of the embedding dimensions. There was also no difference with respect to the odorant concentrations.

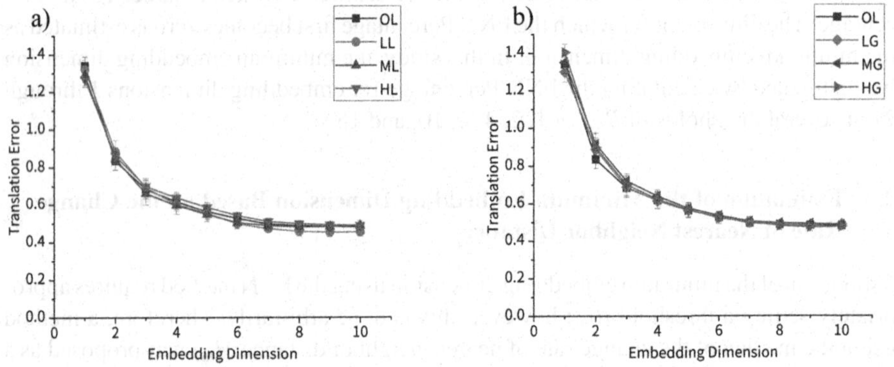

Fig. 3. Translation errors in EGGs during olfactory stimulation (Mean ± SE). a) Lavender odorants, b) Grapefruit odorants.

3.2 Estimation of the Minimum Embedding Dimension Using the FNN Method

The minimum embedding dimension was estimated using the FNN method for the mathematical model that generates the EGG during olfactory stimulation. The FNN method requires the setting a threshold, and in this study, the threshold was set as $R_{tol} = 15$, where the FNN Percentage reached zero for all experimental groups. As shown in Fig. 4, the estimated dimensions were 5 for LL and ML; 6 for OL, MG, and HG; 7 for HL; and 9 for LG.

3.3 Estimation of the Minimum Embedding Dimension Based on the Change Rate of Nearest Neighbor Distance

The minimum embedding dimension was estimated for the mathematical model that generates the EGG during olfactory stimulation based on the change rate of the nearest neighbor distance [13]. As shown in Fig. 5, the minimum embedding dimension for all EGGs was estimated as 2 because M_{tol} was less than 1 when the embedding dimension was 2, when the criterion value for M_{tol} was set to 1. On the other hand, the minimum embedding dimension for all EGGs was estimated as 9 because M_{tol} was less than 0 when the embedding dimension was 9, when the criterion value for M_{tol} was set to 0.

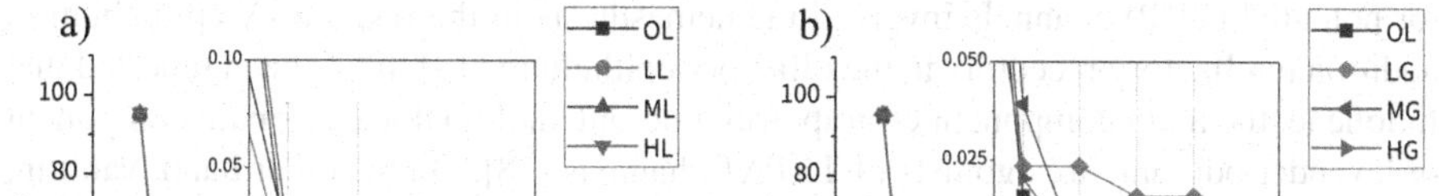

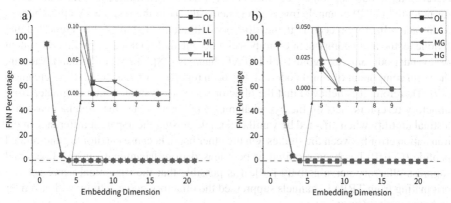

Fig. 4. FNN percentage of EGGs during the olfactory stimulation (Mean ± SD). a) Lavender odorants, b) Grapefruit odorants.

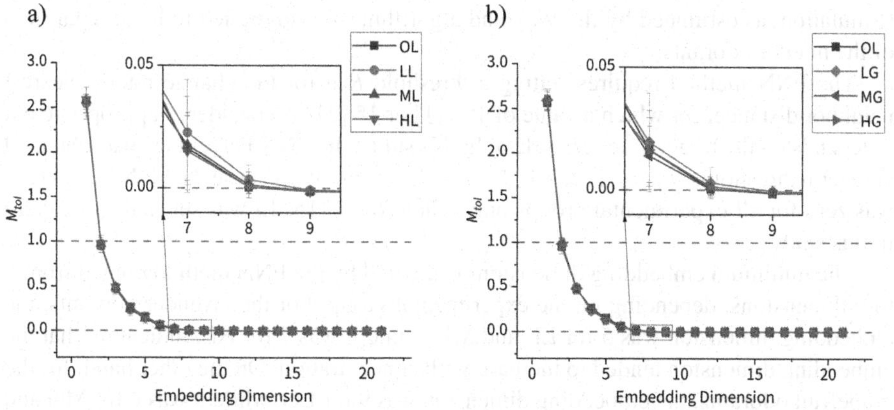

Fig. 5. M_{tol} of EGGs during the olfactory stimulation (Mean ± SD). a) Lavender odorants, b) Grapefruit odorants.

4 Discussion

The effects of different notes and concentrations of olfactory stimulation on the EGG and its mathematical model were investigated. Because a previous study has proven that the mathematical model that generates the EGG is a nonlinear stochastic process [7], we evaluated the EGG by nonlinear analyses as well in this study.

Analysis conducted using the Wayland algorithm demonstrated no significant differences in translation error among all experimental groups. In a previous study using vanilla odorants, the translation error increased proportionally to the concentration of the odorant [16]. Therefore, the result reported in the previous study was inconsistent with the result reported in this study. A possible reason for this could be the difference in the effect of these odorants on chemesthesis. In the nasal cavity, there are transient receptor potential (TRP) channels involved in chemesthesis in the respiratory epithelium in addition to olfactory receptors in the olfactory epithelium [17]. It has been reported that limonene, the main component of grapefruit odorant, and linalool, the main component of lavender odorant, are agonists of TRPA1 channels [18]. On the other hand, vanillin, the main component of vanilla odorant, has been reported not to act on TRPA1 channels [19]. Therefore, it is believed that the olfactory nervous system, which originates from olfactory receptors, acts on the hypothalamus and other organs that regulate gastrointestinal motility when affected by vanilla odorant, causing the apparent difference in the translation error between the studies. On the other hand, because calcitonin gene-related peptide (CGRP) has been reported to be released from trigeminal sensory fibers and suppress olfactory nerve activity [20], it is possible that the trigeminal nerve activity originating from TRPA1 channels suppressed the olfactory nerve activity with lavender and grapefruit odorants.

Because the translation error remained unchanged after embedding dimension 8 for all experimental groups; the embedding dimension of the EGG measured in this study was estimated to be 8. This result was also consistent with that reported in the previous study [16]. Therefore, the embedding dimension of the EGG during olfactory stimulation, as estimated by the Wayland algorithm, was suggested to be 8, regardless of the note of odorants.

The FNN method requires setting a threshold R_{tol} for the change rate of nearest neighbor distance; for which a value of 10 [11] or 15 [21] is considered appropriate but it depends on the target time series data. In this study, the FNN Percentage was obtained at several thresholds ($R_{tol} = 1, 2, 4, 8, 10, 15$). Accordingly, because the FNN Percentage was zero for all experimental groups only when $R_{tol} = 15$, 15 was set as the threshold in this study.

The minimum embedding dimensions estimated by the FNN method ranged from 5 to 9 dimensions, depending on the experimental group. For the lavender odorants, the embedding dimension was 5 for LL and ML, while it was 7 for HL, indicating that the embedding dimension tended to increase with concentration. On the other hand, for the grapefruit odorants, the embedding dimension was 9 for LG, while it was 6 for MG and HG, indicating that the embedding dimension tended to increase at lower concentrations. Intensity can change the impression of an odor [22], and it is possible that this effect was reflected in the embedding dimension results.

Moreover, lavender oil activates the parasympathetic nervous system [1], while grapefruit oil is proven to activate the sympathetic nervous system in studies with rats [2]. In human studies, lavender oil is reported to decrease blood pressure and increase skin blood flow and skin electrical resistance owing to parasympathetic activation [23]. Furthermore, grapefruit oil is reported to increase the low frequency components of blood pressure fluctuations owing to sympathetic activation [24]. Because gastric motility is stimulated by the parasympathetic nervous system and inhibited by the sympathetic nervous system [6], it is possible that the different effects of both odorants on the autonomic nervous system may have affected the embedding dimension results.

Although the FNN method has the advantages of a simple concept and algorithm, it suffers from the problem that no algorithm has been proposed for appropriately setting R_{tol}, which must be set arbitrarily as well. Therefore, we attempted to estimate the minimum embedding dimension using a recently proposed method that estimates the minimum embedding dimension based on the change rate of the nearest neighbor distance as the embedding dimension increases without setting a threshold [13].

The minimum embedding dimension was estimated to be 2 for all experimental groups when the criterion value for M_{tol} was set to 1. This result is reasonable given that the mathematical model that generates the EGG can be expressed as a stochastic differential equation based on the van der Pol equation, which is a second-order differential equation [7]. However, there was a significant difference between the minimum embedding dimension estimated by the Wayland algorithm and that returned by the FNN method. This was assumed to be the overestimated minimum embedding dimension because the Wayland algorithm and FNN method are both affected by noise. Because the transcutaneous EGG has a low potential and there are various organs and muscles near the stomach, noise cannot be prevented from affecting the EGG. Therefore, it was considered that the proposed method, which has been reported to be less susceptible to noise [13], may be more suitable for estimating the minimum embedding dimension with respect to the mathematical model that generates the EGG.

On the other hand, the proposed method did not exhibit differences in the minimum embedding dimension depending on the note and concentration of the odorants, which were observed with the FNN method. One possibility is that the effect of olfactory stimulation on the gastric electrical activity is very small; accordingly, eliminating the effect of noise has resulted in eliminating that small change as well.

The criterion value for M_{tol} was set to 1 to account for the effect of noise, but the EGGs in this study were applied to a bandpass filter. Therefore, the analysis was also conducted with the criterion value for M_{tol} set to 0. The results showed that, unlike when the criterion value for M_{tol} was set to 1, the minimum embedding dimension was estimated as 9 for all experimental groups. This value was close to the minimum embedding dimension estimated by the Wayland algorithm and the FNN method. Thus, because the minimum embedding dimension differed significantly depending on the criterion value for M_{tol}, there may be room for consideration regarding the criterion value for M_{tol} in the proposed method.

5 Conclusion

To investigate the effect of olfactory stimulation on the mathematical model that generates the EGG, nonlinear analyses were performed on the EGGs measured under stimulation of lavender and grapefruit odorants at different concentrations. The translation error estimated by the Wayland algorithm suggested that the determinism of the mathematical model that generates the EGGs did not vary depending on the note and concentration of the odorants. The minimum embedding dimension was estimated by the Wayland algorithm, FNN method, and proposed method using the change rate of the nearest neighbor distance. Accordingly, it was found that each method attained different values. In this study, we used relatively highly palatable odorants but, in the future, we will compare the results obtained from studies using less palatable odorants to elucidate the effects of olfactory stimulation on the mathematical model that generates EGG in more detail and examine the possibility of using the EGG measurement as an odor evaluation technique.

References

1. Shen, J., Niijima, A., Tanida, M., Horii, Y., Maeda, K., Nagai, K.: Olfactory stimulation with scent of lavender oil affects autonomic nerves, lipolysis and appetite in rats. Neurosci. Lett. **383**(1–2), 188–193 (2005)
2. Shen, J., Niijima, A., Tanida, M., Horii, Y., Maeda, K., Nagai, K.: Olfactory stimulation with scent of grapefruit oil affects autonomic nerves, lipolysis and appetite in rats. Neurosci. Lett. **380**(3), 289–294 (2005)
3. MPham, W.S., Siripornpanich, V., Piriyapunyaporn, T., Kotchabhakdi, N., Ruangrungsi, N.: The effects of lavender oil inhalation on emotional states, autonomic nervous system, and brain electrical activity. J. Med. Assoc. Thai **95**(4), 598–606 (2012)
4. Kawai, E., et al.: Increase in diastolic blood pressure induced by fragrance inhalation of grapefruit essential oil is positively correlated with muscle sympathetic nerve activity. J. Physiol. Sci. **70**, 2 (2020)
5. Alvarez, W.C.: The electrogastrogram and what it shows. J. Am. Med. Assoc. **78**, 1116–1118 (1922)
6. Camilleri, M.: Primer on the Autonomic Nervous System Part III Physiology, 2nd edn. Elsevier, Netherlands (2004)
7. Matsuura, Y., Takada, H.: Form and its nonlinear analysis for the use of electrogastrogram as a gastrointestinal motility test. Forma **26**, 39–50 (2011)
8. Takens, F.: Detecting strange attractors in turbulence. In: Rand, D., Young, L.-S. (eds.) Dynamical Systems and Turbulence, Warwick 1980. LNM, vol. 898, pp. 366–381. Springer, Heidelberg (1981). https://doi.org/10.1007/BFb0091924
9. King, G.P., Jones, R., Broomhead, D.S.: Phase portraits from a time series: a singular system approach. Nucl. Phys. B Proc. Suppl. **2**, 379–390 (1987)
10. Fraser, A.M., Swinney, H.L.: Independent coordinates for strange attractors from mutual information. Phys. Rev. A **33**(2), 1134–1140 (1986)
11. Kennel, M.B., Brown, R., Abarbanel, H.D.I.: Determining embedding dimension for phase-space reconstruction using a geometrical construction. Phys. Rev. A **45**(6), 3403–3411 (1992)
12. Kinoshita, F., Fujita, K., Miyanaga, K., Touyama, H., Takada, M., Takada, H.: Nonlinear analysis of electrogastrograms during acute exercise loads. J. Sports Med. Doping Stud. **8**(2), 201 (2018)
13. Nakane, K., Sugiura, A., Takada, H.: Estimating a minimum embedding dimension by false nearest neighbors method without an arbitrary threshold. Adv. Sci. Technol. Eng. Syst. J. **7**(4), 114–120 (2022)
14. Takai, E., Nakane, K., Takada, H.: Estimation of the minimum embedding dimension of a mathematical model describing the electrogastrograms during olfactory stimulation. Bull. Soc. Sci. Form **37**(2) (2022, in Press). (in Japanese)
15. Wayland, R., Bromley, D., Pickett, D., Passamante, A.: Recognizing determinism in a time series. Phys. Rev. Lett. **70**(5), 580–582 (1993)
16. Takai, E., Aoyagi, T., Ichikawa, K., Matsuura, Y., Kinoshita, F., Takada, H.: Effect of olfactory stimulation with vanilla odor on degree of electrical activity to control gastrointestinal motility. In: Antona, M., Stephanidis, C. (eds.) HCII 2021. LNCS, vol. 12769, pp. 519–530. Springer, Cham (2021). https://doi.org/10.1007/978-3-030-78095-1_38

17. Frasnelli, J., Manescu, S.: The Intranasal trigeminal system. In: Buettner, A. (ed.) Springer Handbook of Odor. SH, pp. 113–114. Springer, Cham (2017). https://doi.org/10.1007/978-3-319-26932-0_46
18. Terada, M., et al.: Human TRPA1 activation by terpenes derived from the essential oil of daidai, Citrus aurantium L. var. daidai Makino. Biosci. Biotech. Biochem. **83**(9), 1721–1728 (2019)
19. Premkumar, L.S.: Transient receptor potential channels as targets for phytochemicals. ACS Chem. Neurosci. **5**(11), 1117–1130 (2014)
20. Daiber, P., Genovese, F., Schriever, V.A., Hummel, T., Möhrlen, F., Frings, S.: Neuropeptide receptors provide a signalling pathway for trigeminal modulation of olfactory transduction. Eur. J. Neurosci. **37**(4), 572–582 (2013)
21. Krakovská, A., Mezeiová, K., Budáčová, H.: Use of false nearest neighbours for selecting variables and embedding parameters for state space reconstruction. J. Complex Syst., 932750 (2015)
22. Gross-Isseroff, R., Lancet, D.: Concentration-dependent changes of perceived odor quality. Chem. Senses **13**(2), 191–204 (1988)
23. Yoishida, S., Saeki, Y.: Effects of fragrances on autonomic nervous system. J. Jpn. Soc. Nurs. Res. **23**(4), 11–17 (2000). (in Japanese)
24. Haze, S., Sakai, K., Gozu, Y.: Effects of fragrance inhalation on sympathetic activity in normal adults. Jpn. J. Pharmacol. **90**(3), 247–253 (2002)

An Exploration of Automatic Speech Recognition Within a Nordic Context

Silja Vase[1(✉)] and Gerd Berget[2]

[1] University of Copenhagen, Karen Blixens Plads 8, 2300 Copenhagen S, Denmark
siljavase@hum.ku.dk

[2] Oslo Metropolitan University, Postboks 4 St. Olavs plass, N-0130 Oslo, Norway

Abstract. Automatic speech recognition (ASR) has become a familiar input component for voice user faces, such as texting, preparing structured documents, searching, and voice commands. Inclusive ASR is a premise for a sustainable HCI that supports all types of languages and users. ASR is quite robust for majority languages but still needs to be adequate for smaller languages. Moreover, specific user groups cannot use ASR due to, e.g., speech impediments or accents. This paper discusses the possibilities and limitations of ASR in its current form within a Nordic context raising the following questions: i) What is the state of ASR in terms of usability for smaller and minority languages, and ii) How is ASR discussed regarding future development and inclusion? The current research discusses such topics within the lens of ability-based participatory design established on exploratory data collection. Among other findings, the paper stresses that small and minority languages are neglected in ASR development from an international perspective. Consequently, these languages risk exclusion from the digital development of language technology.

Keywords: Automatic Speech Recognition · Nordic Languages · Assistive Technology

1 Introduction

Language is an essential part of our everyday lives and identity. According to The Universal Declaration of Human Rights [1], all people have the right to their own language. Further, European governments must provide equal possibilities for citizens to participate in society despite one's mother tongue [2]. Governments in the Nordic region risk pushing against these rights by increasing the use of voice user interfaces (VUIs) since such technologies lack robustness for smaller and minority languages [3]. A key aspect of language is how people express written or spoken words, and it is vital in understanding how people interact with computers to produce texts or give commands. Written language has shaped the foundation of how we interact with computers (e.g., [4]) and has, among others, evolved into VUIs. A primary concern towards technologies supporting languages is the societal role of VUIs [5] since these interfaces will affect how citizens interact with and are assisted by the public sector.

M. Antona and C. Stephanidis (Eds.): HCII 2023, LNCS 14020, pp. 288–307, 2023.
https://doi.org/10.1007/978-3-031-35681-0_19

One commonly applied input method is text-based. In specific contexts, however, it is more purposeful to apply alternative input methods, such as automatic speech recognition (ASR), a key component in VUIs. Virtual assistants, smart speakers, and smartphones are all devices using ASR as the primary input. Advanced ASR technologies such as text-to-speech, speech-to-text, and voice command have become common due to the assistive values they provide by the independence enabled from physical body parts such as hands and eyes. ASR is thus often related to assistive technologies as a tool to support people with reduced writing skills [6].

The ability to input textual content can be affected by permanent or temporarily impaired skills or environmental factors. For instance, due to strict hygiene rules, a surgeon performing an operation cannot conduct search queries or acquire patient information from the Electronic Health Record (EHR) using hardware such as a mouse or keyboard. Another example is a person with visual impairments who shall compose a text message on a smartphone with no tactile buttons. A student writing a thesis with a broken hand may also experience challenges with text input. In other words, ASR has considerable potential in many contexts for different purposes and is thus evolving quickly.

While ASR is commonly applied worldwide, there are still huge differences between majority languages on one side and small and minority languages on the other regarding the quality and robustness of the technology. For example, for languages like Danish and Norwegian, ASR is less developed than English [7]. These small languages represent lesser populations to design for, and hence reduced revenue possibilities leaving too modest investments in comprehensive product development [8].

Another challenge in the Nordic countries is the presence of several language forms and dialects. Currently, there are approximately 200 different languages spoken within Nordic countries [9], comprising national and minority languages. ASR is only developed for some of these languages. The technology solitarily supports some of the national languages, and the recognition is not always sufficiently robust [7]. This lack of availability and robustness raises many challenges, such as people needing access to necessary assistive technology who cannot utilize it, or people having to abandon their language or dialect to be able to use ASR. Governments require such technology to be available for all inhabitants but seem unwilling to pay for the necessary technological development. The responsibility of diversity is therefore transferred to the product developers, who do not perceive it as economically beneficial to invest much time and money in smaller and minority languages. This paper discusses the following research questions in a Nordic context, using Denmark and Norway as examples:

RQ_1: What is the state of ASR in terms of usability for smaller and minority languages
RQ_2: How is ASR discussed regarding future development and inclusion?

This study was exploratory in its nature and adopted an empirical research approach to answer the questions of interest. The paper is structured as follows: the background addresses topics such as language, ASR in a Nordic context, user diversity and ability-based design. This is followed by a description of the methods used, an analysis of our findings and a discussion of the research questions. Finally, we address important implications for future research and development.

2 Background

2.1 Language Diversity

Natural language is an interpersonal communication system [10]. Natural language can be regarded as a historically progressed language used to communicate utilizing signs or speech through repetition without conscious planning or premeditation. Almost half of the population on Earth has one of the nine largest languages as their first language. In addition, numerous smaller languages and language forms exist on all continents. To preserve all types of languages, many documents manifest the rights to one's own language, such as The Universal Declaration of Human Rights [1], The UN Convention on the Rights of the Child [11], and the European Charter for Regional or Minority Languages [12].

Language is not a homogeneous unit. In Norway and Denmark, there are approximately 10 million speakers. A language such as Danish could be considered a minority language compared to major languages such as Chinese, Spanish, or English. Danish is an official national language (where The Language Council makes an official dictionary), while Norway only has the two written official languages, Nynorsk and Bokmål, specified as official [5]. The speakers in the two countries represent several linguistic diversities. Neither of the three languages has a clear delimitation of what 'belongs to the language' [5, 13] because all dialectal varieties demonstrate constant interchangeability. Some words are thus evidence of how language reflects cultural and historical changes in society, but they are never admitted as official words [14]. Although Nynorsk and Bokmål are official written languages in Norway, they still encompass a vast range of spellings. To clarify the variation, we highlight the example referred to by Frostad and Schall [15], namely that a longer sentence in Bokmål can be spelled in 165,888 different ways.

The Nordic Language Declaration [9] aims to ensure consistency in the work of the Nordic Council of Ministers regarding democratic language policies and the linguistic rights of Nordic residents. One of the five primary efforts made to ensure language comprehension and language skills is the development of computer translation programs for the languages of the Nordic countries. Programs for multilingual searches in Nordic databases are also created. The efforts encompass national languages in the Nordic countries (Danish, Finnish, Icelandic, Norwegian, and Swedish) and minority languages (Finnish, Yiddish, Karelian, Kven, Meänkieli, Roma, Romani, Russian, Tatar, German, and several Sami languages).

Minority languages are protected by national law and the European Charter for Regional and Minority Languages [12] due to their great importance to the Nordic region. This protection benefits a linguistically diverse society that provides better conditions for knowledge and innovation in democratic and cultural ways [16]. Yet, minority languages in the Nordic countries are vaguely positioned considering language literacy [17]. Digitalization regarding languages in the Nordic region thus encompasses responsibility for upholding minority languages.

Developing robust ASR for smaller languages and minority languages is regarded as essential to ensure language diversity and sustainable protection of a linguistically diverse society [5]. Digital transformation and language are closely linked through the concepts of internationalization and localization. In comparison, internationalization relates to software design for global applications, and localization targets more narrow user groups. Localization can, for example, accommodate for people to apply their native language and the language they are most fluent [18].

2.2 ASR in the Nordic Regions

Citizens in the Nordic region use ASR in everyday life and work-related situations within a broad range of contexts. In short, ASR recognizes people's natural language and translates it into text or a command. The technology can support text-related practices, such as proofreading, dictation, standardized documentation, and voice commands or assistance (e.g., virtual assistants). Consequently, public organizations implement ASR technology due to the expected efficiency and standardized bureaucratic documentation [19].

This paper takes part of departure in linear algorithms not supported by deep learning, which is the fundamental use by public organizations in the Nordic region. ASR is built upon a statistical language model and processes and interprets speech recorded through a microphone. The algorithm converts the speech into recognizable codes and analyses the words and sentences by dividing them into fractions. This information is used to analyze the frequency of words based on pattern recognition. Since ASR is used in various contexts and languages, the modalities of speech differ, which is why the ASR algorithm needs various phonetic dictionaries to interpret all kinds of speech.

ASR receives data from a specific environment, processes this data, and delivers a result back to the environment. In other words, ASR represents an input–process–output structure [20] based on three databases: an overall language model, an acoustic model, and a phonetic dictionary. Depending on the expected use, the language model holds a library of data containing documents and audio files modified for a specific context, such as a medical or an academic domain. The model identifies and translates speech by calculating the probability of words included in a sentence. Several factors contribute to the development of the system's pattern recognition, such as the language model's vocabulary and the amount of data that is decisive for the number of words that can be recognized. Thus, ASR needs big data, such as documents representing what users will say to the system within a specific domain to "make sense" of speech [21]. Such documents could be previous research articles, assignments, EHRs, and reports. Consequently, data are historical, and the digitalization of documents is essential for developing ASR for a language and thus a domain.

For many years there has been a high-level desire for developers to make ASR adapt to individual voices [22]. However, it has proven to be a more significant challenge as languages and voices constantly evolve [23]. Users increase the amount of data by training the system in recording and spelling unknown words and uploading them to the library. ASR is thus user dependent. The acoustic model of the linear algorithm is based on English language, which poses challenges for smaller languages due to their dissimilar characteristics, such as vowel extension and "stød" [24]. The latter refers to "*a suprasegmental creaky voice feature*" [25], which occurs in certain dialects in Denmark. These challenges are linked to preset categorizations by adapting to dialects, accents, and gender [26]. The categories adapt to the user's starting point for the algorithm to achieve an optimized recognition rate. For example, users are divided according to gender because the male pitch is regarded as more profound than the female pitch [27]. Users with dialects, accents, or a different pitch than the average presented by their gender thus risk a lower recognition rate, or no recognition, due to less representative data [28].

The technological maturation of ASR has become more robust for majority languages than smaller languages. The English language model has to a certain degree become independent from users due to deep learning [29, 30] and does not need to keep humans in the loop training the language model in the same time-consuming way as algorithms that are built on more linear models. Inspired by this progress, Nordic national strategies encourage public organizations to increase future use of ASR [31, 32]. This encouragement is tied to an expected establishment of a public grounded open-source language model containing the individual country's languages. These strategic decisions raise questions about which languages will be presented, since countries like Norway have several official and unofficial languages and dialects. Based upon this landscape of several spoken languages, we must acknowledge the need for dense data sets to support each specific language.

2.3 ASR and User Diversity

Speech recognition is often associated with assistive technology, among others, because ASR can replace the use of mouse, and keyboard. ASR can also compensate for lacking or reduced writing skills and is therefore reported to be the most commonly applied assistive technology among people with dyslexia [6]. By using ASR when writing school assignments, for example, pupils and students with dyslexia can become more self-reliant and improve academic performance, which also has a positive impact on self-esteem [33].

For some users, ASR may be a purposeful aid, but due to personal characteristics such as speech impediments it might be difficult to interact with the ASR. For example, for people with Parkinson, keyboard skills are often affected [34], and many people with Down syndrome or other similar conditions may not have developed advanced writing skills [35, 36]. However, both Parkinson and Down syndrome may cause speech impediments [37, 38], which can make it challenging to utilize ASR to the full extent. Previous research indicates an increase in people with speech impairments [39] and a growth in demand for digital tools to facilitate and ease communication for such users [40]. However, today people with speech impediments must adjust their speech to improve recognition so that they can utilize ASR [41].

Assistive technology may be regarded as an add-on between the user and the system [42] and is "*a powerful enabler of participation*" [43]. Consequently, assistive technologies like speech recognition show great potential in contributing to inclusive design development in digitized societies. ASR, however, has a much greater area of application than only representing a type of assistive technology from a disability perspective. Much of this technology is therefore now being utilized by many types of users [44].

Wobbrock and Kane [42] argue that a shift is needed from focusing on disabilities to addressing people's general abilities: "*In making the shift to ability-based design, we move away from assisting human users to conform to inflexible computer systems, and instead consider how systems can be made to fit the abilities of whoever uses them*". The ability-based design perspective acknowledges that people have different abilities in various contexts or settings. For example, a person working in an auto repair shop may find ASR purposeful when searching for information while having greasy hands.

Further development of the ability based approach is the concept of situated abilities. This concept is related to the acknowledgment that human abilities are situated on a continuum, and they may be affected by many different factors. The concept of situated abilities contributes with a useful perspective on ASR because it acknowledges how different abilities affect system interaction. An overarching concept for the ability-based design and situated abilities is universal design. Universal design aims to create inclusive content and to avoid discrimination against anyone, regardless of age, gender identity, cultural background, functional and neurocognitive level [45]. This design perspective can help to locate abilities and, thus, preferences shared among users of a particular technology.

3 Method

Researchers have previously investigated the use of ASR in public organizations in a Nordic context. An exploratory approach to usability has been applied, among others by addressing employees' attitudes towards the technology [7] and data entry [46]. These previous studies have demonstrated a need for future usability considerations that reflect usability. This article discusses such a knowledge gap by addressing future development and inclusion through document analysis and interviews.

3.1 Empirical Material

There is a limited amount of peer-reviewed literature on governmental actions and strategies regarding ASR in the Nordic regions [15, 47]. The methods used in this study were therefore closely aligned with an exploratory data collection inspired by scoping [48], where we mapped out critical concepts of public use encompassing ASR. We found the approach suitable when exploring an incomprehensibly reviewed area to identify possible gaps and efforts made. Based on the review of public policy papers as sources, we applied a synthesis of core concepts found. We clarified central concepts regarding ASR that appeared essential and were shared or repeated across the public policy papers. These concepts encompass barriers towards inclusive ASR, points of interest, usability, and national expectations regarding science and technology.

We conducted a qualitative content analysis [49] of public policy papers comprising the technological development of ASR in Denmark and Norway in the period 2018–2022 [14, 31, 32, 50–55]. The empirical material was coded using NVivo with specific attention to notions of ASR coupled with assistive technology as well as future assumptions of the use of the technology. The documents consist of national strategies and white papers conducted by public institutions such as ministries touching upon ASR and technological considerations regarding assistive development and responsibility.

The content analysis was carried out to shed light on how ASR is discussed regarding future development and inclusion. Further, suppliers' suggestions found through white papers and press releases were analyzed as public institutions within the Nordic countries infrequently allocate technologies such as ASR and thus depend on external suppliers.

This distribution formed an overview of the empirical evidence and led to the realization that we needed more in-depth answers to be able to answer our research questions. We extended our exploratory method empirically through interviews. We will characterize the analysis of public policy papers as the first part of our empirical findings. The interviews contribute with a more saturated data collection and create a better foundation for being able to answer our research questions.

3.2 Interviews

In the second part of our research, we conducted an additional data collection through nine semi-structured interviews. Interviewing as a method is ubiquitous and significantly discussed within HCI [56] and has become a common approach. The participants were ASR suppliers (n = 2) and developers (n = 3) for public use in both Denmark and Norway, IT product managers at public institutions using ASR (n = 2), and digital project managers at ministerial agencies (n = 2). Interviewed stakeholders were located based on their expert knowledge and work with language technology within the public sector. We were led to them by using a snowball effect contacting authors, and other accountable persons who were specified in connection with the previously analyzed policy papers.

The interviews were conducted during 2021 and 2022, when Denmark and Norway had restrictions due to the COVID-19 pandemic. Consequently, four interviews took place online and the rest face-to-face. All interviews lasted between 40 min and two hours and have all been transcribed for analysis. The quotes used in this paper are translated into English.

A coding scheme was developed and divided into 20 text sections contemplating ASR in public use and the science and technology expectations of the technology's development. From here, these sections were divided into further themes regarding future expectations, usability and language inclusion and awareness.

4 Perspectives on Inclusive ASR

4.1 Barriers Towards Inclusive ASR from a User Perspective

Two main barriers to inclusive ASR were identified throughout the analysis: i) linguistic diversity, and ii) speech or pronunciation. The first barrier represents humans who speak a dialect, a minority language, or a divergent accent. Barriers related to speech and pronunciation exemplify humans who have a speech impediment. Given Nordic countries' many languages and dialects [9], ASR must accommodate this linguistic diversity. However, many user representatives are particularly challenged by the use of ASR, which is incompatible with their dialect or mother tongue.

An example of excluded users are students with severe dyslexia who cannot use ASR due to certain dialects. This lack of usability represented a significant barrier during education, a context where ASR could have reduced the workload and cognitive effort related to writing assignments [6]. These students speaking in minority languages or particular dialects relying on writing assistance to complete their degree would be self-reliant if ASR were compatible with their lingo. Also, ASR could positively impact self-esteem and a sense of accomplishment [33].

Potential users who speak Sami (a minority language in the Nordic Region) can use ASR applied in Norwegian municipalities. However, the technology used in many Norwegian municipalities only supports Sami letters and not speech [50]. The lack of Sami linguistic proximity creates additional challenges for streamlined grammatical documentation [15, 17]. ASR could support a more uniform grammatical arrangement, leading to more precise communication and less spelling and typing errors. Since there is no stable norm considering grammar in the Sami language, speech recognition could be applied to standardize terminology, orthography, and syntax and support more stable and precise documentation. Further, enabling people speaking Sami languages to apply ASR at work is also a step in securing the language's viability. Nevertheless, since this technology is not compliant with the Sami language, Sami people cannot utilize the benefits of ASR.

ASR is not always applicable for those who speak with an accent, being non-native speakers. To accommodate such users, ASR must be more robust to translate all words correctly. Presently, workflows regarding EHRs need secretaries to translate doctors' prerecorded health records played from sound recorders. In this context, accents can be tricky to understand by humans, whereas ASR could benefit doctors because it adapts to their individual voices [26]. ASR also allows doctors to produce EHRs in real-time, enabling clinical staff to retrieve information about patients on the same day as examinations.

Another example where ASR could be valuable is humans with conditions affecting their speech, particularly the pronunciation of words. Speech impediments occur in all types of languages. However, due to more robust and better-developed technology, ASR in major languages can potentially recognize unclear pronunciation better than in minor languages [15]. For people who still need to develop sufficient writing skills to utilize, e.g., search systems or text tools, speech may be a purposeful input alternative [36]. Nonetheless, a prerequisite for successful interaction with such systems is that the systems are precise and robust enough to handle unclear pronunciation [36].

There is an increase of people with speech impairments [39] and a higher demand for digital tools to facilitate and ease communication for such users [40]. The demand for such technologies is increasingly influenced by a need for more user-centered designs since people using ASR must adjust their speech to improve recognition [41], being forced to change speech to receive a service. Further, people's speech can change during disease sequences. Due to this progress, speech impairment can improve or deteriorate, demanding further user adaptations. Numerous current ASR options support limited groups of users and need bridging regarding the communication gap between people with speech impairment and society. Even when considering majority languages, there is a gap due to fewer phonetic or written data representing natural language reflecting people with speech impairment. Everyone can therefore use ASR, but the question is to what extent the technology is adapted to smaller user groups at an acceptable level. Official strategies in the field do not specify particular variables for the level of the recognition skill. However, they touch upon many other relevant areas and considerations, which the next section will elaborate on.

4.2 Digital Transformation Requires New Competencies for ASR

According to Danish and Norwegian digital strategies, Nordic countries are undergoing a digital transformation that is in constant motion and must be prepared for significant change [31, 51]. A corresponding point of interest expressed by these governmental policies is the ability to meet and comprehend new digital opportunities and flexibilities that come with digital transformation. As a concept, digital transformation has developed in parallel with the declared fourth industrial revolution. This development creates new and more digital opportunities for societies [51] and requires new competencies concerning governments and citizens. National digital strategies concerning AI communicate "*common goals and focus areas for digitization activities* [...] *and will support digital transformation throughout the entire public sector*" [31]. The outline for Danish and Norwegian national digital strategies acknowledges a societal digital transformation that will require changes and new competencies.

A significant area of interest in Nordic policy documents is the expected increased use of AI that supports the use of ASR in the public sector [31, 52]. Initiatives include establishing sustainable AI solutions that uphold "Nordic values". The task implies developing inclusive solutions for anyone who wants to receive and use the benefits of technologies like ASR that are expected to build on AI. Respectively, AI "*should be built on ethical principles and respect human rights and democracy*" [52]. The use of AI "*takes place with our common values of freedom, liberty, security and equality*" [31]. The development of national language resources is emphasized as a critical prerequisite for the future use of ASR, namely the construction of a structured collection of digital data (audio, text, and words) for free use. Speech recognition represents a critical AI component and must encompass Nordic values. Both Danish and Norwegian governments determine to facilitate the collection of and access to language resources established on written and phonetic data.

Digitalization and data in general are referred to as "*two sides of the same coin*" [53]. Data is repeatedly seen as the link between ASR and the development of AI. As part of the Danish National Strategy for Artificial Intelligence, the Agency for Digitization is commissioned to develop and improve access to a Danish language resource to accelerate the development of commercial and non-commercial Danish AI. Likewise, a Norwegian language resource will be developed to offer expected future advantages to support and assist citizens in using ASR. A national manager for one of the most prominent suppliers of ASR in public organizations in Norway, Sweden, and Denmark expressed a need for data density towards the development of language resources in the Nordic region: "*To improve the performance of ASR and enable a shift to real deep learning and reach a goal of artificial intelligence, a very dense data resource is needed. This counts for all the Nordic countries. So, for Denmark and Norway to get a better system, we need to gather data.*" (Supplier, interview).

Concerning language resources, data density is essential to conduct a sustainable and diverse ASR where citizens are expected "*to take part in increasingly advanced services in their language*" [52]. In this regard, public policy papers express that the public sector has far more language data than those located by the Nordic governments. This concern has led them to raise awareness of language data and resources in the public sector to map out available data [31]. When data is gathered for other interests, legal complications often occur but "*fortunately, there has been much more focus on creating and sharing language data. And language models. In any case, we have seen a big development open-source and sharing in the last few years*" (Project manager, interview). Governments expect citizens to participate in collecting and producing language resources. However, previous projects set up to gather data ran into difficulties regarding funding and legal challenges: "*It is mainly the legal and assets that are the challenge. [...] Previously, we collaborated with other suppliers to create a language resource. However, it is a bit difficult if they do not have the assets to run the project. So, we sit on the edge and wait for them to start again*" (Project manager, interview). How Denmark and Norway collect language data to form open-source language models is not clear from public policy papers.

4.3 Challenges Concerning Data

To a certain extent, ASR built on the English natural language has become independent of users due to the application of multiple deep learning algorithms [30]. The technological maturation of ASR has also become more robust for small languages. Nevertheless, the algorithms for the Nordic languages do not yet have sufficient data density to support deep learning algorithms and AI. ASR built for small languages therefore reflects a slower development than majority languages and is one of the challenges for Danish and Norwegian strategies for AI.

There is a lack of international interest to develop ASR for Nordic countries [19, 47], and public organizations realize such an absence of awareness. During one of the interviews, an IT project manager at a regional hospital in Denmark said: "*It took several years, yes, I actually think it has taken more than ten years to convince* [American providers] *that they should start developing a better engine for the Danish language*" (IT manager, interview). The technology offered in the Nordic market for public use of ASR does not represent a technology that lives up to the level and technological robustness that can be seen in, for example the English market. The slower development of ASR for small languages reflects the lack of economic benefits for these languages compared to majority languages. Consequently, small and minority languages are less attractive regarding future investments in ASR development and speech-related AI. Nevertheless, such developments are required to support the expected future use of ASR algorithms and to apply deep learning, such as natural language processing [31].

The development of algorithms that can support deep learning requires public language resources and must be openly available. These language resources will build on the already available phonetic or written data. It is unclear where these data can be found. One of the initiatives to locate and co-create publicly available language resources is the collaboration between private providers of ASR and the public sector. There is a challenge in establishing some of the collaborations: "*It would be great to have a large common language resource that we could all use. Because then we could also start to support lawyers, and then we could also develop our area and go for new markets* [...] *It's probably not going to happen* [...] *we're very happy to participate in all that work and stuff like that, but I just do not think we're going to carry anything into that pool. Because it has taken us many, many years to build these dictionaries in collaboration with those who use it*" (Supplier, interview).

The public language resources intended to support the possible development of ASR are seemingly dependent on data from private providers. It is challenging for private providers to share this data due to financial reasons as "*suppliers stop and evaluate: 'Is there a business here? Because then we don't want to get rid of it', and it is a huge barrier to progress because we are dealing with small languages*" (Project manager, interview). The lack of international interest in developing ASR for small and minor languages affects current and future use of ASR. Locating and gathering data representing these languages challenge the expected progress of national publicly available language resources expressed by public policy papers.

4.4 Potential for Usability

Despite the challenges associated with ASR, there is great awareness of the potential of this technology in institutions and environments where technology can provide alternative inputs to graphical and text-based interfaces. National strategies in Denmark and Norway express an anticipated increase in the use of ASR in several areas, such as "*process case management, or other use cases such as chatbots, assistance to people with writing difficulties, voice-guided internet search and communication with smart devices and speakers*" [54].

Incomplete datasets represent a challenge for the use of AI and the future expectation for increased use of ASR. The Norwegian Ministry of Local Government and Modernization [31] states that "*Demographic and professional diversity should be guiding parameters in working with artificial intelligence*". Both Danish and Norwegian public digital strategies consider how language resources should be able to represent diversity. Diverse phonetic and written data is regarded due to the risk of developing a future use of AI-based discriminatory data [31]. Data quality is thus an essential consideration in the development of language resources to support ASR.

We have not encountered any government announcements on how usability should be involved in developing ASR or national language resources. However, the attention to a diverse development of language resources helps to create a sustainable development of data that supports the Nordic values that are considered necessary in the development of AI. Since the Nordic regions represent small languages, special efforts are required to ensure that digital solutions are developed [31]. Not all dialects are spoken and documented to the same extent, so some languages will be easier to collect data from and form a denser dataset creating a foundation for possible diverse speech recognition. Norwegian public documents addressing language have a particular focus on the need to offer a wide range of languages represented through data.

4.5 Norwegian Considerations Regarding Future ASR

Norway is a country that contains far more minority languages than Denmark. The national digital strategies reflect a particular focus on the languages Norwegian and Sami, in addition to Bokmål and Nynorsk, two language variants of Norwegian. Ministry of Local Government and Modernization [31] points out that language recognition technologies must be accessible in written Norwegian, Sami, and dialects. The Norwegian government will "*return to the issue of Sami language data and language resources in a report to the Storting on the Sami language, culture and social life. The main theme of the message will be digitization*" [31]. Norwegian policy papers do not clearly show how minority languages are supported or facilitated in the development of language technology. Regardless, the need for both written and phonetic data covering dialects and pronunciation variations is considered.

A unification of languages in Norway should improve the correlation between the state and the citizens. There is a language challenge because "*many residents constantly experience receiving incomprehensible information from the public sector. We who work in the public sector are not free to choose how we want to write*" [55]. An example of an attempt to better unify the language was the Norwegian project "*Clear Language in the State*" [55]. The Norwegian government defined a "clear language" as a correct, clear, and user-adapted language to be applied in written communication from the public sector. The project concluded that creating such a streamlined language is a never-ending story, among others, because of the free choice of many language solutions in the Norwegian language. There seems to be a contradiction between how public institutions demand the unification of languages and the governmental acknowledgment of the various dialects and the need to support these.

4.6 Danish Considerations Regarding Future ASR

A part of the Danish National Strategy for AI is The Government's Vision which expects Denmark to be a front-runner in the responsible development and use of AI, which "*will change the way we work. It will place new demands, but it will also provide opportunities to learn new things and perform tasks more efficiently*" [31]. The terminology indicates an expectation that society must change based on demands represented through technology. How this is related to responsible development is briefly mentioned in connection with a delimitation from USA and China since "*Both countries are investing heavily in artificial intelligence, but with little regard for responsibility, ethical principles and privacy*" [31]. Nonetheless, the American speech recognition company Nuance, owned by Microsoft (USA), delivers the supporting algorithms used by suppliers of ASR in Denmark. Through the public strategies and considerations regarding the future use of AI for ASR, it is not clear how one will delimit the use of this technology, even though it is developed on American principles.

One of five major initiatives in the Danish National Strategy of AI is a Danish language resource that "*will be established to support and accelerate the development of language-technology solutions in Danish*" [31]. The language resource will be freely available, enabling suppliers to build on existing knowledge to create new solutions within voice recognition and language understanding to benefit citizens, authorities, and businesses [31]. Danish Language Center and several Danish media suppliers expect that a language resource must be developed through a collaboration between the private and the public sector. This collaboration must "*create value for potential buyers of language components*", such as the companies that work with developing services and products that include speech recognition [54]. However, the current suppliers do not expect to provide ASR data for this collaboration: "*We will not give anything. we are the ones who are sitting on the gold*" (Supplier, interview).

Due to scarce governmental initiatives for language technology such as ASR and to this extend the development of AI [8] Danish has been ranked as one of the lowest in language technology development of languages in Europe [47]. Besides the small population to produce language data and the specific characteristics of the Danish language such as "stød" [24], the main reasons for the belated development are the lack of i) available linguistic resources, ii) coordination between development, distribution and use and, iii) investments in science and technology of digital language in recent years [8]. Nevertheless, the Danish Agency for Digitization drives to make it easier to create better linguistic Nordic solutions so that it is not only presented by the majority languages: "*Two years ago we launched the sprogteknologi.dk platform, which is a data distribution platform where we exhibit or where we have metadata about a whole lot of language data, so we sort of tried to map what usable data there is because the biggest challenge is the availability of language data and especially spoken data.* [...] *It is mainly a legal challenge that applies as an encounter since all data are licensed or are personal data*" (Project Manager, interview).

Data is often collected for purposes other than the public language resource, so the Danish Agency for Digitization cannot legally use these. Therefore, the Agency must construct a speech resource and follow a written corpus that encounters many work hours. The Agency has applied for funding to develop the language resource and written corpus in a corporation with the privately owned non-profit Alexandra Institute, which works with IT research, development, and innovation. If granted, the Danish Agency for Digitization will harvest data to enable a representation of diverse language use in terms of gender, accents, and dialects (Project Manager, interview).

5 Discussion

In this paper, we wanted to determine how ASR is discussed regarding the future development of the technology while applying an inclusive perspective. Speech is the most natural form of communication for humans. Machines are anything but natural, so interaction with them appears more artificial than human interpersonal speech communication. Since ASR has achieved technological robustness in majority languages, technologies such as this are often equated with natural speech, which leads to expectations for ASR that cannot be met. While ASR is extensively used worldwide, constraints are created for smaller languages such as the Nordic due to homogenized data that support the algorithms on which speech recognition depends. American providers develop the algorithms used in Nordic countries. These algorithms neglect smaller markets based on less revenue potential in relation to the requirements for developing algorithms adapted to small languages such as Danish and Norwegian.

In terms of usability, the majority languages are accommodated relatively well in the development of ASR, but the development is behind in the Nordic countries [15]. Due to the lack of an official spoken language, Norwegian dialects play a significant role compared to other Nordic countries [5], which brings increased expectations for ASR to represent these dialects [15]. These expectations have led to political action plans for future use of ASR in Norway. However, they conflict with the suppliers' lack of attention to dialects and smaller languages in general.

Prior studies have noted a lack of research considering ASR and the importance of how the technology meets and represents smaller languages [15]. Further, reports call for research within HCI to continuously shed light on the area of interest due to the vast development and use of ASR [7]. The development will remain as languages are never static which include spelling, pronunciation and grammar that are all values repeatedly adapted by ASR for it to recognize users' speech in the constant interchangeable Nordic national languages. Also, other values are influential when studying the terms of usability of ASR such as gender, accent, and, dialects all affecting the recognition rate [26] and "stød" which is a noise made special by Danish speakers different to other languages [24].

Very little was found in the literature on the question of ASR being inclusive which is surprising, as the technology increasingly becomes more commonplace in the Nordic countries and thus gradually touches upon various users in need of assistive technology. This will further create complications for the increasing amount of forthcoming users with speech impairments [39]. Public agencies have expressed that they are working towards incorporating deviant values in developing future dictionaries that support the technology's ability to recognize a wide range of voices. Both documents and the people working with public procurement of ASR recognize to encompass dialects, various pitches, accents, and voice changes due to environmental and physical changes. No current language model meets the requirements found and recognized by public agencies and ministries. In this context, opposing understandings of development are seen from private developers' perspectives.

Private providers and associated developers point out that they do not intend to emphasize minor languages. Their raison d'etre is to be able to offer ASR to a profitable user group. Minor languages are thus not developed through the language models offered by private suppliers neutralizing the possible growth in demand for digital tools to facilitate and ease communication for people with speech impairment [40].

Private suppliers do not show cooperation considering giving up their developed dictionaries and the following language models, which is why a versatile and inclusive development of future ASR lies in the hands of public institutions. Consequently, ASR must be developed in collaboration with or ultimately offered by the public sector if the Nordic countries' wishes for sustainability and the maintenance of individual languages are to be met. This view is supported by private providers' neglect of grammatical challenges, where particularly vulnerable users' encounters concerning wording and spelling are not considered profitable areas of work to improve.

This study indicates that minor and smaller languages are facing a major shift in ASR, where the public will, in the future, see it as necessary to develop ASR that is adapted to everyone to not exclude particular users. This finding is consistent with Frostad and Schall [15], who point out that the problematic development requires an increased view of technology's involvement in minor and smaller languages due to data volumes representing various users. Two main barriers towards inclusive ASR are found based on possibly challenged users of the technology illustrated in the analysis: i) linguistic diversity, and ii) speech or pronunciation. This paper questions whether governmental decisions in the ASR area can be implemented. Since private companies do not see a smaller language area as profitable, this discussion leads to an increased focus on future considerations. Future research should examine whether certain users face increased stigmatization.

In the context of ASR, it seems like the business model where the suppliers rely on profitability when developing ASR can result in the exclusion of small languages or more narrow target groups. This lack of inclusion is not in line with the Nordic values that must be included politically in the future technologies. The rapid development of speech technology has led to a political expectation of increased future use of ASR. Public policy documents claim that ASR must be built upon specific values, including ethical principles, human rights, and democracy [52]. To ensure the human rights of being able to use one's language [11], a more inclusive ASR is required for small and minority languages.

Regarding majority languages, speech technology shows weaknesses in meeting people's needs who do not represent the general user [3], e.g., dialects, speech challenges, and temporary impact on one's voice. These technological challenges are only exacerbated if the user applies the technology for small and minority languages. One goal with this paper was to investigate ASR to apply the technology to all types of people. During one of the author's previous research projects on dyslexia [57], common feedback from manuscript reviewers was that this cohort could rely on ASR as an alternative to textual input when a user was struggling with spelling. Consequently, there was less need to focus on a system design that is more supportive of people with spelling challenges. However, based on this study, the shortcomings of ASR for small and minority languages show that this technology cannot support all people in Nordic countries [15] who would benefit from using VUIs rather than providing textual input.

ASR is purposeful in different work contexts because it can be less time-consuming and improve ergonomic conditions. ASR can reduce workload with writing challenges and become an effective assistive technology. The robustness of ASR in majority languages shows this considerable potential. At the same time, the lack of robustness for small and minority languages represents a challenge, which results in the exclusion of user groups, such as people with speech impediments or a speech diverging from the mainstream. Lewis [21] emphasized that significant amounts of data is a premise for building algorithms that enable a technologically robust ASR. These algorithms consist of phonetic and written data and do not consider the diversity of people's speech or how this diversity is entangled in sociocultural identities.

People who differ from the average users in terms of gender, accents, or dialects are less presented in the data, which may result in lower or no recognition rates [28]. There is a need to broaden the user groups included in the development of this technology. By limiting the development of ASR for certain professions, such as medical staff, the needs of for instance people with intellectual impairments are overlooked.

ASR that is not accessible for small or minority languages can result in language endangerment and language loss. The lack of technological robustness can result in people giving up their dialect to get access to such technology. ASR has a usability potential for all types of people if represented in the language data. Considering the importance of representative data, minority languages such as the Sami or Kveen languages are in danger of becoming extinct if the users cannot apply their native language in daily tasks. Based on the situation today, we are hopefully not there yet. However, measures must be taken to preserve small and minority languages. Otherwise, the Nordic region will become a new minority group due to exclusion from ASR based on their mother tongue and further increasing the exclusion of user groups who already are minorities, e.g., people with neurocognitive variations.

Localizing software is a significant effort to motivate speakers of non-dominant languages to apply their native language and consequently help preserve these languages [18]. ASR has often been addressed in the context of assistive technology. By limiting ASR to disabilities, many aspects of this technology are lost, such as everyday use of voice assistance, smart objects, or work-related assistance such as voice commands controlling machines or alternate documentation inputs. Consequently, it seems purposeful to look at ASR through the lens of ability-based design [42].

6 Conclusion

This study set out to research ASR in terms of usability for smaller and minority languages. The technology is commonly applied in the Nordic region and brings forward expectations for its possibilities regarding assistance and future use of AI. This investigation aimed to assess the challenges and possibilities illustrated and discussed regarding development and inclusion in Nordic countries using Denmark and Norway as examples.

From an international perspective, small and minority languages are neglected in ASR development. Consequently, these languages risk exclusion from the digital development of language technology. According to several human rights conventions, it is up to the national state to take care of and support minority languages and dialects that are part of the country. The most apparent finding to emerge from this study is that it seems unclear whether minority languages and dialects other than Sami will be considered in the Nordic countries' future development of ASR. Nevertheless, Danish and Norwegian National Strategies for AI are working towards massively promoting the use of speech recognition with a desire to make use of AI more quickly.

Suppose the stagnant situation regarding the missing inclusion of minority languages and dialects persists. In that case, the Nordic region risks a possible override of the responsibility to support the population's right to their own language. The research has also shown that Sami, Bokmål, Nynorsk, and Danish are all languages that are part of political considerations about future language resources that will promote the future use of ASR. However, it is unclear what actions will ensure that these language resources involve people who fall outside the norm. This study has provided a deeper insight into an absence of responsibility within the inclusive ability of technology. We found a Danish political expectation that suppliers and citizens should build the language resource and expect citizens to adapt to future technologies based on AI such as ASR. Conversely, the State of Norway takes matters into its own hands, where The Government will facilitate the collection of and access to language resources and produce a plan which will be communicated through white papers concerning digitization of languages and the establishment of language resources.

This paper was limited to Norwegian and Danish use of ASR. This study offers some insight into how Nordic values engage in political deliberations. Moreover, there is a lack of clarity in contemplating how these values will be included in the future use of speech-related technologies. This research has introduced many questions in need of further investigation. More work is needed to determine how language resources will be produced in Nordic regions and to follow up on how Nordic values can be included in future language data. Further research is required to determine whether language resources can become more inclusive, as technology has the potential to be helpful in many more contexts and for an increasing amount of users than today.

References

1. UN: Universal declaration of human rights. United Nations, New York (2015)
2. Directorate-General of the UNESCO: Intersectional Mid-Term Strategy on Languages and Multilingualism. United Nations, New York (2007)
3. Sutton, S.J., et al.: Voice as a design material: sociophonetic inspired design strategies in human-computer interaction. In Brewster, S., Fitzpatrick, G. (eds.) Proceedings of the 2019 CHI Conference on Human Factors in Computing Systems. Paper 603, Association for Computing Machinery, Glasgow (2019)
4. Dourish, P.: Where the Action is: The Foundations of Embodied Interaction. MIT Press, Cambridge (2004)
5. De Smedt, K., et al.: The Norwegian Language in the Digital Age = Norsk i den digitale tidalderen. Springer, Berlin (2012)
6. Jing, C.T., Chen, C.J.: A research review: How technology helps to improve the learning process of learners with dyslexia. J. Cognit. Sci. Hum. Dev. **2**(2), 26–43 (2017)
7. Alapetite, A., Boje Andersen, H., Hertzum, M.: Acceptance of speech recognition by physicians: a survey of expectations, experiences, and social influence. Int. J. Hum. Comput. Stud. **67**(1), 36–49 (2009)
8. Kirchmeier, S., et al.: World class language technology: developing a language technology strategy for Danish. In: Calzolari, N. (ed.) Proceedings of the 12th Language Resources and Evaluation Conference 2020, pp. 3297–3301. European Language Association, Marseille (2020)
9. Nordic Council of Ministers: Declaration on a Nordic language policy. Nordisk ministerråd, København (2006)
10. Christensen, L.H., Christensen, R.Z.: Dansk grammatik [Danish grammar]. Syddansk Universitetsforlag, Odense (2019)
11. UN: Convention on the rights of the child. UN, New York (1990)
12. Council of Europe: The European charter for regional and minority languages. Council of Europe, Strasbourg (1998)
13. Hansen, E., Heltoft, L.: Grammatik over det danske sprog [Grammar of the Danish language]. Syddansk Universitetsforlag, Odense (2011)
14. Language Council: Det danske ordforråd [The Danish vocabulary]. https://dsn.dk/sprogets-udvikling/det-danske-ordforrad/. Accessed 05 June 2022
15. Frostad, B.H., Schall, V., Holten, S.M.: Towards ASR that supports linguistic diversity in Norway. In: Choukri, K., Mariani, J., Sakti, S. (eds.) Proceedings of the Language Technologies for All (LT4All) 2019, pp. 328–331. Unesco, Paris (2019)
16. Holmen, A.: Hvorfor styrke og revitalisere små sprog? [Why strengthen and revitalize minor languages?]. In: Niia, K.K. (ed.) Framgång för små språk [Progress for minor languages], pp. 10–15. Uppsala Arkivcentrum, Uppsala (2021)
17. Antonsen, L., et al: Machine translation with North Saami as a pivot language. In: Tiedemann, J., Tahmasebi, N. (eds.) Proceedings of the 21st Nordic Conference of Computational Linguistics 2017, pp. 123–131. Linköping University Electronic Press, Gothenburg (2017)

18. Laxström, N., Wilcock, G., Jokinen, K.: Internationalisation and localisation of spoken dialogue systems. In: Jokinen, K., Wilcock, G. (eds.) Dialogues with Social Robots. Lecture Notes in Electrical Engineering, vol. 427, pp. 207–219. Springer, Singapore (2017). https://doi.org/10.1007/978-981-10-2585-3_16
19. Fournier, H.: New trends in HCI research and development: a cautionary tale. In: Carliner, S. (ed.) E-Learn: World Conference on E-Learning in Corporate, Government, Healthcare, and Higher Education, 2018, pp. 1349–1355. Association for the Advancement of Computing in Education, Waynesville (AACE) (2018)
20. Curry, A., Flett, P., Hollingsworth, I.: Managing Information & Systems: The Business Perspective. Routledge, London (2006)
21. Lewis, J.R.: Practical Speech User Interface Design. CRC Press, Boca Rotan (2016)
22. Rosen, K., Yampolsky, S.: Automatic speech recognition and a review of its functioning with dysarthric speech. Augment. Altern. Commun. **16**(1), 48–60 (2000)
23. Ogundokun, R.O., et al.: Speech recognition system: overview of the state-of-the-arts. Int. J. Eng. Res. Technol. **13**(3), 384–392 (2020)
24. Kirkedal, A.: Danish Stød and Automatic Speech Recognition. Copenhagen Business School, Copenhagen (2016)
25. Hjortdal, A., Frid, J., Roll, M.: Phonetic and phonological cues to prediction: neurophysiology of Danish stød. J. Phon. **94**, 1–15 (2022)
26. Vase, S.: How workarounds occur in relation to automatic speech recognition at Danish hospitals. In: Kurosu, M. (ed.) HCII 2021. LNCS, vol. 12764, pp. 458–472. Springer, Cham (2021). https://doi.org/10.1007/978-3-030-78468-3_31
27. Nass, C.I., Brave, S.: Wired for Speech: How Voice Activates and Advances the Human-Computer Relationship. MIT Press, Cambridge (2005)
28. Koenecke, A., et al.: Racial disparities in automated speech recognition. Proc. Natl. Acad. Sci. **117**(14), 7684–7689 (2020)
29. Singh, A.P., Nath, R., Kumar, S.: A survey: speech recognition approaches and techniques. In: Yadav, D. (ed.) 2018 5th IEEE Uttar Pradesh Section International Conference on Electrical, Electronics and Computer Engineering (UPCON) 2018, pp. 563–567. IEEE, New Jersey (2018)
30. Xiong, W., et al.: The Microsoft 2017 conversational speech recognition system. In: Hayes, M., Hanseok, K. (eds.) 2018 IEEE International Conference on Acoustics, Speech and Signal Processing (ICASSP) 2018, pp. 5934–5938. IEEE, New Jersey (2018)
31. Ministry of Local Government and Modernization: One digital public sector: Digital strategy for the public sector 2019–2025. Ministry of Local Government and Modernization, Oslo (2019)
32. Teknologirådet: Kunstig intelligens: Muligheter, utfordringer og en plan for Norge [Artificial intelligence: Opportunities, challenges and a plan for Norway]. Teknologirådet, Oslo (2018)
33. Lithari, E.: Fractured academic identities: dyslexia, secondary education, self-esteem and school experiences. Int. J. Incl. Educ. **23**(3), 280–296 (2019)
34. Adams, W.R.: High-accuracy detection of early Parkinson's disease using multiple characteristics of finger movement while typing. PLoS ONE **12**(11), e0188226 (2017)
35. Alesi, M., Battaglia, G.: Chapter six: motor development and down syndrome. In: Lanfranchi, S. (ed.) International Review of Research in Developmental Disabilities, vol. 56, pp. 169–211. Academic Press, Cambridge, Massachusetts (2019)
36. Rocha, T., et al.: Usability evaluation of navigation tasks by people with intellectual disabilities: a google and SAPO comparative study regarding different interaction modalities. Univ. Access Inf. Soc. **16**(3), 581–592 (2017)
37. Sanchez, M.M., et al.: Neurobiological elements of cognitive dysfunction in down syndrome: exploring the role of APP. Biol. Psychiatry **71**(5), 403–409 (2012)

38. Dashtipour, K., et al.: Speech disorders in Parkinson's disease: pathophysiology, medical management and surgical approaches. Neurodegener. Dis. Manag. **8**(5), 337–348 (2018)
39. Dua, T., et al.: Speech recognition technology for hearing disabled community. Int. J. Adv. Comput. Res. **4**(3), 882–887 (2014)
40. Balaji, V., Sadashivappa, G.: Speech disabilities in adults and the suitable speech recognition software tools: a review. In: Westphall, C.B., Murugesan, S., Ramesh, T. (eds.) 2015 International Conference on Computing and Network Communications (CoCoNet) 2015, pp. 559–564. IEEE, New Jersey (2015)
41. Cave, R., Bloch, S.: The use of speech recognition technology by people living with amyotrophic lateral sclerosis: a scoping review. Disabil. Rehabil. Assist. Technol. **2021**, 1–13 (2021)
42. Wobbrock, J.O., et al.: Ability-based design: Concept, principles and examples. ACM Trans. Access. Comput. **3**(3), Article no. 9 (2011)
43. Desmond, D., et al.: Assistive technology and people: a position paper from the first global research, innovation and education on assistive technology (GREAT) summit. Disabil. Rehabil. Assist. Technol. **13**(5), 437–444 (2018)
44. Stramondo, J.A.: The distinction between curative and assistive technology. Sci. Eng. Ethics **25**(4), 1125–1145 (2019)
45. Steinfeld, E., Maisel, J.L.: Universal Design: Creating Inclusive Environments. Wiley, New Jersey (2012)
46. Derman, Y.D., Arenovich, T., Strauss, J.: Speech recognition software and electronic psychiatric progress notes: physicians' ratings and preferences. BMC Med. Inform. Decis. Mak. **10**(1), 44 (2010)
47. Pedersen, B.S., et al.: The Danish language in the digital age. In: Rehm, G., Uszkoreitm H. (eds.) META-NET White Paper Series: Europe's Languages in the Digital Age. Springer, Heidelberg (2012). https://doi.org/10.1007/978-3-642-30627-3
48. Arksey, H., O'Malley, L.: Scoping studies: towards a methodological framework. Int. J. Soc. Res. Methodol. **8**(1), 19–32 (2005)
49. Alvesson, M., Sköldberg, K.: Reflexive Methodology: New Vistas for Qualitative Research. Sage, Los Angeles (2017)
50. Kommunal- og distriktsdepartementet: Samisk språk og IT: Språkteknologi [Sami language and IT: Language technology]. https://www.regjeringen.no/no/tema/urfolk-og-minoriteter/samepolitikk/samiske-sprak/samisk-sprak-og-it/id86947/. Accessed 14 Apr 2022
51. Government: Strategi for vækst gennem deleøkonomi [Strategy for growth through a sharing economy]. Ministry of Industry, Business and Financial Affairs, Copenhagen (2017)
52. Kommunal- og moderniseringsdepartementet.: Nasjonal strategi for kunstig intelligens [National strategy for artificial intelligence]. Kommunal- og digitaliseringsdepartementet, Oslo (2020)
53. Government, LGD, The Danish Regions: A coherent and trustworthy health network for all: Digital health strategy 2018–2022. Ministry of Health, Ministry of Finance, Local Government Denmark and the Regions, Copenhagen (2018)
54. Agency for Digitalization and GovTech-Program.: Challenge statement. https://challenges.dk/sites/default/files/2019-09/DIGST%20GovTech-Program%20One%20Pager%20ENG.pdf. Accessed 16 Sept 2022
55. Kvarenes, M.: Klar, men aldri ferdig: En praktisk veileder i klarspråksarbeid [Ready, but never finished: A practical guide to clear language]. Språkrådet og Direktoratet for forvaltning og IKT, Oslo (2010)

56. Abdul, A., et al.: Trends and trajectories for explainable, accountable and intelligible systems: an HCI research agenda. In: Mandryk, R. Hancock, M. (eds.) CHI 2018: Proceedings of the 2018 CHI Conference on Human Factors in Computing Systems 2018, Paper 582. Association for Computing Machinery, Montreal (2018)
57. Berget, G.: Search and Find?: An Accessibility Study of Dyslexia and Information Retrieval. University of Oslo, Oslo (2016)

Understanding the Universal Access User Experience

A Comparison of Form Navigation with Tabbing and Pointing

Bernt Ferner, Adrian Gåsøy, Martin Walberg Nicolaysen, and Frode Eika Sandnes(✉)

Oslo Metropolitan University, 0130 Oslo, Norway
{s346208,s346204,s315519,frodes}@oslomet.no

Abstract. The form is a widely used metaphor in information gathering. Users typically navigate between form elements using a keyboard or a pointing device. This study set out to empirically compare tabbing and pointing in form navigation using keyboards, mouse, and touch. A controlled experiment was conducted with 20 participants. The results show that there was no difference between the input methods for form completion, but the pointing input was significantly faster for correcting mistakes. Yet, most of the participants preferred tabbing over pointing.

Keywords: web · forms · tabbing · pointing

1 Introduction

The form metaphor is widely used in information systems to gather data as users traditionally reused their paper form experience to complete electronic forms without learning. The form metaphor seems effective even as the younger generations of users have less or no background with paper forms. The advantage of a form is that information is entered incrementally in a linear manner, and the completed parts serve as a mnemonic aid to the users after interruptions or pauses. Interactive forms can be implemented with effective error feedback mechanisms that can help users understand and successfully complete complex forms [1].

Traditional form fields are completed using text entry [2, 3], while graphical user interfaces also allow for richer sets of input methods for specific data types such as drop-down menus, date-selectors, time-pickers [4], etc. More abstract types of form input exist such as pointing cameras at QR-codes [5]. In this study we wanted to explore the movement between different form fields. Modern platforms provide several means of moving between form fields, most notably using tabbing with a keyboard-type device, or through direct pointing typically using a mouse, a touchpad or a touchscreen [4, 6]. Accessibility guidelines such as WCAG states that it should be possible to move between form fields with keyboard input, or some similar device, allowing users with reduced motor function access.

In this study we particularly wanted to find out if it takes shorter time to tab between different form fields or by directly clicking on these fields, and what the differences

M. Antona and C. Stephanidis (Eds.): HCII 2023, LNCS 14020, pp. 311–318, 2023.
https://doi.org/10.1007/978-3-031-35681-0_20

between the two are during incremental form field completion, and form correction that involves larger jumps in the form. Also, we wanted to explore if users' preferences are aligned with their performance characteristics.

This paper is organized as follows. The next section reviews related work. Section 3 presents the methodology. The results are presented in Sect. 4 and these are discussed in Sect. 5. The paper is concluded in Sect. 6.

2 Related Works

Various aspects of electronic forms have been studied in the past. Several branches of research have focused on accessibility of forms, in particular the ability to use keyboards in rich internet applications [7–11] and shortcut keys [12]. Others have compared voice-controlled interface navigation to keyboards and mouse [13–15] and the use of autocompletion for users with dyslexia [16]. Studies of general form use on small form-factor devices such as Smartphones suggest that scrolling should be replaced with other navigation mechanisms [17, 18]. Other form issues include error messages [19], speed of form completion [20], what makes respondent succeed or fail in forms [21, 22], and cultural factors [23]. Form error mechanisms has also received attention which have resulted in several explicit advice [1, 24–28].

Other form issues include error messages [19], speed of form completion [20], what makes respondent succeed or fail in forms [21, 22], and cultural factors [23]. Form error mechanisms has also received attention which have resulted in several explicit advice [1, 24–28].

3 Method

3.1 Experimental Design

A within-groups experiment was designed with input method as independent variable and navigation time, correction time, and perceived effectiveness as dependent variables. The input method had three levels, namely tabbing (keyboard), direct pointing (touch) and indirect pointing (mouse).

3.2 Participants

A total of 20 participants were recruited for the experiments using convenience sampling with a balance of females and males. Most of the participants (11 in total) were in their 20 s, but the age range spanned from 19 to 68 (M = 31.6, SD = 13.0). None of the participants reported any reduced motor function, reduced vision [29, 30], or reduced cognition [31].

3.3 Task and Materials

The participants were asked to complete simple forms comprising 16 fields. Each field was labelled with the letter of the alphabet and the participant had to write the letter of the alphabet into the corresponding field. Simply using a letter rather than a word or a sentence was intended to reduce bias caused by differences in reading abilities [32]. For one of the two questionnaires for each conduction an intentional error was inserted into the first field element which was reported once the field was submitted. The participants then had to go back and correct the mistake before resubmitting the form, using the assigned input method.

Six versions of the web form were implemented using HTML and CSS in the Norwegian language (see Fig. 1). The error logic was implemented using JavaScript. Black text on a white background was selected to ensure a high luminance contrast [33].

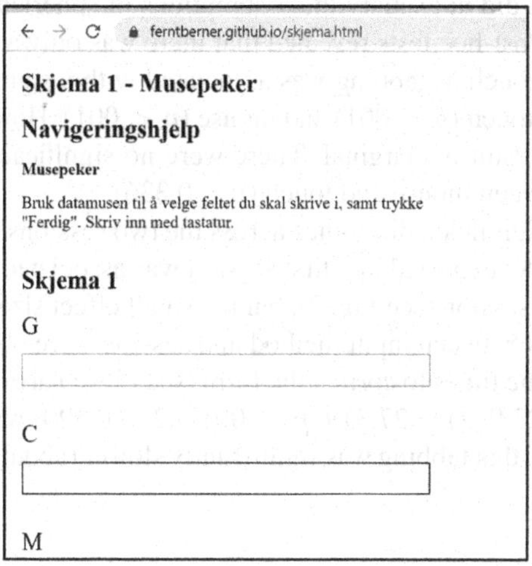

Fig. 1. The form used in the experiments (in Norwegian).

3.4 Equipment

Participants used their own equipment for the experiment and had to use a laptop or a desktop computer with a mouse, and a Smartphone or a tablet. For the tabbing condition task the desktop or laptop keyboard was used, while for the indirect pointing the computer mouse was used. For the direct pointing condition, the Smartphone or tablet touchscreen was used. Of the 20 participants 16 used a laptop (80%), while 4 used a stationary computer (20%). A total of 17 participants (85%) used a Smartphone, while only 3 participants used a tablet (15%).

3.5 Procedure

The experiments were conducted remotely using video/audio conference calls using Discord or FaceTime. The links to the questionnaires were sent via email. The participants were consulted individually. First, each participant was briefed about the experiment. They were asked to complete each condition in two trials, that is, a total of six trials. The participants had to assist with the time-taking, by orally indicating when they started and when they had finished. The experimenters measured the time and recorded the results.

Each session lasted 10–15 min. The experiment was anonymous since all observations were collected in single sessions. There was thus no need to link records across sessions [34]. Statistical analyses were conducted using JASP version 0.16.0.0 [35].

4 Results

The results show that there was a significant difference between the different input methods in terms of form completion times ($F(1.893, 35.974) = 4.9, p = .014, \eta^2 = 0.213$). A Greenhouse-Geisser correction was used since a Mauchly's test of sphericity indicated that the data did not satisfy the assumptions of sphericity although the effect size was very small. Post-hoc tests revealed that there was only a significant difference between tabbing and touch as tabbing was associated with a significantly shorter form completion time than touch ($p < .001$) and mouse ($p < .001$). However, the small effect size signals that this result is marginal. There were no significant differences in form completion times between mouse and touch ($p = 0.336$).

There was also a significant difference across the two sessions ($F(1, 19) = 28.306, p < .001, \eta^2 = 0.243$). As expected, the first session was associated with longer response times than the second session (see Fig. 2), but the small effect size indicates a moderate effect. No interactions between input method and session were observed.

A comparison of the times to correct the form (see Fig. 3) also revealed a significant difference ($F(1.472, 27.972) = 27.319, p < .001, \eta2 = 0.590$) with a large effect size. Post-hoc tests revealed that tabbing was significantly slower (about 50%) than both using

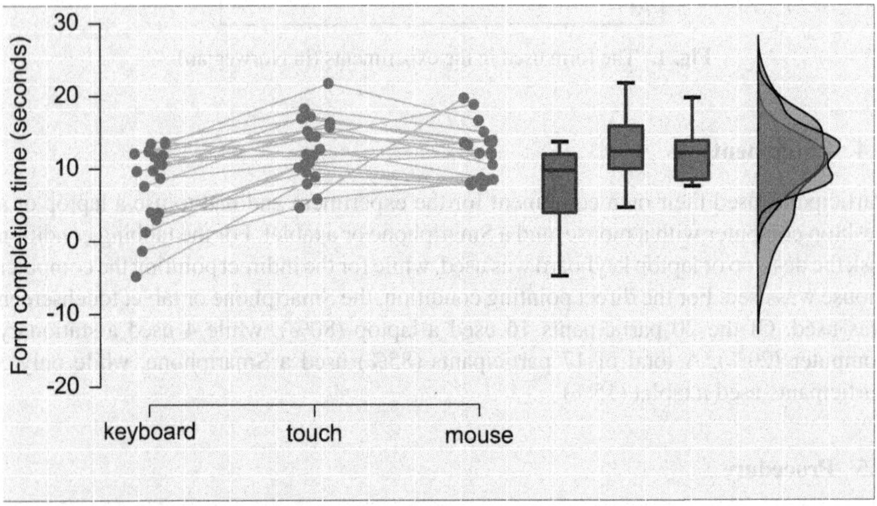

Fig. 2. Raincloud plot showing the form completion times (incremental jumps) for the second session across the three input devices.

mouse ($p < .001$) and touch ($p < .001$). There was no significant difference in correction times for mouse and touch ($p = .990$).

In response to which input method the participants found most effective (see Fig. 4), a majority of 15 preferred tabbing (75%), while 4 participants preferred mouse (20%) and only 1 participant preferred touch (5%).

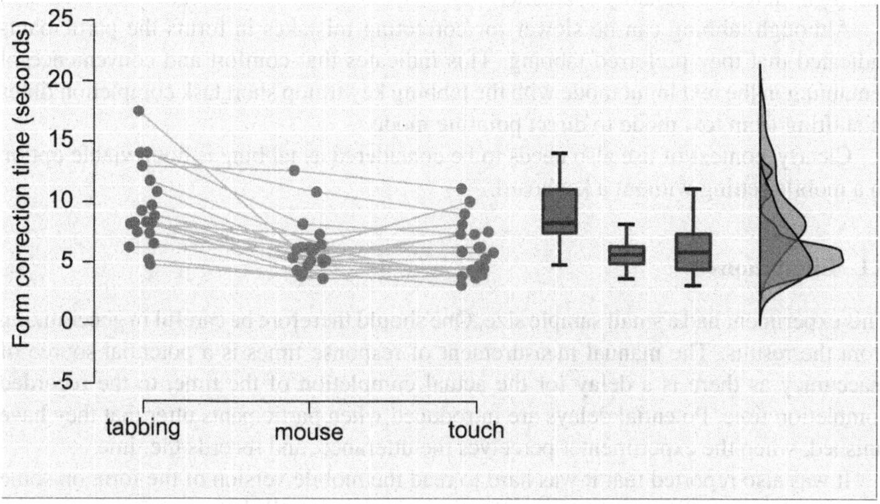

Fig. 3. Raincloud plot showing the distribution of the form correction times (large jumps) for the three input devices.

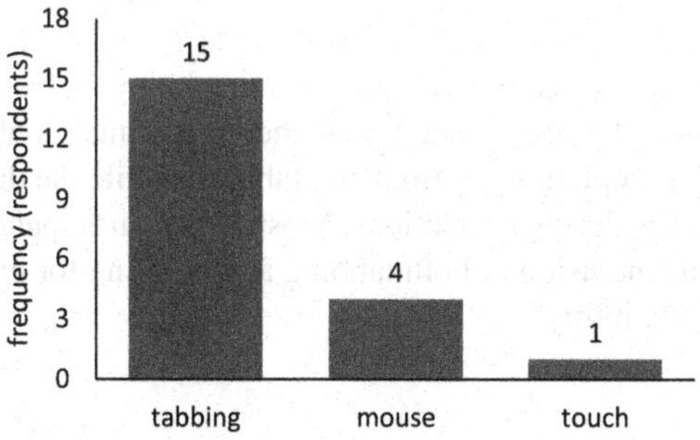

Fig. 4. Form navigation preference.

5 Discussion

The results partially confirmed our hypothesis that it is faster to navigate with tabbing than using either mouse or touch. This is probably because the user can maintain the same input modality for the (text) input and moving (tabbing) to the next field. While with mouse and touch the user will have to switch between virtual-physical text input to the pointing task of the next field. However, the effect sizes show that this difference is marginal.

However, the results showed that tabbing was significantly slower than mouse and touch for correcting errors. Clearly, the time to directly point at the field to be corrected using either mouse or tab was shorter than the repeated pressing of the tabbing key, although more conveniently available.

Although tabbing can be slower for correcting mistakes in forms the participants indicated that they preferred tabbing. This indicates that comfort and convenience of remaining in the text input mode with the tabbing key trump short task completion times of shifting from text mode to direct pointing mode.

Clearly, context of use also needs to be considered as tabbing is not a viable option in a mobile setting without a keyboard.

5.1 Limitations

This experiment had a small sample size. One should therefore be careful in generalizing from the results. The manual measurement of response times is a potential source of inaccuracy as there is a delay for the actual completion of the time, to the recorded completion time. Potential delays are introduced when participants utter that they have finished, when the experimenter perceives the utterance, and records the time.

It was also reported that it was hard to read the mobile version of the form on some devices which may have prolonged the response times. Still the correction times with touch was significantly shorter and it thus seems not to have affected the conclusion.

6 Conclusions

A controlled experiment was conducted to compare tabbing and pointing in form completion and correction. The results show that there were marginally shorter response times associated with completing a form using tabbing, while the direct pointing took a significantly shorter time during corrections. Most of the participants preferred tabbing. The results suggest the inclusion of both tabbing and pointing for navigating forms as it gives the users more flexibility.

References

1. Hofseth, K.Å., Haga, L.K., Sørlie, V., Sandnes, F.E.: Form feedback on the web: a comparison of popup alerts and in-form error messages. In: Chen, Y.W., Zimmermann, A., Howlett, R., Jain, L. (eds.) Innovation in Medicine and Healthcare Systems, and Multimedia. Smart Innovation, Systems and Technologies, vol. 145, pp. 369–379. Springer, Singapore (2019). https://doi.org/10.1007/978-981-13-8566-7_35
2. Sandnes, F.E., Thorkildssen, H.W., Arvei, A., Buverad, J.O.: Techniques for fast and easy mobile text-entry with three-keys. In: Proceedings of the 37th Annual Hawaii International Conference on System Sciences 2004. IEEE (2004)

3. Sandnes, F.E.: Evaluating mobile text entry strategies with finite state automata. In: Proceedings of the 7th International Conference on Human Computer Interaction with Mobile Devices & Services, pp. 115–121. ACM (2005)
4. Skogstrøm, N.A.B., Igeltjørn, A., Knudsen, K.M., Diallo, A.D., Krivonos, D., Sandnes, F.E.: A comparison of two smartphone time-picking interfaces: convention versus efficiency. In: Proceedings of the 10th Nordic Conference on Human-Computer Interaction, pp. 874–879. ACM (2018)
5. Huang, Y.P., Chang, Y.T., Sandnes, F.E.: Ubiquitous information transfer across different platforms by QR codes. J. Mob. Multimedia, 003–014 (2010)
6. Aschim, T.B., Gjerstad, J.L., Lien, L.V., Tahsin, R., Sandnes, F.E.: Are split tablet keyboards better? A study of soft keyboard layout and hand posture. In: Lamas, D., Loizides, F., Nacke, L., Petrie, H., Winckler, M., Zaphiris, P. (eds.) INTERACT 2019. LNCS, vol. 11748, pp. 647–655. Springer, Cham (2019). https://doi.org/10.1007/978-3-030-29387-1_37
7. Watanabe, W.M., Geraldo, R.J., de Mattos Fortes, R.P.: Keyboard navigation mechanisms in tab widgets: an investigation on ARIA's conformance. In: Proceedings of the 29th Annual ACM Symposium on Applied Computing, pp. 721–726. ACM (2014)
8. Carvalho, L.P., Ferreira, L.P., Freire, A.P.: Accessibility evaluation of rich internet applications interface components for mobile screen readers. In: Proceedings of the 31st Annual ACM Symposium on Applied Computing, pp. 181–186. ACM (2016)
9. Antonelli, H.L., Igawa, R.A., Fortes, R.P.D.M., Rizo, E.H., Watanabe, W.M.: Drop-down menu widget identification using HTML structure changes classification. ACM Trans. Access. Comput. **11**(2) (2018)
10. Watanabe, W.M., de Mattos Fortes, R.P.: Automatic identification of drop-down menu widgets using mutation observers and visibility changes. In: Proceedings of the 31st Annual ACM Symposium on Applied Computing, pp. 766–771. ACM (2016)
11. Watanabe, W.M., Geraldo, R.J.E., Fortes, R.P.D.M.: Keyboard navigation mechanisms in widgets: an investigation on ARIA's implementations. J. Web Eng., 041–062 (2015)
12. Dickinson, A.: Is the shortcut the quickest way to go? Translating instructions for keyboard navigation and other stories. ACM SIGCSE Bull. **39**(3), 358–358. ACM (2007)
13. Van Buskirk, R., LaLomia, M.: A comparison of speech and mouse/keyboard GUI navigation. In: Conference Companion on Human Factors in Computing Systems (1995)
14. Christian, K., Kules, B., Shneiderman, B., Youssef, A.: A comparison of voice controlled and mouse controlled web browsing. In: Proceedings of the Fourth International ACM Conference on Assistive Technologies, pp. 72–79. ACM (2000)
15. Rupprecht, D., Etzold, J., Bomsdorf, B.: Model-based development of accessible, personalized web forms for ICF-based assessment. In: Proceedings of the 7th ACM SIGCHI Symposium on Engineering Interactive Computing Systems, pp. 120–125. ACM (2015)
16. Berget, G., Sandnes, F.E.: Do autocomplete functions reduce the impact of dyslexia on information searching behaviour? A case of Google. J. Am. Soc. Inf. Sci. Technol. **67**, 2320–2328 (2016)
17. Harms, J., Wimmer, C., Kappel, K., Grechenig, T.: Design space for focus+ context navigation in web forms. In: Proceedings of the 2014 ACM SIGCHI Symposium on Engineering Interactive Computing Systems, pp. 39–44. ACM (2014)
18. Harms, J., Kratky, M., Wimmer, C., Kappel, K., Grechenig, T.: Navigation in long forms on smartphones: scrolling worse than tabs, menus, and collapsible fieldsets. In: Abascal, J., Barbosa, S., Fetter, M., Gross, T., Palanque, P., Winckler, M. (eds.) INTERACT 2015. LNCS, vol. 9298, pp. 333–340. Springer, Cham (2015). https://doi.org/10.1007/978-3-319-22698-9_21
19. Shneiderman, B.: Designing computer system messages. Commun. ACM **25**, 610–611 (1982)
20. Husser, J.A., Fernandez, K.E.: To click, type, or drag? Evaluating speed of survey data input methods. Surv. Pract. **6**, 1–7 (2013)

21. Cruz-Benito, J., et al.: Improving success/completion ratio in large surveys: a proposal based on usability and engagement. In: Zaphiris, P., Ioannou, A. (eds.) LCT 2017. LNCS, vol. 10296, pp. 352–370. Springer, Cham (2017). https://doi.org/10.1007/978-3-319-58515-4_28
22. Stieger, S., Reips, U.D.: What are participants doing while filling in an online questionnaire: a paradata collection tool and an empirical study. Comput. Hum. Behav. **26**(6), 1488–1495 (2010)
23. Recabarren, M., Nussbaum, M.: Exploring the feasibility of web form adaptation to users' cultural dimension scores. User Model. User Adapt. Interact. **20**, 87–108 (2010)
24. Bargas-Avila, J.A., Orsini, S., Piosczyk, H., Urwyler, D., Opwis, K.: Enhancing online forms: use format specifications for fields with format restrictions to help respondents. Interact. Comput. **23**, 33–39 (2010)
25. Bargas-Avila, J.A., Brenzikofer, O., Tuch, A.N., Roth, S.P., Opwis, K.: Working towards usable forms on the world wide web: optimizing date entry input fields. Adv. Hum. Comput. Interact. 2011 (2011)
26. Bargas-Avila, J.A., Oberholzer, G., Schmutz, P., de Vito, M., Opwis, K.: Usable error message presentation in the World Wide web: do not show errors right away. Interact. Comput. **19**, 330–341 (2007)
27. Pauwels, S.L., Hübscher, C., Leuthold, S., Bargas-Avila, J.A., Opwis, K.: Error prevention in online forms: use color instead of asterisks to mark required-fields. Interact. Comput. **21**, 257–262 (2009)
28. Seckler, M., Tuch, A.N., Opwis, K., Bargas-Avila, J.A.: User-friendly locations of error messages in web forms: put them on the right side of the erroneous input field. Interact. Comput. **24**, 107–118 (2012)
29. Sandnes, F.E.: What do low-vision users really want from smart glasses? Faces, text and perhaps no glasses at all. In: Miesenberger, K., Bühler, C., Penaz, P. (eds.) ICCHP 2016. LNCS, vol. 9758, pp. 187–194. Springer, Cham (2016). https://doi.org/10.1007/978-3-319-41264-1_25
30. dos Santos, A.D.P., Medola, F.O., Cinelli, M.J., Garcia Ramirez, A.R., Sandnes, F.E.: Are electronic white canes better than traditional canes? A comparative study with blind and blindfolded participants. Univ. Access Inf. Soc. **20**(1), 93–103 (2020). https://doi.org/10.1007/s10209-020-00712-z
31. Sandnes, F.E., Lundh, M.V.: Calendars for individuals with cognitive disabilities: a comparison of table view and list view. In: Proceedings of the 17th International ACM SIGACCESS Conference on Computers & Accessibility, pp. 329–330. ACM (2015). https://doi.org/10.1145/2700648.2811363
32. Eika, E., Sandnes, F.E.: Assessing the reading level of web texts for WCAG2.0 compliance—can it be done automatically?. In: Di Bucchianico, G., Kercher, P. (eds.) Advances in Design for Inclusion. AISC, vol. 500, pp. 361–371. Springer, Cham (2016). https://doi.org/10.1007/978-3-319-41962-6_32
33. Sandnes, F.E., Zhao, A.: An interactive color picker that ensures WCAG2. 0 compliant color contrast levels. Procedia Comput. Sci. **67**, 87–94 (2015). https://doi.org/10.1016/j.procs.2015.09.252
34. Sandnes, F.E.: HIDE: short IDs for robust and anonymous linking of users across multiple sessions in small HCI experiments. In: CHI 2021 Conference on Human Factors in Computing Systems Extended Abstracts Proceedings. ACM (2021). https://doi.org/10.1145/3411763.3451794
35. JASP Team: JASP (Version 0.14.1) Computer software (2020)

Using Lean UX in the Design and Evaluation of a Prototype for Automatic Translation Between Sign Languages

Luis Henrique Ferreira Caravalho[1], Soraia Silva Prietch[1](✉), and J. Alfredo Sánchez[2]

[1] Universidade Federal de Rondonópolis, Rondonópolis, MT 78736-900, Brazil
luis.carvalho@aluno.ufr.edu.br, soraia@ufr.edu.br
[2] Laboratorio Nacional de Informática Avanzada, 91090 Xalapa, VER, Mexico
alfredo.sanchez@lania.edu.mx

Abstract. Although an International Sign Language has been created, only a small percentage of people in the world are able to use it. Given this context, it is important to support communication among deaf persons who use different sign languages and who want to meet other deaf persons. A mid- to long-term alternative for accomplishing this is the construction of an automatic system that would translate one sign language into another sign language (SL2SL). Just designing the user experience of such SL2SL translator between sign languages entails a significant challenge. In this paper, we present how proto-personas and user stories specification have been used to foster ideas during user evaluation of a first low-fidelity prototype that explores how deaf persons might communicate via a SL2SL translator. A result of the current stage is the consideration of diverse volunteer profiles, which has helped us learn from different viewpoints, with participants contributing multiple suggestions and highlighting improvements on the proposed interface elements. One of our main contributions is the introduction of conversational proto-personas pairs in our user stories, since we wanted to gain insights into the bilateral needs of users who face the challenge to interact when using different sign languages. This way, we aim to improve our learning curve for designing natural user interfaces for sign language users and to establish the next research stages.

Keywords: Interface design and evaluation · Sign language · Automatic translation

1 Introduction

According to [1], 70 million people identify themselves as deaf persons. Many of these people rely on sign language as their first language to communicate with others. Although an International Sign (IS) – previously called Gestuno or International Sign Language [2] - exists, only a small percentage of people in the world use it [3], since most deaf persons usually have interest in deepening their knowledge on their local sign language.

M. Antona and C. Stephanidis (Eds.): HCII 2023, LNCS 14020, pp. 319–339, 2023.
https://doi.org/10.1007/978-3-031-35681-0_21

Typically, this local sign language refers to the country's official sign language (e.g., Libras (*Língua Brasileira de Sinais*) used in Brazil, or LGP (Língua Gestual Portuguesa) used in Portugal); however, in some locations, more than one sign language can coexist in the same city (e.g., *Langue de Signes Québécoise* and American Sign Language used in Montreal, Canada) or in the same country (e.g., LSM (*Lengua de Señas Mexicana*) and LSMY (*Lengua de Señas Maya Yucateca*) used in Mexico) [4]. Most sign languages are recognized by law as official languages of Deaf communities, since they are full-fledged modes of communication, with grammar and formalisms as any of the oral-written official languages.

Interacting with other deaf persons in the same or other cities, states or countries using their first language is essential to build an identity and to be part of a Deaf culture, in which language and life experience, knowledge, values, sense of community, for instance, can be shared [5]. Perhaps in a small town a Deaf community does not have resources to maintain an association; however, if they can articulate meetings with larger Deaf communities, possibilities are unlimited, in the sense that they can share previous experiences and paths to follow, for example, on promoting sign language courses, celebrating important dates, writing proposals to apply for funding, seeking partnerships.

Our research's main motivation is to offer alternative means to bridge communication between Deaf communities who seek to meet other deaf persons who use different sign languages. This means, a translator from one sign language into another sign language (SL2SL translator) is a unimodal contact [4], in the sense that interaction involves only sign languages (sharing the same modality of communication) as opposed to, for instance, the interaction between a written and a signed language (bimodal contact).

Our research has revealed a gap that should be addressed regarding the user experience (UX) design of SL2SL translator (as discussed in Sect. 2 of this paper). With that in mind, we have been conducting a collaborative study between deaf and hearing researchers and volunteers from Mexico and Brazil, using the Lean UX approach (Sect. 3) to design a SL2SL translator for which the primary target users are deaf persons who are sign language users.

According to [6], the Lean UX process covers four steps carried out in an agile approach: (i) outcomes, assumptions, hypothesis, (ii) design, (iii) creation of an MVP (Minimum Viable Product, in this paper referred to as a prototype) and (iv) research and learning. The process we conducted followed the build-measure-learn feedback loop [6] in each research round: build (prototype), measure (validate internally and test externally) and learn (from users). In Sect. 4, the prototype is briefly described in the light of ten design guidelines for natural sign language interfaces we proposed previously [7]. We then focus on the third round of the Lean UX process, in which we produced proto-personas and user stories specifications (Sect. 5) to foster ideas and conducted user evaluation with our first low-fidelity prototype of an SL2SL translator (Sect. 6). We aimed to improve our learning curve for designing natural user interfaces for sign language users and to establish the next research stages. Since our work involves the collaboration between research groups in Brazil and Mexico, our case study is focused on the design of a translation system that considers the *Língua Brasileira de Sinais* (Libras) and the *Lengua de Señas Mexicana* (LSM) as a starting point. The general idea, however, is that someone could choose any source or target language they would like to translate to or from. In Sect. 7, we discuss our results by analyzing the potential users' interpretation of the interface elements, compared to our design intent, and eliciting alternative designs for future testing. Finally, Sect. 8 presents our conclusions and reports limitations of our work.

Our research contributions include the integration of the proto-personas technique with the specification of user stories that present the interaction of pairs of potential users of the SL2SL translator at the same time. We also advanced in validating a previously proposed set of design guidelines for natural sign language interfaces [7] by obtaining positive feedback from potential users who were representative of relevant proto-personas. We present findings evidenced during the user evaluation with our low-fidelity prototype, which we are confident other researchers can find helpful when working on related projects.

2 Automatic Translation Between Two Sign Languages

As reported by [8], "In spite of the recent advances in Machine Translation (MT) for spoken languages, translation between spoken and Sign Languages (SLs) or between Sign Languages remains a difficult problem." In the case of translation between sign languages, this statement confirms our findings after a thorough literature review: only two incipient works dedicated to the subject [9, 10], which we briefly describe below.

In [9], the authors report image processing experiments to classify letters of a manual alphabet, considering simple and complex backgrounds in videos, and to carry out bidirectional translation between Libras and American Sign Language (ASL). The former experiment consisted of translating three letters of one manual alphabet and a sign from a sign language to another. Results were not promising, but to the best of our knowledge this was the first publication to report an attempt to perform automatic SL2SL translation.

With the goal to design a translation system, [10] presents an investigation on the formalization using gloss writing[1] and image processing studies of two languages, French Sign Language (LSF) and (South) Korean Sign Language (KSL). Some progress has been made indicating paths to avoid and to further explore. Authors mention interaction with deaf persons; however, this was not the focus of their report.

In addition to the two related works found on automatic SL2SL translation, studies have been published that can support research on the field that either investigate relationships between two or more sign languages, though not concerning specifically automatic translation. They focus, for example, on linguistic inquiry (e.g., code-switching, borrowings and loans, studies of Deaf communities in international border areas) [4, 12, 13], lexical measurements (e.g., lexical overlap between languages, (mis)match in meaning, iconicity) [14, 15, 16], and comparable multiple sign languages corpora [17]. We also found investigation on automatic sign language processing systems taking text or speech into account at one of the ends, where processing includes recognition, generation, and translation [18].

[1] A variant to the gloss system has been used to represent sign languages in written form. In a simplified way, the written form "is capitalized as a representation of the manual sign with equivalent meaning. Non-manual signs can be represented by superscript codes, and uses of the sign space can be indicated by subscript letters or numbers" [11].

Moreover, the Thomas Smith-Stark's studies[2] [19] report relations between the *Lengua de Señas Mexicana* (LSM) and the *Língua Brasileira de Sinais* (Libras), since both countries had their first school for the Deaf founded by Eduardo Huet[3], and their sign languages have roots on the French Sign Language (LSF) family. LSF also gave rise to several other sign languages, including ASL[4]. Given these characteristics, one hypothesis is that LSM and Libras may have more similarities when comparing any two other sign languages from the same family [19]. This may as well be a path to research the subject of SL2SL translation.

3 Methodology

In this paper, we report results of the third research round of the Lean UX process (Fig. 1). Previously, in the first round of the build-measure-learn feedback loop, we validated assumptions in a remote session [1] and delivered a set of requirements to build a prototype. In the second round of the loop, we validated internally the prototype and generated translations for interface elements from written to sign language [7]. Researchers, deaf persons and sign language interpreters from Brazil and Mexico participated in both rounds.

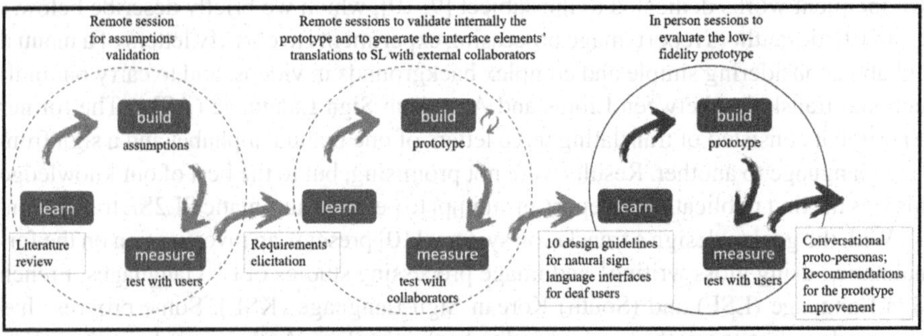

Fig. 1. Three rounds of the build-measure-learn feedback loop.

Our main takeaways from the first two rounds took the form of ten design guidelines for natural sign language interfaces for deaf users [7], around which we built the prototype and conducted user evaluations of the low-fidelity prototype. However, before conducting user evaluations, we wanted to brainstorm about who the potential users would be and in which situations they would find a SL2SL translator useful.

2 Smith Stark, Thomas C. Una comparación de las lenguas manuales de México y Brasil. México: Centro de Estudios Lingüísticos y Literarios, COLMEX, 1990b. [unpublished manuscript].

3 Huet Herrera, Susana Teresa. Datos biográficos del Prof. Eduardo Huet, fundador y primer director de la Escuela Nacional de Sordomudos de México. 1983, unpublished manuscript.

4 Stokoe, W.; Casterline, Dorothy; Croneberg, Carl. A Dictionary of American Sign Language on Linguistic Principles. Washington, D.C.: Gallaudet College Press, 1965.

3.1 Introducing Conversational Proto-personas

In the Lean UX process [6], the Personas technique is not used only once, but it is an ongoing activity. Given this dynamic characteristic, we refer to it as proto-persona profile creation, since it starts from assumptions, and then it goes to research and validation. In this process, we keep a living proto-persona document, which can be adjusted continuously. Moreover, in the Lean UX process, usually hypotheses are proposed instead of (agile) user stories. We chose to create user stories, however, for two reasons: first, to be able to connect two proto-personas in each user story and, second, to maintain the prototype's main goal (to communicate) instead of describing the prototype's features, which would be more suitable to create hypotheses for one single proto-persona at a time.

To create our eight initial proto-persona profiles, we designed a standard template containing data we considered relevant to map potential users' characteristics. In this template, the following fields were included: name, age, gender, country, formal educational level, occupation status, a phrase that best defines the proto-persona, a brief text profile with the proto-persona's characteristics, and a table to rate in a 5-point Likert scale the level (being *none* equals to 1 and *high* equals to 5) of the following 8-statements: (i) Local sign language skills, (ii) Other sign languages skills, (iii) Writing skills (their country's written language), (iv) Reading skills (their country's written language), (v) Technology skills, (vi) Frequency of translator use, (vii) Interest in communicating with people who use different sign languages, and (viii) Have interacted with Deaf persons from other countries. Since we have been conducting research with Sign Language communities for many years [20], proto-persona profiles were created based on several actual individuals from the communities we have interacted with along this period.

3.2 User Stories as a Context for Conversational Proto-Personas

Four user stories described general characteristics of each pair of proto-persona profiles, including, for instance, their nationality and sign languages used, the goal of both proto-personas, and how a SL2SL system can overcome the communication barrier. Our user stories link together pairs of conversational proto-personas, which differ from the existing collaborative personas concept [21], in which a single persona may represent a group of collaborators with specific roles working together–in a project team or in a community of practice—to achieve a collective goal. With our conversational proto-personas, we represent the bilateral needs of two proto-personas who face the challenge to interact with each other using different sign languages.

Note that proto-personas profiles and user stories have been created (and updated) since round two of the Lean UX process while we were collaboratively designing the prototype. This way, in round three we had a clearer scenario about potential users and situations in which they could need to use a SL2SL translator in their lives. Therefore, when planning user evaluation, we wanted to have participants who were representative of the proposed proto-personas. We also invited, for the user evaluation phase, participants with technology or foreign language skills that can help us improve our design proposal for the SL2SL prototype.

In our notion of SL2SL translator we do not intend to provide a dictionary to search for signs in a variety of sign languages. Various interesting options already exist that accomplish that, such as Wikisigns[5] and Spread the sign[6]. Rather, we seek to design interfaces for translating full phrases, lectures, or conversations in sign language, since merely a manual alphabet and isolated signs cannot fully support a fluid communication between deaf or hearing signers (see Sect. 4 to learn about the prototype details).

3.3 User Evaluation Design

Our user evaluation consisted of collecting perceptions and opinions about the prototype from six invited participants with diverse background, gender, and abilities. The prototype evaluation was carried out in six individual sessions with an average duration of 40 min each, taking place at a Brazilian university setting. We used a computer screen to present the interfaces we planned to discuss, an audio recorder to facilitate transcriptions afterwards and, in one user evaluation, a laptop camera to record videos of a deaf participant who provided answers through the interpreter. A standard script was used during each session, following five steps: (i) read and sign an informed consent, (ii) answer a pre-test questionnaire with open questions made out from the fields in the proto-persona profile template, (iii) present the user flow through the seven main interfaces of the SL2SL translator prototype (Fig. 2), (iv) answer the user evaluation questionnaire about the interface elements using a fourteen-slide presentation (see figures in Sect. 6) and, (v) answer one final open question.

The user evaluation questionnaire was designed with open questions to learn about the understanding of every interface element on the screen. Each screen had a different number of interface elements and, consequently, a different number of questions. Two out of fourteen slides presented brief explanations about sign language and automatic translation; the next twelve slides (representing prototype interfaces) presented the user flow with more detail, by expanding the navigation options when an icon or a button was clicked, or when hovering over the interface. The data analysis from user evaluations was conducted using the qualitative approach.

4 A Low-Fidelity SL2SL Prototype

During the prototyping phase of the second round of the Lean UX process, our main goal was to design non-textual interfaces, prioritizing sign language and visual communication. We sought that, primarily, deaf persons who are sign language users could autonomously navigate through the SL2SL prototype. An outcome from this second round was a proposal of ten design guidelines (DG) for natural sign language interfaces for deaf users [7].

In the third (current) round of the Lean UX process, in addition to seeking improvements to the usability and to the user experience design of the prototype, we validate our proposed guidelines. In what follows, we describe the main features of our prototype and how we meet the ten guidelines at design time:

[5] Wikisigns. Mexico. https://www.wikisigns.org/.

[6] Spread the sign. Sweden. https://www.spreadthesign.com/.

- (DG1) *The design should consider the varying characteristics of the target deaf community*. Deaf persons and interpreters participated in the design process, which allowed us to learn about diverse needs. Also, the literature [22, 23] and previous research in the field [24, 25] has shown the diversity in communication needs of Deaf

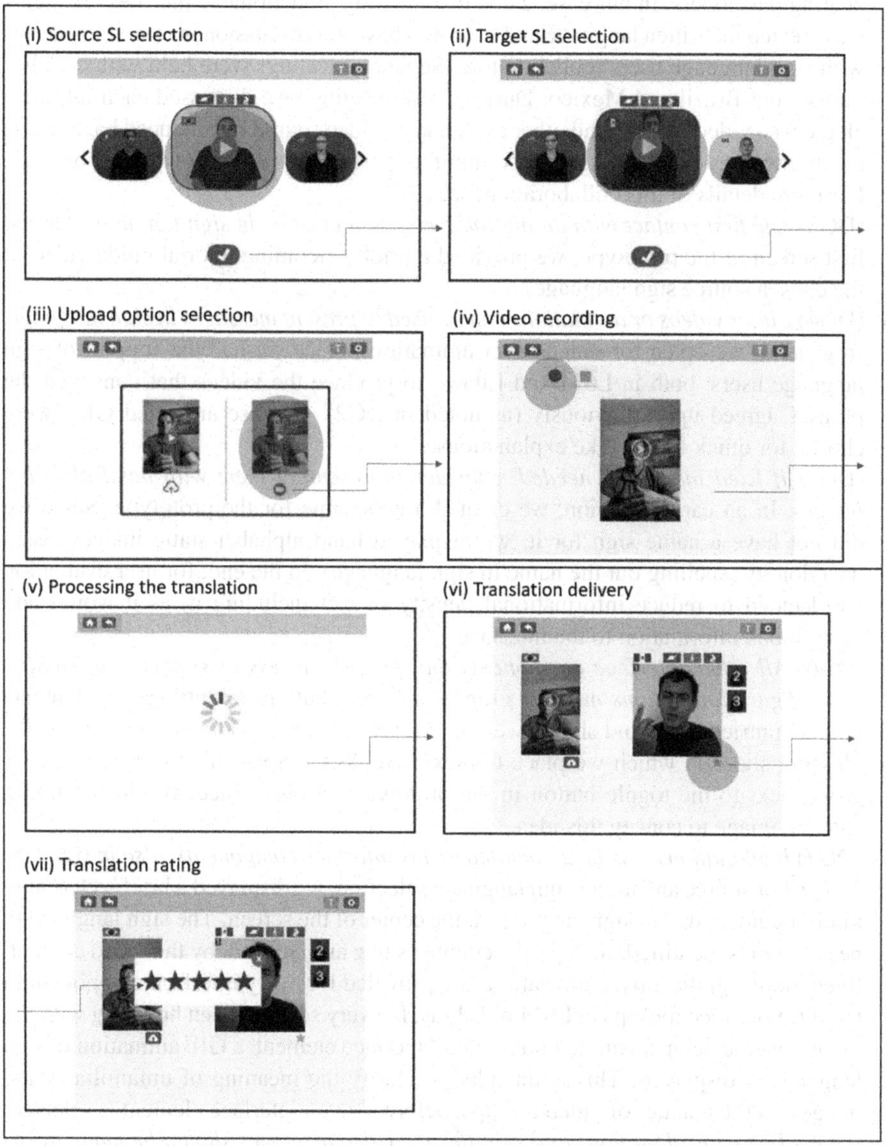

Fig. 2. User flow through seven interfaces of the SL2SL prototype. (Color figure online)

communities. Thus, for example, in our prototype we emphasize non-textual interface elements, but also offer on-demand textual elements.

- (DG2) *All messages presented in the interface must be generated by members of the deaf community.* Typically, interface elements are conceived and implemented by hearing developers. In our case, a document listing all actionable interface elements was created in written language and used as a basis for discussion in remote meetings with sign language users' collaborators. Separate meetings were held with collaborators from Brazil and Mexico. During these meetings we discussed each interface element so video tooltips and other explanatory videos could be produced based upon a consensus reached among deaf community participants prior to video recordings. For more details of this collaboration, see [7].
- (DG3) *The first contact with an interactive system must be in sign language.* On the first screen of the prototype, we provided a brief welcoming tutorial guide video of the chosen source sign language.
- (DG4) *Either videos or animations can be used to present messages in sign language.* In general, we opted for videos over animations, since we had the support of sign language users, both in LSM and Libras, to produce the videos that conveyed the phrases agreed upon previously (as noted in DG2). Concise animated GIFs were chosen for quick tooltip-like explanations.
- (DG5) *If fixed labels are needed, consider representing them with hand alphabet images.* In an earlier version, we created a codename for the prototype. Since we did not have a name sign for it, we displayed hand alphabet static images, as in dactylology (spelling out the name in sign language). In the end, for user evaluation we decided to reduce informational density by not including it, as it would add superfluous information to the interface.
- (DG6) *All other interface components that provide access to system functionality or configuration options must be graphical.* Icons, buttons, identification elements (e.g., countries flags) and sliders were non-textual interface elements, except for the glossing slider in which we place the text "GLOSA" (Spanish and Portuguese for *gloss*) next to the toggle button in the prototype settings, since we did not find a suitable image to convey this idea.
- (DG7) *Explanations may be associated to any interface components, also in sign language.* For source and target sign language selection, we displayed a brief welcoming tutorial guide video in sign language at the center of the screen. The sign language to be selected is identified, first, by the country's flag and, second, by the video content. Even more significantly, explanations are provided for every interface component in the form of video tooltips in LSM or Libras. In every screen, when hovering with the mouse over an icon, a button, or any other interface element, a GIF animation in sign language is displayed. This is intended to clarify the meaning of unfamiliar static images, in the manner of video tooltips, before a given interface element is selected.
- (DG8) *Textual explanations and subtitles for video messages should be made available on-demand.* This guideline is related to DG1, in the sense that we must consider communication diversity within Deaf community, as well as hearing persons who use an oral-written language as their first mode of communication and sign language as a second language. In our prototype, users can enable or disable subtitles by pressing

the capitalized letter "T" button on the top right corner of any screen. Its appearance in natural language or descriptive (glossing) form can be adjusted via the adjacent settings button by switching the glossing option on or off.

- (DG9) *Text subtitles for sign language messages can be expressed in the dominant language.* In our prototype, the written languages used for subtitles are Mexican Spanish, when displaying a video in LSM, and Brazilian Portuguese, when displaying a video in Libras.
- (DG10) *An alternative for presenting text subtitles is a descriptive form (glossing).* A glossing option was referred to in DG6 and DG8. The motivation to include it relates to its usefulness for sign language learners to become familiar with its grammar.

In our first low-fidelity prototype, we relied only on static images that represented videos. For the formative evaluation of this prototype, we included these images in the slide presentation to illustrate how videos would be displayed and used. Thus, we designed the user flow to be presented to participants by means of seven interfaces from our low-fidelity prototype (Fig. 2): (i) source sign language selection (translate from), (ii) target sign language selection (translate to), (iii) selection between video upload or video recording options for sign language input, (iv) video upload (or recording), (v) visual feedback while translating, (vi) translation results delivery and, (vii) translation rating. In Fig. 2, light blue circles on top of selected interface elements and blue arrows indicate the user flow from one screen to the next.

5 Proto-Personas and User Stories

Proto-persona profiles were created to materialize the potential users who would need a SL2SL translator as a communication facilitator. On the top of the potential users list are deaf persons who are sign language users, followed by family members, sign language teachers, professors, and interpreters, as well as various service providers.

Two examples of the instantiated proto-persona profile template are illustrated in Fig. 3. On column (a) we present Fernanda Campos, a Brazilian Deaf designer, whereas on column (b) we present Rosa García, a Mexican hearing CODA (Child Of Deaf Adult) hotel manager.

In total, we created eight proto-persona profiles[7], which included four women, three men and a non-binary proto-persona, five Deaf and three hearing persons, four Mexicans and four Brazilians, with ages ranging from 25 to 50 years old.

[7] Proto-persona profiles: t.ly/NqtS.

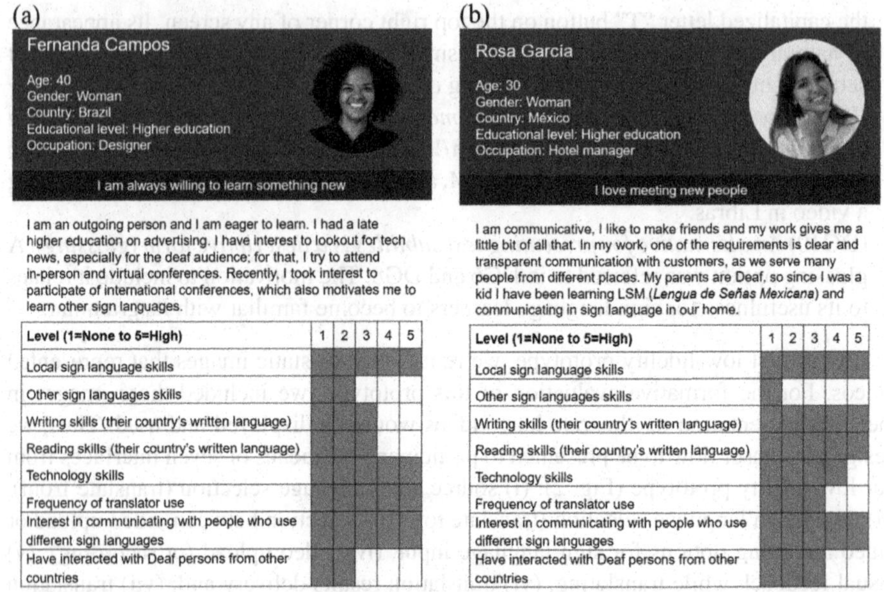

Fig. 3. Two examples of proto-persona profiles: (a) Fernanda Campos, a Brazilian Deaf designer and, (b) Rosa García, a Mexican hearing CODA hotel manager. Credits for pictures: t.ly/CMXX and t.ly/h3me.

We also produced four user stories describing how each pair of proto-persona profiles would need to communicate using different sign languages and how the automatic sign language translator can overcome the communication barrier. In Table 1, we present a potential user story where the proto-persona Fernanda (Fig. 3a) interacts with the proto-persona Rosa (Fig. 3b).

The title of the other three user stories are: (i) Deaf student from Mexico (proto-persona Arturo Herrera) participating in a live broadcasted by Hearing Brazilians who communicate in Libras (proto-persona Carlos Eduardo Pereira); (ii) Brazilian who is deaf (proto-persona Ivo Soares) participates in a meeting of the local Association of the Deaf that has a deaf guest from Mexico participating virtually (proto-persona Guadalupe Gonzalez); and, (iii) Hearing mother from Mexico (proto-persona María Auxilio López) plans her deaf son's trip to Brazil with the help of a Brazilian deaf friend (proto-persona José Ricardo da Silva). The full content of the user stories can be read at t.ly/4veX.

6 User Evaluation of the Prototype

The prototype evaluation consisted of collecting perceptions and opinions about the prototype with six invited participants with diverse backgrounds: two students majoring in information systems, a sign language expert professor, a human-computer interaction researcher, a foreign language professor, and a deaf person who is a Brazilian sign language (Libras) user and is supported by the government. A Libras interpreter mediated the session communication with our deaf participant (Fig. 4).

Table 1. Potential user story where the proto-persona Fernanda Campos interacts with the proto-persona Rosa García.

Brazilian Deaf designer checking in at a hotel in Mexico
For her trip to participate in an international conference, Fernanda Campos decides to stay in a well-rated hotel in the city of Guadalajara, Mexico, and needs to check in when she arrives there. To check in, she must provide a reservation code, confirm her personal data and the duration of her stay. As she already knew the routine of some hotels, Fernanda previously organized the documents that would be requested, and handed them to the hotel receptionist, whose name is Juan José. When checking the reservation data in the hotel system, discrepancies were found. So, Juan José had to ask some questions to Fernanda, who responded in Libras (Brazilian Sign Language) that she is Deaf and asked him to double-check the information. Given the situation, Juan José requests assistance from the hotel manager, Rosa García. Rosa approaches Fernanda and communicates with her using LSM (Mexican Sign Language). However, although some signs of both languages (Libras and LSM) are similar, and the signers perform facial expressions, mimics, and classifiers, significant communication gaps remain. Noting that their forms of communication were insufficient, Fernanda – who has a higher level of technology usage skills and uses translators more frequently - accesses her SL2SL translator to clarify the system's conflicting data and, with the use of the application, her check-in is completed successfully.

Fig. 4. A video frame capture of the recorded user evaluation session.

Out of the proto-persona profiles discussed previously (Sect. 5), only two corresponded to participants in the user evaluations: the deaf participant, and the sign language expert professor. They were invited to provide their point of view on the potential user experience. The other four participants were chosen as experts in their field to give insights about the user interfaces.

Participants' ages ranged from 22 to 44, averaging 31.66 years old. Three were women and three men, whereas three reported high, one medium and two low knowledge level of technology. Four use translators, though only one reported the use a sign language translator. Two participants reported a high knowledge level of sign language, three had only basic knowledge and one never had contact with sign language.

After presenting the user flow of the main interfaces (Fig. 2), we briefed participants about sign language and written language automatic translation. Next, we presented one prototype screen at a time and asked specific questions about their interface elements. Figure 5 to Fig. 8 illustrate the twelve prototype interfaces that were evaluated by participants.

6.1 On Selecting the Source and Target Languages for Translation

On the first screen (Fig.a), five participants said they would start the interaction with the SL2SL prototype by identifying the country flag to select the source language, whereas the other participant would click on the chosen image and then click on the check button at the bottom of the screen. Only one participant did not suggest any change for the source language selection, but the other participants talked about their preferences. Opinions were divided on whether a mouse or a finger should be used to select interface elements on the screen. Except for one participant, they noted that the flag on the videos properly identified the sign language to be selected. Three were concerned about the large number of flags in the world, as some people would not know every option. One suggestion was to display a video in sign language informing the country's name, another was to enlarge the size of the flags.

Another suggestion was modifying the animated GIF's size and position to make it more visible on the screen. One participant suggested a check box on the video, so someone could be sure the appropriate one was selected. Another participant mentioned that a vertical interface would be better and choosing the language could be accomplished by clicking on icons displayed one below the other, with an image or a video associated to each icon.

Since the prototype was presented by means of a slide show, the images on the screen interface were static, so the next questions asked participants about their understanding on the following interface elements: video content, side arrows, buttons, and bubble with an image. Two thought the video content was intended to inform the chosen sign language, two said they cannot guess, one said they showed signs (as in sign language), and one supposed the video would explain what the three buttons above the central video were. Regarding the side arrows we obtained a unanimous response, as all participants said they could be used to navigate to the left or to the right to visualize and select the sign language from which they wish to translate.

The three buttons right above the central video (a turtle, a person and a hare) were understood by three participants as the speed (slow, normal and fast) they would like to play the video; one participant could not understand their intended meaning, one assumed the green button at the center (a person) could be used to listen the video's audio, and one reported that each button could trigger an action.

The button with the capitalized letter "T" had different interpretations: the "T" stands for translation (4 participants), it presents a hint or tip (2 participants), it displays subtitles (2 participants), and it organizes a phrasal sentence. Participants informed the gear button represents settings; however, each participant gave different examples of what could be configured: videos, translations, interfaces, and languages. Concerning the bubble with an image (animated GIF presented when the mouse is over the button "T"), whereas one participant preferred not to answer, each of the other participants had a different interpretation: a quick video, a preview of a video that comes next, an explanation of the button itself, a translation for a phrase typed there, and a confirmation message of the selected source sign language.

We asked participants about the differences they perceived in Fig. 5b with respect to Fig. 5a, of which it is a slight variation (subtitles added). Five of them noticed that text in Portuguese appeared on the screen and one noticed that the background of the button with the capitalized letter "T" changed from grey to black. Four participants who noticed the text, mentioned that it would make it easier to understand what someone should do. Another participant, however, said it would be preferable to watch the video in sign language, since the text explanation would not convey the idea of what to do. This last participant previously reported having medium to low written language knowledge.

Moreover, four participants reported they would navigate through the video carousel, find, and select the target sign language they wish (Fig. 5c), one would double click on the screen and another said that the blue outline around the video means it changed to another language and it will produce a result. Various suggestions were given to improve target sign language selection: displaying different colors to distinguish source and target language selection, presenting the countries' names in sign language, and to increase the videos' sizes. On this screen we also asked what their interpretation was for the "house" and "left arrow" buttons. In both cases, participants had unanimous answers, respectively: back to home screen and back to previous screen.

Fig. 5. Slide for user evaluation 1 to 3. (Color figure online)

6.2 On Sign Language Input

On the interface for providing the sign language expression to be translated (Fig. 6a), three participants said that this interface allows to upload videos, one participant thought it displays results, one said it could save conversations and make calls using the camera, and another one reported that having two sign language videos on the same screen can be confusing. Participants' suggestions included the following: separating the videos, one per screen when possible (3 participants); displaying an animated GIF in sign language explaining the interface elements just like the one presented in the first screen (Fig. 6a); and to revise the interface because it is not clear what one should do (4 participants).

On this screen we also asked how they interpreted the "cloud with an arrow up" and the "camera" buttons. For the cloud button three said it is used for uploading files, one assumed that it is for sharing files externally, one mentioned that the file is within a folder, and one said it suggested a search in a database. For the camera button, four participants thought it could be used to record a video, one supposed someone could click on it to make a videocall, and another one said that after someone uploads a video this button allows for viewing the result.

When asked about what the screen on Fig. 6b has to do with the screen on Fig. 6a, five participants said they both are for recording a video; one out of these five said they also could make a videocall and another thought someone could stop and edit the video in small chunks. We also asked how they interpreted the "red circle" and the "grey square" buttons. For the former, all participants said to record a video; for the latter, three informed to stop a recording, two said to pause a recording, and one said it means a page or a text.

6.3 On Configuration Options

When we asked participants at what point in the prototype can someone access the text settings (Fig. 6c), two said on clicking the gear button without specifying in which screen, two referred to the beginning of the prototype's execution, one said after the video recording, and one noted that the gear button can be accessed in every screen. After that, we asked them to explain each of the elements that can be configured on the text settings screen. The most recurrent answers were the following: changing the font size, the font color, and the background color; four participants mentioned that glossing ("GLOSA") could be enabled, one mentioned this was a GIF option, and another did not understand whether the slider button was enabled or switched off.

Fig. 6. Slide for user evaluation 4 to 6. (Color figure online)

All participants observed a variation in font size when asked what changed from the previous screen (Fig. 6c) to the current screen (Fig. 7a). One participant noticed this screen does not present the GIF in sign language, which they perceived as an aid to use the application. This participant thought we had removed the GIF tooltip; however, we just wanted to show that this is an on-demand option.

6.4 On Sign Language Output

Figure 7b presents the translation delivery screen. When asked about it, participants reported which was the source and the target language, and some of them explained why. Two participants said the source language was the right side one, possibly because it has the number one on it; four informed the source language was on the left side, identifying it by the Brazilian flag; and one participant did not identify which was the target language, not recognizing the flag. About the number 1 on the right-side video and the numbers 2 and 3 on its side (which were intended to refer to translation variants), participants had diverse perceptions: different video speeds, different signs for the same word, orderings to reproduce signs, extra support videos, additional translations to other sign languages, and unopened results. On this screen, we also asked about their interpretation of the "cloud with an arrow up" (save to cloud) button and the "star" (rating) icon. For the former interface element, except for one participant who said it is for saving the file, the other five participants supposed it is intended to upload a video. For the latter, three said it should serve to mark a video as favorite. The rest of the responses varied: it is the result of the translation, the source video is main one, and it defines which one the target language is. When moving from this screen (Fig. 7b) to the next (Fig. 7c), all participants noted the subtitles were enabled and two also noticed the capitalized letter "T" button changes the background color from grey to black.

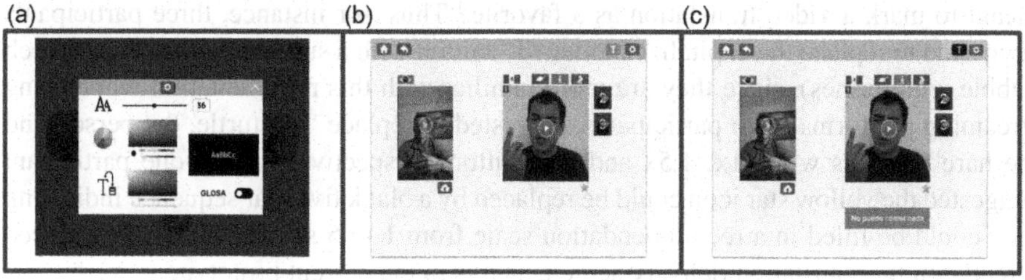

Fig. 7. Slide for user evaluation 7 to 9. (Color figure online)

When shifting from the screen in Fig. 7c to the next (Fig. 8a), five participants perceived changes, except for one who did not notice any change. Two participants noted that the letters of the phrase now are all capitalized; one said the order of the words in the phrase are different, adding that "It is wrong"; and two noticed that this new text is glossing ("GLOSA"), a written form in the Libras grammar. Moving on to the next screen (Fig. 8b), three participants said that now the resulting video with the translation has the number 2 on it, one participant complemented saying that "It is a different translation", whereas the other three did not notice differences from the previous screen (Fig. 8a). To five participants, the last screen (Fig. 8c) conveyed the meaning of an evaluation of the resulting translation.

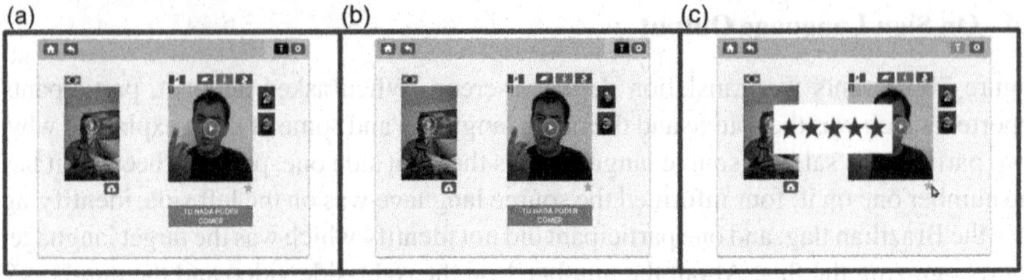

Fig. 8. Slide for user evaluation 10 to 12. (Color figure online)

6.5 Additional User Feedback

In each individual session, after observing that participants' first-glance interpretation of several prototypical interfaces differed from our intended design, we felt the need to go back to each interface element, explained their intent, and asked the participants whether that made sense to them. Their responses varied and included questions such as the following: How does someone choose the source and the target languages? What does the capitalized letter "T" button enable? What do "the turtle, the person and the hare" buttons represent? What is the settings button for? What are the animated GIFs for? Why are two videos needed in the upload or recording screen? What does glossing mean? What are the numbers from 1 to 3 in the translation delivery? Is the star icon in yellow meant to mark a video translation as a favorite? Thus, for instance, three participants suggested to replace the capitalized letter "T" button with a subtitle button (e.g., speech bubble with dashes), since they are more familiar with this representation when using streaming platforms. Two participants suggested to replace "the turtle, the person and the hare" buttons with "1x, 1,5x and 2x" buttons, respectively. Also, one participant suggested the yellow star icon could be replaced by a blank five-star sequence indicating they could be filled in a recommendation scale from 1 to 5 stars; this could be placed directly on the translation delivery screen, as it is in the current prototype.

Finally, we asked one final open question inquiring who the primary users of a SL2SL system could be. One participant said anyone who wants to use it, whereas the other five placed sign language users at the top of their list. These five participants cited a few examples of specific potential users: deaf persons, teachers, professors, interpreters, people who want to learn sign languages, and people who work in immigration offices, in hospitals or in public security.

7 Discussion

Taking a step back and comparing the design ideas with participant perceptions about our first low-fidelity prototype of a SL2SL translator, it is evident that our goal of providing intuitive, straightforward interfaces was not achieved completely. This was compounded at evaluation time by our choice of using static images in our presentation slides, which allowed us to conduct a formative evaluation even while the actual prototype (which included videos and GIF animations) was being constructed but proved to be a limitation in our study. Still, we can report lessons that can be helpful when designing the user experience of an SL2SL translator. In the next paragraphs we further discuss the four main prototype screens evaluated by users, organized as follows: source and target sign language selection, source sign language input, translation results delivery, and additional ideas for a next round of prototype adjustments and user evaluation.

- *Source and target sign language selection.* Most participants would click only on the video with the country's flag to select a source sign language and move directly on to the next screen, describing one-click only interaction. This preference is consistent with experience provided by one of the most used translators for written languages, where one can select the source written language and right after select the destination written language. Our initial design idea was to prevent users from having to go back to the previous screen if they chose a source sign language they did not want. However, sign language presentation poses more dynamic requirements than text. By separating the video controls from the selection button, we ensure user control over welcoming videos navigation (e.g., a given user may wish to watch two or three welcoming videos of different sign languages, exploring the options, before deciding which one they want to select as a source sign language input). Concerning the large number of possible country flags, labeling them with written language would go against our wish to have non-textual interfaces. Alternatively, we could have a sign language welcoming tutorial video about the countries' flags but, in that case, users would need to know the signs for all the listed countries, which is unlikely in general. Another possibility is to include, in addition to the flags, other images in the video, such as the country's map within its continent, or pictures illustrating typical costumes, landscapes, or emblematic places. Yet another idea is to show, separately from the welcoming video, flag icons with their own explanatory video, or an image associated with it. In this case, the icon would be selected, not the video. This alternative interface can be tested in another round of user evaluation. In the current version of the prototype, source and target sign language selection (Fig. 5a and Fig. 5c) share almost identical screen appearance: the only clue that distinguishes the target sign language interface pertains additional buttons (home and back to previous screen). One suggestion to address this concern raised at user evaluation time is the use of distinctive colors for each interface. Alternatively, a visual clue could indicate which source sign language has already been chosen when the user is about to select a target language. One more option to consider is the selection of both source and target sign languages on the same screen.
- *Source sign language input.* This screen (Fig. 5a) was perceived by users as confusing since an image of the same video was displayed on a single screen. By having two videos, one could not be sure if the video was already available in the system or if this enabled a video call between two sign language users. Thus, to disambiguate this interface, one alternative solution could be to redesign the screen by providing only icons, possibly three: upload a pre-saved video, insert a link, or record a video in real-time. These icons can be associated with sign language explanatory animated GIFs to serve as tool tips. This was not a suggestion from participants, but an idea the research team had while discussing users' reactions during evaluation. Also, we could test two different task orders: source sign language video upload, link insertion or video recording before and after target sign language selection. Another alternative

can be the inclusion of a visual user flow fixed on top of the screen to indicate task progress (e.g., breadcrumb navigation, numbered pagination).

- *Target sign language output*. Alternative designs for this interface (Fig. 6b) also can be tested in order to clearly identify between (i) source sign language input and translated sign language delivered, and (ii) alternative translations (videos numbered from 1 to 3) from a single input, taking into account phrase variants, different signers or regionalisms. Participants did not bring up privacy issues of having the translation delivery available for download; however, this was one of ours concern when designing the prototype. We left it out for now, but also can be an alternative interface element for reflection during user evaluation.

In addition to prototype screens, images on buttons, icons, and sliders were a rich source for discussion. The *home, back to previous screen* and *video recording* buttons were easily recognized by participants. Our proposed video speed controls ("the turtle, the person and the hare" – Fig. 5a–c, Fig. 7b–c, Fig. 8a–c) can be tested with an alternative design using a version of "1x, 1.5x and 2x" options, as they have been used in streaming platforms and real-time communication apps which participants are familiar with. This existing scheme is oriented to audio and does not include the option to reduce the playback speed. For SL2SL videos, options such as "0.5x, 1x and 1.5" might be explored. One alternative for placement of the capitalized letter "T" button and the "glossing" slider is to embed them into the video player. Another option is to keep these two elements, in addition to the "settings" button on the top right corner of the screen, since one can use it not only to include subtitles, but also to replace sign language tooltips with written labels while hovering over with the mouse. In both cases, buttons for switching on and off text or glossing should have more suitable icon representations and colors (e.g., a green or blue switched on button, and a gray switched off button). Also, in this first low-fidelity prototype, we chose not to provide audio on-demand since we presented a static version; however, results show that this feature did not come up as a suggestion. In an alternative prototype version, audio control also could be embedded into the video player. *Record* and *stop* buttons outside the camera frame also can be confusing, such those we represented in Fig. 5b, since when someone use the desktop webcam or the smartphone camera those controls usually are placed inside, at the bottom of the camera frame. Once the source sign language video has been translated, users have the option to rate the result by giving it from 1 to 5 stars. Because of the way we represented this functionality, users would take two steps to complete this task, and participants mistook the *star* icon for a *favorite* icon, as if they could save the video for finding (watching) it again later (e.g., as it is used in a well-known real-time communication app). An alternative suggestion is to place the blank five stars in the same screen of the translation delivery video (e.g., as it is used in well-known virtual stores to evaluate their apps), without having to open a pop-up window. The idea behind the "cloud with a upside arrow" button placed on the translation delivery screen was to upload another video for translation without having to select source and destination language all over again; however, this seemed confusing for our user evaluation participants and may need some rethinking.

We can also consider specific, responsive desktop and mobile designs, since participants noted their preference to use the mouse and sometimes tactile interfaces, as well as their wish to scroll horizontally or vertically over the screen. In this case, the alternative designs should also consider how to implement hovering over interface elements to access sign language tooltips or written language labels.

Lastly, we were encouraged by participants coinciding with our view of potential users of SL2SL translators, which are not exclusively for deaf persons, but they also included various service providers as potential users.

8 Conclusion

In this research, we aimed to produce proto-personas and specification of user stories to foster ideas of who the potential users are for SL2SL translators, and in which situations they would feel their need and usefulness. This led us to introduce the notion of conversational proto-personas, which provide us with means to explore how pairs of users interact with each other. In our specific context, conversational proto-personas share the challenge of communicating in different sign languages.

We also conducted a user evaluation of our first low-fidelity SL2SL translator prototype to adjust our learning curve for designing natural user interfaces for sign language users and to establish the next research stages as we learn. This paper presents our achievements, findings and lessons learned. We confirm the importance of involving potential users and collaborators in user experience research in the context of an agile approach. Through our user study, we obtained feedback from participants who were proto-persona representatives, which provided further validation for design guidelines we proposed previously for natural sign language interfaces [7].

The small number of participants in our user evaluation can be regarded as a limitation. More specifically, we need to consider the types of users for whom our results can be applicable. As our proposed proto-personas indicate, the diversity of users and scenarios for SL2SL translators is wide. Regarding our evaluation participants, it would be interesting to have the prototype tested with more users who are representatives of the proto-personas we have designed.

We elicited interesting alternative design ideas that we still need to test, possibly using the A/B testing technique. In future work, we intend to generate and evaluate a mid-fidelity prototype taking participants' suggestions into consideration, as well as to provide videos and animated gifs in sign language which were already recorded and validated by deaf persons.

Finally, it is important to consider, as a next step, the cultural aspects of potential users' preferences and perceptions. We conducted this research with Brazilian volunteers, but we still need to carry out user evaluations with volunteers from Mexico in a subsequent round of research after making the necessary prototype adjustments. In this next round, we will take into account the proto-persona profiles and potential users' suggestions from participants of the current round.

Acknowledgments. We wish to thank José Augusto Fabris, Priscilla Lopes Ferreira, Vanuza Martins Leite, Juan Utrera and Miguel Ángel Preciado for the collaboration with the text translation into Libras and LSM, and video recordings of our prototype's interface elements. Josué Cruz was instrumental in building the prototype. We also appreciate the participation of the volunteers in the user evaluation of the prototype. This study was conducted as part of a project approved by the Research Ethics Committee of the Universidade Federal de Rondonópolis, registered under the CAAE no. 18708619.2.0000.8088.

References

1. United Nations: International Day of Sign Languages, 23 September (2022). https://www.un.org/en/observances/sign-languages-day. Accessed 23 Jan 2023
2. Mesch, J.: Review of international sign: linguistic, usage, and status issues ed. by Rachel Rosenstock and Jemina Napier. Sign Lang. Stud. **17**(3), 403–406 (2017). Project MUSE. https://doi.org/10.1353/sls.2017.0012
3. de Wit, M., Crasborn, O., Napier, J.: Interpreting international sign: mapping the interpreter's profile. Interpret. Transl. Train. **15**(2), 205–224 (2021). https://doi.org/10.1080/1750399X.2020.1868172
4. Quinto-Pozos, D., Adam, R.: Sign languages in contact. Socioling. Deaf Communit., 29–60 (2015). https://doi.org/10.1017/CBO9781107280298.003
5. De Clerck, G.A.M.: Meeting global deaf peers, visiting ideal deaf places: deaf ways of education leading to empowerment, an exploratory case study. Am. Ann. Deaf **152**(1), 5–19 (2007). http://www.jstor.org/stable/26234419
6. Gothelf, J., Seiden, J.: Lean UX - Designing Great Products with Agile Teams, 2nd edn. O'Reilly Media, Sebastopol (2016)
7. Sánchez, J.A., Prietch, S.S., Cruz-Cortez, J.I.: Natural sign language interfaces for deaf users: rationale and design guidelines. In: 2022 IEEE Mexican International Conference on Computer Science (ENC), Xalapa, Veracruz, Mexico, pp. 1–7 (2022). https://doi.org/10.1109/ENC56672.2022.9882905
8. Egea Gómez, S., Chiruzzo, L., McGill, E., Saggion, H.: Linguistically enhanced text to sign gloss machine translation. In: Rosso, P., Basile, V., Martínez, R., Métais, E., Meziane, F. (eds.) NLDB 2022. LNCS, vol. 13286, pp. 172–183. Springer, Cham (2022). https://doi.org/10.1007/978-3-031-08473-7_16
9. Neiva, D.H., Zanchettin, C.: A dynamic gesture recognition system to translate between sign languages in complex backgrounds. In: 2016 5th Brazilian Conference on Intelligent Systems (BRACIS), pp. 421–426. IEEE (2016)
10. Paris, C., Park, J.C., Kim, J.H.: Sign language processing. M1 computer science 2018–2019, internship report: sign language processing. A collaboration between the École Normale Supérieure (ENS) of Lyon and the Korea Advanced Institute of Science and Technology (Kaist), August 26 2019. https://perso.ens-lyon.fr/chloe.paris/assets/docs/2019-CS-m1-internship-report-paris-chloe.pdf. Accessed 17 Jan 2023
11. Mccleary, L., Viotti, E., de Arantes Leite, T.: Descrição das línguas sinalizadas: a questão da transcrição dos dados. ALFA: Revista De Linguística **54**(1) (2010). https://periodicos.fclar.unesp.br/alfa/article/view/2880. Accessed 26 Jan 2023
12. Cruz-Aldrete, M.C., Serrano, J.: La comunidad sorda Mexicana. Vivir entre varias lenguas: LSM, ASL, LSM, Español, Inglés, Maya. Convergencias. Revista de educación **1**(2) (2018)
13. Araújo, P.J.P., Bentes, T.: Línguas de sinais de fronteiras: o caso da LSV no Brasil. Humanidades Inovação **7**(26), 125–135 (2020)
14. Su, S.F., Tai, J.H.: Lexical comparison of signs from Taiwan, Chinese, Japanese, and American sign languages: taking iconicity into account. Taiwan Sign Lang. Beyond, 149–176 (2009)
15. Van Niekerk, A.: A lexical comparison of South African sign language and potential lexifier languages. Doctoral dissertation, Stellenbosch University (2020). https://scholar.sun.ac.za/items/daf7d8fd-5ed1-46f8-b2a9-f457b3e571be. Accessed 19 Jan 2023

16. Fragkiadakis, M.: Assessing an automated tool to quantify variation in movement and location: a case study of American sign language and Ghanaian sign language. Sign Lang. Stud. **23**(1), 98–126 (2022)
17. Kuder, A.: Making sign language corpora comparable: a study of palm-up and throw-away in polish sign language, German sign language, and Russian sign language. In: Proceedings of the LREC2022 10th Workshop on the Representation and Processing of Sign Languages: Multilingual Sign Language Resources, pp. 110–117 (2022)
18. Prietch, S.S., Sánchez, J.A., Guerrero, J.: A systematic review of user studies as a basis for the design of systems for automatic sign language processing. ACM Trans. Access. Comput. **15**, 4, Article no. 36, 33 p. (2022). https://doi.org/10.1145/3563395
19. Cruz-Aldrete, M.: Tras las Huellas del Pasado Común de la LSM y Libras: El Camino de Thomas C. Smith Stark. Humanidades Inovação **7**(26), 9–25 (2020)
20. Cruz-Cortez, J.I., Sánchez, J.A., Prietch, S.S.: Avanços no design da experiência do usuário de um tradutor entre línguas de sinais. In: Escola Regional De Informática De Mato Grosso (ERI-MT), vol. 21 (2021). Evento Online. Anais [...]. Porto Alegre: Sociedade Brasileira de Computação, pp. 108–111 (2021). ISSN 2447-5386. https://doi.org/10.5753/eri-mt.2021.18233
21. Matthews, T., Whittaker, S., Moran, T., Yuen, S.: Collaboration personas: a new approach to designing workplace collaboration tools. In: Proceedings of the SIGCHI Conference on Human Factors in Computing Systems (CHI 2011), pp. 2247–2256. Association for Computing Machinery, New York (2011). https://doi.org/10.1145/1978942.1979272
22. Perlin, G.: As diferentes identidades surdas. In: Revista da Feneis, ano 4, no.14, pp. 15–16 (2002)
23. Huenerfauth, M., Hanson, V.: Sign language in the interface: access for deaf signers. In: Stephanidis, C. (eds.) The Universal Access Handbook, CRC Press (2009). https://doi.org/10.1201/9781420064995
24. Prietch, S.S., Filgueiras, L.V.L.: One assistive technology does not fit all educational strategies: a reflection on deaf students in mainstream classroom. In: Workshop on Rethinking Universal Accessibility: A Broader Approach Considering the Digital Gap, INTERACT 2013, Cape Town, South Africa (2013)
25. Prietch, S.S., de Souza, N.S., Filgueiras, L.V.L.: A speech-to-text system's acceptance evaluation: would deaf individuals adopt this technology in their lives? In: Stephanidis, C., Antona, M. (eds.) UAHCI 2014. LNCS, vol. 8513, pp. 440–449. Springer, Cham (2014). https://doi.org/10.1007/978-3-319-07437-5_42

Study on the Design of Dyslexia-Friendly Drug Instructions

Xin Guan[1](✉), RuiHan Zhang[1], and KaiJun Shi[2]

[1] East China University of Science and Technology, No. 130 Meilong Road, Xuhui District, Shanghai, China
guanxin1098@126.com

[2] Tongji University, No. 1239 SiPing Road, YangPu District, Shanghai, China

Abstract. People with dyslexia are more likely to be unable to understand important information about drugs, which is very likely to cause dangerous phenomena such as misuse. Due to the need to control the sale price of drugs and comply with laws and regulations, the drug instructions are often very compact and dense in the layout design. It is not easy to take care of the dyslexia when designing. This study attempts to introduce product design methods, explore the factors that lead to poor reading experience of instructions, and obtain demand and evaluation characteristics. Through the questionnaire survey, understanding public concern about different forms of content in drug instructions, and classify them. The kano model is used to study user satisfaction, and the user's demand for the function of drug instructions is obtained, which provides data support and theoretical guidance for subsequent design. On this basis, the layout literature in line with the physiological characteristics of dyslexia were studied to complete the design practice of dyslexia-friendly Chinese drug instructions at the lowest possible cost. It is hoped that this design will not only alleviate the distress of readers when reading instructions, but also bring more comfortable and smooth reading experience to the public.

Keywords: Dyslexia · Barrier-free design · Drug instructions

1 Introduction

Developmental dyslexia (DD) refers to individuals who do not have organic brain damage, mental or intellectual disabilities, but still show different degrees of reading difficulties such as inability to accurately and smoothly identify, spell, and decode words under the same educational conditions as their peers [1]. Epidemiological longitudinal data show that dyslexia is highly prevalent, affecting 10–20% of the population regardless of gender [2]. However, the information of the drug instructions is complicated. When the professional terms are concentrated on a thin piece of paper, it is still difficult for young people without dyslexia. For people with dyslexia, the drug instructions are as obscure as 'heavenly books'. The promotion and popularization of barrier-free design, the introduction of relevant laws and regulations around the world, and more designers

M. Antona and C. Stephanidis (Eds.): HCII 2023, LNCS 14020, pp. 340–352, 2023.
https://doi.org/10.1007/978-3-031-35681-0_22

have made some design improvements for people with reading disabilities when arranging various publications. For example, by increasing the font size and increasing the line spacing, the layout is improved to reduce the visual crowding effect [3]. However, the general method is obviously not fully applicable to the commonly used drug instructions. On the one hand, there are strict norms and standards for the text content of the drug instructions, which can not be arbitrarily deleted and changed. On the other hand, for the reasons of ensuring the sale price of commonly used drugs is more pro-people and reducing the use of paper to protect the environment, pharmaceutical factories generally design the sheet sizes of the instructions as small as possible. It is not realistic to develop another version of the commonly used drug instructions for the dyslexia. These limiting factors also bring no small challenge to the layout design of the drug instructions.

In addition, the increasing maturity of digital technology development and the popularity of mobile devices have made the promotion of online drug instructions less difficult to achieve, and in recent years there have been many studies using digital media technologies (virtual reality, augmented reality, etc.) to achieve intervention and treatment for people with dyslexia [4], research has shown that these technologies can provide realistic interactions and real-time feedback that can help people with reading disabilities improve their memory and understanding of vision-related tasks. In this paper, the author not only improves the existing paper version of drug manuals according to the physiological characteristics of dyslexic people, but also makes some preliminary attempts to develop online versions of drug manuals to facilitate dyslexic people to take medications and provide a smoother reading experience for the general public.

2 User Study of Drug Instructions Based on Kano Model

2.1 User Interviews and Initial Demand Acquisition

Based on the Kano model, the user demand process of commonly used drug instructions is as follows. Through in-depth interviews, the user's views and functional requirements on the existing commonly used drug instructions were obtained, and the evaluation dimensions and evaluation characteristics were sorted out. Design a two-way questionnaire, establish a Kano model, and analyze the functional requirements of users for drug instructions design. Through the quality type of demand factors, the user's preferences are studied, and the user's needs are transformed into theoretical support for design.

The original intention of this study is to make appropriate optimization for people with dyslexia on the basis of ensuring the needs of most people. Therefore, we start with the needs of the public. In order to further understand the basic views and demand pain points of the public on the current Chinese instructions of commonly used drugs, screen out the needs with high reliability, and determine the evaluation dimensions and characteristics to make the Kano demand evaluation form. The author took the lead in conducting user interviews on the reading experience of drug instructions. In-depth interviews were invited to a total of 3 patients who needed regular medication, 2 medical workers, 4 elderly people with underlying diseases, and 5 young people in good health. The structure of this interview, the setting of interview questions, the purpose of this interview is to understand the basic information of users, the needs of daily medication, the feelings and problems encountered when reading the instructions, and to sort out the problems that can be improved in reading the instructions.

According the in-depth interviews with users, the user's demand for products is preliminarily obtained and classified. Three evaluation dimensions and eight evaluation features are obtained, and the serial number is marked (as shown in Table 1).

Table 1. Summary of user needs of drug instructions

Properties	Function/Service	Description	
Basic function optimization	Optimize font size	Adjust the font size to read comfortably	1
	Optimize spacing	Adjust overly tight line spacing and character spacing	2
	Content annotation	Differentiate the design of different sections according to the importance, and highlight the key points	3
	Columnar Composing	Layout the different categories of content in the specification in columns to obtain the right length of a single line	4
Appearance form optimization	Add illustration	Add an appropriate amount of illustrations to the specification to help special people understand	5
	Add color	Emotional design according to the type of drug using hue, lightness and saturation changes	6
Adding additional functions	Add online version	Enrich the form of specifications and reduce paper costs	7
	Add voice announcement	Provide voice announcements for people who can't read easily to achieve accessible design	8

2.2 User Interviews and Initial Demand Acquisition

Kano model was proposed by Japanese scholar Noriaki Kano in 1970s. It is an important design method to sort different user demand categories according to user satisfaction [5]. The Kano model divides user needs into five categories: essential needs (M), expected needs (O), charismatic needs (A), indifference needs (I), and reverse needs (R). The correlation between the five types and user satisfaction can be seen in Table 2 below. Under certain circumstances, if the user chooses 'very satisfied' or 'disliked' for both 'the functional requirements are satisfied and the requirements are not satisfied', such results are called suspicious results (Q).

Table 2. The relationship between demand attributes and satisfaction of kano model

Features categories	User satisfaction	
	With these features	Without these features
Attractive features (A)	No change	Down
One-dimensional features (O)	Up	Down
Must-be features (M)	Up	No change
Indifferent features (I)	No change	No change
Reverse features (R)	Down	No change

Based on the KANO model, in the design of the questionnaire, it is necessary to set positive and negative questions on the same evaluation feature. For example, 'if the drug instructions provide key content highlighting design, your feeling is', 'if the drug instructions do not provide key content highlighting design, your feeling is'. All questions have five optional answers, and the views or opinions of the subjects need to be divided into five different levels of satisfaction: 'like', 'should be so', 'does not matter', 'can tolerate' and 'do not like' (Table 3).

Table 3. Comparison table of classification of evaluation results

Participant responses	Non-functional question				
	Like	Must Be	Neutral	Live With	Dislike
Like	Q	A	A	A	O
Must Be	R	I	I	I	R
Neutral	R	I	I	I	R
Live With	R	I	I	I	R
Dislike	R	R	R	R	Q

There is no specific restricted population in this questionnaire, and during the whole questionnaire filling process, all respondents need to read the survey instructions and answer them. The identity of the respondents is confidential, and only basic demographic data such as gender, age and education level are required. The No. 2–8 evaluation features in Table 1 are online using the questionnaire star APP. The No. 1 evaluation feature 'font size', considering that it will be disturbed by the display of mobile devices, can not accurately display the specific size, so the offline paper questionnaire is used for investigation.

2.3 KANO Attribute Classification and Analysis

Reliability Analysis. After excluding some logically contradictory responses, a total of 167 questionnaire data were rearranged and imported into SPSS software for alpha reliability coefficient (Cronbach coefficient) test, and the alpha coefficient was 0.87, which was in the range of 0.7–0.9, implying that the questionnaire research results basically converged and had some reference value.

KANO Attribute Classification and Analysis. Without considering the reverse demand, the statistics of the number of user-selected demand levels are completed and classified, as shown in Table 4.

Table 4. Evaluation scale for Kano questionnaire

	A	O	R	M	Q	I	SII	DDI	
No. 1	29.41%	17.65%	3.26%	31.05%	0.98%	17.65%	49.14%	−50.86%	M
No. 2	26.67%	28.48%	4.85%	16.97%	0.61%	22.42%	58.33%	−48.08%	O
No. 3	33.33%	27.27%	4.24%	10.91%	1.21%	23.03%	64.10%	−40.38%	A
No. 4	22.42%	21.82%	7.88%	9.70%	2.42%	35.76%	49.32%	−35.14%	I
No. 5	36.97%	14.55%	4.85%	10.30%	0.61%	32.73%	54.49%	−26.28%	A
No. 6	35.76%	22.42%	4.24%	8.48%	0.61%	28.48%	61.15%	−32.48%	A
No. 7	28.48%	10.91%	6.06%	12.73%	0.61%	41.21%	42.21%	−25.32%	I
No. 8	36.36%	16.36%	6.67%	7.88%	1.82%	30.91%	57.62%	−26.49%	A

A: Attractive features O: One-dimensional features M: Must-be features
I: Indifferent features R: Reverse features Q: Questionable features

The analysis of the results showed that among the eight design evaluation features, four were classified as charm attributes (A), two were classified as desired attributes (O), zero were classified as essential attributes (M), two were classified as undifferentiated attributes, and zero were classified as reverse attributes (Q).

2.4 SII-DDI Matrix Analysis

User satisfaction coefficient can be divided into Satisfaction Increment Index (SII) and Dissatisfaction Decrement Index (DDI) according to whether a function is available or not, and the following is the formula:

$$SII = (A + O)/(A + O + M + I) \tag{1}$$

$$DDI = (O + M)/(A + O + M + I)(-1) \tag{2}$$

The absolute values of SII and DDI range from 0 to 1, and the larger the value, the greater the improvement benefit; conversely, the smaller the value, the smaller the improvement benefit. Based on the results of SII and DDI calculations, a two-dimensional quadrant diagram is established, with the X-axis located at the average value of SII and the Y-axis located at the average value of DDI, which is used to establish four quadrants to determine the priority of attributes that can be improved, as shown in Fig. 1.

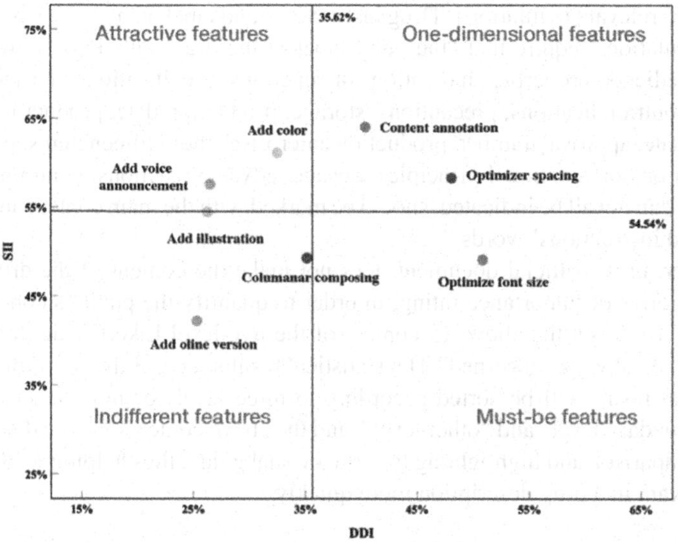

Fig. 1. SII-DDI quadrant images with improved kano model results

3 Improved Design of Chinese Instructions for Dyslexia-Friendly Drugs

After reviewing the literature, I found that due to the differences between the text systems, which leads to dyslexic people to different systems of text reading characteristics are not the same, which also can not form a universal design strategy, this paper chose the Chinese language design, the design of ibuprofen extended-release capsules as the design object, improved Chinese drug instructions for design practice. When understanding the visual characteristics of dyslexic people, the author found that dyslexic people are easily affected by a kind of effect called visual crowding. The visual crowding effect refers to the difficulty in identifying a target object located in the peripheral visual field when other objects are presented around it [6]. Many researchers have verified that visual crowding can be reduced by, for example, changing character spacing, which can alleviate reading impairment [7].

Therefore, the design of dyslexia-friendly Chinese instructions should meet the above-mentioned functional requirements while reducing visual crowding, which requires understanding the degree of public attention to the content categories of drug instructions, so as to make a graded post-design, forming visual guidance to help patients read more quickly and comfortably, so here the author also conducted a survey on the attention to the content categories of drug instructions.

3.1 Drug Instruction Content Category Concern Survey

Writer checked the official website of the National Medical Products Administration of China for the relevant regulations "Drug instructions and label management regulations" [8], the regulations require that "the outer label of the drug must indicate the generic Name, ingredients, properties, indications or functions, specifications, dosage, adverse reactions, contraindications, precautions, storage, production date, product lot number, expiration date, approval number, production enterprise" these fifteen items. In addition, "the indications or functional principles, dosage, adverse reactions, contraindications, precautions can not all be indicated, should be marked with the main content and indicate the 'detailed instructions' words."

However, in the official document does not make the content of the drug specification categories of importance rating, in order to quantify the public's concern about the content, I will set the above 15 content of the five-level Likert scale, from "never concerned" to "always concerned" The statistical results are as follows (Table 5).

The final result will be sorted according to three levels of importance: "primary level", "secondary level" and "other level", and the above contents will be distinguished through comparison and highlighting to form a visual guide, thus helping readers to find what they want in a drug description more quickly.

3.2 Improved Design Practices

Font Size. It is widely accepted that the right font size is crucial for comfortable reading. It is no coincidence that many researchers have also found that font size is an important factor affecting dyslexic readers, and the larger the font size in Chinese characters, the easier it is to recognize the characters [9]. In addition to font size, font type also affects reading speed. The fonts recommended by organizations and associations for dyslexics are mostly sans serif fonts [10]. Common Chinese drug instructions usually have a font size of about 5–6pt (about 2.12 mm), which is obviously also lower than the smallest Chinese font size that the public can comfortably read, and enlarging the text is inevitable. However, under the premise of the same content, the larger the text, the larger the layout will be, which undoubtedly increases the cost of more. Recent studies have shown that the effect of reading speed is not independent, but is usually accompanied by the compounding effect of increased character spacing and line spacing, which improves reading recitation for dyslexics [11]. Therefore, I have made some trade-offs here, using 8–12pt as the common font size of Chinese characters in A5-size publications at a normal reading distance of 30 cm as a reference, and using different font sizes according to importance in the hierarchy for layout design, using 9pt bold for the first level of content, 8pt for the second level, and a slightly smaller font size of 7pt for the third

Table 5. Analysis results of user satisfaction

Content Categories	Never (1 point)	Occasional (2 points)	Don't care (3 points)	Frequently (4 points)	Always (5 points)	Results	
Usage and Dosage	6(3.64%)	10(6.06%)	24(14.55%)	42(25.45%)	83(50.3%)	4.13	First Level
Production date and expiration date	4(2.42%)	3(1.82%)	33(20%)	53(32.12%)	72(43.64%)	4.13	
Indications or functionalities	5(3.03%)	13(7.88%)	25(15.15%)	41(24.85%)	81(49.09%)	4.09	
Contraindications	4(2.42%)	13(7.88%)	26(15.76%)	61(36.97%)	61(36.97%)	3.98	
Precautions	7(4.24%)	14(8.48%)	24(14.55%)	55(33.33%)	65(39.39%)	3.95	
Drug interactions	6(3.64%)	13(7.88%)	37(22.42%)	58(35.15%)	51(30.91%)	3.82	Second Level
Generic Name	5(3.03%)	15(9.09%)	34(20.61%)	75(45.45%)	36(21.82%)	3.74	
Adverse reactions	5(3.03%)	20(12.12%)	33(20%)	65(39.39%)	42(25.45%)	3.72	
Storage conditions	5(3.03%)	26(15.76%)	38(23.03%)	66(40%)	30(18.18%)	3.55	
Specification	11(6.67%)	35(21.21%)	34(20.61%)	54(32.73%)	31(18.79%)	3.36	Third Level
Pharmacological effects	11(6.67%)	31(18.79%)	41(24.85%)	54(32.73%)	28(16.97%)	3.35	
Ingredients	10(6.06%)	34(20.61%)	44(26.67%)	54(32.73%)	23(13.94%)	3.28	
Characteristic	14(8.48%)	30(18.18%)	49(29.7%)	61(36.97%)	11(6.67%)	3.15	
Production companies	21(12.73%)	33(20%)	45(27.27%)	47(28.48%)	19(11.52%)	3.06	
Executive standard and approval number	27(16.36%)	30(18.18%)	42(25.45%)	46(27.88%)	20(12.12%)	3.01	

level in accordance with the concern Table 4. The first level of content uses 9pt bold, the second level uses 8pt, and the third level uses a slightly smaller font of 7pt according to the concern Table 4. As shown in Fig. 2, the first layer of content in concern Table 4 uses 9pt bold Chinese characters, the second layer uses 8pt size, and the third layer uses 7pt size to ensure that important content can be captured quickly and completely by users.

Fig. 2. Font size and thickness at different levels

Characters Spacing and Line Spacing. Although researchers as early as 1982 found that increasing the spacing between words facilitated both types of text by examining the effects of word spacing on static and dynamic text reading in video display terminals [12]. However, the ideographic system of Chinese characters is different from the epigraphic system, and the human brain recognizes the two systems in very different ways, and there is still no consensus on the effects of text spacing on the reading efficiency of dyslexic patients [12]. Similar literature is available that verifies the analysis of the interaction between word spacing and line spacing, and the interaction between inter-character spacing and line spacing is significant, with significant differences between each word spacing under different line spacing conditions, and with increasing line spacing, the requirements of Chinese children with dyslexia for word spacing are reduced as well as the differences between word spacing are decreasing. The difference in line spacing was significant for different word spacing conditions, and as the word spacing increased, the requirement for line spacing width decreased and the difference between line spacing decreased. After validation of the study, it was revealed that the total reading time required by the dyslexic population was shortest for the text formatted with a combination of 1/2 word spacing and 1.5 times the line spacing, so this design was also designed with reference to the results of this experiment The results of this experiment were also used in this design [13].

Content Annotation. In this study, the emphasis is not limited to the common ways such as bolded and highlighted fonts, but adopts a similar "modular" layout design, dividing the entire manual into different sections according to the level of importance of the content categories, either by adding background color, font size contrast, or changing font color, etc. A variety of different combinations are used to produce a continuity of contrast (Fig. 3).

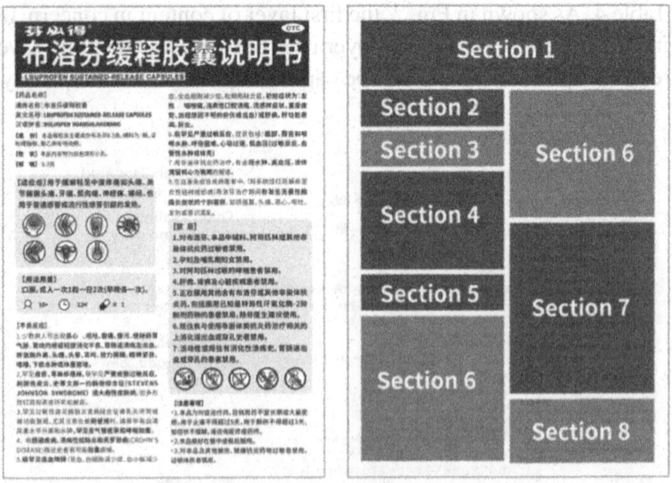

Fig. 3. Modular layout design example

The number of rows and columns of the division of the section is a reference to the survey process "Columnar Composing" needs, although it is a non-differential property, that is, whether it is a single-column or multi-column layout, user satisfaction will not change because of column changes. However, a multi-column design allows for more text in a limited amount of space. In addition, a single line of text that is too long will not allow the reader to follow the line from the end of the previous line to the beginning of the next line, and too short will cause the reader to look back more often, resulting in an increase in reading time. For Pinyin characters, studies have shown that people prefer a reading length of 80 characters per line, which corresponds to about 20 characters for Chinese characters [14]. Based on this, the modular design of the entire layout has two columns vertically, and the number of rows horizontally is determined by the specific text content.

Information Color Design. Color has a strong visual impact, with reference to aesthetic theory and visual experience, the scientific use of color emotions and the use of color information conveying function can coordinate the information framing on the instructions. In terms of color perception, the perceptive ability of dyslexic people is weaker than normal people, so the use of color is not more than three colors as much as possible, and the illustrations try to avoid bright colors, which can reduce the visual burden of dyslexic people [15].

The color of drug packaging should express the characteristics and efficacy of the drug, and it needs to be both scientific and aesthetic disease closely related to the color. In this design, ibuprofen extended-release capsules are analgesic and antipyretic drugs, and "pain" and "heat" are reminiscent of the color red, so the overall color is red, which is used to express the painful point of the disease and emphasize the properties of the drug. The rest is black and gray text, and most of the pages are white, to reduce the color temperature and visual burden, so that the information is clear and affable, and can communicate effectively with patients and help them read the information in the instruction manual.

Graphical Information Design. The graphic design is close to the non-differentiable property of the charm property, but considering the reading characteristics of dyslexic patients, some graphics are still added to the main level of the manual for aiding comprehension. In the recognition of graphics, dyslexic people have certain difficulties, and need to alleviate the interference of graphic crowding effect to be able to analyze the graphics easily, the selection of graphics should not be required to be interesting and ignore the easy to distinguish, the shape design in the form of simple and easy to understand graphics should be as simple as possible to reduce the complex details [16], so that people with dyslexia can visually distinguish the graphics.

As the drug instructions have more pages that need graphic aids to understand, mostly some adverse reactions about body parts are the main ones, so in the author's design, the basic form is outlined using a single line to ensure the recognition of the organ, and a rounded treatment is used to avoid sharp images to make patients uneasy about the drug, fear and other negative psychological implication, the specific illustration style is shown in Fig. 4.

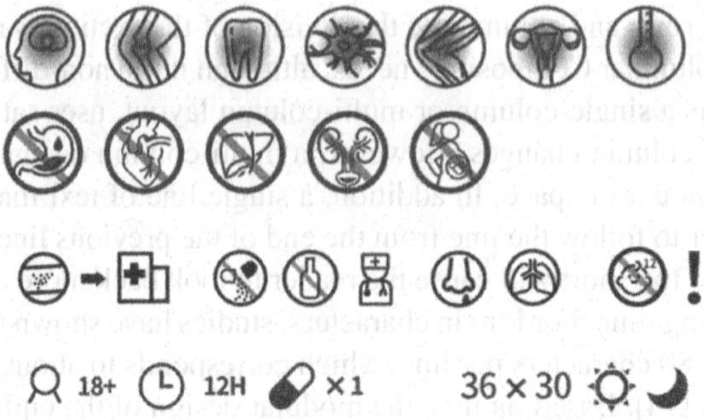

Fig. 4. Part of the graphic design

4 Online Dyslexia-Friendly Manual Design Attempt

Although the online version is a non-differentiated attribute, but "voice broadcast" as a charming attribute exists, taking into account the carrier of voice broadcast is mostly mobile devices, I still added the mobile web design in the design. However, it should be noted that the online version is for the service of voice broadcast, so here I mainly follow the principle of simplicity and ease of use to make a preliminary attempt.

The process of using the voice announcement is as follows: use your mobile device to scan the paper version of the manual or the QR code on the drug package to enter the online manual home page of the mobile web terminal, after the icon of each content category on the home page, there will be an obvious play icon, click the play icon to hear the voice announcement.

And the visual design in accordance with the layout of the above layout in the mobile terminal to do the relevant adaptation processing, categorized can be divided into the following parts.

Font Size: Compared with paper manuals, the biggest advantage of the mobile web terminal is that the original limitations of the size no longer exist, users can personalize the design according to their own needs for font size, the online version of the manual is designed by default with reference to the laws and laws of conventional web design, in the lower right corner of the prominent design of "adjust the layout". This allows users with special needs to customize their own pages and make reading more comfortable.

Characters Spacing and Line Spacing: Although there are differences in the medium of web and paper reading text, the visual characteristics of dyslexic people for reading Chinese characters are unchanged, so the whole text spacing continues in the same way as the previous article, keeping the line spacing 1.5 times and 1/2 word spacing.

Content Annotation: Basically similar to the previous article, in a modular way, the home page is divided into different content panels, panels and panels by changing the visual elements to form differences and levels, so that users can quickly find the key content.

Columnar Composing: Mobile devices are often more moderate width, the length of a single line of text in the normal reading font size is not very long, so in the design of the mobile web side, long text is no longer divided into columns layout.

Color and Illustration: Continue the design of the previous article, keep the same drug design elements the same, maintain the unity of the design (Fig. 5).

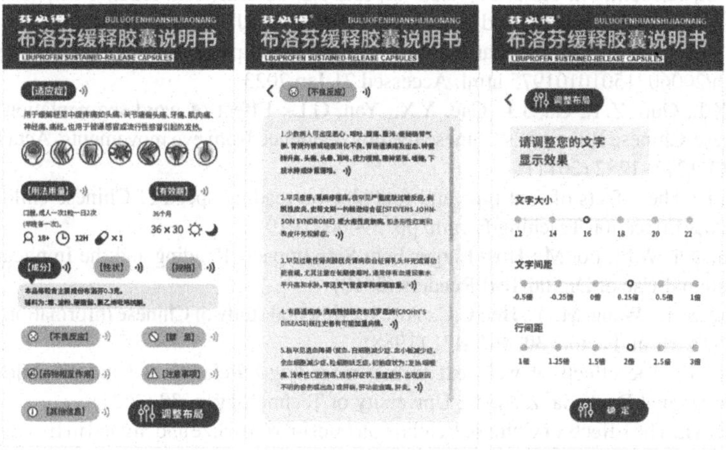

Fig. 5. Part of the mobile web interface design

5 Conclusion

This paper adopts a product design approach to visual design, and proposes design strategies through research and puts them into practice, but unfortunately, the final results have not yet been put into practical use, and their specific utility is yet to be discussed. In addition, the design of the mobile network terminal is not perfect, and the interaction characteristics of visually impaired people need to be further studied for further research and in-depth design. Accessible designers are a hot topic in the design world in recent years, but few designers are special people themselves. We cannot fully empathize with special people, we can only use scientific methods to complete relevant accessibility design as much as possible. We hope the design ideas in this article can provide some reference for accessibility design.

References

1. Lyon, G.R., Shaywitz, S.E., Shaywitz, B.A.: A definition of dyslexia. Ann. Dyslexia **53**, 1–14 (2003)

2. Wu, Y., Cheng, Y., Yang, X., Yu, W., Wan, Y.: Dyslexia: a bibliometric and visualization analysis. Front. Public Health **10**, 915053 (2022)
3. Perea, M., Gomez, P.: Increasing interletter spacing facilitates encoding of words. Psychon. Bull. Rev. **19**, 332–338 (2012)
4. Kalyvioti, K., Mikropoulos, T.A.: Virtual environments and Dyslexia: a literature review. Proc. Comput. Sci. **27**, 138–147 (2014)
5. Kano, N., Seraku, N., Takahashi, F., et al.: Attractive quality and must-be quality. J. Jpn. Soc. Qual. Control **14**, 147–156 (1984)
6. Martelli, M., Di Filippo, G., Spinelli, D., Zoccolotti, P.: Crowding, reading, and developmental dyslexia. J. Vis. **9**, 14 (2009)
7. Gori, S., Facoetti, A.: How the visual aspects can be crucial in reading acquisition? The intriguing case of crowding and developmental dyslexia. J. Vis. **15**, 8 (2015)
8. Drug instructions and label management regulations. https://www.nmpa.gov.cn/xxgk/fgwj/bmgzh/20060315010101975.html. Accessed 21 Jan 2023
9. Bai, X.J., Guo, Z.Y., Gu, J.J., Cao, Y.X., Yan, G.L.: Effect of word segmentation cues on Japanese-Chinese Bilingual's Chinese reading: evidence from eye movements. Acta Psychol. Sin. **43**, 1273–1282 (2011)
10. Yang, F.: The effects of font type and font size on reading speed of Chinese children with Dyslexia. Education Teaching Forum, pp. 59–60 (2019)
11. DeLamater, W.E., Ed, M.: How Larger Font Size Impacts Reading and the Implications for Educational Use of Digital Text Readers (2010)
12. Hwang, S.-L., Wang, M.-Y., Her, C.C.: An experimental study of Chinese information displays on VDTs. Hum. Factors **30**, 461–471 (1988)
13. Yang, F.F.: The effects of web text format n reading efficiency of Chinese children with developmental Dyslexia. Zhejiang University of Technology, p. 38 (2021)
14. Tian, X.H.: The Effects of Chinese Reading on Font or Word Size and Signed in Eye Movement Study. Shenyang Normal University (2019)
15. Wang, X.L.: Visual Design Based on Visual Features of Children with Disabilities Taking Training Book Design as an Example. Central China Normal University (2019)
16. Lin, A.P.: Research on visual emotionalized design for Dyslexia. Industrial Design, pp. 69–70 (2021)

Digital Participation of People with Intellectual Disabilities Living in Residential Institutions – Perspectives, Barriers and Implications

Vanessa Nina Heitplatz(✉) and Christian Bühler

Department of Rehabilitation Technology, TU Dortmund University, Dortmund, Germany
vanessa.heitplatz@tu-dortmund.de

Abstract. In Germany, people with intellectual disabilities often live in total institutions. These are institutions where living places, employment, care, and pedagogical actions are combined and significantly impact residents' quality of life and participation opportunities. This paper aims to analyze the influence of the residential living context on the digital participation opportunities of this group of people. Thus, two studies were conducted between 2018–2019. First is an interview study with 24 caregivers having management responsibility in their institution; second is a focus group study with 50 people with intellectual disabilities. Both studies contain essential findings about the current state of digital participation in the German welfare context. One crucial finding points out communication deficits in the institutions and existing knowledge gaps towards used devices and applications by people with intellectual disabilities. For example, the needs and wishes of people with intellectual disabilities were not recognized by caregivers, and the topic was not considered relevant to the institutions.

Furthermore, people with intellectual disabilities complain about a lack of support from caregivers and the social environment. Caregivers, in turn, need more time and opportunities to address residents' questions and problems. These tensions lead to different coping strategies described in more detail below. Furthermore, this paper presents strategies to combine the contrasting perspectives of involved people and makes suggestions for creating more digital participation opportunities in such institutions.

Keywords: Digital Inclusion · Intellectual Disabilities · Total Institutions

1 Background

Digital participation has become a new key factor for participation opportunities which complements the traditional ways of living. However, unfortunately, they constitute a risk of social exclusion if no access is granted. In this respect, people with intellectual disabilities often living in residential institutions are particularly vulnerable and at risk of digital divides. The following sections introduce information on intellectual disabilities, residential homes, and digital divides in Germany.

M. Antona and C. Stephanidis (Eds.): HCII 2023, LNCS 14020, pp. 353–370, 2023.
https://doi.org/10.1007/978-3-031-35681-0_23

1.1 People with Intellectual Disabilities

The term "intellectual disabilities" is a broad medical term that encompasses various illnesses and syndromes [1]. Intellectual disabilities are internationally defined in the Diagnostic and Statistical Manual of Mental Disorders (DSM-5) [2] and the International Classification of Diseases (ICD-10) [3] of the World Health Organization. Both classification systems are based on the definition of the American Association of Intellectual and Developmental Disabilities (AAIDD) [1], which defines intellectual disability as an impairment that:

- Occurs before the age of eighteen
- Affects mental and adaptive functions (Intellectual Functioning and Adaptive Behavior), and
- Interferes with the performance of activities in daily living contexts [1]

The diagnosis of intellectual disability is not tied to a predetermined age but must be diagnosed in an individual's developmental stage. It is not caused by an accident or a disease in adulthood but is acquired in early childhood [1]. These criteria distinguish it from other diseases or syndromes (e.g., dementia, acquired brain injury) [4]. In addition, as understood in the DSM-5, intellectual disabilities often occur in combination with other disorders, for example, autism spectrum disorders, specific learning disorders, or genetic impairments (e.g., Fragile-X-Syndrome, Rett-Syndrome) [5].

Both classification systems divide intellectual disabilities into four degrees of severity, which are often found in international studies and publications [5]:

a. Mild intellectual disability
b. Moderate intellectual disability
c. Severe intellectual disability, and
d. Profound intellectual disability

The subdivision aims to distinguish the mild forms from severe and profound forms to derive appropriate support for those people in their daily activities [6, 7].

In Germany, intellectual disabilities are also subdivided into degrees of severity using standardized Intelligence-tests to derive needs and financial assistance. However, in practical work and German research, the Model of the International Classification of Functioning, Disability, and Health (ICF) is used for analyzing a person's needs and competencies in all areas of life [2, 7]. This holistic view puts the individual at the center of consideration, not the impairment. For example, a consideration of the intellectual disabilities along the ICF model shows Fig. 1:

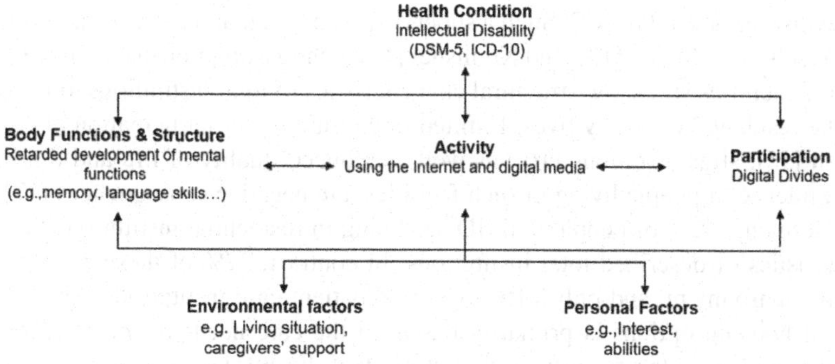

Fig. 1. Adapted ICF Model [8]

In this study, the degree of intellectual disability of the participants is not asked. However, all participants have diagnosed an intellectual disability as a requirement of admission for living in residential facilities (see Sect. 1.2). In addition, from the participants' statements in the focus group study (see Sect. 2), most participants have claimed to have limited memory, reading, and spelling skills.

1.2 The Residential Living Context in Germany

Trescher [9] states that a large proportion of people with intellectual disabilities (ID) live in facilities in which they are dependent on the care in their living facility, their caregivers, or the prevailing conditions and structures. Here, specific living-related assumptions and rules of behavior become present [9]. Such living institutions show characteristics of Goffman's "Total institutions" [10], such as:

- Coincidence of living place and employment
- Cohabitation of similarly situated individuals
- Extended period of residence
- Isolation from the rest of society, and
- System of explicit norms and rules

Living place, employment, care, and pedagogical actions are combined in the residential institution and are offered by only one single source; the residential institution [9].

People with ID often grow up with their peers in such total institutions [11]. Family care is, at least temporarily, outsourced for a certain period of life. A high degree of control (e.g., opening post, access to private living rooms), limited rights of self-determination (e.g., in the design of the living space or access to it), and everyday life of the residents that is oriented to the working hours of the caregivers are characteristics of such forms of accommodation. They differ fundamentally from the kind of living that is taken for granted by the rest of our society [11].

Kremsner [12] also makes clear that even in the 21st century, people with ID are still faced with structural violence and disability-specific abuse (e.g., excessive administration of medication, withholding of care and assistance activities, or demanding gratitude) in those institutions today [12]. Such a supervisory and regulatory structural framework leads Trescher [9], Meuth [13], and Kremsner [12] to the assumption that mainly residential living facilities still show structural characteristics of total institutions today, which harm the residents' everyday lives. Limited opportunities for participation [14], social isolation [15], stigmatizations [16], as well as reduced quality of life and diminished self-confidence of people living in such facilities, are negative consequences [17].

In Germany, 42% of people with ID are living in residential institutions that show characteristics of described total institutions. In contrast, 37% of these people live in a family environment, and only 21% live in outpatient care institutions. The differentiation of housing options is primarily based on the care needs of the residents and, associated with this, the severity of the intellectual disabilities (see Sect. 1.1). People with severe intellectual disabilities are often excluded from outpatient, residential care as they are often unable to adequately address the need for support and care [18]. An international comparison of research in this context is hardly possible because many different terms define the forms of living contexts differently, including terms such as congregated settings [19], group homes [20, 21], supported housing [22], or residential living [23]. Even though residential contexts are named differently in the international context, characteristics of total institutions are often found where people cannot care for themselves. This fact is independent of terminology and housing concepts and allows a certain degree of comparability in international research.

However, according to the UN-Sozialpakt in Germany [24] and the Universal Declaration of Human Rights (Article 25, Paragraph 1), housing and living are fundamental human rights. These articles describe the right of every human to adequate housing. Whether housing is adequate or not is measured by seven criteria by the UN-Sozialpakt, e.g., drinking water, energy for heating, affordability).

Moreover, all member states of the Convention on the Rights of Persons with Disabilities (UN-CRPD) have committed to granting people with disabilities the right to choose a place of residence freely and to decide independently where and with whom they want to live (Article 19) [25]. Nevertheless, such total institutions, which are the context of the study presented in this paper, are not following current rights and laws and are, therefore, important to examine.

1.3 Digital Divides

The term digital divide refers to the differentiation of society into people who use the Internet and those who do not. Recent digital divide research also focuses on the so-called second-level divide, which concerns divides in Internet usage itself [26].

The first group of people profits from various processes and participation opportunities through Internet access and usage. The second group has different opportunities to benefit from the advantages of the digital world. However, they are at risk of exclusion from participation and social empowerment [27, 28]. Recent studies show that people with ID are one of many groups in our society who are often digitally excluded from the Internet and using digital media and technologies [29–32].

Alfredsson Ågren et al. [20] found for example that Internet usage between young people with and without intellectual disabilities (aged between 13–20 years) differed in a significantly lower proportion in terms of "access to internet-enabled devices and performed activities…than the reference group." For this reason, people with ID face some web applications associated with a high degree of cognitive and linguistic skills and arise as barriers for those people. Also, Dobransky, and Hargittai [33] concluded that people with disabilities use the Internet less often than people without disabilities. Missing accessibility and a lack of digital skills are reasons for that [33]. Gomez et al. [34] analyzed smartphone usage by people with Down Syndrome and found a great interest and usage rate of those using smartphone devices. The authors said that people with Down Syndrome still lack digital literacy and need support to train their (digital) skills to use digital devices. At least, recent studies proved that the social environment is important in providing one-to-one support for primary contact and using media and technologies [35]. The relationship between caregivers and people with ID constitutes a critical factor for digital participation, especially in contexts with high dependencies (e.g., residential institutions) [36, 37].

Alfredsson Ågren [38] summarizes that people with ID of different ages have less access to the Internet than the general population. Thus, the Internet represents a new area of life in which those people are excluded. Ramsten et al. [39] identified the following four barriers to the usage of the Internet and digital media:

- Lack of experience in combination with a lack of interest
- Lack of access
- Lack of competencies
- Lack of opportunities for the use

In addition, limited literacy skills, lack of support from the social environment, or technical difficulties in operating the devices can also affect usage opportunities [39–41].

More empowerment is needed to enhance digital participation for disadvantaged groups of people. Therefore, the possibilities of access, active participation in the use of the Internet, new media and technologies, and the acquisition of required (media) competencies is of central importance [16].

The UN-CRPD has highlighted the right of people with disabilities to digital participation. Even though the term "digital participation" is not used in the Convention, the demands for the usage of technologies, free access to information, and equal participation in all social processes and society can be derived from various articles, as Ramsten und Blomberg [42] stated:

> The right to access ICT is stated in the Convention on the Rights of Persons with Disabilities (CRPD) (art. 9). This means that access to ICT becomes highly relevant to achieve further rights set by the CRPD such as; inclusion in community (art. 19), access to information (art. 21), participation in political life, public life (art 29), cultural life, recreation and leisure (art. 30) [42].

In summary, this paper describes an area of tension in which people with ID live in contexts where they are subject to solid control and often cannot decide on their own. Today's digital world provides multiple options for contacting other people, maintaining relationships, and being part of our society. Thus, it is crucial for these people to participate in digital processes and not be excluded.

2 Study

Despite these findings of recent studies, there are gaps in digital participation research. Chadwick et al. [41] stated that more significant insights into how people with ID learn about the Internet, how information is given to them about online risks and how access restrictions are negotiated and implemented would be beneficial. Furthermore, Chadwick et al. [35] argued that there is still no evidence that people with ID need more protection online and that treating them like eternal children constitutes another barrier to Internet access and usage. Also, SafePlace/Disability Rights Texas [43] found that limited research is available specifically on how people with disabilities use and access the Internet and social media. Research also needs to improve access and use in everyday settings where Internet-enabled devices are used [44].

Two studies were conducted between 2018 and 2019 in residential living institutions in Germany to address these research gaps. These studies aimed to learn more about the perspectives and Internet use of people with ID. Also, the caregivers were asked about their views on Internet use in their institutions and the current status quo of digitalization. The first study is an interview study with 24 caregivers having management functions in their residential institutions. The second study presents results from a focus group study with 50 people with ID, living in the caregivers' institutions (called "residents" in the following). Both studies are part of a Ph.D. project finished in 2021 aiming to determine which applications and devices are used by the residents and which factors influence their usage negatively or positively [36]. To analyze the results of both studies, a within-method triangulation was conducted to compare the findings and perspectives [45]. Therefore, both studies were initially individually analyzed using qualitative content analysis. As a result, inductive categories were created for both studies and afterward compared to each other. Similarities and differences were examined to compare the perspectives of caregivers and residents. Finally, a communicative validation was conducted in May 2020 to validate the results of both studies. The whole procedure can be found in Heitplatz [36] and Heitplatz et al. [46].

This paper aims to find out:

(1) How can a digital strategy in residential facilities combine perspectives of all involved people (i.e. residents, caregivers, and pedagogical professionals)?
(2) What steps are necessary for welfare organizations to become more digital and help their clients/residents to realize their rights to digital participation?

All 24 interviewed caregivers worked in residential living institutions, described in Sect. 1.2. The caregivers had expert knowledge and decision-making power in their living institutions, which formally turned the interviews into expert interviews [47]. All persons were asked with the same interview guide about a) their attitudes towards the Internet and digital media, b) the digital infrastructure in their institutions, and c) their opinion about residents' media usage.

All 50 residents were interviewed in 11 focus groups based on other authors' positive experiences with this method in this research field [48, 49]. Because there was no opportunity to meet the participants in advance, Talking Mats [50] was developed to allow all participants to participate regardless of the severity of their intellectual disability or language ability. The interview guideline contained different questions than the guide for the interviews with the caregivers. After the interviews, focus groups were conducted with the residents to expand the first study's results. They lasted approximately 45 to 60 min, depending on the size of the groups (between three to six participants) [46, 51].

3 Results

To answer this paper's research questions and derive implications, the perspectives of caregivers and residents are first described on the basis of selected results. The most contrasting views are summarized in three following inductive categories:

- Communication and knowledge deficits
- Lack of support and help
- Coping strategies

All categories are described in detail in the following section.

3.1 Communication and Knowledge Deficits

The results of both studies show that knowledge gaps and communication deficits appeared among caregivers and residents. The interviews with the caregivers clearly show that knowledge gaps exist regarding the current usage of digital media and the Internet. However, the caregivers' needs and fears regarding this topic must be more evident. The caregivers assume that residents with severe intellectual disabilities cannot use digital media and the Internet. Therefore, they can use it without explaining the usage or selected Internet activities. Furthermore, caregivers expect Facebook and WhatsApp to be the main applications on digital devices by residents with mild forms of intellectual disabilities. The caregivers admitted that, apart from this, they have no idea of what else is used by the residents and what their wishes and needs are, as the following quotation shows:

> "We do not even try to introduce those being older or living longer in our institution to use digital media or to let them try it out. We don't know if it [Internet usage] would make sense for them or if they would benefit from the opportunities of the digital world. So we have a sense of what is needed, but actually we don't know." (quotation of caregiver in Interview 1).

In the interviews, the caregivers had the idea of asking the residents about their needs and wishes for the first time. A second important aspect of the results is communication deficits in residential institutions.

The caregivers only talk to the residents about such topics if conflicts arise with other residents or at work. Apart from that, Internet and media usage is not a current topic for caregivers or is usually negatively associated since it only comes up in the event of problems and conflicts. In addition, for dealing with this topic exists no instrument for accounting or billing in Germany, so everything along this topic is additional, voluntary work of the caregivers. Thus, dealing with digital topics becomes a topic that requires personal commitment, dedication, and voluntariness. One caregiver, for example, reported that he developed materials on his own to support the digital world's first steps because they do not currently exist in plain language (Interview 9). Another caregiver collected private money to buy sim cards and a notebook for his institution to allow the residents to use the Internet (Interview 15). In this context, another result of the study is of central importance. Since the caregivers do not know what applications and devices the residents use, they provide devices that they believe will be used, such as laptops and desktop pc. However, the residents rejected these and were not used as a result. In turn, the caregivers assumed a lack of interest by the residents for the digital world, and the topic was not considered a priority topic by the caregivers.

These communication deficits and knowledge gaps become particularly clear comparing the statements of the residents with those of the caregivers. On the one hand, the applications on the devices are much more diverse than assumed by caregivers. They go beyond WhatsApp and Facebook usage but are often limited to leisure applications [46].

On the other hand, the residents' statements also clearly show that those who do not yet have their device or the possibility of Internet access would like to participate in the digital world to communicate with friends and relatives, make phone calls, or exchange photos. The residents were also asked in the focus groups if they have access to Internet devices in the institutions. As an answer, they often referred to the laptops and desktop PCs that exist. However, residents also clearly stated that they do not want to use these devices because they are "out of fashion." Instead, they would like to use smartphones and tablets, which are currently common in society. In addition, many people would like to learn more about using smartphones and tablets and certain operating functions and security aspects [51]. Unfortunately, this desire for training and further education was absent for the caregivers in the interviews.

These examples are interpreted as two parties' communication deficits and knowledge gaps. This result will continue in the next section when presenting a need for more support and help.

3.2 Lack of Support and Help

A deeper analysis of the data from the focus groups reveals that residents in the evaluation categories "Wishes," "Support," and "Operating problems" repeatedly state that they lack support from their social environment when using the Internet and digital media. For example, one resident says: "I need someone to show me this [using a smartphone]. Then I might be able to do it on my own" (focus group 1). Another quote makes clear that the family lives too far away and that the resident has no one to ask instead: "I would like to learn how to set up the smartphone. My friends don't always have time. And my brother lives so far away" (focus group 3). In this period, when no one is addressing the residents' problems and questions, there is a disruption of use, which can have a long-term impact on skills, competencies, and online relationships.

The residents' perspectives reveal another essential finding. In addition to the perceived lack of support, some residents report taking the caregivers' judgmental statements about competencies so seriously that they do not trust themselves to use the Internet and develop fears about even trying. Fear and low self-confidence are often a result of perceived attitudes from the social environment, such as "you cannot do this" or "I am doing this for you."

> These perceived attitudes seem to make people feel that they are not competent enough to use a smartphone or the Internet. These people trust very much what caregivers or parents tell them and, as a result, do not dare to use new media and technologies and react very anxiously when trying to familiarize [16].

This spiral of negative statements by the social environment and negative feelings about competencies and fears is one reason digital divides exist within people with ID and why opportunities for participation are reduced.

The caregivers often do not realize these strong effects of statements and unintentional judgments on some residents. Therefore, no intent can be assumed. However, the caregivers know they need more time in their daily work to answer all the residents' questions about their devices in detail and deal with the problems more intensively. This aspect becomes particularly clear in the following quote:

> I have employees in my institution who would very much like to do that [helping residents]. But we have not enough employees for that and basic care is more important. What bothers me the most is that we don't create opportunities [for utilization and trying out] and people are excluded from it [digital world]. They even have no opportunity to get to know it (Interview 3).

The caregivers are trapped in their daily work, where staff is often limited, time resources are scarce, and the focus is on daily care. In addition, there is no possibility of financial budgeting for such activities (see Sect. 3.1). The residents' perceived lack of support and help contrasts with the caregivers' difficult day-to-day work, in which deviations from the daily routine are hardly possible, and routines are challenging to interrupt. As a result, different coping strategies emerge on both sides, caregivers and residents.

3.3 Coping Strategies

The coping strategies in the institutions can be described as "closing one's eyes vs. becoming active." On the one hand, there are institutions where caregivers ensure that donations for digital media (tablets) are organized, that materials are developed in plain language, or that funding for digital participation is actively sought. Cooperation with (local) universities or other practical or scientific institutions exists in those institutions to address knowledge deficits and train the media skills of professionals and residents. However, these institutions are rare. In the interview sample, only four out of 24 institutions actively addressed digital inclusion in their institution. The twenty other facilities tended to turn a blind eye to reality, meaning that digital participation was only addressed when urgent problems arose (see Sect. 3.1). Moreover, if the institutions dealt with arisen problems, it was not dealt with sustainably, so the problems often reappeared a few days later. If there is any Internet access in these institutions, it is only made available to the pedagogical staff. Access for residents is often neither permitted nor desired. In some exceptional cases, Internet access is only granted to particular residents who are selected as cognitively fit, and access is heavily regulated. Fears of data misuse and protection by residents, protecting them from complex topics (e.g., pornography) and a high need for control and support, lead caregivers to assume that residents must be protected and kept away from the digital world for their own safety. Institutions still need to be made aware of the fact that this is a postponement or a shift of the issue and that it is, therefore, not resolved.

Whether a facility is more on the active or passive side of digital participation depends to a large extent on the age and attitude towards empowerment and disability of the facility's management, but also on the staff, who can act as a significant transformer and multiplier in the institution. These dependencies become a problem for the residents, who are often helplessly at the mercy of this dependency. Residents also show different coping strategies.

One coping strategy of the residents is to find other ways of accessing the Internet outside their institution. For example, some residents reported that they go to nearby stores in the neighborhood of the institution, which are equipped with free Wi-Fi. Thus, residents spend hours in or in front of the stores surfing the Internet on their smartphones. The residents often make no secret of this behavior, and the caregiver also knows about it, as the results of the interview study show. However, this behavior is accepted and only addressed when problems arise. Sometimes, disputes arise between the store owners, the residents, and the institutions, as "loitering" in front of the stores is not desired. Furthermore, residents reported buying vouchers from online shops at gas stations or supermarkets with their pocket money to do some online shopping afterward. However, most institutions do not desire this, as there is no control over what residents order and when these orders arrive at the institution (see Sect. 1.2).

Another coping strategy is hidden usage, meaning usage beyond caregivers' control and knowledge. Residents use excuses and unsupervised moments to pursue their internet activities. They often use social media or play games. It becomes dangerous when residents communicate with unknown persons, e.g., via social networks or dubious dating platforms, and then go on these dates without the caregivers noticing. This kind of incident was reported several times in the focus groups. The residents often do not dare to talk to the caregivers about it because they know they have done something foolish.

These different strategies and examples show that residents are looking for ways to participate in the digital world. These examples also show that institutions cannot close their eyes to this topic, even if they are still doing so in some cases. The following section will discuss the results and derive implications concerning the research questions.

4 Implications

This paper aims to present strategies to better understand the different perspectives and to help welfare institutions to become more digital. For this purpose, three strategies are presented in the following, which are based on the previously described results.

4.1 Addressing Communication Deficits and Knowledge Gaps

The studies' results clearly show the institutions' communication and knowledge deficits. A first strategy should therefore address these deficits. Thus, the institutions need to understand existing deficits and make them visible. In research, several models exist to understand communication deficits. The four-ear model by Schulz von Thun initially focuses on a sender, who communicates, and a receiver, who receives the communication content [52]. In an adapted form, this model can also be transferred to the context described in this paper and the interacting people.

The sender and receiver can be either the residents or the caregivers. What is significant about this model is to understand what messages a person can send with his or her expressions. These can be factual information, self-disclosure, relationship cues, or appeals. Different types of interference can occur when messages are communicated. The consequence of these disorders are misinterpretations, conflicts, and dissensions. This study's results show that caregivers' misinterpretations lead to districted residents' Internet usage. The following factors can lead to such disorders [52]:

- Different spoken language
- Different Cultures
- Missing knowledge or education to understand the messages
- Background noise (e.g., noise, loud music)
- Ambiguities (one message can have different meanings)
- Interpretation
- Missing interest in the message
- Silent post effect (multiple transmissions change the message until it has a different meaning than the original message)

In the context of this research, additional difficulties and disruptions may occur. The intellectual disability of the residents can be accompanied by speech disorders and might lead to impossible or only partially possible communication. As a result, speech is unclear, and messages might not be understood. Caregivers must create ways to engage residents in conversation and prepare communication pathways along their capabilities and abilities. Talking Mats [50] can provide one opportunity to support such communication (see Sect. 2).

Once awareness of the deficits has been achieved, information offers must be created and taken up. In practice and research, several offers exist that need to be presented to the institutions [51]. These include, for example, the PIKSL labs in Germany, which offer hands-on training in inclusive teams to promote media skills for people with and without disabilities [53]. To assume information about existing apps and websites, a Padlet (an Internet web page) was developed by Pelka and Heitplatz [54], which summarizes various apps and offers in different categories to encourage users to try them out. First, however, the institutions must see and perceive such possibilities and information.

To ensure this, it would be an idea to appoint so-called "lighthouse people." These are people in the institutions who are interested in such topics and actively search for information to pass it on. Such lighthouse people can also motivate other caregivers for such topics and are of central importance for the multiplication of digital topics in the institutions.

Finally, the understanding of communication and the perception of information must be provided with opportunities for use. The results of this and other studies show that there are often no opportunities for testing and experimentation in such regimented contexts [39, 55, 56]. It is, therefore, necessary for institutions to create such learning and experimentation offers and spaces. A concrete instrument could be Coffee Lectures, a method to give short information inputs and get into an exchange about it. Coffee Lectures can be done quickly with coffee and cookies in regular, self-selected intervals [36].

4.2 Addressing the Digital Divide

Another strategy should address digital divides in general and within the group of people with ID in particular because the results of this study and other recent studies still show digital disability divides [27, 31, 57]. In the following, different steps are described to shedding light on this aspect in more detail.

First, it is crucial to conduct more in-depth analyses and research on the Internet usage of people with ID. Although this study showed what applications are used [37], it needs to be shown what problems and barriers arise, where people stop using applications and devices, or what other needs exist. It is also essential to analyze whether people with ID are not interested in the Internet and digital media usage or whether other reasons are barriers to their non-use, e.g., fears, anxieties, or stigmatization. Further research or projects should shed light on those aspects. These findings align with the findings of other studies [35, 43, 44].

In addition, the lack of media literacy of people with ID should be addressed in the future and has been demonstrated in the results of this study and in many other studies [58, 59]. It is essential to consider that every human being, regardless of their impairment or intellectual ability, strives to improve themselves in their competencies (Personal Growth Theory [60]). Therefore, this aspect should also be considered when teaching media skills. Also, it should be considered which activities a person would like to pursue on the Internet, which barriers prevent this and how this Internet access can be individually designed, for example, using the ICF Model (see Sect. 1.3). Baacke [61] defines different levels of media literacy, ranging from simple media usage to active media design. While for some people, swiping pictures on their smartphone can be a success, others may want to become active designers of the Internet and write blog posts or social media entries themselves. Hoppestadt [62] showed that, with some support and practice, people with ID could also independently pursue activities on the Internet using their smartphone or tablet. In addition, devices such as the media dementia tablet [63] can open up options that offer people with ID or other impairments easy Internet access.

Another approach could be to train people as so-called "digital assistants" who help people with special needs exercise their right to participate in the digital world. In German schools, such digital assistants have emerged in the wake of the COVID-19 pandemic as an idea in educational work to support students in their work with digital media [64, 65]. Whether and under what financial and legal conditions such an idea could be transferred to the welfare sector could at least be worth further consideration.

Also, the different Internet user types developed by Heitplatz et al. [16] should also be considered for teaching media skills and enhancing digital participation opportunities in the institutions. These can be used to better familiarize the people in the institutions and to design targeted training or involve some people as experts in inclusive training formats.

4.3 Addressing Lacks of Support

The last strategy is raising awareness of described problems by people with ID, caregivers, and institutions.

As the results show, caregivers need more support and backup from the institution to deal with digital issues and help residents with their questions. Also, the residents need more support from the caregivers, who are often the first contact for the residents. Furthermore, the hands of the institutions are also tied, as there is currently no way to charge for dealing with digital topics (see Sect. 1.3). To resolve this tension, support is needed from policymakers, who must a) create instruments in the institutions to legitimize their involvement with digital topics financially, and b) create funding opportunities on the other side, e.g., through calls for projects and funding. Such solutions would allow the institutions the opportunity to deal with digital participation not only on a voluntary and unpaid basis but also professionally and legitimately.

Residents also need to raise their voices more often and loudly with their concerns and issues. Residents' councils are established in most institutions to represent their interests. This could be an established instrument to draw attention to the lack of access and opportunities for use and sustainably pursue the facility's issue. At the same time, support from the family environment can become important to support the residents in this issue. In some cases, more and more people with ID are also claiming their rights to Internet access and use in institutions, with support from their families or other organizations. The more visible the problems become, the sooner they can be fixed or addressed.

Despite this, the housing situation significantly negatively impacts people with ID participation opportunities. In Germany, there is a need to create further legal frameworks for promoting inclusive housing options for people with ID and to monitor the implementation of regulations and laws that have already been implemented (e.g. through the UN-CRPD). Also, politics can initiate funding programs and projects that enable participatory forms of housing. Good examples already exist, as the SeWo project shows [66].

In the future, it will be necessary for policymakers, academics, and practitioners to solve current problems together.

5 Conclusion

This paper highlights current barriers and difficulties regarding digital participation in German living institutions for people with disabilities. Administrative challenges, communication deficits, and knowledge gaps lead to the assumption that dealing with digital participation is not necessary or taken seriously in residential living institutions. In this study, people with ID share significant concerns regarding their media and Internet use and their needs and wishes, which need to be taken seriously in the future.

As multipliers, caregivers play an essential role as the first and often most important person for questions and problems. First, however, they must be made aware of this role so that unconscious or hurtful comments or stigmatization can be avoided, and instead, an empowering behavior and attitude toward residents can be adopted.

Digitization will continue to be a significant topic in the welfare sector and will be discussed more intensively in the near future. On the one hand, the young people with ID and the young caregivers in the institutions will become important drivers of these digitization processes and are increasingly active in demanding (their) rights to digital participation. On the other hand, the COVID-19 pandemic has shown what and how quickly participation can be made possible in an emergency. These insights and the upwind can help to learn from these experiences and further expand existing options in the institutions [30]. Opening up the facility to digital issues and Internet access for their clients can be an excellent opportunity to eliminate the stigma of total institutions and jump on the "participation train," which is gaining speed in the welfare context. In addition, it gives facilities the option to help shape digital participation, position themselves in this new field, and advertise their facility.

The results of this paper and other presented studies show that German welfare institutions are still at the beginning of these developments and are dependent on support and cooperation with actors and stakeholders on various levels (e.g., science and politics). However, due to their tight bonds with the residents, caregivers in such institutions have the opportunity to contribute to an inclusive and empowering (living) environment for people with disabilities and help them to become active and self-determined Internet users if they wish so.

6 Limitations

The study was conducted at a time when the COVID-19 pandemic did not exist. As briefly discussed earlier, the pandemic lead to short-term participation opportunities for residents in described residential facilities. This was also evident in the validation of the PhD thesis conducted online during the pandemic [36].

An international collaboration with colleagues from a wide range of countries was able to summarize the situation to some extent but was not able to fully analyze it [30]. Therefore, there is a limitation of the results, which should be considered against the current background of the pandemic, which is still ongoing in some countries and regions.

References

1. American Association of Intellectual and Developmental Disabilities: Definition of Intellectual Disability (2020). https://www.aaidd.org/intellectual-disability/definition. Zugegriffen 29 Juli 2020
2. Falkai, P., Wittchen, H.-U. (Hrsg.): Diagnostisches und statistisches Manual psychischer Störungen DSM-5®, 2. Aufl. Hogrefe, Göttingen (2018)
3. Krollner, B., Krollner, D.M.: ICD-Code (2022). https://www.icd-code.de/icd/code/ICD-10-GM.html. Zugegriffen 27 Dec 2022
4. Boat, T.F., Wu, J.T.: Mental Disorders and Disabilities Among Low-Income Children. The National Academies Press, Washington D.C (2015)
5. American Psychatric Association: What Is Mental Illness? (2018). https://www.psychiatry.org/patients-families/what-is-mental-illness. Zugegriffen 29 Juli 2020

6. American Psychatric Association: Intellectual Disability (2013). file:///C:/Users/there/AppData/Local/Temp/APA_DSM-5-Intellectual-Disability.pdf. Zugegriffen 27 Nov 2020
7. Nußbeck, S.: Der Personenkreis der Menschen mit geistiger Behinderung. In: Nußbeck, S., Biermann, A., Adam, H. (Hrsg.) Sonderpädagogik der geistigen Entwicklung. Hogrefe, Göttingen, S 5–17 (2008)
8. German Institute of Medical Documentation and Information: ICF (2019). https://www.dimdi.de/dynamic/en/classifications/icf/index.html. Zugegriffen 30 Januar 2020
9. Trescher, H.: Wohnräume als pädagogische Herausforderung. Springer, Wiesbaden (2017). https://doi.org/10.1007/978-3-658-12846-3
10. Goffman, E.: Asyle. Über die soziale Situation psychiatrischer Patienten und anderer Insassen, 4. Aufl. Suhrkamp, Frankfurt am Main (1981)
11. Mangold, K., Rein, A.: WOHNgruppe – Durchgangspassage vs. Daheim-Sein. In: Meuth, M. (Hrsg.) Wohn-Räume und pädagogische Orte. Erziehungswissenschaftliche Zugänge zum Wohnen, 16. Aufl. VS Verlag für Sozialwissenschaften, Wiesbaden, S 221–244 (2017)
12. Kremsner, G.: Gewalt und Machtmissbrauch gegen Menschen mit Lernschwierigkeiten in Einrichtungen der Behindertenhilfe. Teilhabe **59**(1), 10–15 (2020)
13. Meuth, M.: Theoretische Perspektiven auf Wohnen: Ein mehrdimensionales Wohnverständnis in erziehungswissenschaft licher Absicht. In: Meuth, M. (Hrsg.) Wohn-Räume und pädagogische Orte. Erziehungswissenschaftliche Zugänge zum Wohnen, 16. Aufl. VS Verlag für Sozialwissenschaften, Wiesbaden, S 97–122 (2017)
14. Haage, A.: Das Informaionsrepertoire von Menschen mit Behinderungen. Eine Studie zur Mediennutzung von Menschen mit Beeinträchtigungen (2020)
15. Shpigelman, C.-N.: Leveraging social capital of individuals with intellectual disabilities through participation on Facebook. J. Appl. Res. Intellect. Disabil. **31**(1), 79–91 (2018). https://doi.org/10.1111/jar.12321
16. Heitplatz, V.N., Bühler, C., Hastall, M.R.: I can't do it, they say! – Perceived stigmatization experiences of people with intellectual disabilities when using and accessing the Internet. In: Antona, M., Stephanidis, C. (eds.) HCII 2020. LNCS, vol. 12189, pp. 390–408. Springer, Cham (2020). https://doi.org/10.1007/978-3-030-49108-6_28
17. Nota, L., Ferrari, L., Soresi, S., Wehmeyer, M.: Self-determination, social abilities and the quality of life of people with intellectual disability. J. Interllect. Disabil. Res. **51**(11), 850–865 (2007). https://doi.org/10.1111/j.1365-2788.2006.00939.x
18. Thimm, A., Rodekohr, B., Dieckmann, F., Haßler, T. (Hrsg.): Wohnsituation Erwachsener mit geistiger Behinderung in Westfalen-Lippe und Umzüge im Alter. Erster Zwwischenebricht zum Forschungsprojekt "Modelle für die Unterstützung der Teilhabe von Menschen mit geistiger Behinderung im Alter innovativ gestakten" (MUTIG). Kettler, Bönen (2019)
19. Health Service Executive: Time to Move On from Congregated Settings (2011). https://www.hse.ie/eng/services/list/4/disability/congregatedsettings/
20. Alfredsson Ågren, K., Kjellberg, A., Hemmingsson, H.: Digital participation? Internet use among adolescents with and without intellectual disabilities: a comparative study. New Med. Soc. **22**(12), 2128–2145 (2020). https://doi.org/10.1177/1461444819888398
21. Clement, T., Bigby, C.: Group Homes for People with Intellectual Disabilities: Encouraging Inclusion and Participation. Jessica Kingsley Publishers, London (2009)
22. Hobson, J., Lynch, K., Lodge, A.: Residualisation in supported housing: an organisational case study. Hous. Care Support **23**(1), 1–13 (2020). https://doi.org/10.1108/HCS-09-2019-0019
23. Davidson, A.-L.: Use of mobile technologies by young adults living with an intellectual disability: a collaborative action research. J. Dev. Disabil. **18**(3), 21–32 (2012)

24. Institut für Menschenrechte: Internationaler Pakt über wirtschaftliche, soziale und kulturelle Rechte von 1966 (1966). https://www.institut-fuer-menschenrechte.de/fileadmin/user_upload/PDF-Dateien/Pakte_Konventionen/ICESCR/icescr_de.pdf. Zugegriffen 07 Juli 2020
25. Beauftragte der Bundesregierung für die Belange von Menschen mit Behinderungen: Die UN-Behindertenrechtskonvention. Beauftragte der Bundesregierung für die Belange von Menschen mit Behinderungen (2017). https://www.behindertenbeauftragte.de/SharedDocs/Publikationen/UN_Konvention_deutsch.pdf?__blob=publicationFile&v=2. Zugegriffen 25 Februar 2020
26. Min, S.-J.: From the digital divide to the democratic divide: Internet skills, political interest, and the second-level digital divide in political Internet use. J. Inf. Technol. Polit. **7**(1), 22–35 (2010). https://doi.org/10.1080/19331680903109402
27. Becker, M., et al.: How to design an intervention to raise digital competences: ALL DIGITAL week – Dortmund 2018. In: Antona, M., Stephanidis, C. (eds.) HCII 2019. LNCS, vol. 11572, pp. 389–407. Springer, Cham (2019). https://doi.org/10.1007/978-3-030-23560-4_29
28. Des Power, M.R., Rehling, B.: German deaf people using text communication. Am. Ann. Deaf **152**(3), 291–301 (2007)
29. Borgström, Å., Daneback, K., Molin, M.: Young people with intellectual disabilities and social media: a literature review and thematic analysis. Scand. J. Disabil. Res. **21**(1), 129–140 (2019). https://doi.org/10.16993/sjdr.549
30. Chadwick, D., et al.: Digital inclusion and participation of people with intellectual disabilities during COVID-19: a rapid review and international bricolage. Policy Pract. Intell. Disabil. **22**(12), 2128 (2022). https://doi.org/10.1111/jppi.12410
31. Chadwick, D.D., Chapman, M., Caton, S.: Digital inclusion for people with an intellectual disability. In: Attrill-Smith, A., et al. (Hrsg.) The Oxford Handbook of Cyberpsychology, S 260–284. Oxford University Press, Oxford (2019)
32. Seale, J., Chadwick, D.: How does risk mediate the ability of adolescents and adults with intellectual and developmental disabilities to live a normal life by using the Internet? CP **11**(1) (2017). https://doi.org/10.5817/CP2017-1-2
33. Dobransky, K., Hargittai, E.: Unrealized potential: exploring the digital disability divide. Poetics **58**, 18–28 (2016). https://doi.org/10.1016/j.poetic.2016.08.003
34. Gomez, J.C., Torrado, J.C., Montoro, G.: Using smartphones to assist people with down syndrome in their labour training and integration: a case study. Wirel. Commun. Mob. Comput. **2017**, e5062371 (2017)
35. Chadwick, D., Quinn, S., Fullwood, C.: Perceptions of the risks and benefits of Internet access and use by people with intellectual disabilities. Br. J. Learn. Disabil. **45**(1), 21–31 (2017)
36. Heitplatz, V.N.: Digitale Teilhabemöglichkeiten von Menschen mit intellektuellen Beeinträchtigungen im Wohnkontext. Perspektiven von Einrichtungsleitungen, Fachkräften und Bewohnenden. Eldorado - Repositorium der TU Dortmund (2021)
37. Heitplatz, V.N., Bühler, C., Hastall, M.R.: Caregivers' influence on smartphone usage of people with cognitive disabilities: an explorative case study in Germany. In: Antona, M., Stephanidis, C. (eds.) HCII 2019. LNCS, vol. 11573, pp. 98–115. Springer, Cham (2019). https://doi.org/10.1007/978-3-030-23563-5_9
38. Alfredsson Ågren, K.: Internet use and digital participation in everyday life. Adolescents and young adults with intellectual disabilities. Linköpng University Medical Dissertations No. 1734. Department of Health, Medical and Caring Sciences Linköping University, Linköping (2020)
39. Ramsten, C., Dag, M., Martin, L., Marmstal Hammar, L.: Information and communication technology use in daily life among young adults with mild-to-moderate intellectual disability. J. Intellect. Disabil. **24**(3), 289–308 (2018)

40. Dobransky, K., Hargittai, E.: The disability divide in internet access and use. Inf. Commun. Soc. **9**(3), 313–334 (2006)
41. Chadwick, D., Fullwood, C., Wesson, C.J.: Intellectual disability, identity, and the Internet. In: Luppicini, R. (Hrsg.) Handbook of Research on Technoself, Bd 8, S 229–254. IGI Global, Pennsylvania (2013)
42. Ramsten, C., Blomberg, H.: Staff as advocates, moral guardians and enablers – using ICT for independence and participation in disability services. Scand. J. Disabil. Res. **21**(1), 271–281 (2019). https://doi.org/10.16993/sjdr.608
43. SafePlace/Disability Rights Texas: How People with Disabilities use social media. Report (2016)
44. Alfredsson Ågren, K., Kjellberg, A., Hemmingsson, H.: Access to and use of the Internet among adolescents and young adults with intellectual disabilities in everyday settings. J. Intellect. Dev. Disabil. **45**(1), 89–98 (2020). https://doi.org/10.3109/13668250.2018.1518898
45. Flick, U.: Triangulation. VS Verlag für Sozialwissenschaften, Wiesbaden (2011)
46. Heitplatz, V.N., Bühler, C., Hastall, M.R.: Usage of digital media by people with intellectual disabilities: contrasting individuals' and formal caregivers' perspectives. J. Intellect. Disabil. **26**, 420–441 (2021). https://doi.org/10.1177/1744629520971375
47. Kaiser, R.: Qualitative Experteninterviews. Springer, Wiesbaden (2014). https://doi.org/10.1007/978-3-658-02479-6
48. Buchholz, M., Ferm, U., Holmgren, K.: Support persons' views on remote communication and social media for people with communicative and cognitive disabilities. Disabil. Rehabil. **42**(10), 1439–1447 (2018). https://doi.org/10.1080/09638288.2018.1529827
49. Löfgren-Mårtenson, L., Sorbring, E., Molin, M.: "T@ngled Up in Blue": views of parents and professionals on Internet use for sexual purposes among young people with intellectual disabilities. Sex. Disabil. **33**(4), 533–544 (2015). https://doi.org/10.1007/s11195-015-9415-7
50. Tracey, O.: The use of Talking Mats to support people with dementia and their careers to make decisions together. Health Soc. Care Commun. **21**(2), 171–180 (2013)
51. Heitplatz, V.N.: Fostering digital participation for people with intellectual disabilities and their caregivers: towards a guideline for designing education programs. SI **8**(2), 201–212 (2020). https://doi.org/10.17645/si.v8i2.2578
52. Hilsenbeck, T.: Die 4 Ohren stellen sich vor. Das 4-Ohren-Modell von Schulz von Thun in einer etwas anderen Form (2010)
53. In der Gemeinde leben gGmbH: PIKSL mobil - PIKSL (2020). https://piksl.net/bildungsangebote/piksl-mobil/. Zugegriffen 29 Dezember 2020
54. Pelka, B., Heitplatz, V.N.: Digitale Tools für die Soziale Arbeit (2020). https://padlet.com/BastianPelka/t3uvigzejspmx6ga
55. Abel, J., Hirsch-Kreinsen, H., Steglich, S., Wienzek, T.: Akzeptanz von Industrie 4.0 (2019). https://www.plattform-i40.de/PI40/Redaktion/DE/Downloads/Publikation/akzeptanz-industrie40.pdf?__blob=publicationFile&v=6. Zugegriffen 27 November 2020
56. Pelka, B.: Digitale Teilhabe: Aufgaben der Verbände und Einrichtungen der Wohlfahrtspflege. In: Kreidenweis, H. (Hrsg.) Digitaler Wandel in der Sozialwirtschaft. Grundlagen - Strategien - Praxis, S 57–80. Nomos, Baden-Baden (2018)
57. Fischer, K.W., Williamson, H., Guerra, N.: Technology and social inclusion: technology training and usage by youth with IDD in the national longitudinal transition study of 2012. Inclusion **8**(1), 43–57 (2020)
58. Ayres, K.M., Mechling, L., Sansosti, F.J.: The use of mobile technologies to assist with life skills/independence of students with moderate/severe intellectual disability and/or autism spectrum disorders: considerations for the future of school psychology. Psychol. Schs. **50**(3), 259–271 (2013). https://doi.org/10.1002/pits.21673
59. Bosse, I.: Standards der Medienbildung für Menschen mit Behinderung in der Schule. Ludwigsburger Beiträge zur Medienpädagogik, pp. 1–6 (2012)

60. Jain, C.R., Apple, D.K., Ellis, W.E.: What is self-growth? Int. J. Process Educ. **7**(1), 41–52 (2015)
61. Baacke, D.: Medienkompetenz - Begrifflichkeiten und sozialer Wandel. In: von Rein, A. (Hrsg.) Medienkompetenz als Schlüsselbegriff, Bonn, S 112–124 (1996)
62. Hoppestad, B.S.: Current perspective regarding adults with intellectual and developmental disabilities accessing computer technology. Disabil. Rehabil. Assist. Technol. **8**(3), 190–194 (2013)
63. Mediadementia (o.J.) Unser Tablet für die Demenzbetreuung
64. Bildungsserver Sachen-Anhalt: Digitalassistenz (2022). https://www.bildung-lsa.de/informationsportal/schule/schulentwicklung/digitalassistenz.htm
65. Hochschule Merseburg: Digitalcoach für Schulen und weitere Bildungskontexte (2023). https://www.hs-merseburg.de/hochschule/information/weiterbildungsangebote/highlights/zertifikatskurs-digitalcoach-fuer-schulen-und-weitere-bildungskontexte/
66. SeWo GmbH: SeWo—Selbstbestimmtes Wohnen für Menschen mit Behinderung (2021). https://sewo-nrw.de/. Zugegriffen 02 Januar 2023

Interactive Design of Auxiliary Makeup APP for People with Abnormal Color Perception Based on the Concept of "Inclusive Design"

Keke Huang and Yongyan Guo(✉)

School of Art Design and Media, East China University of Science and Technology, Shanghai, People's Republic of China
g_gale@163.com

Abstract. With at least 70 million men and 7 million women in China suffering from colour blindness, there is a huge demand for make-up colour aids. Make-up requires an overall control of colour, but people with abnormal colour vision are unable to judge and select their own make-up and colour combinations when applying make-up, which can greatly affect the effect of make-up, so this research has huge potential for application.

This paper firstly collects user needs for supplementary make-up products by means of secondary data surveys and user interviews, secondly uses the AHP method to obtain a weighting of user needs, and finally transforms user needs through an inclusive design method and outputs a final solution. By optimising the experience, functionality and visual requirements, the app scans faces and distinguishes colours for colour entry and contrast correction through face recognition technology, and provides colour matching solutions and make-up tips based on colour diagnosis to help people with colour vision abnormalities solve their make-up problems.

Keywords: Inclusive design · Demand analysis · AHP · Abnormal color perception · Auxiliary makeup

1 Research Background

Colour vision abnormalities refer to the lack or inability of the visual organs to perceive colour, and are classified as either colour weakness or colour blindness. According to statistics, the prevalence of colour vision abnormalities is about 6–9%, and the number of people with colour vision abnormalities in China is as high as 70 million, with at least 70 million men and 7 million women being colour blind. Research on special groups such as people with colour vision abnormalities in China is relatively weak compared to developed countries in terms of research data and practical applications. As society becomes more concerned about people with colour vision, research on people with colour vision abnormalities is increasing and is spread across many fields, but designs for people with colour vision abnormalities in the field of lifestyle make-up have yet to be developed. Make-up requires total colour control, but people with colour vision

M. Antona and C. Stephanidis (Eds.): HCII 2023, LNCS 14020, pp. 371–389, 2023.
https://doi.org/10.1007/978-3-031-35681-0_24

are unable to judge and choose their make-up and colour combinations when applying make-up, and many people with colour vision disorders choose to give up make-up. Make-up is not just for the masses; people with colour vision abnormalities also have their own quest for beauty. There is a growing trend towards diversity and individuality in the pursuit of beauty, and more and more technology is being put into make-up to provide new experiences and designs for the beauty industry. Many beauty apps have emerged to provide users with a wealth of beauty information and services online, which are more instant, convenient and accurate. This research will both consider the characteristics of people with colour vision abnormalities and help them to shape their lives with more confidence by using smart products to assist them with their make-up. It also fills a gap in the existing design of make-up aids for people with colour vision abnormalities, which is important for the development and improvement of the field of make-up aids for people with colour vision abnormalities.

2 Research Theory and Methodology

2.1 Inclusive Design

Coleman first used the term inclusive design in 1994 and it has gradually become widely used [1]. Inclusive design improves the quality of life for the general public and special groups by reducing the requirements for user capabilities, expanding the target audience and the environment in which the product can be used, and increasing the degree of inclusiveness. Inclusive design aims to meet the needs of a wide range of users, including mainstream users and those with special needs, and often aims to include more people with lower levels of sensory, motor and cognitive abilities [2].

Inclusive design products or services need to be as accessible as possible to the majority of people and need to be human-centred. Design thinking that incorporates modern design concepts places more emphasis on equality in the development of things, flexibility of use and comprehensive applicability [3]. Through the summary of design methods to propose design principles for design application and guidance, and the design principles of inclusive theory can basically be summarised in the following aspects.

(1) People-centred principle
In the design process of inclusive design, the design needs of a wide range of people are met as far as possible, so that each group of people is treated without discrimination, which requires the concept of inclusive design to adhere to the principle of "people" as the centre of the user experience. In the process of considering special groups of people, the corresponding design needs are changed due to their specific functional barriers.
(2) Principle of diversity and difference
Products should consider the diversity of user groups in the design process, recognise design differentiation and take into account the diverse needs of users. In a diverse and differentiated user group, it is essential to accommodate the differences between users, to understand the needs of the general public for the product and to take into account the difficulties faced by other people with functional abnormalities in their daily lives.

(3) Principle of flexibility
It is important not only to understand the purpose and function of the product and the users it is intended for, but also to ensure that the use of the product is as simple and flexible as possible, easily adaptable to the evolving needs of use. In the design according to the needs of special groups of people, due to the existence of physical defects of the user, it is also necessary to adhere to the principle of simple operation and flexible use according to the user's way of use.
(4) Principle of optionality
When a single design solution does not satisfy all users, it is necessary to consider offering different options to users. In the product design process, a single design solution cannot meet the needs of all users, it is necessary to consider giving users different options, putting everyone on an equal footing, by meeting higher design standards and thus meeting the needs of all users, at the same time, such products should not be limited by technical conditions, but should take the initiative to inspire users so that the product can ensure the ability to reach a wider range of users Inclusion.

Inclusive design is a flexible and resilient process. As a comprehensive design concept in modern design, it is based on the idea that design should meet the needs of the majority of users as far as possible in the process of use and treat the majority of people in society equally in the design process. It advocates that the design approach should be adapted to treat the needs of the able-bodied, the disabled and the elderly equally, that the design should meet the needs of the general public while taking into account the special needs of groups outside the scope of use of the product, and that the design for special groups should be designed not only for their special needs but also for the general public to participate in and use. The product is designed to meet the needs of each individual as far as possible and to achieve the goal of fair and equal access.

2.2 Interaction Design System for Makeup APP for People with Colour Vision Abnormalities

With the development of production technology, people's demand for products has risen to a more emotional stage, and user satisfaction has become a major concern and prerequisite, and user experience is an important indicator of user satisfaction and the merits of design solutions [4]. Therefore, starting from user needs can further realise the user's emotional appeal to the product [5]. User needs can help designers to explore the possibilities of optimising the user experience from its essence. User needs are multi-layered and include functional, physical/psychological and subjective-emotional dimensions.

User research generally begins with the collection of secondary data, from which the extent to which the problem has been solved can be judged, before moving on to primary data. The purpose of collecting secondary data is to assist in the design of a solution, to understand the overall market environment, usage environment, key metrics or key audiences, and to complement the primary data (interview results) to better research the problem, interpret the findings and identify the audience. The purpose of the interviews is to restore the true perspective of the audience, to analyse abstract ideas through concrete information and to verify the accuracy of the definition of secondary data collection.

Secondary data research, also known as indirect data research, requires a short period of time, costs less, is faster, and provides a preliminary understanding of the nature, scope, content and focus of the target audience through newspapers and other literature. User interviews are used to understand the psychological needs and behavioural characteristics of users through face-to-face conversations with the target users and are a qualitative research method with good flexibility and adaptability.

2.3 Analytic Hierarchy Process

Analytic Hierarchy Process (AHP) is a method combining qualitative and quantitative analysis proposed by the American scholar Scary in 1971 [6]. It is a convenient and versatile framework capable of solving multi-criteria decision problems, evaluating alternatives and deriving final priorities [7]. Hierarchical analysis is the analysis of objectives as a system, dividing the objective level into a number of evaluation indicators and calculating the weights of the evaluation indicators by means of qualitative fuzzy quantitative calculation methods as a basis for decision making [8]. The AHP method is introduced to evaluate the requirements, calculate the priority of the requirement elements and check the logical consistency of their judgement, thus deepening the understanding of the user requirements and helping the designer to make a choice on the solution.

The experts used the scaled scale (Table 1) to make a two-by-two comparison of the criterion level and sub-criterion level indicators to derive the judgement matrix and indicator weights. The following formula was used for the calculation of the indicator weight values (Formulas 1–7).

Table 1. Scaling table

Comparison of scale values between two	Relative importance meaning
9	Very important
7	Important
5	More important
3	General importance
1	Equally important
1/3	General secondary
1/5	Lesser importance
1/7	Secondary
1/9	Very secondary
Note: 2, 4, 6, 8, 1/2, 1/4, 1/6, 1/8, as adjacent intermediate values of the above scales	

The judgement matrix H consists of individual scale values, element h_{ij} is the significant scale value of indicator H_i relative to indicator H_j, and n is the number of indicators in the matrix.

$$H = (h_{ij})_{n \times n} = \begin{bmatrix} h_{11} \cdots h_{1n} \\ \vdots \ \ddots \ \vdots \\ h_{n1} \cdots h_{nn} \end{bmatrix} \tag{1}$$

Different expert evaluations yielded different scale values, and the opinions of the experts were integrated using geometric averaging, i.e. h_{ij} aggregated to h'_{ij} and formed an aggregated judgment matrix H'.

$$h'_{ij} = \sqrt[10]{\prod_{m=1}^{10} h_{ij}^{m}} \tag{2}$$

In the formula: h_{ij}^{m} is the scale value obtained from the evaluation of the mth expert.

The aggregated judgement matrix H' is normalised using the square root method to obtain the matrix row vector, i.e. the weight value of each indicator, expressed as W_i.

$$W_I = \overline{W}_i / \sum_{i=1}^{4} \overline{W}_i \tag{3}$$

$$\overline{W}_i = \sqrt[4]{\prod_{i=1}^{4} h'_{ij}} \tag{4}$$

The reasonableness of the indicator weights is assessed in terms of whether the matrix passes consistency validation.

$$\lambda_{\max} = \sum_{i=1}^{4} \frac{\sum_{i=1}^{4} h'_{ij} \times W_i}{4W_i} \tag{5}$$

$$CI = (\lambda_{max} - n)/(n - 1) \tag{6}$$

$$CR = CI/RI \tag{7}$$

In the formula: λmax is the maximum characteristic root; *CI* is the consistency verification index; *CR* is the consistency ratio, when $CR \leq 0.1$, the weight consistency verification passes.

2.4 Research Framework

The research idea of this paper is shown in Fig. 1. Firstly, taking user needs as the core, through secondary data survey and user interview, focusing on user information, product needs, experience optimization, and collecting user suggestions for assisted make-up products; secondly, using AHP to process user needs and get user needs weighting; finally, through the case of assisted make-up app interaction design for people with abnormal colour vision to transform user needs and output the final solution.

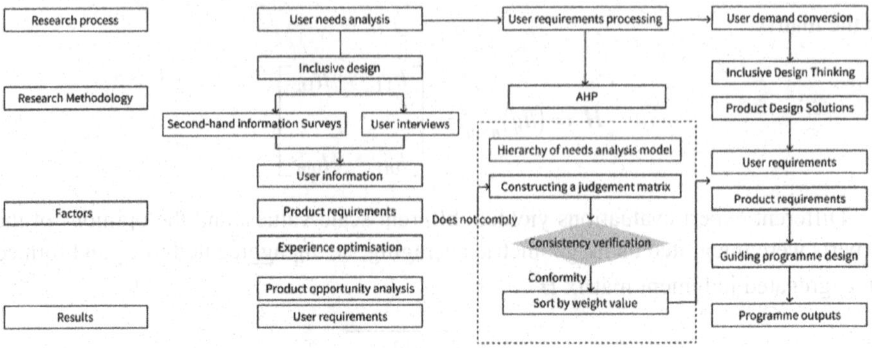

Fig. 1. Interaction Design System Framework

3 User Research and Requirements Collation

3.1 User Surveys and Interviews

Study 1: A second-hand survey on make-up for people with colour vision abnormalities was conducted on b-site, Zhihu and Douban, and a total of five videos of users with colour vision abnormalities were collected. The user experience of make-up for people with colour vision abnormalities was mainly summarised as follows: (1) make-up is difficult, for example, make-up does not feel colourful, they cannot grasp the intensity of red, they do not wear blush, they only wear one colour of lipstick, etc.; (2) the attitude of people with colour vision abnormalities towards make-up is not avoidance, but encouragement to learn make-up. Some people think that not being able to wear make-up because of colour weakness is bad and affects their mood, and that they need to understand or learn about make-up to help them become confident. (3) In terms of solutions, the advice for most people with colour vision is to seek help from friends and rely on them to recommend the right colours.

Some people with abnormal colour vision have been trained to become make-up artists. Tomlin is a colour-blind make-up artist who went from being afraid to take on the job to actively discussing colour balance with her trainer. Through the encouragement and help of many friends, she gradually learned more make-up techniques and became more confident. Although she cannot distinguish between different reds, she has a strong sense of light and dark colours and her efforts and hobby have kept her going. For people with colour vision abnormalities, make-up is a beautiful thing, a process of accepting oneself.

Study 2: User interviews are a qualitative research method that can be used to pinpoint product usage problems and uncover the user needs behind the problems. When designing an internet product, using this method helps product practitioners to understand information about users' experiences and habits, usage scenarios, existing experiences and so on.

The target users of this study are people with abnormal colour perception, so 10 users with abnormal colour perception were recruited for one-on-one interviews through friends' recommendations and online software channels such as posting and Douban. The purpose of the interviews was to understand the subjective feelings and preferences of users with colour vision abnormalities when accessing beauty information and services, as well as when using beauty software, and to analyse the pain points and difficulties encountered by users in the process of using mobile software and make-up, as well as the solutions. During the user interviews, the user's statements are recorded through notes and audio recordings to facilitate the subsequent summarisation of user needs.

Through typical user interviews (Table 2), user needs are explored in depth from the psychological and physical aspects of the users, which paves the way for the next product architecture.

After obtaining the user's consent, the user is given the background to the project and is then interviewed on a line by line basis according to the interview outline, with key words recorded during the interview. In the process of getting to know the user better, it is also possible to follow up on a particular point of view to find out the deeper reasons for it.

Table 2. Outline of user interviews.

Part 1: Basic user information questions
1. Occupation, gender, age, hobbies 2. Basic information on colour vision abnormalities 3. How many hours a day do you use your mobile phone? 4. What mobile applications do you use on a daily basis? – How much time do you spend on these mobile apps? – Do you actively try new mobile apps? 5. do you experience any problems using mobile apps? – Does the colour of the mobile interface assist with operation? Do the colours of the function buttons have an impact? – Is there any inconvenience due to the high number of colours in the interface? What are the perceived inconveniences? Can you give me an example? – When you look at the phone, do you feel the psychological effect of the colours? For example, the green colour of antivirus software means "safe" 6. What do you think impresses you most about the mobile app - the colours, the graphics or the text?
Part 2: Product-related issues

(continued)

Table 2. (*continued*)

Before using
1. Do you know your skin type? What are the problems or dissatisfactions of your skin type and features?
2. What is your attitude towards make-up?
3. Do you know the beauty products you are going to use before you use them? How do you find out about beauty products?
In use
1. Do you know the correct procedure for applying make-up?
– How do you usually apply your own make-up and which areas do you apply? How long do you spend on your make-up each time?
What problems do you encounter every time you apply your own make-up?
2. Does colour vision make it difficult to apply make-up on a daily basis? (distinguishing, choosing and matching colours) For beauty tutorials, do you have problems with choosing beauty products of similar colours?
3. How often do you access beauty information and services online and what are your habits? What software do you prefer to use to access beauty information and services? What kind or forms of beauty information do you like to read most, such as text, pictures and videos?
4. Have you ever bought beauty products that are not suitable for you?
Have you ever encountered any problems in skincare or make-up? Are there any parts that are difficult to master? Do you ask friends for help?
After use
1. Do you share your experiences with friends about products that you feel good about using? Will you continue to repurchase products that suit your needs? Will you try other products?
2. Do you feel that make-up has made a big difference to you? What are the main aspects?
– Is there any difference between your daily and work situation when you wear make-up?
Part 3: Experience-related issues
1. Would you use a software (app) designed for people with colour vision disorders that would help you choose the right make-up, select your make-up and teach you how to apply it?
2. What do you think should be taken into account when designing an app for people with colour vision disorders to assist with make-up? What kind of features would you expect from a product?
3. What do you think are the disadvantages of the existing (beauty) apps? Is the interface friendly? Is it easy to understand the textual information content, icons, categories, etc. in the interface?
4. What are the benefits of getting beauty information and services through beauty app than other kinds of app?

3.2 User Requirements Collation

At the end of the interview, the interview notes are textualised to summarise and sort out the user's views and provide supporting content for the interview conclusions (Table 3).

The interview viewpoints were recorded to summarise the interview findings.

(1) The target users are women with colour vision abnormalities aged 18–30: the interviews revealed that the target users use their mobile phones for entertainment and leisure for more than one hour a day. Although there are different degrees and types

Table 3. Transcript of interview views

Questions	Answer keyword/sentence
Occupation, gender, age, hobbies	Student oriented; 18–30 young female; sunny and active; wide range of hobbies, love shopping, talking about fashion, etc.
Colour vision abnormalities	Red blindness; colour blindness; blue blindness; green blindness
Skin Type/Facial Problems	oily skin; combination skin; dry skin; sensitive skin Swollen eyeballs; asymmetrical or stray shapeless eyebrows; poorly shaped face; poorly proportioned features; dark skin
Frequency and habits of mobile phone use	Uses mobile phone daily, very frequently; likes to swipe it at leisure time/before bed
Effects of colour vision abnormalities on the use of mobile phones	Some images are difficult to judge; the captcha code is indistinguishable; use the function by habit; poor reading experience when there are many colours
Frequency and habits of accessing beauty advice and services online	For fragmented time; before bedtime; for boredom; when learning to apply make-up for the first time; when you want to change your style; when learning how to use a product; when making pre-purchase decisions
Software for accessing beauty advice and services	Little Red Book; Beauty Fix; You Look Good Today; Weibo; youtube; b-site; Taobao; Sephora
Which form of beauty advice do you prefer to see (text/photo/video)	Preference for video or a combination of graphics and text Too much text for a poor reading experience, easy visual fatigue, difficult to concentrate
The effect of colour vision abnormalities on make-up	Can't grasp shades; afraid to wear blush; can't match colours; don't know what products suit you; afraid to try new products
Problems encountered when applying make-up	Poor choice of foundation shades; not being able to match makeup colours; not being able to choose eye shadows poor grasp of eye shadow, easy to find the wrong position; favourite make-up does not suit you after painting; not knowing how make-up really looks afterwards; difficulty in finding the right position of blush

(*continued*)

Table 3. (*continued*)

Questions	Answer keyword/sentence
How to choose your own cosmetics	Recommendations from friends; find online advice
What beauty advice and services do you like to get with beauty apps	Skin texture detection; accurate pushing of products and precautions based on user's skin texture; beauty community for users to share and view tips; virtual online makeup trials; product reviews; product data lists; product ingredient search; popular product recommendations; makeup tutorials; buying products
Experience suggestions for existing beauty apps	Personalised recommendations; enhanced professionalism; aesthetically pleasing interface; enhanced attention to special groups such as people with colour vision disorders
Expected features/requirements for a make-up app to assist people with abnormal colour vision	Avoidance of judgement by colour; assistance in matching colours; personalised recommendations for make-up and products; judgement of make-up success; guidance on make-up techniques
The effect of make-up on them	Confident; wants to try more on his own but has difficulty
Get beauty information and services through beauty APP, which is better than other kinds of APP	More focused beauty information and services; some more professional articles and analysis; more functionality: you can test skin quality, check product ingredients, etc. Search is more precise and saves users time

of colour vision abnormal conditions, the general attitude towards life can be summarised as being curious, having a wide range of hobbies and being positive. Six of the users interviewed said that they were more concerned with the quality of life. The target users also have the following characteristics and therefore have a demand for the use of supplementary beauty apps.

① The change in status or stage of life has led users to focus on the beauty sector. Seven of the interviewees said that after they entered university or postgraduate studies, they had more time for themselves and began to pay attention to their image and skin quality. Four of the interviewees said that when they were looking for a job or when they first joined the workforce, they actively sought help from friends, checked product reviews and beauty teaching videos to learn about make-up in order to make a good impression on others.

② They spend a lot of time online and are curious about new things. Ten of the users interviewed said that they spend more than an hour a day on their mobile phones for entertainment and leisure, sometimes three or four hours. Six of them said that watching beauty videos is sometimes relaxing, pleasing to the eye and satisfying their curiosity. When it comes to products they want to buy, the detailed product analysis in beauty apps can also satisfy their curiosity and help them choose products more rationally. Users have a positive outlook on beauty consumption and attitude towards life. All 10 users interviewed showed their approval of beauty product purchases during the interview. Beauty products make users more beautiful while enhancing their own sense of well-being.

(2) The target users like to use mainstream social, entertainment or beauty software to get beauty information and services, where the favorite beauty software is basically consistent with the results of the preliminary market research. The target users' favorite software to get beauty information and services are Weibo, Xiaohongshu, Beauty Fix, You Look Good Today, Youtube, bilibili, Taobao, Sephora, Meitou Beauty The most popular apps are Weibo, Xiaohongshu, Beauty Fix, You Look Good Today, Youtube, bilibili, Taobao, Sephora, Meitou Beauty, Beauty Camera and Zhihu. Among them, Little Red Book, Beauty Fix, You Look Good Today, Beauty Camera and Meitou Beauty are beauty software. However, there is no beauty software for people with abnormal colour vision, only functional software such as colour blindness tests and colour blindness cameras.

① Existing beauty software allows users to access a wide range of information and services in the beauty vertical. According to interviewed users, beauty software represented by Beauty Fix is more specialised in its content, allowing users to check the ingredients of products and thus judge their availability more precisely, effectively preventing them from choosing beauty products that are not suitable for them. Beauty software represented by "Xiaohongshu", in its content community, users can, on the one hand, meet people with the same hobby and exchange beauty tips with each other, and on the other hand, learn about the availability of skincare products or cosmetics through other users' sharing and reviews. Beauty software such as "You look great today" has a skin quality measurement function that allows users to quickly understand their own skin quality, and according to the characteristics of their skin type, products and precautions are precisely pushed, so that users can take fewer detours in the process of skincare. Some beauty software offers virtual online makeup trials to meet the needs of users who can experience the effects of cosmetics without leaving home.

② The low authenticity of the software content, poor accuracy of the features and the ease of use of the interface are the shortcomings of the existing beauty software user experience. While existing beauty communities showcase a large number of user tips and product reviews for those in need of beauty, the authenticity of the content cannot be determined. As beauty software is a must for major beauty brands to place advertisements and marketing, it is also a gathering place for internet celebrities and beauty experts to bring their products to the public. Users say that some beauty software has too many promotional and marketing advertisements, and the overall picture is cluttered with colours and indistinguishable information. Some beauty software has a deeper functional hierarchy, with the same sections appearing over and over again, making it difficult to distinguish the information hierarchy and making it more complicated for users to get started. Others are more skincare oriented and do not cover colour cosmetics, which is not functional enough and leads to single content. Other users say that although AI skin quality measurement is effective, the results are sometimes inaccurate.

③ There are no make-up products on the market for this group of people, and too many software programs have too many colours that are difficult to distinguish from each other, making it difficult to use.

People with colour vision problems are unable to choose the right products on their own and need help from friends. The intensity and variety of colours can change a lot in make-up, so they cannot rely on their friends for every aspect of the process. There are no complementary make-up products on the market for this group of people, and too many software programs have too many colours that are difficult to distinguish from each other, making it difficult to use.

(3) The problem that users still have in seeding products and learning make-up sessions is the lack of planning guidance. The target users say that most of the existing beauty software can only be used as information software for product shopping and comparison before purchase, and for people with abnormal colour vision, most of the other people's colour trials and comparisons are meaningless, and they cannot find the products that really suit them on the online app. The majority of users say they like to get their beauty information from Weibo and Xiaohongshu. They are more inclined to learn make-up techniques and receive product recommendations from beauty bloggers, but their inability to recognise colours leads them to blindly follow the trend and buy products that are not suitable for them. At the make-up stage, users say that there are many problems with their make-up: for example, they are too heavy on the eyeshadow, they are afraid to wear blush, their make-up colours are confusing, and so on. This can lead to them being embarrassed to go out with strange make-up or not knowing it at all, needing help from friends to find the right make-up style for them, and rarely trying new products because it takes more time to match them and they all wear the same make-up with the same products they are used to.

3.3 Modelling the Hierarchy of User Requirements

According to the research results, the user needs of the assisted make-up app for people with abnormal perception and the requirements of the AHP method were collated, and the evaluation problem was hierarchised according to the target layer, criterion layer and sub-criterion layer, and a hierarchical model of user needs was established (see Fig. 2). Guideline level indicators are denoted by H1, H2, H3 and H4, sub-criterion level indicators contained in H1 are denoted by H11, H12 and H13, and the same applies to the rest of the indicators.

A brief analysis of the requirements in the model shows that people with colour vision disorders are looking for an "inclusive visual representation" (H1) of the product, in terms of colour, visualisation of information and hierarchical differentiation to improve the visual experience. In the "reliable and practical functions" (H2) indicator, users' needs for software functionality are mainly focused on colour matching and contrast aids. "Auxiliary colour schemes" (H21) helps users to personalize their makeup

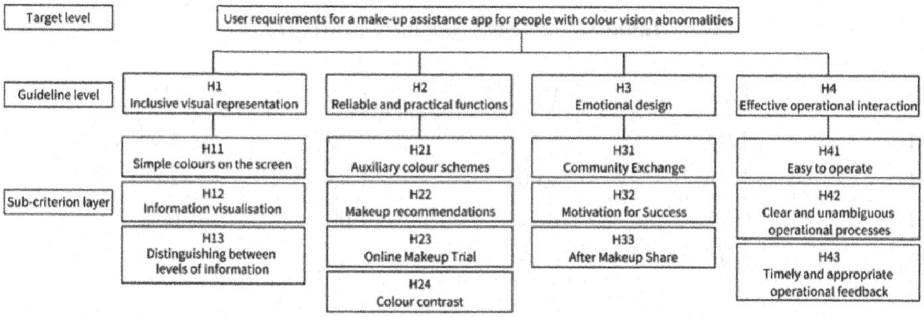

Fig. 2. Hierarchical structure model of user requirements.

with the right colour. "Makeup recommendations" (H22) helps to learn different makeup looks according to the occasion, giving the user a reliable and professional experience. "Online makeup trial" (H23) provides users with a more intuitive look, making it easy and intuitive to choose a look. "Colour contrast" (H24) assists in correcting the effect of the user's make-up and intelligently suggests the intensity of the colours, solving the user's make-up problems. For this particular group of users with colour vision abnormalities there is a need for "emotional design" (H3), including community communication, success motivation and post-makeup sharing. Acknowledging the user's make-up and encouraging sharing, sharing with friends, building positive emotions and enriching the make-up experience. This type of practical software requires "effective operational interaction" (H4) to guide the user through its use. Simple operation, clear procedures and timely feedback will make it less difficult for the user to use.

3.4 AHP-Based Demand Importance Analysis

The analysis of the importance of the demand for assisted make-up for people with colour vision abnormalities is a process of calculating the weights of the indicators of the hierarchical model of demand using AHP, and the weights are verified for consistency to obtain the importance of the demand for assisted make-up for people with colour vision abnormalities.

Ten designers, ophthalmologists, were invited to rate the guideline layer and sub-criterion layer indicators based on the scaling scale (Table 1) to derive the judgement matrix and indicator weights. The process of calculating the indicator weights is explained here, using indicator layers H1, H2, H3 and H4 as examples.

The opinions of the 10 experts were integrated using the geometric mean method, i.e. the 10 hij were aggregated into $h'ij$ and formed into an aggregated judgement matrix H', see Table 4. After processing the expert evaluation, the weights corresponding to the indicators are calculated according to the judgement matrix.

Table 4. Aggregate judgment matrix H'

H	H_1	H_2	H_3	H_4
H_1	1.00	0.82	2.03	1.05
H_2	1.21	1.00	1.83	2.30
H_3	0.49	0.54	1.00	0.41
H_4	0.95	0.43	2.43	1.00

The indicator weights from formulas (2)–(3) are W1 = 0.275 2, W2 = 0.355 6, W3 = 0.149 7 and W4 = 0.2262. Calculate the maximum characteristic root of the aggregate judgment matrix H' from formula (5) λmax is 4.09. According to Table 5, when n = 4, the corresponding *RI* is 0.89. According to formula (6)–(7), the consistency verification ratio *CR* is 0.037, which is less than 0.1, indicating that the consistency verification passed and the calculated index weight value is reasonable. In the same way, the sub-criterion level index weight is also calculated according to the above steps, and the comprehensive weight of each index is finally obtained (Table 6).

Table 5. Average stochastic consistency index RI (partial)

n	1	2	3	4	5	6	7	8	9
RI	0	0	0.52	0.89	1.12	1.26	1.36	1.41	1.46

The analysis of requirements importance results is as follows. Indicator weights help designers to capture the core needs of users, and the following data will be combined to further analyse the results of the importance of assisting people with colour vision abnormalities in their make-up needs.

(1) Reliable and practical functions are the primary needs that users expect to be met. The reliable and practical function (H2) in Table 4 has a weight of 0.355 6, and its subindicators auxiliary colour matching (H21) and colour contrast (H24) have higher weights, indicating that users prefer practical functions that can address make-up needs.
(2) Inclusive visual performance is the base point for aiding make-up and enhancing user experience. Inclusive visual representation (H1) is weighted second only to reliable and practical functionality (H2). Throughout the entire process of assisting people with colour vision abnormalities to apply make-up, inclusive visual representation focusing on the visual characteristics of the people is present in all aspects of the user's psychological and physical needs. Among its sub-indicators, information visualisation (H12) is given a high weighting.
(3) Intelligent services and pleasant visuals are the main psychological needs of users and are key to increasing the added value of the product and user pleasure. Effective interaction (H4) has a higher weighting than emotional design (H3), while timely

Table 6. Combined weights of demand indicators for the design of an app to assist make-up for people with colour vision abnormalities

	Guideline level	Weights	Sub-criterion layer	Partial weights	Combined weights	Sort
Complementary make-up needs for people with colour vision disorders	H1 Inclusive visual representation	0.2722	H11 Simple colours on the screen	0.1878	0.0612	9
			H12 Information visualisation	0.5418	0.1275	2
			H13 Distinguishing between levels of information	0.2703	0.0836	5
	H2 Reliable and practical functions	0.3556	H21 Auxiliary colour schemes	0.2418	0.0846	4
			H22 Makeup recommendations	0.1649	0.0785	6
			H23 Online Makeup Trial	0.1639	0.0498	10
			H24 Colour contrast	0.4294	0.1427	1
	H3 Emotional design	0.1360	H31 Community Exchange	0.2641	0.0357	12
			H32 Motivation for Success	0.5119	0.0696	7
			H33 After Makeup Share	0.2240	0.0305	13
	H4 Effective operational interaction	0.2362	H41 Easy to operate	0.2010	0.0475	11
			H42 Clear and unambiguous operational processes	0.2736	0.0647	8

(*continued*)

Table 6. (*continued*)

	Guideline level	Weights	Sub-criterion layer	Partial weights	Combined weights	Sort
			H43 Timely and appropriate operational feedback	0.5252	0.1241	3

and appropriate feedback (H43) is in 3rd place in the overall indicator weighting, above the remaining 10 sub-indicators.

4 Interactive Design Practice of Auxiliary Makeup APP for People with Abnormal Color Perception Based on the Concept of "Inclusive Design"

Firstly, an inclusive design idea is proposed based on a preliminary analysis of the need for assisted make-up for people with colour vision abnormalities. Then, the interaction design is developed by using the more important user requirements as the main reference for the design solution and combining them with other requirements.

4.1 Inclusive Design Thinking

Inclusive visual presentation is the 2nd ranked need in the overall indicator weighting, so the visual characteristics of people with colour vision disorders need to be taken into account in the design of the content of the screen in terms of colour, information and hierarchy. Even for people with colour vision impairment, colour remains an easy and quick way to differentiate between different types of data. The recognisability and legibility of information graphics is improved by

(1) Not relying exclusively on colour to differentiate information, while using multiple visual variables to encode information.
(2) Choosing a safe colour scheme.
(3) Use of textual annotations.

The user research shows that the target users are unable to correctly perceive and distinguish the colour of certain areas, and that even if the colour is changed so that the user can distinguish it, the true visual effect cannot be restored. The make-up is categorised and pushed in a targeted way, with colour comparison and correction assistance after the user has applied the make-up. The main functions of the product are divided into three main sections: intelligent entry of make-up and skin type information, colour matching recommendations and after make-up comparison assistance.

4.2 Interaction Design for a Make-Up Aid for People with Colour Vision Disorders

The interaction design of the make-up aid app for people with colour vision abnormalities is based on user needs and their prioritised results to achieve an upgraded user experience. The user requirements of high importance "colour contrast" (H24), "information visualization" (H12) and "timely and operational feedback" (H43) are taken as the main reference for the design and combined with other requirements for the solution design (see Fig. 3).

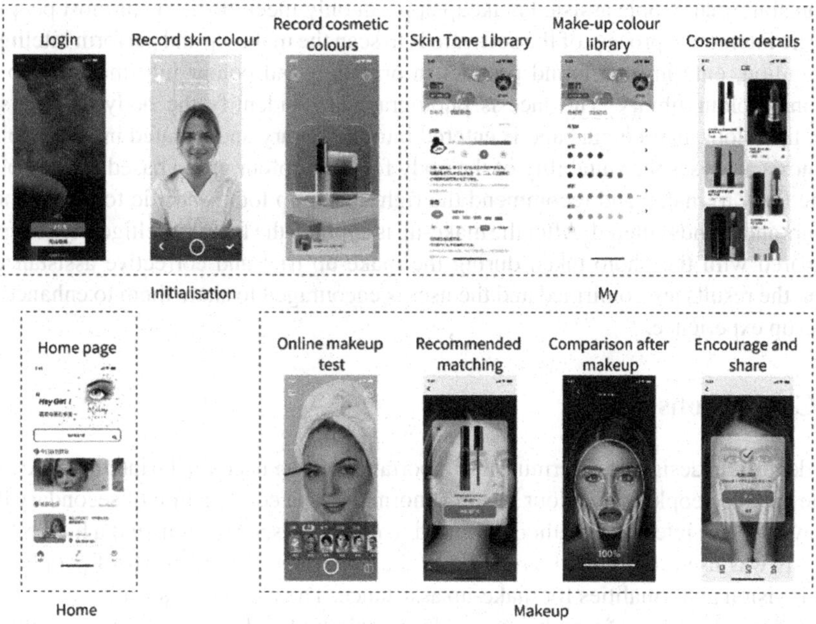

Fig. 3. APP interface (partial)

The software is divided into 4 modules: "Initialisation", "Home", "My" and "Make-up". Body colour includes skin tone, hair colour and pupil colour, while cosmetic information includes brand and brand colour number, and the colour will be entered into the App's colour library to provide colour matching during the make-up process. The "Home" section includes: search for make-up styles, make-up recommendations and a community forum. It mainly provides users with information and services related to beauty products, recommends various styles of make-up daily and provides a search function and a collection of favourite make-ups. The community forum provides a platform for users to share beauty content and to exchange makeup styles through friends' sharing. On the "My" page, users can manage their personal information, including their skin tone and lip colour, in addition to their basic information. The colour library includes the cosmetic colours entered by the user, in addition to which the user can add new cosmetic information by clicking on the "+" button. The make-up interface is based on the principles of inclusive design, with people at the heart of the design process. The main focus is on the make-up needs of people with abnormal colour perception, with targeted functions such as auxiliary colour matching and colour contrast to assist make-up application, personalised make-up recommendations and the diversity of user needs. Through an inclusive visual performance and practical functions to address user needs. Step 1: Users can choose their favourite make-up to try on; Step 2: After choosing the make-up, the interface will display specific information about the make-up match; Step 3: After the make-up is done, the system compares the colour of the trial make-up and the make-up afterwards and reminds to correct it, after the comparison is confirmed to be successful, go to Step 4: Users can choose the make-up to share. Such a colour vision abnormal people assisted makeup app can only meet the needs of most people.

The interactive process of the software is to scan the make-up and perform intelligent recognition, entering the brand product information and colour information into the personal colour library. The face is photographed to identify the body colour (skin tone, lip colour, hair colour) and is entered into the library and updated in time. Colour diagnosis analyses the suitability of the body for each colour group based on the colour of the body to match and recommend the right make-up look, specific to the cosmetic colours and brands entered. After the make-up is applied, the face is intelligently scanned, compared with the photo taken during the make-up trial and corrective assistance is given, the results are confirmed and the user is encouraged to share them to enhance the make-up experience.

5 Conclusions

In order to help designers determine the importance of user needs in the interaction design of the app for people with colour vision abnormalities, a combination of secondary data survey and user interview method was used to conduct user research, and a hierarchical analysis was used to obtain the ranking of the importance of the needs of people with colour vision abnormalities for make-up assistance. The method was validated by using the interaction design of a make-up app for people with colour vision abnormalities as an example. The results show that the method is able to determine the importance of design factors and is applicable to the interaction design of an app for people with colour vision abnormalities. The main conclusions are as follows.

(1) In this paper, an interaction design method for a make-up app for people with colour vision abnormalities is proposed based on user needs. A combination of secondary data survey and user interview method is used to derive user requirements, and the AHP method is used to quantitatively analyse and calculate the weighting of user requirements, determine the weighting and ranking of each design element in user requirements, and obtain the key design factors to guide the solution design.

(2) With the aim of exploring user needs and improving user experience, this method partially fills the gap that exists in the field of make-up assistance design for people with colour vision abnormalities, fully explores the psychological and physiological needs of people with colour vision abnormalities in make-up, and establishes a systematic system of make-up assistance user needs for people with colour vision abnormalities.

(3) Guided by the concept of "inclusive design", this paper distils the design factors that influence make-up assistance for people with colour vision disorders, and provides new ideas and theoretical support for the interaction design of make-up assistance apps for people with colour vision disorders. The results of this study will help developers and designers of human-computer interaction interfaces to make decisions and optimise human-computer interaction solutions for people with colour vision disorders.

The design analysis has only been carried out on a limited number of research samples and will be expanded to refine the design and further adapt the solution in conjunction with market research. The design will also be tested with an HCI eye-tracking device to verify that the design is working effectively and to make improvements to better suit the needs of users.

References

1. Coleman, R.: The case for inclusive design-an overview. In: Proceedings of the 12th Triennial Congress. International Ergonomics Association and the Human Factors Association, Canada (1994)
2. Goodman-Deane, J., Ward, J., Hosking, I., et al.: A comparison of methods currently used in inclusive design. Appl. Ergon. **45**(4), 886–894 (2014)
3. Zhao, C.: Design for ageing: an inclusive stance and critical attitude. ZHUANGSHI **09**, 16–21 (2012)
4. Chen, M.Y., Chen, D.P., Chu, X.N.: Identification for product service system redesign modules based on user experience. Comput. Integr. Manuf. Syst. **22**(11), 2522–2529 (2016)
5. Zhang, B.C., Wang, Y.Q., Yang, Y.L., et al.: Role modeling design of ASD children's picture books based on visual tips. Packag. Eng. **41**(22), 244–250 (2020)
6. Zhang, D.F.: Usability evaluation method of human computer interface of stereoscopic garage based on FAHP. J. Mach. Des. **31**(4), 97–100 (2014)
7. Kulakowski, K.: Understanding the Analytic Hierarchy Process. CRC Press, Boca Raton (2020)
8. Hou, S.J., Liu, J.C., Sun, K.: Design and evaluation of hospital escort beds based on AHP-FCE. Packag. Eng. **40**(24), 174–178 (2019)

A Novel Experiment Design for Vision-Based Fatigue Detection

Doreen Jirak[1(✉)], Giulia Belgiovine[1], Omar Eldardeer[1], and Francesco Rea[2]

[1] Contact Unit, Istituto Italiano di Tecnologia, Genoa, Italy
doreen.jirak@iit.it
[2] RBCS, Istituto Italiano di Tecnologia, Genoa, Italy

Abstract. Manufacturing companies continuously integrate robots for collaboration with human workers. That challenges the design of a safe and ergonomic worker's place to avoid collisions with the robot or other possible accidents that can severely injure a human. As many tasks in manufacturing premises entail repetitive tasks like carrying heavy loads back and forth over a long period, one critical aspect that the industry focuses on is the detection of human fatigue state. While the literature targets bio-markers like the arousal state or measures deviations in the walking or carrying pattern using inertial measurement units (IMU) or other body sensors, studies considering a vision-based approach are sparse. Additionally, the usage of specific body devices demands individual calibration and is prone to errors in the sensor readings. Therefore, we introduce and explain in detail a novel experimental protocol for fatigue induction in humans performing a bucket load-carry task. The experimental design considers only a camera setup (RGB and neuromorphic) that records the face and posture of each participant, delivering data applicable for feature extraction and the development of a fatigue detection module at a later stage. Finally, we provide some preliminary evaluation from the pilot study obtained from the Swedish Occupancy Fatigue Inventory (SOFI) questionnaire.

Keywords: Human-Robot Collaboration · Experimental Design · Muscular Fatigue

1 Introduction

Among various definitions, the Canadian Center for Occupational Health and Safety (CCOHS)[1] [4] defines fatigue as follows: "Fatigue is often thought of as the state of feeling very tired, weary or sleepy resulting from various sources such as insufficient sleep, prolonged mental or physical work, or extended periods of stress or anxiety. Boring or repetitive tasks can intensify feelings of fatigue. Fatigue can be described as either acute or chronic". Fatigue can be separated into *active* fatigue when, e.g., working with a heavy load, *passive* fatigue when performing repetitive tasks (e.g. working at a conveyor belt), and *sleep-related* fatigue which is present when working in shifts that disrupt the circadian rhythm.

[1] https://www.ccohs.ca/.

M. Antona and C. Stephanidis (Eds.): HCII 2023, LNCS 14020, pp. 390–398, 2023.
https://doi.org/10.1007/978-3-031-35681-0_25

The consequences of fatigue are manifold [13,16] and can be summarized as follows:

- Decline in physical condition
- Musculoskeletal disorders (MSD): Muscles stress, chronic pain in bones (e.g., lower back pain) and joints (knee)
- Decline in reaction times and attention
- Decline in other cognitive functions like memory
- Impact on cardiovascular functions: increased heart rate and variability
- Other clinical aspects: burnout, depression, etc.

Especially in the industrial context where workers are exposed to heavy machinery and collaborate with robots, fatigue can lead to severe accidents, faulty operations of machines, and errors in the production line. Also, fatigue and its consequences can have a prolonged impact on an employee's health status. Therefore, it is essential to determine the kinematic and physiological parameters that characterize fatigue. Standard approaches to detect fatigue in humans comprise applying body sensors to measure electrodermal activity, muscle activity, acceleration patterns using inertial measurement units, and the heart rate variability. For instance, [15] recorded muscular activity from IMU and heart rate from a Shimmer device[2] in a manufacturing environment from 8 participants performing low to high fatigue-inducing task such as material assembling, pick up&insertion objects in a box, and manual material handling using two hands. The authors extracted features from jerk and acceleration computations, which revealed that the wrist and torso features provide the most descriptive information to distinguish a fatigued state from non-fatigued state (fatigue detection). For the selection of a predictive model, the wrist, hip, and ankle movements showed the best discriminative features and were used for the long term prediction of fatigue levels. [14] analysed the muscle activity using surface electromyogram (sEMG) and motion capturing during repetitive lifting tasks. The authors focused on identifying activity patterns before and in a fatigued state specific to the lower back as this are is vulnerable to pain and might need attention for the development of injury prevention strategies. While the authors confirm certain level of fatigue based on the heart, respiration, and perspiration, the sEMG data could not suggest fatigue level differences. The obtained results suggest some limitations to the sensor capacity resulting in a low signal-to-noise ratio and selectivity of body areas that impact the sensor recordings (low-fat areas, muscle bundles). [9] presented a study on manual handling tasks over a long period of standing (up to 5 h) and revealed significant differences in the muscular twitch force (MTF) and center of pressure (COP) displacement speed. The results indicate posture variability in a muscular fatigue state which, consequently, may alter the movements in the hip and lower-back region, causing muscular disorders in the long term. As fatigue parameters can differ among humans based on their health status and disposition, fatigue studies also rely on self-reports using, e.g., the Borg rating of perceived exertion (RPE) [3] or

[2] https://shimmersensing.com/wearable-sensor-products/.

the Swedish Occupational Fatigue Inventory questionnaire (SOFI) [1] that we selected for our paper. However, the sensor calibrations necessary for each individual, cables, and on-body devices hinder the application of fatigue detection in real industrial use cases. Hence, a contactless, vision-based approach would be a better candidate. Our literature search revealed that vision-based studies analyzing fatigue in humans are sparse and rather dedicated to driver's fatigue [7,17] As a consequence, no publicly available datasets exist until now. Therefore, we set up a novel experiment for fatigue detection in an industrial setting using only RGB cameras and a neuromorphic camera. We hypothesize that with the camera setup we are able to detect relevant fatigue parameters in the human body and face, for example:

1. Face:
   - Eyes: closing patterns, blink frequency ([6])
   - Mouth: yawning, strained lips ([11])
   - Arousal-Valence level obtained from compositional facial expressions ([2])
2. Body ([8]):
   - Deviations in body posture (especially shoulder, hips, knees)
   - "crouche" posture
3. Gait ([12]):
   - Increase/decrease of step width, step width variability
   - Discontinuous walking pattern, walking variability

2 Experimental Design and Setup

As the present research is embedded within the greater scope of the VOJEXT project[3], we defined the experimental task to be a typical use case and simulate a worker's routine task, specifically carrying heavy buckets with two hands back and forth and lifting them on a table. The selected load weights were within the range of most lifting tasks, according to an assessment of over 1000 lifting tasks in workplaces in the United States [5]. Each participant was asked to perform the experiment with a specific weight defined during the "user profile" phase. Figures 1 and 2 demonstrate the lab settings.

The designed protocol consisted of the following phases:

1. **Baseline and users-profiling:** We started the experimental session by asking participants for personal information such as age, biological sex, height and weight, sports practiced, and training habits. Then we asked them to stand in front of the cameras to record their "natural" posture and walking style.
2. **Familiarization phase (no weights):** Each participant had a 5-minute familiarisation or warm-up period, which consisted of performing the main task without loads. Specifically, they had to walk between two desks carrying two empty buckets (one in each hand); once at the desk, participants had to place the buckets on the floor and lift them onto the table (one by one). In this lifting phase,

[3] https://vojext.eu/.

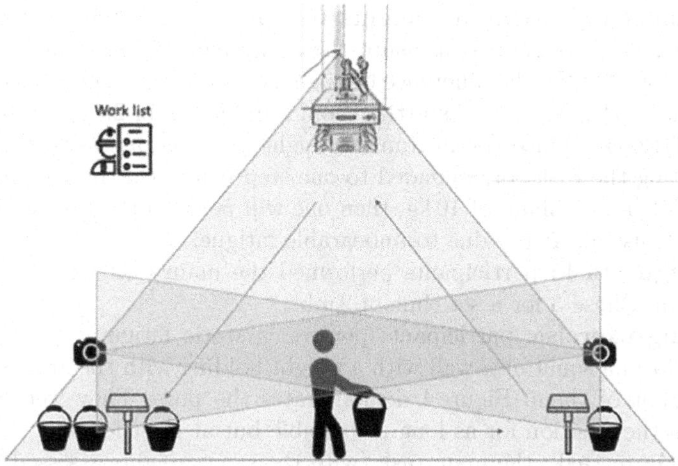

Fig. 1. Sketch of the experimental setup in the lab showing the cameras that record the participant's face and a (neuromorphic) camera mounted on a robot capturing the body pose.

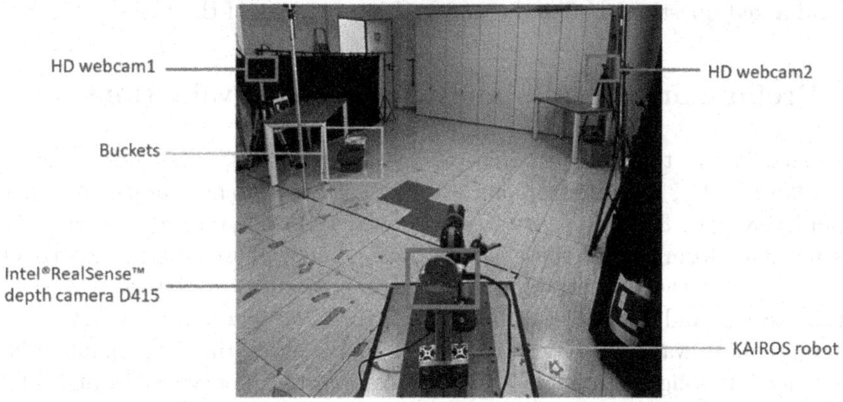

Fig. 2. Experimental setup in the real lab (lateral view) showing the KAIROS robot used in manufacturing environments for human-robot collaborative tasks.

participants had to use a particular strategy, i.e., grab the bucket by the handle with both hands and lift it in the squat position. The same applies when dropping the buckets from the desk to the floor. Figure 3 shows one image from the recorded data for this phase for one participant. They must repeat this operation for the set time of 2 min. The standardization of the motor strategy was necessary to avoid fatigue features being dependent on that, but also to prevent accidents due to incorrect postures/movements. This phase also helped the participants to familiarise themselves with the task.

3. **Assessment of maximum weights to carry:** Participants were asked to lift incremental weights to measure the equivalent of Maximum Voluntary Contraction (MVC); the difference between two successive weights to be lifted was set at 2.5 kg (per arm), starting from a minimum of 2.5 kg up to a maximum of 12.5 kg. Once the maximum weight has been assessed, the weights used during the task corresponded to one step before this maximum (e.g., if one can lift a maximum of 10 kg, then one will perform the task with 7.5 kg) to avoid muscle collapse due to unbearable fatigue.
4. **Pre-fatigue task:** participants performed the main task with the weights assessed in Phase 3 for a set time of 2 min.
5. **Fatiguing exercise**: participants perform a static fatiguing task in which they perform a squat at a wall with a weight holding with the arms stretched out in front of them. Figure 4 demonstrates the pose. They were asked to maintain the position for as long as possible but at least for 30 s.
6. **Post-fatigue task:** the main task (with the same weights assessed in Phase 3) was repeated for other 2 min.
7. **Questionnaires and debriefing:** each participant self-evaluated the fatigue level by filling in the Swedish Occupational Fatigue Inventory (SOFI) questionnaire [1]. Then, the experimenter explained the aim of the experiment and asked questions about the personal impressions of the task.

3 Preliminary Results and Qualitative Evaluations

Ten participants took part in this pilot study (5 males, 5 females, mean age 26.6 years $\pm$ 1.96), recruited among students and researchers at the IIT institution. However, 3 participants were dropped from the dataset as there were missing data from one of the cameras during some phases of the experiment. The weights of the buckets used during the pre and post-fatigue phases varied between 5 and 12.5 kg each bucket (8.75 $\pm$ 2.53). The bucket weight in the fatiguing phase was 2.5 or 5 kg (4.255 $\pm$ 1.25). We asked the participant to hold the weight as long as possible and this phase varied between 37 s and 1 min. Additionally, we also collected qualitative feedback from the participants about their experience with the task and which part they feel fatigued more. After the exercise of the fatiguing phase, some of the participants reported feeling more fatigued in the arms, while some others reported being more fatigued in the legs.

Fig. 3. Example image from the recorded dataset showing a participant during the familiarization phase (no weights).

Fig. 4. Example image showing the physical exercise (squats) between the pre and the post-fatigue phase.

The SOFI questionnaire is a self-reporting questionnaire that examines physical and mental fatigue. It is one of the most popular fatigue evaluations in the research and industry of ergonomics [10]. It consists of 20 items categorized into

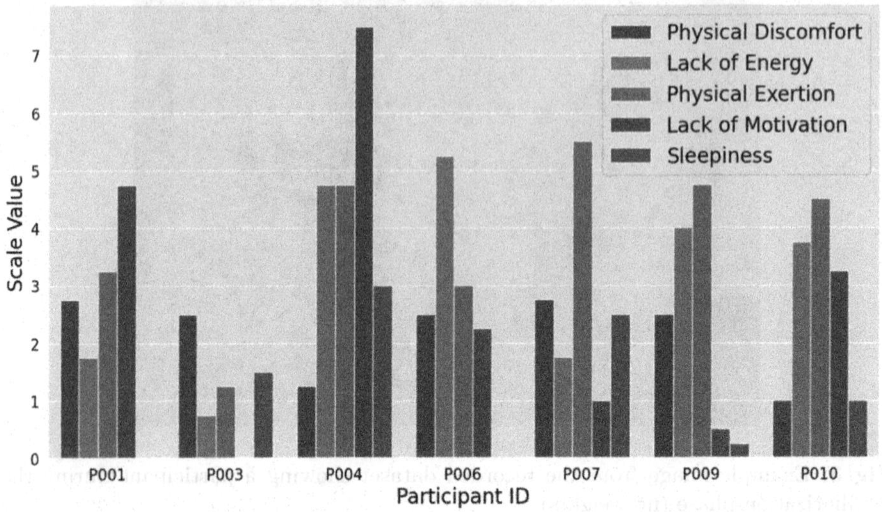

Fig. 5. Scores obtained from each participant for each item in the SOFI questionnaire. Note that for participant P003 the "lack of motivation" is 0.

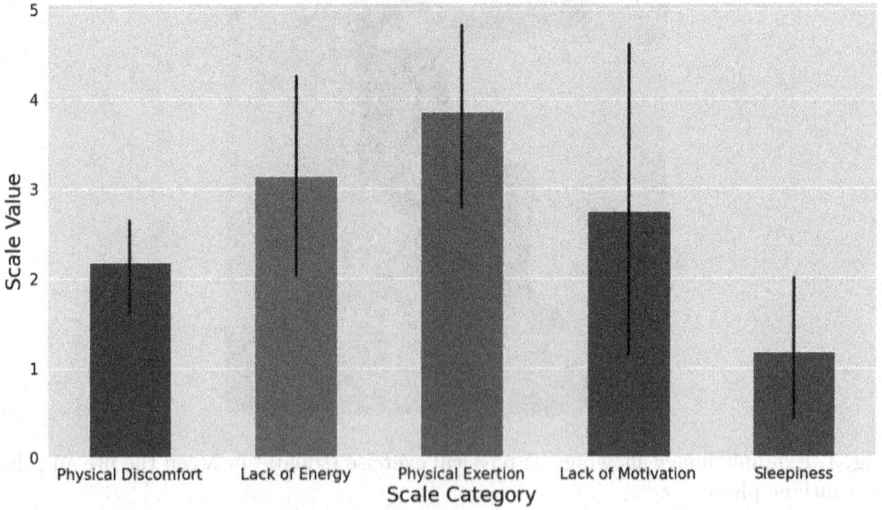

Fig. 6. Average score for each sub-scale of the fatigue questionnaire across all the participants.

five sub-scales (4 items each) corresponding to different fatigue categories. The categories are: *Lack of Energy*, *Physical Exertion*, *Physical Discomfort*, *Lack of Motivation*, and *Sleepiness*. The response format for each item was a 10 points Likert scale. Figure 5 shows the scores reported by each participant at the end of the experiment for each sub-scale of the questionnaire. As can be observed, there was quite a variability in the way participants reported feeling fatigued, with some of them (e.g., participants 1 and 4) reporting higher scores for *Lack of Motivation* item, and others reporting higher scores for more physical-related factors, such as *Lack of Energy* (e.g., participant 6) or *Physical Exertion* (e.g., participants 7, 9, 10). On average, these last two factors seem to have been the most descriptive of the overall state of the participants, as can also be appreciated from Fig. 6, which shows the average scores of each fatigue subscale among all participants.

4 Discussion and Conclusion

Fatigue in workers performing physically demanding and repetitive work negatively impacts the human's health status and can potentially increase the risk of errors and accidents during a work shift. Especially in the industrial context, where collaborative tasks with robots become a daily routine, the detection of fatigue is crucial for safe and ergonomic interactions. The majority of studies on physical fatigue in the current research literature focus on wearable sensors which need individual calibrations and are error-prone to noise or cost-intensive motion capture systems. Additionally, both settings can not be implemented beyond laboratory settings. In contrast, our research aims to identify critical facial and body parameters showing the onset and evolution of fatigue states in humans performing repetitive tasks with heavy loads similar to real manufacturing settings. Therefore, we presented a novel experiment for fatigue detection using only a camera setup that allows the extraction of face and posture features. Our experiment design includes clear explanations of the task and the selection of weights to avoid overcompensation strategies. Our preliminary results on the SOFI questionnaire confirm a higher level for *Lack of Energy* and *Physical Exertion* among the participants. However, we also obtained high variance across the participants, which can be explained by their low number (N=7) and some limitations observed during and post hoc the experiment. For instance, the experimental protocol defined a fixed time for the performance in the pre and post-fatigue phases. The participants' speed while performing the task varied (i.e., some were faster than others and performed the single round of carrying and lifting tasks more times). Thus, the starting point in the pre and post-fatigue phases was sometimes not the same (e.g., a participant started at one table with camera 1 in the pre-fatigue phase and at another table with camera 2 in the post-fatigue phase), which caused asynchronous data between participants. Consequently, when evaluating features from the data, e.g., the head or eye gaze directions, additional computations of respective offsets between the starts and the cameras are needed. Furthermore, we believe that the SOFI scores show some levels of fatigue which might have been induced only by the exercise between the pre and post-fatigue, i.e. the scores do not necessarily reflect substantial muscle fatigue as the experiment duration was rather short. Therefore, we suggest implementing longer physical exercises and task sessions for the fatigue induction, which would also allow the extraction of fatigue levels (e.g., mild, medium, high) that are easier to monitor and resemble better real scenarios for human workers than a binary fatigue detection task. Finally, a larger number of participants is necessary in order to validate our experimental protocol and find patterns that can generalize the fatigue state of a user, irrespective of subjective and personal factors.

References

1. Åhsberg, E., Fürst, C.J.: Dimensions of fatigue during radiotherapy-an application of the Swedish Occupational Fatigue Inventory (SOFI) on cancer patients. In: Acta Oncologica 40.1, pp. 37–43 (2001)
2. Balasundaram, A., et al.: Computer vision based fatigue detection using facial parameters. In: IOP Conference Series: Materials Science and Engineering, vol. 981. 2, p. 022005. IOP Publishing (2020)
3. Borg, G.: Borg's perceived exertion and pain scales. Human kinetics (1998)
4. Caldwell, J.C., et al.: Fatigue and its management in the workplace. Neurosci. Biobehav. Rev. **96**, 272–289 (2019)
5. Dempsey, P.G.: A survey of lifting and lowering tasks. Int. J. Ind. Ergon. **31**(1), 11–16 (2003)
6. Divjak, M., Bischof, H.: Eye blink based fatigue detection for prevention of computer vision syndrome. In: MVA, pp. 350–353 (2009)
7. Du, G., et al.: Vision-based fatigue driving recognition method integrating heart rate and facial features. IEEE Trans. Intell. Transp. Syst. **22**(5), 3089–3100 (2020)
8. Fuller, J.R., et al.: Posture-movement changes following repetitive motioninduced shoulder muscle fatigue. J. Electromyograph. Kinesiol. **19**(6), 1043–1052 (2009)
9. Garcia, M.-G., Läubli, T., Martin, B.J.: Longterm muscle fatigue after standing work. Hum. Factors **57**(7), 1162–1173 (2015)
10. González Gutiérrez, J.L., et al.: Spanish version of the Swedish occupational fatigue inventory (SOFI): factorial replication, reliability and validity. Int. J. Ind. Ergon. **35**(8), 737–746 (2005)
11. Haque, M.A., et al.: Facial video-based detection of physical fatigue for maximal muscle activity. IET Comput. Vis. **10**(4), 323–330 (2016)
12. Hu, X., et al.: Effects of backpack load on spatiotemporal turning gait parameters. Int. J. Ind. Ergon. **95**, 103443 (2023)
13. Lerman, S.E., et al.: Fatigue risk management in the workplace. J. Occupational Environ. Med. **54**(2), 231–258 (2012)
14. Li, X., et al.: A framework for evaluating muscle activity during repetitive manual material handling in construction manufacturing. Autom. Construct. **79**, 39–48 (2017)
15. Maman, Z.S., et al.: A data-driven approach to modeling physical fatigue in the workplace using wearable sensors. Appl. Ergon. **65**, 515–529 (2017)
16. Sadeghniiat-Haghighi, K., Yazdi, Z.: Fatigue management in the workplace. Ind. Psychiatry J.**24**(1), 12 (2015)
17. Yao, K.P.: Real-time vision-based driver drowsiness, fatigue detection system. In: IEEE 71st Vehicular Technology Conference. IEEE, vol. 2010, pp. 1–5 (2010)

Data Visualization Accessibility for Blind and Low Vision Audiences

Chloe Keilers, Garreth W. Tigwell, and Roshan L. Peiris(✉)

School of Information, Rochester Institute of Technology, Rochester, NY 14623, USA
{cmk4967,garreth.W.Tigwell,roshan.peiris}@rit.edu

Abstract. While data visualizations have the potential to convey vast quantities of information, they are not always accessible to audiences with vision impairments. We prepared and distributed an online survey to blind and low vision adults to investigate the accessibility of data visualizations across the following five mediums—computers, phones, tablets, paper, TVs. After analyzing 45 survey responses, we identified that the inaccessibility is pervasive and that people want to interpret data independently. At present, data visualizations are largely inaccessible to blind and low vision users; however, it is possible to improve accessibility with intentional design.

Keywords: BLV · blind · low vision · graphics · visualization · accessibility

1 Introduction

Data visualizations are ubiquitous, from our paper's bar charts to the latest health department pandemic statistics [11,26]. Visualizations use visual features to convey meaningful information to an audience [20,29]. People who are blind, have low vision, color vision deficiency, etc. might not be able to access or perceive visualization features, and, therefore, miss what the visualization conveys, which could be a critical communication barrier. An inaccessible pandemic graph released by a newspaper or health outlet may deprive blind and low vision people of vital information in the middle of a health crisis [11]. Designing accessible visualizations and tools not only make this information available to a wider audience but may even be required to meet legal and Americans with Disabilities Act (ADA) requirements [1]. For visualizations to be accessible, they must first be detectable and then provide summaries of data trends, freedom to explore details, and meaningful context [17].

Some options for blind people to access graphs include screen readers, tactile charts, and magnification. Screen reader users could access data visualization via a high level summary in alternative text (alt text) [16] or by navigating tabular data [25]. Accessing charts with screen readers takes twice as long for users to understand when compared to non-screen reader users [24]. Tactile devices convey charts through embossment, haptics, and braille annotations [14]; however,

M. Antona and C. Stephanidis (Eds.): HCII 2023, LNCS 14020, pp. 399–413, 2023.
https://doi.org/10.1007/978-3-031-35681-0_26

these are expensive, difficult to find, and time-consuming to create or automate [9].

In this research, we investigate the current state of data visualization accessibility across several mediums from a Blind and Low Vision (BLV) users' perspectives and propose several recommendations for approaching accessible data visualization. For this purpose, we created and distributed a survey to answer the research question "What are the accessibility perspectives of a BLV users on access data visualizations across different mediums?". As our main contributions, in our findings with 74 BLV survey participants, we found that blind and low vision people consider data visualizations across all mediums to be inaccessible and poorly designed and, these users desire more independent alternatives to access data visualizations.

2 Related Work

Data visualization is the visual representation of a data set [29]. Data visualizations appear everywhere from daily newspapers to online scientific papers, ranging from simple line graphs to complex interactive graphs with multiple axes. There are many approaches to make data visualization accessible for blind or low vision audiences, both technological and methodological. While there are many studies that investigate the specific technologies and methods used to access a data visualization, there are few qualitative studies that investigate the current practices and perspectives of blind and low vision people.

2.1 Data Visualization

Many data visualizations appear in professional settings such as scientific literature, business reports, and engineering diagrams, and those visualizations are powerful tools that have become more available with the rise and increasing prevalence of computer graphics and mass media [10]. Data visualizations are used to inform and enhance what the data is saying, from a phone's battery status icon to a timeline graph of stocks to the seven day rolling average of COVID-19 cases [11,26]. Data visualizations have informed populations, highlighted issues, and help changed health care throughout history [7,23]. Two early examples include John Snow's map of 1854 cholera outbreaks that showed a link between the disease and water [10] and Florence Nightingale's 1858 pie chart showing preventable deaths as a result of lack of sanitation as the leading cause of army fatalities [10]. Outside of healthcare, data visualizations help people make better informed decision in everyday life, such as the New York City metro map transporting commuters and tourists alike efficiently [21].

Ware [29] describes comprehending data visualization first by having a "problem to be solved," then carrying out a "visual search" to answer the initial query. A graph exists to display data for the users to draw their own conclusions. The user's comprehension and conclusion rely heavily on the visual characteristics of the graphs [20]. To make data visualizations more accessible to blind people, the format and visual characteristics of the graph must be available, while also providing blind people the freedom to explore the graph to answer their own questions.

2.2 Current Technology for Accessibility

Numerous methods and technologies aim to make data visualizations accessible to BLV people by using either tactile or aural interfaces. Kim et al. [17] surveyed available literature and put forward a visualization accessibility model where accessible is "notifying the existence of a chart, providing an overview of the chart, offering details only when requested, [and] conveying the context when necessary and helpful." Several methods use combinations of these technologies. When viewed under the accessibility model, each technology has different strengths and weaknesses.

Screen Readers: Alt Text: Screen readers are widely available as they need no particular hardware beyond a computer and speaker. The most common method used by screen readers to handle images is to read the image's alt text. Jung et al. [16] surveyed and interviewed blind people on how alt text is currently used and could be improved for data visualizations by testing four styles of alt text: brief descriptions, detailed descriptions, data trends, and raw data points. Jung et al. concluded that more detailed alt text and access to raw data points were the preferred options. Participants mentioned their desire to access data freely and to know the chart type and visual features [16]. A single alt text may not provide sufficient freedom to explore a chart on its own; however, it could provide a high-level summary while being leveraged with other methods to explore the data.

Screen Readers: Others Screen readers in combination with other tools increase opportunities to read graphs. A study by Godfrey et al. [12] explores the creation and exploration of data visualization by screen reader users in the R statistical programming language. Using R and screen readers, participants could not only create graphs but also explore the data interactively. While their study showed screen readers' important utility, they are not perfect. Sharif et al. [24] found that if screen readers detect a graph it takes twice as long for users to understand, and with less accuracy, when compared to non-screen reader users. This is due to screen readers, relatively one-dimensional devices, reporting every label and x-y coordinate for each data point. Additionally, the performance and capabilities of screen readers can have an impact on the user's understanding. Beal et al. [2] studied an iPad math app and noted that VoiceOver screen readers read fraction "1/4" as "one slash four" as opposed to "one over four" or "one fourth". Screen readers do not read or speak the same as humans do. While screen readers are widely available, they alone cannot provide full access to data visualizations.

Tactile Devices. Tactile devices convey graphs through textures, embossments, braille annotations, and 3-D prints [14]. Unfortunately, tactile charts are not only expensive and more difficult to find, but they are also more time-consuming to create as Engel and Weber [9] show when attempting to automate the task.

Touch screens are also popular due to their widespread commercial availability. They open more visualizations opportunities, especially when combined with audio or haptic methods. Beal and Rosenblum [2] tested an iPad app with tactile graphs to teach blind and low vision students mathematics, taking advantage of Apple's VoiceOver to help students interact with the display. In this case, the tablet functions as a screen reader with a touch interface to provide more details about graphs.

Low Vision Aids. Low vision aids include various magnification devices which may improve accessibility for low vision users [18]. Additionally, most computers and phones have built-in zoom options or accessibility features to change the colors of a screen. Low vision and color blind users use magnifiers to enlarge or enhance the image.

Optical Recognition. Optical character recognition (OCR) pulls text from pictures to make it accessible to computers and by extension to people with screen readers. The U.S. Government Printing Office found that, for images with printed text, the OCR accuracy rate hovers above 98% [3]. For more complicated images and environments, artificial intelligence (AI) has been applied to improving image processing and recognition. Granquist et al. [13] tested two AI vision aids to read warped text, such as a soup can label, from images with 13-57% accuracy.

2.3 Creation of Data Visualization

When creating data visualizations, there are two ways to make them accessible: first, give the power and tools to blind and low vision audience to create data visualizations themselves from raw data, second, educate and support creators to design more accessible visualizations. In addition to Godfrey et al.'s [12] R statistical programming language, there are several tools that enable screen readers to interpret code that create and read data visualizations [5,27].

Heer et al. [15] discussed a wide array of different data visualization types and what considerations should take place when choosing how to visualize and present data. They strongly encourage simpler data visualizations when possible and emphasized that "the DNA underlying all visualizations remains the same; the principled mapping of data variables to visual features such as position, size, shape, and color" [15]. While complex and interactive data visualizations are harder to make accessible, this "mapping" of data to visual features is also an important consideration to making any visualization accessible. [6] recommended some design guidelines based on how blind "Orientation & Mobility" instructors build a mental model of space.

After a data visualization is created, a set of heuristics principles could be applied to check and fix inaccessible designs. Web Content Accessibility Guidelines (WCAG) 2.0 have been adopted by U.S. courts as the website accessibility standards [28]. The first WCAG originated when the internet was less media heavy and has been slow to adapt to changing technology and internet usage [19]. More recently, Elavsky et al. [8] created a set of heuristic principles for visualization accessibility called Chartability. Chartability starts with four heuristics principles from WCAG: Perceivable, Operable, Understandable, and Robust (POUR); while introducing three more principles: Compromising, Assistive, and Flexible (CAF).

2.4 Summary

As observed here, accessible data visualizations is a topic that has been explored widely. In summary, while many researches have explored the usability of existing methods for BLV people accessing data visualizations, several studies have proposed methods that use techniques such as haptics for presenting accessible data visualizations to BLV people. Thus, in our research, we examine BLV peoples' perspectives on the accessibility of data visualizations across several mediums and discuss their preferences and requirements, as well as present recommendations for when developing new methods in the future.

3 Survey

To determine the most popular, accessible, and user-friendly method to access graphs, we created and distributed a survey for adult blind and low vision participants. Our survey gathered information on current technology usage and data visualization practices. We had 25 questions—five multiple-choice and 20 text. We scrubbed text responses and grouped shorter quantitative answers into appropriate categories. Longer text fields required more qualitative thematic analysis [4]. We posted and emailed the survey to various internet groups and organizations for blind and low vision people. The survey was anonymous, but the respondent could enter a $15 USD lottery if they chose to.

We collected 74 responses over two months. Out of the 74, 45 valid responses were identified where, the rest were removed due to being incomplete, repeated or was identified as spam. All participants were adults, 18 and over, with a median age 45-54 and a mode age 65 or older. The gender split was 56% male and 44% female. There were 14 totally blind participants, 19 legally blind participants. Of the rest, 5 identified as totally/legally blind and 7 as either low vision. At least 19 participants have been blind since early childhood. Educational backgrounds ranged from high school to doctoral degrees; three-quarters had some post-secondary education. Half (24) reported having no science, technology, engineering, or math (STEM) experiences; ten currently work or study STEM; eight previously worked or studied STEM; and three were unsure if they had any STEM experiences. All but two participants use smartphones. One-third (14) of participants reported using tablets. Over 85% (39) of participants use computers. Two-thirds (30) of participants used screen readers, including JAWS (25), VoiceOver(9), NVDA(8), and others. Thirteen participants used more than one screen reader, i.e. JAWS on computers and VoiceOver on iPhones.

4 Findings

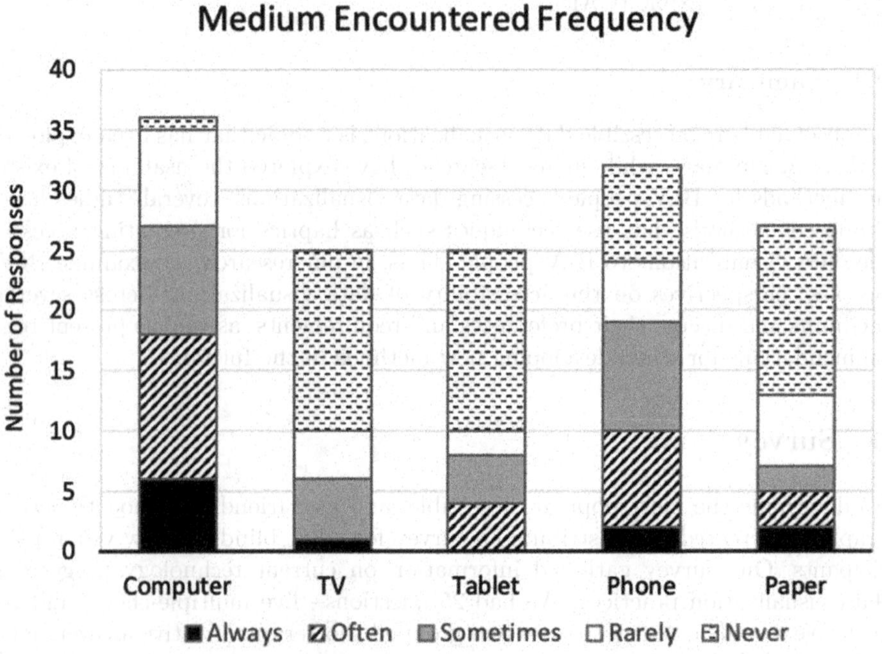

Fig. 1. Frequency of graph encounters on different mediums by number of responses.

We asked participants about their usage of the following five mediums—computers, phones, paper, tablets, and TVs. Participants rated how often they encounter data visualizations on each medium (Fig. 1); computers and phones have the most frequent encounters. Participants rated how often graphs are accessible and inaccessible on a scale of "1 Never" to "5 Always". We calculated net rating by comparing accessibility "Always" responses to inaccessibility "Never" responses (Fig. 2). Based on net rating, all mediums appear largely inaccessible; however, computers and phones might be considered the most accessible. Methods used by each type of medium include:

- Computers were the most popular with 31 answers. Screen readers via alt text, optical character recognition (OCR), or third-party extension such as

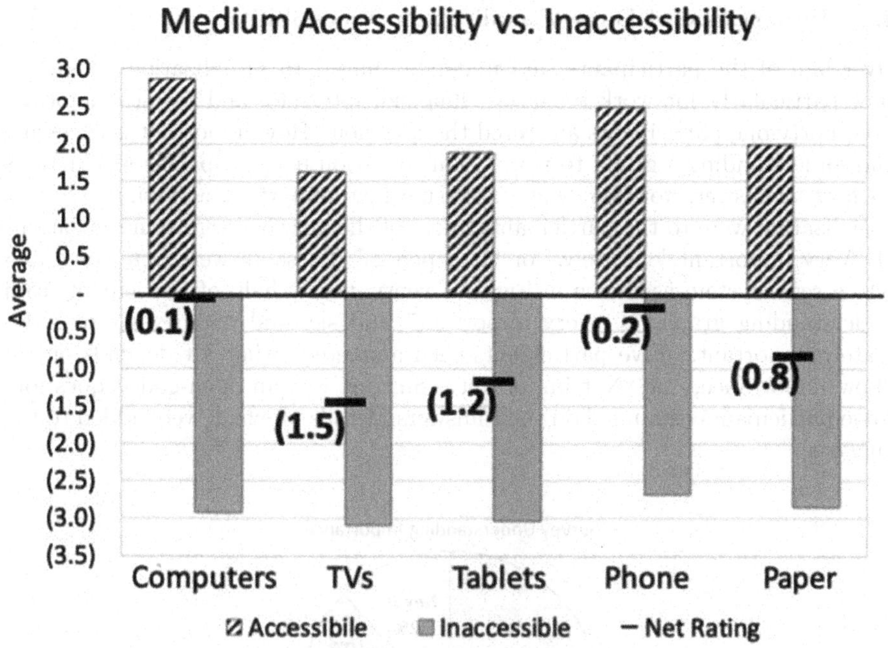

Fig. 2. Average accessibility where on a scale, positive 5 indicates always accessible and negative (5) indicates never accessible. The average figure is shown as the net rating where within brackets indicate a negative value

SAS Accelerator are the primary method used to access visualizations on computers. People without screen readers may use large monitors that adjust magnifications. Other responses mentioned braille display, zoom software, sighted help, and spreadsheet data.

- Phones had 24 responses. Ten used screen readers using either alt text, OCR, or image description. Other responses mentioned sighted help, audio chart descriptions, and sonic graphs in a weather app. People without screen readers do not consider phones as accessible as people with screen readers due to smaller screens.
- Paper had nine responses: three used braille or tactile graphs; four asked for sighted help; two scanned graphs. One of the tactile responses described an old device from the '70s that traced the shape of a graph. For people with low vision who use a magnifying tool, paper also reduces eye fatigue.
- Tablets were the second least popular medium with only five responses. Four used a screen reader, and one used an audio chart description.
- TVs were the least popular medium, with only four responses. Each person used something different: audio description, Roku, Google Chromecast, or Amazon Firestick.

4.1 Importance of Data Visualization Accessibility

Over half of the participants said understanding data visualizations is important particularly for work scenarios, financial interests, and medical information. Forty-one participants answered the question "How important is accessing and understanding a graph to you?". This question had no specific instructions on how to answer; however, when assessing how important accessing the data visualization were to the participants, most of the answers were some variations of "Very Important," "Rarely," or "It depends." These answers were converted into a scale system as shown in Fig. 3. Twenty, nearly half, of participants said understanding graphs is "Very important" and six said "Somewhat or moderately important." Five participants each answered either "It depends on...," "Low importance," or "Not important." Since it was an open-ended question, some participants expanded on their answers, details of which were added to the analysis.

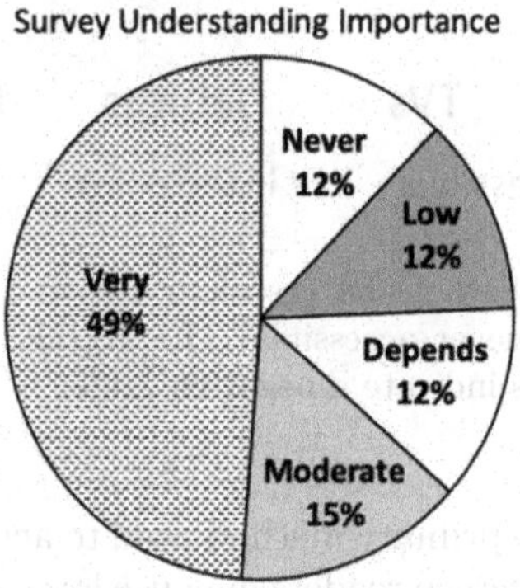

Fig. 3. Responses of how important accessing and understanding is a graph from "Never" to "Very Important."

Thirty-six responses provided examples of when accessing data visualization is most important. Nine participants mentioned on the job scenarios; six mentioned understanding financial, investment, and banking information; and others mentioned accessing medical information, temporal data, and mass communication. Participants really care about the data visualization when the context is important to them and their personal interests. Some comments emphasized the importance of context and access to information: "*Very important as these are often where the core information of reports are presented.*" (P02) where as P23 said, "*If I need to obtain information from said graph to answer questions.*" Furthermore, P24 added "*When there are not other ways to get the data or if trying to understand trends.*"

Participants are invested when the context is important to their personal interests. P44 said, "*It is very important to read chart when data is not available in text format. If I cannot get data, chart remains only available option to read data.*" Another (P37) said, "*When I deem the information important, such as COVID stats, etc.*" A participant (P05) concluded, graphs are "*very important as these are often where the core information of reports are presented.*"

The desire for more accessible data is related to the desire for inclusion and independence. P08 called for more open and accessible data, saying "*Democratization of knowledge and finding ways to be more inclusive through quantitative or qualitative research.*" Another (P06) emphasized how useful visualizations are as a "visual shorthand" and said, "*A graph exists to convey information...A good presentation should be able to convey all the information in the graph in words and text with minimal loss of emotional impact.*"

4.2 When a Data Visualization Is Inaccessible

When a data visualization is not easily accessible, many participants attempt more than one technique. One participant, P25, listed their options: "*Ignore it, look for a text description, get someone to summarize, or emboss it in Braille.*" Twenty-two participants said they would ask for sighted help, though 16 said this is not their first choice. P32 said, "*I ask somebody to describe it or try to understand the content without it.*" A few mentioned advocating for themselves by contacting the creator for either an alternate format or access to the raw data. This takes additional time and may not provide enough information to interpret graphs. As one participant, P05 said, "*Seek information in another format e.g. the raw data from which the chart was created. However, the charts often interpret the raw data so getting the raw data does not highlight the key message that the chart is presenting.*" Eleven participants said they would skip or ignore the visualization, but this is their last resort. Here, P26 said, "*If I can, I skip over it.*"

4.3 Suggested Areas of Improvements

Participants are frustrated by poor designs that hinder their access to data visualization. As such, there were 36 responses and of those only five said "None" or "Don't know." The most common suggested responses were:

- Include better screen reader support across all software and mediums. "*I would like screen readers to have support for it*" (P23)
- Create narrative summaries, either in alt text or context of the article, "*Better descriptions of graphs or charts. Alt text would also be useful*" (P26).
- Provide an audio format, either descriptions or sonic graphs, "*Better alt text or descriptions that can be interacted with to pay better attention to numbers choice of audio representation*" (P45).
- Make data navigation easier, "*Would like more independent way to access them without sighted assistance*" (P31).
- Design with accessibility and inclusiveness in mind, i.e. choose high contrasts colors and textures; use large fonts; label axes, rows, and columns "*Various, especially thin lines, are usually difficult to discern. Maybe alternative methods to distinguish lines on a graph would help*" (P24).

- Enhance tactile graphics, "*...Make tactile displays which can show graphs really affordable (and refreshable)*" (P29).
- Provide raw data, Excel or spreadsheet version, "*Always build in excel so that data can be navigated easily...*" (P29).

4.4 Other Comments

At the end of the survey there was a text box for participants to share closing thoughts and comments about the subject. One participant emphasized how useful graphs are as a "visual shorthand" and said that a good presentation or article should equally convey all the information in the text itself.

> "*A graph exists to convey information, not emotion. It's not art that needs to be seen to be appreciated. It's just visual shorthand, a model to convey information in an easy way. A good presentation should be able to convey all the information in the graph in words and text with a minimal loss of emotional impact.*" (P06)

A few other participants expressed the desire to read graphs without help and their frustration that creators do not provide accessible format for the data.

> "*It would be great to be able to do them without help.*" (P19)
> "*Most graphic and charts can be created in Excel and then provided in an accessible form, but most sighted folks do not do this.*" (P31)

5 Discussion

We found BLV people use many methods and technologies to access data visualizations. We gauged which of the five mediums (computers, phones, paper, tablets, TVs) are most accessible. Types of methods and technologies vary according to the user's level of vision, access to technology, and available mediums. These methods may be divided between screen reader users (SRUs), who are predominantly legally or totally blind, and non-SRUs, who generally have low vision.

SRUs use third party screen reader extensions, audio descriptions, and occasionally sighted help to access data visualizations. They do not consider data visualizations on any medium very accessible. Non-SRUs generally use various magnification approaches and sighted help as well. They perceive all mediums to be slightly more accessible. TVs and tablets are not popular among either group, perhaps due to few users or due to visualizations on these mediums being especially challenging. Five participants mentioned using tactile and braille methods in addition to screen readers.

Multiple alternatives to provide access are important because there is no one universal method that works for everyone. Redundant non-visual measures to access graphs include: alt text descriptions, figure captions, tabular forms of data, and possibly tactile, haptic, or sonic forms of graphs. Sharif, et al., recommends auto-generated alt text via artificial intelligence [24]. When auto-generated text is accurate, this both relieves pressure on the graph's creator and also enables independent exploration for users. Jung suggested creating hidden HTML data tables and mentioning their location in the graph's alt text [16]. This does not work in all circumstances, especially when there is too much data. Not every user appreciates having access to tabular data.

5.1 Pervasive Inaccessibility

Inaccessibility is pervasive; data visualizations are not free from their environments. Users who are blind or have low vision must navigate past challenging obstacles to recognize there is a graph in the first place. There are physical, mental, and emotional tolls from inaccessibility. Participants who encounter graphs spend both time and effort trying to understand a graph and advocating for better support. When the graph is not important, it is easier to skip.

5.2 Independent Interpretation

Everyone has multiple methods for accessing data visualizations, but many emphasize the desire to interpret data independently. Half of the participants ask for sighted help; however, for three quarters of those it is a final resort, only to be used when the data is important. Sighted help is also not always reliable. Those who have experience with braille charts also prefer them for the power and independence they provide. Frequently, participants express the desire for easier navigation and the power to manipulate the graph in order to access information.

Tactile charts provide independent access to visualizations; however, they are difficult to find for adult users. Although 3-D printing is becoming more accessible to commercial markets, it is still rare [14]. Haptic devices are becoming more widespread in modern smartphones and could apply to a variety of visualizations [22]. Current tactile graphs and haptic prototypes require investment to buy equipment, and neither technology is as prevalent as screen readers.

5.3 Design Frustration

Poor visualization design hinders access. Participants feel this could be avoided with more mindful planning. Most frustrations with design could be avoided if graph creators check their visualizations using heuristic guidelines. Web Content Accessibility Guidelines have been adopted by U.S. courts as the website accessibility standards [28] and might be a good place to start for guidance. More recently, Elavsky, et al., created a set of heuristic principles for visualization accessibility called Chartability [8], which can help creators avoid and fix inaccessible design.

6 Recommendations

Creators should use heuristics to improve data visualizations and provide alternate ways of accessing data such as ensuring adequate text descriptions, providing access to data tables, and investigating more versatile tactile means.

6.1 Heuristics Checklist

Poor visualization design hampers access. Most design obstacles could be avoided if creators intentionally design and check their visualizations using heuristic guidelines. Existing and future heuristics should be verified with end users to ensure results meet expectations.

Taking an heuristic approach might start with Web Content Accessibility Guidelines (WCAG) 2.0. These were adopted by the U.S. courts as website accessibility standards [28]. More recently, Elavsky et al. created a set of heuristic principles for visualization accessibility called Chartability [8]. Chartability expands on WCAG 2.0's four heuristics principles–Perceivable, Operable, Understandable, and Robust–while introducing three additional principles–Compromising, Assistive, and Flexible.

6.2 Alternate Access

Data visualizations are most commonly shared through images or interactive codes; however, there are redundant non-visual measures to access graphs, including alt text descriptions, caption descriptions, tabular forms of data, and possibly tactile, haptic, or sonic forms of graphs. Jung et al. recommends comprehensive alt text measures [16].

Sharif et al. recommends auto-generated alt text via artificial intelligence [24]. When auto-generated text is accurate, this both relieves pressure on the graph's creator and also increases independent exploration for users. Jung et al. suggested creating hidden HTML data tables and mentioning their location in the graph's alt text [16]. This does not work in all circumstances, especially when there is too much data. Not every users appreciates having access to tabular data.

Tactile charts provide independent access to visualizations; however, they are difficult to find for adult users. Although 3D printing is becoming more accessible to commercial markets, it is still rare [14]. Haptic devices are becoming more widespread in modern smartphones and could apply to a variety of visualizations [22]. Current tactile graphs and haptic prototypes require investment to buy equipment and neither technology is as prevalent as screen readers.

7 Conclusion

Blind and low vision users consider the current state of data visualization to be unsatisfactory-most users consider visualizations easier to skip. Methodologies and technologies vary according to the user's level of vision, access to technology, and available mediums. Blind participants typically rely on screen readers, but show an interest in tactile formats. Low vision participants use magnification tools, but cannot control how well graphs are designed. Both groups will skip visualizations, ask sighted people for help, or contact graph creators for details when initial methods fail. Graph creators should be more intentional. By researching heuristics, alternatives, and new modes of accessing graphs, it is possible to make data visualizations more accessible.

References

1. Administration, G.S.: Section 508 of the Rehabilitation Act (1973). https://www.section508.gov/
2. Beal, C.R., Rosenblum, L.P.: Use of an accessible iPad app and supplemental graphics to build mathematics skills: feasibility study results. J. Vis. Impairment Blindness (Online) **109**(5), 383 (2015)
3. Booth, J.M., Gelb, J.: Optimizing OCR accuracy on older documents: a study of scan mode, file enhancement, and software products (2006)
4. Braun, V., Clarke, V., Hayfield, N., Terry, G.: Thematic analysis. In: Liamputtong, P. (ed.) Handbook of Research Methods in Health Social Sciences, pp. 843–860. Springer, Singapore (2019). https://doi.org/10.1007/978-981-10-5251-4_103
5. Center, S.H.: Introduction to the SAS graphics accelerator. https://documentation.sas.com/doc/en/gracclug/1.0/p04o83muel10yen12ptmogjpapez.htm (2021)
6. Chundury, P., Patnaik, B., Reyazuddin, Y., Tang, C., Lazar, J., Elmqvist, N.: Towards understanding sensory substitution for accessible visualization: an interview study. IEEE Trans. Visual Comput. Graphics **28**(1), 1084–1094 (2022). https://doi.org/10.1109/TVCG.2021.3114829
7. Crisan, A.: The importance of data visualization in combating a pandemic. Am. J. Public Health **112**(6), 893–895 (2022)
8. Elavsky, F., Bennett, C., Moritz, D.: How accessible is my visualization? evaluating visualization accessibility with chartability. Eurograph. Conf. Visualiz. (EuroVis) 2022 **41**(3), 14522 (2022)
9. Engel, C., Weber, G.: Improve the accessibility of tactile charts. In: Bernhaupt, R., Dalvi, G., Joshi, A., K. Balkrishan, D., O'Neill, J., Winckler, M. (eds.) Human-Computer Interaction - INTERACT 2017, vol. 10513, pp. 187–195. Springer International Publishing, Cham (2017). https://doi.org/10.1007/978-3-319-67744-6_12
10. Friendly, M.: A brief history of data visualization. In: Handbook of Data Visualization, pp. 15–56. Springer, Heidelberg (2008). https://doi.org/10.1007/978-3-540-33037-0_2
11. Gleason, C., et al.: Disability and the Covid-19 pandemic: using twitter to understand accessibility during rapid societal transition. In: The 22nd International ACM SIGACCESS Conference on Computers and Accessibility, pp. 1–14. ACM, Virtual Event Greece (2020). https://doi.org/10.1145/3373625.3417023

12. Godfrey, A.J.R., Murrell, P., Sorge, V.: An accessible interaction model for data visualisation in statistics. In: Miesenberger, K., Kouroupetroglou, G. (eds.) Computers Helping People with Special Needs, vol. 10896, pp. 590–597. Springer, Cham (2018). https://doi.org/10.1007/978-3-319-94277-3_92
13. Granquist, C., Sun, S.Y., Montezuma, S.R., Tran, T.M., Gage, R., Legge, G.E.: Evaluation and comparison of artificial intelligence vision aids: Orcam MyEye 1 and seeing AI. J. Vis. Impairment Blindness **115**(4), 277–285 (2021)
14. He, L., Wan, Z., Findlater, L., Froehlich, J.E.: Tactile: a preliminary toolchain for creating accessible graphics with 3D-printed overlays and auditory annotations. In: Proceedings of the 19th International ACM SIGACCESS Conference on Computers and Accessibility, pp. 397–398. ACM, Baltimore Maryland USA (2017). https://doi.org/10.1145/3132525.3134818
15. Heer, J., Bostock, M., Ogievetsky, V.: A tour through the visualization zoo. Commun. ACM **53**(6), 59–67 (2010). https://doi.org/10.1145/1743546.1743567
16. Jung, C., Mehta, S., Kulkarni, A., Zhao, Y., Kim, Y.S.: Communicating visualizations without visuals: investigation of visualization alternative text for people with visual impairments. IEEE Trans. Visual Comput. Graphics **28**(1), 1095–1105 (2022). https://doi.org/10.1109/TVCG.2021.3114846
17. Kim, N.W., Joyner, S.C., Riegelhuth, A., Kim, Y.: Accessible visualization: design space, opportunities, and challenges. Comput. Graph. Forum **40**(3), 173–188 (2021). https://doi.org/10.1111/cgf.14298
18. Latham, K.: Benefits of low vision aids to reading accessibility. Vision. Res. **153**, 47–52 (2018). https://doi.org/10.1016/j.visres.2018.09.009
19. Lazar, J., Dudley-Sponaugle, A., Greenidge, K.D.: Improving web accessibility: a study of webmaster perceptions. Comput. Hum. Behav. **20**(2), 269–288 (2004). https://doi.org/10.1016/j.chb.2003.10.018
20. Lee, S., Kim, S.H., Hung, Y.H., Lam, H., Kang, Y.A., Yi, J.S.: How do people make sense of unfamiliar visualizations?: a grounded model of novice's information visualization sensemaking. IEEE Trans. Visual Comput. Graphics **22**(1), 499–508 (2016). https://doi.org/10.1109/TVCG.2015.2467195
21. Lloyd, P.B., Rodgers, P., Roberts, M.J.: Metro map colour-coding: effect on usability in route tracing. In: Chapman, P., Stapleton, G., Moktefi, A., Perez-Kriz, S., Bellucci, F. (eds.) Diagrams 2018. LNCS (LNAI), vol. 10871, pp. 411–428. Springer, Cham (2018). https://doi.org/10.1007/978-3-319-91376-6_38
22. Paneels, S., Roberts, J.C.: Review of designs for haptic data visualization. IEEE Trans. Haptics **3**(2), 119–137 (2010). https://doi.org/10.1109/TOH.2009.44
23. Segel, E., Heer, J.: Narrative visualization: telling stories with data. IEEE Trans. Visual Comput. Graphics **16**(6), 1139–1148 (2010). https://doi.org/10.1109/TVCG.2010.179
24. Sharif, A., Chintalapati, S.S., Wobbrock, J.O., Reinecke, K.: Understanding screen-reader users' experiences with online data visualizations. In: The 23rd International ACM SIGACCESS Conference on Computers and Accessibility, pp. 1–16. ACM, Virtual Event USA (2021). https://doi.org/10.1145/3441852.3471202
25. Torres, M.J.R., Barwaldt, R.: Approaches for diagrams accessibility for blind people: a systematic review. In: 2019 IEEE Frontiers in Education Conference (FIE), pp. 1–7. IEEE, Covington, KY, USA (2019). https://doi.org/10.1109/FIE43999.2019.9028522
26. Valencia, S., Kirabo, L.: Twitter, Covid-19, and disability: what worked and what didn't. XRDS **28**(2), 20–23 (2022). https://doi.org/10.1145/3495255

27. Yu, W., Kangas, K., Brewster, S.: Web-based haptic applications for blind people to create virtual graphs. In: 11th Symposium on Haptic Interfaces for Virtual Environment and Teleoperator Systems, 2003. HAPTICS 2003. Proceedings, pp. 318–325. IEEE Comput. Soc, Los Angeles, CA, USA (2003). https://doi.org/10.1109/HAPTIC.2003.1191301
28. Walker, K.: Modern day technology: not accessible to all, but necessary to navigate this society. Syracuse J. Sci. Tech. L. **35**, 98 (2018)
29. Ware, C.: Information visualization: perception for design. MA, third edn, Interactive technologies, Morgan Kaufmann, Waltham (2013)

On Time Reading Performance: A Comparison of the Clock Face and Digit Representations

Martine Amanda Dahl Knapskog, Frida Lines, Erik Semb Maalen-Johansen, Evelyn Eika, and Frode Eika Sandnes(✉)

Oslo Metropolitan University, 0130 Oslo, Norway
frodes@oslomet.no

Abstract. Time plays an essential part of our lives. We are typically surrounded by two types of time representation, clock faces and digits. Previous work focused on children's ability to read time, but adults' ability to read time have received less attention especially considering recent technological paradigm shifts and altered technology usage patterns. We therefore designed a simple time reading experiment. Our results show that participants read digit representations of times more rapidly with a lower error rate than clock face representations. These patterns were also exhibited by participants who preferred clock faces. Most errors were associated with the hands at angles of 60 and 30°. Most of the participants also reported that they prefer digit representations. Implications of these results are that the choice of time representation can be an important factor in time critical context where there is a low tolerance for error.

Keywords: time representation · analog time · digital time · clock face · digit times · age factor

1 Introduction

Time is a widely used point of reference that regulates our lives in many ways. Time was traditionally represented using clock faces when timepieces were mechanical devices. It was practical to represent hours, minutes, and seconds using hands. With the emergence of mainstream computing, time became straightforward to represent using strings of digits without the need for graphics. Yet, the traditional clock face from the mechanical era has survived and is commonly used within the current graphical user interface paradigm. For instance, most smartwatches allow the user to choose if they want a traditional clock face or a digit representation.

Colloquially, clock face time representations are commonly referred to as analog time and digit representations are commonly referred to as digital time. Although practical in everyday usage, they are also somewhat misleading as a clock face in a graphical user interface is a digital representation of time – at the same degree as the digit representation is digital. From another perspective, there are also mechanical timepieces that display time using digits. There are even analog designs for sundials that show time using digits [1, 2].

M. Antona and C. Stephanidis (Eds.): HCII 2023, LNCS 14020, pp. 414–427, 2023.
https://doi.org/10.1007/978-3-031-35681-0_27

Reading clock faces involves a level of indirection where the viewer first must perceive the angles of hour- and minute hands and interpret their meaning, while digits are read directly. With practice one would expect viewers to recognize clock hand shapes and digit configurations.

Modern society comprises a diverse mix of individuals. The older segment of the population grew up without easy access to computers and therefore mostly used clock faces. The young segment of the population has been exposed to computers from an early age, and clock faces may be merely an entertaining or eccentric oddity. The number of people with a deep background clock face usage will diminish in the years to come. Based on this we designed an experiment to probe the participants proficiency in reading time. Clock reading is particularly relevant as time plays an integral part of human life. In some contexts decisions must be made rapidly and users need to read information rapidly with low tolerance for error. This study focuses on the visual presentation of time and does not address issues related to low vision [3, 4], reduced cognitive function [5], alternative modalities [6, 7], and other modes of information transfer [8].

The rest of this paper is organized as follows. The next section reviews related works while Sect. 3 presents the methodology. The results are presented in Sect. 4 followed by a discussion in Sect. 5. The paper is concluded in Sect. 6.

2 Related Work

Several studies have addressed the reading of time [9]. Several of these have focused on children. Friedman and Laycock [10] found that pupils in first grade successfully were able to read digit time, while clock faces posed bigger challenges. Typically, pupils were only able to read the full hour. Their study, involving 240 participants, observed this situation up to fifth graders. Similarly, Boulton-Lewis, Wilss and Mutch [11] also found that schoolchildren found it easier to read digit times, although they did not necessarily understand the meaning of the times. They also observed that at fourth grade pupils start to develop systematic strategies for utilizing the fact that there are 60 min in an hour. Ali, Singh and Sandnes [12] found that school children preferred clock faces over digit representations, while adults preferred digit representations. Vacali [13] found that children found it more difficult to encode time than decode time and that this difficulty negatively correlated with age. Burny, Valcke and Desoete [14] found that pupils' ability to read time were related to their mathematics abilities. Burny, Valcke, Desoete and Van Luit [15] compared the time reading abilities of Flemish schoolchildren to Chinese schoolchildren and found that the Chinese school children's abilities were two year ahead of the Flemish schoolchildren. The authors attributed this difference to differences in the curriculum. Reading level in general is often connected to education level [16–18] and one may speculate that reading skills and mathematical skills are interrelated when solving such tasks.

On the other side of the demographic scale Bodner et al. [19] studied clock face reading and setting in elderly with dementia. They claimed that reduced clock setting abilities could be a predictor to be used when screening dementia. Along similar lines, several studies refer to clock face drawing tests [20–22]. Clock setting interfaces has also been studied in the human computer interaction domain [23–25].

The debate about the strength and weaknesses of clock faces versus digit times share similarities with the debate about pie charts versus bar graphs [26], and they are similarly relevant when such information is used in critical visualizations [27]. The renowned visualization expert makes some valuable comments about circular visualizations in the aptly titled text “Our Irresistible Fascination with All Things Circular” [28].

Many studies point out that when the reading task involves assessing part of a whole, the pie chart is more effective than other chart types [29], while if searching for the smallest or the smallest portion the bar chart is more effective than pie charts [30]. Several studies within cognitive psychology have explored the perception of angles. Xu, Chen and Kuai (31) showed that the size of the just noticeable angle depends on the angle itself, and that our sensitivity to angles is more sensitive when the angles are nearly vertical or horizontal and less sensitive around 60° (degrees). For pie charts, it is not the angle per se, but rather the area and arc lengths that is most prominent in affecting viewers’ judgements [32, 33]. It has also been shown that small portions often are underestimated, and large portions are overestimated [34]. The literature has also explored other more exotic circular graphs such as radar plots [35], petal plots [36], and polar plots [37].

3 Method

3.1 Experimental Design

A within groups experimental design was chosen. Time representation was the independent variable with two levels, namely clock-face and digits. Dependent variables included response time, error rate and preference. Such parameters are often used in such experiments [38–40].

3.2 Participants

A total of 16 participants were recruited with a mean age of 40.2 years ($SD = 17.6$). The youngest participant was 22 year and the oldest was 68 years. Participants were recruited using convenience sampling.

3.3 Materials

A total of 24 random times rounded to the nearest 5-min timestamp were generated. Half of these were represented using a clock face (see Fig. 1), and the other half were represented using a digit format (see Fig. 2). Positive polarity [41] was used with maximum contrast [42–45], that is black foreground on a white background to maximize legibility. The timestamps were randomized, and the sequence of clock face and digit times were presented in alternating order. The times were put into a PowerPoint presentation with one time at each slide. There was a separating page in between each time in the presentation so that each time measurement could be separated.

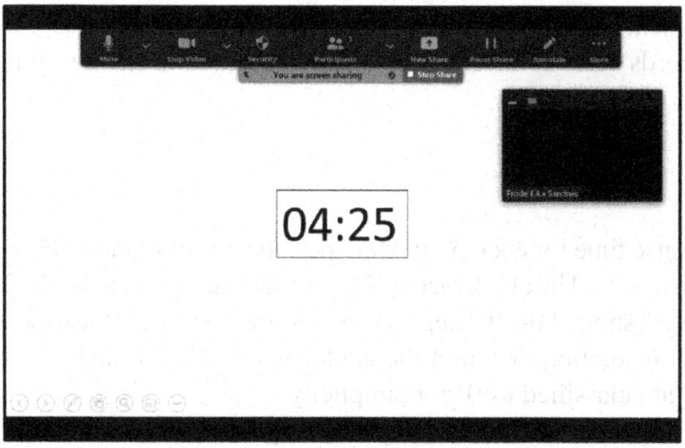

Fig. 1. Example of digit time task (viewed in zoom) used in the experiment

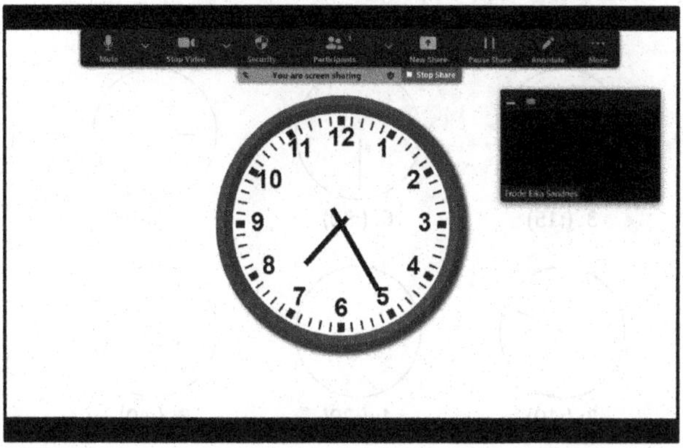

Fig. 2. Example of clock face time task (viewed in zoom) used in the experiment

3.4 Procedure

The experiment was conducted remotely using zoom (see Figs. 1 and 2). The participants were first sent the link to the zoom meeting. After connecting the participants were informed about the experiment. The PowerPoint presentation was shared with each of the participants and when shown the time, the participants were asked to read the time and speak it out aloud. The experimenters noted down the response and measured the time to provide the response using a smartphone stopwatch. After the experiment, the participants were asked complementary questions including their preferred time representation, what they typically used and their age. Participants were tested individually, and each session lasted between 15 to 20 min.

The experiment was conducted in single sessions and there was therefore no need to link data records across sessions [46]. The experiment could therefore be conducted anonymously.

3.5 Analysis

The mean response time for each participant per time representation type was computed as well as the error rate. The clock face types were also analyzed according to the angle of the hands. Figure 3 shows how the angles were interpreted. Since the time representations had a minimum resolution of 5 min the angles where 0°, 30° and 60° (degrees). Note that 90° angles are classified as 0° for simplicity.

The responses were statistically analyzed using JASP version 0.13.1.0 [47]. Shapiro-Wilks tests showed that the observed response times and error rates were not normally distributed. Non-parametric tests, namely Wilcoxon signed-rank tests and Spearman correlations, have therefore been employed herein.

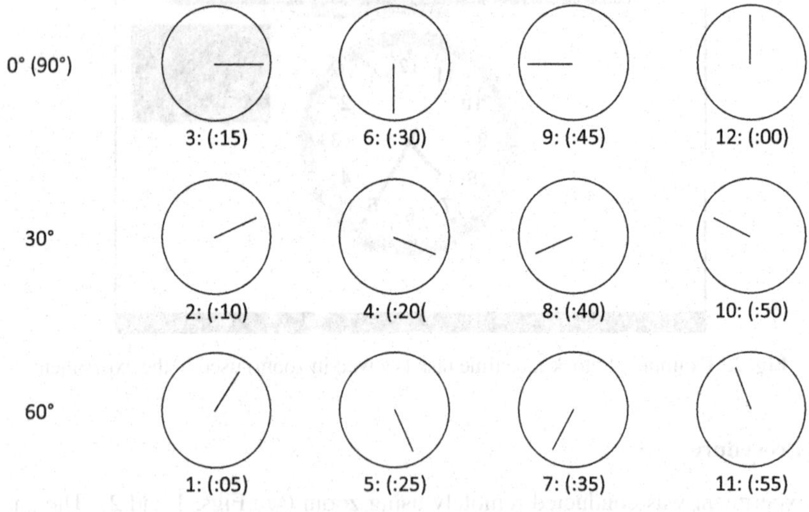

Fig. 3. Clock face hand angle interpretations for hours: (:minutes).

4 Results

Figure 4 shows that the time in seconds to read the digit time representation ($M = 2.5$, $SD = 0.5$) was shorter than the time to read the clock face representation ($M = 3.3$, $SD = 1.3$) and the difference was statistically significant ($W = 130$, $p < .001$).

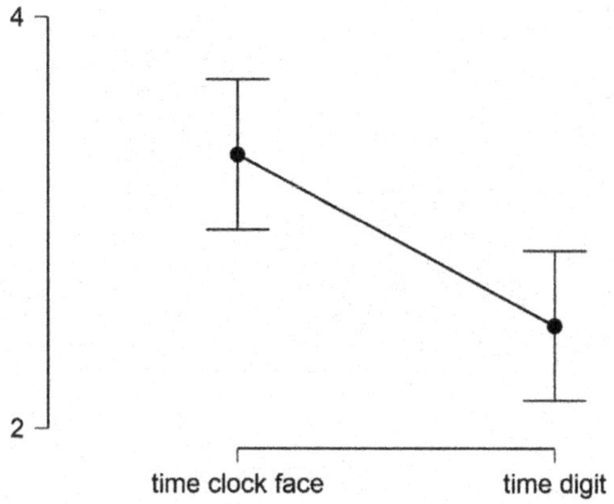

Fig. 4. Mean response times in seconds. Error bars show 95% confidence intervals.

We also correlated the response times for clock face against age and found a significant strong negative correlation ($r_s(16) = -0.717$, $p = .002$), that is older participants were faster at reading the clock face time than younger participants. No significant correlation was found for the digit representation ($r_s(16) = -0.364$, $p = .166$).

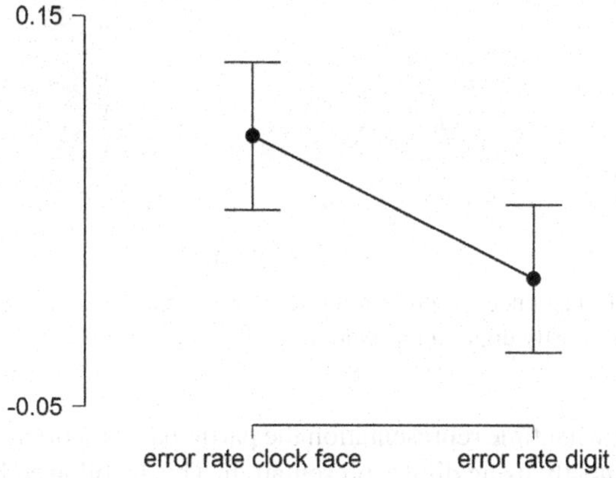

Fig. 5. Error rates. Error bars show 95% confidence intervals.

Figure 5 shows that the error rates associated with reading the digit time representation ($M = 1.6\%$, $SD = 3.4\%$) was lower than the error rates associated with reading the clock face representation ($M = 8.9\%$, $SD = 10.7\%$) and the difference was statistically significant ($W = 36.0$, $p = .012$).

Similarly, the error rates associated with the clock face showed a significant negative correlation with age ($r_s(16) = -0.859$, $p < .001$). No significant correlation between age and error rates of the digit representation was detected ($r_s(16) = 0.296$, $p = .266$).

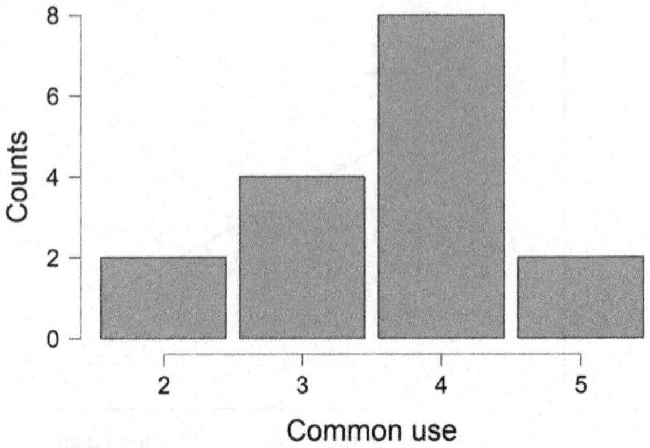

Fig. 6. Distribution of respondents' usual time representation. 1: Only clock face, 2: mostly clock face, 3: both, 4: mostly digit representation, 5: only digit representation.

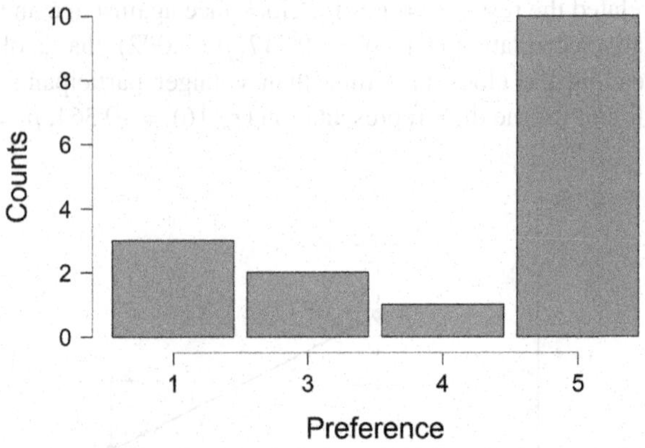

Fig. 7. Distribution of respondents' preferred time representation. 1: Only clock face, 2: mostly clock face, 3: both, 4: mostly digit representation, 5: only digit representation.

Figure 6 shows what time representation the participants report as typically using. A majority reported mostly using digit representation. This is followed by using both, and the same number of participants reported using only digit representation and mostly clock face. None of the participants reported that they only used the clock face representation. There was no correlation between age and typical use ($r_s(16) = -464, p = .070$).

Figure 7 shows the participants preferred time representation. Clearly, a majority indicated a strong preference for digital representation, while 3 participants indicated a strong preference for clock face. None of the participants indicated a preference for clock faces. The results in Figs. 3 and 4 are quite similar, which is confirmed by a significant strong positive correlation between what time representation the participants usually use and what they prefer ($r_s(16) = 0.792, p < 0.001$). In other words, participants who prefer clock face will typically also use clock face and vice versa.

A significant negative strong correlation was found between time representation preference and age ($r_s(16) = -0.535, p = .033$).

Table 1. Clock face time tasks and associated errors (presented in chronological order).

Time	Errors	Angle (degrees)	
		Hours	Minutes
10:20	5	30°	60°
07:55	4	60°	60°
04:40	3	30°	30°
10:55	3	30°	60°
01:30	1	60°	0°
07:25	1	60°	60°
02:30	0	30°	0°
05:00	0	60°	0°
06:45	0	0°	0°
08:00	0	30°	0°
11:05	0	60°	60°
12:15	0	0°	0°

There were more errors associated with the clock face (a total of 17) than the digit representation (a total of 3). We therefore analyzed the clock face errors in more detail. Table 1 shows the clock face task and the respective errors. By inspecting Table 1 it seems that the errors are higher if the clock face hands are not horizontal or vertical. The error seems especially high if the hands are at an angle of 60°. To explore this further, Table 2 was generated which lists the number of errors in relation to the angle of the hour and minute hands. According to this table most errors were associated with minute hands at a 60° angle and hour hand at a 30° angle, followed by both hands at 60° angles.

Table 2. Clock face errors according to angle of the hour- and minute hands.

Hours	Minutes		
	0°	30°	60°
0°			
30°		15.0%	55.0%
60°	5.0%		25.0%

Table 3. Clock face errors according to angle of the hour- and minute hands.

Type of error	Percentage
closer to nearest quarter hour	45.0%
5 minutes off	15.5%
Digit reading error (misreading 15 as 16)	10.0%
after closest quarter	5.0%
Unknown	5.0%

To get insight into what may have caused these errors we tried to classify the mistake by analyzing the time set by the participant and the intended time. These results are summarized in Table 3. The errors could be classified into several distinct categories. The largest category comprising 45% of the cases involved misreading the hour hand as being closest to the nearest quarter hour, that is 3, 6, 9 or 12 h. This was followed by misreading the minute hand by 5 min (15.5%) of the cases. Two of the digit task mistakes involved misreading the hour 15 as 16.

5 Discussion

The results show that the performance of the digital time representation was significantly better in terms of time to read time and errors in reading time. The time to read the time as digits was nearly one second shorter than reading the clock face (30%). The error rate with the clock face was more than 450% higher than the digit representation. In a time-critical context with no tolerance for error these differences can be what determines success from failure.

One possible explanation for this result could be that most of the participants also reported that they usually used digital time representations and preferred digital time representations. In this sense the observations could be considered biased towards the digit representation. It would have been relevant to have repeated the experiment with carefully balanced groups with the same number of participants with practices and preferences for each of the two time representations. Although relevant this scenario is not practical as we argue that the skew in preference for the digital representation is likely representative of the general population. It is thus difficult to find young participants with a preference for the clock face representation. The correlations between age and positive abilities to read clock face time further support this view. This could suggest that reading clock faces require more training and skill than digit time reading and that younger participants have been less exposed to clock faces compared to the older cohort. One may wonder if the skill to read clock faces will diminish and disappear in the decades to come in a similar manner as certain icons become less recognizable as the objects they represent become obsolete [48]? On the other hand the digit time representation did not correlate with age which indicates that the expected performance characteristics may be more robust and balanced. Another relevant observation is that those who preferred the clock face also exhibited better performance with the digital representation.

Although the use and preference patterns correlated positively, there was an interesting difference between what participants typically used and preferred. The responses to the question on what the participants typically used were centered around neutral and mostly digital, while the preferences were more extreme with most participants indicating digits, or clock face.

The observation that more errors are associated with clock hands at 60° and 30° angles is consistent with the literature which shows that assessments of angles are most accurate for 0° and 90° angles and less accurate in between [31]. The reading of the two dials requires some interpretation while digits can be read directly.

It is also interesting to observe that participants tended to round up the reading of the hour hand to the nearest quarter hour on the dial (3:00, 6:00, 9:00 and 12:00). The hour hand is shorter than the minute hand and therefore possibly harder to read. This speculation is supported by the observations which revealed a higher portion of incorrect hour interpretation compared to minute interpretations.

Our observed shorter reading times and lower error rates with digits compared to clock faces agree with the literature on clock reading among children (see for instance [10, 11]). However, the age-related preference for clock faces does not agree with Singh et al.'s study of school children's preference of time reading [12]. One key difference between the works is that children were not part of the cohort studied herein and naturally we would be able to make similar observations. Perhaps children fall in a separate category where the visual clock face is more visually interesting than the sequence of digits? Also, as noted by Boulton-Lewis et al. [11] children may not fully comprehend the meaning of time, even though they are able to read time.

5.1 Limitation

One weakness of the current experiment is the small sample size and ad-hoc cohort. The experiment was conducted during the COVID-19 pandemic and the lockdown and physical distancing complicated the recruitment of participants. There are also some errors introduced by Internet delays as it could take some time before a participant read out the time before it was recorded by the experimenters. Moreover, some participants reported a delay from when we said "go" until they could see the time task on their screen. One possible way to have reduced this problem would be to send the PowerPoint file to the participants and asked them to share the screen and control the progress, while we recorded the session. We would then have a more accurate measurement of time from the stimuli was presented to an answer was given. However, storing participants audio would mean the experiment no longer would be anonymous. The remote experiment also meant that we could not control the environment and there is a chance that some participants may have been exposed to local disturbances.

We should therefore be careful in generalizing too much from the results. However, the results give indications of challenges with the clock-face paradigm with the current technological paradigms in society that should be considered in future work.

The results indicated that the hand of the clock face angle may be related to the error rate. It is thus possible that the results are affected by the distribution of the clock face time tasks. We therefore tallied the number of clock face time tasks according to the hand angle combinations (see Table 4). The time tasks are relatively evenly distributed with approximately two tasks per configuration, but the 60–60° task have three tasks and there are no tasks associated with full and half past tasks for 0° and 60° hour angles (for example 18:30, or 11:00). It is thus possible that this may have affected the results. Future work should carefully design time tasks that uniformly represent the clock face hand angle combinations.

Table 4. Distribution of clock face time tasks and potential bias.

Hour hand	Minute hand		
	0°	30°	60°
0°	2		0
30°	2	1	2
60°	2		3

6 Conclusion

A simple experiment was conducted to assess participants ability read time represented using clock faces and digits. The results show that both the time to read the time was shorter and the associated error rate was smaller with digit time representation compared to the clock face representation. Most participants also preferred the digit representation. We also observed an effect of age as older participants were more likely to prefer the clock face, and demonstrated shorter response times and lower error rates with the clock face compared to younger participants. Despite this the response times were shorter and error rates lower with the digit representation, regardless. Implications of this work is that digit representation is preferable over clock faces especially in time-critical context with low or no tolerance for error.

References

1. Falconer, K.J.: Digital sundials, paradoxical sets, and Vitushkin's conjecture. Math. Intell. **9**(1), 24–27 (1987). https://doi.org/10.1007/BF03023569
2. Scharstein, H., Krotz-Vogel, W., Scharstein, D.: Digital sundial. Renew. Energy **12**(1), 118 (1997)
3. Sandnes, F.E.: What do low-vision users really want from smart glasses? faces, text and perhaps no glasses at all. In: Miesenberger, K., Bühler, C., Penaz, P. (eds.) ICCHP 2016. LNCS, vol. 9758, pp. 187–194. Springer, Cham (2016). https://doi.org/10.1007/978-3-319-41264-1_25
4. Sandnes, F.E., Eika, E.: Head-mounted augmented reality displays on the cheap: a DIY approach to sketching and prototyping low-vision assistive technologies. In: Antona, M., Stephanidis, C. (eds.) UAHCI 2017. LNCS, vol. 10278, pp. 167–186. Springer, Cham (2017). https://doi.org/10.1007/978-3-319-58703-5_13

5. Sandnes, F.E., Lundh, M.V.: Calendars for individuals with cognitive disabilities: a comparison of table view and list view. In Proceedings of the 17th International ACM SIGACCESS Conference on Computers and Accessibility, pp. 329–330. ACM (2015). https://doi.org/10.1145/2700648.2811363
6. Huang, Y.P., Chang, Y.T., Sandnes, F.E.: Ubiquitous information transfer across different platforms by QR codes. J. Mob. Multimedia 003–014 (2010)
7. dos Santos, A.D.P., Medola, F.O., Cinelli, M.J., Garcia Ramirez, A.R., Sandnes, F.E.: Are electronic white canes better than traditional canes? a comparative study with blind and blindfolded participants. Univ. Access Inf. Soc. **20**(1), 93–103 (2020). https://doi.org/10.1007/s10209-020-00712-z
8. Lin, M.W., Cheng, Y.M., Yu, W., Sandnes, F.E.: Investigation into the feasibility of using tactons to provide navigation cues in pedestrian situations. In: Proceedings of the 20th Australasian Conference on Computer-Human Interaction: Designing for Habitus and Habitat, pp. 299–302 (2008). https://doi.org/10.1145/1517744.1517794
9. Williams, R.F.: Image schemas in clock-reading: latent errors and emerging expertise. J. Learn. Sci. **21**(2), 216–246 (2012). https://doi.org/10.1080/10508406.2011.553259
10. Friedman, W.J., Laycock, F.: Children's analog and digital clock knowledge. Child Dev. 357–371 (1989). https://doi.org/10.2307/1130982
11. Boulton-Lewis, G., Wilss, L., Mutch, S.: Analysis of primary school children's abilities and strategies for reading and recording time from analogue and digital clocks. Math. Educ. Res. J. **9**(2), 136–151 (1997). https://doi.org/10.1007/BF03217308
12. Ali, H., Singh, G., Sandnes, F.E.: Towards accessible representations of time: learning from the preferences of children and adults. In: Proceedings of the 12th ACM International Conference on Pervasive Technologies Related to Assistive Environments, pp. 317–318. ACM (2019). https://doi.org/10.1145/3316782.3322736
13. Vakali, M.: Clock time in seven to ten year-old children. Eur. J. Psychol. Educ. **6**(3), 325–336 (1991). https://doi.org/10.1007/BF03173154
14. Burny, E., Valcke, M., Desoete, A.: Clock reading: an underestimated topic in children with mathematics difficulties. J. Learn. Disabil. **45**(4), 351–360 (2012). https://doi.org/10.1177/0022219411407773
15. Burny, E., Valcke, M., Desoete, A., Van Luit, J.E.H.: Curriculum sequencing and the acquisition of clock-reading skills among Chinese and Flemish children. Int. J. Sci. Math. Educ. **11**(3), 761–785 (2013). https://doi.org/10.1007/s10763-012-9362-z
16. Kaushik, H.M., Eika, E., Sandnes, F.E.: Towards universal accessibility on the web: do grammar checking tools improve text readability? In: Antona, M., Stephanidis, C. (eds.) HCII 2020. LNCS, vol. 12188, pp. 272–288. Springer, Cham (2020). https://doi.org/10.1007/978-3-030-49282-3_19
17. Eika, E., Sandnes, F.E.: Authoring WCAG2.0-compliant texts for the web through text readability visualization. In: Antona, M., Stephanidis, C. (eds.) UAHCI 2016. LNCS, vol. 9737, pp. 49–58. Springer, Cham (2016). https://doi.org/10.1007/978-3-319-40250-5_5
18. Eika, E., Sandnes, F.E.: Assessing the reading level of web texts for WCAG2.0 compliance—can it be done automatically?. In: Di Bucchianico, G., Kercher, P. (eds.) Advances in Design for Inclusion. Advances in Intelligent Systems and Computing, vol. 500. Springer, Cham (2016). https://doi.org/10.1007/978-3-319-41962-6_32
19. Bodner, T., Delazer, M., Kemmler, G., Gurka, P., Marksteiner, J., Fleischhacker, W.W.: Clock drawing, clock reading, clock setting, and judgment of clock faces in elderly people with dementia and depression. J. Am. Geriatr. Soc. **52**(7), 1146–1150 (2004). https://doi.org/10.1111/j.1532-5415.2004.52313.x
20. Berger, G., Frölich, L., Weber, B., Pantel, J.: Diagnostic accuracy of the clock drawing test: the relevance of "Time Setting" in screening for dementia. J. Geriatr. Psychiatry Neurol. **21**(4), 250–260 (2008). https://doi.org/10.1177/0891988708324939

21. Mazancova, A.F., Nikolai, T., Stepankova, H., Kopecek, M., Bezdicek, O.: The reliability of clock drawing test scoring systems modeled on the normative data in healthy aging and nonamnestic mild cognitive impairment. Assessment **24**(7), 945–957 (2017). https://doi.org/10.1177/1073191116632586
22. Cohen, J., et al.: Digital clock drawing: differentiating 'thinking' versus 'doing' in younger and older adults with depression. J. Int. Neuropsychological Society: JINS **20**(9), 920 (2014). https://doi.org/10.1017/S1355617714000757
23. Skogstrøm, N.A.B., Igeltjørn, A., Knudsen, K.M., Diallo, A.D., Krivonos, D., Sandnes, F.E.: A comparison of two smartphone time-picking interfaces: convention versus efficiency. In: Proceedings of the 10th Nordic Conference on Human-Computer Interaction, pp. 874–879. ACM (2018). https://doi.org/10.1145/3240167.3240233
24. Hemmert, F., Hamann, S., Wettach, R.: The digital hourglass. In: Proceedings of the 3rd International Conference on Tangible and Embedded Interaction, pp. 19–20. ACM (2009). https://doi.org/10.1145/1517664.1517672
25. Zekveld, J., Funk, M., Bakker, S.: The tumble clock: bringing users in touch with their snooze time. In: Proceedings of the 2016 ACM Conference on Designing Interactive Systems pp. 900–904. ACM (2016). https://doi.org/10.1145/2901790.2901857
26. Spence, I.: No humble pie: the origins and usage of a statistical chart. J. Educ. Behav. Stat. **30**(4), 353–368 (2005)
27. Sandnes, F.E., Dyrgrav, K.: Effects of graph embellishments on the perception of system states in mobile monitoring tasks. In: Luo, Y. (ed.) CDVE 2014. LNCS, vol. 8683, pp. 9–18. Springer, Cham (2014). https://doi.org/10.1007/978-3-319-10831-5_2
28. Few, S.: Our irresistible fascination with all things circular. In: Perceptual Edge Visual Business Intelligence Newsletter, pp. 1–9 (2010)
29. Hollands, J.G., Spence, I.: Judging proportion with charts: the summation model. Appl. Cogn. Psychol. Official J. Soc. Appl. Res. Mem. Cogn. **12**(2), 173–190 (1998). https://doi.org/10.1002/(SICI)1099-0720(199804)12:2%3C173::AID-ACP499%3E3.0.CO;2-K
30. Sandnes, F.E., Flønes, A., Kao, W.-T., Harrington, P., Issa, M.: Searching for extreme portions in distributions: a comparison of pie and bar charts. In: Luo, Y. (ed.) CDVE 2020. LNCS, vol. 12341, pp. 342–351. Springer, Cham (2020). https://doi.org/10.1007/978-3-030-60816-3_37
31. Xu, Z.X., Chen, Y., Kuai, S.G.: The human visual system estimates angle features in an internal reference frame: a computational and psychophysical study. J. Vision **18**(13), 10 (2018). https://doi.org/10.1167/18.13.10
32. Bertini, E., Elmqvist, N., Wischgoll, T.: Judgment error in pie chart variations. In: Proceedings of the Eurographics/IEEE VGTC Conference on Visualization, pp. 91–95. IEEE (2016)
33. Skau, D., Kosara, R.: Arcs, angles, or areas: individual data encodings in pie and donut charts. Comput. Graph. Forum **35**(3), 121–130 (2016). https://doi.org/10.1111/cgf.12888
34. Hollands, J.G., Dyre, B.P.: Bias in proportion judgments: the cyclical power model. Psychol. Rev. **107**(3), 500–524 (2000). https://psycnet.apa.org/doi.org/10.1037/0033-295X.107.3.500
35. Burch, M., Weiskopf, D.: On the benefits and drawbacks of radial diagrams. In: Huang, W. (ed.) Handbook of Human Centric Visualization, pp. 429–451. Springer, New York (2014). https://doi.org/10.1007/978-1-4614-7485-2_17
36. Sandnes, F.E.: On the truthfulness of petal graphs for visualisation of data. In: Proceedings of NIK 2012 the Norwegian Informatics Conference, pp. 225–235. Tapir Academic Publishers (2012)
37. Redford, G.I., Clegg, R.M.: Polar plot representation for frequency-domain analysis of fluorescence lifetimes. J. Fluoresc. **15**, 805 (2005). https://doi.org/10.1007/s10895-005-2990-8
38. Aschim, T.B., Gjerstad, J.L., Lien, L.V., Tahsin, R., Sandnes, F.E.: Are split tablet keyboards better? a study of soft keyboard layout and hand posture. In: Lamas, D., Loizides, F., Nacke, L.,

Petrie, H., Winckler, M., Zaphiris, P. (eds.) INTERACT 2019. LNCS, vol. 11748, pp. 647–655. Springer, Cham (2019). https://doi.org/10.1007/978-3-030-29387-1_37
39. Sandnes, F.E., Thorkildssen, H.W., Arvei, A., Buverad, J.O.: Techniques for fast and easy mobile text-entry with three-keys. In: Proceedings of the 37th Annual Hawaii International Conference on System Sciences 2004. IEEE (2004). https://doi.org/10.1109/HICSS.2004.1265675
40. Sandnes, F.E.: Evaluating mobile text entry strategies with finite state automata. In: Proceedings of the 7th International Conference on Human Computer Interaction with Mobile Devices and Services, pp. 115–121. ACM (2005). https://doi.org/10.1145/1085777.1085797
41. Pedersen, L.A., Einarsson, S.S., Rikheim, F.A., Sandnes, F.E.: User interfaces in dark mode during daytime – improved productivity or just cool-looking? In: Antona, M., Stephanidis, C. (eds.) HCII 2020. LNCS, vol. 12188, pp. 178–187. Springer, Cham (2020). https://doi.org/10.1007/978-3-030-49282-3_13
42. Sandnes, F.E., Zhao, A.: An interactive color picker that ensures WCAG2. 0 compliant color contrast levels. Proc. Comput. Sci. **67**, 87–94 (2015). https://doi.org/10.1016/j.procs.2015.09.252
43. Sandnes, F.E.: Understanding WCAG2.0 color contrast requirements through 3D color space visualization. Stud. Health Technol. Inform. **229**, 366–375 (2016). https://doi.org/10.3233/978-1-61499-684-2-366
44. Hansen, F., Krivan, J.J., Sandnes, F.E.: Still not readable? an interactive tool for recommending color pairs with sufficient contrast based on existing visual designs. In: The 21st International ACM SIGACCESS Conference on Computers and Accessibility, pp. 636–638. ACM (2019). https://doi.org/10.1145/3308561.3354585
45. Brathovde, K., Farner, M.B., Brun, F.K., Sandnes, F.E.: Effectiveness of color-picking interfaces among non-designers. In: Luo, Y. (ed.) CDVE 2019. LNCS, vol. 11792, pp. 181–189. Springer, Cham (2019). https://doi.org/10.1007/978-3-030-30949-7_21
46. Sandnes, F.E.: HIDE: short IDs for robust and anonymous linking of users across multiple sessions in small HCI experiments. In: CHI 2021 Conference on Human Factors in Computing Systems Extended Abstracts Proceedings. ACM (2021). https://doi.org/10.1145/3411763.3451794
47. JASP Team (2020). JASP (Version 0.14.1) [Computer software]
48. Berget, G., Sandnes, F.E.: The effect of dyslexia on searching visual and textual content: are icons really useful? In: Antona, M., Stephanidis, C. (eds.) UAHCI 2015. LNCS, vol. 9177, pp. 616–625. Springer, Cham (2015). https://doi.org/10.1007/978-3-319-20684-4_59

Users' Opinions When Drawing with an Eye Tracker

Andreas Mallas(✉), Michalis Xenos, and Maria Margosi

Computer Engineering and Informatics Department, Patras University, Patras, Greece
{mallas,xenos}@ceid.upatras.gr, mmargosi@upatras.gr

Abstract. Eye tracking is interwoven with the research in the field of Human-Computer Interaction as a tool that examines the user's visual attention in their interactions with computing devices and can reveal behaviors and factors that could otherwise remain unnoticed. In this paper, we take a novel approach by examining the use of an eye tracking system as an input method by developing a drawing application that the users can draw with their gaze. The application was developed to address the need for drawing software accessible to all individuals using commercially available and affordable hardware. An evaluation experiment (n = 25) was conducted, with results showing that although participants felt drawing with their gaze had a degree of difficulty, they enjoyed the experience and thought that drawing with their gaze was an exciting and fun experience. Furthermore, comments were made that could constitute a meaningful improvement for future application iterations. Finally, a longitudinal study showed that users' drawing skills markedly improved each time they used the application while also feeling more inclined to use it daily.

Keywords: Eye-gaze Based Interaction · Interaction Techniques · Eye Tracking · Drawing · User Study

1 Introduction

Eye tracking technology has become increasingly popular in the Human-Computer Interaction (HCI) research community. However, in the last few years, its usage as a research tool is also spreading outside of the field of HCI. From eye tracking research examining the visual and cognitive processes during reading [1] to using eye tracking for studying economic theory [2]. Other works focus on health disorders and include examining visual attention with eye tracking in people with affective disorders [3], autism [4], and neuropsychiatric disorders [5].

While these types of studies provide crucial data on the range and utility of eye tracking, the research questions that the HCI investigates are frequently unique and distinct within the context of the opportunities that arise because of technological evolution. A typical use of eye tracking data in HCI research would be to enhance the design process; for example, by improving students' designs in a HCI course with the use of eye tracking data [6]. Futhermore, eye tracking has also been used as an input method. For

M. Antona and C. Stephanidis (Eds.): HCII 2023, LNCS 14020, pp. 428–439, 2023.
https://doi.org/10.1007/978-3-031-35681-0_28

example, Murata et al. compared four character input methods in a gaze input interface with results indicating differences between the examined input methods regarding speed and accuracy [7]. Murata and Moriwaka examined the effectiveness of eye gaze input methods regarding click, drag, and menu selection tasks and concluded that the best input method relates to the task type [8].

Onishi et al. presented a combination of input modalities for pointing and selecting, using eye gaze and breathing [9]. The eye gaze was utilized for pointing and breathing to alternate between the two input phases (pointing and selection), with their results showing that it achieved almost comparable performance to conventional methods. Regarding drawing, multiple input methods that deviate from the typical keyboard and mouse interfaces have been examined with Folgieri et al. developing BrainArt, which interprets the user's cerebral rhythms to allow the creation of drawings by utilizing EEG -based BCI (Brain-Computer Interface) [10].

Additionally, Harada et al. examined the use of voice as an input modality by developing VoiceDraw, a free-form drawing application for people with motor impairments that does not require typical forms of input methods (e.g., keyboard and mouse) [11]. Furthermore, Drey et al. presented VRSketchIn, which uses a pen and tablet with 6 degrees of freedom as input devices for VR (Virtual Reality) sketching by combining "unconstrained 3D mid-air with constrained 2D surface-based sketching" [12].

In this paper, we present a drawing application that uses the user's gaze as an input method that does not target a specific group of users but aims to provide an easy-to-use and easy-to-learn application that everyone can use without requiring expensive hardware. An evaluation experiment was conducted where 25 participants were asked to draw a predefined illustration, and their perspective was assessed regarding their experience with the application.

Section 2 presents work related to eye tracking drawing, while Sect. 3 presents the application and details about the implementation. Section 4 describes the methodology of the evaluation experiment, followed by the results and the discussion in Sect. 5. Finally, Sect. 6 provides the conclusions and future research directions that could be pursued.

2 Related Work

One of the first uses of eye tracking for drawing was EagleEyes [13], which operated by attaching electrodes on the head of the user to measure the electro-oculographic potential (EOG) and interpret the signals to coordinates on the screen. EagleEyes focused on being utilized as an input device by persons with disabilities, and among other applications, it was employed with a painting program similar to finger painting but with users using their eyes.

EyeArt is an application for producing images with gaze interactions utilizing an eye tracker [14]. The application can be used solely with gaze or alternatively with a mouse and keyboard to enable the operation by disabled and non-disabled users, respectively.

Kamp and Sundstedt developed and evaluated a drawing application that combines input modalities by utilizing the user's gaze and voice to cater to the needs of disabled users [15]. Specifically, the gaze of the user corresponds to the position of the cursor, and the user's voice is employed for activating when the gaze is used for drawing lines or positioning the cursor on the canvas. Compared with a typical mouse and keyboard setup, results indicated that using gaze and voice resulted in less control, speed, and precision, but the users find it more enjoyable and that, given enough time to practice, "it would get significantly easier".

EyeSketch is an application with gaze control also targeted at disabled users but, contrary to other works, allows editing of the objects [16]. Objects can be moved and resized after their creation, while their attributes can be modified at any time. Dwell buttons enable the tool and object selection, while gaze gestures and closing of the eyes allow the moving and resizing of objects. Dwell buttons are buttons that can be selected by gazing at them for a predefined time period and gaze gestures are performed by moving your eyes from a certain point of the screen to another, with each gesture associated with a predefined operation (e.g., move or resize). A follow-up of the previous work focused on utilizing the EyeSketch application to compare gaze gestures and dwell buttons as different editing tool implementation methods and found that "gaze gestures were an equally good input method as dwell buttons" and that gaze gestures are a viable alternative if implemented correctly [17].

Similar to the aforementioned work, Pfeuffer et al. examined three techniques for menu selection: dwell time, gaze button, and cursor, but in the context of VR [18]. The authors found comparable user performance between gaze techniques to pointer-based menu selection but requiring less physical effort.

Creed et al. developed and evaluated the application "Sakura," allowing people with disabilities to create visual design work [19]. Sakura combines eye tracking with the use of a mechanical switch as input methods and enables extended editing capabilities such as object selection and manipulation, creative typography, and a technique for element alignment. The system has achieved a high score regarding usability with non-disabled users, with a small group of physically impaired participants also reporting a good level of usability.

A different approach to utilizing eye tracker data was proposed by [20], where the goal was to create artistic renderings by performing abstract transformations of images. Using the user's eye tracking data, a perceptual model of the image was created, and the system then used that data to apply brush strokes to the image to create abstract painterly paintings.

Scalera et al. presented a novel architecture for eye tracking assisted drawing by employing a robotic arm that directly draws on a canvas based on the user's gaze that draws in the virtual canvas on the screen [21]. Since the actual process of drawing is assigned to the robot, the user's gaze is somewhat disconnected by the end result allowing the filtering and preprocessing of the eye tracking data that enables the smoothing of the lines drawn and the removal of noisy data enabling "cleaner" drawings. The authors mention that their application can be used by people with disabilities or artists seeking novel art forms.

What all the aforementioned works related to drawing using an eye tracker have in common is that their applications focus on people with disabilities. The research idea of the application presented in this paper arose to address the need for drawing software accessible to all by using affordable hardware.

3 The Application

An application that uses data from an eye tracker was developed to enable users to draw with their gaze. The application uses the Tobii Eye Tracking Core Software[1] driver that allows access to the eye tracking features of Tobii 4C Eye Tracker, which was the eye tracker used in the experiment. The application targeted the Windows platform as the required driver is only available for Windows. However, since it was developed using java, it can run on any operating system (Windows, MacOS, Linux, Unix, and BSD) in the case of a future release of Tobii Eye Tracking Core Software that provides support for other platforms.

The user interface comprises two sections; the canvas, which covers the largest portion of the UI area and is where the user can draw, and the UI buttons that provide the required functionality for a drawing application (Fig. 1).

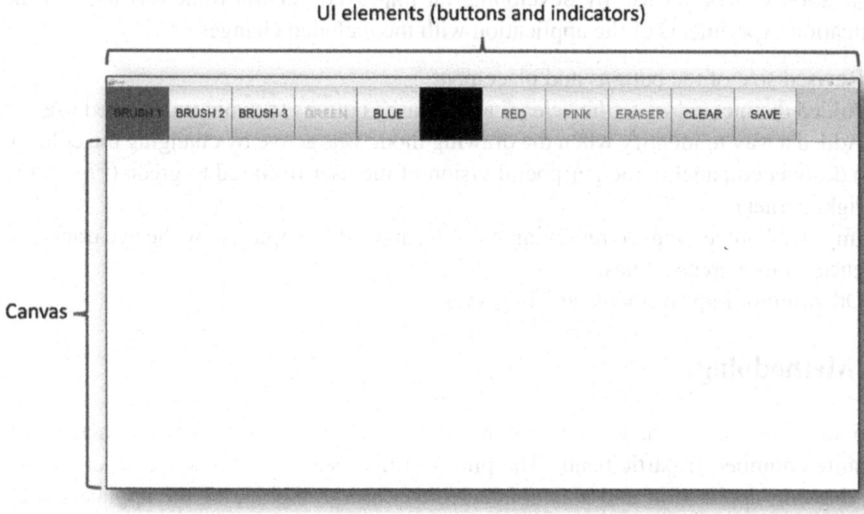

Fig. 1. The UI of the drawing application consists of the canvas area and the buttons and indicators.

Careful consideration was given to avoiding the "Midas Touch problem" [22], which can be introduced when utilizing the user's gaze as an input method -since the gaze also enables visual perception, e.g., when the user scans the UI- resulting in unintended inputs. To circumvent the "Midas Touch problem", the application implements a drawing mode and a viewing mode; in the first mode, the users can draw with their eyes, and in the second, the users can view all the UI elements, including the canvas and buttons without resulting in an action. Several alternatives were evaluated to alternate between the two modes; however, in the final design of the application, the user can alter modes by utilizing any key (keyboard or mouse button), giving more freedom to choose the preferred hand placement. Additionally, dwell buttons were used (a dwell button is

[1] https://gaming.tobii.com/getstarted/.

activated when the user dwells for a predefined period of time on them), eliminating unintended "clicks" when the user just glimpsed at them.

An iterative process for the application development was followed where initially, a version with a core set of features was created, then the researchers evaluated the application, and with the feedback acquired, the next version with additional features and modifications to the original specifications was released.

When the application development progressed to a stage where it was suitable for testing (e.g., having a complete feature set and the necessary stability and performance), a pilot phase for testing the application was conducted, and a small number of users evaluated the application regarding usability, functionality, and performance.

During the pilot phase and based on the user feedback and the analysis of the data captured by the application, several application weaknesses were identified, both in terms of the way it operates and the user requirements regarding the features it offers. Additionally, steps were taken to avoid possible problems that would arise from the application's incorrect use by developing an improved version (that was used in the evaluation experiment) of the application with the included changes:

- Revised size of the buttons and placement
- Added distinct colors to the "clear" and "erase" buttons to avoid unintended use
- Added a way to identify when the drawing mode was active by changing the color of a designated panel in the peripheral vision of the user from red to green (Fig. 1, top right corner)
- Improved processing for removing noise from the data captured by the eye tracker to ensure more precise lines
- Other minor improvements and bug fixes

4 Methodology

Initially, to assess the early version of the application, pilot testing was conducted with a limited number of participants. The pilot testing assessed the practical operation of the drawing application and was conducted to observe the use of the application by actual users. Then, suggestions and user feedback gathered from the pilot testing were incorporated into the final version of the application, and a more extensive evaluation experiment followed. The goal of the evaluation experiment was to assess the usage of eye tracking technology in a painting application in real-world situations and by actual users.

4.1 Experiment Setup and Participants

The evaluation experiment (including the piloting) was conducted in a controlled environment of a Human-Computer Interaction laboratory. A laboratory was deemed appropriate for the experiment because the controlled conditions that it provides ensure the consistency of the results. An announcement was made to the social media accounts of the laboratory to attract volunteers and inform them about the subject of the experiment. Additionally, contact information for scheduling an appointment for the experiment was provided. Booking an appointment was necessary to avoid overcrowding the laboratory, as well as avoid long waiting times. A total of 25 Greek participants took part in the experiment, 18 males and 7 females, aged between 20 to 37 (Mean = 25.76 and SD = 4.72), whereas for the piloting, a total of 5 users participated.

4.2 Piloting

In conjunction with the Tobii 4C Eye Tracker gaze tracking equipment, a laptop computer was used for the piloting. The laptop had the drawing application installed, and the task of the participants was to draw a face out of their imagination. After the piloting process, an interview was conducted with each participant, where users were invited to express their feedback on the application's usability and functionality and suggest ways of improvement. Due to the unique way the user interacts with the program (e.g., eye gaze), it was critical to discover possible issues during use and apply relevant changes that would help improve the user's experience. Additionally, a recording of the drawing process was captured for each user to uncover problems that the users may not have observed. The following data were collected for each user: data on task execution time, percentages of successful and unsuccessful attempts, and the user's dead time, i.e., the time interval during which the user interrupted the process of interacting with the application because they encountered some difficulty during the operation of the application. A more extensive evaluation experiment followed the pilot phase, where a larger number of users evaluated the final version of the application.

4.3 Equipment and Tools

During the evaluation experiment, the Tobii 4C Eye Tracker was used similarly to the piloting. However, a desktop computer was used instead of a laptop to facilitate more comfortable viewing by utilizing a 21.5-inch monitor (Fig. 2). Before conducting the experiment, participants had to answer an open question to self-evaluate their drawing abilities. The pre-question was (translated from Greek):

- Do you think that you're good at drawing?

In addition, after finishing the experiment, a semi-structured interview was conducted that included the following questions (translated from Greek):

- How would you describe the experience of designing with an eye tracker?
- Did you enjoy the designing process?
- How would you rate the application?
- Are there any suggestions for improving the application?
- Are there any suggestions for improving the designing process?

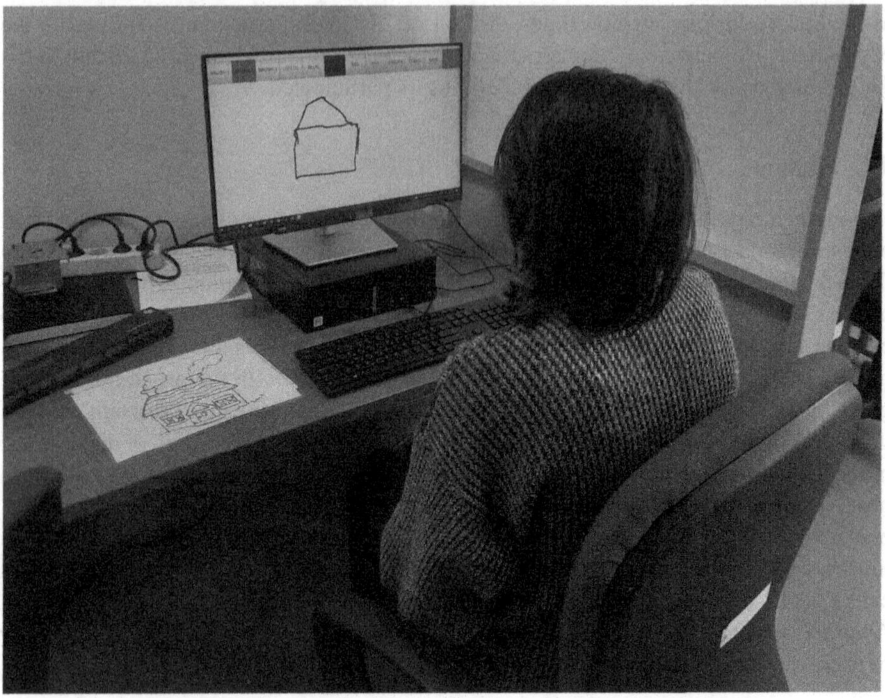

Fig. 2. A user that is drawing with their gaze during the experiment.

4.4 Experiment Protocol

Before the experiment commenced, each participant was informed about the experiment and was asked to sign a consent form. In addition, they were asked to self-assess their drawing abilities. Afterward, participants had to take a seat in front of the screen where the eye tracker was attached, and they were asked to follow the calibration instructions of the eye tracker. After the successful calibration of the eye tracker, participants were ready to use the drawing application. At this point, the researcher guided the participant through the application by presenting the available options and their functionalities and how to change between the two modes: drawing and viewing. After the application's presentation and the clarifications when needed, participants were asked to take some time to familiarize themselves with the application. After the participant was acclimated with the application and its function, they were given a simple house drawing that they could examine for a few minutes and were asked to try to recreate it as close to the original as they could. An identical drawing was given to each participant and is depicted in Fig. 3. The house depicted in the drawing was chosen as it has a combination of straight and curved lines that would present a certain level of difficulty, even for users with some drawing experience. The task was considered complete when the participants felt satisfied with their result or deemed that it was 'the best they could do'.

Fig. 3. The house that was used as a model for the participants to try and replicate with their drawing.

Although there were no time limitations, it was observed that the acclimation phase took no longer than 2 to 3 min for each participant, while, on the other hand, the drawing phase ranged from 10 to 15 min. At the end of the experiment, participants participated in a semi-structured interview regarding their experience with the application.

Moreover, a small sample of the participants was selected to participate in a longitudinal study where they used the application frequently to examine if this could have any meaningful improvement in their eye tracking drawing skills. The procedure followed by those participants after their first attempt was different as they were already familiar with the application, and no further instructions were needed. Furthermore, another distinction from the first time they participated in the experiment is that after finishing their drawing, they were only asked if they felt that their drawing skills had improved.

5 Results and Discussion

The qualitative analysis of the semi-structured interviews mainly revealed positive results concerning the participants' experience with the application. In the question regarding the participants' self-evaluation of their drawing abilities, only 6 out of 25 participants stated that there were competent at drawing, while 5 reported average drawing skills, with the rest noting that they felt poor at drawing. Even though most of the participants stated that they were not talented in drawing (19 out of 25), the post-experiment interview responses showed that the majority of the participants (21 out of 25) enjoyed the drawing process with an eye tracker; only 4 participants stated that they did not enjoy the process with 1 of them stating that they did not want to try it again. Moreover, all the participants thought that the application was interesting and easy to learn, and they provided constructive feedback for improvements for a future version of the application. For example, 5 participants highlighted the importance of adding an 'undo' button to the application. At the same time, 3 participants mentioned that instead of a plain white canvas, there should be a faded grid or aligned dots that would help the drawing process by guiding the gaze to predefined positions. In addition, 9 participants stated that the 'eraser' tool should be improved by adding different sizes to be more precise when erasing, as sometimes they felt that it was too large to accurately perform the erasing of fine details. In this context, 5 participants asked for a greater selection of colors and brush alternatives, while the option of moving the toolbar sideways to have more drawing space was also mentioned by a participant.

Furthermore, there were some noteworthy comments regarding certain implementation details and the peculiarities of gaze drawing. For example, 3 of the participants felt there should be better control of the speed of the marker, while 2 participants felt it was challenging to draw a curved line and proposed "autocorrection" features (where the line drawn is reshaped to the perfect version of the line/curve that most closely resembles) for a smoother result. The sensitivity of the marker was also an issue widely discussed, with several participants proposing that the sensitivity should be higher (3 out of 25) while others that it should be lower (5 out of 25).

Regarding the comments about the drawing sensitivity and the speed of the marker, it should be noted that the application does not set these parameters, and instead, they are directly controlled by the eye movement (e.g., a sudden movement of the eye from the left to the right of the screen area results in a line that covers the entire width of the screen). A potential modification in the speed and responsiveness of the marker would be to add a time delay (the current version is optimized for maximized responsiveness given the hardware used), but that would result in lines that are drawn with a delay giving the user time to look back on the line that is yet to be drawn resulting in potentially unintended inputs.

Overall, participants, despite that they felt that it was not so easy to draw with their eyes, enjoyed the experience and thought that drawing with their gaze was an exciting and fun experience.

The participants who took part in the longitudinal study revealed that their drawing skills markedly improved each time they used the application and mentioned that their confidence in drawing increased as they spent more time with the application. Additionally, all participants of the longitudinal study revealed that, given their improvement, they felt more inclined to use the application daily than when they had used it only once. Figure 4 shows from screenshots (1) to (4) the progress in the drawings of a participant that stated that he had poor drawing skills. Comparing the first attempt (1) with the last (4) reveals an increased detail in the drawing of the house while being a step closer to the original (for someone with no drawing experience).

Fig. 4. The figure depicts the progress in the drawing skills of a user participating in the longitudinal study where (1) is the first drawing and (4) is the last.

6 Conclusion, Limitations and Future Work

The paper presents a drawing application that employs the user's gaze as an input method for drawing while utilizing affordable and commercially available eye tracking hardware. An evaluation experiment investigated the users' opinions expressed in a semi-structured interview regarding their experience with the application and potential suggestions for improvements. A qualitative analysis of the results revealed that -even though most users had self-evaluated as not competent in drawing- they liked drawing with their gaze and found it particularly interesting. Additionally, despite most of them mentioning that it was not so easy to draw with their eyes, the overwhelming majority of the users said that the application was easy to learn. The latter point was also corroborated by the findings of the longitudinal study, with participants stating that they felt they improved in drawing while using the application repeatedly for a longer period of time and with some of them mentioning that they could utilize it in their daily lives. Finally, the participants made suggestions that could be integrated into a future version of the application that also highlight some limitations of the application, with some notable mentions being to include drawing assists in the form of grid lines or dots as well as an "autocorrection" feature that draws the ideal version of the line that the user designed. Another potential shortcoming is that the current application version does not offer advanced features such as moving and resizing objects which can be considered for inclusion in subsequent versions. Our work presents the first -to our knowledge- longitudinal study for a drawing application that uses gaze as an input method for non-disabled individuals, with results showing that, given enough practice time, it can be a viable alternative to typical drawing applications.

Acknowledgements. The authors would like to thank Konstantinos Benakis for developing an early version of the application.

References

1. Schroeder, S., Hyönä, J., Liversedge, S.P.: Developmental eye-tracking research in reading: introduction to the special issue. J. Cogn. Psychol. **27**, 500–510 (2015). https://doi.org/10.1080/20445911.2015.1046877
2. Lahey, J.N., Oxley, D.: The power of eye tracking in economics experiments. Am. Econ. Rev. **106**, 309–313 (2016). https://doi.org/10.1257/aer.p20161009
3. Armstrong, T., Olatunji, B.O.: Eye tracking of attention in the affective disorders: a meta-analytic review and synthesis. Clin. Psychol. Rev. **32**, 704–723 (2012). https://doi.org/10.1016/j.cpr.2012.09.004
4. Chita-Tegmark, M.: Attention allocation in ASD: a review and meta-analysis of eye-tracking studies. Rev. J. Autism Dev. Disord. **3**(3), 209–223 (2016). https://doi.org/10.1007/s40489-016-0077-x
5. Itti, L.: New eye-tracking techniques may revolutionize mental health screening. Neuron **88**, 442–444 (2015). https://doi.org/10.1016/j.neuron.2015.10.033
6. Xenos, M., Rigou, M.: Teaching HCI design in a flipped learning M.Sc. course using eye-tracking peer evaluation data. In: 17th European Conference on e-Learning, pp. 611–619, Athens, Greece (2019)
7. Murata, A., Hayashi, K., Moriwaka, M., Hayami, T.: Study on character input methods using eye-gaze input interface. In: 2012 Proceedings of SICE Annual Conference (SICE), pp. 1402–1407 (2012)
8. Murata, A., Moriwaka, M.: Effectiveness of eye-gaze input method: comparison of speed and accuracy among three eye-gaze input method. In: Ahram, T.Z., Falcão, C. (eds.) AHFE 2018. AISC, vol. 794, pp. 763–772. Springer, Cham (2019). https://doi.org/10.1007/978-3-319-94947-5_75
9. Onishi, R., et al.: GazeBreath: input method using gaze pointing and breath selection. In: Augmented Humans 2022, pp. 1–9. Association for Computing Machinery, New York, USA (2022). https://doi.org/10.1145/3519391.3519405
10. Folgieri, R., Lucchiari, C., Granato, M., Grechi, D.: Brain, technology and creativity. BrainArt: a BCI-based entertainment tool to enact creativity and create drawing from cerebral rhythms. In: Lee, N. (ed.) Digital Da Vinci, pp. 65–97. Springer, New York (2014). https://doi.org/10.1007/978-1-4939-0965-0_4
11. Harada, S., Wobbrock, J.O., Landay, J.A.: VoiceDraw: a hands-free voice-driven drawing application for people with motor impairments. In: Proceedings of the 9th International ACM SIGACCESS Conference on Computers and Accessibility, pp. 27–34. Association for Computing Machinery, New York, USA (2007). https://doi.org/10.1145/1296843.1296850
12. Drey, T., Gugenheimer, J., Karlbauer, J., Milo, M., Rukzio, E.: VRSketchIn: Exploring the design space of pen and tablet interaction for 3D sketching in virtual reality. In: Proceedings of the 2020 CHI Conference on Human Factors in Computing Systems, pp. 1–14. Association for Computing Machinery, New York, USA (2020). https://doi.org/10.1145/3313831.3376628
13. Gips, J., Olivieri, P.: An eye control system for persons with disabilities. In: Computer Science Department, The Eleventh International Conference on Technology and Persons with Disabilities, Los Angeles, California (1996)

14. Meyer, A., Dittmar, M.: Conception and development of an accessible application for producing images by gaze interaction-EyeArt. Presented at the (2007)
15. van der Kamp, J., Sundstedt, V.: Gaze and voice controlled drawing. In: Proceedings of the 1st Conference on Novel Gaze-Controlled Applications, pp. 1–8. Association for Computing Machinery, New York, USA (2011). https://doi.org/10.1145/1983302.1983311
16. Heikkilä, H.: EyeSketch: a drawing application for gaze control. In: Proceedings of the 2013 Conference on Eye Tracking South Africa, pp. 71–74. Association for Computing Machinery, New York, USA (2013). https://doi.org/10.1145/2509315.2509332
17. Heikkilä, H.: Tools for a gaze-controlled drawing application – comparing gaze gestures against dwell buttons. In: Kotzé, P., Marsden, G., Lindgaard, G., Wesson, J., Winckler, M. (eds.) INTERACT 2013. LNCS, vol. 8118, pp. 187–201. Springer, Heidelberg (2013). https://doi.org/10.1007/978-3-642-40480-1_12
18. Pfeuffer, K., Mecke, L., Delgado Rodriguez, S., Hassib, M., Maier, H., Alt, F.: Empirical evaluation of gaze-enhanced menus in virtual reality. In: Proceedings of the 26th ACM Symposium on Virtual Reality Software and Technology, pp. 1–11. Association for Computing Machinery, New York, USA (2020). https://doi.org/10.1145/3385956.3418962
19. Creed, C., Frutos-Pascual, M., Williams, I.: Multimodal gaze interaction for creative design. In: Proceedings of the 2020 CHI Conference on Human Factors in Computing Systems, pp. 1–13. Association for Computing Machinery, New York, USA (2020). https://doi.org/10.1145/3313831.3376196
20. Santella, A., DeCarlo, D.: Abstracted painterly renderings using eye-tracking data. In: Proceedings of the 2nd International Symposium on Non-Photorealistic Animation and Rendering, pp. 75-ff. Association for Computing Machinery, New York, USA (2002). https://doi.org/10.1145/508530.508544
21. Scalera, L., Seriani, S., Gallina, P., Lentini, M., Gasparetto, A.: Human-robot interaction through eye tracking for artistic drawing. Robotics **10**, 54 (2021). https://doi.org/10.3390/robotics10020054
22. Jacob, R.J.K.: What you look at is what you get: eye movement-based interaction techniques. In: Proceedings of the SIGCHI Conference on Human Factors in Computing Systems, pp. 11–18. Association for Computing Machinery, New York, USA (1990). https://doi.org/10.1145/97243.97246

A Practical CAD Method for the Visually Impaired: A Case of Modeling the Leaning Tower of Pisa

Kazunori Minatani(✉)

National Center for University Entrance Examinations,
Komaba 2-19-23, Meguro-ku, Tokyo 153-8501, Japan
minatani@rd.dnc.ac.ip

Abstract. The visually impaired, who cannot see graphics displayed on a screen, are not capable of 3D modeling using commonly used CAD software. On the other hand, the significance of digital fabrication using 3D CAD is enormous in satisfying their needs. Based on this awareness of the problem, the author, who is himself visually impaired (totally blind), has promoted the direction of programmable CAD and devised a form of CAD modeling that does not require confirmation of the modeled object on a screen. CAD is used not only for designing practical machine parts but also for modeling 3D models. As part of a study of CAD modeling methods for the visually impaired, a model of the Leaning Tower of Pisa was made, together with devising the programmable CAD processing system used and the method of modeling. Through subjective evaluation, it was confirmed that the model was comparable to models modeled by sighted people with regard to similarity to the real object and the beauty of the models. The method proposed by the author can be expected to function as a CAD modeling method for the visually impaired. The method can be improved so as to enable use of the system by a wider range of visually impaired people, taking into account their unique needs.

Keywords: Visually impaired people · 3D CAD · 3D modelling · Programmable CAD · Method of first-person research · Assistive technology

1 Introduction: The Objective and Its Significance

The visually impaired, who cannot see graphics displayed on a screen, are not capable of 3D modeling using commonly used CAD software. Severely visually impaired people operate computers using screen reader software, which presents character information displayed on the screen by the operating system to the user (the visually impaired). Voice output using a text-to-speech engine or Braille output to a refreshable Braille display is used as a means of presentation, but character information is still the target of presentation. A practical means has

M. Antona and C. Stephanidis (Eds.): HCII 2023, LNCS 14020, pp. 440–450, 2023.
https://doi.org/10.1007/978-3-031-35681-0_29

not been established for the visually impaired to represent graphics displayed on a screen as they are (without converting them into character information). By way of example, CAD software used to perform 3D modeling on a computer makes it essential to see the graphics in order to grasp the object being modeled. Therefore, such CAD software is not available for the visually impaired who operate computers using screen reader software.

On the other hand, the visually impaired have many needs for products that assist their daily living (self-help devices), but because they are a minority, such products are not mass-produced and must be tailor-made. The significance of digital fabrication using 3D CAD is enormous in satisfying these needs. Such utilization of digital fabrication is called DIY assistive technology [1] and is attracting attention from people with disabilities and their supporters [2–4].

In the use of 3D objects for the visually impaired, attempts to provide such objects to them are abundant, but research on the production of these objects by the users themselves is extremely scarce. Research and practice in providing information to visually impaired people by semi-3D [6] (2.5D) or 3D objects [5] is active in many realms, [7] including maps, [8] paintings [9,10], and museum exhibits. [11] These are recognized for playing a fundamental role in their social life, such as education, cultural access, and mobility. [12] On the other hand, research on how visually impaired people can produce 3D objects is extremely limited. Inquiries into the CAD methods available to them have been limited to research aimed at proof of concept, with the main focus on experimental device inventions [13,14].

It must also be noted that the absence of such a versatile means of 3D production for visually impaired people is a severe barrier to the provision of semi-3D and 3D-based information to them in a user-participatory manner. If visually impaired people themselves can prototype maps and replicas that are easy for them to recognize, the efficiency of the creation process and the quality of the produced products should improve.

Based on this awareness of the problem, the author, who is himself visually impaired (totally blind), has promoted the direction of programmable CAD and devised a form of CAD modeling that does not require confirmation of the modeled object on a screen. [15,16] The practicality of this method has been confirmed in the production of simple-shaped machine parts required for self-help equipment [15].

On the other hand, CAD is used not only for designing practical machine parts but also for modeling 3D models. In such modeling using CAD, the reproduction of an actual thing and the realization of beauty are generally pursued. This paper evaluates the effectiveness of the author's proposed CAD modeling method for the visually impaired in the production of 3D models. In general, models are more complex in shape than the mechanical parts of self-help devices. Therefore, this effectiveness assessment will verify whether the method in question can withstand more advanced applications.

How to evaluate the achievement of such research is itself an issue that must be examined. This modeling method was proposed by the author himself, and it is also he who performs the modeling using this method. Therefore, the task of developing a CAD modeling method for the visually impaired, which the author is promoting, can be regarded as a first-person research project. In a previous study that examined the effectiveness of this method for the production of simple-shaped machine parts required for self-help devices, it was evaluated by verifying whether the devices produced by this method were useful for their purpose. [15] The target of the study in this paper is the effectiveness of this method for the production of models, and this evaluation method cannot be applied. There is no precedent for a study that evaluates the quality of models made by visually impaired people using CAD. Therefore, proposing and applying a valid evaluation method also forms part of the task of this paper.

2 Established Modeling Tasks and Production Methods

For this purpose, the author created a 3D model of the Leaning Tower of Pisa (Fig. 1). This famous tower was selected as the target for the following reasons: the regularity of the shape changes from the second to the seventh floors and the effective use of loop processing; similarities and differences between the geometry of the first and second to fourth floors, allowing the use of programmable methods; high consistency of shapes with no addition of irregular decorations, thus keeping the program code relatively logical; and the actual object is widely known, and subjective evaluation is easy.

Fig. 1. The created 3D model of the Leaning Tower of Pisa.

From the point of view of utilizing the characteristics of programmable CAD, several policies were adopted. The modeling was attempted by utilizing logical sums, differences, and logical products of geometrical solids without pursuing free-form modeling. As the data is described using programmable CAD methods, the inclination of the tower, the number of floors, the number of columns, the number of bells, and so on can be easily changed numerically. This allows flexible modification and adjustment of the shape based on the printed results.

As the programmable CAD processor, JSCAD [18] was used, which is written in JavaScript. In previous studies [15,16], OpenSCAD [19] was used. From the perspective of this paper, JSCAD has the following advantages over other programmable CAD software, including OpenSCAD. Firstly, it can be executed from the command line, and (if computing resources permit) parameters can be intuitively adjusted by entering numerical values into a Web form from a browser. This allows even users who are not CAD experts to adjust the geometry to their liking in the future. Secondly, the processing system can be extended by utilizing the rich assets of the JavaScript language, including the implementation of functions for debugging. Specifically, by verifying numerical data such as the size of objects when compiling from source code to STL data, it is possible to check to a certain extent whether the products are in line with the user's intentions. This function is of great significance for visually impaired people who cannot check the shape of the product by looking at the graphics. The development potential of these two benefits is discussed in more detail in the conclusions.

The modeling work was carried out in a similar way to coding by programmers in general: the source code was written in a general-purpose editor and compiled in a programmable CAD processor to generate STL data. Many programmable CAD software packages have a built-in source code editor, which allows modeling to be performed while checking the objects generated from the source code being input in real time as graphics (Fig. 2). However, the inability to see such graphics is similar to general CAD software, which is not available to visually impaired people. Because the visually impaired do not benefit from the ability to check the objects generated by programmable CAD software as graphics in real time, general-purpose editor software with excellent source code editing functions was used instead (Fig. 3).

The author, the creator of this model, is not able to grasp the shape by looking at the real object or photographs, so the challenge is how to ascertain the shape of the original Leaning Tower of Pisa. The means used by the author are described below.

First, the author made use of his memory of tactile observation of a model. The Spanish Association for the Visually Impaired (ONCE) runs an institution called the Museum of Touch. This facility, located in Madrid, Spain, houses models of many architectural monuments that have been selected as World Heritage Sites, including a model of the Leaning Tower of Pisa, which is about 60 cm in height (Fig. 4). The author has experience of having observed this, but this observation remains purely in his memory. It is totally inadequate for modeling the architectural form, especially if the lack of memory of details is taken into account.

Second, 3D models of the Leaning Tower of Pisa from the 3D model data-sharing service Thingiverse were also utilized. These 3D models are to be used as comparison objects for subjective evaluation. For parts of the shape that were too detailed to be confirmed by touch, the STL data conversion function of JSCAD was used, and the returned data was cut out and enlarged using programmable CAD and 3D printed for confirmation.

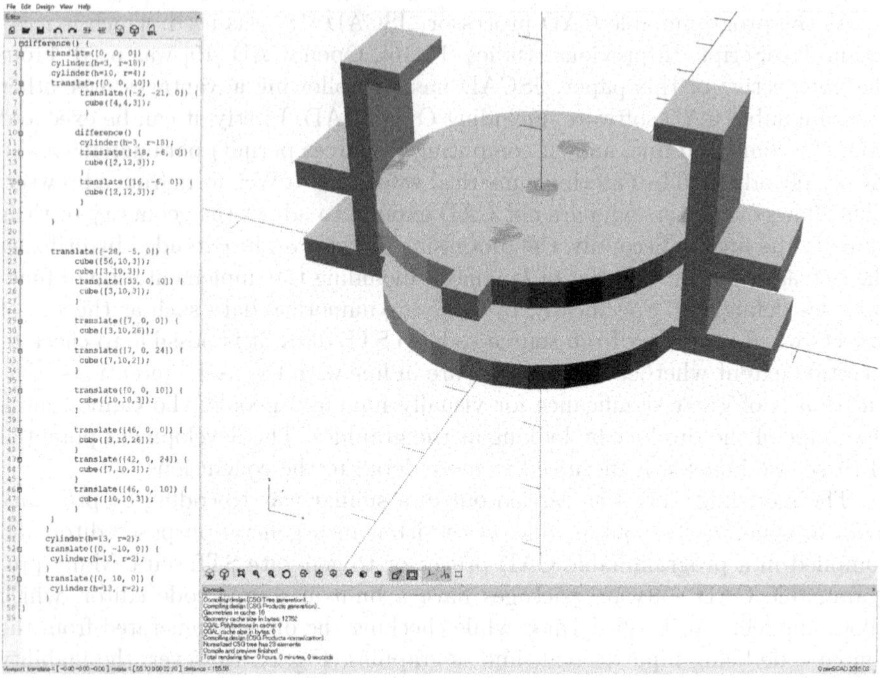

Fig. 2. OpenSCAD editing screen with a graphic representation of the current modeling.

Third, he searched for information that needed to be supplemented from documents on the Web, including Wikipedia. Such texts can be easily read with screen reader software. Specifically, he attempted to confirm the number of stories of the tower and investigate the number of columns, because even between 3D models submitted to Thingiverse, the number of columns does not always match.

3 Evaluation

3.1 Design of the Evaluation

With the aim of verifying whether the CAD method proposed by the author for the visually impaired can be used for the production of models, an evaluation of the above-mentioned model of the Leaning Tower of Pisa was carried out.

In designing the evaluation, the method was examined. Previously, no method had been formulated to evaluate the quality of models made by visually impaired people using CAD. On the other hand, the viewpoint that models are evaluated according to their visibility is well established. Verifying the social understandability of the produced models is essential for evaluating the effectiveness of this

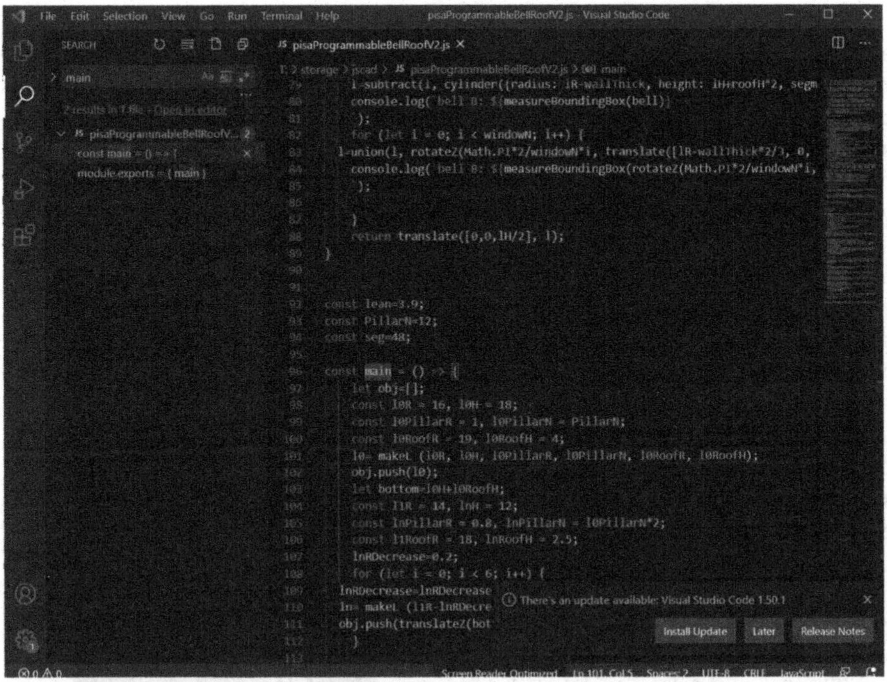

Fig. 3. The editing screen of this paper showing some of its source code.

method, and this perspective of verifying the visibility of the models was followed. Specifically, a subjective evaluation was carried out by sighted persons without visual impairment. If the perspective of utilizing the model for the visually impaired is taken into account, there is a certain significance in conducting a subjective evaluation in which a visually impaired person is a participant in the experiment and observes the model by touching it. However, this evaluation is not an evaluation of model making by visually impaired people, but an evaluation of models that are meaningful to visually impaired people, which was not deemed to be appropriate for the present purpose.

Generally, the quality of a model is discussed in terms of its similarity to the actual object - in this case, the Leaning Tower of Pisa as an actual building - but often the beauty of the model is also a subject of discussion. Therefore, in this evaluation, in addition to similarity to the real thing, beauty was also a subject of evaluation.

The objects for comparison by participants were four models: the top three 3D model data found by searching for "Pisa tower" on the 3D data-sharing website Thingiverse [21], and the 3D model data made for this paper (Fig. 5). There is sufficient rationale for assuming that the models uploaded to Thingiverse were created by sighted persons, and not created by the visually impaired.

In a preliminary experiment, participants were asked to rate the similarity and beauty of each of the models on a five-point scale. The majority of the participants' answers gave the same rating of 5 or 4 for all four models. This tendency in the way the answers were given may mask deviations from the perspective of comparing the modeled objects in this paper with other 3D models. In interviews with participants conducted after the answers were given, scores were also given based on absolute ratings based on each respondent's everyday senses, and there was little interest in making relative comparisons between the four scores. Therefore, it was decided to re-examine the evaluation method.

The subsequent experiment took the form of asking participants to rank the four 3D models relative to each other. Participants in the experiment were asked to score the four 3D models on a scale of 3, 2, 1, and 0, starting with the one with the highest resemblance to the real object. In other words, the higher the score, the higher the relative similarity was rated. The same scoring was also sought in the evaluation of aesthetics. The four models were labeled A, B, C, and D, respectively. The model created in this paper, that is, the model produced by the CAD method proposed by the author for visually impaired people, was labeled C. The experiment took the form of presenting these models printed by a 3D printer to the participants and asking them to fill in the rankings in a questionnaire.

Fig. 4. Model of the Leaning Tower of Pisa in the Museum of Touch of the Spanish Association for the Visually Impaired.

Prusa MINI [20] was used as the 3D printer for printing the models and PrusaSlicer as the slicer software. Black PLA materials were used for 3D printing. When printing, the height was adjusted to be between 10 cm and 17 cm, considering the maximum print size of the Prusa MINI and simplicity of observation, while taking into account the respective precautions for printing in the provisos attached to the 3D data.

Eight adult participants in their 20 s to 60 s, two males and six females, participated in the experiment. The presence or absence of visual impairment must be noted as an attribute that influences the perspective and means of evaluation of the models, especially considering the task of this study. None of the participants had visual impairments and all were sighted.

One of the participants declared that two of the four models would result in the same evaluation and give the first rank to them. Originally, 3 points were

Fig. 5. Four 3D models used for the evaluation (C is the author's work, partly differing from the final version).

awarded to the model that was given the first rank, but for this response, 2.5 points were awarded to each of the two first-place models. This process resulted in a total score of 5 points for the participant in question, as well as for the other participants, and avoided over- or under-influencing the results.

3.2 Results

GNU R [22] version 3.3.3 was used for all of the following validations. It should be noted that the purpose of this evaluation is to verify whether there is a significant difference between the models produced by the CAD method for the visually impaired proposed by the author and those produced by sighted people in terms of similarity to the real object and aesthetics. In other words, it is not to verify whether the former is superior to the latter.

Similarity to the Real Object. The median additive scores given to models A, B, C, and D were 2.25, 0, 2, and 1, respectively. The results of multiple comparisons by Wilcoxon's rank sum test with Holm's adjusting method between A, B, C, and D, respectively, are shown below.

```
␣␣␣␣␣␣␣␣Pairwise␣comparisons␣using␣Wilcoxon␣signed␣rank␣test

data:␣␣melted_r$value␣and␣melted_r$variable
```

```
␣␣a␣␣␣␣␣b␣␣␣␣␣c
b␣0.067␣-␣␣␣␣␣-
c␣0.319␣0.139␣-
d␣0.260␣0.260␣0.573

P␣value␣adjustment␣method:␣holm
```

For the model created in this paper and for all three remaining models created by sighted persons, the median of scores given was 2 for the former, as mentioned above, and 1 for the latter. A Mann-Whitney U test between the former and the latter showed no significant differences (p=0.3715).

On the Beauty of the Models. The medians of the additional points given to models A, B, C, and D were 2, 1, 1.5, and 1, respectively. The results of multiple comparisons by Wilcoxon's rank sum test with Holm's adjusting method between A, B, C, and D, respectively, are shown below.

```
␣␣␣␣␣␣␣␣Pairwise␣comparisons␣using␣Wilcoxon␣signed␣rank␣test

data:␣␣melted_b$value␣and␣melted_b$variable

␣␣a␣␣␣␣b␣␣␣␣c
b␣0.18␣-␣␣␣␣-
c␣1.00␣1.00␣-
d␣0.53␣1.00␣1.00

P␣value␣adjustment␣method:␣holm
```

For the model created in this paper and for all three remaining models created by sighted persons, the median of scores given was 1.5 for the former, as mentioned above, and 1.5 for the latter. A Mann-Whitney U test between the former and the latter showed no significant differences (p=0.4716).

4 Conclusions and Future Challenges

A model of the Leaning Tower of Pisa was made as part of a study of CAD modeling methods for the visually impaired. Through subjective evaluation, it was confirmed that the model was comparable to models modeled by sighted people. The method proposed by the author can be expected to function as a CAD modeling method for the visually impaired.

Researchs aimed at developing experimental devices that can be used by visually impaired people to perform CAD [13,14] assume relatively simple shapes as objects to be modeled. Such research should be conducted on more complex shapes, such as the one shown in this paper, from the point of view of drawing out the full potential of the visually impaired and of practicality.

The method examined in this paper, which has been validated as a modeling tool in addition to a self-help device production tool, should be made readily available to a wider range of visually impaired people. To achieve this, it will be necessary to reduce the difficulty of this method. In contrast to intuitive modeling, which is done by looking at graphics, in this method as currently devised, the user has to perform many calculations accurately and memorize the shape. To reduce this burden, the debugging functionality mentioned in the second advantage of JSCAD could be useful.

It would also be desirable to develop this method into a modeling method for visually impaired people without CAD knowledge. As mentioned in the introduction, visually impaired people in general have more needs for 3D modeling than sighted persons, especially in terms of the production of self-help devices. Moreover, CAD modeling is a valued skill with preferential salaries, and its use is restricted to personnel with a certain level of training. Therefore, the approach described in the previous paragraph of reducing the difficulty of CAD methods alone does not allow visually impaired people in general to perform modeling that meets their needs. Programmable CAD is also referred to as parametric CAD. This is an expression that focuses on the characteristic of it which allows the objects generated to be varied by adjusting the parameters that are given. It is desirable to develop a mechanism that makes use of this characteristic to enable flexible object generation that fits the user's needs from a given source code by simple parameter input.

Acknowledgments. This work was supported by KAKENHI (21H04419) and JST RISTEX Grant Number JPMJRX21I5, Japan.

References

1. Hurst, A., Tobias, J.: Empowering individuals with do-it-yourself assistive technology. In: Proceedings of The 13th International ACM SIGACCESS Conference on Computers and Accessibility, pp. 11–18. (2011)
2. Hurst, A., Kane, S.: Making making accessible. In: Proceedings of the 12th International Conference on Interaction Design and Children, pp. 635–638 (2013)
3. Hook, J., Verbaan, S., Durrant, A., Olivier, P., Wright, P.: A study of the challenges related to DIY assistive technology in the context of children with disabilities. In: Proceedings of the 2014 Conference on Designing Interactive Systems, pp. 597–606 (2014)
4. Steele, k., Blaser, B., Cakmak, M.: Accessible making: designing makerspaces for accessibility. Int. J. Des. Learn. **9**(1), 114–121 (2018)
5. Karbowski, C.-F.: See 3D: 3D printing for people who are blind. J. Sci. Educ. Stud. Disabil. 23 (2020)
6. Shinohara, M., Shimizu, Y., Mochizuki, A.: Three-dimensional tactile display for the blind. IEEE Trans. Rehabilit. Eng. **6**(3), 249–256 (1998)
7. Butler, M., Holloway, L., Reinders, S., Goncu, C., Marriott, K.: Technology developments in touch-based accessible graphics: a systematic review of research 2010–2020. In: CHI 2021: Proceedings of the 2021 CHI Conference on Human Factors in Computing Systems, pp. 1–15. (2021)

8. Holloway, L., Butler, M., Marriott, K.: Accessible maps for the blind: comparing 3D printed models with tactile graphics. In: CHI 2018: Proceedings of the 2018 CHI Conference on Human Factors in Computing Systems, pp. 1–13 (2018)
9. Stangl, A., Hsu, C., Yeh, T.: Transcribing across the senses: community efforts to create 3D printable accessible tactile pictures for young children with visual impairments. In: Proceedings of the 17th International ACM SIGACCESS Conference on Computers and Accessibility, pp 127–137 (2015)
10. Dao, S.D., Truong, T., Pissaloux, E., Romeo, K., Djoussouf, L.: Semi-automatic Contour "Gist" Creation for Museum Painting Tactile Exploration. In: Miesenberger, K., et al. (eds.) ICCHP 2022. LNCS, vol. 13341, pp. 270–277. Springer, Heidelberg (2022). https://doi.org/10.1007/978-3-031-08648-9_31
11. Reichinger, A., Carrizosa, H.G., Travnicek, C.: Designing an interactive tactile relief of the Meissen table fountain. In: Miesenberger, K., Kouroupetroglou, G. (eds.) ICCHP 2018. LNCS, vol. 10897, pp. 209–216. Springer, Cham (2018). https://doi.org/10.1007/978-3-319-94274-2_28
12. Gual, J., Puyuelo, M., Lloverás, J., Merino, L.: Visual impairment and urban orientation. Pilot study with tactile maps produced through 3D printing. Psyecology **3**(2), 239–250 (2012)
13. Siu, A.-F., Kim, S., Miele, J.-A., Follmer, S.: ShapeCAD: an accessible 3D modelling workflow for the blind and visually-impaired via 2.5D shape displays. In: The 21st International ACM SIGACCESS Conference on Computers and Accessibility, pp. 342–354 (2019)
14. Lieb, S., Rosenmeier, B., Thormahlen, T., Buettner, N.: Haptic and auditive mesh inspection for blind 3D modelers. In: The 22nd International ACM SIGACCESS Conference on Computers and Accessibility, pp. 1–10 (2020)
15. Minatani, K.: Finding 3D CAD data production methods that work for people with visual impairments. In: Stephanidis, C. (ed.) HCI 2017. CCIS, vol. 713, pp. 548–554. Springer, Cham (2017). https://doi.org/10.1007/978-3-319-58750-9_76
16. Minatani, K.: A proposed method for producing embossed dots graphics with a 3D printer. In: Miesenberger, K., Kouroupetroglou, G. (eds.) ICCHP 2018. LNCS, vol. 10897, pp. 143–148. Springer, Cham (2018). https://doi.org/10.1007/978-3-319-94274-2_20
17. Introduction? Web de la ONCE. https://www.once.es/otras-webs/english. Accessed 23 Jan 2023
18. JSCAD - JavaScript CAD. https://openjscad.xyz/. Accessed 23 Jan 2023
19. OpenSCAD - The Programmers Solid 3D CAD Modeller. https://openscad.org/. Accessed 23 Jan 2023
20. Original Prusa MINI+ — Original Prusa 3D printers directly from Josef Prusa. https://www.prusa3d.com/category/original-prusa-mini/. Accessed 23 Jan 2023
21. Thingiverse - Digital Designs for Physical Objects. https://www.thingiverse.com/. Accessed 23 Jan 2023
22. R Core Team: R: A language and environment for statistical computing, R Foundation for Statistical Computing, Vienna, Austria (2017)

Inclusion Through Accessibility. Handi Bot, a Translator for Portuguese Sign Language

Sónia Rafael[1,2(✉)], Francisco Rebelo[1,2], Beatriz Pinto[3], Andreia Gil[3], Catharina Lima[3], Joana Chitas[3], Marta Pascoal[3], and Lúcio Simões[3]

[1] CIAUD, Research Center for Architecture, Urbanism and Design, Lisbon School of Architecture, University of Lisbon, Rua Sá Nogueira, Pólo Universitário, Alto da Ajuda, 1349-063 Lisbon, Portugal
srafael@campus.ul.pt, frebelo@fa.ulisboa.pt

[2] ITI – Interactive Technologies Institute/LARSyS, Faculty of Fine-Arts, University of Lisbon. Largo da Academia Nacional e Belas Artes, 1249-058 Lisbon, Portugal

[3] Faculty of Fine-Arts, University of Lisbon. Largo da Academia Nacional de Belas Artes, 1249-058 Lisbon, Portugal
{andreiagil,catharinalima,joanachitas, marta.pascoal}@edu.ulisboa.pt, lucio.simoes@campus.ul.pt

Abstract. The project described in this paper is based on the concepts of accessibility and inclusion, with a special focus on the online experience of deaf people. Digital inclusion is inevitably linked to accessibility, as technologies allow for better integration into society through their association with opportunities, citizenship, and knowledge. A significant part of people with hearing impairment have difficulty understanding textual information, as Portuguese is not their first language and, being a phonetic language, it is difficult to learn since a profoundly deaf person cannot associate sounds with characters. That said, the first language of a deaf person is sign language and they prefer online communication in sign language through video, thus avoiding writing or reading. Most sites still do not legitimize sign language, creating a barrier in communication since accessing any information requires knowledge of Portuguese. Our project is therefore trying to eliminate these barriers and thus improve the online experience of these people. We start from the concept of Assistive Technology, which are resources and services that aim to facilitate the daily activities of people with disabilities. They seek to increase functional capacities and thus promote the independence and autonomy of those who use them. To this end, we developed Handi, a translator bot that works through a browser extension and translates into sign language any content that appears in the browser, be it text or video. Handi Bot contains accessibility options responding to most user needs. To develop the bot, extensive user research was carried out, with interviews with deaf people and the entire UX design methodology was followed to reach a sustained result.

Keywords: Interaction Design · Accessibility · Inclusion · Deafness · Bot · Browser Extension

M. Antona and C. Stephanidis (Eds.): HCII 2023, LNCS 14020, pp. 451–466, 2023.
https://doi.org/10.1007/978-3-031-35681-0_30

1 Introduction

One of the concerns of designers should be to conceive, develop and implement accessible digital and physical artefacts. For this reason, they must include, in their projects, inclusion concerns that integrate all individuals regardless of their race/ethnicity, economic situation, class, gender, or their disabilities.

Accessibility must always be considered in any project, so that everyone has an equal opportunity to access information.

Nowadays there are already several accessible and inclusive websites that opt for a simplified language – descriptive images with alt-text, audio text reading, option to adjust the contrast and size of the font, etc. Despite these concerns, we know that the interaction and experience of a person who is blind or deaf can never be the same as that of other users.

Digital artifacts are normally designed for people without limiting conditions and then adapted for users with disabilities. For this reason, it is difficult to cover all the needs to make them inclusive and accessible if this has not been designed in advance.

The project presented in this article seeks to address the needs of a group with hearing impairment, and seeks to answer the following question: how can the digital experience of deaf people be made more accessible? What are their main difficulties and needs? What strategies and tools exist, how do they work and how can they be adapted and implemented for the benefit of people with hearing impairment?

It was then necessary to start by understanding the target audience. We noticed that most people with hearing impairment have difficulty understanding textual information. This evidence is since Portuguese is not its mother tongue, but sign language.

Portuguese is more difficult for the deaf to learn because, as it is a phonetic language, each character corresponds to a sound. Only individuals who become deaf after learning the Portuguese language have greater ease in understanding it.

After understanding the target audience, we performed a benchmarking, and some applications were analysed. From these applications we extract relevant formal and conceptual information for our project. A questionnaire was then carried out with a set of questions to understand the difficulties, the levels of written and read Portuguese, and the level of education of deaf people.

Then, the Handi project was defined – a translator bot that works through a browser extension and translates into sign language any content that appears in the browser, whether text or video in Portuguese. The UX Design methodology was used to develop the project prototype and a video that works as a proof of concept.

1.1 Accessibility and Inclusion

Accessibility in the physical world is defined as the degree to which a space is usable by the greatest possible number of people [1]. Accessibility in the digital world is also measured by the degree to which "space" can be used by most people. Today we understand accessibility as a basic requirement of usability in the use of physical and digital spaces.

International Organization for Standardization (ISO) defines accessibility as an "extent to which products, systems, services, environments and facilities can be used by people from a population with the widest range of needs, characteristics and capabilities to achieve identified goals in identified contexts of use" [2].

We can conclude that accessibility is the path to inclusion and turns out to be a subclass of usability, although it should not be confused with it. The definition of the term usability is an attribute related to the ease of use of a product, how quickly people learn to use it, how efficient it is, how memorable is its interaction pattern, how prone to errors and how much users like to use it [3]. Usability is concerned with all potential users, while accessibility seeks to include all its users regardless of whether there are limitations that may prevent the performance of some task. The term accessible implies both physical and communication accessibility. The concept of accessibility directly highlights conditions related to buildings; transport; equipment and furniture; and communications systems [4].

There continues to be a great need for investment in accessibility and inclusion, as design itself can exclude a large proportion of people. Kat Holmes, former director of inclusive design at Microsoft, argues that designing for inclusion starts with recognizing exclusion [5]. When considering accessibility in design, design is much more likely to be the source of exclusion than of inclusion. It is necessary to rethink the way it is created in the digital environment, because while design can encompass all people, it can itself exclude them.

Designers are constantly influenced by their own biases when creating solutions that they can see, hear, touch, and understand. The designer, when creating a solution from his own point of view, without adequate user research, tends to design only for people with similar circumstances or preferences [6].

We believe that most people have felt excluded at some point, and as the individual moves further away from what is socially considered the normative standard, this exclusion will occur more regularly. This fact can be observed from race, class, or gender and from different physical and psychological dispositions, which may involve some type of disability. Inclusion appears in many forms, but exclusion has only one meaning. Holmes [5] suggests asking a hundred people what inclusion means and you will get hundreds of different answers. If we ask the same people what it means to be excluded, the answer will be clearly homogeneous – "that's when I get left out". Daily, people feel excluded in a variety of situations when designers do not pay due attention to certain details: a computer mouse that does not work for left-handed people, vending machines that do not accept multiple payment options, a chair that does not hold obese people, etc. These questions end up proving in practice the way in which society builds the world without thinking about inclusion.

1.2 Universal and Inclusive Design

Accessibility must be integrally related to universal design, in which the process of using a product, service or system can be used by everyone. This relationship between accessibility and universal design puts users on an equal footing, regardless of whether they have any disability.

It is also necessary to remember that a large percentage of the population suffers from some type of limitation that may or may not affect the ability to use technologies and technological products [7]. At the same time, the average age and life expectancy are increasing and with advancing age, human capacities are decreasing [8] "facing problems such as reading on the screen when vision deteriorates or use of a mouse when dexterity decreases" [9].

In this context, universal design and inclusive design are identified, and the barrier that differentiates them is very narrow. We can call inclusive design, the creation of products aimed at a target audience that needs specific equipment that mitigates its limitations and allows ensuring its integration into daily activities. Universal design is characterized by an equitable nature and by being a process of creating products that can be used by people with the widest variety of situations [10].

A design process that is primarily concerned with the user will be the one that will best be able to create an artifact that responds to their needs and requirements.

The term "universal" may connote a "one size fits all" approach with the aim of designing one product that satisfies all types of users [11]. To create accessibility through universal design, empathy is the first step. What makes design, design is creating artifacts for others, understanding their problems, and creating solutions to their needs" [12].

Universal design is the best path to inclusion – while accessible design creates products that can be used by people with disabilities – universal design creates products for the widest possible audience, which includes, but is not limited to, people with disabilities [1]. Therefore, the gateway to universality in design is empathy with the other.

1.3 Assistive Technologies

Assistive technology (AT) is a broad term that integrates assistive, adaptation and rehabilitation devices for people with disabilities. AT artifacts are designed for easy interaction with people and offer additional accessibility to individuals with reduced abilities or disabilities. It's not just restricted to the digital world but is also found in physical artefacts and spaces.

There are many people who are not aware that they use assistive technologies, for example, when wearing glasses and contact lenses, or hearing aids, wheelchairs, canes, tactile maps [6].

Okumura, Rudek and Canciglieri [12] talk about the process of creating assistive technologies and how to understand aspects of universal design, ergonomics, and usability, to serve the largest number of people, considering, in the process of design, the type of persona, the activity and the scenario involved.

Advances in technology and investment in areas of communication and information have been important as technological possibilities have been increasingly developed as instruments for inclusion and interaction across the entire planet.

1.4 Accessibility Rules

For the development of accessibility in assistive technology, it is necessary to comply with legislative requirements. In many countries, from this need, several rules, regulations, and initiatives have emerged to provide universal access to digital space and communication systems for all.

There are a set of recommendations that make web content more accessible. They are the ADA – Americans with Disabilities Act [14] and WCAG 2.1. Web Content Accessibility Guidelines [15].

The ADA recommendations that regulate the rights of citizens with disabilities in the United States of America are established as laws so that people with disabilities can have equal access to public services. In the country, the Department of Justice has already concluded that the lack of accessibility to websites may be a violation of this law. While in the USA the rules are already laws, in Europe the issue is on the public agenda for legislation that will make adherence to accessibility guidelines for web content mandatory.

Portugal was the first Member State of the European Union, in 1999, to adopt accessibility requirements for the contents and services provided by the Public Administration on the Internet. The Portuguese website ecosystem accessibility.gov.pt [16] aims to disseminate, share, and promote best accessibility practices for web content and mobile applications. It provides tools to support accessibility and usability, to ensure the promotion of good practices and improve the experience of using digital services. In "about us" you can read the information for the Web and Mobile Applications Accessibility Directive (Directive 2016/2102), and its respective transposition into the national legal system (DL nº 83/2018, of 19 of October, the XXI Constitutional Government), which brought together in the Agency for Administrative Modernization [17] the technical competences of accessibility and usability.

Today there are strict standards for web accessibility that designers and developers follow when building digital products, services, or systems. The most used model is formulated by the WAI-AGE [18]. The guidelines cover standards for content such as natural information: text, images, and sounds; page structure definitions; code; presentations etc. WAI-AGE Project ended in 2010 and Updated Resources on Web Accessibility for Older Users and Web Accessibility [19] were introduced.

In fact, there needs to be laws to meet basic accessibility needs, but essentially for designers and developers involved in creating accessible products.

2 Characterization of the Hearing-Impaired Population in Portugal

Statistical data are not very accurate about deaf people in Portugal. According to the National Survey of Disabilities, Disabilities and Disadvantages – published by the National Institute for Rehabilitation in 1996 – there were at that time around 115,066 people with hearing impairment and 19,172 with deafness.

The Statistics Portugal (INE) website does not have conclusive data on deafness in Portugal. There is only one study on deaf blindness, from 2015, and another study of people with disabilities, from 2001. The 2001 Census registered 84,172 hearing-impaired people, and ten years later they were even less clear in disability and particularly on deaf people since they only distinguish the population with difficulties in carrying out some daily activities such as "listening to" and which can be caused by health or age reasons.

The study carried out in 2001 [20] presents some relevant data, although they are not updated, they present a general picture of the panorama of the deaf in Portugal. This study reveals that according to data from the 2001 Census, the population with at least one type of disability represented 6.1% of the total resident population. Of this percentage, 13.2% of the Portuguese population is hearing impaired. We can see in Fig. 1 how the various types of disability are distributed by gender and age.

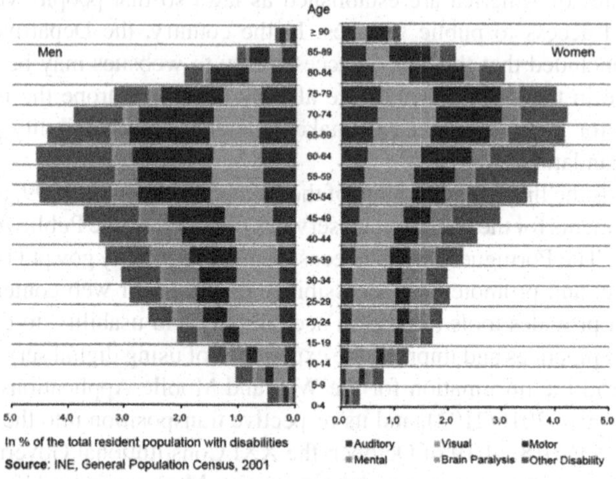

Fig. 1. Age structure of the population with disabilities, by type of disability. Portugal, 2001

2.1 Portuguese Sign Language in the Digital Environment

Portuguese Sign Language (LGP) is a language of the deaf community, it has its own grammatical structure, culture, and identity. This language has a very rich lexicon and linguistic variety, it has several dialects, it is constantly evolving like any other language. In this course, it is understood that the language has been in constant evolution, subject to social changes, cultural influences, and socio-regional experiences.

In recent years, the deaf community has watched with anticipation the evolution of information technologies. For them, what they found most important in information technologies was communication with the computer and the ideal way to process communication for a deaf person: through visual communication.

Thus, the evolution of technology is essential for this community, as it improves the experience that these people have on the internet. Websites, videos, and programs that previously seemed to be inaccessible, now have access to technologies, gadgets and functionalities that can allow the inclusion of tools that facilitate the experiences of a deaf person.

2.2 Project Target Audience

Most hearing impaired/deaf people have difficulty understanding textual information, as Portuguese is not their first language, only those who become deaf after learning Portuguese have greater understanding.

Since most of the words in the Portuguese language do not exist in sign language, huge barriers are created in the interaction of the deaf with digital content, such as not being able to understand some content.

It should be noted that the presentation of content through sequential images helps this group a lot to understand what is being communicated, thus integrating keywords written in Portuguese to facilitate and try to eradicate a barrier in integration and communication. These images and captions must be well contextualized, being extremely important when designing the interfaces.

3 The Project for the Handi Bot

3.1 Benchmarking with the Most Relevant Applications

The references addressed aim to make the online experience more accessible to users with disabilities and seek to include people with special needs in society to adapt to their needs.

The applications that are presented offer services for converting content available on Portuguese-language sites into sign language. These sites are mostly paid.

Hand Talk is an application/platform that simultaneously translates text or voice that aims at the social inclusion of deaf people. It works with the help of a virtual 3D interpreter that reacts to a text voice command, converting the content in Portuguese to Libras (Brazilian Portuguese Sign Language).

ProDeaf developed since 2011, it recognizes the listener's voice, translates the speech, and shows the deaf what was said through the animation of a 3D animated agent. The opposite can also be done shortly, with the deaf person making the signs with a special glove whose movement is captured by the cell phone camera and translated to the listener.

Live Transcriber in order to help people with hearing loss, launched this accessibility application in 2019 that transforms the voice captured by the smartphone's microphone into subtitles in real time on the device's screen. The app is available in over 70 languages and dialects.

Librol is developed to translate Portuguese texts into Libras. The project was created in 2013, in a university context. The idea came after an analysis carried out in the accessibility scenario on the Campus, where hearing impaired students became increasingly rare. Librol was created to facilitate the understanding of deaf students. Through its tools it is possible to translate operating systems, news websites, social networks, texts in general and all academic material on and off the internet.

Giulia was created in 2014, it captures the gestures of the deaf and hard of hearing in Libras and transforms them into text and audio in Portuguese. The idea for this application came with a bracelet that recorded users' movements for use in electronic games.

Spread the sign gathers gestures from different sign languages from around the world. In a search box, type the word or phrase you want to search for. The site is managed by the non-profit European Sign Language Centre, and the project is an ongoing process.

There are other applications, but we have listed those that we believe are most promising in terms of making the lives of people with hearing loss more accessible.

3.2 Audience Test

To understand the target audience, a questionnaire was developed. The questions helped to understand the difficulties of deaf people; the levels of written and read Portuguese; the level of education, your type of interaction with online content.

The sample is made up of 165 Portuguese deaf people, aged between 15 and 65 years, in which 50.9% are male and 49.1% female. 78.8% of respondents have profound deafness and 21.2% have non-profound deafness.

Regarding the level of education, 13 have a master's or doctorate, 27 have a degree, 19 are higher education students, 48 have secondary education, 5 have basic education, 36 have a job, 16 are unemployed and 1 is retired.

Through the questionnaire, we noticed that most of them have profound deafness; the average level of Portuguese read is 4 (on a scale of 1–5); the average level of written Portuguese is 3 (on a scale of 1–5). The most used apps are Instagram, Facebook and WhatsApp and the least accessible apps are YouTube, WhatsApp, and Facebook. The difficulties are revealed due to the lack of concise, correct subtitles and unclear information. Most respondents prefer sign language in the digital environment.

In Fig. 2 we can see that the level of Portuguese read for 43% of the participants is 4 (scale 1–5). Figure 3 shows the level of written Portuguese, which for 44.8% of the participants is 3 (scale 1–5).

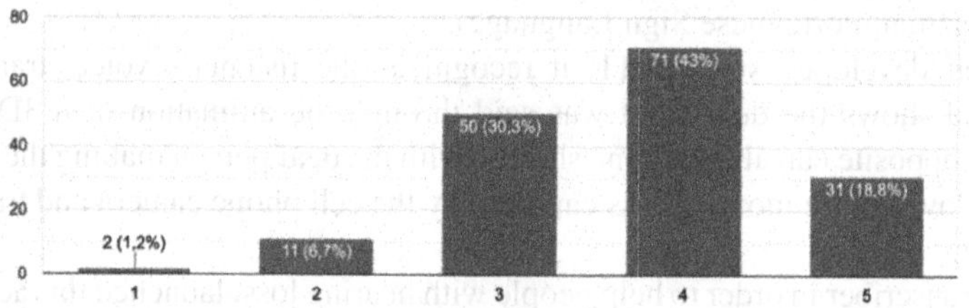

Fig. 2. Portuguese reading level by people with hearing impairment (165 participants)

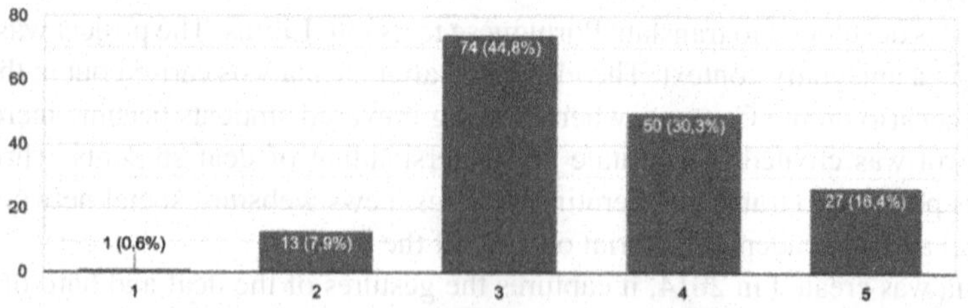

Fig. 3. Written Portuguese level by people with hearing impairment (165 participants)

The frequency of internet access in number of hours per day was also questioned, in which of the 165 participants, 33.3% answered more than 5 h a day, 25.5% answered from 3 h to 5 h a day and 28.5% answered responded 1h to 3h per day. The most used device to access the internet is the cell phone, according to 67.9% of the participants. In Fig. 4 we can see that the applications that are most used are those that allow video calling. Facebook is used by 85.5% of participants, WhatsApp by 80%, Instagram by 77% and Messenger by 69.1%

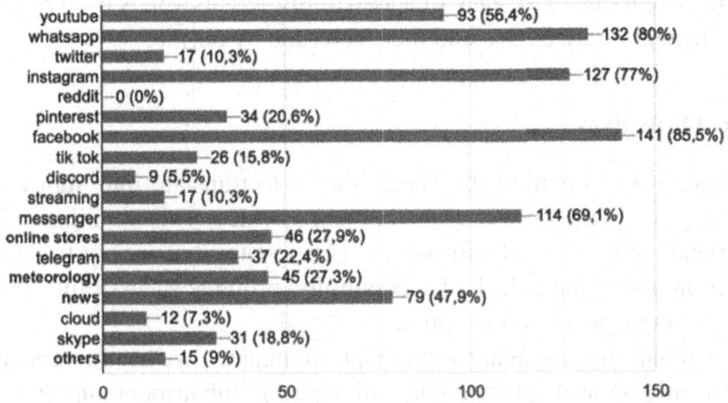

Fig. 4. Apps and/or websites that are most used by people with hearing impairment (165 participants)

It was also asked if the participants used auxiliary sign language applications/websites. Most deaf people do not use any auxiliary app (82.4%), but those who answered yes (17.6%) mentioned Spread the Sign (65.5%).

Regarding the most difficult Applications/sites to navigate/use (Fig. 5) the most mentioned apps are those that contain a lot of text. YouTube was indicated, which most of the time lacks subtitles in the videos. Informative sites (23%), YouTube (18.8%) Facebook/WhatsApp (17%) are the ones that have the greatest difficulty in using and the reason for this is due to the lack of subtitles.

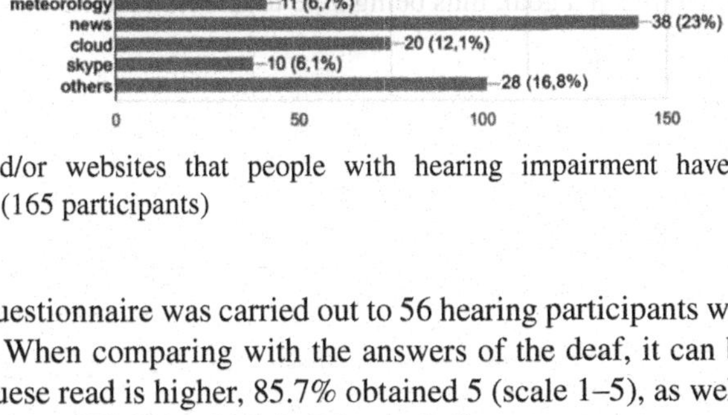

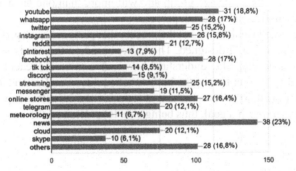

Fig. 5. Apps and/or websites that people with hearing impairment have more difficulty using/navigating (165 participants)

A second questionnaire was carried out to 56 hearing participants without any auditory condition. When comparing with the answers of the deaf, it can be seen that the level of Portuguese read is higher, 85.7% obtained 5 (scale 1–5), as well as the level of written Portuguese of 73.2%, which is 5 (scale 1–5).

The frequency of internet access for hearing and deaf people is practically the same. The most used device continues to be the cell phone (78.6%). The applications that are most used are the same as those for the deaf but including YouTube. Which shows that the deaf do not use it due to the lack of accessibility. WhatsApp is used by 87.5% of the participants, Instagram by 64.3% and then YouTube by 60.7%.

3.3 Project Objectives

The main objective of creating the Handi Bot is to translate into sign language any content that appears in the browser, whether text or video. This bot aims to improve the online experience of deaf people; improve access to sites that are not frequently visited by the deaf community due to lack of accessibility; promote accessibility and inclusion; and make sign language an online option.

After benchmarking and analysing the questionnaires, we tried to understand what kind of tool would be useful for people with hearing impairment and that was not yet available and implemented. We realize the need to make applications such as YouTube, (videos), more accessible, as well as the translation into sign language as humanized as possible. To fulfil this objective, the bot is anthropomorphic and allows customization, it also allows adding new gestures, recorded on video, that are not available, and it also allows changing the translation speed. This bot is available on a website, as a browser extension and as a bot.

3.4 Personas, User Journey and Flow Chart

The personas profiles for the project were based on the questionnaire that was developed to be able to understand the type of interaction that deaf people have with online content. Through the various responses obtained, it was possible to create the profile of users covering more than one age group and with more than one need, thus having an orientation in the user-centred design process.

User journeys are visualizations of the process that personas must go through to fulfil the experience that is being designed. Therefore, based on the needs of each persona, the user journey is developed to understand how each user would react to the use of the Handi Bot and if the perception of the bot's functionality is understandable.

The flow chart (Fig. 6) allows the visualization of the complete experience that the user goes through to reach a goal, thus being able to understand the integral interaction.

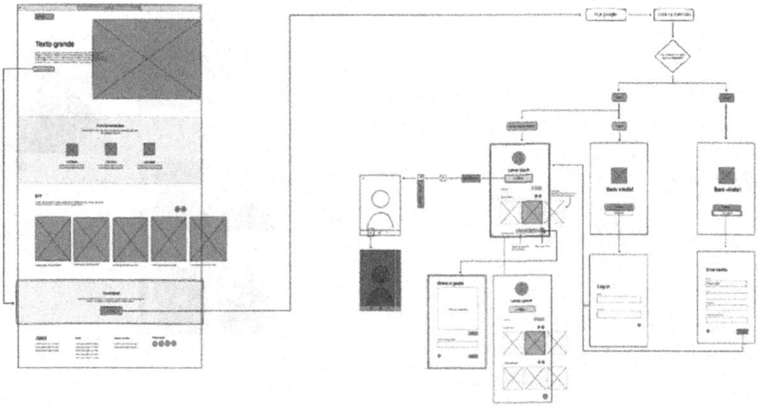

Fig. 6. Flowchart of the experience

3.5 Wireframes and Prototyping

The wireframes consist of the presentation of the diagram and the visual structure (Fig. 7). The bot was developed in a way that encompassed all the necessary tools that improve and help the interaction that deaf users have with online content.

Thus, the prototype (Fig. 8) is a realistic view of what the final performance of the project will be, allowing to test the functionalities of each tool. User testing was performed to assess usability. It can be consulted at: https://app.usabilityhub.com/do/88e5209dbc5/d26c.

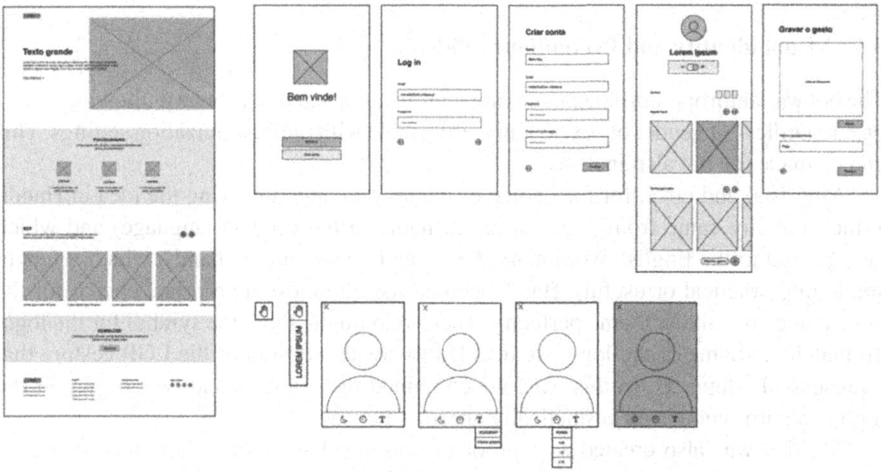

Fig. 7. Wireframes of the website structure, browser extension and Handi Bot (respectively)

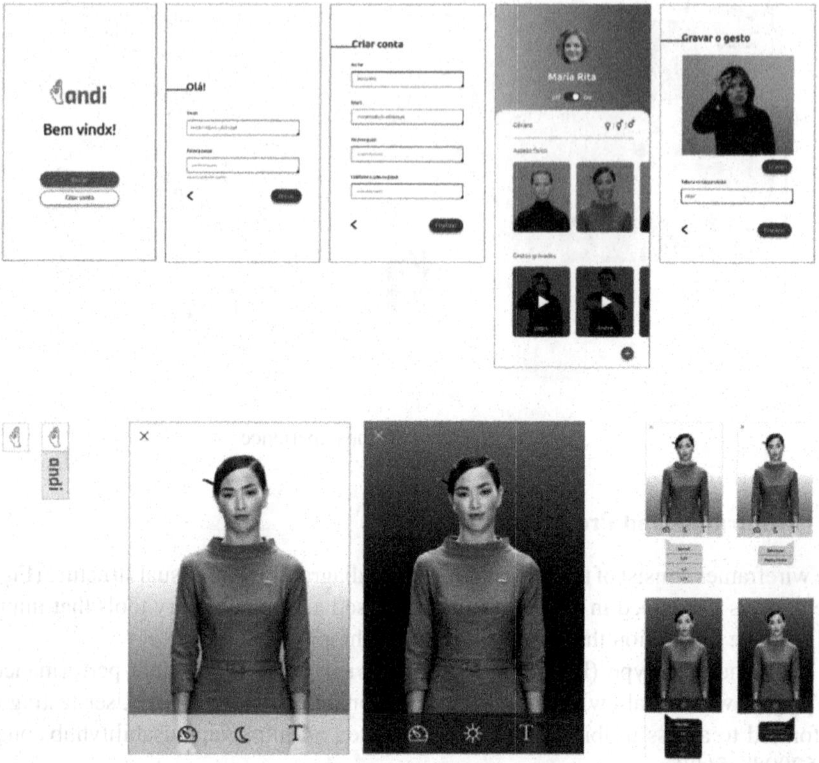

Fig. 8. Prototype of the browser extension and the Handi Bot

3.6 Visual identity and Promotional Video

The bot was anthropomorphized, making it more human and non-binary, allowing everyone, regardless of gender or sex, to feel comfortable with the customization settings. This choice made the bot also inclusive.

After trial and error, for the choice of name, we ended up fixing the idea in Handi. Which initially came from Andi (a unisex name in the English language) and which later passed to the English word hand (hand) and its variations (handy, which refers to something practical or useful). Handi seemed like the most appropriate choice for the bot's name, as it fit the theme perfectly. Then we thought about the symbol for the logo. To match the name of the logo, we decided to create a design of the LGP gesture that represents the letter H. In this way, we combined the graphics and typography of the logo in a harmonious and aesthetically appropriate way.

A video was also created as a proof of concept that explains how the bot works (Fig. 9). The video can be seen at: https://youtu.be/1BzQC5iUcTw.

Fig. 9. Storyboard of the presentation video of the Handi Bot

4 Conclusion

The need to integrate people with this type of limitation for ethical and social reasons is understood. The great involvement of technologies in our daily lives requires constant evaluation and development of equipment, such as applications and extensions that help to reduce inequality in access to online content. With the development of this extension, we make sign language an online option and therefore a significant improvement will be given to the online experience of this group. This proposal differs from others already implemented by the ability to have a bot like a human figure, customizable, which follows principles of gender inclusion, and which allows adding gestures by recording them on video. We believe that this proposal could significantly improve the accessibility of people with hearing impairment to information content that is not available to them.

The questionnaire carried out to 165 Portuguese individuals with hearing loss was very relevant to understand their limitations and particular needs, and we believe it to be a contribution to the advancement of knowledge in this area.

References

1. Kalbag, L.: Accessibility for Everyone. A Book Apart, New York (2017)
2. International Organization for Standardization. ISO 9241-112:2017. Ergonomics of human-system interaction — Part 112: Principles for the presentation of information. https://www.iso.org/standard/64840.html. Accessed 15 Sep 2022
3. Nielsen, J., Loranger, H.: Prioritizing Web Usability. New Riders, Indianápolis (2006)
4. Manzini, E.J.: Inclusão e Acessibilidade. Revista da Sobama **10**(1), Suplemento, 31–36 (2005)
5. Holmes, K.: Mismatch. How Inclusion Shapes Design. MIT Press, Massachusetts (2020)
6. Gilbert, R.M.: Inclusive Design for a Digital World: Designing with Accessibility in Mind (Design Thinking). Apress, Switzerland (2019)
7. Henry, S.L.: Understanding web accessibility. In: Web Accessibility. Apress, Switzerland (2006). https://doi.org/10.1007/978-1-4302-0188-5_1
8. Norman, D.: The Psychology of Everyday Things. Basic Books, New York (1988)
9. European Commission – Commission wants a more efficient internet for the disabled. IP/08/1074, Brussels (2008)

10. Henry, S.L., Abou-Zahra, S., Brewer, J.: The role of accessibility in a universal web. In: Proceedings of the 11th Web for All Conference (W4A 2014), Article 17, pp. 1–4. Association for Computing Machinery, New York (2014). https://doi.org/10.1145/2596695.2596719
11. Persad, U., Langdon, P., Clarkson, P.J.: A framework for analytical inclusive design evaluation. In: International Conference on Engineering Design, ICED 2007. Cite des Sciences et de L'Industrie, Paris (2007)
12. Keates, S., Clarkson, J.: Countering design exclusion. In: Clarkson, J., Keates, S., Coleman, R., Lebbon, C. (eds.) Inclusive Design. Springer, London (2003). https://doi.org/10.1007/978-1-4471-0001-0_27
13. Okumura, M.L.M., Rudek, M., Junior, O.C.: Application of assistive technology in a concurrent engineering environment for the special products development: a case study. In: Stjepandić, J., Rock, G., Bil, C. (eds.) Concurrent Engineering Approaches for Sustainable Product Development in a Multi-Disciplinary Environment. Springer, London (2013). https://doi.org/10.1007/978-1-4471-4426-7_79
14. Ada.gov – United States Department of Justice Civil Rights Division. https://www.ada.gov
15. Web Content Accessibility Guidelines (WCAG) 05 June 2018. 2.1. W3C Recommendation. https://www.w3.org/TR/WCAG21
16. Acessibilidade.gov.pt. https://www.acessibilidade.gov.pt
17. Agência para a modernização administrativa (AMA). https://www.ama.gov.pt/web/agencia-para-a-modernizacao-administrativa/acessibilidade
18. Web Accessibility Initiative WAI-AGE Project (IST 035015). Web Accessibility Initiative: Ageing Education and Harmonisation. https://www.w3.org/WAI/WAI-AGE
19. W3C. Web Accessibility Initiative WAI. Older Users and Web Accessibility: Meeting the Needs of Ageing Web Users. https://www.w3.org/WAI/older-users
20. Gonçalves, C.: Family framework of people with disabilities: an exploratory analysis of the results of the 2001 census. Revista de Estudos Demográficos **33**, 69–94 (2001)
21. Dam, R., Siang, T.: Design thinking: getting started with empathy. Interaction Design Foundation (2020). https://www.interaction-design.org/literature/article/design-thin-king-getting-started-with-empathy. Accessed 16 Jan 2022
22. Maia, J.J.M.: Transumanismo e pós-humanismo: descodificação política de uma problemática contemporânea (2018). Ph.D. Thesis. http://hdl.handle.net/10316/80671. Accessed 01 Feb 2022
23. Renaut, A.: O indivíduo. Reflexão acerca da filosofia do sujeito. Difel, Rio de Janeiro (2004)
24. Heidegger, M.: Letter on humanism. In: Krell, D.F. (ed.) Basic Writings. Harper Collins Publishers Inc., New York (2008)
25. Junges, J.R.: Ética Ecológica: Antropocentrismo ou Biocentrismo? Perspectiva Teológica, 33(89). Faculdade Jesuíta de Filosofia e Teologia, Brasil (2001). https://doi.org/10.20911/21768757v33n89p33/2001. http://www.faje.edu.br/periodicos/index.php/perspectiva/article/view/801. Accessed 20 Jan 2022
26. Elkington, J.: Towards the sustainable corporation: win-win-win business strategies for sustainable development. Calif. Manage. Rev. **36**, 90–100 (1994). https://doi.org/10.2307/41165746
27. ISO – International Organization for Standardization. https://www.iso.org
28. Earthy, J., Jones, B., Bevan, N.: The improvement of human-centred processes –facing the challenge and reaping the benefit of ISO 13407. Int. J. Hum. Comput. Stud. **55**, 553–585 (2001). https://doi.org/10.1006/ijhc.2001.0493
29. Norman, D.A., Draper, S.: User Centered System Design: New Perspectives on Human-Computer Interaction. Lawrence Erlbaum Associates, New Jersey (1986)
30. ISO 13407:1999 Human-Centred Design Processes for Interactive Systems. https://www.iso.org/standard/21197.html. Accessed 15 Jan 2022

31. Verganti, R.: User-Centered Innovation is not Sustainable. Harvard Business Review (2010). https://hbr.org/2010/03/user-centered-innovation-is-no. Accessed 21 Jan 2022
32. ISO 9241-210:2010 Ergonomics of Human-System Interaction – Part 210: Human-Centred Design for Interactive Systems. https://www.iso.org/standard/52075.html. Accessed 28 Jan 2022
33. Cruhl, M., Diehl, J.: Design for sustainability, a step-by-step approach. UNEP, United Nations Publications. D4S Publication (2009). https://wedocs.unep.org/handle/20.500.11822/8742. Accessed 18 Jan 2022
34. Blevis, E.: Sustainable interaction design: invention and disposal, renewal and reuse. In: Proceedings of the SIGCHI Conference on Human Factors in Computing Systems, CHI 2007, pp. 503–512. Association for Computing Machinery, NY (2007). https://doi.org/10.1145/1240624.1240705
35. Brown, A.S.: A model to integrate sustainability into the user-centered design process (2011). Electronic Theses and Dissertations (1830). https://stars.library.ucf.edu/etd/1830. Accessed 19 Jan 2022
36. Van Der Ryn, S., Cowan, S.: Ecological Design: 10th Anniversary Edition. Island Press, Washington D. C (1996)
37. IDEO.org: The field guide to human-centered design. Design Kit (2015). https://www.designkit.org. Accessed 29 Dec 2021
38. Giacomin, J.: What is human centred design? Des. J. **17**(4), 606–623 (2014). https://doi.org/10.2752/175630614X14056185480186
39. Maguire, M.: Methods to support human-centred design. Int. J. Hum.-Comput. Stud. **55**(4), 587–634 (2001). https://doi.org/10.1006/ijhc.2001.0503
40. Cross, N.: Designerly ways of knowing: design discipline versus design science. Des. Issues **17**(3), 49–55 (2001). https://doi.org/10.1162/074793601750357196
41. Papanek, V.: Design for the Real World, 3rd edn. Thames & Hudson Ltd, London (2019)
42. Fry, T.: The scenario of design. Des. Philos. Pap. **3**(1), 19–27 (2005). https://doi.org/10.2752/144871305X13966254124158
43. Mau, B.: Massive Change. A Manifesto for The Future Global Design Culture. Phaidon Press Ltd, New York (2006)
44. Dunne, A., Raby, F.: Speculative everything: Design, Fiction, and Social Dreaming. The MIT Press, Massachusetts (2013)
45. Stegall, N.: Designing for sustainability: a philosophy for ecologically intentional design. Des. Issues **22**(2), 56–63 (2006)
46. Vallet, F., Eynard, B., Millet, D., Mahut, S.G., Tyl, B., Bertoluci, G.: Using eco-design tools: an overview of experts' practices. Des. Stud. **34**(3), 345–377 (2013). https://doi.org/10.1016/j.destud.2012.10.001
47. Holt, D., Cameron, D.: Cultural Strategy: Using Innovative Ideologies to Build Breakthrough Brands. Oxford University Press, UK (2010)
48. Brown, T.: Change by Design: How Design Thinking Transforms Organisations and Inspires Innovation. HarperCollins, New York (2009)
49. Manzini, E.: New design knowledge. Des. Stud. **30**(1), 4–12 (2009)
50. Roshko, T.: The pedagogy of bio-design: methodology development. WIT Trans. Ecol. Environ. **135**, 545–558 (2010). https://doi.org/10.2495/DN100491
51. Findeli, A.: Rethinking design education for the 21st century: theoretical, methodological, and ethical discussion. Des. Issues **17**, 5–17 (2001). https://doi.org/10.1162/07479360152103796

52. Cooke, P.: Green design aesthetics: ten principles. City Cult. Soc. **3**(4), 293–302 (2012)
53. Pazmino, A. V.: Uma reflexão sobre Design Social, Eco Design, e Design Sustentável. In: International Symposium on Sustainable Design (2007)
54. Fallman, D.: The interaction design research triangle of design practice, design studies, and design exploration. Des. Issues **24**(3), 4–18 (2008). https://doi.org/10.1162/desi.2008.24.3.4
55. Schon, D.: The Reflective Practitioner: How Professionals Think in Action. Basic Books, New York (1983)

Revisiting Redundant Text Color Coding in User Interfaces

Fredrik Strømsvåg Sandvold[1], Thomas Schuller[1], Andreas Rolfsvåg[1], Knut-Erik Sikkerbøl[1], Fausto Orsi Medola[2], and Frode Eika Sandnes[1](✉)

[1] Department of Computer Science, Faculty of Technology, Art and Design, Oslo Metropolitan University, 0130 Oslo, Norway
frodes@oslomet.no

[2] School of Architecture, Arts, Communication and Design, Sao Paulo State University (UNESP), Bauru, SP, Brazil

Abstract. Practices for using redundant text color in user interfaces vary. Some designers have carefully incorporated redundant coding in their design, while in other instances redundant coding is not utilized. There is a vast body of research on the effects of color on visual search. In this study we wanted to corroborate earlier findings in the current context. A simple recognition experiment was configured. The results agreed with the literature in that color has a significant effect on response time when the color is known, while it has no effect on recall. The results support the use of redundant color coding in interfaces, especially for time-critical applications where the user must act rapidly.

Keywords: redundant color coding · text color · user interface

1 Introduction

Color display technology [1, 2] has become an expected low cost and widely available technology on many types of electronic devices during the last two decades from desktop computers [3] to mobile devices such as smartphones [4–6]. Many user interfaces utilize these color capabilities to achieve aesthetic qualities [7–12], establish trust [13–18], create groupings [19], and facilitate visual search [20–22]. For instance, color harmonies [23, 24] are often used to evoke various emotions and moods [25, 26]. Color is also used in interfaces to create groupings [19] where different groups of related elements such as menu items have certain colors [27]. In context of searching, color can be used to direct the users' attention such as using red color in form fields that have been completed incorrectly [28], or indicate a form submit button using a color that contrasts the other colors of the interface.

It is an established practice that hues should not be used on their own to communicate important information as users with reduced color perception might be unable to discriminate between certain colors [29]. Instead, color should be used as a redundant coding together with other information, most notably text and images, but also position, size, and shape, or non-visual cues such as haptics [30, 31].

M. Antona and C. Stephanidis (Eds.): HCII 2023, LNCS 14020, pp. 467–476, 2023.
https://doi.org/10.1007/978-3-031-35681-0_31

There is a vast body of work that has explored the effects color can have on visual searching, that is, color can shorten the time to identify a specific target [32]. Still, many interfaces do not exploit the opportunities to use color to facilitate search. One may imagine a designer constrained by a corporate color profile of a customer, limiting the choices of colors for effective visual communication.

Seminal studies on redundant color coding (see for instance [33]) were conducted more than 50 years ago, at which time color coding only could be found on printed material. Color print was also more expensive to produce and therefore not as common as black and white printing. We wanted to verify if these observations still hold with current users highly accustomed to color display and user interfaces in color. Are current users exhibiting different traits than users of the past? We therefore conducted an experiment inspired by previous research on redundant color coding.

2 Related Work

Early and often referred to work on effects on color was conducted by Stroop [33], who showed that peoples' response times were slowed down when the words of different colors do not match the color of that word. Stroop tests are commonly used as part of cognitive test batteries and one can conduct a simple experiment to experience the Stroop effect. However, the Stroop effect is not directly related to search. Green and Andersson [32] is an early study which showed that redundant color coding can speed up the time to locate a target during search. However, they also found that color did not influence recall. Similar work was conducted subsequently [34–36]. The study of Keller et al. [35] showed how color can be used to help viewers with interpreting information visualizations. Lindsey et al. [37] claim that it is not the appearance of a color that influences visual search but rather the physical color channels in the human visual system. In practical terms of facilitating visual search on the web, colors are claimed to be the most effective cue for communicating the presence of hyperlinks [38].

Research studies into color and aesthetics on the web have explored the relationship between the perception of aesthetics and visual complexity [7], and color and gender differences [8]. Especially how aesthetics can affect first impressions of web sites [10] and decisions, and online shopping have received some attention [11, 12]. Also, several studies have addressed how colors affect users' trust in websites [13, 14], the products represented [15], and the organization they represent such as higher education institutions [18]. For instance, it has been found that highly saturated colors can have a negative effect on trust [14].

Visualization is yet another field where color has been studied extensively [39, 40] (see for instance the survey by Silva et al. [41]). Examples include affective use of colors [42], color scales [43], color maps [44], and color palette design [45].

Other research directions have included diverse topics such as how color coding affects learning [46], and how color use affects power consumption with certain display technologies [47].

3 Method

3.1 Experimental Design

A within-groups experimental design was chosen with two independent variables, stimuli type and session, and two dependent variables, response time, recall rate (as opposed to error rate [48–50]. The stimuli type had two levels, namely black and white and color, and the session variable had two levels, first and second. We also asked the participants about their preferred stimuli type.

3.2 Participants

A total of 20 participants were recruited for the experiment of which 7 were identified as female and 13 were identified as male. Most participants (70%) were in the 20–34-year age range, one person was between 35–49 years of age, and 5 participants were 50 years or older. Convenience sampling was conducted due to the covid-19 pandemic involving students at the authors' university and acquaintances of the authors. All the participants were native Norwegian speakers who had completed a minimum of lower secondary education. Participants were not questioned regarding previous reading challenges.

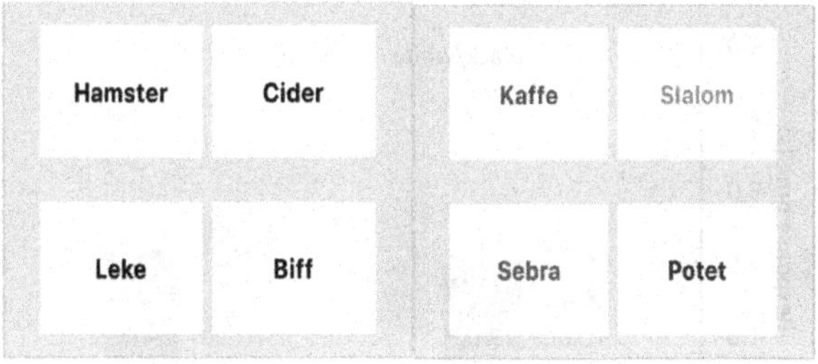

Fig. 1. Example of experiment software challenges in black and white and color, respectively. The user selects the word in a predetermined category. Black-and-white words: hamster, cider, play, and steak. Color words: Coffee, slalom, zebra, and potato.

3.3 Materials

A remote experiment platform was implemented for the browser using React. The experiment software presented words in four categories in black and white and in colors, respectively (see Fig. 1). The words were presented in Norwegian. Each category was assigned a unique color that was used consistently throughout the experiment. The four categories included animals, food, drink, and activity. A total of 10 challenges were created for each category. The participant had to click on the word belonging to a given category (a different category for each condition), and the software logged the time it took for the participants to respond.

3.4 Procedure

Due to the pandemic the experimental sessions were conducted remotely using Microsoft Teams. The participants were first briefed about the task. Next, the participants were asked to share their screen with the experiments. The session was split into four parts. The two first parts were a trial session with the color and black and white condition, and the two last parts were the second session with both the color and black and white stimuli. The user was told to recognize a specific category and then click on the word representing that category in the software. After the software session, the user was directed to an online form implemented in Google form, where they had to recall the words related to each category. The presentation orders (black-white vs color) were balanced to prevent bias. Participants were tested individually. Each session lasted approximately 10 min.

The experiment was conducted during a single session and participation was therefore anonymous as there was no need to link records across sessions [51].

3.5 Analysis

The successful recall rate was manually computed based on the responses in the online form. These results were combined with the time measurements obtained by the experiment software. Statistical analyses were performed using JASP version 0.13.1.0 [52].

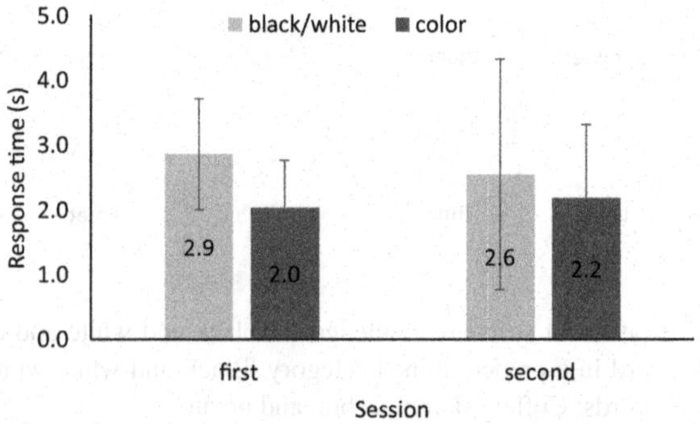

Fig. 2. Mean response times per task (in seconds) per condition. Error bars shows standard deviation.

4 Results

A two-way repeated measures ANOVA shows that the observations of response times (see Fig. 2) showed a significant difference between black and white and color ($F(1, 19) = 13.376$, $p = .002$, $\eta^2 = 0.116$). The time to recognize categories with color took shorter time in seconds for the first ($M = 20.4$, $SD = 7.4$) and second ($M = 21.9$, $SD = 11.3$) session, than the first ($M = 28.7$, $SD = 8.6$) and second ($M = 25.5$, $SD = 17.9$) session with black and white. No significant difference could be found across the two sessions ($F(1, 19) = 0.084$, $p = .775$). Moreover, no interaction between the type of stimuli and the session was detected ($F(1, 19) = 1.923$, $p = .182$).

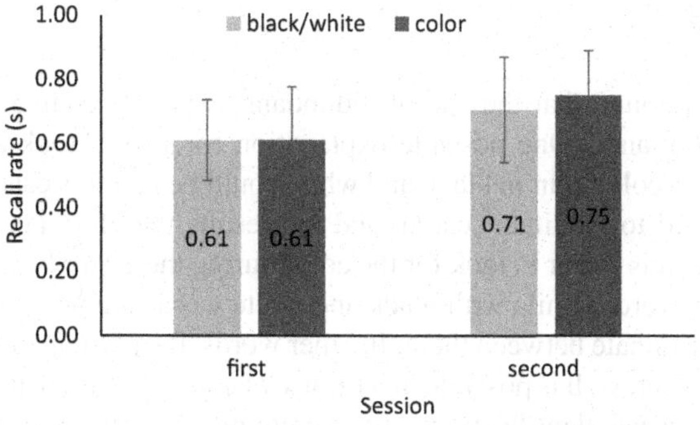

Fig. 3. Recall rates per condition. Error bars show standard deviation.

When observing the recall rate (see Fig. 3), the situation is reversed, i.e., the two-way repeated measures ANOVA did not reveal any significant difference in recall related to the use of color ($F(1, 19) = 0.951$, $p = 0.342$). However, an effect of session on the recall rate was observed ($F(1, 19) = 31.533$, $p < .001$, $\eta^2 = 0.322$). In both conditions, the participants on average managed to recall one more item in the second session: most participants recalled 7 of the 10 items in the second, while in the first session most participants only recalled 6 out of 10 items. No interaction between the presentation type and session was identified ($F(1, 19) = 1.000$, $p = .330$).

We also combined the recall rate and response times by computing the recalls per second (Fig. 4). A two-way ANOVA shows that this combined measure gave a significant difference of both visual presentation ($F(1, 19) = 23.742$, $p < .001$, $\eta^2 = 0.258$) and session ($F(1, 19) = 25.581$, $p < .001$, $\eta^2 = 0.199$), but without any interaction between the two ($F(1, 19) = 0.062$, $p = 0.805$). Clearly, the recalls per second is higher with colors than with black and white, and higher for the second session.

When asked about their preference, a majority responded that they preferred color (60%), a minority preferred black and white (10%), while 30% expressed that they had no opinion. No correlations were found between preference and performance.

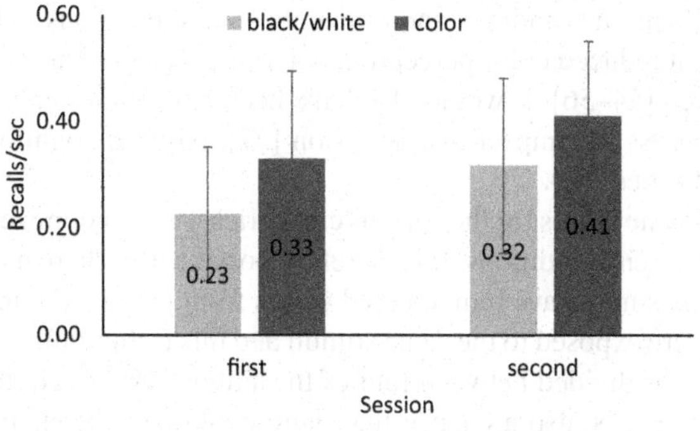

Fig. 4. Recalls per second. Error bars show standard deviation.

5 Discussion

The current study found that the use of redundant text color-coding improved words recognition performance. One possible explanation for why it took a shorter time to recognize words in color than in black and white could be that it is easier to spot a color as color is believed to facilitate search, and the results therefore agree with previous work [33]. Hence, it is easier to look for the color during the 10 trials rather than reading the content of the words, while with black and white words the participants had to read the words to discriminate between them. In other words, the participants established this strategy from the context. It is possible that the use of color speeds up the search as it adds a feature of faster visual identification to the communication interface. When comparing the two sessions it seems that the task of identifying colors of text did not improve with practice, probably because we already have developed our skills to recognize words in various contexts.

The results showed that the text color had no effect on recall. If it is the case that participants indeed recognized the color categories using color only, one may even have observed a lower recall rate for the color categories. Practice had an effect, which makes sense as the learning is strengthened through retention during the second session.

As our observations agree with similar studies conducted before color displays were commonplace it seems that how users respond to color has not changed much because of increased exposure to such color stimuli.

As redundant color coding indeed facilitated visual search one may ponder why it is not used more extensively. Is it so that corporate color schemes and visual identity trumps effective visual communication mechanisms? Another explanation could be that if redundant color coding is overused the user may be fatigued by the competing visual signals. In this sense, redundant coding should probably only be used for important interface elements in terms of urgency, frequency of use and impact.

5.1 Limitations

A shortcoming of the current experiment is the small sample size although it is within the norms of human computer interaction experiments [53]. One should therefore be careful in generalizing the findings and utilize these as indications. Another limitation of this study is that reduced color perception was not considered, as color vision would affect visual search [54–56]. It would also have been relevant to repeat the experiment with cohorts to assess the impact of low vision [57], reduced cognitive function [58], and reading disabilities [59].

Although the same words for the various categories were randomized, they were also repeated in the different conditions. It is therefore possible that there has been a learning effect as participants may have remembered words from previous rounds. However, all the participants were exposed to the same stimuli and this is thus unlikely to have caused bias. The testing was divided between four of the authors. Although the procedure was clearly specified there is also a chance that there could have been small variations in how the sessions were conducted.

6 Conclusion

A simple experiment was conducted to reassess the effects of text color-coding on recognition and recall. The results indicate that the recognition response time is significantly faster when the item to be recognized has a specific color. Color did not have any effect on subsequent recall rate. In conclusion, our findings support the established practice of facilitating visual search through redundant coding using color. The results suggest that the effect on color in information processing is similar with current day users as in the past. In time-critical applications [60] where the user must respond rapidly to changes in a user interface the time saved through such redundant coding may make a large difference.

References

1. Christ, R.E.: Review and analysis of color coding research for visual displays. Hum. Factors **17**(6), 542–570 (1975). https://doi.org/10.1177/001872087501700602
2. Sabnis, R.W.: Color filter technology for liquid crystal displays. Displays **20**(3), 119–129 (1999). https://doi.org/10.1016/S0141-9382(99)00013-X
3. Humar, I., Gradis, M.: The impact of color combinations on the legibility of a Web page text presented on CRT displays. Int. J. Ind. Ergon. **38**(11–12), 885–899 (2008). https://doi.org/10.1016/j.ergon.2008.03.004
4. Chino, E., et al.: Development of wide-color-gamut mobile displays with four-primary-color LCDs. In: SID Symposium Digest of Technical Papers, pp. 1221–1224. Blackwell Publishing Ltd, Oxford (2006). https://doi.org/10.1889/1.2433197
5. Dong, M., Zhong, L.: Chameleon: a color-adaptive web browser for mobile OLED displays. In: Proceedings of the 9th International Conference on Mobile Systems, Applications, and Services, pp. 85–98 (2011). https://doi.org/10.1145/1999995.2000004
6. Lee, M.Y., Son, C.H., Kim, J.M., Lee, C.H., Ha, Y.H.: Illumination-level adaptive color reproduction method with lightness adaptation and flare compensation for mobile display. J. Imaging Sci. Technol. **51**(1), 44–52 (2007). https://doi.org/10.2352/J.ImagingSci.Technol.(2007)51:1(44)
7. Michailidou, E., Harper, S., Bechhofer, S.: Visual complexity and aesthetic perception of web pages. In: Proceedings of the 26th Annual ACM International Conference on Design of Communication, pp. 215–224. ACM (2008). https://doi.org/10.1145/1456536.1456581
8. Coursaris, C.K., Swierenga, S.J., Watrall, E.: An empirical investigation of color temperature and gender effects on web aesthetics. J. Usability Stud. **3**(3), 103–117 (2008)
9. Kuo, L., Chang, T., Lai, C.C.: Color aesthetics with regard to product design and multimedia web pages. Multimedia Tools Appl., 1–19 (2023). https://doi.org/10.1007/s11042-023-14580-1
10. Reinecke, K., et al.: Predicting users' first impressions of website aesthetics with a quantification of perceived visual complexity and colorfulness. In: Proceedings of the SIGCHI Conference on Human Factors in Computing Systems, pp. 2049–2058. ACM (2013). https://doi.org/10.1145/2470654.2481281
11. Cai, S., Xu, Y.: Designing not just for pleasure: effects of web site aesthetics on consumer shopping value. Int. J. Electron. Commer. **15**(4), 159–188 (2011). https://doi.org/10.2753/JEC1086-4415150405
12. Wang, Y.J., Hernandez, M.D., Minor, M.S.: Web aesthetics effects on perceived online service quality and satisfaction in an e-tail environment: The moderating role of purchase task. J. Bus. Res. **63**(9–10), 935–942 (2010). https://doi.org/10.1016/j.jbusres.2009.01.016

13. Alberts, W.A., Van Der Geest, T.M.: Color matters: color as trustworthiness cue in web sites. Tech. Commun. **58**(2), 149–160 (2011)
14. Skulmowski, A., Augustin, Y., Pradel, S., Nebel, S., Schneider, S., Rey, G.D.: The negative impact of saturation on website trustworthiness and appeal: a temporal model of aesthetic website perception. Comput. Hum. Behav. **61**, 386–393 (2016). https://doi.org/10.1016/j.chb.2016.03.054
15. Pengnate, S.F., Sarathy, R.: An experimental investigation of the influence of website emotional design features on trust in unfamiliar online vendors. Comput. Hum. Behav. **67**, 49–60 (2017). https://doi.org/10.1016/j.chb.2016.10.018
16. Pengnate, S., Sarathy, R., Lee, J.: The engagement of website initial aesthetic impressions: an experimental investigation. Int. J. Hum.-Comput. Interac. **35**(16), 1517–1531 (2019). https://doi.org/10.1080/10447318.2018.1554319
17. Ku, E.C.S., Chen, C.-D.: Flying on the clouds: how mobile applications enhance impulsive buying of low cost carriers. Serv. Bus. **14**(1), 23–45 (2019). https://doi.org/10.1007/s11628-019-00407-3
18. Stefko, R., Fedorko, R., Bacik, R.: Website content quality in terms of perceived image of higher education institution. Pol. J. Manage. Stud. **13**(2), 153–163 (2016). 10.17512%2Fpjms.2016.13.2.15
19. Marcus, A.: Principles of effective visual communication for graphical user interface design. In: Readings in Human–Computer Interaction, pp. 425–441. Morgan Kaufmann (1995). https://doi.org/10.1016/B978-0-08-051574-8.50044-3
20. Wolfe, J.M.: Visual search: how do we find what we are looking for? Annu. Rev. Vis. Sci. **6**, 539–562 (2020). https://doi.org/10.1146/annurev-vision-091718-015048
21. D'Zmura, M.: Color in visual search. Vis. Res. **31**(6), 951–966 (1991). https://doi.org/10.1016/0042-6989(91)90203-H
22. Carter, R.C.: Visual search with color. J. Exp. Psychol. Hum. Percept. Perform. **8**(1), 127 (1982). https://doi.org/10.1037/0096-1523.8.1.127
23. Sik-Lanyi, C.: Choosing effective colours for websites. In: Colour Design, pp. 600–621. Woodhead Publishing (2012). https://doi.org/10.1533/9780857095534.4.600
24. Nazar, M., Khan, R.Q., Perveen, M., Khan, W.Q.: Web branding harmonizer: need of color harmonies and its solution in website development. In: Proceedings of the 2017 International Conference on Infocom Technologies and Unmanned (ICTUS), pp. 346–350. IEEE (2017). https://doi.org/10.1109/ICTUS.2017.8286030
25. Pelet, J.É., Papadopoulou, P.: The effect of colors of e-commerce websites on consumer mood, memorization and buying intention. Eur. J. Inf. Syst. **21**(4), 438–467 (2012). https://doi.org/10.1057/ejis.2012.17
26. Demir, Ü.: Investigation of color-emotion associations of the university students. Color. Res. Appl. **45**(5), 871–884 (2020). https://doi.org/10.1002/col.22522
27. Cyr, D., Trevor-Smith, H.: Localization of Web design: an empirical comparison of German, Japanese, and United States Web site characteristics. J. Am. Soc. Inform. Sci. Technol. **55**(13), 1199–1208 (2004)
28. Hofseth, K.Å., Haga, L.K., Sørlie, V., Sandnes, F.E.: Form feedback on the web: a comparison of popup alerts and in-form error messages. In: Chen, Y.-W., Zimmermann, A., Howlett, R.J., Jain, L.C. (eds.) Innovation in Medicine and Healthcare Systems, and Multimedia. SIST, vol. 145, pp. 369–379. Springer, Singapore (2019). https://doi.org/10.1007/978-981-13-8566-7_35
29. Sandnes, F.E., Zhao, A.: An interactive color picker that ensures WCAG2.0 compliant color contrast levels. Procedia Comput. Sci. **67**, 87–94 (2015). https://doi.org/10.1016/j.procs.2015.09.252

30. Lin, M.W., Cheng, Y.M., Yu, W., Sandnes, F.E.: Investigation into the feasibility of using tactons to provide navigation cues in pedestrian situations. In: Proceedings of the 20th Australasian Conference on Computer-Human Interaction: Designing for Habitus and Habitat, pp. 299–302 (2008). https://doi.org/10.1145/1517744.1517794
31. dos Santos, A.D.P., Medola, F.O., Cinelli, M.J., Garcia Ramirez, A.R., Sandnes, F.E.: Are electronic white canes better than traditional canes? A comparative study with blind and blindfolded participants. Univ. Access Inf. Soc. **20**(1), 93–103 (2020). https://doi.org/10.1007/s10209-020-00712-z
32. Green, B.F., Anderson, L.K.: Color coding in a visual search task. J. Exp. Psychol. **51**(1), 19–24 (1956). https://doi.org/10.1037/h0047484
33. Stroop, J.R.: Studies of interference in serial verbal reactions. J. Exp. Psychol. **18**(6), 643–662 (1935). https://doi.org/10.1037/h0054651
34. Luder, C.B., Barber, P.J.: Redundant color coding on airborne CRT displays. Hum. Factors **26**(1), 19–32 (1984). https://doi.org/10.1177/001872088402600103
35. Keller, T., Gerjets, P., Scheiter, K., Garsofky, B.: Information visualizations for knowledge acquisition: The impact of dimensionality and color coding. Comput. Hum. Behav. **22**(1), 43–65 (2006). https://doi.org/10.1016/j.chb.2005.01.006
36. Kanarick, A.F., Petersen, R.C.: Redundant color coding and keeping-track performance. Hum. Factors **13**, 183–188 (1971). https://doi.org/10.1177/001872087101300211
37. Lindsey, D.T., Brown, A.M., Reijnen, E., Rich, A.N., Kuzmova, Y.I., Wolfe, J.M.: Color channels, not color appearance or color categories, guide visual search for desaturated color targets. Psychol. Sci. **21**(9), 1208–1214 (2010). https://doi.org/10.1177/0956797610379861
38. Carlson, J.R., Kacmar, C.J.: Increasing link marker effectiveness for WWW and other hypermedia interface: an examination of end-user preferences. J. Am. Soc. Inf. Sci. **50**(5), 386–398 (1999)
39. Rhyne, T. M.: Applying color theory to digital media and visualization. In: Proceedings of the 2017 CHI Conference Extended Abstracts on Human Factors in Computing Systems, pp. 1264–1267. ACM (2017). https://doi.org/10.1145/3027063.3076594
40. Wang, L., Giesen, J., McDonnell, K.T., Zolliker, P., Mueller, K.: Color design for illustrative visualization. IEEE Trans. Visual Comput. Graphics **14**(6), 1739–1754 (2008). https://doi.org/10.1109/TVCG.2008.118
41. Silva, S., Santos, B.S., Madeira, J.: Using color in visualization: a survey. Comput. Graph. **35**(2), 320–333 (2011). https://doi.org/10.1016/j.cag.2010.11.015
42. Bartram, L., Patra, A., Stone, M.: Affective color in visualization. In: Proceedings of the 2017 CHI Conference on Human Factors in Computing Systems, pp. 1364–1374. ACM (2017). https://doi.org/10.1145/3025453.3026041
43. Silva, S., Madeira, J., Santos, B. S.: There is more to color scales than meets the eye: a review on the use of color in visualization. In: Proceedings of the 2007 11th International Conference Information Visualization (IV 2007), pp. 943–950. IEEE (2007). https://doi.org/10.1109/IV.2007.113
44. Zhou, L., Hansen, C.D.: A survey of colormaps in visualization. IEEE Trans. Visual Comput. Graphics **22**(8), 2051–2069 (2015). https://doi.org/10.1109/TVCG.2015.2489649
45. Gramazio, C.C., Laidlaw, D.H., Schloss, K.B.: Colorgorical: creating discriminable and preferable color palettes for information visualization. IEEE Trans. Visual Comput. Graphics **23**(1), 521–530 (2016). https://doi.org/10.1109/TVCG.2016.2598918
46. Ozcelik, E., Karakus, T., Kursun, E., Cagiltay, K.: An eye-tracking study of how color coding affects multimedia learning. Comput. Educ. **53**(2), 445–453 (2009). https://doi.org/10.1016/j.compedu.2009.03.002

47. Dong, M., Choi, Y. S. K., Zhong, L.: Power-saving color transformation of mobile graphical user interfaces on OLED-based displays. In: Proceedings of the 2009 ACM/IEEE International Symposium on Low Power Electronics and Design, pp. 339–342. IEEE (2009). https://doi.org/10.1145/1594233.1594317
48. Sandnes, F.E., Thorkildssen, H.W., Arvei, A., Buverad, J.O.: Techniques for fast and easy mobile text-entry with three-keys. In: Proceedings of the 37th Annual Hawaii International Conference on System Sciences 2004. IEEE (2004). https://doi.org/10.1109/HICSS.2004.1265675
49. Sandnes, F.E.: Evaluating mobile text entry strategies with finite state automata. In: Proceedings of the 7th International Conference on Human Computer Interaction with Mobile Devices and Services, pp. 115–121. ACM (2005). https://doi.org/10.1145/1085777.1085797
50. Aschim, T.B., Gjerstad, J.L., Lien, L.V., Tahsin, R., Sandnes, F.E.: Are split tablet keyboards better? A study of soft keyboard layout and hand posture. In: Lamas, D., Loizides, F., Nacke, L., Petrie, H., Winckler, M., Zaphiris, P. (eds.) INTERACT 2019. LNCS, vol. 11748, pp. 647–655. Springer, Cham (2019). https://doi.org/10.1007/978-3-030-29387-1_37
51. Sandnes, F.E.: HIDE: Short IDs for robust and anonymous linking of users across multiple sessions in small HCI experiments. In: CHI 2021 Conference on Human Factors in Computing Systems Extended Abstracts Proceedings. ACM (2021). https://doi.org/10.1145/3411763.3451794
52. JASP Team (2020). JASP (Version 0.14.1) [Computer software]
53. Caine, K.: Local standards for sample size at CHI. In: Proceedings of the 2016 CHI Conference on Human Factors in Computing Systems, pp. 981–992. ACM (2016). https://doi.org/10.1145/2858036.2858498
54. Brown, A.M., Lindsey, D.T., Guckes, K.M.: Color names, color categories, and color-cued visual search: sometimes, color perception is not categorical. J. Vis. **11**(12), 2 (2011). https://doi.org/10.1167/11.12.2
55. Simon-Liedtke, J.T., Farup, I.: Evaluating color vision deficiency daltonization methods using a behavioral visual-search method. J. Vis. Commun. Image Represent. **35**, 236–247 (2016). https://doi.org/10.1016/j.jvcir.2015.12.014
56. Cole, B.L., Maddocks, J.D., Sharpe, K.: Visual search and the conspicuity of coloured targets for colour vision normal and colour vision deficient observers. Clin. Exp. Optom. **87**(4–5), 294–304 (2004). https://doi.org/10.1111/j.1444-0938.2004.tb05058.x
57. Sandnes, F.E.: what do low-vision users really want from smart glasses? Faces, text and perhaps no glasses at all. In: Miesenberger, K., Bühler, C., Penaz, P. (eds.) ICCHP 2016. LNCS, vol. 9758, pp. 187–194. Springer, Cham (2016). https://doi.org/10.1007/978-3-319-41264-1_25
58. Sandnes, F.E., Lundh, M.V.: Calendars for individuals with cognitive disabilities: a comparison of table view and list view. In: Proceedings of the 17th International ACM SIGACCESS Conference on Computers and Accessibility, pp. 329–330. ACM (2015). https://doi.org/10.1145/2700648.2811363
59. Eika, E., Sandnes, F.E.: Assessing the reading level of web texts for WCAG2.0 compliance-can it be done automatically?. In: Advances in Design for Inclusion, pp. 361–371. Springer, Cham (2016). https://doi.org/10.1007/978-3-319-41962-6_32
60. Sandnes, F.E., Eika, E.: Head-mounted augmented reality displays on the cheap: a DIY approach to sketching and prototyping low-vision assistive technologies. In: Antona, M., Stephanidis, C. (eds.) UAHCI 2017. LNCS, vol. 10278, pp. 167–186. Springer, Cham (2017). https://doi.org/10.1007/978-3-319-58703-5_13

Usage of Self-Motivating Achievements to Collect Accessibility Information of Indoor Environments

Jan Schmalfuß-Schwarz(✉), Claudia Loitsch, and Gerhard Weber

Technical University Dresden, Nöthnitzer Straße 46, 01187 Dresden, Germany
jan.schmalfuss-schwarz@tu-dresden.de
https://tu-dresden.de/ing/informatik/ai/mci

Abstract. Orientation and finding ways in buildings are particular challenges for people with disabilities. To cope with these obstacles, open accessible indoor maps enriched with accessibility information are required. To generate these is both a time-consuming and knowledge-intensive task [6] One possible solution is the use of volunteers who collect freely accessible map data. To support so-called mappers in this process, appropriate user-centered applications are needed, that guide and motivate those who collect them in the acquisition. Therefore, we present the results and their conclusions from a study carried out in the German-speaking area, which was primarily aimed at active mappers from the OpenStreetMap community.

Keywords: indoor maps · accessibility · people with disabilities · inclusive mobility · crowdsourcing · volunteered geographic information

1 Introduction

Mobility is a crucial part of our daily life and also includes the ability to orientate ourselves inside buildings [8]. At the same time, people with disabilities face many diverse barriers within buildings [3,9]. Therefore, it is essential to provide accessibility information about indoor environments to enable people with disabilities the planning of trips and on-site navigation [6,8,14,17]. However, the current amount of indoor information, including basic structure as well as barriers and additional accessibility information supported by existing maps, or orientation and navigation systems is sparse [6,14]. Crowdsourcing-based approaches can be a solution to collect those specific data. Hence, it is essential to understand the motivation of people who voluntarily gather georeferenced data and to support them in this process as they can cause a huge contribution to overcome the gap.

The objective of this work is to develop a user-centered application that supports mappers to provide more information about indoor accessibility. Therefore, we conducted a user study to understand the variety of incentives, how motivational aspects influence the collection of data and how we can encourage the

M. Antona and C. Stephanidis (Eds.): HCII 2023, LNCS 14020, pp. 477–488, 2023.
https://doi.org/10.1007/978-3-031-35681-0_32

volunteers to collect as much as possible. Moreover, we examined differences in current approaches to indoor and outdoor map data collection. This is important because the number of people who voluntarily collect indoor data is significantly lower.

2 State of the Art

Problems in providing basic information about a building and barriers or accessibility information (e.g. if a speech output inside an elevator exists) are already described in various publications. Existing scientific work range from overview papers describing different research gaps [6,8,17], to analyzes of the quantity and quality of mapped indoor data [14], to the analyzes of potential barriers for different user groups [5,9], and the classification of barriers according to different criteria (e.g. surmountable, individually surmountable, insurmountable) [12]. A subsequent problem, which was also discussed by Froehlich et al. [6] is the acquisition of accessibility-related indoor data, in particular the large amount of information required and the number of different contexts in which they have to be collected. This is also reflected in the analyzes by Striegl et al. [14], which examines both commercial and freely accessible GIS systems and shows, that the number of mapped buildings is low and the number of collected information inside these buildings is limited. The acquisition can be divided into two areas. The first aspect is the recording of building floor plans, which has already been addressed, for example by Tschorn et al. [15] and De las Heras et al. [7]. The second element is the collection of further required information regarding accessibility, which is complex. A possible approach for this gap is to involve volunteers who make the required indoor map data freely available. In this regard, OpenStreetMap[1] is a suitable platform, since it already has the option of capturing indoor map data in the Simple Indoor Tagging[2] format and can also be freely expanded on the basis of the simple data scheme of OSM in form of key-value pairs[3].

Furthermore, other open source projects be predicated on OpenStreetMap and add different information to the database like the accessibility for wheelchairs by the wheelmap[4] project. As early as 2014, Ding et al. [4] have discussed various open source projects - some of them are also based on OpenStreetMap - and the possibility of referencing them using Linked Data.

Moreover, one of the main aspects of using crowdsourcing is to understand how volunteers collect data efficiently and correctly and what their encourages is. In this regard, Budhathoki et al. [1,2] presented different intrinsic and extrinsic motivators for volunteered geographic information like OSM. Furthermore, Qin

[1] OpenStreetMap: https://openstreetmap.org (Last Access: 2023-02-10).

[2] OSM-Wiki for Simple Indoor Tagging: https://wiki.openstreetmap.org/wiki/Simple_Indoor_Tagging (Last Access: 2023-02-10).

[3] OSM-Wiki for Tags: https://wiki.openstreetmap.org/wiki/Tags (Last Access: 2023-02-10).

[4] Wheelmap.org: https://wheelmap.org/ (Last Access: 2023-02-10).

et al. [10] and Rice et al. [11] offered a crowd-sourcing application to collect barriers in outdoor environments, in particularly to address the difficulty to map dynamic data. Finally, Zeng et al. [16] discussed the opportunity that people with disabilities collect and map accessibility-related data by themselves.

In addition to current research on using volunteers to increase the count of accessibility information, with StreetComplete[5] an outdoor application that accumulate different data already exist and is freely accessible[6]. Depending on the user position, missing information on physical objects - also regarding accessibility - are visualized by icons and can be recorded by using a simplified question-and-answer user interface.

SITMapChecker. With SITMapChecker[7] an application was presented to record accessibility information within indoor environments, which shows an overview of a selected indoor map and displays missing information based on achievements [13] (see Fig. 1). However, these are solely focused on the acquisition of information about specific objects and do not take other motivations into account, which can lead to an exclusion of potential mappers. Moreover, the current implementation is limited by showing the missing information but doesn't support the editing of the objects.

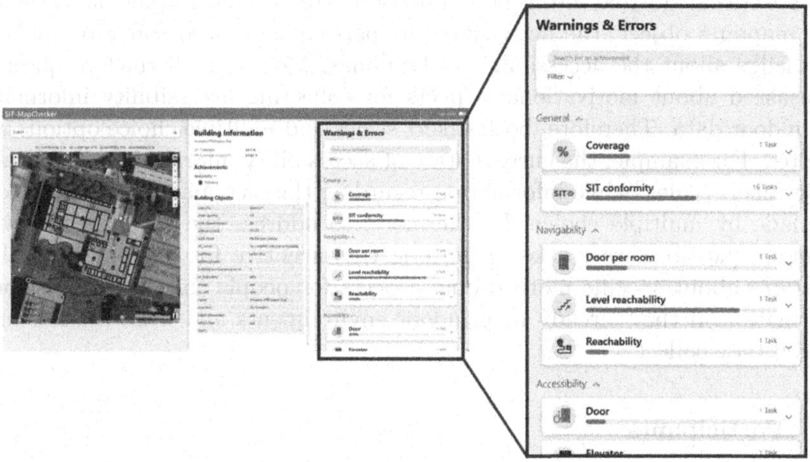

Fig. 1. Screenshot of the current state of SITMapChecker, which shows object based achievements on the right side [13]

[5] OSM-Wiki for StreetComplete: https://wiki.openstreetmap.org/wiki/DE:StreetComplete (Last Access: 2023-02-10).

[6] Google PlayStore for StreetComplete: https://play.google.com/store/apps/details?id=de.westnordost.streetcomplete&hl=de&gl=US (Last Access: 2023-02-10).

[7] GitHub for SITMapChecker: https://github.com/AccessibleMaps/SITMapChecker (Last Access: 2023-02-10).

In summary, the problem regarding the collection of accessibility information is well known and can be resumed to various factors, such as the variety and richness of information, as well as limited knowledge about the information needed. One possible approach to address the information gap is to use volunteers to collect such data. The necessary extent to reach this goal requires a more detailed analysis of the collectors and their support and motivation. A first starting point is the SITMapChecker.

3 User Study

The application SITMapChecker already uses achievements but is still limited in the way how information are gathered. To address the described gap, a study was conducted to discuss the current activity regarding the collection of indoor map data as well as the generation of user-centered achievements to support the collection of accessibility information in buildings based on individual motivations.

3.1 Methodology

The study was realized in form of an online questionnaire with 41 questions, which were categorized into general questions about demographic data, the current mapping object, the activity of the participants, used software and their knowledge about the accessibility of buildings. Moreover, distinctive questions were asked about motivational aspects for collecting accessibility information and indoor data. Therefore, both Likert scales and multiple choice options were inserted. For example, the current state of accessibility information was assessed using Likert scales, while information regarding the own mapping content could be made by multiple choice. Furthermore, to address the key aspect, several common questions were asked regarding the incentive for mapping as well as questions about specific motivational aspects for people collecting accessibility information, if they already map indoor environments and what kind of information they collect.

3.2 Participants

The questionnaire was distributed via various mailing lists in German-speaking countries and addressed the OSM community as well as communities based on it (see Fig. 2). Overall, 47 people took part in the study. 41 stated that they were male, 3 female, 1 person diverse and 2 participants remained unspecified (see Fig. 3). The ages range from younger than 18 years to 70 years or older, while 40 of the participants are between 25 and 69 years old. Moreover, 38 people from Germany, 7 from Austria and 2 people from Switzerland took part (see Fig. 4).

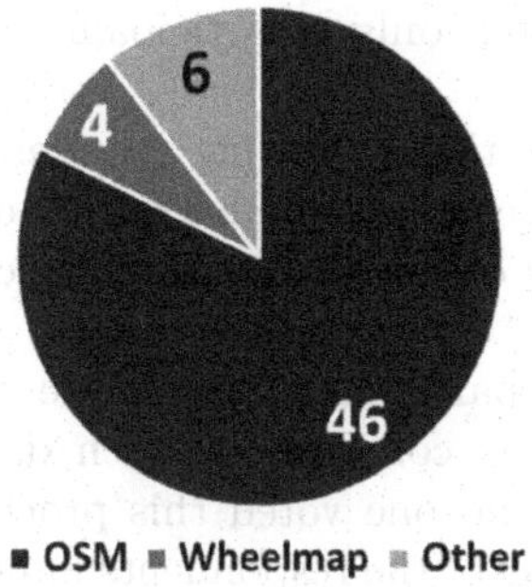

Fig. 2. Overview community

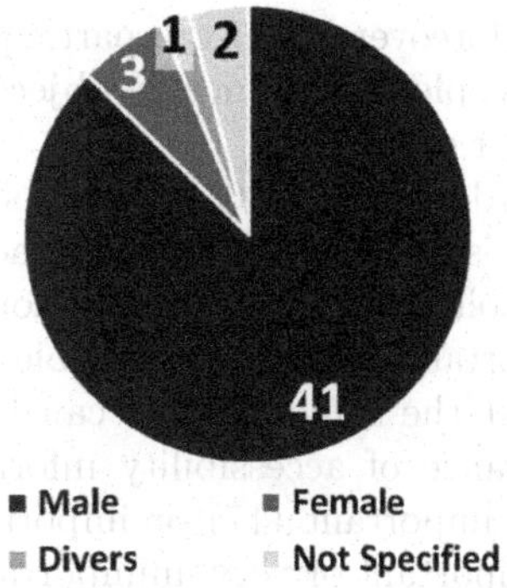

Fig. 3. Overview gender

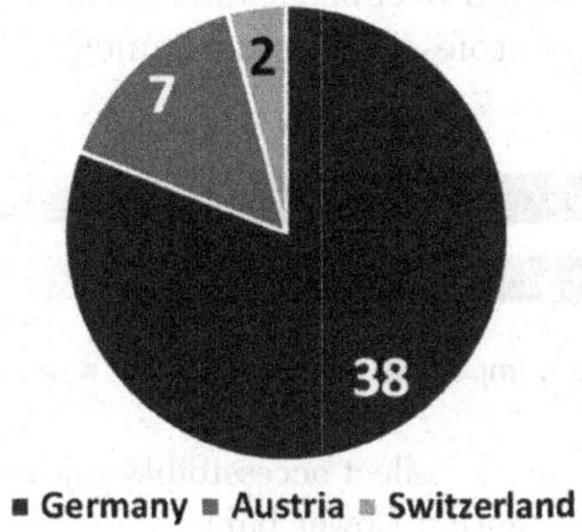

Fig. 4. Overview countries

17 of the participants map several times a week, 15 of them several times a month, and 12 people several times a day. Only 3 of the respondents mentioned, that they collect data less often (see Fig. 5).

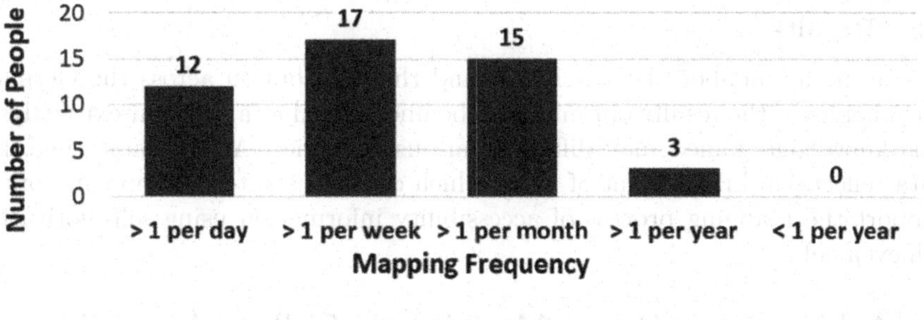

Fig. 5. Overview mapping frequency

Moreover, 41 of the participants accumulate data within cities and 6 of the 41 people map primarily objects in urban areas, but only 9 participants collect indoor data.

Additionally, 46 of the 47 surveyed people say that collecting georeferenced data is a hobby for them. In addition, 21 of the respondents also contribute to the collection of data for personal reasons, and 34 of the participants notice the importance of freely accessible information.

At the same time, it can be stated that the participants are aware of the relevance of accessibility information and rate the collection of such data as very important (17) or important (21). In turn, no one voted this process as unimportant or very unimportant. Furthermore, 39 of the respondents indicated that they also collect accessibility information. Referring to this, 7 of the 8 people, who did not collect accessibility information, rated it as important or moderate. (see Fig. 6) In this regard, 11 of the participants indicated that they collect accessibility information because it affects them personally or at least one person in their personal or professional environment.

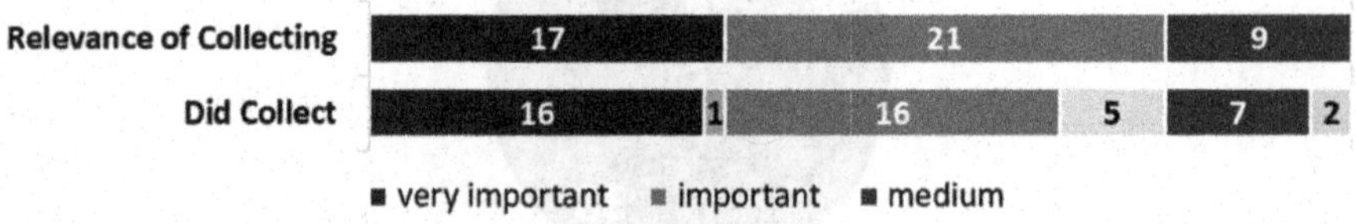

Fig. 6. Assessment of relevance to collect accessibility information (top bar) and people who collect accessibility information (lower bar)

Only 9 of the respondents collect building data, with 5 mainly entering building outlines. In contrast, only 4 people of all respondents also record further building elements such as rooms, stairs, elevators or others. They state, for example, that they want to improve orientation in buildings and specifically support people with disabilities in planning and implementing routes in buildings.

3.3 Results

Based on the number of participants and the distribution across the German-speaking area, the results obtained can be understood as a first context analysis. The knowledge gained may differ in various countries. At the same time, the data reflects an initial point of view, which can be used to develop concepts to support the mapping process of accessibility information using self-motivating achievements.

4 Achievement Based Mapping to Collect Accessible Information for Buildings

In regard to the gained knowledge, it can be assumed that a large number of mappers are willing to actively contribute to the collection of accessibility information. At the same time, the collection of indoor map data and the knowledge about required information for people with disabilities inside buildings is not yet widespread. To improve this, it is necessary to motivate data collectors to collect accessibility information in indoor map data. Furthermore, a handout is required to enable the mapper to enter the needed data correctly. In the best case, it can be achieved that no lengthy familiarisation of the subject area is necessary and that data can be recorded without much preliminary effort by mappers.

In this regard, the achievement approach offers a way to motivate mappers to collect indoor map data and accessibility information using specific achievements. In order to implement this in the best possible way, an analysis of the various motivational aspects and a division of the group into various subgroups is required. In turn, these can be used to adapt achievements to the needs of the individual person and to support the recording process in the best possible way.

From the information obtained in the survey, we divide mappers into the main groups of people who already collect indoor data and such who do not. The first group contains only 9 participants who were split into subgroups based on the following three facts:

1. If they or a person in their environment is affected by a disability.
2. If they collect mostly one kind of object/subject or structure in a building.
3. If they already collect accessibility information.

This leads to a tripartite division of the group, which shows that people who do not have a disability themselves or who do not have a person with a disability in their immediate environment usually perceive very specific objects in buildings (6). Furthermore, this group can by divided into 4 people who collect accessibility information and 2 people who did not collect such data. In contrast to this, the three participants who are personally affected by an impairment or in whose environment a person is affected mostly do not have a pronounced preference regarding the data collection. (see Table 1).

Table 1. Overview about the subgroups for people, who collect indoor data

Environment	Self affected	Specific mapping subject	Collecting accessibility features	Number of people	Group name
Indoor	no	yes	yes	4	GroupIn A21
			no	2	GroupIn A22
	yes	no	yes	3	GroupOut B11

In comparison, the larger group, which only collects outdoor data, shows greater diversity. At the same time, the largest subgroup - taking into account the same aspects as in the indoor area - with 22 out of 38 volunteers represents those who neither have an impairment themselves nor have a person with an impairment in their environment (see Table 2).

Table 2. Overview about the subgroups for people, who collect outdoor data

Environment	Self affected	Specific mapping subject	Collecting accessibility features	Number of people	Group name
Outdoor	no	no	yes	22	GroupOut A11
			no	3	GroupOut A12
		yes	yes	3	GroupOut A21
			no	2	GroupOut A22
	yes	no	yes	7	GroupOut B11
			no	1	GroupOut B12

Moreover, they don't collect very specific data, but at the same time map accessibility information. Furthermore, this group is not represented in the indoor subgroups, which can probably be attributed to the newer and mostly less known collection of indoor data or the higher complexity in the collection of indoor data. (see Figs. 7 and 8)

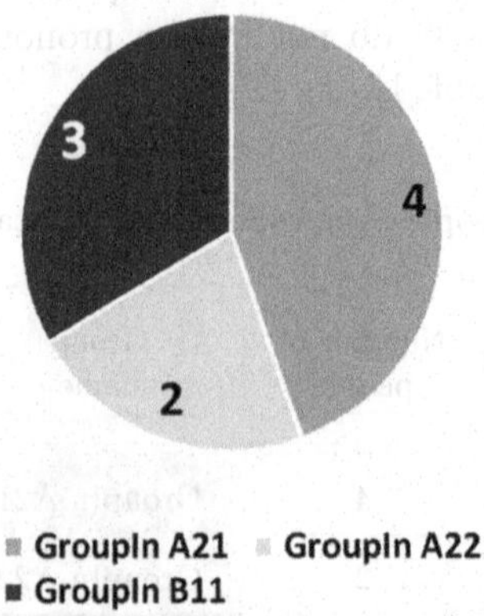

Divided subgroups (3) for indoor mapping

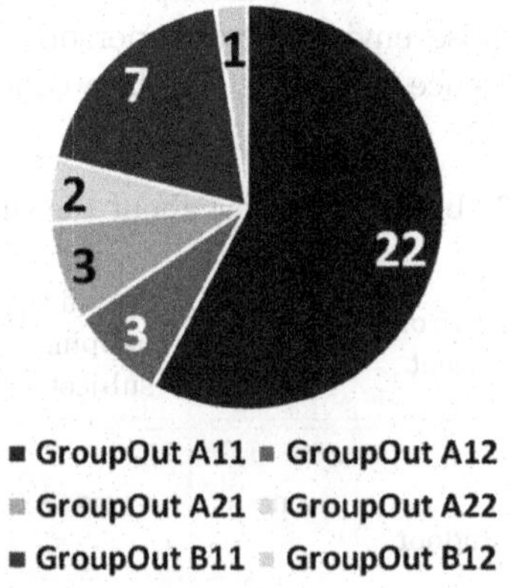

Divided subgroups (6) for outdoor mapping

Fig. 7. Overview of people who mapping indoor and outdoor

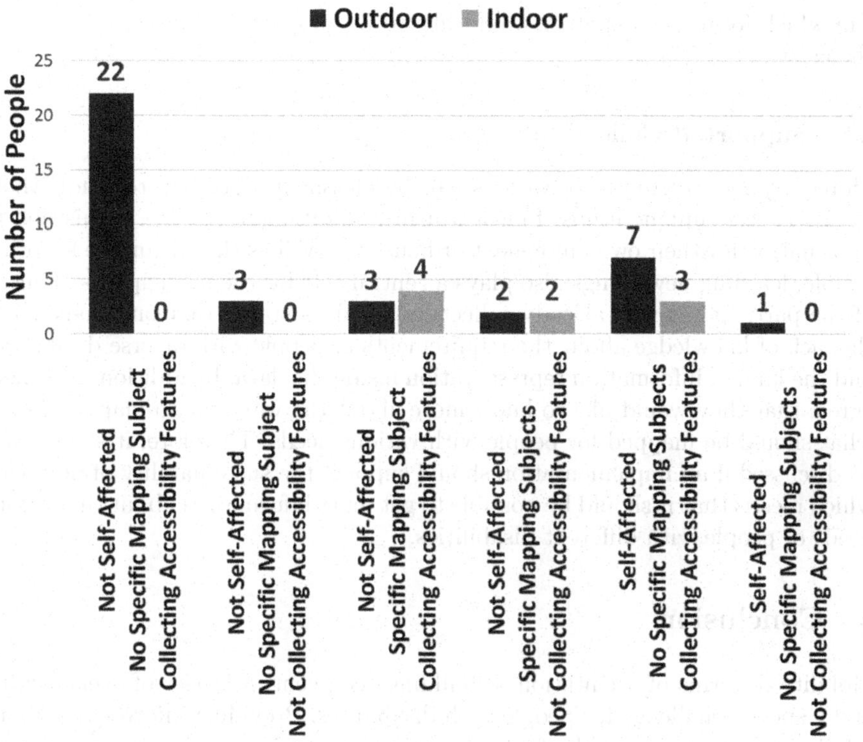

Fig. 8. Comparison of people who mapping indoor and outdoor

Based on the facts presented, different aspects can fundamentally play a central role in the collection of general indoor data as well as accessibility information.

4.1 Individual Achievements

Most of the mappers collect accessibility information. The reasons to do this reach from personal impairment, an impairment of a person in their social environment to general social commitments. In addition, there are differences what kind of objects will be mapped. For example, in indoor environments, mainly specific things like elevators are recorded by the volunteers. In contrast, most people who map outdoor data, collect general georeferenced data. Since such a procedure is also conceivable indoors, user-centered achievements must be made available that enable the collector to describe specific objects more precisely or generally display all the information that is still required in an environment. In the latter case, it can also make sense to subdivide the achievements based on the different needs of people with different impairments, to reduce the amount of information on the one hand, but also to specifically support mappers who want to collect data explicitly for a group of people on the other hand. The choice

- in which form the volunteer would like to be supported - should be made by themselves.

4.2 Supported Collection

Moreover, the different motivations can be classified according to Budhathoki et al. [1] (e.g. unique ethos, fun, altruism). Additionally to the acquisition of information for their own enjoyment or benefit as well as the advantage for other people, learning new things also plays a central role for the participants. Thus, 5 of the participants who already collect indoor data stated that one challenge is the lack of knowledge about the requirements of people with diverse disabilities and the kind of information representation inside the data. In addition, 2 of them agree, that they would like to know more about the way how to map as well as what should be mapped for people with various needs. Therefore, it should also be discussed if an implementation should support the sustainability of mappers, which means that it should be possible to get more information about the various needs of people with different disabilities.

5 Conclusion

Mobility in terms of orientation in buildings is a central aspect of everyday life and a special challenge for people with disabilities. Providing information about a building in advance in the form of an indoor map is therefore a fundamental prerequisite for improving mobility. The creation of such maps as well as their updating and enrichment with accessibility information is time-consuming and knowledge-intensive. This can be circumvented, for example, by using volunteers to help collect the required data. In order to accomplish this, an appropriate user-centered approach is needed that motivates the collectors and supports them in the correct collection of the data. A first foundation for this process is the study discussed here, which represents a rudimentary context analysis for the German-speaking area for the open-source project OpenStreetMap. On the one hand, the study shows that only a small proportion of the currently active mappers (9 out of 47) record indoor environments. On the other hand, the collected data can be used to show that there is a broad awareness of accessibility and the information required for it. Furthermore, both social backgrounds and personal interests in specific objects can be motivating aspects. In connection with this, achievements can be developed, which collect object-specific information and associated accessibility information (e.g. about an elevator) or directly address a target group - such as the collection of data for people in wheelchairs. In addition, some of the participants - who collect indoor data - would like to know more about the needs of people with disabilities to understand why certain information are needed and should be collected. Therefore, it is essential to provide a way to give more extensive information. Such a supportive approach must be designed and validated in the next step. Therefore, the focus has to be on an user-centered design to evaluate the practicability in form of a prototype-based user study.

Acknowledgement. This work was partially funded by the Federal Ministry of Labour and Social Affairs (BMAS) under the grant number 01KM151112.

References

1. Budhathoki, N., Nedovic-Budic, Z., Bruce, B.: An interdisciplinary frame for understanding volunteered geographic information. Geomatica **64**, 11–26 (2010)
2. Budhathoki, N.R., Haythornthwaite, C.: Motivation for open collaboration: crowd and community models and the case of openstreetmap. Am. Behav. Sci. **57**(5), 548–575 (2013). https://doi.org/10.1177/0002764212469364
3. Constantinescu, A., Müller, K., Loitsch, C., Zappe, S., Stiefelhagen, R.: Traveling to unknown buildings: accessibility features for indoor maps. In: Miesenberger, K., et al. (eds.) ICCHP-AAATE 2022. LNCS, vol. 13341, pp. 221–228. Springer, Heidelberg (2022). https://doi.org/10.1007/978-3-031-08648-9_26
4. Ding, C., Wald, M., Wills, G.: A survey of open accessibility data. In: Proceedings of the 11th Web for All Conference, W4A '14. Association for Computing Machinery, New York, NY, USA (2014). https://doi.org/10.1145/2596695.2596708
5. Engel, C., et al.: Travelling more independently: a requirements analysis for accessible journeys to unknown buildings for people with visual impairments. In: The 22nd International ACM SIGACCESS Conference on Computers and Accessibility, ASSETS '20. Association for Computing Machinery, New York, NY, USA (2020). https://doi.org/10.1145/3373625.3417022
6. Froehlich, J.E., et al.: Grand challenges in accessible maps. Interactions **26**(2), 78–81 (2019). https://doi.org/10.1145/3301657
7. De las Heras, L.P., Ahmed, S., Liwicki, M., Valveny, E., Sánchez, G.: Statistical segmentation and structural recognition for floor plan interpretation: notation invariant structural element recognition. Int. J. Doc. Anal. Recogn. **17**(3), 221–237 (2014)
8. Loitsch, C., Müller, K., Engel, C., Weber, G., Stiefelhagen, R.: AccessibleMaps: addressing gaps in maps for people with visual and mobility impairments. In: Miesenberger, K., Manduchi, R., Covarrubias Rodriguez, M., Peňáz, P. (eds.) ICCHP 2020. LNCS, vol. 12377, pp. 286–296. Springer, Cham (2020). https://doi.org/10.1007/978-3-030-58805-2_34
9. Müller, K., Engel, C., Loitsch, C., Stiefelhagen, R., Weber, G.: Traveling more independently: a study on the diverse needs and challenges of people with visual or mobility impairments in unfamiliar indoor environments. ACM Trans. Access. Comput. **15**(2) (2022). ISSN 1936-7228, https://doi.org/10.1145/3514255
10. Qin, H., Aburizaiza, A.O., Rice, R.M., Paez, F., Rice, M.T.: Obstacle characterization in a geocrowdsourced accessibility system. ISPRS Ann. Photogram. Remote Sens. Spatial Inf. Sci. **2**(3W5), 179–185 (2015)
11. Rice, M.T., et al.: Crowdsourcing techniques for augmenting traditional accessibility maps with transitory obstacle information. Cartogr. Geogr. Inf. Sci. **40**(3), 210–219 (2013)
12. Schmalfuß-Schwarz, J., Loitsch, C., Weber, G.: Considering time-critical barriers in indoor routing for people with disabilities. In: Miesenberger, K., Manduchi, R., Covarrubias Rodriguez, M., Peňáz, P. (eds.) ICCHP 2020. LNCS, vol. 12377, pp. 315–322. Springer, Cham (2020). https://doi.org/10.1007/978-3-030-58805-2_37

13. Schmalfuß-Schwarz, J., Striegl, J.: Analyse tool für simple indoor tagging. Anwenderkonferenz für Freie und Open Source Software für Geoinformationssysteme, Open Data und OpenStreetMap, pp. 26–30 (2021). https://www.fossgis-konferenz.de/2021/data/FOSSGIS_Tagungsband_2021.pdf
14. Striegl, J., Lotisch, C., Schmalfuss-Schwarz, J., Weber, G.: Analysis of indoor maps accounting the needs of people with impairments. In: Miesenberger, K., Manduchi, R., Covarrubias Rodriguez, M., Peňáz, P. (eds.) ICCHP 2020. LNCS, vol. 12377, pp. 305–314. Springer, Cham (2020). https://doi.org/10.1007/978-3-030-58805-2_36
15. Tschorn, G., Kray, C., Broelemann, K.: Extracting Indoor Map Data From Public Escape Plans on Mobile Devices (2013)
16. Zeng, L., Kühn, R., Weber, G.: Improvement in environmental accessibility via volunteered geographic information: a case study. Univ. Access Inf. Soc. **16**(4), 939–949 (2016). https://doi.org/10.1007/s10209-016-0505-9
17. Zlatanova, S., Sithole, G., Nakagawa, M., Zhu, Q.: Problems in indoor mapping and modelling. In: International Archives of the Photogrammetry, Remote Sensing and Spatial Information Sciences - ISPRS Archives, vol. 40, pp. 63–68. International Society for Photogrammetry and Remote Sensing, Cape Town (2013). https://doi.org/10.5194/isprsarchives-XL-4-W4-63-2013

Modification of the Brief Measure of Technology Commitment for People with Aphasia

Bianca Spelter[1(✉)], Sabine Corsten[2], Lara Diehlmann[2], Mirjam Gauch[1], Marie Hoffmann[3], Sven Karstens[3], Almut Plath[2], and Juliane Leinweber[1]

[1] Faculty of Engineering and Health, Health Campus Göttingen, University of Applied Sciences and Arts Hildesheim/Holzminden/Göttingen, Hildesheim, Germany
{bianca.spelter,mirjam.gauch,juliane.leinweber}@hawk.de

[2] Faculty of Healthcare and Nursing, Catholic University of Applied Sciences Mainz, Mainz, Germany
{sabine.corsten,lara.diehlmann,almut.plath}@kh-mz.de

[3] Department of Computer Science, Therapeutic Sciences, Trier University of Applied Sciences, Trier, Germany
sven.karstens@hochschule-trier.de

Abstract. People with aphasia (PWA), an acquired communication disorder, benefit from speech and language therapy (SLT). SLT can be conducted as telepractice, which requires a certain level of technology commitment (TC). Neyer et al. (2012) developed an assessment for TC for older adults. Due to its high linguistic complexity, this study aimed to: (1) adapt the brief measure of TC to the PWA´s needs, (2) add and evaluate items regarding the commitment to telepractice. The modification was an iterative process, alternating piloting, and modification phases. In the piloting, PWA answered the questions of the assessment using verbal probing. The original measure was conducted during the first piloting phase (n = 6). After the first modification and addition of items on telepractice, a second piloting (n = 5) followed. After further modification, the third piloting (n = 3) started. The data were analysed using behaviour coding and qualitative content analysis. Based on the first piloting phase, the layout was adjusted, and visual support (i.e., smileys) was added. Synonyms replaced words with higher word frequency. Subordinate clauses were reduced. The second piloting showed improved accessibility. However, difficulties arose with the added items, and smileys were misleading on some items. Results of the third piloting phase showed that the change of the visual support (i.e., red cross, yellow circle, green checkmark) was helpful. General comprehensibility was further improved. However, not all rules of official plain language could be followed, as items would lose discriminatory power. In future studies, the modification must be tested for its psychometric properties.

Keywords: Technology commitment · telepractice · aphasia · speech and language therapy

M. Antona and C. Stephanidis (Eds.): HCII 2023, LNCS 14020, pp. 489–509, 2023.
https://doi.org/10.1007/978-3-031-35681-0_33

1 Background

In the UN Convention on the Rights of Persons with Disabilities (UNCRPD) [1], accessibility and technology are considered a precondition for the full participation of people. New technologies provide novel options for the support of people including people with disabilities. Therefore, from an ethical point of view, it is essential to consider all people when implementing new technologies, also in the area of health care. The UNCRPD demand "to undertake or promote research and development, and to promote the availability and use of new technologies" [1].

Given the importance of this topic, it is relevant to identify the individual characteristics that might influence the successful and intentional use of technology. Different technology commitment models depict factors influencing attitudes towards technologies and the willingness to use them. The Technology Acceptance Model (TAM) [2] is a widely used theoretical model that explains how users come to accept and use technology. It is proposed that a user's acceptance of technology is based on their perceptions of its usefulness and ease of use. Technology can lead to increased acceptance and perceived usefulness, creating a positive feedback loop. Neyer et al. (2012) assume that the successful use of technology depends, among other things, on whether people are willing to value technological progress as a personal gain and are convinced that they can handle and control technology competently. They propose an integrative model of technology commitment to predict technology use that includes such personality traits as technology acceptance, technology competence, and control [3].

Technology acceptance is a reflection of the subjective evaluation of technological progress. In particular, the personal relationship to modern technologies is considered rather than the evaluation of their significance for the society. Thus, technology acceptance manifests primarily in personal interest in technical innovations [3].

Technology competence is the subjective expectation of possible behavioural options in technology-relevant situations. It includes both, biographically gathered experiences with familiar technologies and the expected flexibility to as-yet-unknown technological innovations [3].

Technology control is a person's subjective expectation of the outcome of their technology-relevant actions. It thus reflects the extent of the perceived controllability of technology [3].

Combining the aim to improve the participation of people with disabilities and the knowledge of technology commitment, it seems highly relevant to be able to examine all persons' technology commitment. This includes people with aphasia (PWA), an acquired communication disorder that occurs in 20% of stroke survivors and can affect speaking, listening, reading, and writing modalities. PWA are often excluded from studies due to their communication disorder [4, 5].

Aphasia impacts the quality of life more than any other impairment [6]. Speech and language therapy is traditionally delivered face-to-face. However, recent scoping reviews demonstrated that telepractice for PWA is comparable to face-to-face treatment regarding naming skills [7] and can improve the quality of life, depending on the intervention used [8]. Further, people with aphasia are shown to benefit from the use of new technologies as Virtual Reality [9]. In addition, telepractice can facilitate patient access and increase treatment frequency [10]. For implementing technology in speech and language therapy with PWA, the assessment of technology commitment (TC) is relevant.

While there is a lot of research on technology commitment in older adults or other patient groups, such as people with dementia, little is known about PWA. Menger et al. (2020) found that Internet use in people after stroke with and without aphasia ranged from fully independent to by proxy (i.e., access via someone who uses the Internet on their behalf). Most participants perceived their aphasia as a barrier. Aphasia was related to difficulties with technology-based written communication. Nevertheless, for the majority, it was not the only reason for failing to acquire or improve skills. While the impact of aphasia was meaningful, the analysis revealed that age was a stronger predictor of Internet use. Further, the level of education was related to participants' feelings about their skills. Therefore, this research demonstrates that it is essential to consider the influence of factors such as age, proxy use, education, and previous technology use and experience [11].

User-centred design workshops with PWA in the project TELL[1], in which this study was also realised, showed the unique needs of PWA when using technology, i.e., a platform for telepractice. For example, large font sizes and a distraction-free screen were significant. Difficulties with technology-based written communication arose as well. PWA stated that they need short and easy sentences and a feature to read aloud text to support their reading. They also expressed the need for further support, i.e., always-visible support buttons and explanatory videos [12].

As Menger et al. (2020) showed, aphasia is an essential factor influencing technology use. However, other personal factors, as described in several models for technology use, need to be considered. Therefore, assessments for technology commitment are relevant since they help to understand people's level of support and engagement toward new technology. This understanding is crucial for the successful implementation and adoption of new technology. TC assessments can reveal key areas of resistance or lack of knowledge that may impede implementation success.

The brief measure of TC by Neyer, Felber and Gebhardt (2012) is a time-efficient instrument created explicitly for older adults. The authors developed an integrative model for TC that considers the components of technology acceptance, technology competence, and control. The brief measure TC consists of an introductory instruction and a total of 12 items, which are rated according to the agreement on a five-point Likert scale (1 = "*strongly disagree*"; 5 = "*strongly agree*"). The sub-scales with examples of items are shown in Table 1 [3]. No validated assessments capture the commitment to use technology and the acceptance of speech and language telepractice with special consideration of the respondents' linguistic limitations, as they exist with PWA. The future benefit of such an instrument can be found in research and practice and improve participation in speech and language telepractice. With such an instrument, patient commitment can also be identified before application. Using an already existing, validated instrument to determine the commitment of PWA to technology seems evident for the time being. When selecting such a transferable survey tool, the brief measure TC has the advantage that it has already been validated and has good psychometric properties. In addition,

[1] The current work is supported by a grant of the German Federal Ministry of Education and Research [BMBF, 01IS19039].

according to the authors, the construct of technology commitment can be used to record the successful use of new technologies, especially in older age groups [3]. As stroke and the occurrence of aphasia are associated with age [13], this assessment seems promising for use with PWA.

Table 1. Subscales and examples of items of the brief measure of TC [3].

Subscale	Items	Example item (German)	English translation
Technology acceptance	1–4	Ich bin stets daran interessiert, die neuesten technischen Geräte zu verwenden. (Item 3)	I am always interested in using the latest technical devices. (Item 3)
Technology competence	5–8	Den Umgang mit neuer Technik finde ich schwierig – ich kann das meistens einfach nicht. (Item 8)	I find dealing with new technology difficult - I just can't do it most of the time. (Item 8)
Technology control	9–12	Es liegt in meiner Hand, ob mir die Nutzung technischer Neuentwicklungen gelingt – mit Zufall oder Glück hat das wenig zu tun. (Item 10)	It is in my own hands whether I succeed in using new technical developments - it has little to do with chance or luck. (Item 10)

From a speech and language therapy point of view, however, it must also be taken into consideration that the brief measure TC may only be comprehensible to PWA to a limited extent. Hence, simplifications or adaptations might be necessary. Another aspect to be considered when adopting the brief measure TC is that it asks about commitment in general and not more specifically in speech and language telepractice. Therefore, it is relevant to formulate new items that measure commitment for telepractice in speech and language services.

With the brief measure of TC by Neyer et al. (2012), TC can be measured in older adults. Due to the high linguistic complexity of the brief measure, the study aimed to: (1) adapt the brief measure of TC to the needs of PWA, (2) add and evaluate items regarding the commitment to telepractice.

2 Methods

The modification of the brief measure of TC was an iterative process (see Fig. 1), alternating piloting and modification phases following the guidelines of Tafforeau et al. (2019) [14]. In each piloting phase, cognitive interviews were conducted. The participants answered the items of the brief measure and were asked for feedback via verbal probing. Cognitive interviews are beneficial for checking the comprehensibility of items, identifying respondents' problems in responding to the assessment, revealing the causes of these problems, and generating suggestions for improvement [15, 16]. Verbal probing was used, as it requires less verbal expression than the Think Aloud method [15] and could be adapted for people with aphasia. Behaviour Coding was added as an evaluation method to include the (non-verbal) reactions to the items [17], especially for participants with difficulties in language production.

During the first piloting phase (n = 6), the original measure was conducted to identify difficulties in intelligibility. After the first modification and adding four items on telepractice, further piloting (n = 5) followed. Based on the results, the brief measure was modified and tested again (n = 3) resulting in the third version of the modified brief measure.

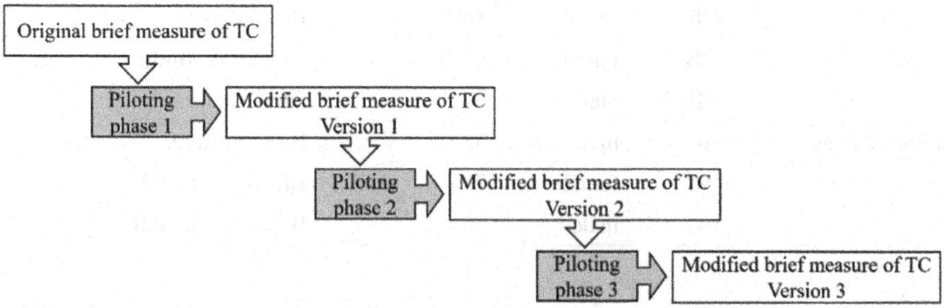

Fig. 1. Overview of modification and piloting phases.

2.1 Participants

For each piloting phase, people with chronic aphasia, who had not previously participated, were included. Persons (age > 18 years) with chronic aphasia (at least 6 months post onset) were included. The type and severity of aphasia were reported by the treating therapist with the consent of the participants. Since cognitive interviews were used to collect data, people with severe language comprehension disorders were excluded. Regarding speech production, participants should at least be able to verbalise short utterances in a simple sentence structure. As a result, PWA ranging widely in severity of aphasia participated. The presence of a written language disorder or apraxia of speech was not an exclusion criterion. Individuals with other psychiatric-neurological disorders (especially major depression or onset of dementia judged by a physician) were excluded.

Table 2. Participants' characteristics.

	ID	Sex	Age (years)	Type of aphasia (severity)
Piloting Phase 1	AA	female	83	Broca (mild)
	BA	female	93	Amnestic (mild)
	CA	male	76	Wernicke (mild)

(continued)

Table 2. *(continued)*

	ID	Sex	Age (years)	Type of aphasia (severity)
	DA	male	66	Amnestic (moderate)
	EA	female	56	Broca (moderate)
	FA	male	63	Broca (moderate)
Piloting Phase 2	AB	female	91	Broca (moderate)
	BB	male	59	Amnestic (mild)
	CB	female	56	Broca (mild)
	DB	female	66	Amnestic (mild)
	EB	male	67	Amnestic (mild)
Piloting Phase 3	AC	male	52	Broca (severe)
	BC	female	35	Broca (moderate)
	CC	male	50	Broca (moderate)

An overview of the included participants can be seen in Table 2. In the first piloting (n = 6), the mean age was 72 years, in the second (n = 5), 67.8 years, and in the third (n = 3), 45.6 years. The ratio of men to women was balanced in all piloting phases.

2.2 Data Retrieval

In cognitive interviews, the participants answered the items of the brief measure of TC. The researchers used an interview guide to provide similar questions for the participants. The assessment was pre-structured into four sections. After each section, verbal probes (e.g. "*Were there any sentences that were difficult for you?*") were asked about previous items. This prevented asking an additional question after each item, thus influencing the respondents' answers [17]. In addition, further general questions on handling the brief measure TC (e.g., "*How was the questionnaire for you?*") were formulated in the guideline, which were asked after processing the brief measure TC. All interviews were recorded. The recordings were used for the behaviour coding as well as transcripted verbatim for a qualitative content analysis.

2.3 Data Analysis

The data were analysed using behaviour coding [17] and qualitative content analysis [18].

In behaviour coding, the participant's answering reaction is evaluated in a structured way with a coding system [19]. The underlying assumption is that unclear items lead to noticeable response behaviour, and thus difficulties with items can be identified [17]. For this purpose, the frequency of coded behaviours of the participants for each item was considered [19]. The investigator conducted the behaviour coding based on the recordings. Only the immediate responses and reactions to the items were coded. Responses to the verbal probes or other statements made by the respondents were not considered since they were evaluated in the qualitative content analysis. For this study's coding, the code system of Oksenberg et al. (1991) was adopted (see Table 3). Codes (1)–(5) are evaluated as direct indications of difficulties with the items. If none of the codes (1) – (5) were applied, the answer was coded as adequate. However, this cannot be equated with a confirmed comprehension of the item but merely indicates that no conclusions about non-understanding can be drawn from the response behaviour. If the behaviour corresponded to code (6), the behaviour was assessed in respect of the response scale. Only then was code (6) or code (7) assigned. Code (7) intends to identify specific difficulties that occur in answering the scale. This procedure was chosen because sometimes participants name a corresponding answer category directly and immediately after the item presentation but first categorised their agreement with the items by saying "*yes*" or "*no*".

Table 3. Adapted coding system based on Oksenberg et al. (1991) [17].

Code	Definition (Participant...)
Before item presentation:	
(1) Interruption	... answers ahead of time or interrupts
Immediately after item presentation:	
(2) Refusal to answer	... refuses to answer; gives no, or only para-verbal answer (e.g., sigh)
(3) Don't know	... indicates he/she does not know the answer
(4) Clarification	... wants repetition or explanation of an item or indicates a problem in understanding
(5) Inadequate answer	... gives an answer that does not meet the item objective or is unrelated
(6) Adequate answer	... gives satisfactory answer that meets item objective (e.g., "*strongly agree*")
After adequate answer:	
(7) Qualified answer	... answers adequately and, when grading the answer on the scale, makes an additional remark suggesting uncertainty, asks a question about grading, or corrects the answer immediately

The transcripts of the interviews were analysed by conducting a qualitative content analysis. With the verbal probes, it was possible to record indications of the subjects' difficulties, which thus also allowed us to conclude the suitability of the assessment for the target group. For the instruction and each item, there was a category "direct indication of difficulties" (i.e., a participant describes the item as difficult) and "indirect indication of difficulties" (e.g., a participant shows insecurities in the verbal probing). Further, one category included all statements on formal aspects of brief measure TC.

The results of the behaviour coding and qualitative content analysis were combined to identify challenging items (see Table 4).

Table 4. Criteria for the identification of challenging items.

Behaviour Coding	Qualitative Content Analysis	
Item rated with one of the codes (1) to (5)	Direct indication of difficulties: - Participant identifies an item as difficult	Indirect indication of difficulties: - Participant shows insecurities in verbal probing

2.4 Criteria for Modification

Plain language is aimed at people with intellectual disabilities, learning difficulties, dementia, or aphasia [20]. It is, therefore, a suitable means of adapting test instruments for PWA. Whether a text complies with the rules of plain language can be examined using comprehensibility testing procedures [20]. The criteria are presented in Fig. 2.

Level	Domain	Fulfilment criteria
Layout	Font	– sans serif – min. size 14 – font markup: underlining or boldface preferred
	Text layout	– each sentence on a new line – no word separation at the end of the line – left-justified
Word level	Word structure	– short words: max. ten letters – separation of complex words by media point – no abbreviations – avoid passive voice
	Vocabulary	– easily understandable words – as far as possible, no foreign terms – explain foreign terms
Sentence level	Sentence structure & sentence meaning	– short sentences: max. 12 words, not more than two sentence parts – simple sentences: not more than one unit of information – avoid nominal style – avoid negation
Text level	-	– same words for the same things – relevant information at the beginning – subheadings desirable

Fig. 2. Overview of rules for German plain language according to Bredel & Maaß (2019) [20].

3 Results

In the following, the results of the three piloting and modification phases are presented. Afterward, an overview of the modification process is given. The participants' utterances were translated (if possible and relevant, with aphasic symptoms) for this paper. The examples sometimes contain the German item to illustrate the linguistic modifications. However, an English translation of the items is always included.

3.1 First Piloting and Modification Phase

In the first piloting phase, the original brief measure of TC was tested to identify intelligibility. The participants expressed difficulties regarding the instruction, like one participant (AA) saying, "*I don't know anything yet.* ". Based on the criteria for identifying problematic items (see Table 4), six items (4, 6, 9, 10, 11, and 12) were assessed as unsuitable in their original form. It can be noted that the items of the subscale technology control were affected most. One example is item 10: "*It is in my own hands whether I succeed in using new technical developments - it has little to do with chance or luck.* ". For this item, difficulties were identified via the behaviour coding for three participants (see Table 5). All six participants labelled it directly or indirectly as challenging, with four participants expressing direct difficulties, e.g., "*(sighs) This is difficult*" (EA). Participant BA contradicted her previous answer concerning the response scale. She repeated the item to herself and expressed that the negation was complex for her.

Table 5. Frequency distribution of codes per item in Behaviour Coding of piloting phase 1.

Sub-scale	Item	Frequency distribution of codes						
		(1) Interruption	(2) Refusal to answer	(3) Don't know	(4) Clarification	(5) Inadequate answer	(6) Adequate answer	(7) Qualified answer
technology acceptance	1				**1**		5	
	2						3	**3**
	3				**1**		4	**1**
	4			**1**			3	**2**
technology competence	5						2	**4**
	6		**1**				4	**1**
	7						3	**3**
	8						5	**1**

(continued)

Table 5. *(continued)*

Sub-scale	Item	Frequency distribution of codes						
		(1) Interruption	(2) Refusal to answer	(3) Don't know	(4) Clarification	(5) Inadequate answer	(6) Adequate answer	(7) Qualified answer
technology control	9			**1**	**1**	**1**	2	**1**
	10			**1**	**3**		2	
	11			**1**	**1**		2	**2**
	12		**1**	**1**	**2**		1	**1**

Printed in bold: Codes 1 – 5 indicate difficulties with the item; Code 7 indicates difficulties with the response scale.

In addition, participants provided some general feedback. For example, the subordinate clauses caused difficulties ("*There are so many "ifs" uh (.) there are so many yeses and noes that it always jumps.* "; FA). One participant added, "*The shorter, the better.*" (FA). Aspects of the layout, such as font size and presentation of the response scale, were also considered limited in their manageability for PWA. One participant said, "*Oh, it's written so small, I can't even read it.*" (AA). All in all, the suitability of the original brief measure TC for PWA was assessed as restricted.

Based on the first piloting phase, the layout (e.g., font size) was adjusted following the guidelines for plain language [20]. Visual support (i.e. smiley markers) was added and the possible responses were written under every item to reduce the cognitive challenge while answering. In all items, individual words were replaced by more frequent synonyms and inconsistently used terms were unified. For example, there were many terms like new *technical developments, technical devices, technical products*, or *modern technology.* In the modification, they are uniformly called *(latest) technical devices.* Subordinate clauses were reduced in 6 of the 12 items and the introduction. Examples of changes can be seen in Sect. 3.4.

3.2 Second Piloting and Modification Phase

The second testing phase with the modified and extended version showed that linguistic simplification improved accessibility for the participating PWA.

Concerning the instruction of the scale, four of the five participants were able to reproduce the topic appropriately. Due to the severity of her aphasia, participant AB could not respond in complete sentences. Still, she answered simple choice questions on the subject adequately and gave examples of technical devices.

An improvement in comprehensibility seems to have been achieved for the items as well, especially concerning the subscale technology competence (see Table 6). However, the results also show the necessity of another revision. The items of the subscale technology control still proved to be the most difficult. As a result, the complexity should be further reduced. Bredel and Maaß (2019) state that nominalisations make some texts even more complex than sentence structures [20]. In a new adaptation, nominalisations, among other things, should be further reduced. Item keywords could be underlined in the text layout.

The piloting of the four added items demonstrated difficulties in understanding. For example, one participant (AB) mentioned in the verbal probing "*television*" as a technical device in speech and language therapy. This indicates that she did not understand the topic of the added items since television is not a typically used technical device in speech and language therapy. The differentiation between telediagnostics and teletherapy became only clear after further explanation.

The visual support via smileys improved accessibility. Code (7), which indicates difficulties with the response scale, could be reduced compared to the first piloting. However, the visual support via smileys did not seem helpful to all participants. For some negatively polarised items, the happy smiley for "*strongly agree*" did not correspond to the associated emotions. For example, for the item "*I find it difficult to deal with technical devices. I usually can't do it.*", the participants had to select the happy smiley to agree strongly. One participant (EB) explained, "*When he (…) laughs, that's actually something positive for me, but for me, it's negative because I can't use it.*". The larger font compared to the original was perceived positively by the participants, as participant DB says, "*The writing was clear. Not too small, not too big. I thought it was great*".

Table 6. Frequency distribution of codes per item in Behaviour Coding of piloting phase 2.

Sub-scale	Item	Frequency distribution of codes						
		(1) Interruption	(2) Refusal to answer	(3) Don't know	(4) Clarification	(5) Inadequate answer	(6) Adequate answer	(7) Qualified answer
technology acceptance	1						4	**1**
	2						5	
	3		**1**			**1**	3	
	4			**1**			4	
technology competence	5						5	
	6						5	
	7						5	
	8						4	**1**
technology control	9				**1**	**1**	3	
	10		**1**	**1**			3	
	11		**1**				3	**1**
	12			**2**			3	

(continued)

Table 6. *(continued)*

Sub-scale	Item	Frequency distribution of codes						
		(1) Interruption	(2) Refusal to answer	(3) Don't know	(4) Clarification	(5) Inadequate answer	(6) Adequate answer	(7) Qualified answer
telepractice in speech and language therapy	13						4	**1**
	14					**1**	3	**1**
	15				**1**	**1**	3	
	16				**1**		3	**1**

Printed in bold: Codes 1 – 5 indicate difficulties with the item; Code 7 indicates difficulties with the response scale.

As a result of the second piloting phase, important keywords were underlined in the text layout, e.g., "*I find it interesting to use the <u>newest</u> technical devices.*". In addition, further linguistic modifications (e.g., starting all sentences with the subject) were realised. The visual support was changed to a red cross for "*strongly disagree*", a yellow circle for "*partly agree*" and a green checkmark for "*strongly agree*" to avoid a conflict of emotions not corresponding with the response (see Fig. 5). The red cross and green checkmark were chosen following the visual support of the Stroke and Aphasia Quality of Life Scale-39 (SAQOL-39) [21] which was developed for and evaluated with PWA.

3.3 Third Piloting and Modification Phase

The third piloting phase showed that the linguistic modifications further improved comprehensibility.

The instruction, which was not adapted compared to the first modified version, was also well comprehended by the participants in this piloting phase. For example, participant BC answered the question about the topic with: "*ehm..technical devices.*". After completing the scale, the same respondent reported difficulties with the term "*technical devices*". It was sometimes difficult for her to answer the items because the answers varied for different technical devices: "*Well, the mobile phone works great, the tablet works great, and the food processor works so-so.*"

Regarding the items, the results varied between the participants. Participant BC expressed no difficulties with the items except for the challenge of different technical devices. On the contrary, she often explained how she came up with the answer without being asked. For the item "*I have a problem with a technical device: I have to solve it alone.*", she described, "*(...) then ehm I have to manage it ehm alone.*". Participant AC identified challenges with two items because of the negation. Participant CC also showed difficulties with negations in items. In addition, he was challenged by the items of the subscale technology control because he interpreted the phrases "*I control*" and "*I influence*" regarding the companies behind the technical devices or software. He explained that he worked for a tech company and said, "*I don't check my app for the email on my phone... The software (...) don't check anymore. I only look for the response for the email.*" He could not transfer the technology control to himself despite the interviewer explaining the items.

Although there were more codings of *(7) qualified answer* in the piloting of this version (see Table 7), in contrast to the first modification, two participants (AC, BC) named the visual support as a positive aspect ("*Symbols really help*"; AC). This shows a discrepancy between the behaviour coding results and the participants' qualitative feedback. The visual support via a cross, circle, and checkmark had the advantage that one PWA (BC) could use the symbols as gestures to support communication when word-finding problems occurred: "*Yes ehm sometimes so (shows a circle with thumb and index finger) ehm yes*". However, one participant (CC) was confused by the yellow circle "*I don't know, what that is*".

All participants in this piloting phases are experienced with telepractice. BC said that the "*tablet is always there*" and she sometimes uses video therapy, e.g., when a Covid-19 infection is suspected. AC replied to the introduction of telepractice with "*zoom*". They showed no difficulties understanding the two telepractice items.

As a result, only one item was modified in the modification process. The instruction and visual support stayed as in the second version of the modification. In addition to the keywords, indicators of negations were underlined (e.g., "This is no coincidence."). It is impossible to avoid negations altogether within this assessment, but highlighting the rebuttals is intended to draw attention to it to improve the understanding.

Table 7. Frequency distribution of codes per item in Behaviour Coding of piloting phase 3.

Sub-scale	Item	Frequency distribution of codes						
		(1) Interruption	(2) Refusal to answer	(3) Don't know	(4) Clarification	(5) Inadequate answer	(6) Adequate answer	(7) Qualified answer
technology acceptance	1						2	**1**
	2						3	
	3						3	
	4						3	
technology competence	5						1	**2**
	6						2	**1**
	7				**1**		1	**1**
	8						2	**1**
technology control	9					**1**	2	
	10				**1**		2	

(continued)

Table 7. (*continued*)

Sub-scale	Item	Frequency distribution of codes						
		(1) Interruption	(2) Refusal to answer	(3) Don't know	(4) Clarification	(5) Inadequate answer	(6) Adequate answer	(7) Qualified answer
	11						3	
	12				**1**		1	**1**
telepractice in speech and language therapy	13					**1**	2	
	14					**1**	1	**1**

Printed in bold: Codes 1 – 5 indicate difficulties with the item; Code 7 indicates difficulties with the response scale.

3.4 Overview of the Modification Process

The results of the piloting phases lead to a modification of the original brief measure of TC. In the following, an overview of the modification process is given. Throughout the modification process, the number of words was reduced in the items as well as in the instruction (see Fig. 3). Only from the second to the third modification was a word added to one item to simplify the sentence structure.

In addition, the items were linguistically simplified. Some examples of simplification can be seen in Fig. 4. Some words were exchanged for shorter and more frequently used synonyms according to the Frequency Dictionary German [22] leading to a reduction of long terms. The decline in the mean length of sentences was achieved through syntactic structure adjustments. It was further reduced by dividing the contents into several sentences, especially in the second modification. As a result, the number of long sentences and subordinate clauses also decreased.

An example of the modification process of item 12, which was perceived as very challenging in the first and second piloting phases, is provided in Fig. 5. The conditional sentence was replaced in the first modification by a nominal construction. The nominalised phrase "*is ultimately under my control*" was reduced by the verb "*to control*". Further, "*new technological developments*" was replaced by "*new technical devices*" as inconsistently used words were unified throughout the brief measure. In the second modification, the content of the items was divided into two sentences. Consequently, the nominal construction was replaced, and the words per sentence decreased. Due to the unification process of the sentence structures, the item now begins with the subject of the sentence. The number of long words (> ten letters) decreased from three to two but could not further be reduced without changing the item's content.

As described earlier, the response scale of the original brief measure caused problems for the PWA. One modification was to write the possible responses under every item

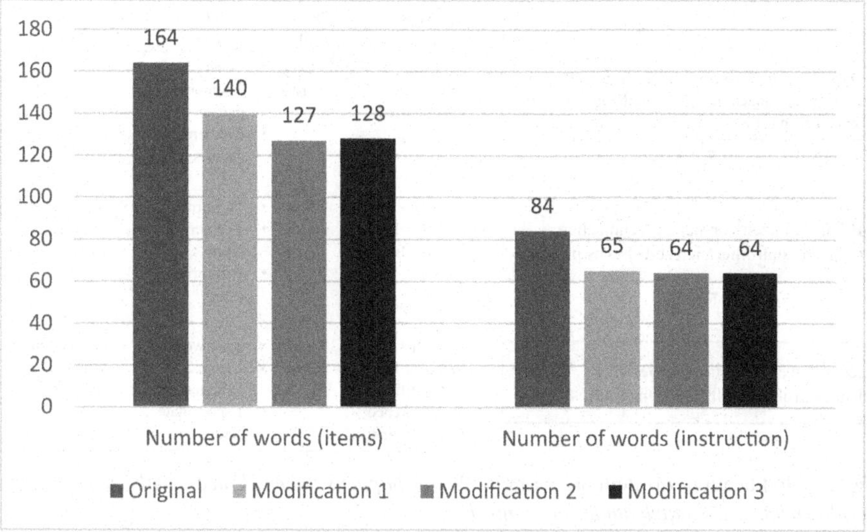

Fig. 3. Reduction of words in items and instruction from original to the modifications.

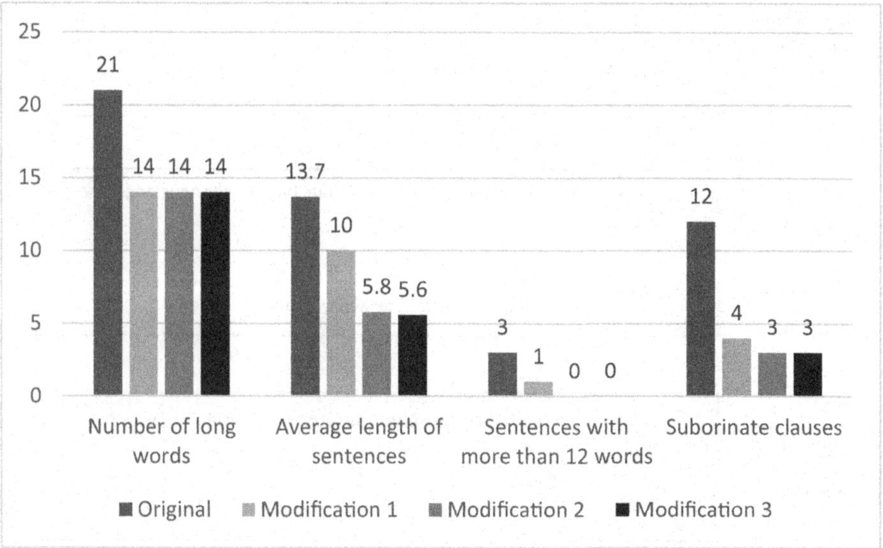

Fig. 4. Reduction of the number of long words, mean length of sentences in words, long sentences (> 12 words), and subordinate clauses in items from original to the modifications.

to reduce the cognitive challenge while answering the scale. In addition, visual support was added and modified throughout the modification process (see Fig. 6).

	Layout	Word level	Sentence level	Text level
Das, was passiert, wenn ich mich mit technischen Neuentwicklungen beschäftige, obliegt letztlich meiner Kontrolle.	✓ sans serif • font size 10 ✓ left-justified	• 3 long words	• 14 words • 3 sentence parts • 2 subordinate clauses	
Beim Benutzen von neuen technischen Geräten kontrolliere ich selbst, was passiert.	✓ sans serif ✓ font size 14 ✓ left-justified	• 2 long words	• 11 words • 3 sentence parts • 1 suborinate clause	✓ inconsistently used terms were unified
Ich nutze ein technisches Gerät. Ich kontrolliere selbst, was passiert.	✓ sans serif ✓ font size 14 ✓ left-justified ✓ each sentence on a new line	• 2 long words	✓ 2 x 5 words ✓ 1 resp. 2 sentence parts • 1 suborinate clause	✓ unification of sentence structures

Fig. 5. Modification of item 12 (Eng.: "*What happens when I deal with new technical developments is ultimately under my control.*").

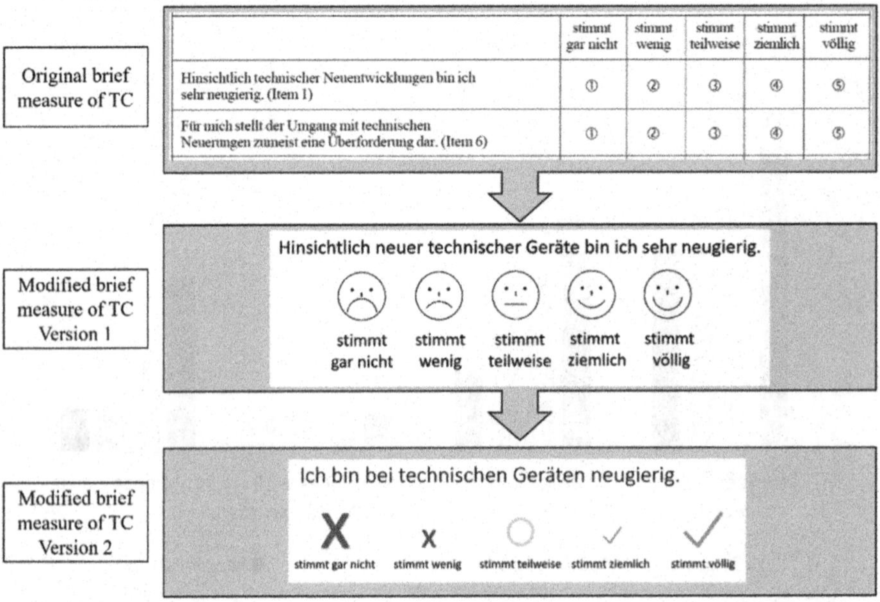

Fig. 6. Modification of the response scale including visual support. (Color figure online)

4 Discussion

Modifying the brief measure of TC, including linguistic simplification and visual support, was essential to meet PWA's needs. The three piloting and modification phases increased accessibility for PWA, noticeable in the results of the behaviour coding as well as the qualitative content analysis. Further, linguistic simplification is visible when comparing the original and the modifications regarding the criteria for official plain language. The results underline the importance of plain language, also named by the UNCRPD as a tool to increase the accessibility of people with disabilities [1].

However, not all rules of official plain language could be followed, as the items would lose discriminatory power. Comparable to the translation process of assessments, linguistic simplification should not only pay attention to the equivalence between original and target wording but rather strive for the modified item to primarily convey the original content [14]. The resulting distance to the original should be accepted to provide an adequate measurement instrument for PWA.

Dalemans et al. (2009) proposed increasing PWA participation in research by adjusting the assessment. Therefore, they suggest using pictograms, placing only one question per page, bolding the key concepts in items, using a large font, visualising the answering possibilities in words and pictures, reducing the question length, and excluding negatives in the question [4]. This is consistent with the adjustments made in this study based on participant feedback. A large number of the code *(7) qualified answer,* as well as the input of the participants in the piloting of the original, showed that the response scale original brief measure of TC was not suitable for PWA. Reducing code *(7) qualified answer* in the second piloting can be interpreted as improving the response scale. The qualitative feedback showed that the response scale written above every item, and the visual support via the smiley markers were considered helpful. Nevertheless, for the negatively polarised items, the happy smiley for "*strongly agree"* did not correspond to the associated emotions. For this, the smiley markers, which are widely used in the literature [23], seemed to be not suitable for the modification of the brief measure TC. There is a wide variety of visual support for Likert scales available. It was chosen to use a red cross for "*strongly disagree"*, a yellow circle for "*partly agree"* and a green checkmark for "*strongly agree"* leading to a further reduction of the code *(7) qualified answer* and positive feedback of the participants. The decision was based on the findings of Hilari & Byng (2001), who evaluated different response formats with 12 PWA. In their study, most participants preferred the visualisation with cross and checkmark. Still, some participants found it confusing [24], which was also shown in our research. Overall, these findings stress the importance of adequate visual support in questionnaires for PWA and the inclusion of PWA in the development process.

However, changing the response scale's graphic design might influence participants' answers. Experimental studies have shown that graphical elements of rating scales can systematically influence response behaviour. When interpreting and answering questions, respondents use not only verbal but also visual aspects of the assessment [25]. Thus, the visual presentation of questions must be considered when designing such measurements and, especially when comparing results across assessments in which the visual representation of response scales varied [26]. It is recommended that non-task-related graphical elements such as colours, shading, or symbols are used with caution since they may lead to undesirable effects [25]. Thus, a balance must be struck between possible factors influencing response behaviour and the need for visual support for PWA. However, if visual support is used consistently in the validation of the modified version of the brief measure TC, it should not affect the comparability of the results.

This study also aimed to evaluate new items on speech and language telepractice. The piloting of the first added items showed difficulties in understanding specialist terms and the general use of technical devices in therapy. The reduction from four to two items and the linguistic modification seemed successful.

For the subscales of technology acceptance and competence, the descriptions of the participants were consistent with the definitions of the concepts of Neyer et al. (2012). However, one participant (CC) had difficulties with the concept of technology control. Instead of understanding items like "*I use a technical device. I control what happens myself.*" as the expectation of the outcome of his technology-relevant actions, he interpreted it as controlling the companies behind the technical devices or software. It is relevant to note that this participant used to work for a big tech company before his stroke. There might be an influence of his technology biography on the understanding of this item. Therefore, it may be helpful in future studies to collect biographical information relevant to technology.

Methodological Reflection. The iterative modification process with alternating piloting and modification phases following Tafforeau et al. (2019) was initially developed for the translation into different languages. In this study, we used the approach to modify the German brief measure of TC into German plain language. It allowed us to adapt and re-test the assessment according to the results between the piloting phases. The qualitative content analysis gave insight into the validity of the brief measure. As some participants with mild aphasia explained their answers (even when not explicitly asked), their explanations revealed how they understood the items. This matches the Think Aloud method in which participants are asked to verbalise the thought processes that led to their answer [16]. This shows that this method is applicable to people with mild aphasia and can be added in future piloting.

The selection of appropriate piloting methods for questionnaires was reduced due to the communication disorder of the target group. Most common piloting methods, such as the Think Aloud approach, work with meta-language, which already represents a high demand for linguistically healthy participants [19]. Even though some participants were able to verbalise their thought processes, for others, the method of verbal probing proved too abstract. In these cases, the questions had to be supplemented by closed ones, generating less information. Nevertheless, verbal probing as a qualitative method was crucial to identify reasons for difficulties, general framework conditions, and mainly only apparently adequate answers. Especially in participants with more severe aphasic symptoms, the advantage of behavioural coding became apparent: conclusions about the quality of the items could be drawn by observing the response behaviour. Generally, behaviour coding is well suited for identifying some problems but does not always explain why they exist and may miss other significant issues. Therefore, the combination of cognitive interviews and behaviour coding is crucial.

The sample was too small to analyse the response distributions in Behaviour Coding. In addition, only one coder performed the behaviour coding for each participant. Therefore, it cannot be confidently assumed that the results are independent of the investigators. In future studies, interrater reliability should therefore be evaluated.

Besides the small number of participants, a strength of the study is the variety of types and severity of aphasia, reflecting the heterogeneity of this patient group. Furthermore, participants who did not participate earlier were included in every piloting phase. While this makes it more difficult to compare the piloting results, a learning effect can be prevented.

The participants in the third piloting phase were significantly younger than in the previous two. In principle, age should not affect comprehensibility, but the scale does include several technical terms. Since age is strongly related to being online [27], younger respondents might have less difficulties understanding the items.

In addition, it would have been helpful to assess the severity of the comprehensive skills of the participating PWA. The information on the type and severity of aphasia is a vital indication. However, detailed test results on language skills would improve the interpretation of the results.

5 Conclusion

Translating into plain language is essential to assessing TC in people with communication impairments such as aphasia. This way, barriers to access to telepractice can be discovered and subsequently reduced. Furthermore, people with communication disorders can be included in research when according assessments exist.

In a follow-up project, the modification of the brief measure must be tested for its psychometric properties. The properties of the original scale cannot be adopted because of the apparent deviations from the original version. Therefore, the quality of the test properties should be surveyed and tested again.

References

1. United Nations Convention: United Nations convention on the rights of persons with disabilities. UNCRPD (2022)
2. Davis, F.D.: Perceived usefulness, perceived ease of use, and user acceptance of information technology. MIS Quarterly (1989). https://doi.org/10.2307/249008
3. Neyer, F.J., Felber, J., Gebhardt, C.: Entwicklung und Validierung einer Kurzskala zur Erfassung von Technikbereitschaft. Diagnostica (2012). https://doi.org/10.1026/0012-1924/a000067
4. Dalemans, R., Wade, D.T., van den Heuvel, W.J.A., de Witte, L.P.: Facilitating the participation of people with aphasia in research: a description of strategies. Clinical rehabilitation (2009). https://doi.org/10.1177/0269215509337197
5. Shiggins, C., et al.: Towards the consistent inclusion of people with aphasia in stroke research irrespective of discipline. Arch. Phys. Med. Rehabil. **103**, 2256–2263 (2022). https://doi.org/10.1016/j.apmr.2022.07.004
6. Lam, J.M.C., Wodchis, W.P.: The relationship of 60 disease diagnoses and 15 conditions to preference-based health-related quality of life in Ontario hospital-based long-term care residents. Med. Care (2010). https://doi.org/10.1097/MLR.0b013e3181ca2647

7. Cordes, L., Loukanova, S., Forstner, J.: Scoping Review über die Wirksamkeit einer Screen-to-Screen-Therapie im Vergleich zu einer Face-to-Face-Therapie bei Patient*innen mit Aphasie auf die Benennleistungen. Zeitschrift für Evidenz, Fortbildung und Qualität im Gesundheitswesen (2020). https://doi.org/10.1016/j.zefq.2020.08.002
8. Gauch, M., Leinweber, J., Plath, A., Spelter, B., Corsten, S.: Quality of life outcomes from aphasia telepractice: a scoping review. Aphasiology (2022). https://doi.org/10.1080/02687038.2022.2079604
9. Devane, N., Behn, N., Marshall, J., Ramachandran, A., Wilson, S., Hilari, K.: The use of virtual reality in the rehabilitation of aphasia: a systematic review. Disabil. Rehabil. (2022). https://doi.org/10.1080/09638288.2022.2138573
10. Nichol, L., Pitt, R., Wallace, S.J., Rodriguez, A.D., Hill, A.J.: "There are endless areas that they can use it for": speech-language pathologist perspectives of technology support for aphasia self-management. Disabil. Rehabil. Assistive Technol. (2022). https://doi.org/10.1080/17483107.2022.2037758
11. Menger, F., Morris, J., Salis, C.: The impact of aphasia on internet and technology use. Disabil. Rehabil. **42**, 2986–2996 (2020). https://doi.org/10.1080/09638288.2019.1580320
12. Spelter, B., Corsten, S., Diehlmann, L., Plath, A., Leinweber, J.: The user-centred design in the development of a platform for Teletherapy for people with Aphasia. In: Antona, M., Stephanidis, C. (eds.) Universal Access in Human-Computer Interaction. Novel Design Approaches and Technologies. Lecture Notes in Computer Science, vol. 13308, pp. 342–359. Springer, Cham (2022). https://doi.org/10.1007/978-3-031-05028-2_23
13. Ellis, C., Urban, S.: Age and aphasia: a review of presence, type, recovery and clinical outcomes. Top. Stroke Rehabil. **23**, 430–439 (2016). https://doi.org/10.1080/10749357.2016.1150412
14. Tafforeau, J., Cobo, M.L., Tolonen, H., Scheidt-Nave, C., Tinto, A.: Guidelines for the development and criteria for the adoption of Health Survey instruments. O. fn statistics, Luxembourg, European Commission (2005)
15. Collins, D.: Pretesting survey instruments: an overview of cognitive methods. Qual. Life Res. Int. J. Qual. Life Aspects Treat. Care Rehabil. **12**(3), 229–238 (2003). https://doi.org/10.1023/A:1023254226592
16. Lenzner, T., Neuert, C., Otto, W.: Kognitives Pretesting (2014)
17. Oksenberg, L., Kalton, G.: New strategies for pretesting survey questions. J. Offi. Stat. **7**, 349 (1991)
18. Kuckartz, U.: Qualitative Inhaltsanalyse. Methoden, Praxis, Computerunterstützung. Beltz Juventa, Weinheim, Basel (2012)
19. Nápoles-Springer, A.M., Santoyo-Olsson, J., O'Brien, H., Stewart, A.L.: Using cognitive interviews to develop surveys in diverse populations. Med. Care (2006). https://doi.org/10.1097/01.mlr.0000245425.65905.1d
20. Bredel, U., Maaß, C.: Leichte sprache. Maaß, C., Rink, I. (eds.) Handbuch Barrierefreie Kommunikation, pp. 251–271. Frank & Timme, Berlin (2019)
21. Hilari, K., Byng, S., Lamping, D.L., Smith, S.C.: Stroke and Aphasia Quality of Life Scale-39 (SAQOL-39): evaluation of acceptability, reliability, and validity. Stroke **34**, 1944–1950 (2003). https://doi.org/10.1161/01.STR.0000081987.46660.ED
22. Quasthoff, U. (ed.): Frequency dictionary German. DEU = Häufigkeitswörterbuch Deutsch, 1st edn. Frequency dictionaries, vol. 1. Leipziger Univ.-Verl., Leipzig (2011)
23. Jäger, R.: Konstruktion einer Ratingskala mit Smilies als symbolische Marken. Diagnostica **50**, 31–38 (2004). https://doi.org/10.1026/0012-1924.50.1.31
24. Hilari, K., Byng, S.: Measuring quality of life in people with aphasia: the stroke specific quality of life scale. Int. J. Lang. Commun. Disord. **36**, 86–91 (2001). https://doi.org/10.3109/13682820109177864

25. Menold, N., Bogner, K.: Design of rating scales in questionnaires. GESIS Survey Guidelines. Leibniz Institute for the Social Sciences: Mannheim, Germany, pp. 1–13 (2016)
26. Christian, L.M., Dillman, D.A.: The influence of graphical and symbolic language manipulations on responses to self-administered questions. Public Opin. Q. **68**, 57–80 (2004). https://doi.org/10.1093/poq/nfh004
27. van Deursen, A.J., Helsper, E.J.: A nuanced understanding of Internet use and non-use among the elderly. Eur. J. Commun. **30**, 171–187 (2015). https://doi.org/10.1177/0267323115578059

Accessible Indoor Orientation Support by Landmark-Based Navigation

Julian Striegl(✉), Julius Felchow, Claudia Loitsch, and Gerhard Weber

Chair of Human-Computer Interaction, TU Dresden,
Nöthnitzer Straße 46, 01187 Dresden, Germany
{julian.striegl,claudia.loitsch,gerhard.weber}@tu-dresden.de

Abstract. Unassisted visits to unfamiliar buildings can be an insurmountable barrier for people with visual impairments and blindness. Depending on their individual needs and preferences, people with visual impairments and blindness need specific information regarding indoor barriers, accessibility features, landmarks, temporal relations, etc. to find their way. While research in the field of accessible indoor navigation has been going on for several years, proposed systems need a huge amount of localization beacons, rely on proprietary map data, and mostly follow a classical turn-by-turn navigation approach, resulting in high installation and maintenance costs and presumably do not lead to accurate cognitive maps in users. This paper introduces the concept of app-based, accessible indoor orientation support through automatically generated landmark-based route descriptions utilizing open-source map data. A user study is conducted with 4 blind participants, interacting with both a working app-based high-fidelity prototype for indoor orientation support and a classical turn-by-turn indoor navigation system using Wizard-of-Oz to traverse through an unfamiliar building, followed by backtracking to a starting point. Cognitive maps, performance during backtracking, perceived usability, and acceptance are measured after execution of the route-finding. Additionally, an expert interview is conducted with a blind guide dog user. Results indicate a good acceptance and usability of the system. Furthermore, measured cognitive maps are closer to ground truth when using the proposed system in comparison to the control condition.

Keywords: Indoor Orientation · Indoor Navigation · Accessibility · Screen Reader · Barriers · Cognitive Maps · OpenStreetMap · Visual Impairments · Blindness

1 Introduction

Indoor mobility and specifically orientation and navigation in unknown buildings is a huge hurdle for people with visual impairments (VI). While there are common solutions for outdoor navigation, established accessible solutions for indoor environments are still sparse. Reasons for that are, among others, the high hardware installation and maintenance cost of needed indoor localization technologies

M. Antona and C. Stephanidis (Eds.): HCII 2023, LNCS 14020, pp. 510–524, 2023.
https://doi.org/10.1007/978-3-031-35681-0_34

in general, the challenge of accurate indoor localization itself [25], and the sparse availability of indoor data - especially regarding accessibility information [7,21]. Furthermore, indoor navigation systems for people with VI have to fulfil the specific requirements and information needs of this diverse target group [13,16]. Depending on individual needs and preferences, people with VI need, among others, information about indoor barriers, accessibility features, landmarks, and temporal relationships to find their way independently and without assistance [16].

Previous work has presented different approaches to indoor navigation and orientation for people with VI [3,6,11,22]. It has been shown that the required localization based on Bluetooth Low Energy (BLE) beacons is sufficient to support users in exploring indoor spaces. However, these systems either use proprietary map data to create route descriptions or need a high number of BLE beacons [11,18]. In addition, architectural constraints often make it difficult to equip buildings with additional hardware. Technical solutions for indoor localization that require as little hardware as possible are therefore particularly important. Furthermore, existing indoor navigation approaches often follow a classic turn-by-turn navigation approach, although it has already been shown that people with VI can better remember and confirm their path using landmarks and points of interest (POIs) [16,24]. Applications such as BlindSquare[1], and Soundscape[2] apply outdoor navigation for this target group. However, research is still necessary to investigate what kind of landmarks and level of detail help to navigate and successfully orientate within an indoor environment and how those information needs differ from individual to individual as recent research showed that landmarks such as stairs, elevators, toilets, temporary barriers, and POIs are differently prioritized by people with VI and people with mobility impairments during indoor wayfinding [16].

Therefore, we present a new indoor orientation support system for people with VI that facilitates route finding and backtracking of unknown routes through accessible, location-based route descriptions generated from open-source indoor map data. The core concept is a landmark-based route description, tailored to the needs of people with VI to create a better cognitive map of the environment than it is possible with traditional indoor turn-by-turn navigation. This is motivated by the fact, that people who frequently rely on turn-by-turn navigation systems tend to have a lower sense of direction [9]. Additionally, our proposed system needs a lower amount of beacons for indoor localization and uses open source data, resulting in lower installation and maintenance costs in comparison to alternative systems. We conducted a pilot study and an expert interview to assess created cognitive maps and backtracking performance and to evaluate perceived ease of use and acceptance while using the proposed system. We hypothesized that by providing on-demand landmark-based route descriptions at key locations in buildings, users with VI will have a better cognitive

[1] BlindSquare, http://www.blindsquare.com/, retrieved: October 15, 2022.

[2] Soundscape, https://apps.apple.com/us/app/microsoft-soundscape/id1240320677?ls=1, retrieved: October 15, 2022.

map of their surroundings compared to a classical turn-by-turn indoor navigation approach resulting in better backtracking performance.

In Sect. 2 state-of-the-art related work is presented and analyzed. Section 3 introduces the overall concept and the developed high-fidelity prototype. The methodology and results of the conducted user study are laid out in Sect. 4 and discussed in Sect. 5. Section 6 draws a conclusion and proposes future work.

2 State of the Art

There is a variety of research in the field of accessible outdoor navigation, for instance, using vibration [17,19], sonification [4,27], text-to-speech [10], tactile maps [1,5,20], or pin-matrix displays [8,26] but research on accessible solutions for indoor navigation is still scarce. Nevertheless, some promising systems have been proposed in the past.

Calle-Jimenez et al. [3] presented a prototype that uses scalable vector graphics (SVG) for storing accessibility descriptions, such as information on spatial layout, etc., for indoor rooms and objects. By interacting with the SVG through a screen reader, related information is read out to the user. Additionally, their system provides a route planning functionality does not include indoor tracking functionalities. A user study conducted with blind participants showed that users liked the approach and assessed the system to be helpful for everyday life. However, the study did not measure specific usability.

Su et al. [22] proposed a sonification approach that employs three-dimensional sounds to guide the user's finger on a touch screen in order to convey indoor floor plans to users with VI. Users can interact with the system by moving their fingers on the screen to follow paths or recognize certain shapes. Consequently, the system replays directional sound cues. Moreover, the system supports different gestures for panning, zooming, and getting information on POIs. A user study with blind participants has shown that the system can communicate geometric shapes, floor plans, directions, and information about landmarks to users.

Kim et al. [11] developed a turn-by-turn, beacon-based indoor navigation system, capable of delivering information on surroundings or predefined route descriptions at chosen landmarks inside a building. In a user study, participants with VI were able to explore an unknown indoor environment with the help of the developed system. However, route descriptions were created manually and not generated automatically.

Cheraghi et al. [6] presented a similar beacon-based indoor navigation system. In their system, beacons are placed at chosen landmarks and modeled as nodes in a graph. Edges between nodes are weighted based on the quality of the path between nodes, and pathfinding is implemented using a Dijkstra algorithm. Manually constructed three-dimensional indoor maps are used as map data. Users receive feedback by text-to-speech and vibration signals through a smartphone. Cheraghi et al. demonstrated that users with VI who used the application could find certain destinations faster and at shorter distances. However, users' cognitive maps were not investigated, and navigation followed a classical turn-by-turn approach.

Sato et al. [18] developed a smartphone-based conversational indoor navigation assistant for people with VI called *NavCog3*. While their application utilizes classical turn-by-turn navigation, it also provides information on landmarks and POIs while tracking the location of users based on BLE beacons and particle filter-based dead reckoning. The authors investigated the perceived usefulness and effectiveness of the system in a user study with people with VI. In their study, most participants with VI were able to complete given tasks with the system successfully and information on landmarks and POIs was rated as helpful by participants. The system, however, needs a high number of BLE beacons and a pre-created fingerprint map to work accurately. The accuracy of created cognitive maps of participants was not measured in the scope of the study.

Lüders et al. [13] presented an accessible, adaptable indoor routing algorithm for people with disabilities. Their system takes the individual information needs of people with VI and mobility impairments into account and generates landmark-based routes accordingly by leveraging OpenStreetMap (OSM) data. The authors focused their work on the routing itself and did not implement a high-fidelity prototype, thereby testing their system merely in a Wizard-of-Oz approach to investigate the perceived usefulness and acceptance of the system. The results of their study indicated a good acceptance among the target group of users with VI and mobility impairments.

In summary, related work shows that accessible indoor navigation systems can successfully be used to assist blind and visually impaired people during indoor exploration. However, previous studies have not investigated the cognitive maps of users created by using respective indoor navigation systems. Furthermore, existing systems either follow a classical turn-by-turn navigation approach, use manually created route descriptions, proprietary indoor maps, or did not implement a fully working system for indoor orientation support. Therefore, the next section introduces the concept and prototypical implementation of an accessible system to support the orientation of users with VI through auto-generated landmark-based route descriptions based on open-source map data.

3 Design and Prototype of an Accessible Indoor Orientation Support Application

The work described in this paper follows a user-centred design approach. The requirements of the target group for route descriptions and interactions were analytically investigated in the context of indoor navigation while taking into account related research (see Sect. 2). Based on the results, a orientation support system was designed and implemented as a high fidelity prototype.

3.1 Concept

The system proposed in this work aims to provide informative landmark-based route descriptions. This facilitates independent wayfinding by providing users with appropriate information about their surroundings and thus enhancing their sense of direction. This approach has two advantages. Firstly, users have to familiarize themselves with the building instead of merely following instructions, which leads to a better cognitive map of the building. Secondly, the need for precise localization is reduced. Consequently, the proposed system can be employed in a greater variety of buildings with lower installation costs. Following the information for orientation support delivered through the system, the user will be able to explore an unknown building without the need for a sighted guide. For this, they will be able to listen to descriptive route directions that contain contextual information about the environment through an accessible smartphone app. That information includes the location of POIs, such as toilets, doorways, elevators, or stairs and landmarks. In addition to the route descriptions, a BLE beacon-based localization approach is used to locate users at specific key locations to be able to support them in case they lose orientation. This will allow users to find their way back on the correct path (backtracking) or to explore a building without the necessity of human assistance.

The proposed concept does not aim to bring users to their destination in the fastest way possible but to give them the necessary information to find the way themselves, get to know the environment better and get contextual information so that they will be able to build a better cognitive model of the building they explore. A typical envisioned use case is a person that will regularly visit a currently unfamiliar building in the future. Since they do not know the building yet, they won't be able to easily explore and get to know the building without any guidance. The system promotes a better sense of direction and confidence in one's mobility. People with VI can thus explore a building more independently and with less fear of getting lost. We hypothesize that users who use the proposed system for the first time will take longer to reach a destination in a building but will develop a more accurate cognitive map of the building, allowing them to find their way more confidently on revisits.

3.2 Implementation

We implemented a high-fidelity, screen reader-optimized prototype as a cross-platform smartphone application using Flutter[3]. The application interacts with EMBC22 BLE beacons[4] to determine the approximate position of the user. Based on information stored in publicly available OSM indoor map data, the system generates route descriptions that guide users to specific locations and supply them with additional information on their environment.

Generation of Route Descriptions. The needed map data is retrieved from OSM using the Overpass API[5]. Landmarks, POIs, and rooms are extracted per building level and stored in the GeoJSON format. For the prototype, we require

[3] Flutter Framework, https://flutter.dev/, retrieved: February 2, 2023.

[4] EMBC22 - Beacons, https://www.emmicroelectronic.com/product/beacons/embc22, retrieved: February 2, 2023.

[5] Overpass API, https://overpass-turbo.eu/, retrieved: February 2, 2023.

that indoor map data is available in OSM in sufficient quantity and quality. If this is not the case, additional information, such as important POIs or the location of stationary landmarks for VI users, must be enriched in OSM indoor data. This can be done either locally on the pre-parsed data or preferably on the OSM data itself, thereby making it accessible for other applications. For path-finding, a weighted Dijkstra algorithm is used. The routing graph is created based on the parsed OSM data. For the algorithm, a landmark adjacency list is created. Landmarks are used as nodes and the neighbor information in the tag field builds up the undirected graph edges. The weighting is based on the distance of landmarks. The distance is calculated based on the latitude and longitude values of the landmark, using Vincenty's formula [14]. Route descriptions are generated by sorting objects in order of appearance on the generated route, by calculating on which side the objects appear in relation to the user on the route, and by calculating on which landmarks a turn occurs with which angle, in order to generate corresponding directions. Generated route descriptions contain information about the path the user has to take, locations of objects (e.g. doors, bins, doorways) they will encounter on their way, and other information about the environment, such as specific noises or smell that may help the user with orientation. For the conducted user study, route descriptions are automatically generated and are then manually reviewed to ensure they are suitable for the study. In later productive systems, this manual step should be omitted.

Localization. To get the distance to the next BLE beacon, the Received Signal Strength Indicator (RSSI) is used. Based on Wang et al. [23], the average of the most recent signal strength values per beacon is used to determine a more accurate distance. Since this work does not aim to track the precise position of the user, no triangulation is employed, instead, the only information used is the distance to a singular beacon.

User Interface and User Experience. The interface is designed to be usable via a screen reader and to allow for one-handed interaction. The interface mainly presents route descriptions to the user (see Fig. 1). Additionally, the app bar contains two buttons. The first button allows the user to get context information on the current screen in case they get lost in the interface of the application. The second button gives the user information on the last landmark the device has been close to. In that way, users can reconfirm their position and track or correct their progress along the route. Both buttons trigger a snackbar[6] message so that the screen reader focus is not reset. Thus, this message is read out by the screen reader but create no major context change for the user, to minimize the distraction from the route-finding. Route descriptions are organized into route stages. Each route stage contains a list of route descriptions, which is hidden by default. This allows the user to quickly move the focus of the screen

[6] Material Design - snackbar, https://m2.material.io/components/snackbars/android, retrieved: February 6, 2023.

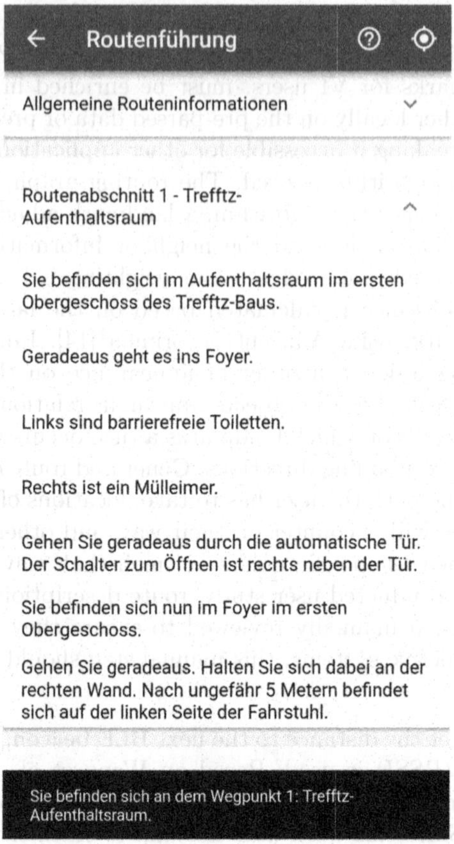

Fig. 1. Implemented accessible user interface. A snackbar message with information on the nearest landmark is shown at the bottom of the screen. As the user study was conducted in Germany, route descriptions were generated in German.

reader between the route stages and to get a better overview of the progress and the route stages. Additionally, if the focus of the screen reader was moved to a different route stage, for example by an unintended tap, the user can find back to the current route stage without having to skip through all of the route descriptions and instructions. At any given time, only one route stage can be extended. In that way, the user interface will not be filled with all the route descriptions and the focus of the screen reader can be moved quickly between the route stages. When a route stage is extended, the route descriptions for this route stage are shown and the user is informed that the route stage is extended. Thereby, the route instructions are shown that the user has to follow to reach the next landmark. Additionally, enhanced information on the environment is given. This information can be accessed by double-tapping on the route description items that contain more details. The screen reader announces to the user if a route description element has more details. The details are shown as a snackbar message. Such information could be on functional elements, such as if a door opens automatically or where the control panel of the elevator is. When the user gets close to the next landmark, a snackbar message is given to the user. All visual elements exceed the minimum contrast value threshold of 4.5:1, thereby meeting the contrast accessibility requirements of the WCAG[7].

4 Evaluation

To evaluate the concept, a user study was conducted with 4 blind participants. The aim of this evaluation was to investigate how the developed high-fidelity prototype for accessible indoor orientation support (experimental condition) affects the cognitive map and the backtracking performance of participants in comparison to a classical turn-by-turn indoor navigation (control condition using Wizard-of-Oz). Furthermore, we wanted to investigate the acceptance and usability of the created system. Cognitive maps, backtracking performance, perceived ease of use, and acceptance were measured after reaching a specific destination for both conditions.

4.1 Participants

Four people with blindness (two male, and two female) between the ages of 30 to 60 years participated in the study. One participant had some residual light perception, however, they were not able to observe shapes or distinguish contours from each other. All of the participants were accustomed to using a white cane for orientation, were able to read Braille, and were familiar with using a smartphone by interacting with a screen reader. Additionally, all participants reported that they used common outdoor navigational systems before. None of the participants was familiar with the indoor environment and the routes that were selected for the study. All participants had to sign a privacy policy and consent form to comply with data protection provisions.

4.2 Methodology

An A/B-testing experiment with a within-subjects study design was chosen to account for the low number of participants. Therefore, all participants tested the experimental and the control condition sequentially. Next to demographic information, the familiarity with navigation systems and with the explored environment during the user study, as well as with smartphone and screen reader usage was inquired at the beginning of the study. Afterward, participants were asked to find their way along two different routes. To ensure the comparability of the two testing conditions, routes were preselected to be equally complex and around 200 m long. Participants were given the high-fidelity prototype for the

[7] WCAG 2.1 Contrast Minimum, https://www.w3.org/WAI/WCAG21/Understanding/contrast-minimum.html, retrieved: February 6, 2023.

experimental condition for one route (see Fig. 2a) and were guided by a classic turn-by-turn indoor navigation system using Wizard-of-Oz for the control condition for the second route. To avoid any bias due to the complexity of the routes and to account for possible learning and fatigue effects, the order of routes and the assignment to experimental/control condition for an individual route was semi-randomized per participant.

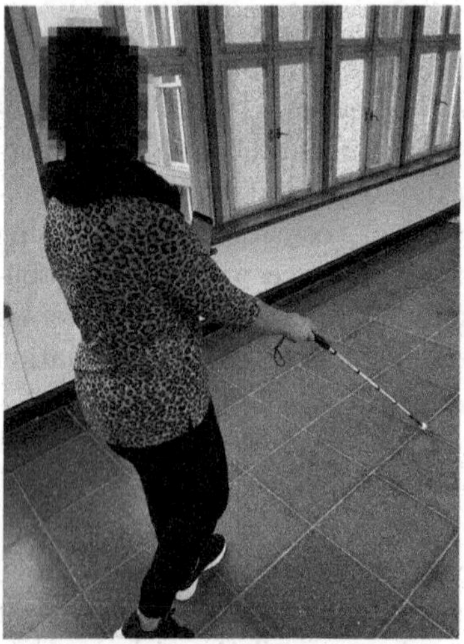

(a) Usage of the high-fidelity prototype for route finding.

(b) Measuring of cognitive maps using magnet stripes.

Fig. 2. Pictures from the conducted user study.

After successful route finding, participants were asked to backtrack their way to the start without any help from the navigational methods. The facilitator gave hints when requested by participants or when necessary to ensure the safety of test subjects. The number of given hints, the time needed, and the number of detours taken by participants during route finding and backtracking were tracked. After each route-finding session, participants had to answer a questionnaire on the usability of the system using the System Usability Score (SUS) [2]. Additionally, users were asked to model the cognitive map of the traversed route on a metal surface using magnet strips to represent paths taken [15] (see Fig. 2b). They were also asked to mention any milestones and POIs they remember. Finally, a conclusive questionnaire was conducted as a formative evaluation to gather feedback about the system, suggestions for improvements, and assessments of the general usability and usefulness of the approach.

In addition, a semi-structured expert interview with a guide dog user with VI that is highly proficient with navigational systems was conducted as a phone call. The designed concept was explained to the interviewee to get feedback about possible additional information and interaction modalities a guide dog user may need while using the system.

4.3 Results

Task Performance. All participants completed the route-finding tasks as well as the following backtracking. The average time it took the participants to find the route with the prototype (17.38 min) was more than double the time it took with the Wizard-of-Oz navigation (6.85 min). This was highly influenced by the user listening to and understanding the route instructions, as opposed to just following the turn-by-turn instructions during Wizard-of-Oz. Additionally, the users had to actively search for the path, objects, and entrances to corridors during exploration. Opposed to that, the average time needed for backtracking after route finding with the prototype (8 min) was quicker compared to Wizard-of-Oz (8.85 min). During route finding, the participants needed hints and corrections to successfully find their way to the destination. An average of 2.5 hints were needed for route finding with the prototype, as opposed to 0.5 corrections during the Wizard-of-Oz navigation. During backtracking, the participants needed a smaller number of hints for the experimental condition (2.25 hints average) than for the control condition (2.5 hints average). To compare the cognitive maps of the participants, the weighted city-block distance was used, based on the works of Miao [15]. Thereby, map features were weighted differently based on their significance for route finding (intersections 0.29, length: 0.21, orientation: 0.13). The results show, that the cognitive map for the experimental condition is closer to the original in comparison to the control condition. The respective mean distance to the ground truth is 0.573 for the prototype (standard deviation (STD): 0.43), which is less than half the mean distance of the maps resulting from the control condition (mean: 1.16, STD: 0.55). Furthermore, the participants remembered a larger number of milestones after route finding using the prototype and were able to name significantly more landmarks (mean: 4.5, STD: 0.58) than after Wizard-of-Oz (mean: 1.25, STD: 1.26).

Usability. The SUS results show, that the users preferred the prototype over the turn-by-turn Wizard-of-Oz approach. The mean SUS for the prototype is 82.5 (STD: 9.84), compared to 75.63 (STD: 28.31) for the Wizard-of-Oz. Using the SUS grading based on Lewis, this attributes the grade A to our prototype compared to grade B to the Wizard-of-Oz approach [12]. The high standard deviation is mainly influenced by one user that was highly unsatisfied with turn-by-turn navigation. They did not like the plain turn-by-turn navigation with less information about the environments and expressed that they did not feel safe during navigation since they had to rely on the correctness of the instructions, especially since they were given too little additional information to self-verify the path.

Acceptance. The results of the final questionnaire show, the participants were more inclined to use the high-fidelity prototype (mean: 4.75, STD: 0.43) as opposed to the turn-by-turn navigation (mean: 3.75, STD: 1.09). The rationale given was the depth of information, the ability to look ahead, and the general possibility to get an overview of the environment. All participants mentioned the cognitive effort to use the prototype was higher but acceptable. In addition, participants confirmed that they got to know the building better due to the more exploratory and active navigation, which also helped them with backtracking. All participants reported that the backtracking was easier after route finding with the prototype. Most of the participants expressed interest in using the system as a preparation tool to familiarize themselves with the route before visiting an unknown location and all participants expressed a high demand for such a system as an on-site orientation support.

Formative Feedback. Two of the participants expressed that it would be better if the system would be accurate enough so that you do not need to prepare for the route at all. An important factor for the participants was that the system should be usable hands-free. Therefore, different interaction possibilities such as voice interaction support, smartwatch gestures, or the play/pause hardware buttons of headphones as inputs were proposed. One participant also added, that for users with light perception, additional information on light conditions could be added.

Expert Interview Results. Results of the expert interview with the guide dog user comprise that route descriptions should include POIs the guide dog is familiar with such as elevators, stairs, and corridors. For directions, the general location of the nearest landmark is crucial so that the user can nudge the dog in that direction and rely on the dog to find it and guide them there. Since guide dogs are trained to avoid escalators and rotating doors (as they are hazardous areas for dogs), pathfinding should be adjustable to avoid routes with these objects and find alternative routes. Interaction-wise, hands-free usability is important since guide dog users often fall back on having the dog on the one hand, and holding the cane with the other hand.

5 Discussion

Overall, results indicate a good acceptance and usability of the system. Participants expressed a high interest in a system that supports them during indoor wayfinding and measured cognitive maps were closer to ground truth when using the proposed system than in the control condition. Thereby, the results confirm that providing more information on landmarks in the environment, instead of turn-by-turn instructions, supports conscious exploration and leads to a better understanding and thus more independent and save orientation and way finding indoors. Consequently, some result areas will be examined in more detail:

- **Performance during Backtracking:** Results showed a time improvement during the backtracking process for the experimental condition in comparison to the Wizard-of-Oz control. In line with related research [9], this could be

explained by the lack of decision-making while following turn-by-turn instructions and by the statements of test subjects, who mentioned that they did not concentrate on the route during turn-by-turn navigation, even though they knew that backtracking was a part of the conducted experiment.
- **Cognitive Maps:** The cognitive maps that participants were able to reproduce after backtracking were more accurate for the experimental condition than for the turn-by-turn control. More specifically, the calculated distance between the cognitive map and ground truth was half the distance for the experimental than for the control condition, giving a strong indication that participants were able to get to know and remember the building better using the landmark-based orientation support through the prototype than through following the turn-by-turn instructions. Moreover, participants were able to remember more milestones after using the prototype, which might facilitate the backtracking process.
- **Usability:** While the usability was rated as good by participants, some room for improvement could be identified for future iterations. As the screen reader is not usable one-handed, most of the participants held the smartphone in their left hand and performed the screen reader gestures with the right hand. That led to subjects either holding the white cane uncomfortably in the right hand or putting it away for smartphone interaction, which is not ideal. Furthermore, all participants were used to iOS instead of Android devices and had some problems using the native Android screen reader. A follow-up study should therefore be conducted with an iPhone since this seems to be the preferred device for most users in the VI community and the system should be optimized for single-handed or hands-free usage.

5.1 Limitations

With four participants with VI during the hands-on user study and one additional expert interview with a VI person using a guide dog, the size of the study was too small to obtain significant results. Therefore, a follow-up study should include a larger amount of test subjects. Furthermore, a between-subject study design could be used in a single-blind randomized A/B-testing experiment setup to account for any effects of fatigue or of route complexity.

During route finding and backtracking, the facilitator had to intervene in some occasions to ensure the safety of participants or when participants went too far off the route in both the experimental and control condition. In a follow-up study in a safe environment, no hints should be given to the user to see if they are able to find the way without any interference from the facilitator.

While the focus of the presented concept and study was on indoor areas, one of the used routes partially crossed an outdoor area due to the constraints of the available localities. During the outdoor section, all participants needed additional information to find their way, as the area had too few objects that could be used as landmarks, showing a possible weak spot of the landmark-based approach - at least for the outdoors. Follow-up studies should therefore use indoor routes of similar complexity exclusively and include indoor areas with wide open spaces (such as foyers) to better test the usefulness and usability of the proposed system in those environments.

6 Conclusion

This study investigated how landmark-based route descriptions support the orientation, wayfinding, and backtracking process of people with VI in unknown buildings. We hypothesized that landmark-based descriptions, tailored to the information needs of people with VI, result in better cognitive maps compared to classical turn-by-turn navigation in indoor spaces. Results of the conducted user study indicate, the usage of the proposed prototype led to a better comprehension of the building and more accurate cognitive maps than the turn-by-turn navigation control condition. The proposed concept was well received by participants and the implemented high-fidelity prototype showed good usability for the target group of people with VI.

While results were promising and in line with related work, several improvements to the concept and prototype could be made in follow-up studies. Route descriptions should be adjustable by the end user to his/her individual information needs. Additionally, information on the complexity of a path and on the accessibility of individual route sections for a specific user group should affect the routing graph weights to create more intelligent path-finding (similar to the works of [13]). Furthermore, the system should be able to detect when a user deviates too far from a set route. Additionally, the support of hand-free interactions via a voice user interface and the support of smartwatches could be added. The localization accuracy could be improved through hybrid localization approaches (e.g., using WiFi or ultra-wideband) and supplemented by dead reckoning. Follow-up studies could, furthermore, investigate how well created cognitive maps stay in long-term memory. Finally, the usefulness and usability of the system for other user groups (e.g., people with mobility impairment or cognitive impairment) should be explored in a user study of larger scale.

Acknowledgements. This work was partially funded by the Federal Ministry of Labour and Social Affairs (BMAS) under the grant number 01KM151112.

References

1. Brock, A., Truillet, P., Oriola, B., Jouffrais, C.: Making gestural interaction accessible to visually impaired people. In: Auvray, M., Duriez, C. (eds.) EUROHAPTICS 2014. LNCS, vol. 8619, pp. 41–48. Springer, Heidelberg (2014). https://doi.org/10.1007/978-3-662-44196-1_6
2. Brooke, J.: SUS-a quick and dirty usability scale. 1996 (1996)
3. Calle-Jimenez, T., Luján-Mora, S.: Accessible online indoor maps for blind and visually impaired users. In: ASSETS 2016 - Proceedings of the 18th International ACM SIGACCESS Conference on Computers and Accessibility, pp. 309–310 (2016)

4. Carroll, D., Chakraborty, S., Lazar, J.: Designing accessible visualizations: the case of designing a weather map for blind users. In: Stephanidis, C., Antona, M. (eds.) UAHCI 2013. LNCS, vol. 8009, pp. 436–445. Springer, Heidelberg (2013). https://doi.org/10.1007/978-3-642-39188-0_47
5. Červenka, P., Břinda, K., Hanousková, M., Hofman, P., Seifert, R.: Blind friendly maps. In: Miesenberger, K., Bühler, C., Penaz, P. (eds.) ICCHP 2016. LNCS, vol. 9759, pp. 131–138. Springer, Cham (2016). https://doi.org/10.1007/978-3-319-41267-2_18
6. Cheraghi, S.A., Namboodiri, V., Walker, L.: GuideBeacon: beacon-based indoor wayfinding for the blind, visually impaired, and disoriented. In: 2017 IEEE International Conference on Pervasive Computing and Communications, PerCom 2017, pp. 121–130 (2017)
7. Froehlich, J.E., et al.: Grand challenges in accessible maps. Interactions **26**(2), 78–81 (2019)
8. Holloway, L., Marriott, K., Butler, M.: Accessible maps for the blind: Comparing 3D printed models with tactile graphics. In: Conference on Human Factors in Computing Systems - Proceedings, vol. 2018-April (2018)
9. Ishikawa, T.: Satellite Navigation and Geospatial Awareness: Long-Term Effects of Using Navigation Tools on Wayfinding and Spatial Orientation. Professional Geographer **71**(2), 197–209 (2019)
10. Kaklanis, N., Votis, K., Tzovaras, D.: A mobile interactive maps application for a visually impaired audience. In: W4A 2013 - International Cross-Disciplinary Conference on Web Accessibility (2013)
11. Kim, J.E., Bessho, M., Kobayashi, S., Koshizuka, N., Sakamura, K.: Navigating visually impaired travelers in a large train station using smartphone and Bluetooth Low Energy. In: Proceedings of the ACM Symposium on Applied Computing, vol. 04–08-Apri, pp. 604–611 (2016)
12. Lewis, J.R.: The system usability scale: past, present, and future. Int. J. Hum.-Comput. Interact. **34**(7), 577–590 (2018)
13. Lüders, F., Striegl, J., Schmalfuß-Schwarz, J., Loitsch, C., Weber, G.: Accessible adaptable indoor routing for people with disabilities. In: Miesenberger, K., et al. (eds.) ICCHP-AAATE 2022. LNCS, vol. 13341, pp. 169–177. Springer, Cham (2022). https://doi.org/10.1007/978-3-031-08648-9_20
14. Mahmoud, H., Akkari, N.: Shortest path calculation: a comparative study for location-based recommender system. In: 2016 World Symposium on Computer Applications & Research (WSCAR), pp. 1–5. IEEE (2016)
15. Miao, M.D.I.: Blindenspezifische Methoden für das User-Centred Design multimodaler Anwendungen. TU Dresden (2014)
16. Müller, K., Engel, C., Loitsch, C., Stiefelhagen, R., Weber, G.: Traveling more independently: a study on the diverse needs and challenges of people with visual or mobility impairments in unfamiliar indoor environments. ACM Trans. Access. Comput. **15**(2) (2022)
17. Poppinga, B., Magnusson, C., Pielot, M., Rass-mus Gröhn, K.: TouchOver map: Audio-tactile exploration of interactive maps. In: Mobile HCI 2011–13th International Conference on Human-Computer Interaction with Mobile Devices and Services, pp. 545–550 (2011)
18. Sato, D., Oh, U., Naito, K., Takagi, H., Kitani, K., Asakawa, C.: NavCog3: an evaluation of a smartphone-based blindindoor navigation assistant with semantic features in a large-scale environment. In: ASSETS 2017 - Proceedings of the 19th International ACM SIGACCESS Conference on Computers and Accessibility, pp. 270–279 (2017)

19. Schmitz, B., Ertl, T.: Making digital maps accessible using vibrations. In: Miesenberger, K., Klaus, J., Zagler, W., Karshmer, A. (eds.) ICCHP 2010. LNCS, vol. 6179, pp. 100–107. Springer, Heidelberg (2010). https://doi.org/10.1007/978-3-642-14097-6_18
20. Senette, C., Buzzi, M.C., Buzzi, M., Leporini, B., Martusciello, L.: Enriching graphic maps to enable multimodal interaction by blind people. In: Stephanidis, C., Antona, M. (eds.) UAHCI 2013. LNCS, vol. 8009, pp. 576–583. Springer, Heidelberg (2013). https://doi.org/10.1007/978-3-642-39188-0_62
21. Striegl, J., Lotisch, C., Schmalfuss-Schwarz, J., Weber, G.: Analysis of indoor maps accounting the needs of people with impairments. In: Miesenberger, K., Manduchi, R., Covarrubias Rodriguez, M., Peňáz, P. (eds.) ICCHP 2020. LNCS, vol. 12377, pp. 305–314. Springer, Cham (2020). https://doi.org/10.1007/978-3-030-58805-2_36
22. Su, J., Rosenzweig, A., Goel, A., De Lara, E., Truong, K.N.: Timbremap: enabling the visually-impaired to use maps on touch-enabled devices. In: ACM International Conference Proceeding Series, pp. 17–26. Association for Computing Machinery (2010)
23. Wang, Y., Yang, X., Zhao, Y., Liu, Y., Cuthbert, L.: Bluetooth positioning using RSSI and triangulation methods. In: 2013 IEEE 10th Consumer Communications and Networking Conference, CCNC 2013, pp. 837–842 (2013). https://doi.org/10.1109/CCNC.2013.6488558
24. Williams, M.A., Galbraith, C., Kane, S.K., Hurst, A.: "Just let the cane hit it": How the blind and sighted see navigation differently. In: Proceedings of the 16th International ACM SIGACCESS Conference on Computers & Accessibility, pp. 217–224. ASSETS 2014, New York, NY, USA. Association for Computing Machinery (2014)
25. Zafari, F., Gkelias, A., Leung, K.K.: A survey of indoor localization systems and technologies. IEEE Commun. Surv. Tutor. **21**(3), 2568–2599 (2019)
26. Zeng, L., Weber, G.: Exploration of location-aware you-are-here maps on a pin-matrix display. IEEE Trans. Hum.-Mach. Syst. **46**(1), 88–100 (2016)
27. Zhao, H., Plaisant, C., Shneiderman, B.: "I hear the pattern" - Interactive sonification of geographical data patterns. In: Conference on Human Factors in Computing Systems - Proceedings, pp. 1905–1908 (2005)

Designing for Children with Autism Spectrum Disorders

User Requirements for Accessible Digital Pretend Play Interventions for Children with Autism Spectrum Disorders: A Human Centered Design Approach

Louisa Bremner[1](✉), Duke Gledhill[1], and Jo Jolliffe Wood[2]

[1] University of Huddersfield, Huddersfield, UK
louisabremner@gmail.com
[2] Schooling Re-Engineered, Lancley Consulting, Salford, UK

Abstract. Pretend play is a stage in early childhood development where children learn and develop language and social skills through acting out imaginary scenarios. Pretend play skills are typically delayed for children with Autism Spectrum Disorders (ASD). Digital technology has been successfully used to engage children with ASD in pretend play, however research around the needs and requirements of the user is often omitted in these designs. Human Centered Design (HCD) provides a way of including these needs and making interventions suitably accessible to the target user. This paper presents the results of a multi-stage HCD process including observations, interviews and a Delphi study, using both the primary group (children with ASD) and their proxies (professionals who work closely with the group). The final result is a set of User Requirements which emerged from the data in the HCD stages. The User Requirements and guidelines presented provide researchers with a tool for developing digital pretend play interventions for children with ASD. Future research could benefit by incorporating the User Requirements when designing digital pretend play interventions, which is a small but growing area of research.

Keywords: Human Centered Design · User Requirements · Autism Spectrum Disorder · pretend play

1 Introduction

1.1 Pretend Play

Play is an essential part of childhood development as it is where children, at a subconscious level, "can attempt to make sense of the world around them", [1]. A lack of play in childhood can lead to a delay in developing key concepts and play level can be a guide for measuring cognitive maturity and social growth [2].

A particularly important type of play in early childhood development is pretend play. Pretend play is where children learn through acting out imaginary scenarios related to their social surroundings. It is a powerful way for children to develop language and

M. Antona and C. Stephanidis (Eds.): HCII 2023, LNCS 14020, pp. 527–545, 2023.
https://doi.org/10.1007/978-3-031-35681-0_35

various social skills. As pretend play skills can be an indicator of an individual's life success, happiness, and ability to form strong relationships, it is essential to avoid delays to forming this skill. A wealth of data indicates a strong correlation between engaging in pretend play, development of social skills and the ability to empathize [3, 4].

Children with ASD tend to be naturally disinclined towards certain play activities, including pretend play or role-play, and cooperative play. They may additionally experience difficulty in conceiving non-literal situations and objects. In general, play for children with ASD may need more structured teaching compared to the intrinsically motivated and open play of typically developing children [5]. Some common features of autism can include difficulties with joint attention (i.e., shared focus on an object), pretend play, delayed verbal and nonverbal communication, motor delay, unusually repetitive behaviors and inflexibility in disengaging visual attention [6]. Pretend play is an activity that tends to expose some of the difficulty experienced in these deficits. A lack of pretend play is considered as an early indicator in the diagnosis of ASD.

Increasing opportunities for pretend play can therefore be of particular benefit to children with ASD and wider society. Hence, it is of key importance to find novel ways of using pretend play and look for ways to enhance its impact.

1.2 Digital Pretend Play Interventions for ASD

Pretend play is frequently a focus of child therapy, partly because of its capacity to allow children to practice models of the world around them in a safe familiar environment. Teachers have long used non-interactive mediums to teach pretend play to children with ASD, for example video clips and play scripts like 'Identiplay' [5].

An increasing number of digital technologies such as augmented reality, virtual reality and interactive virtual environments have been used successfully to help children to engage in forms of pretend play and role play. New technology mediums such as Virtual Reality (VR), Augmented Reality (AR) and Artificial Intelligence (AI), can be leveraged for special education. Research suggests that these technologies support increased mastery, information retention and generalization of new knowledge by being actively involved in constructing knowledge through a learning-by-doing situation [7]. Certain aspects of technology make it a great medium to support children with ASD in engaging with pretend play. Research shows that, 'computer or video games were the most enjoyed activity among children with ASD' [8]. Individuals with ASD are purported to have an affinity for technology due to its 'safe' and 'predictable' nature [9].

An increasing body of research shows positive results in digital pretend play intervention for individuals with ASD [9]. Game based technologies such as robots, augmented reality, virtual environments and interactive story books have been successfully used in pretend play interventions to promote, among other things, social interaction, sensory processing and adaptation to change [10].

1.3 Stakeholder Design Input

Considering the voice of stakeholders, whilst developing digital interventions, is key to creating something that will be engaging and successful for the end user. Although this is an integral step of the design process, it can be time consuming and laborious, and thus is sometimes omitted. Since children with ASD are a group who interact with the world differently to their typically developing peers, researchers and developers could benefit from research that reflects their needs when designing digital interventions. Despite an increasing trend in researchers creating digital pretend play interventions for children with ASD, User Requirements or guidelines have not yet been established.

Consulting the user base is a long process, which studies address to varying degrees. Although some employ approaches to take input from users such as co-design or participatory design, some studies do not implement the voice of users in their designs as reported in a systematic review on AR interventions for children with ASD [11]. The creation of a standard toolkit or guidelines, based on the needs and requirements of the user, could help other researchers to design more accessible, more suitable digital pretend play interventions for children with ASD, without needing to repeat the whole consultation process.

1.4 Human Centered Design

The field of HCI provides several approaches to involving the user, one such way is to adopt a Human Centered Design process (HCD), formerly known as User Centered Design (UCD). HCD is a multi-stage process where users are involved in the design, providing input and feedback on design choices. Human-centered design is 'an approach to interactive systems development that aims to make systems usable and useful by focusing on the users, their needs and requirements' [12].

HCD is simultaneously a philosophy and a methodology. As a philosophy, the core principles are to involve users early; often and in the real world context; to know the users well; to give them control and to discover before designing and continue to discover even after delivery. As a method, HCD is characterized by a multi-stage process that allows input and feedback, as the developers create the product [13–15].

There are many methods that may be associated with HCD which can be borrowed from different research domains. The methods can range from user observations, focus groups, persona development, rapid prototyping and design guidelines [16]. The selected steps as a whole, add up to a HCD process.

One of the cornerstones of HCD is that you should not design from the perspective of emphasizing the features of a system and then expect the user to adapt. Instead, systems should be designed to meet the psychological, situational, emotional, and intellectual needs of users [16].

Effective and engaging experiences of socio-dramatic role play need to be carefully designed since children with ASD have very specific needs. Any supporting AR system needs to strongly consider the user's very particular needs. Researchers have advocated for and developed Human-Centered approaches as appropriate methods of designing applications for children with ASD [17, 18]. HCD is "a multidisciplinary design approach based on the active involvement of users to improve the understanding of user and task requirements, and the iteration of design and evaluation" [19]. Users are involved as key stakeholders from start to end of the design and development of an application, to ensure that the needs of the end-user are genuinely met.

This study therefore adopts a HCD process to design an application for a digital role play activity, reflecting the needs of the user group, by establishing User Requirements and a conceptual system framework for the application design which are transferable to other role play activities and similar interventions for children with ASD.

1.5 Aim

This study explores the creation of User Requirements as a product of a HCD approach which can support the design and development of digital pretend play interventions that can meet the needs of children with ASD.

2 Methodology

The process followed several stages of a HCD process to involve stakeholders including the primary user and special education professionals. Input from key stakeholders generated a picture of the main user and the activity in question. A theoretical framework was used throughout, which was based on a combination of activity theory [22] and self-determination theory [21]. The following stages of stakeholder involvement were undertaken. The study adhered to a code of ethics which was approved by the University of Huddersfield ethics committee.

Stage 1: Observations. Observations of the primary user group were conducted at two schools in the UK. Unstructured Naturalistic Observations took place to observe the target group in their natural environment. Two schools were recruited to take part in the observations which the researcher attended. The schools were selected using convenience sampling. Two classes were observed in each school. The teachers in each classroom directed the researcher to a number of children who matched the target user criteria for the study for observation. The observations adopted an ethnographic approach which meant that the presence of the researcher was minimized using no additional equipment for recording purposes other than a notebook, and the children were observed in their natural state. Field notes of the children's play activities were gathered based on a template analysis coding system [23] and temporally recorded by the researcher. These notes were then analyzed using the theoretical framework which primarily categorized enablers and inhibitors of the activities with some further categorization based on characteristics of the teaching strategies and the observed children. The a priori categories used to develop a matrix for analysis of the observations, were updated after use in the first school leading to minor improvements. The analysis was checked by a second researcher. The observations provided an opportunity to look for the challenges, the techniques used to support children with ASD and the structure of play activities which were coded into enablers and inhibitors of pretend play activity.

Stage 2: Interviews. Semi structured interviews were conducted with 23 special education and pretend play experts (proxy users) such as teachers and educational psychologists. The purpose was to discover the challenges, benefits and strategies for motivating children with ASD in pretend play. Interviewees were recruited through convenience sampling, and selected using the following criteria:

a. Professional experience of teaching, supporting or caring for children with ASD

b. Professional experience of developing/supporting children's language and social skills through pretend play or play-related strategies

The interview questions were created and tested in advance using the theoretical framework and reviewed by two researchers. The key strategies and needs identified in the interviews were coded into enablers and inhibitors of such activities using the same a priori categories as the data from the observations. A Template Analysis (King, 2012) was carried out by researcher A and validated by researcher B. This was followed by a second analysis in which inductive categories were formed from the transcripts. Quantitative analyses were performed to determine how frequently inhibiting and enabling factors were mentioned. Factors were deemed important depending on the number of people/times mentioned, as well as the qualitative emphasis. Differences were resolved by discussion. A third researcher checked the analysis using a random sample.

Stage 3: Generation of User Requirements. Using the extracted information from the observations and interviews, 23 User Requirements were generated to support the design of a digital pretend play intervention for children with ASD. The requirements included guidance around the use of 'Steps/sequencing', 'Personalisation' and 'Sensory input/features' amongst others.

Stage 4: Delphi Study. The User Requirements were validated through a Delphi method. Delphi methods have been in use since the 1950's and are a process for gaining consensus on how well experts agree with a given issue [20]. The study involved 18 experts who were selected based on a set of defined criteria and lasted for two rounds. At each round, the experts rated the user requirement and then added feedback for their selection. Any requirements that did not meet the consensus threshold were then modified using the expert feedback. After the two rounds, all 23 User Requirements reached a strong consensus rate. The Delphi method led to User Requirements that better reflected the voices of experts in the domain.

Stage 5: Restructuring of the User Requirements into Guidelines. Following the Delphi study, the 23 User Requirements were placed in a logical order for the further use by researchers who may want to use them. Each requirement was translated into generic guidance for creating a digital intervention.

3 Results

3.1 Observations

A non-temporal condensed version of notes taken across the four classrooms is presented. Table 1 presents each of the enabling factors of the observed activity. Table 2 presents the inhibiting factors of the observed activities. The categories emerged during the observations where multiple instances of the same categorizations could be observed across either the same class or multiple classes.

Table 1. Observations Enabling Factors of observed activities.

Enablers	School 1, Class 1	School 1, Class 1	School 2, Class 1	School 2, Class 2
iPad:	Very proficient with iPad Executed all actions independently	Looking at iPad, pressing random, swiping	iPad used as a reward for good behaviour	
Adult guidance:	Adult pressed a musical key to suggest a new game Adult guidance - "which one?", "You do it"	Mirroring and down on same level	Tasks differ depending on the child's verbal and reading skills i.e. reading or pointing Finite number of options given on PowerPoint slide to help with choice	Progressive difficulty of task – line up, now sort by size Teacher encouragement/ suggestions – 'do you want…?'
Adult Instruction:	Tells the child to stop Use picture cards	Child asks for help	Counts down from 5	Teacher repetition of instruction Avoidance of undesirable behaviour '3, 2, 1, stand up and count' Verbal prompts for moving to next activity
Rewards	Choice for children e.g. which toy		Use of reward/disadvantage if child behaves as intended Whiteboard makes it easy to select a positive behaviour and log this for tracking	Reward of free play with the item purchased
Signing/symbols	Child signing for adult help Struggles to sit and shows signs to help Use the "finished" sign to signal activity end Adults sign for "outside" to signal outdoor play	Signing guided by adult	Signing with pecs cards and sign language to avoid undesirable behaviour	Pecs cards used to signify next activity

(*continued*)

Table 1. (*continued*)

Enablers	School 1, Class 1	School 1, Class 1	School 2, Class 1	School 2, Class 2
Interactive elements –	Interactive elements on physical books buttons which make sounds Pushing buttons to hear sounds		Use of interactive whiteboard to select correct object Physical pennies given to count	
Positive praise	Positive feedback on brick arranging activity		High five for good work Clapping/high fives Teacher encouragement for skills	
Music/Singing	Song to signal start and end of activities Goodbye song		Song for finishing the activity Song to signify going back to the classroom	Teachers all join in singing and making actions to accompany the words Tidy up song to transition between tasks
Structure of activity	Fast changing pace	Fast changing pace Repeats instructions on lanyard Repeat signs		Repetition and catchy jingle make children join in
Setting			Takes place in quiet space with limited numbers and one staff member Small groups are easier to manage	Map of sitting positions is on whiteboard when staff and students return to class Quiet room – less distractions

3.2 Interviews

Enablers. The enablers were split into five main groups which were characteristics of the child; interactions; objects; properties and environmental conditions. Within each group, there were several enablers which were raised creating subcategories. The number of times an enabler was mentioned was recorded including how many individual people mentioned the item. The results are shown in Table 3.

Inhibitors. Inhibitors of activity had four of the same categories, characteristic; interactions; properties and environmental conditions. The category "objects" did not emerge from the results. The same process as described in the enablers section was followed. The results are shown in Table 4.

Table 2. Observations Inhibiting Factors of observed activities.

Inhibitors	School 1, Class 1	School 1, Class 1	School 2, Class 1	School 2, Class 2
Difficulty completing tasks leading to frustration	Struggling to sit		PowerPoint technology difficult to use	Can't find name of child on the UI – whiteboard Not being able to see all cards at once – frustrated when they can't find them
Emotional regulation	Not happy – adults use pressure to help Child crying – removed with use of signs for "finished"		Behaviours which challenged the supporting adults	Behaviours which challenged the supporting adults
Distractedness Focus on unrelated objects:	Pushes blu-tack.around	Drops to play with wool ball and pot Child loses interest in sitting down for food	Getting distracted, running around room and throwing chairs/cleaning up Distracted behaviour – walking around the room, running around	Distracted behaviour – Running around out of seats iPad takes attention Child distracted and playing with toys instead
Lack of interest	In books - Pushes book off the table that weren't interactive		Some children display disinterest in colouring in task	Child puts toys away instead of playing with the items
Motor control		Struggled with motor task		Child needs assistance to execute sticker task due to motor skills
Noisy/distracting environment			One child copies another child	Busy space full of equipment

(*continued*)

Table 2. (*continued*)

Inhibitors	School 1, Class 1	School 1, Class 1	School 2, Class 1	School 2, Class 2
Circumstantial events				Child lost ball at playtime Child not engaging because he is ill

3.3 Delphi Study

After round one, 17 out of 23 items reached a clear consensus of above 90%. Items that had reached consensus were removed from the following round to prevent repetition and fatigue for the participants. The consensus reaching rate for the first round was 73.91%. Regardless of consensus, all comments and suggestions were analyzed and considered. The analysis method used for the comments matched that of the earlier UCD process used to generate the initial set of User Requirements. Additional clarification was made to three additional items, UR8, UR9 and UR16 as shown in Table 5.

In round two of the survey, the participants were asked to rate their level of agreement with the changes made to the remaining nine requirements. For each re-rated item, participants received statistical results and comments from the previous round. The participants were asked to review the comments before re-rating the items. Space was given for participants to add additional comments to support their ratings.

Of the nine requirements that were re-rated, eight reached a clear consensus above 90%. The only requirement which was under the 90% bar was UR15 "Modelling". After a review of the comments, it was clear that the issue was the use of one word which was not determined as the correct terminology by the experts. Following this feedback, the terminology was updated and the two participants who had noticed the issue were contacted for their revised agreement. As 22 of the 23 requirements had passed and the issue with the 23rd requirement had been resolved, it was deemed that a further round of Delphi survey was not required. In Delphi methodology, once consensus of the research items has been achieved, the study can be terminated.

3.4 User Requirements

A set of 23 User Requirements for digital pretend play activities were established based on the results from the observation and interview stages. The User Requirements aim to represent the needs of children with ASD. The User Requirements came from four basic categories emerging from the data, these were 'interactions', 'objects', 'properties' and 'environmental conditions'. The categories represent, at a high level, basic elements of structure within an activity. The Delphi study was then used to validate the requirements using expert feedback, making improvements based on the results.

The final set of User Requirements were operationalized into guidelines to help designers create supportive pretend play interventions for children with ASD. The User

Table 3. Interviews Enablers

Interviews - Enablers		No. of people	Overall Mentions
Charac-teristics	Interest In Technology	1	1
	Specific Individual Interest	7	14
	Peer/Paired Work	5	9
Interactions	Key/Deep Questioning	4	7
	Language/conversation	7	18
	Prompts/Cues	5	6
	Actions	6	6
	Adult Guidance	9	23
Objects	Technological artefacts (e.g. iPad)	6	12
	Props (Objects of Reference)	6	9
	Rewards/Motivators	4	10
	Story books (visual)	3	5
	Dressing Up/Masks	4	9
	Visual Aid (e.g.picture cards)	6	10
	Preparation/Familiarization	4	7
Properties	Practice/Repetition	4	7
	Routine, structure and consistency	7	13
	Steps/Sequencing	6	13
	Modelling	4	5
	Choice (e.g. of character)	1	1
	Levelled Difficulty/appropriateness	5	6
	Precise language (e.g. closed Qu's)	7	12
	Adult training	3	6
	Personalisation	5	6
	Realistic environment/situation	3	4
Environmental Con-ditions	Quiet Environment/Space	5	10
	Familiar/Safe Environment	5	9
	Sensory	8	25

Table 4. Interviews Inhibitors

	Characteristics of the child							Interactions						Properties			Environmental Conditions		
Interviews - Inhibitors	Fixated Behaviors	Difficulty Processing Information	Literal/comprehension skills (lack of)	Poor attention/ concentration	Poor Memory	Mood/Behavior/ motivation	Imagination (lack of)	Sensory difficulties	Relationships / interrelating	Difficulties with loss of control	Language/ communication skills	Do not understand emotions	Do not understand reactions	Task complexity	Ease of use (Technological artefact)	Lack of Consistency	New/unfamiliar environments	Imaginary situations/contexts	Busy/ overstimulating spaces
No. of people	9	2	1	2	1	7	7	8	12	10	6	5	4	3	1	4	2	1	3
Overall Mentions	21	2	1	2	1	11	14	13	21	18	8	7	6	3	1	4	4	1	6

Requirements were reorganized to provide a logical format for designers and developers to understand and follow. The final User Requirements and related guidelines are presented in Table 6.

4 Discussion

Observations. In the observations, the environment in which tasks took place was very important. This was true across both schools and classes. For focused activities, children were taken to a separate quiet environment or sensory room. Signs/prompts were used to signal the transition between activities, this could be in the form of music or counting down from 3. Catchy songs were frequently used and children were encouraged to join in. Individual activities were short and often used sequencing to progress to a further task. There were many instances of repetition across all schools and classes, this frequently came from teachers in the form of scheduling and use of song and picture prompts. Books were a primary focus in School 1. Some of the children were disengaged with the idea of reading, therefore the teacher used books with sensory elements such as buttons to engage the children and try to increase their interest. Due to the teacher's knowledge of each of the children, they were able to target the children at an appropriate level and this was tailored to children across each class. From the observations, it was clear that:

1. The environment where the activity takes place has to be defined - calm quiet place with few distractions.
2. Activities should be kept short with a clear start, end and transition e.g., via music or sound.
3. Frustrations due to learning materials must be minimized to avoid task rejection.
4. Positive reinforcement appears to motivate the children and should be taken into consideration.

Table 5. Delphi Study Results, round 1 & round 2

#	User Requirement	Round	%	Mean	Median	Sum	IQR	Outliers
UR1	Key questions/questioning	1	94.74	4.737	5	90	1	none
UR2	Language and vocab suited to task/story	1	94.74	4.737	5	90	1	none
UR3	Prompts/cues	1	89.47	4.473	5	85	1	none
		2	98.88	4.944	5	89	0	unknown
UR4	Actions	1	93.68	4.684	5	89	1	none
UR5	Adult guidance	1	90.53	4.526	5	86	1	2
UR6	Peer/Paired work	1	87.37	4.368	4	83	1	none
		2	96.66	4.833	5	87	0	unknown
UR7	Stories/Books	1	95.79	4.789	5	91	0	unknown
UR8	~~Objects of reference~~	1	92.63	4.632	5	88	1	none
	Digital Objects of Reference	2	95.55	4.778	5	86	0	unknown
UR9	~~Dressing up/masks or mirrors~~	1	93.68	4.684	5	89	1	none
	Digital and physical dressing up or mirror mechanics	2	95.55	4.778	5	86	0	unknown
UR10	Rewards/ motivators	1	90.53	4.526	5	86	1	2
UR11	Preparation/ familiarization	1	91.58	4.579	5	87	1	2
UR12	Practice/ repetition	1	93.68	4.684	5	89	1	none
UR13	Routine/ consistency	1	92.63	4.632	5	88	1	none
UR14	Steps/sequencing	1	96.84	4.842	5	92	0	unknown
UR15	Modeling	1	89.47	4.474	5	85	1	none
		2	88.88	4.444	5	80	1	none
UR16	Choice	1	91.58	4.579	5	87	1	none
		2	96.66	4.833	5	87	0	unknown
UR17	Levelled (according to difficulty)	1	95.79	4.789	5	91	0	unknown
UR18	Adult Training	1	96.84	4.842	5	92	0	unknown
UR19	Feedback	1	89.47	4.474	5	85	1	none
		2	95.55	4.778	5	86	0	unknown
UR20	Personalisation	1	89.47	4.474	5	85	1	none
		2	94.44	4.722	5	85	1	none
UR21	~~Realistic environment~~	1	82.11	4.105	5	78	2	none
	Relatable Scenarios	2	97.77	4.889	5	88	0	unknown
UR22	Quiet/Familiar Environment	1	93.68	4.684	5	89	0	unknown
UR23	Sensory input/features	1	92.63	4.632	5	88	1	none

Table 6. Instructional User Requirements

#	User Requirement	System design guidelines
UR22	Quiet/familiar environment	The optimum environment for the proposed activity is: • familiar to the child e.g., school/nursery • in a quiet space which is calm and has low sensory input
UR7	Stories/Books	Use a (preferably familiar) book scheme or other kind of narrative story with a developed "universe" as a basis for the activity
UR21	Relatable scenarios	Using familiar age-appropriate story narratives will provide reasonable guarantee that content is relatable for children in the age group If creating novel content, relatable scenarios must be selected, i.e., going to the doctor
UR17	Levelled (according to difficulty)	Provide a minimum of three difficulty levels for the child to begin the activity
UR20	Personalisation	Provide individual profiles for customization of: • Profile pictures - can be of the child or a library of themes e.g., train/dinosaur • Adaptations for sensory needs (audio/visual) • Additional supports i.e., visual cues • Difficulty levels
UR23	Sensory input/features	Within each child's profile save settings which reflect the needs of the child, including: • Preferred volume • Turning sound cues on/off • Removing additional text
UR5	Adult guidance	Adults should have access to the child's profile and help the child to set this appropriately at the beginning and throughout use of the activity. Additional supports should be provided to the adults to help the child extend the activity

(*continued*)

Table 6. (*continued*)

#	User Requirement	System design guidelines
UR18	Adult training	Include a section for guiding adult training including: · Written and video instructions on how to use the app · Suggestions of how to extend the activities
UR16	Choice	Give children limited choice over what story or character to play i.e., between 3 and 10 choices at one time. Use achievements per story/character completed to encourage a diverse choice of character or story
UR14	Steps/sequencing	Split the activity into task blocks which are between 5–10 min each. Sequence the learning into steps. The recommendation is: Block 1 – Familiarization with the narrative Block 2 – Context i.e., delivery of the narrative Block 3 – Pretend/role play activity
UR3	Prompts/cues	Optionally (depending on individual needs of child) signal the start and end of activities using a sound cue or song If child attention can be tracked, use voice prompts when attention has been lost
UR13	Routine/ consistency	Repeat the same structure throughout activities Use the activity blocks in UR14 and cues in UR3 to ensure the routine is clear
UR11	Preparation/ familiarization	Build in a step which familiarizes the user on characters, their relationships with each other and key ideas
UR8	Digital objects of reference	When introducing a new or unfamiliar object, provide a "digital objects of reference" i.e., 3D form of an object that must be able to be interacted with, e.g. rotated through interaction with the device

(*continued*)

Table 6. (*continued*)

#	User Requirement	System design guidelines
UR9	Digital & physical dressing up or mirror mechanics	Provide props or visual aids to help the child get into role, e.g., stethoscopes/masks Provide children the opportunity to see themselves 'in role'. (This could be in the form of pictures or live views.)
UR4	Actions	Build in actions to activities, e.g., playing with snowball or making expressions
UR1	Key questions/ questioning	Build a regular/consistent pattern of questioning of the character/role. This should focus on what a character might say or do or to recognize and understand responses and expressions of other characters in the story
UR2	Language and vocab suited to task/story	Language used should be checked by an appropriate education professional to ensure appropriate language and vocabulary are used for the user group Consider visual language of the app to suit the target group, i.e. simple and clear design
UR10	Rewards/ motivators	Provide positive reinforcement for appropriate behaviors through a reward structure including small rewards for tasks and "achievements" for completing full sessions. All rewards should have optional audio (sounds/music/animated voices) Do not have a "fail" state
UR12	Practice/ repetition	Build in opportunities for practice through repeated themes or knowledge building in the content, e.g., in the "familiarization" step Give clear opportunities for children to play again Ensure that activities are repeatable (without using predictable answers)
UR15	Modelling	Provide supports that can be turned on/off that can help children to model behaviors, e.g., videos, animation, or visual feedback

(*continued*)

Table 6. (*continued*)

#	User Requirement	System design guidelines
UR19	Feedback	Live visual feedback can be given where task appropriate Metrics that can help to understand progress should be recorded for viewing by teachers or children, aim to present these positively Experiences may be recorded and watched back, as a fun reward and for reflection of the activity
UR6	Peer/Paired work	As well as a version that can be played alone, give an option for a second player child to join the activity with a second device. This should be used at the discretion of the child

5. Adult involvement can help to extend the themes and learning in an activity
6. Structure, sequencing and repetition can support children's engagement.

Interviews. The interviews reflected the findings of the observations. In line with the observations, the interviews reported enablers of 'adult guidance', 'quiet environment', 'prompts' (e.g. songs or signing), and 'rewards'. 'Levelled difficulty/appropriateness' was mentioned frequently which aligns to the observations, where learning was customized to the individual. Some new categories emerged such as 'Dressing Up/Masks' and the use of 'story books' to inspire and guide the play scenarios. A lot of emphasis was placed on 'routine, structure and consistency', as well as 'steps/sequencing'. This essentially means that the tasks should be broken down and consistently delivered. Some of the participants extended that for some children with ASD, it may take more repetition before learning is acquired. For example, they recommended getting children familiar with a story book before attempting to extend the activity further. The use of 'precise language' was also given significant importance, using finite rather than vague expressions was deemed as necessary. For example, inviting a child with ASD to lunch by saying "Let's go for lunch" may be misinterpreted, instead you could use, "Do you want to come for lunch with us?".

For inhibitors, similar reports were made to the observations. The most frequently mentions inhibitors were, 'fixated behaviors', 'relationships/interrelating' and 'difficulties with loss of control'. Three categories of inhibitors emerged from environmental conditions, 'new/unfamiliar environments', and 'busy/ overstimulating spaces' which were both reported in the observations and additionally 'Imaginary situations/contexts'.

It was clear from the overlap between the observations and interviews that certain enabling factors could help to manage inhibiting factors. At this stage, each of the main themes which emerged through the template analyses were extrapolated and then converted into requirements.

Delphi Study. The Delphi study's main purpose was to validate that the user requirements matched the perspective of experts in the area of pretend play for ASD. Most of the User Requirements passed on the first round and the few that failed needed clarification rather than removal. From the comments given by the experts, it was clear that some did not understand whether these would be real elements or digital, therefore UR8, 'Objects of reference' was changed to 'Digital Objects of Reference' and UR9, 'Dressing up/masks or mirrors' was changed to 'Digital and physical dressing up or mirror mechanics'. Another item that was contested was UR21, 'Realistic environment'. This User Requirement was suggesting that content should be realistic and relatable to the child and not involve too much fantasy. Some experts contested this as they felt imaginary situations could work well depending on the child. It was therefore changed to 'Relatable Scenarios' instead, to reflect being in line with the child's current understanding of the world. The wording of the requirements was reflected to incorporate the expert feedback, after which the User Requirements were all either stable or above the consensus reaching threshold.

User Requirements. The final result of this work is the codification and dissemination of User Requirements for Role Play and Pretend Play activities. Each User Requirement carefully reflected both the data collected from the observations, interviews and Delphi study. The requirements extrapolated the most important and frequently mentioned or emphasized information from each of these stages. In the final stage, the requirements were restructured logically so that they formed guidelines that could be adapted and followed by other practitioners.

5 Conclusion

In answer to the aim of the study, User Requirements were generated for digital pretend play-based interventions for children with ASD, contributing to HCI knowledge and tools. A unique group such as children with ASD needs a set of established User Requirements to assist developers, to avoid problems and increase usability for the application. This study provides a deeper understanding of the target user needs and their context. It also provided an important opportunity to see how children in the target group responded in play scenarios.

These User Requirements could support many different designs and products, using different types of technology. The contribution to knowledge is through providing researchers with a set of rigorously tested User Requirements which can ground their designs in human-centered research. The research could also have potential for wider applicability beyond this group, for example children with language delay as well as typically developing children. The research suggests that the trend towards the creation of digital pretend play interventions for children with ASD will continue. Making User Requirements available for other researchers to is therefore a worthwhile contribution to this small but ever growing space.

5.1 Limitations

The HCD process involved a combination of adult proxy feedback and primary observations. This was partly due to challenges around access to the children with ASD, communication barriers and this group being vulnerable.

The User Requirements generated in this study focus on a narrow activity setting, pretend play for children with ASD. Using these User requirements as a base for creating more general User Requirements for all digital interventions for children with ASD could also be of benefit. Some of the requirements and recommendations found in this work have wider applicability across other activities so to extract these and conduct further work to produce more general User Requirements would be a logical next step to contribute to HCD generated knowledge.

5.2 Future Research

Future research could focus on more direct feedback from primary users and looking for instruments that could be used to overcome communication challenges where necessary, to enhance designs.

To extend and support this knowledge, further research is recommended to test the efficacy of the tool through evaluation of digital interventions created using the requirements. This is the next step that the authors took in the wider study.

An evaluation of each individual requirement of the system would help to show how much each of the requirements makes a difference to the usability of such digital interventions for children with ASD. Carrying out further evaluation would help strengthen the tool and allow for any adjustments arising from further study. Additionally, evaluation of continued input from the involvement of users, especially from primary use, would help to strengthen both the tool and requirements.

References

1. Canning, N.: Children's empowerment in play. Eur. Early Child. Educ. Res. J. **15**(2), 227–236 (2007)
2. Goncu, A., Gaskins, S.: Play and Development: Evolutionary, Sociocultural, and Functional Perspectives. Taylor and Francis (2012, 2007)
3. Ten Eycke, K.D., Müller, U.: Brief report: new evidence for a social-specific imagination deficit in children with autism spectrum disorder. J. Autism Dev. Disorders, **45**(1), 213–220 (2014, 2015)
4. Baron-Cohen, S.: Autism and symbolic play. Br. J. Dev. Psychol. **5**(2), 139–148 (1987)
5. Phillips, N., Beavan, L.: Teaching Play to Children with Autism: A Practical Intervention Using Identiplay, 2nd edn. Sage, Newcastle upon Tyne (2012)
6. Lai, M., Lombardo, M.V., Baron-Cohen, S.: Autism. Lancet (British Edition), **383**(9920), 896–910 (2014)
7. Anderson, A.: Virtual Reality, Augmented Reality and Artificial Intelligence in Special Education: A Practical Guide to Supporting Students with Learning Differences, 1st edn. Routledge, London (2019)
8. Eversole, M., et al.: Leisure activity enjoyment of children with autism spectrum disorders. J. Autism Dev. Disorders, **46**(1), 10–20 (2015, 2016)

9. Boucenna, S., et al.: Interactive technologies for autistic children: a review. Cogn. Comput. **6**(4), 722–740 (2014). https://doi.org/10.1007/s12559-014-9276-x
10. Bremner, L., Fabricatore, C., Lopez, X.: Using game based technology as a mediating function in interventions to develop pretend play skills in children with autism spectrum disorder. In: Elbæk, L., Majgaard, G., Valente, A., Khalid, S. (eds.) Proceedings of the 13th International Conference on Game Based Learning ECGBL 2019, pp. 846–853. Academic Conferences and Publishing International, Reading (2019)
11. Khowaja, K., et al.: Augmented reality for learning of children and adolescents with autism spectrum disorder (ASD): a systematic review. IEEE (2020)
12. ISO.: ISO 9241-210:2019(en) Ergonomics of human-system interaction—Part 210: Human-centred design for interactive systems (2019). https://www.iso.org/obp/ui/#iso:std:iso:9241:-210:ed-2:v1:en. Accessed 24 May 2022
13. Andrews, C., et al.: A new method in user centered design: collaborative prototype design process. J. Tech. Writ. Commun. **42**, 123–142 (2012)
14. De Leo, G., Gonzales, C.H., Battagiri, P., Leroy, G.: A smart-phone application and a companion website for the improvement of the communication skills of children with autism: clinical rationale, technical development, and preliminary results. J. Med. Syst. **35**, 703–711 (2011). https://doi.org/10.1007/s10916-009-9407-1
15. De Leo, G., Leroy, G.: Smartphones to facilitate communication and improve social skills of children with severe autism spectrum disorder: Special education teachers as proxies. In: Cassell, J. (ed.) 7th International Conference on Interaction Design and Children, pp. 45–48 (2008)
16. Still, B., Crane, K.: Fundamentals of User-Centered Design: A Practical Approach. CRC Press Taylor & Francis Group, Boco Raton (2017)
17. Cañete, R., Peralta, M.E.: ASDesign: a user-centered method for the design of assistive technology that helps children with autism spectrum disorders be more independent in their daily routines. Sustainability (Basel, Switzerland) **14**(516), 516 (2022)
18. Kerawalla, L., Luckin, R., Seljeflot, S., Woolard, A.: "Making it real": exploring the potential of augmented reality for teaching primary school science. Virtual Reality: J. Virtual Reality Soc. **10**(3), 163–174 (2006)
19. Mao, J.Y., Vredenburg, K., Smith, P.W., Carey, T.: The state of user-centered design practice. Commun. ACM **48**, 105–109 (2005)
20. Jones, J., Hunter, D.: Consensus methods for medical and health services research. BMJ (Online) **311**(7001), 376–380 (1995)
21. Ryan, R.M., Deci, E.L.: Self-determination theory and the facilitation of intrinsic motivation, social development, and well-being. Am. Psychol. **55**(1), 68–78 (2000)
22. Bedny, G.Z., Seglin, M.H., Meister, D.: Activity theory: history, research and application. Theor. Issues Ergon. Sci. **1**(2), 168–206 (2000)
23. King, N.: Doing template analysis. In: Symon, G., Cassell, C. (eds.) Qualitative Organizational Research: Core Methods and Current Challenges, pp. 426–450. SAGE Publications, Inc. (2012)

User Experience Evaluation in Virtual Reality for Autism: A Systematic Literature Review

Aulia Hening Darmasti(✉), Niels Pinkwart, and Raphael Zender

Department of Computer Science, Humboldt University of Berlin, Berlin, Germany
darmasta@hu-berlin.de

Abstract. Virtual reality (VR) used for people with autism spectrum disorder (ASD) is gaining a place among researchers lately. The rich interactivity provided by VR makes it a powerful tool for various purposes, one of which is to support interventions for people with ASD. Since people with ASD have a different sensory experience, the user experience (UX) within VR applications for ASD becomes a crucial aspect. There have been past literature reviews of VR applications for ASD. However, to the best of our knowledge, there is hardly one that focuses on the methods used in evaluating the users' experience towards interaction techniques or interface elements incorporated in various VR applications. In this review, 24 studies met predetermined PICo (Population, Interest, Context) criteria from the search based on three relevant databases, namely Pubmed NCBI, Dimensions.ai, and IEEE Xplore. Direct examination from observers appears as the most popular method used to assess experiences of people with ASD in using VR and followed by self-report questionnaire method. In addition, although all relevant literatures mentioned their UX evaluation method, only a few studies whose evaluation is relevantly subjected towards their interaction techniques or user interface elements. This review is expected to provide insights and considerations in designing UX evaluation method for VR applications for people with ASD in the future.

Keywords: Virtual reality · Autistic spectrum disorder · User experience · Interaction technique · User interface elements

1 Introduction

In recent years, the utilization of virtual reality (VR) in autism spectrum disorder (ASD) intervention has attracted huge interest among researchers and practitioners. VR provides a rich exploration for ASD intervention, such as multisensory experience, social scenarios, and virtual worlds. As people with ASD are experiencing difficulties in two core domains: (1) social communication and social interaction, and (2) restricted, repetitive, and sensory behaviors or interests [1], interacting with computers and mobile phones will by some means don't demand them to interact with a real society, which is one of their biggest challenges. Thereof, a person with ASD enjoys playing games that provide a safe environment to explore or express themselves [2].

M. Antona and C. Stephanidis (Eds.): HCII 2023, LNCS 14020, pp. 546–568, 2023.
https://doi.org/10.1007/978-3-031-35681-0_36

On the other side, researchers and developers have recently started to introduce UX element as one of the substantial matters within the development process of a digital application, including VR applications. Since people with ASD experience a different sensory experience from neurotypical people [3], it is interesting to look more closely into how people with ASD perceive and experience VR as compared to neurotypical people.

Several studies of VR applications for people with ASD have been reported [4–7]. Lal Bozgeyikli et al. conducted a review on the design considerations of VR for individuals with ASD [4]. They presented design issues accumulated in previous literature based on user studies exploring the usefulness of VR as a training tool for ASD. They further classified past studies into two categories, namely immersive/non-immersive VR systems and the targeted skill. Meanwhile, Valencia et al. summarized the impact of technology on people with ASD [5]. The report highlighted three research questions about the use of technology in educational contexts; to know the ways technology contributes to the education of people with ASD, to know which UX and accessibility elements/methods are considered by researchers in analyzing the impact of the technology, and to know which game elements are considered in designing the gamification in the education of people with ASD. Their study suggested considering accessibility and usability tests to ensure positive experiences for users with ASD in future studies, as only a handful of research took it into account. In a similar aim, MesaGresa et al. performed an evidence-based systematic review on the effectiveness of VR for children and adolescents with ASD [6]. Though their review evaluated the effectiveness of the VR applications and included both clinical and technical perspectives, little to no discussion was found on UX evaluation methods used for reviewed reports. Lastly, Glaser et al. carried out a literature review on the design characteristics of VR systems designed as a training tool for individuals with autism with an emphasis on analyzing how VR systems had been described by past studies, including the technologies used, subjects, contexts, available supports and type of tasks [7].

However, none of the studies looked closely into how part studies evaluated their participants' experience and how the experience correlated with VR elements. Although researchers have worked on creating useful applications utilizing VR, it is important to also understand better which interaction techniques are more effective for population with ASD, so that the benefit of VR applications can be gained optimally. The present review particularly aims to analyze the state of the art of how software developers and researchers evaluate the UX on VR applications for people with ASD with two main guiding questions:

- **RQ1**: How do researchers of VR applications for people with ASD evaluate the UX on their system?
- **RQ2**: Are those UX evaluation methods specifically intended to assess VR elements (Interaction techniques/UI elements)?

To answer these questions, a systematic review method was chosen because it allows a systematic evaluation of current knowledge using a predetermined selection framework [8], resulting in a more comprehensive and unbiased analysis. Understanding this subject at hand would provide valuable insights and considerations in the future exploration of

Human-computer Interaction areas, especially for VR designers and developers who serve people with ASD.

2 Definition, Theoretical Framework, and Methodology

2.1 Virtual Reality (VR) and User Experience (UX)

Virtual reality (VR) has been defined in several ways. Literally, Merriam-Webster Dictionary defines VR as an artificial environment which is experienced through sensory stimuli (such as sights and sounds) provided by a computer and in which one's actions partially determine what happens in the environment [9]. Steuer defines VR as a real or simulated environment, in which a perceiver experiences telepresence [10]. Telepresence refers to being able to feel present somewhere different from your real location. Brooks defines virtual reality as an experience where the user is effectively immersed in a responsive virtual world [11]. VR is also described as a set of technologies that allow people to immerse in a world beyond reality [12]. One of the first virtual reality systems is the one designed by Morton Heilig in 1962 [13] which enabled the user to a multi-sensory experience, also known as a multi-modal experience. Besides VR, the terms Augmented Reality (AR), Mixed Reality (MR), and Extended Reality (XR) are also widely known. While AR takes place in the physical world, MR is a hybrid system of AR and VR [14], and XR is the superset of those three.

Today, VR comes in various hardware and software configurations. For instance, Standalone Head-mounted Display (HMD) like Oculus Quest and HTC VIVE, Google Cardboard + smartphone, and Cave Automatic Virtual Environment (CAVE) [15]. These VR applications could provide distinct multi-sensory experience to their users since the VR environment allows the designers and developers to entirely custom its storyboard and interaction techniques into UI elements. The high interactivity degree provided by virtual reality makes it a great tool for a wide variety of purposes, e.g., entertainment [16, 17], educational platform [18], training [19], medical aid [20–22], to intervention for person with ASD.

UX is also substantial in the development of 3D space. According to Nielsen Norman Group, UX comprises all aspects of the end-users interaction with its products, services, and company [42]. As defined in ISO 9241–11:2018 [23], UX is defined as users' perceptions and responses including the users' emotions, beliefs, preferences, comfort, behaviours, and accomplishments that occur before, during, and after using a system, product, or service. UX encompasses User Interface (UI) and its usability, how easy a UI is to use [24]. Researchers have been working on evaluating the user experience of digital applications, but to date, the popular UX evaluations are of 2D products. To examine UX in a 3D environment is another story and hence it comes up as an interesting topic for the researchers.

2.2 Literature Searching Procedure and Analysis

To get a systematical, well-ordered review process, PRISMA (Preferred Reporting Items for Systematic Reviews and Meta-Analyses) flow diagram was utilized [25]. This framework was utilized due to its ability to retrieve reliable relevancy from the reviewed studies.

Past reports analyzed in the current study were gathered from three databases, namely Dimensions.ai, IEEE Xplore, and Pubmed NCBI. These databases were selected based on following considerations. Dimensions.ai is an independent scholarly search database that provides free access to a vast collection of curated research outputs. It contains more than 126 million publications and provides a wide range of filtering options to facilitate specific searches [26]. Meanwhile, IEEE Xplore comprises publications on computer science, electrical engineering, electronics, and associated areas. It provides access to more than 5 million documents in related fields [27]. Lastly, Pubmed NCBI is a free database that supports the search of biomedical and life science literature, containing more than 33 million references and abstracts from biomedical fields [28]. This database supports an in-depth and inclusive view of ASD by providing a search from the biomedical area.

Moreover, a precise search term throughout literature collection is deemed critical in a systematic literature review. Thus, PICo (Population, phenomenon of Interest, Context) tool was applied to construct a fine research focus. PICo is beneficial for qualitative reviews because there is no comparator to be considered [29]. The determined PICo components are as follows.

- Population (P): Studies with focus on VR applications for users with ASD,
- Interest (I): UX evaluation method, interaction techniques, and UI elements,
- Context (Co): Research projects that mention their evaluation method, interaction techniques, and UI elements on their VR application for ASD.

The search terms *("Virtual Reality" OR VR) AND (Autism OR Autistic OR ASD) AND (Usability OR Comfort OR Safety OR Experience)* were therefore implemented to draw relevant studies from the large pools of databases.

2.3 Selection Strategy

Inclusion/Exclusion Criteria. The inclusion criteria were reasoned as the following:

- Only studies from 1 January 2011 - 31 May 2021 are included,
- Only studies written in English,
- Only studies that specified their evaluation method, interaction techniques or UI elements on their VR application for ASD.

Exclusion criteria:

- Publications in the forms of book or short report.
- Studies that are on AR, MR, and XR. Even though theoretically VR subsumes under XR, the literature which focuses on XR is excluded in this study to avoid including other XR subsumes.

Selection Steps and Analysis. Taking the inclusion and exclusion criteria into account, the selection process then proceeded as the following:

1. *Literature collation.* A search with the pre-defined terms was conducted in chosen databases, namely Dimensions, IEEE Xplore, and Pubmed NCBI,

2. *Exclusion.* Collated publications categorized as books or short reports were excluded.
3. *Title and abstract check.* Title and abstract checks were carried out to verify the relevance of collated studies. Only studies which mentioned terms, such as user experience, usability testing, and experience relation, were then read fully.
4. *Full-text reading.* As a final step, a thorough reading was conducted for reports that satisfied previous points.

Furthermore, during the last step, the authors looked for the following points within the selected studies:

- The research discusses in-depth about development, design, or test towards VR applications for people with ASD,
- The literature discusses user experience or similar terms, e.g., usability, accessibility, feasibility, or other terms that imply user experience but could only be understandable with context.
- The report mentions any interaction techniques or UI elements they used on the VR application.

The data drawn from respective studies was then analyzed and organized using the following structure:

1. *Key Finding*
    - UX evaluation method. The identified UX evaluation methods were divided into two: data acquisition method and data processing method. The data processing method is collected to support better understanding towards the evaluation method. Meanwhile, data acquisition methods with similar characteristics were then classified into five groups:
        - Observer's observation,
        - Participant fills self-report,
        - Physiological data,
        - Concurrent Thinking Aloud,
        - Caregiver's viewpoint.
    - User interface/interaction technique.
2. *Secondary data.* Secondary data accommodates interesting data but not highlighted as key findings, for instance, data about devices used and participant demographic.
3. *Meta-data.* Since reviewed studies were multidiscipline, meta-data such as publication type and publication field were also collected.

3 Results

3.1 Search and Study Selection Result

Using the predefined search terms, the total studies obtained were 125, 48, and 49 from Dimensions, IEEE Xplore, and Pubmed NCBI, respectively. After removing duplicates, 155 distinct records were listed as dataset (Fig. 1).

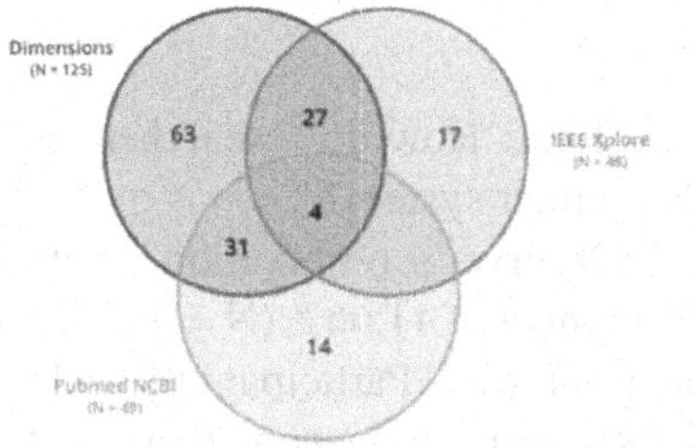

Fig. 1. Venn diagram of the total records obtained from the search.

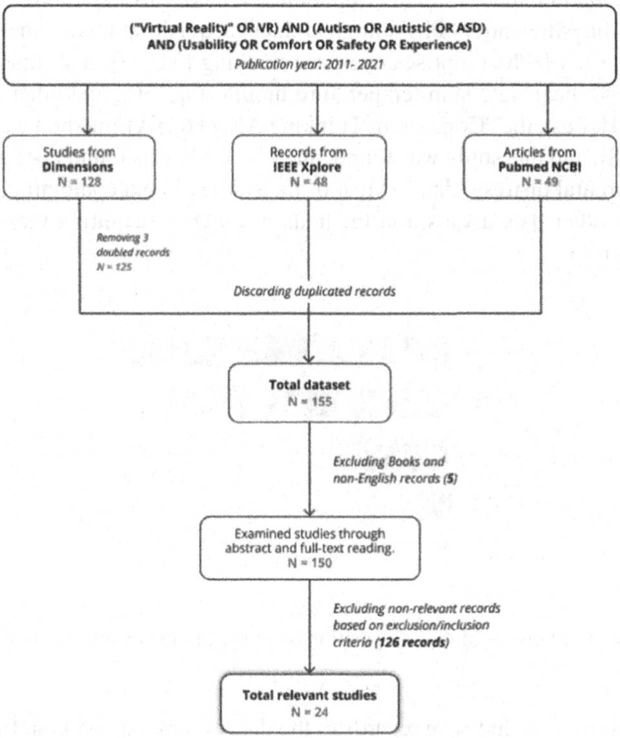

Fig. 2. Diagram flow of the searching and selection process.

From the 155 studies, another five publications either books or not written in English were excluded from the dataset, so only 150 studies will be investigated further (Fig. 2). Afterward, the abstract and full-text examination was carried out to identify studies that met all the inclusion criteria. During the literature review process, 26 studies met the selection criteria, but there were three studies from one research group that had the same user experience assessment method. In this case, only one study with more complete evidence and analysis was considered to represent those three studies. In the end, in total, only 24 studies were left to be analyzed. The general result from the full-text review is presented in Appendix.

3.2 Key Findings

UX Evaluation Methods. "RQ1: How do researchers of VR application for people with ASD evaluate the UX on their system?".

As seen in Fig. 3, the "Observer's observation" method was the most used data acquisition method with the number of 41.66% (N = 17). Meanwhile, the second popular method on data acquisition group was "Participant fills self-report" N = 15 (36.58%) in which those studies asked participants to respond to a list of survey questions. However, one study by Ravindran et al. [30] only took the participant questionnaire without using it because the responses were not consistent with what was noted by the observers. Moreover, the participants' limited communication skill also affecting their ability in filling out the questionnaire. "Physiological data" acquisition then come in third place 14.63% (N = 6), which comprises eye-gaze tracking [31–34], real-time brain signals monitoring [35], heart rate skin temperature monitoring [36], and other physiological signals [33, 34]. Last, the "Concurrent Thinking Aloud (CTA)" method was used by two studies [37, 38], and one study was found, and one study was found taking "Caregiver's viewpoint (parental distress) data". Most of the studies found combining these two top methods with other data acquisition methods in order to acquire a more reliable and sound observation.

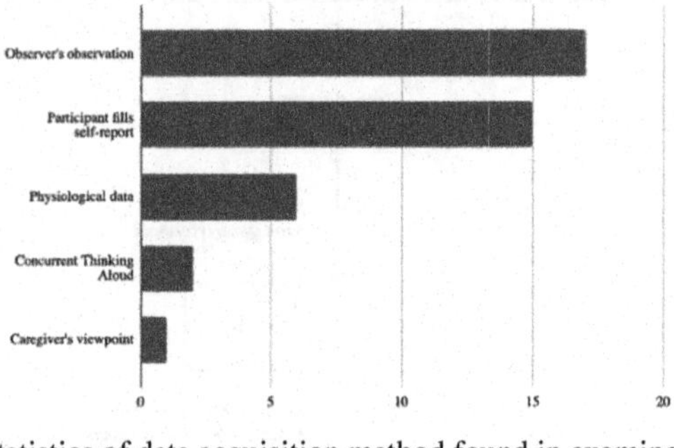

Fig. 3. Statistics of data acquisition method found in examined studies.

There is no trend found with regards to the data processing method. Each study has its own data processing method, depending on the data acquisition method and each study objective. For instance, Malihi et al. [32] utilized Machine Learning algorithm such as elastic nets, random forest, AdaBoost, and NN to predict the user-reported ratings of sense after obtaining self-report data from users. Luca et al. [12] also recorded psychometric assessments from their participants. On the other hand, Bozgeyikli and co-workers [4, 39–41] applied ANOVA and Mauchly tests to analyse their questionnaire results.

It is interesting to note that the user experiences in reviewed studies were described using greatly varied terms, such as comfortability, accessibility, acceptability, usability, safety, physical experience, and even cybersickness. The variables measured from each evaluation method were also quite diverse since they depend greatly on the respective evaluation method and study focus. One great example is Bozgeyikli et al.'s work [39] whereby the study clearly listed the measured variables, namely difficulty in understanding, difficulty in operating, difficulty in control, enjoyment, effort, tiredness, overwhelmed-ness, and frustration. The participants in this study were asked to scale their rating for those variables through a questionnaire, in which the data was then processed using ANOVA methods.

The physiological response also appears as one of the parameters measured among the listed studies. Feng et al. tracked the Region of Interest (ROI) from the participant's eye movement by showing virtual faces on a DesktopVR [31]. Mei et al. compared VR with Customizable Virtual Human (CVH) to VR applications without CVH and measured the participants' total joint attention achieved through eye tracking on participant's ROI [42]. The study concluded that the presence of CVH helped ASD to gaze less at unimportant areas and could improve user performance in 3D interaction tasks (such as locomotion) and result in a more pleasant user experience. On the other side, Lahiri et al. created a system that provides feedback based on the participant's viewing pattern [33]. The same group also measured physiological data (Biopac, CV, EDA, EMG) and the affective states of the participants' [34]. Their work resulted in a system that could predict the user's affective states from objective measures through physiological signals. Additionally, Finkelstein et al. measured the participant's total energy consumed through an armband and tracking equipment [43]. Lastly, Halabi et al. captured the participant's verbal response (speech recognition) and physical motion [44].

User Interface/Interaction Technique. "RQ2: Are those UX evaluation methods specifically intended to assess VR elements (Interaction techniques/UI elements)?".

Of all reviewed studies, only six studies could answer this re- search question, where three of them were produced by Bozgeyikli et al. [39–41], two by Mei et al. [42], and one by Lal Bozgeyikli et al. [45]. *Firstly*, Bozgeyikli et al. specifically evaluated 3D interactions towards ASD users' experience, such as tangible object manipulation, haptic device, touch and snap, touchscreen (Object selection Manipulation), and real walking and walk in place (Locomotion) [39]. In their another study [40], Bozgeyikli et al. examined the same interactions as in the previous one, yet with a different display method. In another study, they particularly assessed locomotion techniques (redirected walking, walk-in-place, joystick, stepper machine, point teleport, flying, flapping and trackball) [41]. *Secondly*, Mei et al. examined the effect of Customizable Virtual Human (CVH) on ASD users' experience and compared its efficacy with the VR application without a CVH [32, 42]. *Lastly*, Lal Bozgeyikli et al. specifically evaluated the effect of five user interface attributes (Instruction methods, visual fidelity, view zoom, clutter, and motion) towards ASD users' experience [45]. Meanwhile, the rest of the studies only mentioned their system's interaction techniques or UI elements, without providing further explanation if the evaluation was really intended for those specific VR elements.

Secondary Data

Devices. Devices listed here are the ones that the authors clearly indicated in their report. Most of the studies used more than one device on their system. As shown in Fig. 4, standalone HMD was shown to be the most preferable display method used among the relevant studies by 50% (N = 15). It comprises Oculus Rift (N = 6), HTC Vive (N = 2), Class VR (N = 1) and Google Daydream (N = 2) and not-specified standalone HMD

(N = 4). DesktopVR took the second place in 26.66% (N = 8) and followed by Google Cardboard (HMD + smartphone) in 13.33% (N = 4). One study used CAVE [44] and the 'Other' group utilized a curtain screen [39] and stereoscopic screen with 3D glasses [43].

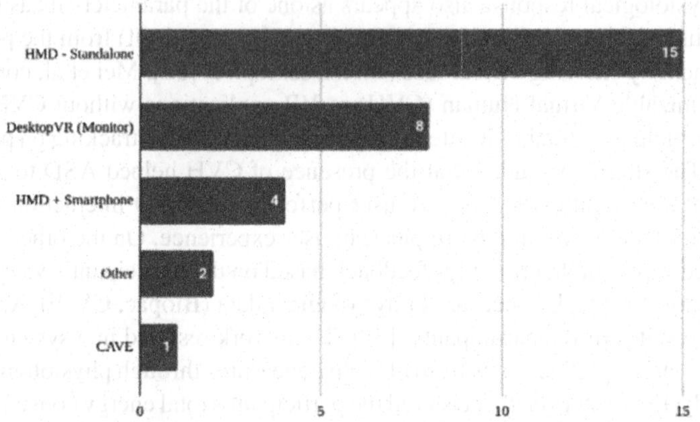

Fig. 4. Statistics of display method found in relevant studies.

Besides display method, some studies also use controllers and trackers in their experiments. Three studies were found using Leap Motion, three others using mouse, one using a hand-held controller and oculus-rift controller as inputs from the users. Six studies employed motion trackers in their systems, four used eye-trackers, and two tracked physiological signals. One study also mentioned microphone and speaker as their I/O devices.

Participant Demography. Participant demography was summarized in Table 1. From the sorted 24 studies, the average number of participants was 9–10 persons, with 6–7 persons as the median. The minimum number of participants who joined was one person, and the largest number of participants was 32. It was also found that ten studies did not reveal the participants' gender information. Hence, the gender percentage was calculated only based on 14 studies that provided gender information. The result shows that 84.38% of participants who joined the study were male.

Table 1. Participant demography from 24 studies

Feature	Number
Number of participants	
Mean from 24 studies	9.66
Median from 24 studies	6.5

(continued)

Table 1. (*continued*)

Feature	Number
Max number of participants	32
Min number of participants	1
Gender	
Male	84.38%
Female	15.62%
Age	
Adult	34.8%
Adolescence	26.1%
Children	26.1%
N/A	13.0%

Furthermore, not every study gave detailed information about the age of the participants. Even though all studies provide their total number of participants, only a few provided the participant age range and mean. Hence, the age data were classified into three age ranges, namely Children (6–13 years), Adolescents (14–19 years), and Adults (older than 19 years) following the age classification by Robert V. Kail [1]. Our analysis shows that 34.8% of studies had Adults as their participants, followed by Children and Adolescence in the same number, 26.1% from 24 studies. The classification of 'High-functioning' and 'Low-functioning' was not used since a large number of studies supports stopping the use of the function-labeling system to categorize ASD individuals. Although the distribution of numbers between each age group is almost even, we could see an opportunity to include more children and adolescents in future studies since the exploration number in this age group is not as high as in adult age group. Nevertheless, it can also be a prompt to future studies this eld to always indicate participants' age group.

Meta-Data. Among 24 studies, 58.33% (N = 14) studies are proceedings, 16.66% (N = 4) were journals, and 4.16% (N = 1) was a transaction. The publishers of respective studies were also categorized to infer the authors' publication field preferences. As shown in Fig. 5, the most popular field to publish user experience evaluation on VR for ASD was the Technology field by 54.16% (N = 13). Other relevant fields include Psychology, Medicine, Virtual Rehabilitation, Education and Technology, and Education.

4 Discussion

Each of reviewed studies utilized different intervention or treatment approach towards ASD population, from social scenarios, games, vocation, training, to static scenes where the ASD users were only able to sightsee without having to interact with the environment. Hence, each study used different levels of interactivity and built various combinations of user interface elements and interaction techniques, including 3D interaction. For the

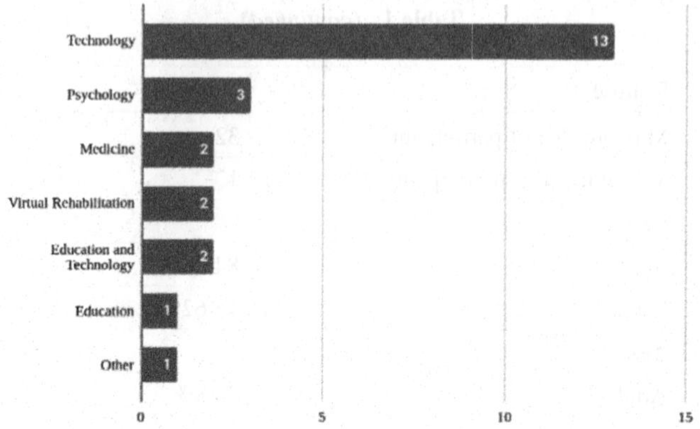

Fig. 5. Statistics of publication field

same reason, each study also applied a specific method to evaluate the user experience in their study.

To answer the first research question, "How do researchers of VR applications for people with ASD evaluate the UX on their system?", direct examination from observers was found as the most common data acquisition method used to assess the ASD users' experience in using VR and followed by self-report questionnaire (filled by the participant). However, according to Pearl [46] and Newbutt [47], self-report questionnaires in people with ASD/ID appeared to produce a more vulnerable or biased result. The self-reporting method is not recommended for ASD users since they may have difficulty reflecting or reporting their feelings or emotions. Accordingly, Bozgeyikli et al. who used both methods stated that their results should not be generalized since they might not be applicable to medium or low-functioning ASD individuals [39, 40] who have more limitations in expressing their emotions. Ravindran et al. [30] also asked participants to fill in survey data, but the data was not included in the process since the responses were not consistent with the observer's observation result. Additionally, some of their participants were also impacted by their limited communication skills in completing the questionnaire independently.

Almost all the data acquisition methods used by the relevant studies involved either third-party observation or required participant's verbal expression. Looking at the subject limitation in the social communication [1], future research might involve more exploration of physiological response in evaluating the users' experience of VR applications for ASD users. Six relevant studies found have already started the exploration of using biofeedback. For instance, Lahiri et al. used electrocardiogram (ECG), cyclic voltammetry (CV), electrodermal (EDA), and electromyographic (EMG) to predict user's affective states such as anxiety, enjoyment, and engagement of participants [34] and Mei et al. which measured participants' total joint attention through eye tracking [3]. Further research in this field would be a great help in obtaining more equitable users' voices.

It is also interesting to note that although all selected studies were able to address the first research question, only six studies were able to answer the second research question, "Were the UX evaluation methods intended for specific VR elements (Interaction techniques/UI elements)?". The works of Bozgeyikli et al. [39–41] thus become increasingly relevant to the present research questions. They straightforwardly discussed the user experience evaluation based on specific various interaction techniques on VR training applications for people with ASD. Their studies lead to conclusions about the sample population's preference for VR display methods and interaction techniques. Lal Bozgeyikli et al. also investigated the UI attributes of VR training applications for people with ASD [45]. Both groups focused on VR training applications for high-functioning ASD. On the other hand, Mei et al. evaluated the effect of using Customizable Virtual Human (CVH) on VR application with a VR hand-eye coordination training game. The differences in the user's 3D interaction performance, game performance, and user experiences while playing with CVH and without CVH were assessed. However, there are only a handful of studies that have specifically aimed to evaluate the UX of VR interaction techniques and UI elements. This could be an indication that this topic is still not popular in the research field. Thus, future studies could be directed to visit and investigate the UX of the interaction techniques and UI elements of VR for people with ASD.

5 Conclusion

This review aims to answer the guiding question "How do researchers of VR application for people with ASD evaluate the UX on their system?" and the succeeding question "Are these UX evaluation methods intended for specific VR elements (Interaction techniques/UI elements)?". From three databases (Pubmed NCBI, IEEE Xplore, and Dimensions.ai), 24 relevant papers were selected using PRISMA framework. The review established that most of the studies used a direct observation method. Although the efficacy and reliability of self-report questionnaires by participants with ASD remain debatable, the self-report questionnaire appeared to be the second most used method among the studies. It is suggested that researchers might start exploring the involvement of physiological response in evaluating the users' experience of VR applications for ASD users.

It also became apparent that only a small number of studies correlated a UX evaluation to specific VR elements (Interaction techniques/UI elements) when VR application was tested on people with ASD. The comfortability of using VR applications not only belongs to neurotypical but also to people with ASD whose sensory system is more sensitive than the average. In order to gain to maximize the benefit of the therapies, training, or education in VR, understanding the population response towards various interaction techniques is essential. Having said that, more reports and investigations on this topic are expected in the future. Lastly, this review hopefully adds valuable considerations for future design and development of VR applications, especially in designing the UX evaluation method for VR applications for people with ASD.

Acknowledgments. Aulia would like to sincerely thank Indonesian Endowment Fund for Education/*Lembaga Pengelola Dana Pendidikan* (LPDP) for the financial support during the work of this article.

Appendix

Author, Year	Intervention/Therapy/Treatment	User interface/Interaction technique	UX Evaluation Method	Output/Variable Measured	Interesting Insights
Li et al. (2019) [48]	Social stories using Kolb's experiential learning model	- Interface components: Visual hints, task list - Interaction: Verbal response - 3D Interaction: Selecting object (Tapping the in-VR rating button)	- Observation from observer; onsite and video. Direct interview to participant	- Output: Case report per individual (qualitative)	Enabling in-VR task lists, hints, and real-time feedbacks are effective for providing in-VR facilitations, which is needed in delivering treatment for ASD users
Junaidi et al. (2020) [49]	Social scenario; selecting food menu, seating, and putting the dirty dishes	- Interface comp: Visual hints, task list - Interaction: Verbal response	- Observation from observer and observer filling questionnaire	- Variables measured: Borg and Gall; convenience of using HMD, object readability in VR, understanding the instructions in VR - Output: Statistics of user experience (quantitative)	- The VR content used has not been able to address LFA problems - LFA users want to use VR devices, but with some limitations
Di Mascio et al. (2020) [37]	Scenes (space, forest, historic site) and games (virtual blocks)	- Interface comp: Scenes - Interaction: Remote control, gamepad, virtual hand (leap motion) - 3D Interaction: Selecting and manipulating an object	- Concurrent Think Aloud (CTA), - Observation from observer. Direct interview to participant - Self-report questionnaire/survey (but not used)	- Output: Acceptability and usability data (quantitative), and engagement (qualitative)	- The evaluation framework could represent the foundations for an innovative IVE evaluation framework

(continued)

(*continued*)

Author, Year	Intervention/Therapy/Treatment	User interface/Interaction technique	UX Evaluation Method	Output/Variable Measured	Interesting Insights
Malihi et al. 2020 [50]	Social scenario (in school bus) and scenes (Blue Planet)	- Interaction: Exploring the VR scene by moving their head (VR) or mouse control	- Self-report questionnaire/survey - Using elastic nets, random forest, AdaBoost, and NN to predict the user-reported ratings of sense	- Variable measured: Demography, sense of presence (Spatial presence, naturalness, engagement) and safety (cybersickness, anxiety) - Output: correlation between IQ and anxiety to sense of presence and safety	- The most accurately predicted target is spatial presence, followed by engagement - IQ and anxiety traits are identified as critical predictors of spatial presence and engagement
Ravindran et al. (2019) [30]	Social scenario consists of reciprocal interaction	- Interface comp: Scenes, Avatar - Interaction: Verbal response	- Observation from observer; onsite and video. Observer filling questionnaire and do a direct interview to participant - Self-report questionnaire/survey	- Variables measured: Joint attention, participant's mood, self-report condition (Alertness, eye discomfort, clarity of vision, headache, stomachache, balance, enjoyment), and observation result (participant's tolerance of HMD, enjoyment, adverse side effects, value from Floreo)	- Observations from the observer is the primary evaluation method - Participant's questionnaire response was not consistent as the observer's note due to limited communication skills
Feng et al. (2018) [31]	Showing virtual faces on the screen	- Interface comp: Avatar with varying realism degree and pupil size - Interaction: Mouse control	- Tracking participant's eye movement (ROI) and combining the user's preference between two different faces with different realism and eye size	- Variables measured: - Region of Interest (ROI) from participant's eye-gaze - Participant's preference	ASD children rather indifferent towards facial features manipulation
Newbutt et al. (2020) [51]	Scenes (Moon, Historical Place) and Game (Throwing Ball)	- Interface comp: Scenes - Interaction: virtual hand (controller) - 3D Interaction: Selecting object	- Observer do the direct interview to participant - Self-report questionnaire/survey	- Variables measured: Enjoyment/Usefulness, physical experience, and preference	The most preferred device is the high-end HMD

(*continued*)

(*continued*)

Author, Year	Intervention/Therapy/Treatment	User interface/Interaction technique	UX Evaluation Method	Output/Variable Measured	Interesting Insights
De Luca et al. (2021) [52]	Scenario games with CBT	- Interface comp: Scene - 3D Interaction: Full-body movement	- Observation from observer, using GARS - Psychometric assessment - Parental distress (Self-report questionnaire)	Variables measured: Psychometric (Nonverbal fluid intelligence, attention process, visual-spatial functions)	Combined rehabilitation using CBT with VR may be promising in improving cognition
Schmidt et al. (2021) [53]	Train public transportation skills	- Interface comp: Scenes - Interaction: Selecting object	- Expert review, observation from observer. Observer filling questionnaire - Self-report questionnaire/survey	- Variable measured: Usability question set using SUS and adjective scale by Bangor	The spherical video-based virtual reality (SVVR) is easy-to-use and has positive user-experience feedback in general
Bozgeyikli et al. (2019) [39]	Vocational: cleaning, shelving, environmental awareness, loading, money management, and social	- Interface comp: Scenes - 3D interaction: -- Object selection & manipulation; Tangible object manipulation, Haptic Device, Touch and Snap, Touchscreen -- Locomotion; Real Walking, Walk-in Place	- Observation from observer - Self-report questionnaire/survey - Participant's questionnaire response is processed using ANOVA,	- Variables measured: user experience (difficult in understanding, difficult in operating, in control, enjoyment, effort, tiredness, overwhelmedness, frustration) and task completion	- Participants prefer touchscreen and tangible interaction techniques and real walking - Participants had more difficulty in gesture and more abstract interaction
Bozgeyikli et al. (2018) [40]	Vocational: cleaning, shelving, environmental awareness, loading, money management, and social	- Display method: HMD, curtain screen - 3D interaction:, -- Object selection & manipulation; Tangible object manipulation, Haptic Device, Touch and Snap, Touchscreen -- Locomotion: Real Walking, Walk-in Place,	- Observation from observer - Self-report questionnaire/survey - Questionnaire with a Likert scale is processed using one-way ANOVA	- Variables measured: preference, cybersickness, user experience (ease of interaction, enjoyment, frustration, tiredness, immersion)	- (Same points from preliminary result) - Curtain display is more preferred than HMD - Participants prefer more realistic and real-life linkable interaction techniques

(*continued*)

(continued)

Author, Year	Intervention/Therapy/Treatment	User interface/Interaction technique	UX Evaluation Method	Output/Variable Measured	Interesting Insights
Bozgeyikli et al. (2018) [45]	Scene in virtual warehouse with a realistic appearance, the user asked to go without colliding obstacles	- Interface comp: Avatar - Interface attribute: Instruction methods, Visual fidelity, View zoom, Clutter, Motion	- Observation from observer - Self-report questionnaire/survey - Questionnaire is processed using ANOVA, Mauchly sphericity test	- Variables measured: user experience, presence, motion sickness, user comment	To use animated instructions and avoid verbal instructions, use low visual fidelity and standard view zoom, and use no clutter and no motion in VR training application for HF ASD
Bozgeyikli et al. (2016) [41]	Scene in virtual warehouse with a realistic appearance, user asked to go without colliding obstacles	- Interface comp: Avatar - 3D interaction: -- 3 commonly used: redirected walking, walk-in-place, joystick, -- 2 unexplored techniques: stepper machine, point & teleport -- 3 selected techniques for ASD: flying, flapping, and trackball	- Observation from observer - Self-report questionnaire/survey (Likert scale) - Questionnaire is processed using ANOVA, Mauchly sphericity test	- Variables measured: ease of understanding, ease of operating, required effort, tiredness, being in control, enjoyment, being overwhelmed and frustrated, motion sickness, and presence	- Joystick, point & teleport, redirected walking, and walk-in place are suitable for VR locomotion techniques - Hand gesture-based and automatic movement locomotion are not convenient for HD ASD
Mei et al. (2015) [42]	Game: Imagination soccer (Hand-eye coordination)	- Interface comp: Customizable Virtual Human (CVH) & NonCVH	- Self-report questionnaire/survey - Question set using PIFF2 and Likert scale	- Variables measured: task success rate, user experience (presence, involvement, and flow)	- CVH can increase hand-eye-coordination performance - CVH improved the UX (presence, involvement, and flow) of ASD users
Nuguri et al. (2021) [35]	Social scenario in Orientation Day; recognizing facial expressions, sharing ideas, turn-taking in conversations	- Interface comp: Scenes, bubbles, pop-up boxes, status bars - 3D Interaction: Locomotion (teleportation in VR)	- Self-report questionnaire/survey (using SUS) - Observation from observer towards the app - Observation from observer towards user's real-time brain signals	- Variables measured: immersiveness, frustration, engagement, task completion	- Teleportation in VR is preferred than moving with a mouse & keyboard - VR is preferred than desktop - Network speed affects the satisfaction of UX

(continued)

(*continued*)

Author, Year	Intervention/Therapy/Treatment	User interface/Interaction technique	UX Evaluation Method	Output/Variable Measured	Interesting Insights
Mei et al. (2018) [32]	Game: Imagination soccer (Hand-eye coordination)	- Interface comp: Scenes, avatar (CVH)	- Eye-gaze logging - Paired t-test (CVH-NCVH comparison) using Bonferroni correction	Variable measured: Total acquired joint, time gazing at Regions of interest (ROI)	- Including CVH results on slower reaction to do the joint attention request - CVH helps ASD to gaze less at unimportant areas
Zhao et al. (2016) [54]	Puzzle game, collection game, and delivery game	- 3D Interaction: Object manipulation (hold, move, and drop)	- Participants fill a questionnaire/survey	Variable measured: user experience, task performance	- Participants are engaged and motivated to play well - Not really adapted to use Leap Motion device
Finkelstein et al. (2013) [43]	Game with physical activity; - Dodging, ducking, jumping - Collecting points	- Interface comp: Scene - 3D Interaction: Full-body movement	- Self-report questionnaire/survey - Observation from observer	Variables measured: demographic, total energy burnt, user experience (enjoyment, replayability, amount of exercise, preference)	- Two non-verbal participants cannot provide feedback; some participants received parental assistance in filling questionnaire - Participants show more interest in familiar themes
Schmidt et al. (2019) [55]	Training to use public transportation (Applied Behavior Analysis + immersive technologies + special education curriculum)	- Interface comp: Scene	- Observation from observer. Direct interview to participant - Self-report questionnaire/survey (SUS) - Cluster semantics coding categories using affinity mapping techniques	Output: Affect (joy/fun/excitement, willingness to return), Accessibility (physical, cognitive, cybersickness), General (usefulness, realism, real-world connections)	The qualitative codes categorization (on output) and operationalizations
Bernardes et al. (2015) [38]	Traveling training; validating the ticket, sitting in the right place, pressing the stop button	- Interface comp: Scene	- Concurrent Think Aloud (CTA) - Task performance (completion time)	Variables measured: Technology acceptance, interface comprehension, task performance	- ASD group takes longer on finishing the task compared to the control group (TD) - Serious game intervention is needed

(*continued*)

(continued)

Author, Year	Intervention/Therapy/Treatment	User interface/Interaction technique	UX Evaluation Method	Output/Variable Measured	Interesting Insights
Kuriakose et al. (2012) [36]	Bidirectional social conversation	- Interface comp: Scene, Avatar	- Observation from observer towards user performance - Observation from observer towards physiological response (Heart Rate and Skin Temperature)	Variables measured: affective states (engagement and likeness) through physiological features (HR & SKT)	- The use of wired physiological sensors possibly induces additional anxiety factors and limiting the user's movement freedom
Halabi et al. (2017) [44]	Conversation (Role-play and turn-taking)	- Interface comp: Scene, Avatar - Interaction: Verbal response (speech recognition), waving (gesture recognition)	- Self-report questionnaire/survey	- Variables measured: voice and physical motion, time in task completion	- Level of immersion: CAVE > HMD > Desktop - The most liked display method: CAVE
Lahiri et al. (2012) [33]	Bidirectional social conversation	- Interface comp: Scene, 3D Avatar - Interaction: mouse	- Observation from observer - Physiological signal acquisition	- Variables measured: ROI (face, context-relevant objects, and other) and attention duration	This system provides feedback based on quantitative measurement of user's performance and viewing pattern
Lahiri et al. (2011) [34]	Bidirectional social conversation	- Interface comp: Scene, Avatar	- Observation from observer - Physiological signal acquisition	Variables measured: Physiological data and Affective states (anxiety, enjoyment, and engagement of participants)	The system can predict user's affective states from objective measures (physiological signals)

References

1. Kail, R.V.: Children and Their Development, 6th edn. Pearson, Upper Saddle River (2011)
2. Kapp, K.M.: The Gamification of Learning and Instruction. John Wiley & Sons, Nashville (2012)
3. Leekam, S.R., Nieto, C., Libby, S.J., Wing, L., Gould, J.: Describing the sensory abnormalities of children and adults with autism. J. Autism Dev. Disord. **37**(5), 894–910 (2007). https://doi.org/10.1007/s10803-006-0218-7
4. Bozgeyikli, L., Raij, A., Katkoori, S., Alqasemi, R.: A survey on virtual reality for individuals with autism spectrum disorder: design considerations. IEEE Trans. Learn. Technol. **11**(2), 133–151 (2018)
5. Valencia, K., Rusu, C., Quiñones, D., Jamet, E.: The impact of technology on people with autism spectrum disorder: a systematic literature review. Sensors (Basel) **19**(20), 4485 (2019)
6. Mesa-Gresa, P., Gil-Gómez, H., Lozano-Quilis, J.-A., Gil-Gómez, J.-A.: Effectiveness of virtual reality for children and adolescents with autism spectrum disorder: an evidence-based systematic review. Sensors (Basel) **18**(8), 2486 (2018)
7. Glaser, N., Schmidt, M.: Systematic literature review of virtual reality intervention design patterns for individuals with autism spectrum disorders. Int. J. Hum. Comput. Interact. **38**, 1–36 (2021)
8. Yuan, Y., Hunt, R.H.: Systematic reviews: the good, the bad and the ugly. Am. J. Gastroenterol. **104**(5), 1086–1092 (2009)
9. Merriam-Webster: Virtual reality definition' (2022). www.merriam-webster.com/dictionary/virtual%20reality. Accessed 13 Mar 2022
10. Steuer, J.: Defining virtual reality: dimensions determining telepresence. J. Commun. **42**(4), 73–93 (1992)
11. Brooks, F.P.: What's real about virtual reality? IEEE Comput. Graph. Appl. **19**(6), 16–27 (1999)
12. Berg, L.P., Vance, J.M.: Industry use of virtual reality in product design and manufacturing: a survey. Virtual Reality **21**(1), 1–17 (2016). https://doi.org/10.1007/s10055-016-0293-9
13. Branda, E.: Review: oculus rift. J. Soc. Archit. Hist. **74**(4), 526–528 (2015)
14. Milgram, P., Kishino, F.: A taxonomy of mixed reality visual displays. In: IEICE Transactions on Information Systems, vol. E77-D, no.12, pp. 1321–1329 (1994)
15. Cruz-Neira, C., Sandin, D.J., DeFanti, T.A., Kenyon, R.V., Hart, J.C.: The CAVE: audio visual experience automatic virtual environment. Commun. ACM **35**(6), 64–72 (1992)
16. Vargas Gonzalez, A.N., Kapalo, K., Koh, S., LaViola, J.: Exploring the virtuality continuum for complex rule-set education in the context of soccer rule comprehension. Multimodal Technol. Interact. **1**(4), 30 (2017)
17. Diaz, D., Boj, C., Portalés, C.: HybridPLAY: a new technology to foster outdoors physical activity, verbal communication and teamwork. Sensors (Basel) **16**(4), 586 (2016)
18. Oyelere, S.S., Bouali, N., Kaliisa, R., Obaido, G., Yunusa, A.A., Jimoh, E.R.: Exploring the trends of educational virtual reality games: a systematic review of empirical studies. Smart Learn. Environ. **7**(1), 1–22 (2020). https://doi.org/10.1186/s40561-020-00142-7
19. Chan, J.C.P., Leung, H., Tang, J.K.T., Komura, T.: A virtual reality dance training system using motion capture technology. IEEE Trans. Learn. Technol. **4**(2), 187–195 (2011)
20. Lee, S.: A showcase of medical, therapeutic and pastime uses of virtual Reality (VR) and how VR is impacting the dementia sector. Adv. Exp. Med. Biol. **1156**, 135–141 (2019)
21. Leeb, R., Pérez-Marcos, D.: Brain-computer interfaces and virtual reality for neurorehabilitation. Handb. Clin. Neurol. **168**, 183–197 (2020)

22. van Bennekom, M.J., de Koning, P.P., Gevonden, M.J., Kasanmoentalib, M.S., Denys, D.: A virtual reality game to assess OCD symptoms. Front. Psychiatry **11**, 550165 (2020)
23. ISO, ISO 9241-11:2018: Ergonomics of, human-system interaction—Part 11: Usability: Definitions and concepts. pub-ISO:adr: pub-ISO (2018)
24. Norman, D., Nielsen, J.: The definition of user experience (UX) (2022). https://www.nngroup.com/articles/definition-user-experience/. Accessed 13 Mar 2022
25. Moher, D., Liberati, A., Tetzlaff, J., Altman, D.G., PRISMA Group: Preferred reporting items for systematic reviews and meta-analyses: the PRISMA statement. PLoS Med. **6**(7), e1000097 (2009)
26. Dimensions: Dimensions (2022). https://www.dimensions.ai/. Accessed 28 Mar 2022
27. I. Xplore: About IEEE Xplore (2022). https://ieeexplore.ieee.org/Xplorehelp/overview-of-ieee-xplore/about-ieee-xplore. Accessed 28 Mar 2022
28. P. NCBI: PubMed.gov (2022). https://pubmed.ncbi.nlm.nih.gov/.Accessed 28 Mar 2022
29. Stern, C., Jordan, Z., McArthur, A.: Developing the review question and inclusion criteria. Am. J. Nurs. **114**(4), 53–56 (2014)
30. Ravindran, V., Osgood, M., Sazawal, V., Solorzano, R., Turnacioglu, S.: Virtual reality support for joint attention using the floreo Joint attention module: usability and feasibility pilot study. JMIR Pediatr. Parent. **2**(2), e14429 (2019)
31. Feng, S., et al.: The uncanny valley effect in typically developing children and its absence in children with autism spectrum disorders. PLoS ONE **13**(11), e0206343 (2018)
32. Mei, C., Zahed, B.T., Mason, L., Ouarles, J.: Towards joint attention training for children with ASD - a VR game approach and eye gaze exploration. In: 2018 IEEE Conference on Virtual Reality and 3D User Interfaces (VR), Reutlingen, March 2018
33. Lahiri, U., Trewyn, A., Warren, Z., Sarkar, N.: Dynamic eye gaze and its potential in Virtual Reality based applications for children with autism spectrum disorders. Autism Open Access **1**(1) (2011)
34. Lahiri, U., Welch, K.C., Warren, Z., Sarkar, N.: Understanding psychophysiological response to a Virtual Reality-based social communication system for children with ASD. In: 2011 International Conference on Virtual Rehabilitation, Zurich, Switzerland, June 2011
35. Nuguri, S.S., et al.: vSocial: a cloud-based system for social virtual reality learning environment applications in special education. Multimed. Tools Appl. **80**(11), 16827–16856 (2020). https://doi.org/10.1007/s11042-020-09051-w
36. Kuriakose, S., Sarkar, N., Lahiri, U.: A step towards an intelligent human computer interaction: physiology-based affect-recognizer. In: 2012 4th International Conference on Intelligent Human Computer Interaction (IHCI), Kharagpur, India, December 2012
37. Di Mascio, T., Tarantino, L., De Gasperis, G., Pino, C.: Immersive virtual environments: a comparison of mixed reality and virtual reality headsets for ASD treatment. In: Gennari, R., et al. (eds.) Methodologies and Intelligent Systems for Technology Enhanced Learning, 9th International Conference, pp. 153–163. Springer, Cham (2020). https://doi.org/10.1007/978-3-030-23990-9_19
38. Bernardes, M., Barros, F., Simoes, M., Castelo-Branco, M.: A serious game with virtual reality for travel training with Autism Spectrum Disorder. In: 2015 International Conference on Virtual Rehabilitation (ICVR), Valencia, Spain, June 2015
39. Bozgeyikli, E., Bozgeyikli, L., Raij, A., Katkoori, S., Alqasemi, R., Dubey, R.: Virtual reality interaction techniques for individuals with autism spectrum disorder: design considerations and preliminary results. In: Kurosu, M. (ed.) HCI 2016. LNCS, vol. 9732, pp. 127–137. Springer, Cham (2016). https://doi.org/10.1007/978-3-319-39516-6_12

40. Bozgeyikli, E., Bozgeyikli, L.L., Alqasemi, R., Raij, A., Katkoori, S., Dubey, R.: Virtual reality interaction techniques for individuals with autism spectrum disorder. In: Antona, M., Stephanidis, C. (eds.) UAHCI 2018. LNCS, vol. 10908, pp. 58–77. Springer, Cham (2018). https://doi.org/10.1007/978-3-319-92052-8_6
41. Bozgeyikli, E., Raij, A., Katkoori, S., Dubey, R.: Locomotion in virtual reality for individuals with autism spectrum disorder. In: Proceedings of the 2016 Symposium on Spatial User Interaction, New York, NY, USA, October 2016
42. Mei, C., Mason, L., Quarles, J.: "I Built It!"—Exploring the effects of customizable virtual humans on adolescents with ASD. In: 2015 IEEE Virtual Reality (VR), Arles, Camargue, Provence, France, March 2015
43. Finkelstein, S., Barnes, T., Wartell, Z., Suma, E.A.: Evaluation of the exertion and motivation factors of a virtual reality exercise game for children with autism. In: 2013 1st Workshop on Virtual and Augmented Assistive Technology (VAAT), Lake Buena Vista, FL, USA, March 2013
44. Halabi, O., Abou El-Seoud, S., Alja'am, J., Alpona, H., Al-Hemadi, M., Al-Hassan, D.: Design of immersive virtual reality system to improve communication skills in individuals with autism. Int. J. Emerg. Technol. Learn. **12**(05), 50 (2017)
45. Bozgeyikli, L.L., Bozgeyikli, E., Katkoori, S., Raij, A., Alqasemi, R.: Effects of virtual reality properties on user experience of individuals with autism'. ACM Trans. Access. Comput. **11**(4), 1–27 (2018)
46. Pearl, A.M., Edwards, E.M., Murray, M.J.: Comparison of self-and other-report of symptoms of autism and comorbid psychopathology in adults with autism spectrum disorder. Contemp. Behav. Health Care **2**(1), 1–8 (2017)
47. Newbutt, N., Sung, C., Kuo, H.-J., Leahy, M.J., Lin, C.-C., Tong, B.: Brief report: a pilot study of the use of a virtual reality headset in autism populations. J. Autism Dev. Disord. **46**(9), 3166–3176 (2016). https://doi.org/10.1007/s10803-016-2830-5
48. Li, C., Ip, H.H.S., Ma, P.K.: A design framework of virtual reality enabled experiential learning for children with autism spectrum disorder. In: Cheung, S.K.S., Lee, L.-K., Simonova, I., Kozel, T., Kwok, L.-F. (eds.) Blended Learning: Educational Innovation for Personalized Learning: 12th International Conference, ICBL 2019, Hradec Kralove, Czech Republic, July 2–4, 2019, Proceedings, pp. 93–102. Springer, Cham (2019). https://doi.org/10.1007/978-3-030-21562-0_8
49. Junaidi, A.R., Alamsyah, Y., Hidayah, O., Mulyawati, N.W.: Development of virtual reality content to improve social skills in children with low function autism. In: 2020 6th International Conference on Education and Technology (ICET), Malang, Indonesia, October 2020
50. Malihi, M., Nguyen, J., Cardy, R.E., Eldon, S., Petta, C., Kushki, A.: Data-driven discovery of predictors of virtual reality safety and sense of presence for children with autism spectrum disorder: a pilot study. Front. Psychiatry **11**, 669 (2020)
51. Newbutt, N., Bradley, R., Conley, I.: Using virtual reality head-mounted displays in schools with autistic children: views, experiences, and future directions. Cyberpsychol. Behav. Soc. Netw. **23**(1), 23–33 (2020)
52. De Luca, R., et al.: Innovative use of virtual reality in autism spectrum disorder: a case-study. Appl. Neuropsychol. Child **10**(1), 90–100 (2021)
53. Schmidt, M., Schmidt, C., Glaser, N., Beck, D., Lim, M., Palmer, H.: Evaluation of a spherical video-based virtual reality intervention designed to teach adaptive skills for adults with autism: a preliminary report. Interact. Learn. Environ. **29**(3), 345–364 (2021)

54. Zhao, H., Swanson, A., Weitlauf, A., Warren, Z., Sarkar, N.: A novel collaborative virtual reality game for children with ASD to foster social interaction. In: Antona, M., Stephanidis, C. (eds.) Universal Access in Human-Computer Interaction. Users and Context Diversity: 10th International Conference, UAHCI 2016, Held as Part of HCI International 2016, Toronto, ON, Canada, July 17-22, 2016, Proceedings, Part III, pp. 276–288. Springer, Cham (2016). https://doi.org/10.1007/978-3-319-40238-3_27
55. Schmidt, M., Beck, D., Glaser, N., Schmidt, C., Abdeen, F.: Formative design and evaluation of an immersive learning intervention for adults with autism: design and research implications. In: Beck, D., et al. (eds.) Immersive Learning Research Network: 5th International Conference, iLRN 2019, London, UK, June 23–27, 2019, Proceedings, pp. 71–85. Springer, Cham (2019). https://doi.org/10.1007/978-3-030-23089-0_6

A Tool to Assess the Attention of Children with Autism Spectrum Disorder (ASD): from Design to Evaluation

Zied El Houki(✉), Dena Al Thani, Belikis Banire, Marwa Qaraqe, and Maryam Aziz

College of Science and Engineering, Hamad Bin Khalifa University, Ar-Rayyan, Qatar
zelhouki@hbku.edu.qa

Abstract. According to recent studies, good learning implies paying attention, which is crucial for each child, especially for those with autism spectrum disorder (ASD) who are known to usually experience attention deficit. Basically, the attention deficit has caused concerns among stakeholders (teachers and parents) regarding their academic achievements. Due to the importance and relevance of attention in productive and personalized learning, many research have studied the different technologies present nowadays that help to assess the attention. In this work, we present a tool that automatically detect attention for children with ASD when viewing learning materials online. Additionally, the process of developing a user-friendly platform is important. Thus, this paper presents the design, the development, and the evaluation phases of the interface. The latter was done using the Heuristic method of Nielsen and the System Usability Scale (SUS).

Keywords: Autism · Autism Spectrum Disorder · Usability · Heuristic evaluation · System Usability Scale

1 Introduction

Autism Spectrum Disorder (ASD) is a neurodevelopmental disorder characterized by a deficit in social communications and repetitive patterns of behavior [1]. According to reports from the Center of Disease Control and Prevention (CDC) of the United States, the frequency of this disorder is high and has been increased from 1 in 110 children in the year 2000 to 1 in 54 children in the year 2020 [2]. Among the unusual patterns of behaviors exhibited by the children with ASD, are the attentional behaviors, such as problems in preserving attention which is a fundamental element in ensuring good learning outcomes, especially for children with ASD. In fact, the lack of this attention increases the concerns between the different stakeholders (such as parents and teachers) about their academic achievements [3].

Despite the prevalence of this disorder, there are no known treatments for the symptoms of ASD yet, however, education can provide important support for children which ASD and can serve as a relative cure for their deficit [4]. Therefore, several studies have explored multiple technologies for educational and behavioral interventions. Children

M. Antona and C. Stephanidis (Eds.): HCII 2023, LNCS 14020, pp. 569–580, 2023.
https://doi.org/10.1007/978-3-031-35681-0_37

with ASD are characterized by attention deficit, and they exhibit a range of attentional behaviors due to heterogeneity in the spectrum. The current state-of-the-art of engagement assessment in ASD is through subjective methods, which require a long year of experience [5]. Our previous review shows that researchers often focus on how technology innovations can improve the engagement level of children with ASD, but the application of this technology for engagement assessment is still in its infancy [6–18]. The method that is commonly applied is based on subjective evaluation, which requires high expertise and time-consuming. However, few studies have explored the objective assessment of engagement level during learning by utilizing existing sensing technologies for typically developing individuals [7]. The few existing engagement assessments are based on generalized attention, which is not suitable for children with ASD due to their heterogeneity. Our recent experimental study with children with ASD shows the potential of sensing technologies such as face tracking using artificial intelligence (AI) in assessing the engagement level of children with ASD [4]. A web-based application has been developed using sensing technologies and AI to detect visual, auditory and social attention. Also, the engagement assessment can be used remotely than in-person, which is essential for the unprecedented online learning due to the Covid-19 pandemic and beyond. The engagement assessment platform generates personalized student reports after each learning session. Similarly, the platform will record the facial and gaze movement of the users using a webcam that relies on a frame-to-frame analysis during the learning process. Webcam is generally ubiquitous with mobile devices and cheap to purchase—the data collected during the attention task in a secured server. Using webcam will also support the remote setting approach undertaken in this research. The aim is for this platform to be used by teachers, specialists, and parents. Therefore, it is important for such a platform to be easy to use.

Also, it is important that this type of platforms that are used in education to be developed in a proper and effective way through taking in consideration the usability aspects. The aim of this paper is to present the platform design and development phases, and to discuss the evaluation phase that took place with experts in heuristic evaluation.

2 Importance of Attention in the Current Context

The currently available technological solution for children with ASD is frequently centered on basic deficiencies such as speech and social interaction; yet there are very few research that study how these children pay attention [8]. Some parents of children with ASD have reached the conclusion that the underlying reason of their children's core deficits is an attention impairment. Atypical attention is one of the core deficits that characterize children with ASD [8]. Because of this, attention evaluation becomes the first and most important step in the process of developing any kind of learning intervention for children who have autism spectrum disorder (ASD). In addition, attention assessment offers answers coming from two distinct points of view. One of these is the fact that attention evaluation determines the efficiency of any learning intervention and how well children with ASD adapt to it [9]. The assessment of an individual's level of attention to the intervention to develop adaptive learning is the other perspective. Adaptive learning is vital for supporting the cognitive ability of children who have autism spectrum disorder (ASD) [10].

3 Usability in the Context of Web-Application

The development of the internet and new technologies in the last two decades has contributed to a new era of education, and it's important that these new interfaces must be well designed and effectively evaluated in a proper way. Usability is a key issue in HCI since it is the aspect of the quality of the user interface [11]. The International Standards Organization (ISO-9241) [12] defines usability as: "the extent to which a product can be used by specified users to achieve specified goals with effectiveness, efficiency and satisfaction in a specified context".

4 Methodology

4.1 Pre-study

This study was initiated by conducting a semi-structured interview with seventeen experts from different professions to have an overview about the attention of children with ASD during learning activities [4]. For this, a purposive sample was used to recruit the participants [13] from different ASD specialties to guarantee the triangulations of the data sources. The participants consisted of a special educationist, speech-language pathologist, psychologist, occupational therapist, behavioral specialist, faculty members of ICT-ASD and parents, in order to obtain an overview of the attention of children with ASD during the learning activities. The use of theme analysis was necessary in order to determine the primary considerations that went into the development of the attention evaluation tool. The nature of attention, tactics for getting attention, attentional behaviors, and quantifying attention level are the five primary themes that emerged as key factors for objective attention assessment in children with ASD. According to the findings, taking into account parallel attentional behaviors provides an improved paradigm for the creation of an attention evaluation system for children with ASD.

4.2 System Architecture

The objectives of this research are to develop an objective engagement assessment.

using machine learning models to detect the attention and engagement level of children with ASD in a lab setting, as well as to provide generated reports on engagement level of the child which can be interpreted by the teacher. The engagement assessment platform will consist of teachers and parents' views. The teacher can sign in with the credentials to assess their student's engagement level during learning. The platform uses a novel and intelligent approach for personalized engagement assessment using an integrated webcam for face and eye-tracking, as illustrated in Fig. 1. The application will be presented in four modules. In the first one, we present attention tasks for the initial calibration of personalized behavior during learning engagement. The attention task consists of target stimuli (social, nonsocial and auditory) simulating typical classroom distractions such as social, nonsocial, audio and audiovisual distractions. The distraction levels will be two different levels (baseline and hard) to capture the degree of the engagement level of each user. The second module will consist of feature extraction from facial and gaze features during the attention task to train the machine learning model. The third module consists of machine learning models to detect when the user pays attention to the target stimuli in the attention task and when they are inattentive. In the fourth module, the personalized attentional model developed will be used to assess their engagement level in other learning tasks, which can be interpreted by the teacher or parents as depicted in Fig. 2 illustrating overall attention, visual attention, auditory attention, and social attention.

Three different forms of visual results are also generated. The first one, presented in Fig. 2 is the 'Attention Frequency' result that displays a bar chart which shows the count of inattention and attention measured through the activity. The second result, presented in Fig. 3, is the 'Attention with time' result which displays a scatter plot that shows the child's attention span with time. The third result, presented in Fig. 4, is the 'Attention Gaze' result that shows a video of the heatmap of the child's gaze which can be used by the teacher to determine the points of interest of the child during the entire activity.

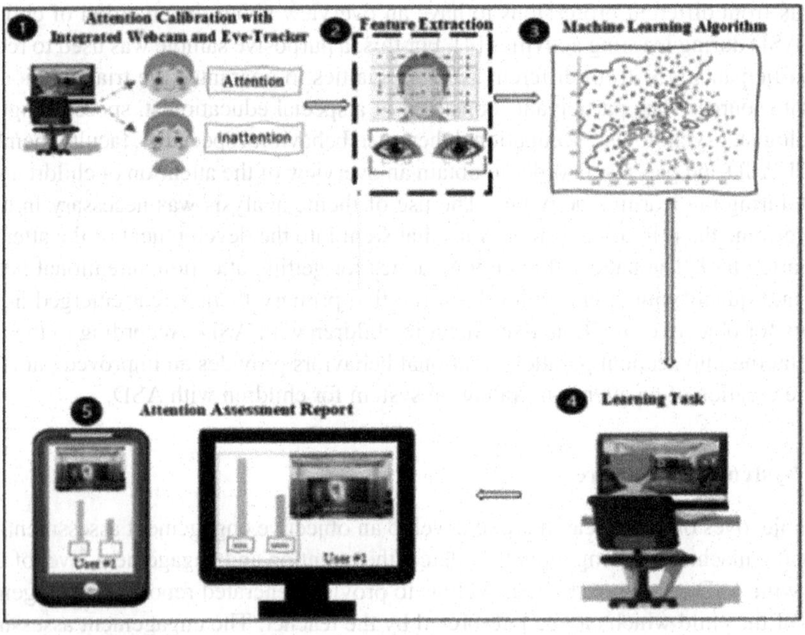

Fig. 1. Methodology describing the five modules of the application.

For the parents, they can add their children to the platform and assist them in performing the activities. For the students' view, they are able to access the learning materials uploaded by the teacher. The webcam is be used to conduct face and eye calibration before starting the activity. This calibration provides accurate data related to the engagement level on areas of interest (AOIs) on the material as well as the facial expression of the student, which could detect engagement or boredom. The platform development undergoes an iterative prototyping process to achieve the desired design. In addition, its architecture is scalable to adapt new content for different subject to make it accessible to individuals with and without special needs.

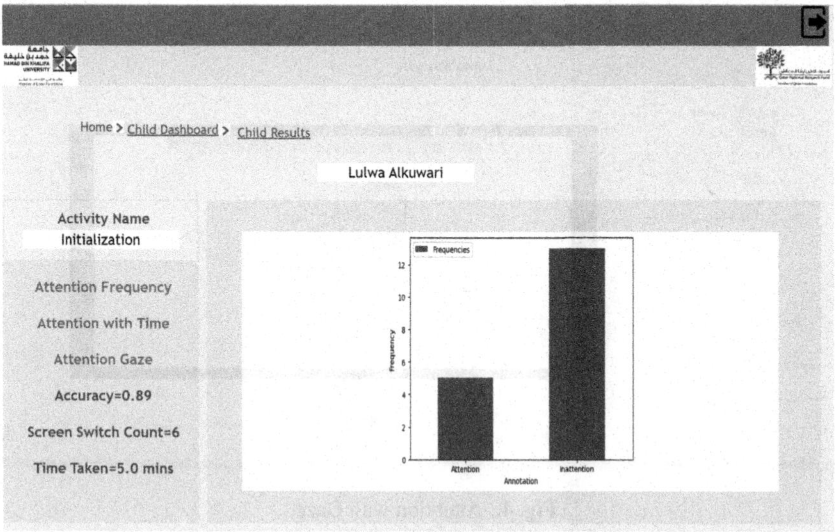

Fig. 2. Attention frequency.

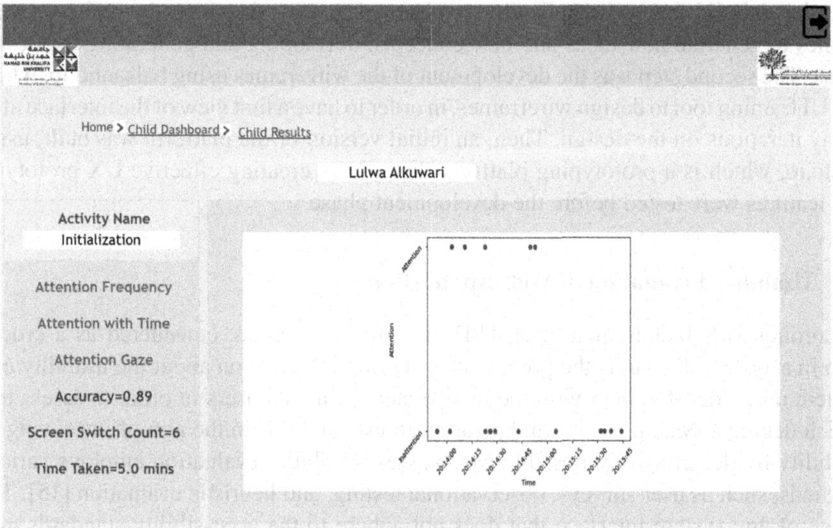

Fig. 3. Attention with time.

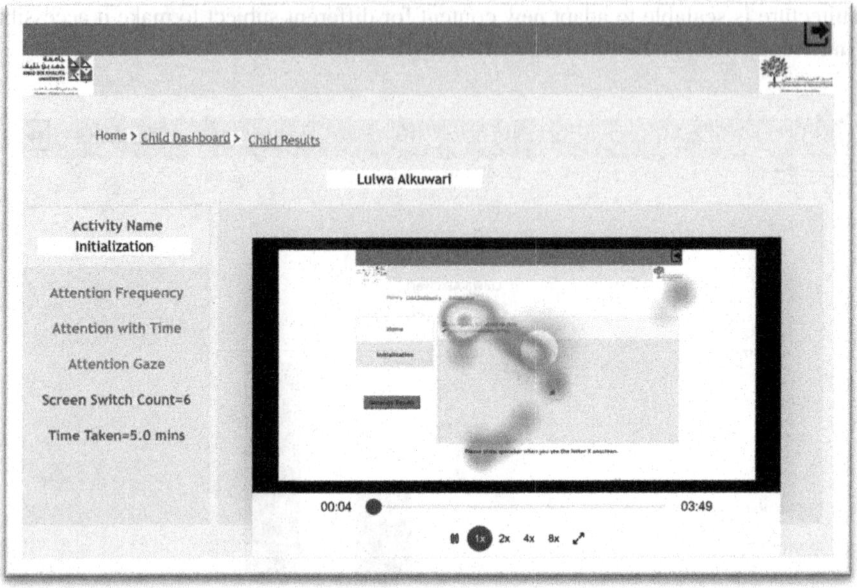

Fig. 4. Attention with Gaze.

4.3 Prototype Design

In order to build this web application, we started first by sketching the different wireframes to generate new ideas and new concepts, developing and generating the design ideas. The second step was the development of the wireframes using balsamiq.io, which is a UI framing tool to design wireframes, in order to have a first view of the interface after many iterations on the design. Then, an initial version of the platform was built, using proto.io, which is a prototyping platform that allows creating effective UX prototype. All features were tested before the development phase.

4.4 Usability Evaluation of Web-Application

According to Schneiderman et al. [14], usability evaluation, considered as a crucial step in a system design, is the process of gathering information about the usability of a system under development with the involvement of actual users in order to assess to a which degree a system is easy and pleasant to use, and this in the aim of improving its usability by detecting any possible weaknesses. Usability evaluation employs various methods, such as user surveys, observational testing, and heuristic evaluation [15]. The usage of any system interface that does not adhere to the accessibility standards may be difficult for people with impairments. The World Wide Web Consortium's (W3C) Accessibility Initiative (WAI) [20] has published several recommendations, including the Web Content Accessibility Guidelines.

The evaluation method employed in our study is the Heuristic Evaluation (HE) method, which was developed by Nielsen and Molich in 1990.

4.5 Heuristic Evaluation

Nielsen and Molich (1990) [16] devised an initial set of guidelines, which they referred to as heuristics, in order to determine whether or not all of the elements that are present in the interface adhere to the guidelines. These heuristics, often known as principles, are more like general rules of thumb than precise sets of directions to follow for usability. The first set had a total of nine different heuristics. In later years, Nielsen developed a set of ten heuristics [17] that were based on the work done on an individual level. The following is a list of these ten heuristics that were developed by Nielsen and Molich (1990):

1. Visibility of system status;
2. Match between system and real world;
3. User control and freedom;
4. Consistency and standards;
5. Error prevention;
6. Recognition rather than recall;
7. Flexibility and efficiency of use;
8. Aesthetic and minimalist design;
9. Help users recognize, diagnose, and recover from errors;
10. Help and documentation.

5 Study Design

5.1 Participants and Recruitment Process

According to Nielsen and Molich (1990) at least three to five evaluators could identify 75 per cent of the problems in a system. Four experts were invited to conduct the heuristic evaluation. For this purpose, we used an approach of convenience sampling which is known as a non-probabilistic sampling that refers to collecting data from conveniently available people [15]. Additionally, the data collection using such an approach to recruitment is not time consuming [16]. The invited participants were researchers, graduate students and had used the heuristics of Nielsen.

5.2 Study Protocol

The following protocol was used to conduct this study:

1. An email was sent to the evaluators. They were informed that the data collected will remain anonymous and there is no correct or false answer. They were requested to respond to the email and inform about their consent to be part of this study;
2. A Convenience sampling was used to easily recruit the participants;
3. The evaluation is carried online. Each participant received a link to the web interface and a survey as well as a brief description of the purpose of the evaluation and the usability heuristics. During the evaluation process, participants were asked to write down the number of the broken heuristic or guideline, a brief description of the problem, and their proposal to overcome the broken heuristic or guideline, with

severity ratings ranging from 0 to 4. The severity grade ranges from 0 to 4, with 0 representing "not a problem", 1 representing "cosmetic problem only", 2 representing "moderate", 3 representing "major" and 4 representing "usability catastrophe";
4. After the system had been explored and evaluated, the participants were sent a form that consist of the System Usability Scale [17], on which they were asked to explain their feelings regarding each of the ten statements that were made about the system. On a scale from 1 (strongly disagree) to 5, the criteria for assessing each point were based on how strongly you felt about it (strongly agree).

6 Data Analysis

To carry out the evaluation, two data sets were collected as part of the study: one related to the usability problems identified through the heuristic evaluation exercise in the web application while the second one is related to the responses collected from the SUS questionnaire.

Nielsen's heuristics evaluation [17] is a usability inspection method that uses predetermined criteria, which are based on Nielsen and Molich's experience with usability engineering and backed by research, to evaluate the usability of a system. It is a data-driven approach to discover usability issues, their sources, and the severity of their impacts. During heuristics evaluation, evaluators review a system and document any issues that violate the criteria.

The criteria are derived from ten usability principles based on the collective experience of usability professionals. They are divided into categories such as Visibility of System Status, Match Between System and the Real World, User Control and Freedom, and others. During the evaluation, the evaluator looks for issues that fall into each of these categories. If issues are found, they are documented in a report including the issue, level of severity and recommendations for improvement. Once the evaluation is complete, the report is used to help design a better product. In the context of this project, it is crucial to produce a system that works smoothly with the different stakeholders.

A system usability study questionnaire [17] is a document used to help evaluate the usability of computer systems, software, websites, and apps. The questionnaire is typically filled out by users of the system. It includes questions about how easy or difficult it is to use the system and the quality of the system's design. The answers from users can help identify areas for improvement. The questionnaire might also be used as part of a larger usability study, such as a focus group or usability test. According to Brook (1995) [17] the SUS questionnaire proposes a specific method that calculates the obtained results. To interpret the data, a simple formula of the number is applied. For the even statements q2, q4, q6, q8 and q10, we need to subtract 5. Then, for the statements q1, q3, q5, q7 and q9, we need to subtract 1. Then, we multiply the sum of the scores by 2.5 to obtain the overall value of SU. It's noted that SUS scores have a range of 0 to 100.

7 Results

According to Nielson, it is advised that at least three users take part in a heuristic evaluation in order to reveal 75% of the usability issues. As we have used a convenience sampling method, email invitations were sent to seven participants. However, only four of them accepted to perform the evaluation.

The results of this heuristic evaluation study are presented in the following subsections.

7.1 Demographic Information

The researcher, and the postgraduate who conduct research and evaluation in HCI or interface design experience were taken into consideration when selecting the experts who would participate in the project. They have the necessary work experience to conduct the heuristic evaluation, as they have worked in the field of interface and web design. Invitations were extended to seven eminent figures, only four of them have confirmed their attendance at this meeting.

The table below shows the demographic information of all the experts who participated in the study (Table 1).

Table1. Demographic information of all the experts who participated in the study.

Participant	Gender	Highest degree	Employment status	Level of HCI
Expert 1	Male	Master	PHD student	Proficient
Expert 2	Female	Master	Employed	Proficient
Expert 3	Female	Master	PHD student	Expert
Expert 4	Female	Bachelor	Master student	Competent

*HCI: Human Computer Interaction.

7.2 Usability Problems

Figure 5 shows the usability problems and the average severity rating of the identified problems for each heuristic. The number of the identified problem for each heuristic is represented by the left axis, and the right axis represents the average severity ratings. The cumulative number of the 10 heuristics is 86, and each heuristic in usability heuristics is represented by a stacked column generated by Microsoft Excel, which represents the number of usability problems identified for one or more severity rating (from one to four) using multiple colors (green for cosmetic, light blue for minor, grey for major and red for catastrophe), and the line linking the different points represents the average severity ratings of all usability problems identified. The most commonly broken heuristics are visibility of system status, consistency and standards, and flexibility and efficiency of use (each has $N = 11$), followed by error prevention (each has $N = 10$). Some comments of the experts for the most frequently violated/broken heuristics are given in the table below (Table 2).

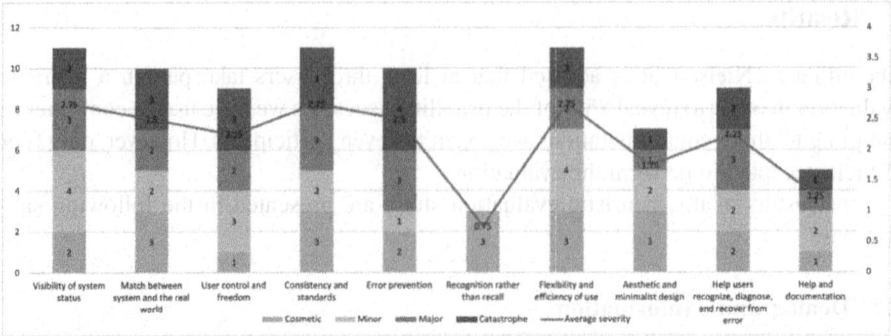

Fig. 5. Usability problems identified using the ten heuristics of Nielsen.

Table 2. Experts' comments based on Nielsen's heuristics.

Heuristic broken	Problem description	Severity rating
Visibility of system status	The tabs are not showing for me as centered in the screen, it is on the side of the screen and thus some tabs are not accessible	4
Aesthetic and minimalist design	The design is quite simple and straight forward, it is not complex nor chaotic	2
Consistency and Standards	Navigating the website through the keyboard (tabs and arrows) is not user-friendly. When adding a parent, the flow by using the tab button is email -> add button -> choose file -> upload button -> parent name. However, it should be: email - > parent name -> add button -> choose file -> upload button	3

7.3 System Usability Scale (SUS)

Table 3 shows the SUS for each participant for our web application following Brook's methods, it's noted that the SUS is ranged between 0 and 100, where higher score indicates a better usability.

According to the results in Table 3, we can observe that the scores are ranged between 55 and 82.5 with an average of 65. Sauro J [18] stipulates that there are multiple ways to analyze the SUS scores. These ways include percentiles, grades, adjectives, acceptability and promoters and detractors. In our study, we adopt the method of acceptability to interpret the scores in a way of what is "acceptable" and "inacceptable".

According to the grading score of Bangore et al. (2008) the average score of our web application is 65 which means that our web application is good but needs some improvements.

Table 3. System usability scale for each participant.

Participant ID	SUS score
1	62.5
2	55
3	60
4	82.5

8 Interface Enhancement

After generating the different results from the heuristic evaluation and the system usability scale, our interface needs some improvements in order to fulfil all the user needs, which include:

- The page size needs to be adjusted so that users can see all the content on the screen;
- The possibility of adding more options for the parents' view that enable the parent to access their child's individual page in order to track the performance;
- The option of creating a dashboard for each child in order to track the child's activity;
- The inclusion of a return button to home page on all pages
- The conformance of web accessibility standards;
- The Implementation of a confirmation step prior to proceeding through the application views to insure validity and correctness of the entered data.

9 Conclusion

This paper highlights the different steps used to design and to evaluate a web application designed for children with autism spectrum disorder, using the heuristic evaluation method of Nielsen, by measuring the usability problems that can affect the user experience. First, a prototype was designed to have an overview on how the features of this web application will be working. Then, after the development of this web application, a heuristic evaluation was conducted to detect the different usability problems. Suggestions to enhance the web application are then provided with an emphasis of making the interface ease to use to a variety of users. One of the main goals of this web application is to tell whether the child is attentive while performing learning activities.

Acknowledgement. "This contribution was made possible by Rapid Response Call cycle 2 Grant from the Qatar National Research Fund (a member of Qatar Foundation) under Grant RRC02-0706-210003. The statements made herein are solely the responsibility of the authors".

References

1. Patten, E., Watson, L.R.: Interventions targeting attention in young children with autism. Am. J. Speech-Lang. Pathol. **20**(1), 60–69 (2011)

2. Knopf, A.: Autism prevalence increases from 1 in 60 to 1 in 54: CDC. Brown University Child Adolescent Behavi. Lett. **36**, 4 (2020)
3. Eaves, L.C., Ho, H.H.: School placement and academic achievement in children with autistic spectrum disorders. J. Dev. Phys. Disabil. **9**, 277–291 (1997)
4. Banire, B., Al Thani, D., Qaraqe, M.: Informing the design of attention assessment system for children with autism spectrum disorder: a thematic analysis approach. In: International Conference on information and Communication Technology and Accessibility (ICTA), pp. 1–6 (2021)
5. Patten, E., Watson, L.R.: Interventions targeting attention in young children with autism
6. .Banir, B., et al.: Attention assessment: evaluation of facial expressions of children with autism spectrum disorder
7. Chen, et al.: Reflecting on, and planning to use learning resources improved performance in statistics among undergraduate students (2017)
8. Kerns, K.A., Macoun, S., MacSween, J., Pei, J., Hutchison, M.: Attention and working memory training: a feasibility study in children with neurodevelopmental disorders. Appl. Neuropsychol.-Child **6**(2), 120–137 (2017). https://doi.org/10.1080/21622965.2015.1109513
9. Kinnealey, M., Pfeiffer, B., Miller, J., Roan, C., Shoener, R., Ellner, M.L.: Effect of classroom modification on attention and engagement of students with autism or dyspraxia. Am. J. Occup. Ther. **66**(5), 511–519 (2012). https://doi.org/10.5014/ajot.2012.004010
10. Szafir, D., Mutlu, B.: Pay attention!: designing adaptive agents that monitor and improve user engagement. In: Proceedings of the SIGCHI Conference on Human Factors in Computing Systems (2012)
11. Parlangeli, O., Marchigiani, E., Bagnara, S.: Multimedia systems in distance education; effects of usability on learning. Interact. Comput. **12**(1), 37–49 (1999)
12. ISO 9241-210:2010 Ergonomics of human-system interaction- Part 210: Human-centered design for interactive systems
13. Tongo, M.D.C.: Purposive sampling as a tool for informant selection. Ethnobot. Res. Appl. **5**, 147–158 (2007)
14. Shneiderman, B., Plaisant, C., Cohen, M., Jacobs, S.: Designing the User Interface: Strategies for Effective Human-Computer Interaction. Pearson, London (2016)
15. Minocha, S., Sharp, H.: Learner-centered and evaluation of web-based e-learning environments. In: The 7th HCI Educators Workshop: Effective Teaching and Training in HCI. Preston, United Kingdom (2004)
16. Nielsen, J., Molich, R.: Heuristic evaluation of user interfaces. In: Proceedings of SIGCHI Conference on Human Factors Computing System Empowering People (CHI), pp. 249–256 (1990). J. Mankoff, A. K. Dey, G. H
17. Brook, J.: SUS – a quick and dirty usability scale. In: Jordan, P.W., Thomas, B., McClland, I.L., Weerdmeestrer, B. (eds.) Usability Evaluation in Industry, pp. 189–194. CRC Press, Boca Raton (1996)
18. Sauro, J., Lewis, J.R.: Chapter 8: Standardized usability questionnaire. In: Sauro J., Lewis, J.R., (eds.) Quantifying the User Experience, 2nd edn. pp 185–248. Morgan Kaufmann, Boston (2016)
19. Bangor, A., Kortum, T., Miller, J.: An empirical evaluation of the system usability scale, pp. 574–594 (2008)
20. W3C Web Accessibility Initiative [W3C WAI]: W3C-WAI (2023). https://www.w3.org/WAI/fundamentals/accessibility-intro/. Accessed 15 Jan 2023

Multimodal Interaction for Persons with Autism: The 5A Case Study

Mattia Gianotti, Alberto Patti(✉), Francesco Vona, Francesca Pentimalli, Jessica Barbieri, and Franca Garzotto

Politecnico di Milano, Piazza Leonardo da Vinci, 32, 20133 Milan, Italy
{mattia.gianotti,alberto.patti,francesco.vona, francesca.pentimalli,jessica.barbieri,franca.garzotto}@polimi.it
https://i3lab.polimi.it/

Abstract. Persons with Autism Spectrum Disorder (ASD) experience, in general, cognitive rigidity and behavioral and communication problems. These issues dramatically affect their everyday life abilities, such as interacting with others or being autonomous in most daily tasks. 5A project aims at supporting ASD individuals by exploiting the combination of Virtual Reality (VR), Augmented Reality (AR), and Conversational Agents (CA). Using low-cost headsets and smartphones, 5A offers a unique intervention for ASD people. The VR training allows the user to learn how to perform daily tasks in a safe and controlled environment. The AR experience enables the generalization of the acquired skills in real-world settings. Finally, the customizable CA assists and prompts the user at every step in both experiences. As a first use case for 5A applications, we report its use in urban mobility with trains. A case study evaluation was conducted, measuring the effect of 5A apps on 5 ASD users. Our preliminary results showed that users had improved their autonomy level (perceived and measured by external caregivers). The first lessons learned by this study are also reported as a set of guidelines about technology usage, design, and experimentation for immersive technologies in support of persons with ASD.

Keywords: Augmented Reality · Virtual Reality · Conversational Agents · Daily Living Skills · Autism Spectrum Disorder

1 Introduction

Autism Spectrum Disorders (ASD) is a broad group of neurodevelopmental disabilities that affects approximately 80 M persons (1% of the world population) [2]. ASD is characterized by different degrees of impairments in reciprocal social interactions, verbal and non-verbal communication, restricted interests, and repetitive patterns of behavior [2]. There are different severity degrees in ASD, leading to different levels of autonomy in everyday life activities. Interactive technologies have been receiving increasing attention for ASD treatments

M. Antona and C. Stephanidis (Eds.): HCII 2023, LNCS 14020, pp. 581–600, 2023.
https://doi.org/10.1007/978-3-031-35681-0_38

and interventions. They have been explored for a variety of purposes: to provide new assessment techniques for ASD, to support the development of specific social or cognitive skills, and to help persons in specific tasks [6,9,16,18,21]. Our research focused on the latter goal and is characterized by a novel multimodal approach in which different paradigms of interaction - Virtual Reality, Augmented Reality, and Conversational interaction - are smoothly integrated. In this paper, we exemplify the approach by presenting project 5A ("Autonomy for Autisms Achieved by means of virtual and Augmented reality and conversational Agents") as a case study. 5A has been designed and developed as a set of VR and AR applications for low-cost devices aimed at helping subjects with ASD become more autonomous in everyday life. Virtual Reality experiences are 3D interactive digital environments shown on head-mounted displays that provide a training space for the user to simulate specific tasks, e.g., related to the use of public transportation for urban mobility (Fig. 1 left). AR applications are meant to support the users in the autonomous execution - in the real world - of the same activities experienced in VR (e.g., "taking the metro"). This is achieved by showing interactive elements on the mobile phone - that appear superimposed on the view of the surrounding physical world to provide contextualized visual hints ("facilitators") during the activity (Fig. 1 right). Additionally, to provide a consistent "continuum" between the virtual and the real world, the "trans-media elements" are used in the experience. These are interactive digital elements that are present in both the VR and the AR applications, with the same visual properties and interaction features (Fig. 1 middle) to help persons with ASD to transpose what they learn in the simulated VR environment to the more complex and variegated space of the real world. Conversational interaction complements and enhances the traditional interaction paradigms and contents of wearable VR and mobile-phone-enabled AR. A customizable Conversational Agent embodied in a virtual character is integrated into all VR and AR applications and plays the role of user companion during the virtual or on-site experience. It provides individualized prompts, suggestions, and feedback in natural language (using text, speech, or both) to respond to explicit requests for help by the user and to support him/her at some crucial steps in the activity or when potentially problematic behaviors of the user are detected (e.g., the user does not perform any interaction for a long time). The paper discusses the design process adopted in 5A, the design and technology challenges induced by the need for strong coordination of the design of VR and AR experiences in terms of content and interactive behavior, the rationale of the solutions adopted, and the ongoing empirical evaluation, involving 20 young adults with ASD. Reported results involve only the 5 users who have completed the procedure so far. We also report the lessons learned in the project, which has been distilled into a set of design, technology, and evaluation guidelines for multimodal interactive applications that smoothly integrate VR, AR, and Conversational Interaction for ASD persons.

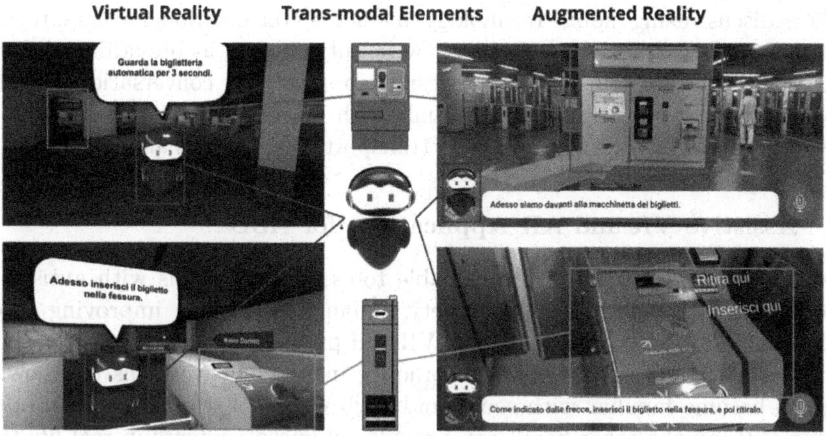

Fig. 1. On the left: two examples of the Virtual Reality experience in the subway scenario; in the middle: three examples of trans-modal elements: the ticket machine, the conversational agent, and the turnstile; on the right: two examples of Augmented Reality experience in the subway scenario

2 Related Work

Persons with autism often face various difficulties in urban mobility, such as sensory overload, routine changes, social interactions, difficulties with time management, and fear of running into unforeseen problems [15]. It's important to note that these difficulties can vary greatly from person to person and that some individuals with autism may have little or no difficulty navigating urban environments. Nevertheless, understanding the common challenges faced by individuals with autism can help cities and transportation providers design more inclusive and accessible systems that support everyone's mobility needs. To our knowledge, there are several examples in the literature showing how immersive technologies can support people with autism in these tasks, but 5A is the first use case where Virtual Reality, Augmented Reality, and Conversational Agents are integrated together to support these users in public transport scenarios.

2.1 Assistive Conversational Agents for ASD

Voice-based Conversational Agents (VCA) can support people with special needs by acting as their personal assistants. The use of VCAs by adolescents with ASD can help them manage their daily difficulties, from self-care to social interactions [7] to improve their independence and quality of live [11]. Examples can be found in the literature where VCAs assist individuals with autism in areas such as social skills training [19], communication skills development [20] and stress and anxiety management [13]. There were some attempts to support individuals with autism also in their urban mobility by providing real-time information, customized support, and improved access to transportation options. For example, in [7], the authors discuss using mobile technology, including conversational agents, to support independent travel for individuals with autism, such as providing guidance and support during trips. In [1], a design approach for conversational agents is presented that can support individuals with autism in their urban mobility, providing real-time information about transportation options and routing.

2.2 Assistive VR and AR Applications for ASD

The use of VR/AR can provide valuable tools for individuals with autism by improving social skills, reducing anxiety, enhancing learning, improving accessibility, and increasing independence. VR can provide virtual and safe environments where persons with ASD can practice in real-life situations by allowing them to become familiar with social and environmental stimuli in a controlled setting. AR, on the other hand, can provide enhanced contents in real life that can help individuals with autism to learn and understand complex information and concepts by improving motivation, attention, and the learning of new tasks [4] Many VR training applications have been created recently to instruct people with ASD how to use public transportation, such as buses and airplanes. In [5], for example, users can learn all the steps required to travel by bus, including arranging a route, waiting for the appropriate bus, selecting a seat, and determining when to stop to exit the vehicle. The applications of [12] and [14] instead focus on the plane scenario. In these experiences, 360 video simulations are used to explain to users how to take a flight. Each intervention is guided by a narrative script based on Social Stories, but users are unable to interact with the scene's objects and may only pause the video. In [17], ASD individuals can learn what to do in an airport by freely moving into the setting, engaging with the objects, and acting as they would in the real world. About Augmented Reality, there are a few examples in the literature regarding the help of ASD individuals in public transportation. The work of [10], who built a navigation app with visually-oriented navigation, is the most representative. It collects Google Street View photographs of a calculated path to identify unique locations connected with waypoints. Hence delivering a more human-centric and visually-oriented navigation application. No examples of VR or AR applications that assist ASD individuals in train or subway scenarios have been found.

3 The Design Process of 5A's Applications

The design of all 5A applications has been performed as a participatory process. Six ASD and neurodevelopmental disorder specialists (psychologists from 2 top-level care institutions in Italy) have worked with the development team on: i) the specification of the tasks to be simulated in VR and to be supported in AR; ii) the definition of the visual contents and the dialogues between the Conversational Agent and the user; iii) the expert-based usability evaluation of the progressive prototypes. The approach followed in each meeting was as follows: the psychologists were presented with concepts, helpful information, and prototypes/examples to provide them with a base knowledge of how they would interact with the applications. There was then a discussion of ideas and functionalities, each followed by an analysis of the feasibility and usability of the proposals, considering both technological complexity and end users' needs. Finally, the choices taken were implemented and shown during the next meeting. An exercise was also proposed to the therapists regarding the dialogues of the CA: each psychologist was given post-it notes of different colors, representing the user and the CA. S/He was free to develop the possible conversation flows in some situations. This was used to categorize the possible VCA replies (e.g., positive reinforcement and explanation of the tasks). For each category found, the therapists were then asked to provide us with multiple sentence instances to propose different options to the user. Following this approach, multiple focus groups were organized to define the requirements and functionalities of the different experiences. The final design choices made during the meetings with therapists are presented in Table 1.

4 The 5A Applications

We have created two different applications to create the environment of 5A training: the first application manages all Virtual Reality scenarios and VR tutorials. In contrast, the second manages all the AR scenarios and AR tutorials. This decision has been taken to avoid confusing the users between the two technologies and setups.

4.1 The VR Application

The VR application is an Android app developed through Unity Game Engine and Cardboard SDK designed to immerse the user into a digital replica of the world. To work correctly, the mobile phone must have access to the Internet and needs to be connected to a pair of headphones provided with a microphone to have a clear voice signal from the user (see Sect. 8 for further details), and a Bluetooth controller. The caregiver can then configure the application, place the device inside the visor and help the user wear the equipment. Throughout the experience, the user is seated on a swivel chair and what he sees is shown to the caregiver through a projector using a screen mirroring device (Fig. 2).

VR Tutorial. The tutorial part is designed to help the user practice the fundamental interactions to use the applications. It is divided into two parts: one is to exercise the interactions available in the space using the controller: look at things, select an item, pick it up, choose between items, and move in the space. Given our design constraints requiring low-cost visors, we had limited interactions.

- Gaze: The user must turn the head so that the center of the face is pointing towards the target object. The user then has to keep the position for five seconds to confirm the intention to act.

Table 1. Summary of codesign sessions

Codesign Session	Summary
Requirements	– The project should provide a linked experience to the user – The trans-media elements aid the link between experiences: objects that can create a link between concepts of the virtual worlds and the augmented/real one – The VR application represents the first step of the learning process, where the user can review the tasks in a safe and controlled environment – The AR application has no control over the natural environment and can only provide support during the execution of the tasks.
VR Application	– Slow and continuous movement was preferred over the teleport – Interaction with buttons was preferred to the gaze-and-dwell paradigm – Arrows and the "spotlight" (lowering the visibility of the environment other than the target element) were chosen to help the user
AR Application	– The device should be used in landscape mode – The VCA should occupy the bottom left corner of the screen together with the audio transcription – Pointing hands and arrows were chosen to help the user
VCA Dialogues	– The VCA should be proactive by prompting the user in case of no interaction or conversation – The VCA should talk using short sentences with simple and direct instructions – The VCA should provide positive reinforcement at the end of every completed task

- Select: The user must look at an interactable object (as through gaze) and then press on the controller's top buttons (any key is fine).
- Pick up: It is similar to the selection with the addition of a visual hint that the user will need his hand in real life to act (e.g., pick up a ticket from the stamp machine after validation).
- Choose: It is similar to the selection, but the user can choose between two or more alternatives to interact with (e.g., between two vending machines, select one to use).
- Move: In this interaction, the user has to move in the virtual space. As reported in Table 1, a continuous slow movement was implemented. The activation of the movement is given by looking at the target location and keeping the trigger on the controller pressed. While the conditions are met, the user moves slowly in a straight line at a constant speed otherwise the motion stops.

The second part of the tutorial instead focuses on the vocal interaction with the conversational agent. In this case, the VCA explains the type of vocal interactions recognized by the system (affirmative and negative responses, help requests, and exit requests). Then the VCA provides some questions, and the user has to use the sentence the VCA just provided (or a similar one) to show he comprehended the interaction.

Fig. 2. Render samples of the VR world (left) and the user playing (right)

Fig. 3. A user in the station framing the automatic vending machine.

VR Experience. The core of the VR app is the experience part. For the training in the train scenario, the user has to select the departing and arrival stations from a list, the type of payment (cash or credit card), and the number of intermediate stops. The experience takes place in a digital replica of a country train station specifically realized through 3D modeling from the blueprints and photos of a real example. We decided on this solution for two reasons: it is the kind of station most frequent in our territory (even if every station is unique in some aspects), and it was modeled over the station where the exploratory study will occur. Further developments may include the definition of different stations. The VCA guides the user in a step-by-step sequence of actions throughout all the tasks: from the street outside the station to the exit in the following station. The experience is subdivided into several steps, each using one of the interactions described previously. Table 2 report all the tasks and the interaction method required to continue in the experience. The VCA always listens to the user's vocalization so that s/he can always respond to the VCA's question, ask for help or exit the system. If the user does not interact with the system for some time, it prompts the user to ask if s/he needs help.

4.2 The AR Application

The AR application is a mobile app developed through Unity Game Engine that is designed to use the phone's camera intensively to retrieve contextual information and provide specific localized help. We used Vuforia SDK to recognize the different interaction points (automatic vending machine, timetable, stamp machine, platform) through 3d models and photos. However, given the difficulties due to illumination, reflection, poor details of the objects, and many others that will be discussed in Sect. 8, we needed to create some additional target images. Those images must be placed close to the interaction point. When the camera frames it, even if the recognition of the object fails, the images will be recognized, and the experience will continue transparently for the user (Fig. 3).

Table 2. Table of tasks in the VR experience.

Task	SubTask	Interaction
Task 1 - Reach the station's entrance	1.1 Find the entrance door	Gaze
	1.2 Select the entrance door	Select
	1.3 Reach the entrance	Move
Task 2 - Buy the Ticket	2.1 Find the vending machine	Gaze
	2.2 Choose one vending machine	Choose
	2.3 Reach the selected vending machine	Move
	2.4 - 2.11 Interact with the vending machine screen	Select
	2.12 Retrieve the ticket	Pick up
Task 3 - Find the platform	3.1 Find the timetable	Gaze
	3.2 Reach the timetable	Move
	3.3 Identify the train in the timetable	Select
	3.4 Identify the platform	Select

Task	SubTasks	Interaction
Task - 4 Stamp the ticket	4.1 Find the stamp machine	Gaze
	4.2 Reach the stamp machine	Move
	4.3 Insert the ticket	Select
	4.4 Pick up the ticket	Pick up
Task 5 - Reach the platform	5.1 Move to the door for the platforms	Move
	5.2 Identify the right platform sign	Select
	5.3 Move below the selected platform sign	Move
Task 6 - Use the train	6.1 Enter the train door	Move
	6.2 Exit the train door	Move
Task 7 - Exit the station	7.1 Move to the door to enter the station	Move
	7.2 Move to reach the exit door	Move

AR Tutorial. The AR tutorial is divided into two moments. The first part consists of a sequence of instructions correlated with explanatory images that gives information about the application's functionalities. In the second part, the user is invited to test the four actions available throughout the experience: frame an object, speak with the system, Use a quick-response button, and use the help button. The key interaction of the AR experience is to frame some objects, called interaction points. In the tutorial, we defined two images that will never appear in the experience. The user must learn to visualize the target completely on the screen. One key difference between the VR app and the AR app is the listening mode of the CA: while in VR, the environment is controlled and silent. The AR case is crowded, full of noises and other people talking. For this reason, the VCA is no longer always listening, but the user has to activate the microphone, press the activation button once, speak, and then press it again to end the recording. Context-dependent quick-response buttons have been added to let the user respond to the VCA's questions with the most common response available. Additionally, to reinforce the idea of the VCA helping the user, the picture of the VCA can be pressed to easily send a help request, making it a simple and intuitive interaction.

AR Experience. The experience, differently from the VR experience, does not follow a linear flow. We designed the application to respond to the interaction with any of the different interaction points during the experience. Whenever the system identifies an interaction point, it asks the user if s/he intends to interact with it. In case of a positive answer, the system verifies if all the mandatory previous steps had been completed; some steps may be automatically confirmed if the user has followed the system's instructions; otherwise, a confirmation is asked of the user directly from the VCA. If all the steps are confirmed, the user will be provided with specific help on interacting with an interaction point (e.g., which button to press on a screen in the automated vending machine). Otherwise, the VCA informs the user of the first step in the queue he had to do before interacting with that interaction point. If the user does not interact with the system for some time, it prompts the user to ask if s/he needs help.

4.3 Voice-Based Conversational Agent and Experience Control

The VR and AR applications are powerful "general purpose" systems. The VR app offers a set of predefined environments, a vocal interaction interface, a dialogue manager, and a set of available control. The AR app offers a general mechanism to recognize images, a vocal interface, and a dialogue manager. Nevertheless, the applications' backbone is the chatbot engine executed in the shared server. The application keeps sending information about the user's activity to the server through a secure WebSocket. Once decoded (directly from the message or with Speech-To-Text technology and Natural Language Processing in case of audio messages), the user interaction's intent is used to decide the response behavior of the system as a whole: triggering a response of the CA, an effect in VR or AR or a new step in the experience, or a combination of those.

5 The Case Study

We have conducted a case study involving 5 ASD young adults with the collaboration of clinical and therapeutic centers specializing in ASD and neurodevelopmental disorders The goal is to measure the usability, utility, and effect that VR and AR assisted by VCA technologies can have on ASD people in improving daily living skills, such as being able to use the train for interurban mobility. The ethical committee of Politecnico di Milano and the care centers approved the experimental protocol and authorized its execution.

Research Variables. We posed three research questions (RQ1, RQ2, and RQ3) and defined some research variables to evaluate them better. For each research variable, we indicate the collection tool used (Table 3).

To measure V1.1, V1.2, V1.3, and V1.4, we used a simplified version of SUS questionnaire [3] repeated four times, one for each of the experiences. To measure V2.1, we used a custom questionnaire. We decided to tailor the questionnaires to meet the capabilities of our target users. All the modifications to standard questionnaires had been performed following suggestions of the caregiver to maintain the inquired content of the questionnaire in a language our user can understand.

Table 3. Research questions, variables, and data collection methods associated.

Research Question	Research Variable	Data collection method
RQ 1] Usability: are the applications developed for 5A usable?	V1.1)] Usability of VR Tutorial	Questionnaire
	V1.2)] Usability of VR Experience	Questionnaire
	V1.3)] Usability of AR Tutorial	Questionnaire
	V1.4)] Usability of AR Experience	Questionnaire
RQ 2] Utility: did the users perceive the 5A apps as useful?	V2.1)] Perceived utility for ASD users	Questionnaire
RQ 3] Effectiveness: the training with 5A's apps (VR and AR) is it helpful to improve the autonomy of ASD people in using the train for interurban mobility?	V3.1)] Autonomy perceived by the ADS user	Questionnaire
Secondly, what part of the experience benefits best from our training, and where is the training ineffective?	V3.2)] Autonomy perceived by the caregivers	Ecological Observation Grid

In addition, during all sessions, a qualitative report has been filled out by the caregiver to annotate peculiar behaviors or situations.

5.1 Materials and Methods

Participants. The study involves five users with a diagnosis of Autism Spectrum Disorder (ASD) (age $\mu : 22.4y.o, \sigma : 3.01$) (3 male and 2 females). Their profile is reported in Table 4. Three out of five present a mild-to-moderate intellectual disability. All participants had never experienced the use of AR, and only one had few previous experiences with a VR visor. We profile the users according to their attitude toward testing new technology using a simplified ATI [8] test, and all users showed a positive attitude. Simplifications were used according to the same principles described above. Participants could withdraw at any moment in the experimentation. All participants and their caregivers agreed to the protocol with informant content.

Table 4. Table of user profiles

User	Gender	Age	Presence of Aggressive behavior	Presence of Sensory Ipersensibility	Presence of Anxiety issues	Previous VR Experiences	Previous AR Experience
1	M	23	None	Very high	Few	No	No
2	F	15	None	High	High	No	No
3	F	16	None	None	Few	No	No
4	M	18	None	Very High	High	Few	No
5	M	20	None	None	Few	No	No

Table 5. Table of the tasks to be completed. For each task is also indicated the average level of autonomy measured by caregivers at T0, T1, and T2

Task	Autonomy at T0	Autonomy at T1	Autonomy at T2
Task 1) Identify the train station's entrance	0.4	0	0
Task 2) Buy a ticket at the automated vending machine	1.2	0.8	0.6
Task 3) Identify on the timetable the departure platform	0.2	0.2	0.6
Task 4) Validate the ticket	0.8	0.65	0.4
Task 5) Reach the correct platform	0	1	0.2
Task 6) Enter the train and exit at the right stop	0	0.2	0.2
Task 7) Exit the destination station	0.2	0.6	0.2

Procedure. Participants underwent a two-step training protocol. Initially, they were asked to perform, with the supervision of a caregiver, a preliminary evaluation session (called hereafter T0) to measure the starting level of autonomy in using the train to move from two non-adjacent cities. During the evaluation, the user had to undergo the tasks reported in Table 5. Caregivers annotate for each task the degree of autonomy shown by the user on a 4-value Likert scale: task completed autonomously by the user (0), The user needed help to complete the task (1), completed by substituting the user (2), a task not reached (3). In the first training session, users test VR visors to verify they have no rejection behavior and no motion sickness. The setup was prepared as described in Sect. 4.1.

For this purpose, the users see a 360 video played from YouTube. After 5 min, the therapists verify the user's condition. Then the user performs one session with the VR tutorial. Once both parts of the tutorial (Interaction and Conversation) are completed, the user is asked to answer the Usability Questionnaire on the VR tutorial. Then the user is asked to perform the first training session with the VR application; at the end, another Usability Questionnaire is compiled for the VR application. Finally, the user performs the AR tutorial experience and fills out the last Usability Questionnaire on the AR tutorial.

At the end of the session, a team member delivers the parent a kit containing a phone, visor, headphones, controller, and instruction manual and explains how to start the experience at home. The user will perform seven sessions at home in the following week. During each session, the caregiver notes the user's behaviors. At the end of the experience, the user will also compile the questionnaire on the perceived Utility of the experience with VR.

At the end of the week, the user and the caregiver meet again in a fixed train station (Station A) where the user performs the experience without support (called hereafter T1) to measure the starting level of autonomy in using the train to reach another destination (Station B) avoiding descending at the intermediate station. The caregiver takes notes on the autonomy level shown by the user on the same scale as T0.

Once reached Station B, the user performs the AR tutorial again. Then s/he and the caregiver perform the trait backward (from station B to Station A) with the support of the AR application (called hereafter T2). The caregiver takes notes on the autonomy level shown by the user on the same scale as T0.

6 Results and Discussion

6.1 Usability

As discussed in Sect. 5, we simplified the SUS questionnaire to adapt it to our target users' needs by using only five questions (number 1,2,3, 4, and 9) [3]. We asked the users to answer on a 5-point scale: 1) strongly disagree, 2) disagree, 3) undecided, 4) agree, and 5) strongly agree. The questionnaire's replies obtained for all 5A experiences are summarized in Fig. 4. We then used the collected data to calculate the overall usability score of each task which is expressed on a scale of 50 points and has been calculated by applying the equation used by the original SUS questionnaire: $Score = ((Score_1 + Score_3 + Score_9 - 3) + (10 - Score_2 - Score_4)) * 2.5$. The adapted SUS score that we used to indicate the overall usability of 5A is summarized in Table 6.

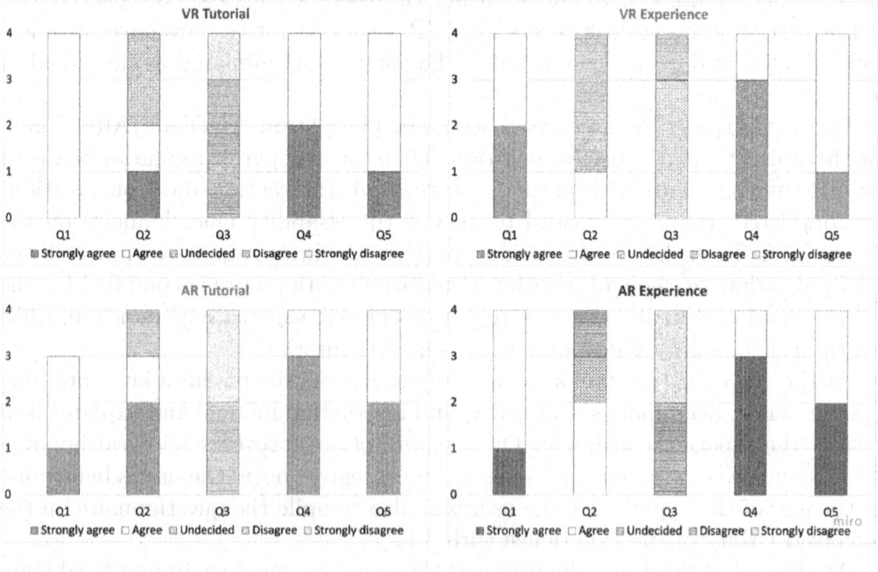

Fig. 4. The graphs represent the results of the modified SUS questionnaire for VR training, VR experience, AR training, and AR experience. Q1-Q2-Q3-Q4-Q5 symbolize the questions that have been asked to the participants. These are Q1) Do you think the system is easy to use? Q2) Do you think you would need help to use this system alone? Q3) Did you find the tool complicated to use? Q4) Do you feel confident using the system? Q5) Did you like using this system?

Table 6. Adapted SUS score.

Adapted SUS score	Adjective relating
>40	Excellent
36–40	Good
35	Ok
26–34	Poor
<25	Awful

Table 7. Usability scores obtained during each 5A experience.

Task	Adapted SUS score
VR tutorial	35.6
VR experience	40.6
AR tutorial	36.3
AR experience	39.4

From Table 7, we can observe that all our tasks have an adapted SUS score greater than 35, meaning that 5A is usable and well-perceived by the users. Specifically, the AR experience scores were slightly below excellent, while the VR experience was considered excellent on average by our participants. It is interesting to notice that in all cases, users thought they needed help to use the system after the tutorial and not after using the application itself. None encountered usability issues in either the tutorials or the experiences. This could mean that the step-by-step learning-by-doing walkthrough of the interactions available in the tutorials has successfully taught the users the mechanics of the experience. It is also worth noting that the participants said they would need more help with the AR applications than the VR. This might be an environmental effect (e.g., they are more scared of using the app in the real world than in the safety of their homes) or an effect on the nature of the technology. Further research is needed to confirm either possibility.

Usability of the CA. In addition, we asked the users three direct questions about how easily they found prompting and interacting with the CA. Those are: while interacting with the VCA is it easy to interpret the written instructions? while interacting with the VCA is it easy to interpret the vocal instructions? is it easy to interact with the avatar? Everyone reported that the VCA was easy to comprehend in written form, and only User3 reported was undecided over the clarity of the vocal form of the instructions (only during the VR tutorial). Furthermore, all the participants agreed or strongly agreed that interacting with the VCA was easy. These results confirm that the VCA could be a viable tool for interaction for ASD people.

6.2 Utility

For each of the seven tasks of the experienced, we asked the participants to indicate how much the app helped them learn how to complete each step. The replies have been expressed on a 5-point scale: 0) it was beneficial, 1) it was helpful, 2) I am not sure, 3) it was not useful, and 4) it was not useful at all. Regarding the VR applications, 50% of the users indicated that the app was very helpful for all tasks, while the other 50% reported it was helpful. On the other hand, for the AR tasks, 75% of the participants found the app very useful in learning how to find the station, find the automated vending machine, find the platform, enter and exit the train, and find the exit. The app was judged very helpful to use the automated vending machine by 50% of the people, while 50% found it useful. The app, instead, served a lesser purpose in learning how to use the timetable: 50% found it very useful, 25% found it useful, and 25% were not sure. Overall, the results suggest that the users found using 5A apps advantageous for learning purposes. Moreover, AR seems to be slightly more useful in this context, this is probably because it allows a better engagement with the environment. However, the points in which the app has more difficulty (i.e., identifying the timetable) have also been evaluated as less usable. Possibly more precise help offered by the system would have increased the user's performance.

It is important to mention that both the usability and utility analyses described above do not consider User1; this participant reported having had headaches during the experience and experienced several technical difficulties that made the experience very different from the experience of the other testers.

6.3 Autonomy

Autonomy Perceived by Caregivers. The core research question we want to analyze is the effectiveness of the training with 5A with the ultimate goal of investigating whether combining VR and AR experiences can improve the users' autonomy. The following section describes how we analyzed task-per-task results and differentiated them according to the technology thus, we will use task numeration, which you can find in Table 2's (first column) to describe this analysis.

First, we looked at which tasks were the most complex for the user at T0 (Fig. 5). We computed a "complexity score" by associating a numeric value to the autonomy level shown by the users: 0 for users that completed the task autonomously, 1 for users who needed help, and 2 for users who had to be substituted by caregivers. The most complex task, on average, was Task 2, with a complexity score of 1.2 ($\sigma 0.4$); Secondly, Task 4 had an initial score of 0.8 ($\sigma 0.4$). Thirdly, Task 1 scored 0.4 ($\sigma 0.5$). Finally, Tasks 3 and 7 showed a score of 0.2 ($\sigma 0.4$), and Tasks 5 and 6 had a score of 0 (i.e., all users completed the task in autonomy). For Task 1, results showed the best improvement: all users become autonomous in the task by the end of the experience ($\Delta_{T2-T0} = -0.3, \sigma 0.4$). Interestingly, this result is completely dependent on the VR training ($\Delta_{T1-T0} = -0.3, \sigma 0.4, \Delta_{T2-T1} = 0, \sigma 0$). For Task 2, the improvement registered is comparable to Task 1 ($\Delta_{T2-T0} = -0.33, \sigma 0.3$), and also, in this case, most of the improvement can be registered in the VR part of the training ($\Delta_{T1-T0} = -0.27, \sigma 0.37, \Delta_{T2-T1} = -0.067, \sigma 0.14$). For Task 3, the overall result is a slight increase in the difficulty measured ($\Delta_{T2-T0} = 0.1, \sigma 0.4$). Interestingly, at T1, users needed less help in this task ($\Delta_{T1-T0} = -0.1, \sigma 0.27$), while the AR part of the experience seemed to make the task harder for them ($\Delta_{T2-T1} = 0.2, \sigma 0.27$). For Task 4, the training seemed to help the users ($\Delta_{T2-T0} = -0.2, \sigma 0.27$); this improvement seems to be equally shared between the VR and AR parts

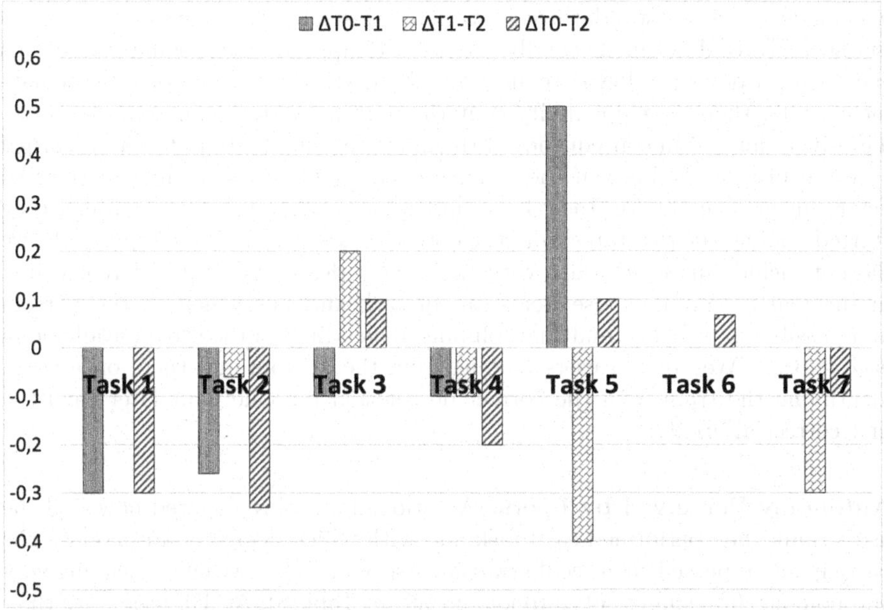

Fig. 5. Autonomy perceived by the caregivers. The tasks are: Task1) identify the train station entrance, Task2) by a ticket at the automated vending machine, Task3) identify on the time table the departure platform, Task4) validate the ticket, Task5) reach the correct platform, Task6) enter the train and exit at the right stop, Task7) exit the destination station.

($\Delta_{T1-T0} = -0.1, \sigma0.4, \Delta_{T2-T1} = -0.1, \sigma0.22$). For Task 5, the overall result is a slight increase in the difficulty registered ($\Delta_{T2-T0} = 0.1, \sigma0.2$). Inversely to Task 3, at T1, users needed more help in this task ($\Delta_{T1-T0} = 0.5, \sigma0$), while the AR part of the experience seemed to make the task easier for them ($\Delta_{T2-T1} = -0.4, \sigma0.2$). Task 7 followed closely Task 5, with a slight decrease in measured difficulty ($\Delta_{T2-T0} = -0.1, \sigma0.5$). At T1, users needed more help in this task ($\Delta_{T1-T0} = 0.2, \sigma0.27$), while the AR part of the experience seemed to make the task easier for them ($\Delta_{T2-T1} = -0.3, \sigma0.57$). Task 6, instead, was invariant in the measures. The reason is simply that users needed no help in completing the task.

Further, we looked at our notes and the ones taken by the caregivers during the sessions to contextualize the obtained data. While interpreting the results, it is important to remember that tasks 2 and 4 involve learning a more or less complex procedure completely unfamiliar to the users. We can hypothesize that VR application is more useful for memorizing sequences of steps, while AR is more helpful in case of "specific" localized doubts during the experience. During Tasks 5 and 7, the VR training seemed to have made the users less autonomous, while AR provided them more autonomy. Three reasons could have led to a lower performance than expected in VR. The first is that the virtual simulation was made inside a "standardized" station. This may have confused the users in the real-world setup. Secondly, in the VR app, we used some visual aids (i.e., arrows pointing down) to indicate the destination point of intermediate movements; there is a possibility that this hinting system confused the users. Thirdly, to answer in consequence of the movement interaction, the user learned to move in straight lines in the space, which could be misleading in the real environment. Finally, for Task 3, we noticed a peculiar habit of all users: they started reading the timetable from the bottom instead of from the top. In VR, we did not include multiple trains with the correct destinations at different times; in the real timetable, those items are present and positioned at the bottom and possibly in either of multiple columns, depending on the screen available in each station. We noticed users reading from the bottom and then, once tired, identifying the train with the correct destination but one hour later than the first correct alternative.

Autonomy Perceived by Users. Additionally, we investigated how well the users think they performed each task and with which degree of autonomy - the participants reported their feedback using a 4-point Likert scale (3 meaning very autonomous, 0 meaning not autonomous at all, Table 8). At T0, users rate their autonomy very low: no task overcomes the 1.25 on average, except for Task 6, which emerged to be the one in which they are more autonomous. At T1, the perceived autonomy improved, where all tasks were rated between 2.5 and 2.25. We can deduce that several VR task repetitions significantly boosted the user's confidence in their skills. This information, combined with the improvement registered by an external observer, could signify that VR is a powerful preliminary training. At T2, the rating is even higher, with all scores at 2.75 over 3 and a low standard deviation. We can deduce that AR is perceived as a powerful tool for the support of the user that felt, on average, almost completely autonomous in performing the task. From this analysis, we had to exclude User 5 because he/she was accustomed to performing the exercise in her/his routine.

Table 8. Perceived user's autonomy at T0, T1 and T2 in completing alone the tasks

	Task1	Task 2	Task 3	Task 5	Task 6	Task 7
T0	$\mu 1, \sigma 1.4$	$\mu 0.5, \sigma 0.79$	$\mu 1, \sigma 0.82$	$\mu 1.25, \sigma 0.96$	$\mu 1.625, \sigma 1.1$	$\mu 1.25, \sigma 0.95$
T1	$\mu 2.5, \sigma 1$	$\mu 2.4, \sigma 0.79$	$\mu 2.5, \sigma 1$	$\mu 2.5, \sigma 1$	$\mu 2.25, \sigma 0.96$	$\mu 2.5, \sigma 1$
T2	$\mu 2.75, \sigma 0.5$	$\mu 2.75, \sigma 0.32$	$\mu 2.75, \sigma 0.5$	$\mu 2.75, \sigma 0.5$	$\mu 2.75, \sigma 0.5$	$\mu 2.75, \sigma 1$

7 Limitations

The 5A exploratory study shows the great potential that our tool can have in the scope of supporting therapies for young adults with autism. However, all these results are preliminary and further research is needed to confirm them. Moreover, this study faces three main limitations. First, we looked at participants with very specific profiles: with a diagnosis of ASD (high functioning), over 15 years old, able to verbalize with intelligible words, and not completely autonomous in the urban mobility tasks. For this reason, our subject population is small, and to overcome this issue, we keep recruiting more subjects to increase the sample size of our study. Another critical point present in our study is that our targets were able to complete some of the tasks autonomously from the very start. This is a consequence of having selected young adults with high-functioning ASD conditions. Furthermore, studies on lower functioning levels or younger users need to be conducted to verify our claims further. Second, our research faces many challenging factors typical of "working in the wild": the public transportation entities were uncooperative since they firmly opposed letting us put the tags in the real environment. This unfortunate situation negatively affected our schedule and the users' experience. Also, since we could not obtain the planimetry of the stations, the VR stations had been modeled to be realistic but not the replica of the space, which could have impacted the learning of the more "space navigation" tasks. Finally, 5A apps required a constant high-quality network connection and were designed with 5G technology in mind. Nevertheless, in the real world, network quality could be scarce. This has been a big challenge for trials in AR since some users felt stuck because the app could not connect to the server for minutes.

8 Design Guidelines

A second important contribution we want to bring with our work is the collection of guidelines distilled from the positive and negative lessons we learned in designing, creating, and testing the 5A apps.

- The use of Trans-media Elements: Use elements that allow the user to make references between the experience in VR and later in AR. It will help them remember the sequences of tasks to use that object. The design we suggest is to be a "low-detail" version of the real objects. Keep the right proportions, color, and distinctive elements, but use plain color backgrounds and bold black lines for contour. Another trans-media element is the VCA's Avatar, which needs to keep the same functional structure.
- Step-by-step active walkthrough tutorial effectively supports the learning process of how to use the app. We suggest creating tutorials that involve one mechanic at a time and where the users can test it immediately.
- VR activity has proven to be ideal for performing pre-training. It is ideal for memorizing sequences of steps to interact with specific items. It can also be a very powerful confidence boost for the users.
- AR activity has proven ideal for performing spot-on tasks, spatial orientation, and mobility.
- AR experience is useful for on-demand spot-on support. The important aspect is to provide direct and precise information.

- ASD users have found the VCA a useful and viable tool to support them. We have seen that users prefer written text over voice because they can be distracted by the environment (digital or real).
- ASD users showed difficulties when the VCA responded slowly or had difficulty interpreting the audio signal.
- Simulating spaces that present a very large variability distilling a standardized setup has not been beneficial for the users, who had been confused by the modification in the disposition of the objects in the real world. Whenever possible, use simulations from real space.
- Virtual aids can be very useful to help users in virtual reality; however, users get confused or, at worst, expect to find them in the real world.
- The use of the microphone was necessary for the VR setup: most visors are designed with sponges or plastic boxes to cover the one inside the phone.
- AR technology is not mature enough for the field with ASD, especially where network problems arise. Space Mapping is too error-prone in repositioning items (we measured position errors in the order of meters) as much as GPS localization in indoor spaces (not to mention underground). Models or image recognition instead have limits on the material of the surfaces (e.g., highlights, reflections) and the variability of the elements in the real-world panorama (e.g., too few details or too many details for screen reading, ticket machines with a different disposition of buttons). CAs can be a viable tool to support AR technology when it fails.
- AR is as useful as precise in providing help on the sport to the users.
- Use video tutorial instead of the user manual for delivering the devices at home to the users.

9 Conclusion

Project 5A ("Autonomy for Autisms Achieved by means of virtual and Augmented reality and conversational Agents") is characterized by a novel multimodal approach in which different interaction paradigms - Virtual Reality, Augmented Reality, and Conversational interaction- are smoothly integrated. This paper describes how we co-designed, implemented, and empirically evaluated it. To the best of our knowledge, our project is among the first developed that merge the three technologies to support fragile people. Although preliminary, the results of the empirical study indicated that the combined use of VR, AR, and VCA Technologies is usable by ASD people. Data also hint that the combined training based on VR experiences and AR in loco support is a viable tool to support the users in gaining autonomy in public mobility tasks. We believe that our work could be the beginning of a strand of research on the role of Mixed Reality applications in supporting users in developing autonomy, confidence, and skills for their daily life. We also have distilled our experiences providing guidelines on designing, implementing, and evaluating such combined mixed reality solutions.

Our research is still at an early stage. Hence many aspects need to be explored further. We are currently continuing the recruitment and testing with new users with this protocol; By increasing the sample size, we want to measure more solid results to confirm our observations. We also started a parallel study in a different public mobility scenario (i.e., the underground) to verify eventual biases due to the setup. We will also work on improving the limitations that emerged during the empirical evaluation (e.g., network dependency, latency)

Acknowledgment. This research has been developed in the context of the project "5A-Autonomie per l'Autismo Attraverso realtà virtuale, realtà Aumentata e Agenti conversazionali", thanks to the contribution of TIM Foundation, expressing TIM's social commitment and its mission to promote digital innovation and to support inclusion, communication, and social and economic growth. We thank our project partners "Fondazione Sacra Famiglia" and "IRCCS Eugenio Media" for contributing to the application design activities. We would like to thank also TIM S.p.A. that partially funds this work through its UniversiTIM granting program.

References

1. Allouch, M., Azaria, A., Azoulay, R.: Conversational agents: goals, technologies, vision and challenges. Sensors **21**(24) (2021). https://doi.org/10.3390/s21248448, https://www.mdpi.com/1424-8220/21/24/8448
2. American Psychiatric Association: Diagnostic and statistical manual of mental disorders: DSM-5, 5th edn. Autor, Washington, DC (2013)
3. Bangor, A., Kortum, P.T., Miller, J.T.: An empirical evaluation of the system usability scale. Intl. J. Hum.-Comput. Interact. **24**(6), 574–594 (2008)
4. Berenguer, C., Baixauli, I., Gómez, S., Andrés, M.d.E.P., De Stasio, S.: Exploring the impact of augmented reality in children and adolescents with autism spectrum disorder: a systematic review. Int. J. Environ. Res. Publ. Health **17**(17), 6143 (2020)
5. Bernardes, M., Barros, F., Simoes, M., Castelo-Branco, M.: A serious game with virtual reality for travel training with autism spectrum disorder. In: 2015 International Conference on Virtual Rehabilitation (ICVR), pp. 127–128. unknown, June 2015
6. Bozgeyikli, E., Bozgeyikli, L., Raij, A., Katkoori, S., Alqasemi, R., Dubey, R.: Virtual reality interaction techniques for individuals with autism spectrum disorder: design considerations and preliminary results. In: Kurosu, M. (ed.) HCI 2016. LNCS, vol. 9732, pp. 127–137. Springer, Cham (2016). https://doi.org/10.1007/978-3-319-39516-6_12
7. Cha, I., Kim, S.I., Hong, H., Yoo, H., Lim, Y.K.: Exploring the use of a voice-based conversational agent to empower adolescents with autism spectrum disorder. In: Proceedings of the 2021 CHI Conference on Human Factors in Computing Systems. CHI '21, Association for Computing Machinery, New York, NY, USA (2021). https://doi.org/10.1145/3411764.3445116
8. Franke, T., Attig, C., Wessel, D.: A personal resource for technology interaction: development and validation of the affinity for technology interaction (ATI) scale. Int. J. Hum.-Comput. Interact. **35**(6), 456–467 (2019)
9. Gelsomini, M., Garzotto, F., Montesano, D., Occhiuto, D.: Wildcard: a wearable virtual reality storytelling tool for children with intellectual developmental disability. In: 2016 38th Annual International Conference of the IEEE Engineering in Medicine and Biology Society (EMBC), pp. 5188–5191. IEEE (2016)

10. Gonzalez, L.: Clarifai featured hack: Spectrum navigator is a GPS app that helps people navigate by landmark (2018). https://www.clarifai.com/blog/clarifai-featured-hack-spectrum-navigator-is-a-gps-app-that-helps-people-navigate-by-landmark
11. Ladner, R.E.: Design for user empowerment. Interactions **22**(2), 24–29 (2015). https://doi.org/10.1145/2723869
12. Miller, I.T., Miller, C.S., Wiederhold, M.D., Wiederhold, B.K.: Virtual reality air travel training using apple iPhone X and google cardboard: a feasibility report with autistic adolescents and adults. Autism Adulthood **2**(4) (2020)
13. Nadel, J., Grynszpan, O., Martin, J.C.: Autism and Socially Interactive Agents, 1st edn, pp. 437–462. Association for Computing Machinery, New York, NY, USA (2022), https://doi.org/10.1145/3563659.3563673
14. Parris, J.: Boise airport virtual reality experience will help children with autism, September 2019. https://www.ktvb.com/article/news/local/bois-airport-virtual-reality-experience-boise-state-university/277-7cbff515-3e08-48f7-aa21-40579cbf60c0
15. Rezae, M., Mcmeekin, D., Tan, T., Krishna, A., Lee, H., Falkmer, T.: Public transport planning tool for users on the autism spectrum: from concept to prototype. Disab. Rehabil. Assis. Technol. **16**, 1–11 (2019). https://doi.org/10.1080/17483107.2019.1646818
16. Schmidt, M.M., Glaser, N.: Piloting an adaptive skills virtual reality intervention for adults with autism: findings from user-centered formative design and evaluation. J. Enab. Technol. **15**(3), 137–158 (2021)
17. Soccini, A.M., Cuccurullo, S.A.G., Cena, F.: Virtual reality experiential training for individuals with autism: the airport scenario. In: Bourdot, P., Interrante, V., Kopper, R., Olivier, A.-H., Saito, H., Zachmann, G. (eds.) EuroVR 2020. LNCS, vol. 12499, pp. 234–239. Springer, Cham (2020). https://doi.org/10.1007/978-3-030-62655-6_16
18. Stewart Rosenfield, N., Lamkin, K., Re, J., Day, K., Boyd, L., Linstead, E.: A virtual reality system for practicing conversation skills for children with autism. Multimodal Technol. Interact. **3**(2), 28 (2019)
19. Tanaka, H., Negoro, H., Iwasaka, H., Nakamura, S.: Embodied conversational agents for multimodal automated social skills training in people with autism spectrum disorders. PLOS ONE **12**(8), 1–15 (2017). https://doi.org/10.1371/journal.pone.0182151
20. Tanaka, H., Negoro, H., Iwasaka, H., Nakamura, S.: Embodied conversational agents for multimodal automated social skills training in people with autism spectrum disorders. PLoS ONE **12**(8), e0182151 (2017)
21. Vona, F., Torelli, E., Beccaluva, E., Garzotto, F.: Exploring the potential of speech-based virtual assistants in mixed reality applications for people with cognitive disabilities. In: Proceedings of the International Conference on Advanced Visual Interfaces, pp. 1–9 (2020)

Using Technology-Based Augmentative and Alternative Communication to Develop Adaptive Behavior in a Child with Autism Spectrum Disorders – An Intervention Program

Eleni Koustriava(✉) and Maria Koutsmani

University of Macedonia, 54636 Thessaloniki, Greece
{elkous,mea21026}@uom.edu.gr

Abstract. Individuals with autism face lots of difficulties in developing their communication skills, which affect their socialization while also increase their challenged behavior. Consequently, many individuals with autism are candidates for Augmentative and Alternative Communication systems (AAC) which will enable them communicate their needs and feelings, and thus to diminish their maladaptive behavior. The present study explored the impact of using an AAC software to develop communication and socialization skills in a boy with autism in the context of an intervention program. Additionally, it was aimed to improve his adaptive behavior by diminishing his maladaptive behavior that could be a result of the boy's inability to communicate his needs. Initial and final assessments conducted using the Vineland Adaptive Behavior Scales, Second Edition (VABS-II). The intervention program was based on the AAC technological tool GRID 3. The results showed that the boy's communication and socialization skills were improved, while his maladaptive behavior was reduced as a result of his ability to communicate his needs more successfully.

Keywords: Augmentative and Alternative Communication · Autism · Vineland Adaptive Behavior Scales · Socialization · Maladaptive Behavior

1 Introduction

Lots of individuals with autism never develop their verbal speech, which is very unhelpful for them to improve or even use their communication skills [14]. According to the literature, the success factor for someone to develop effective communication is to have the opportunity to speak about his needs and his feelings. If someone is not able to do that, it could be possible to develop a challenged behavior [13], present low academic skills, and have poor job opportunities [14].

All the evidence shows that children with disabilities are struggling with their behavior, very often misbehave, and face difficulties in socializing with their peers [31]. The rate of those individuals is quite big, around 10%–40% of young children [12]. In this

M. Antona and C. Stephanidis (Eds.): HCII 2023, LNCS 14020, pp. 601–613, 2023.
https://doi.org/10.1007/978-3-031-35681-0_39

regard, many children, because of their inability to communicate effectively with their peers and integrate into the whole, are easily socially isolated [1].

Consequently, many individuals with autism are candidates for Augmentative and Alternative Communication systems (AAC). Augmentative is the system that targets the improvement of an individuals' communication by contributing to their speech, while alternative is the system that provides different means for communication by bypassing speech [18]. One of the positive things of AAC is that provides the information visually, which is something that affects positively the user with autism who can process anything new better when they can see it [19, 28]. Conforming to Flippin et al. [10], a very useful instrument of AAC is the Picture Exchange Communication System (PECS) that helps in making real requests and interacting with people from the main environment through the exchange of pictures [30]. The use of picture exchange in combination with Speech Generating Devices (SGD), such as tablets, mobile phones, and other handled devices can be even more successful [16]. According to Frea et al. [13], AAC helps individuals with autism who cannot speak to develop their ability to express personal choices and to improve their impairment in communication, while at the same time, helps them to reduce their challenging behavior.

There have been many types of research that examined how those interventions are valuable for children's speech production and development, using aided communication [11, 20, 29]. Specifically, O'Neill et al. [20] investigated the effects of AAC using aided language modeling and aided language stimulation. The outcomes revealed an improvement in children's communication, in both the comprehension and expression domains. They also used strategies like expectant delay, direct prompting, and open-ended questions. Similarly, the study by Meer et al. [29] proved the value of AAC in children with autism. According to the same researchers, the participants of their study succeed to use technological items of AAC, when a few months before they could not do it. Since the intervention started, they preferred working with AAC using computers as AAC through technology seems to be more interesting for them [25]. In another remarkable intervention [11], children with Down syndrome, practiced the COMPIC system of computerized pictographs. The results showed that they had been much better with their social interaction, language development, decision-making, and their will to communicate [11].

Special emphasis has been given on the techniques that should be used to introduce AAC tools. For instance, when the VOCA tool (communication aid) was introduced in four individuals with autism, the researchers used the expectant delay, questioning looks with eye contact, and physical approach techniques with significant results. Individuals with autism had been much more motivated so their communication reactions were highly increased [4]. Another technique that combined with AAC lead to significant results in peer support in school [3]. In the study of Young et al. [32], iPads were provided to the students to experiment with typing words and speaking through the device. All the children could ask Alex, a boy with autism and nonverbal speech, many things such as his news from the weekend. Alex was using the iPad to respond to questions with pictures and words. The abovementioned method seems that attracted Alex and motivated him a lot to communicate with his peers [32]. Furthermore, Biggs et al. [3], support that when more than one in class uses the AAC, it makes it more convenient for the child with communicational difficulties. That confidence creates an inclusive environment, where more and more opportunities are being in place for the children to socialize and make friendships [9, 17].

Furthermore, it had been proved that the use of AAC helps individuals to make big progress with their improper behaviors [5]. Battaglia et al. [2] and Charlop-Christy et al. [5] investigated the effect of AAC on children with autism who had severe communicational difficulties. Both of the above-mentioned studies succeed to increase an individual's verbal speech in daily routine and during playtime. The consequences of that progress were that their social-communication behaviors had increased and their challenged behavior had been decreased. The second study referred, in addition, improvements in maladaptive behavior such as biting, kicking, and screaming. Those behaviors had been reduced after many interventions with AAC [2]. According to Van Der Meer & Rispoli [30], when a child cannot speak is unable to express his desires, which is what causes aggressiveness in his communication. AAC builds a functional relationship between children with autism and their environment [6].

This functional relationship with the environment appears to be corroborative with the results of Son et al. [26], who refers to more examples that AAC had a positive impact on challenging behaviors. Picture exchange pictures and voice-output communication aids (VOCAs) has been used for non-verbal speech children with autism. All the participants stopped reacting aggressively and learned for the first time to express their desires and to communicate effectively. In addition, on the same study, another very important issue regarding the interventions of AAC is that children would be permitted and encouraged to choose the tool or the program they wanted to use. Choosing the instrument of AAC that is more suitable to the participant can be very effective to him [26]. Another very similar study to the previous ones refers to a 4 year-old boy with non-verbal autism. That boy was very aggressive while he was trying to communicate with his peers. After introducing ACC to him, he found a way to express his wants and needs through the picture exchange. The results were impressive as his aggressive behavior saw a dramatic decline, proving that AAC allowed him to improve his communication by reinforcing his ability to express himself [13].

In order to evaluate the advantages resulted by the use of AAC, Vineland Adaptive Behavior Scales (VABS), Survey Edition Sparrow et al. [27] have been suggested. VABS is the most common instrument to measure Adaptive Behavior [23]. People with Autism Spectrum Disorder present difficulties in their communication, socialization, and living skills [8]. All these domains compose Adaptive Behavior, which is the ability to take care of personal and common needs independently [21]. Sparrow et al. [27] recommend Vineland-II, as a well-designed tool that is capable to assess an individual's functional skills. The validity of this measurement is undeniable and it can be used for both children with disabilities and those without [27].

In consonance with Chatham et al. [8] who used VABS to evaluate children with autism, Socialization is the most challenged domain to them and after comes Communication, Daily living skills, and Motor skills. It is also very impressive that children with autism are fallen behind in these categories of Adaptive Behavior even if their intelligence hasn't been impaired [7]. The first time that VABS had been used on children with autism but without any kind of intellectual disability was on 64 individuals and proved that IQ is not the most important factor, which influences adaptive behavior [24].

2 Study

The aim of this study was a) to develop a boy's Communication and Socialization skills using a technology-based AAC tool (GRID 3), and b) to improve his adaptive behavior by diminishing his maladaptive behavior that could be a result of the boy's inability to communicate his needs.

3 Method

3.1 Participant

The research focused on M., a boy thirteen years old who has autism. M. was a non-verbal speaker who occasionally vocalized speech-like sounds. For instance, he couldn't say any words or sentences to describe his needs. More specifically, he was using an informal type of communication which was common only to his family, moving his hands to show «yes» by touching his knee or «no» by touching his shoulder. M. was very nervous every time he tried to explain to an adult or a peer what he was saying. His behavior had a variety of reactions such as making loud noises to attract others attention or pulling his surroundings from their sleeves to show them pictures and phrases in books giving them a clue to guess his thoughts. He was so disappointed when nobody could understand him and, consequently, he was negative to participate to any kind of activity in the school.

In the past he had received additional learning practicing his communication through PECS. However, he had not succeeded to use this method to communicate effectively with the people of his environment. In the case of M., PECS seemed to be very restricted to his needs because the vocabulary that used was focused on improving his knowledge and not on expressing his wants and desires. As a result, he didn't really want to use PECS anymore.

3.2 Instruments

The basic instrument used to develop the communication and socialization skills in M. was GRID 3 (Smartbox), a complete communication software that enables people to have a voice, control their environment and live more independently. It has been designed for anyone with complex communication or access needs and includes a wide range of resources that you can control by touching your screen. It provides a core vocabulary that somebody can use in a useful way according to a person's needs (Smartbox Assistive Technology, 2022).

For the initial (baseline) and the final assessment of the communication and socialization skills of M., as well as his adaptive behavior, the Vineland Adaptive Behavior Scales (VABS-II) was used. Specifically, two domains have been used, a) the Communication Domain with its three sub-domains, 1) Receptive, 2) Expressive, 3) Written

Communication, and b) the Socialization Domain with its three sub-domains, 1) Interpersonal Relationships, 2) Play and Leisure Time, 3) Coping Skills. In addition, the Maladaptive Behavior Index with the Internalizing, Externalizing and Other items, and the Maladaptive Behavior Critical Items. Sparrow et al. [27] were used to assess the level of misbehavior, his deviating behavior. In VABS, each item within the set is scored as 0 (never), 1 (sometimes), 2 (usually) and added the total score separately [22].

Last but not least, semi-structured interviews consisted of six open-ended questions. The questions concerned about M.'s improvement on his Communication and his general progress after the intervention. Moreover, both the mother and the teacher have been asked to do any further recommendations on how AAC could be used as an educational tool to the individuals with autism, and how they want to use that instrument in the future to help M. on his daily life.

3.3 Procedure - Intervention Program

As it was necessary to assess and reassess the boy's adaptive behavior, his mother and his teacher filled out the same form twice, one for the baseline assessment and another one for the final one. All the domains and sub domains have been measured and age equivalents for each set were derived from Vineland standardization data [22].

The intervention took part on a daily basis at school and 2–3 times at home for about six weeks. All the process started teaching GRID 3. First, the boy was practicing the communication through picture exchange using cards which were printed by the environment of GRID 3. After the child's familiarization with the printed cards, he was introduced to GRID 3 with the use of a notebook. The chosen vocabulary was relative to the prioritized topics that the pupil was going to learn to communicate effectively: A) starting introducing himself b) talking more about his needs and preferences, and c) expressing his feelings. The intervention program was based a language escalation with the child starting to a) answer questions in one word, b) answer using full sentences (from simple ones of "verbal + object" to more complex ones like "verbal + object *and* verbal + object"), and continuing to c) make his own questions and sentences, and d) use polite sentences.

The different types of teaching methods used to introduce the child in AAC were 1) Question & Prompting 2) Modeling, 3) Motivation & Target, and 4) Time Delay.

4 Results

In the first place, the participant was evaluated by addressing to his mother and his teacher the manual packages of the respective record forms of VABS-II. To analyze the results, initially, the chronological age of M. was calculated according to the guidelines of VABS-II. Based on the chronological age, the raw scores for each domain (communication, socialization) and each sub-domain were calculated as well. Based on the raw score in each case, the match up with v-scale and the age equivalent was completed. Based on the v-scales core in each domain and sub-domain, the match up with the typical score, the confidence interval, and the level of adaptive behavior was completed. Similarly, the values for the index of maladaptive behavior and its sub-domains were calculated (Table 1).

Table 1. The score of Communication and Socialization domains and sub-domains before the intervention according to Mother's (M) and Teacher's (T) answers.

		Raw score	v-scale score	Standard score domain	90% Confidence interval	Level of Adaptive Behavior	Age equivalence
Receptive Communication	M	12	2		±2	low	1:1
	T	18	4		±2	low	1:6
Expressive Communication	M	18	1		±2	low	1:0
	T	14	1		±2	low	0:9
Written Communication	M	1	4		±2	low	2:1
	T	13	6		±2	low	5:1
Communication	M	**Total: 7**		**31**	±7	low	
	T	**Total: 11**		**40**	±7	low	
Interpersonal Relationships	M	17	2		±2	low	0:6
	T	16	2		±2	low	0:5
Play and leisure time	M	5	1		±3	low	0:6
	T	7	2		±3	low	0:8
Coping Skills	M	9	6		±2	low	1:1
	T	7	6		±2	low	1:9
Socialization	M	**Total: 9**		**36**	±8	low	
	T	**Total: 10**		**38**	±8	low	

In consonance with all the results of the first evaluation, M. was in a low level of Adaptive Behavior in his both main domains, Communication and Socialization Skills. The standard deviation on his communication ability was between 4 and 4.5, whilst it had been counted around 4.1 and 4.2 on his Socialization activity.

Comparing with the typical population, his score had shown that his adaptive behavior is equivalent with the behavior of a boy on age between 9 months old and 1.5 years old on his Communication and between 5–8 months old on his Socialization. The homogeneity of their answers shows that both the mother and the teacher agreed that he had a variety of difficulties in his Communication and Socialization. The results were indicative for the boy's needs. According to both the mother's and the teacher's answers, M. had more severe problems in his Receptive Communication and his Expressive Communication, as well as in Interpersonal Relationships and in Play and Leisure Time. More precisely, M. was more obsessive with objects or some activities like singing favorite songs or watching favorite films and less interested on people and the interaction between him and his peers.

Later, after the intervention and the reassessment with VABS-II, M. remained in a low level on his Adaptive Behavior for both of his Communication and Socialization Skills. However, his mother noticed that he made progress in his receptive and expressive communication, as his score was almost double after the intervention. Similar are the results based on the teacher's answers.

Table 2. The score of Communication and Socialization domains and sub-domains after the intervention according to Mother's (M) and Teacher's (T) answers.

		Raw score	v-scale score	Standard score domain	90% Confidence interval	Level of Adaptive Behavior	Age equivalence
Receptive Communication	M	23	6		±2	low	1:11
	T	27	7		±2	low	2:10
Expressive Communication	M	36	2		±2	low	1:11
	T	25	1		±2	low	1:4
Written Communication	M	1	4		±2	low	2:1
	T	13	6		±2	low	5:1
Communication	M	**Total: 12**		**40**	±9	low	
	T	**Total: 14**		**43**	±9	low	
Interpersonal Relationships	M	38	6		±2	low	2:6
	T	33	5		±2	low	2:0
Play and leisure time	M	25	4		±2	low	2:7
	T	29	5		±2	low	3:1
Coping Skills	M	14	7		±2	low	2:6
	T	14	5		±2	low	2:6
Socialization	M	**Total: 17**		**52**	±9	low	
	T	**Total: 15**		**49**	±9	low	

Composing all the above-mentioned domains, Communicational Domain of Vineland had become greater for 94% as reported by the mother of the boy and 44% according to his teacher. In addition, both the teacher and the mother reported on the form that he had been much better in his interpersonal relationships and his play and leisure time, as his equivalent age according to VABS-II was 2–3 years old after the reassessment. In addition, according to his mother, M.'s coping skills had been increased 56% while for the teacher this score had been two times higher (Table 2).

Furthermore, he had a better score on his maladaptive behavior which was one of the main targets of the present research. According to the results, the index of Maladaptive Behavior was clinically important before the intervention, which was very high (Table 3). However, it turned to a lower level (high) after the intervention, which shows that according to his mother he made progress on the reassessment (Table 4). In the past, the way that M. was communicating was by screaming, tapping his hands on the table, and being very nervous. After the intervention it has been estimated that M. was more able to express his needs and that helped him to improve his Communication and

Socialization Skills. He learned how to communicate using the technological program of AAC and there were few times that he tried to use it independently, to say something to one of his peers.

Table 3. The score of Maladaptive Behavior and its sub-domains before the intervention according to mother's (M) and the teacher's (T) answers.

		Raw score	V-Scale score	90% Confidence Interval	Level
Maladaptive Behavior	M	28	21	±1	Clinically high
	T	23	20	±1	High
Internalizing	M	12	22	±2	Clinically high
	T	10	21	±2	Clinically high
Externalizing	M	10	20	±1	High
	T	8	19	±1	High

Table 4. The score of Maladaptive Behavior and its sub-domains after the intervention according to mother's (M) and the teacher's (T) answers.

		Raw score	V-Scale score	90% Confidence Interval	Level
Maladaptive Behavior	M	25	20	±1	High
	T	22	20	±1	High
Internalizing	M	10	21	±2	Clinically high
	T	10	21	±2	Clinically high
Externalizing	M	8	19	±1	High
	T	5	18	±1	High

The general level of the Maladaptive Behavior and its sub-domains Internalizing and Externalizing remains the same according to the mother's and the teacher's answers. Although, according to the measurement of the raw scores, M.'s Maladaptive Behavior presents improvement on both sub-domains. The only excuse is the Internalizing sub-domain which shows stability conforming to the teacher's answers.

The evidence had been reported on the reevaluation by VABS-II which showed higher score on his Receptive and Expressive Communication sub-domains and his Leisure and Play time, Interpersonal relationships and his Coping Skills on his Socialization sub-domains (Fig. 1). According to the results, the boy's Adaptive Behavior had been increased while his Maladaptive Behavior had been decreased (Table 4). Technically M. was happier to communicate with the technological tool and he was more willing to participate during the learning. According to his teacher, M. started to be more interested to play with the children or even to cooperate with them. Another important achievement was also that the boy started to communicate more independently using the app as he felt more confident. He didn't expect the teacher to prompt him to use the computer anymore.

Additionally, M. was very enthusiastic with Grid 3, for two reasons: he was a very good user on computers, so he was happy when he was using the app, and he reacted very positive on the digital voice that had replaced his own. Using AAC, M. had been able to have the control of his talking and he succeeded with a lot of practice to communicate with his peers and adults in a productive way.

In the interviews, both the mother and the teacher admitted that the intervention helped the child to improve his Socialization and Expressive Communication. They agreed that his confidence had increased and he was more active to communicate his needs. This is because he felt that he would be clear about what he said and that made him very confident. Due to his new way of communication, the teacher reported that he was more interested in participating in classroom (team) activities and he started trying to interact with his peers. In addition, the most significant improvement was that M. was able to express his desires and occasionally some of his feelings.

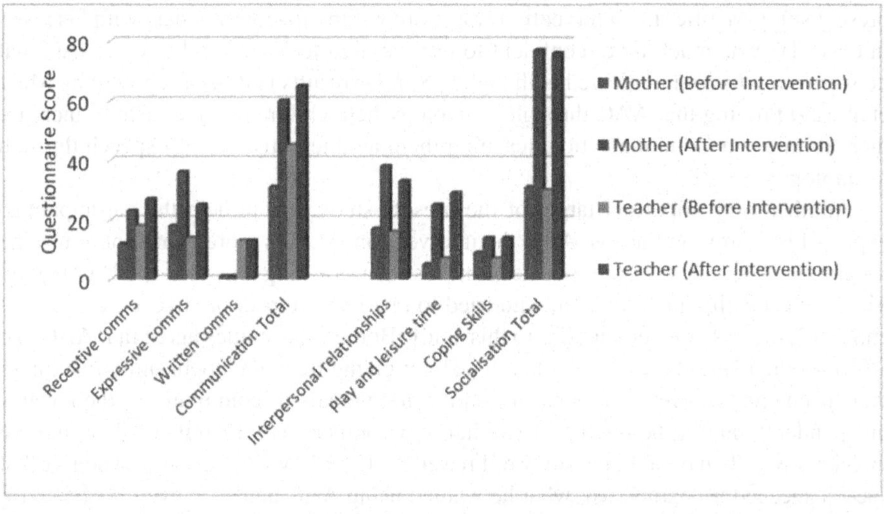

Fig. 1. The total score of the two main domains of VABS-II a) Communication and its subdomains (Receptive, Expressive and Written Communication) and Socialization and its subdomains (Interpersonal relationships, Play and leisure time, Coping Skills) before and after the assessment from the mother and the teacher.

All the adults in this study wish to could have more interventions like the aforementioned. The mother of the boy said that "Children with nonverbal speech have the right on communication skills and this is a tool which makes it accessible for them". On the same page, the teacher wondered if the school could buy the program for her class, so she was interested to learn the price and more information for the best use of it. Parents tried to do the intervention at home, as they noticed that since he is using this, he's more willing to speak.

5 Discussion

This case study highlights the impact of AAC on individuals with autism who hadn't developed their verbal speech and it shows the effect on reducing their challenging behavior. In the present study the way that M. was communicating was by screaming and making loud noises regardless where he was. In a very similar study there was a boy, whose reactions were unpredictable and he couldn't manage to control his tantrums and his aggressive behavior every time when people didn't understand what he was saying [13]. After the intervention using AAC, it has been estimated that M. – similarly to the boy in the above-mentioned study – made an important progress in his Communication and Socialization Skills, which also helped him to reduce their challenge behavior.

One more study show that AAC and especially AAC through technology attracted individuals' interest and motivated them to communicate effectively. The results in the present study suggest that communication through technology-based on AAC system such as GRID 3 was very effective on M. exactly in the same way as happened to the study of O'Neill et al. [20] using another technological tool of AAC. Also, in the present study M. after the intervention was more willing to communicate with his peers in class. He was much more confident to use the high technological tool of AAC that he was trying to communicate his thoughts. Similar results had been reported by Meer et al. [29] proving that AAC through technology help children with autism to increase their abilities on Communication, teaching them an alternative way of speech through technology.

Another very important target of the present study was to help the participant to express his desires and needs. After the intervention, M. was more confident to use the program of AAC and to communicate his needs such as asking for water, food or playing. The results of Flippin et al. [10], who tried to prove the impact of AAC on expressing children's desires, are very similar to this study. Both of the studies agree that AAC can affect productively the children when it's about giving them the opportunity to express their needs and desires. The idea of helping individuals to communicate their wants independently and to be intelligible to their environment is to help them also improve their challenge behavior. In the study of Frea et al. [13], a boy with autism and non-verbal speech succeed to learn to ask what he wanted using AAC and as a result his behavior had been changed positively. In the present study there was also a positive result on challenging behavior as M.'s Maladaptive Behavior had been reduced significantly.

Moreover, what also helped M. to improve his Communication and Socialization domains was the inclusive environment that had been created in school as he could talk through AAC with some of his peers. As it has been proved lots of the children with typical speech want to be involve using AAC and to communicate with the non-verbal children in class [3, 9, 15]. That environment motivates also the children with autism to communicate with their peers as they feel more confident the same way as M. felt. That is why he tried many times to invite his friends to listen his digital voice through the program, Grid 3 and to communicate with him. Last but not least, for an intervention like that it is very important to find an instrument that is suitable for the participant [26]. The choice of the technological tool of AAC in M.'s case study was really successful as it could be easily adapted to his needs and he seemed to be confident while he was using it.

5.1 Limitations

The present study involved only one participant. To see its impact on communication, socialization and the adaptive behavior of children with autism, the AAC intervention would provide more valid results if the sample was more extensive. Furthermore, as AAC is meant to develop communication and social skills, it would be more effective if the child results were continued to be monitored over a longer period of time to assess whether these skills have been embedded. The continuation and development of the AAC results in similar studies are essential in ensuring that AAC has a real affect and impact on children with autism. Also, generalization is another very crucial fact that it has to be succeeded and the children have to learn to use AAC in more than one environment. More studies need to prove that children can use a technological tool of AAC indoors and outdoors, perhaps providing a tablet instead of a computer.

References

1. Barker, R.M., Akaba, S., Brady, N.C., Thiemann-Bourque, K.: Support for AAC use in preschool, and growth in language skills, for young children with developmental disabilities. Augment. Altern. Commun. **29**(4), 334–346 (2013). https://doi.org/10.3109/07434618.2013.848933
2. Battaglia, D., McDonald, M.E.: Effects of the picture exchange communication system (PECS) on maladaptive behavior in children with autism spectrum disorders (ASD): a review of the literature. J. Am. Acad. Spec. Educ. Prof. **8**, 20 (2015). ISSN EISSN-2325-7466
3. Biggs, E.E., Carter, E.W., Gustafson, J.: Efficacy of peer support arrangements to increase peer interaction and AAC use. Am. J. Intellect. Dev. Disabil. **122**(1), 25–48 (2017). https://doi.org/10.1352/1944-7558-122.1.25
4. Campbell, P.H., Milbourne, S., Dugan, L.M., Wilcox, M.J.: A review of evidence on practices for teaching young children to use assistive technology devices. Topics Early Childhood Spec. Educ. **26**(1), 3–13 (2006). https://doi.org/10.1177/02711214060260010101
5. Charlop-Christy, M.H., Carpenter, M., Le, L., LeBlanc, L.A., Kellet, K.: Using the picture exchange communication system (PECS) with children with autism: assessment of PECS acquisition, speech, social-communicative behavior, and problem behavior. J. Appl. Behav. Anal. **35**(3), 213–231 (2002). https://doi.org/10.1901/jaba.2002.35-213
6. Charlop, M.H., Malmberg, D.B., Berquist, K.L.: An application of the picture exchange communication system (PECS) with children with autism and a visually impaired therapist. J. Dev. Phys. Disabil. **20**(6), 509–525 (2008). https://doi.org/10.1007/s10882-008-9112-x
7. Charman, T., Pickles, A., Simonoff, E., Chandler, S., Loucas, T., Baird, G.: IQ in children with autism spectrum disorders: data from the Special Needs and Autism Project (SNAP). Psychol. Med. **41**(3), 619–627 (2011). https://doi.org/10.1017/S0033291710000991
8. Chatham, C.H., et al.: Adaptive behavior in autism: minimal clinically important differences on the Vineland-II. Autism Res. **11**(2), 270–283 (2018). https://doi.org/10.1002/aur.1874

9. Chung, Y.C., Carter, E.W., Sisco, L.G.: A systematic review of interventions to increase peer interactions for students with complex communication challenges. Res. Pract. Persons Severe Disabil. **37**(4), 271–287 (2012). https://doi.org/10.2511/027494813805327304
10. Flippin, M., Reszka, S., Watson, L.R.: Effectiveness of the picture exchange communication system (PECS) on communication and speech for children with autism spectrum disorders: a meta-analysis (2010). https://doi.org/10.1044/1058-0360(2010/09-0022)
11. Foreman, P., Crews, G.: Using augmentative communication with infants and young children with Down syndrome. Down Syndrome Res. Pract. **5**(1), 16–25 (1998). https://doi.org/10.3104/reports.71
12. Fox, L., Smith, B.J.: Promoting social, emotional and behavioral outcomes of young children served under IDEA. Issue Brief. Tech. Assist. Center Soc. Emotional Intervention Young Children (2007)
13. Frea, W.D., Arnold, C.L., Vittimberga, G.L.: A demonstration of the effects of augmentative communication on the extreme aggressive behavior of a child with autism within an integrated preschool setting. J. Posit. Behav. Interv. **3**(4), 194–198 (2001). https://doi.org/10.1177/109830070100300401
14. Ganz, J.B.: AAC interventions for individuals with autism spectrum disorders: State of the science and future research directions. Augment. Altern. Commun. **31**(3), 203–214 (2015). https://doi.org/10.3109/07434618.2015.1047532
15. Ganz, J.B., Sigafoos, J., Simpson, R.L., Cook, K.E.: Generalization of a pictorial alternative communication system across instructors and distance. Augment. Altern. Commun. **24**(2), 89–99 (2008). https://doi.org/10.1080/07434610802113289
16. Iacono, T., Trembath, D., Erickson, S.: The role of augmentative and alternative communication for children with autism: current status and future trends. Neuropsychiatric Disease Treatment **12**, 2349 (2016). https://doi.org/10.2147/NDT.S95967
17. Koegel, L.K., Camarata, S.M., Valdez-Menchaca, M., Koegel, R.L.: Setting generalization of question-asking by children with autism. American J. Ment. Retardation **102**(4), 346–357 (1997). https://doi.org/10.1352/08958017(1998)102%3C0346:SGOQBC%3E2.0.CO;2
18. Mirenda, P.: A back door approach to autism and AAC. Augment. Altern. Commun. **24**(3), 220–234 (2008). https://doi.org/10.1080/08990220802388263
19. Mirenda, P.: Autism, augmentative communication, and assistive technology: what do we really know? Focus Autism Other Dev. Disabil. **16**(3), 141–151 (2001). https://doi.org/10.1177/108835760101600302
20. O'Neill, T., Light, J., Pope, L.: Effects of interventions that include aided augmentative and alternative communication input on the communication of individuals with complex communication needs: a meta-analysis. J. Speech Lang. Hear. Res. **61**(7), 1743–1765 (2018). https://doi.org/10.1044/2018_JSLHR-L-17-0132
21. Papadopoulos, K., Metsiou, K., Agaliotis, I.: Adaptive behavior of children and adolescents with visual impairments. Res. Dev. Disabil. **32**(3), 1086–1096 (2011). https://doi.org/10.1016/j.ridd.2011.01.021
22. Paul, R., et al.: Adaptive behavior in autism and pervasive developmental disorder-not otherwise specified: microanalysis of scores on the Vineland Adapt. Behav. Scales (2004)
23. Perry, A., Factor, D.C.: Psychometric validity and clinical usefulness of the Vineland adaptive behavior scales and the AAMD adaptive behavior scale for an autistic sample. J. Autism Dev. Disord. **19**(1), 41–55 (1989)
24. Pugliese, C.E., et al.: Longitudinal examination of adaptive behavior in autism spectrum disorders: influence of executive function. J. Autism Dev. Disord. **46**(2), 467–477 (2015). https://doi.org/10.1007/s10803-015-2584-5

25. Shane, H.C., Laubscher, E.H., Schlosser, R.W., Flynn, S., Sorce, J.F., Abramson, J.: Applying technology to visually support language and communication in individuals with autism spectrum disorders. J. Autism Dev. Disord. **42**, 1228–1235 (2012). https://doi.org/10.1007/s10803-011-1304-z
26. Son, S.H., Sigafoos, J., O'Reilly, M., Lancioni, G.E.: Comparing two types of augmentative and alternative communication systems for children with autism. Pediatr. Rehabil. **9**(4), 389–395 (2006). https://doi.org/10.1080/13638490500519984
27. Sparrow, S.S., Balla, D.A., Cicchetti, D.V.: Vineland adaptive behavior scales: survey form. Am. Guid. Serv. (1984)
28. Taylor, B.A., Harris, S.L.: Teaching children with autism to seek information-acquisition of novel information and generalization of responding. J. Appl. Behav. Anal. **28**(1), 3–14 (1995). https://doi.org/10.1901/jaba.1995.28-3
29. Van der Meer, L., et al.: Teaching multi-step requesting and social communication to two children with autism spectrum disorders with three AAC options. Augment. Altern. Commun. **29**(3), 222–234 (2013). https://doi.org/10.3109/07434618.2013.815801
30. Van Der Meer, L.A., Rispoli, M.: Communication interventions involving speech-generating devices for children with autism: a review of the literature. Dev. Neuro Rehabil. **13**(4), 294–306 (2010). https://doi.org/10.3109/17518421003671494
31. Walker, V.L., Snell, M.E.: Effects of augmentative and alternative communication on challenging behavior: a meta-analysis. Augment. Altern. Commun. **29**(2), 117–131 (2013). https://doi.org/10.3109/07434618.2013.785020
32. Young, A., Clendon, S., Doell, E.: Exploring augmentative and alternative communication use through collaborative planning and peer modelling: a descriptive case-study. Int. J. Inclus. Educ. 1–16 (2021). https://doi.org/10.1080/13603116.2020.1867383

Multimodal Interaction in ASD Children: A Usability Study of a Portable Hybrid VR System

Luna Maddalon[1](✉), Maria Eleonora Minissi[1], Sergio Cervera-Torres[1], Amaia Hervás[2], Soledad Gómez-García[3], and Mariano Alcañiz[1]

[1] Instituto Universitario de Investigación en Tecnología Centrada en el Ser Humano (HUMAN-Tech), Universitat Politécnica de Valencia, Valencia, Spain
lmaddal@i3b.upv.es

[2] Fundació de Docencia Y Recerca Mútua Terrassa (MTA) - Grup Salut Mental Infanto Juvenil, Terrassa, Barcelona, Spain

[3] Facultad de Magisterio y Ciencias de la Educación, Universidad Católica de Valencia, Valencia, Spain

Abstract. Recently, virtual reality (VR) has gathered a growing attention for treatment and intervention of autism spectrum disorder (ASD). However, few studies have attempted to use a portable VR system that can provide a good sense of presence. The aim of this article was to introduce a usability study aimed at exploring two interaction modes in virtual tasks presented in a portable hybrid VR system. The interaction modes were using a virtual hand reflecting the user's hand movements and a Wii remote controller. Four children with ASD of level 1 and five children with typical development (TD) aged between 7–8 experienced both modes of interaction (Wii remote controller and virtual hand) through two different tasks (selection and dragging) presented in a randomized order. Behavioural responses in terms of response time were measured within each task. Additionally, qualitative measures regarding the perceived difficulty and preferences for using the two interaction modes were evaluated. Finally, the efficiency of task action and the sense of presence perceived in the VR system were reported. The findings indicated that the virtual hand mode interaction was the most efficient in terms of response time and perceived difficulty. Moreover, the TD group reported a faster response time than the ASD group in the four tasks. In addition, the system has been shown as capable of transmitting a high sense of presence. Future studies are needed to replicate the results in a larger sample.

Keywords: Portable Hybrid VR System · Usability · Virtual Reality · Interaction · Autism Spectrum Disorder · Children

1 Introduction

Autism Spectrum Disorder (ASD) is a neurodevelopmental disorder characterized by social, communication, and behavioral deficits. In recent years, research on ASD has shown increasing interest in adopting technologies for treatment, such as computer applications and especially virtual reality (VR) [1–5]. In contrast to standard computer-based

M. Antona and C. Stephanidis (Eds.): HCII 2023, LNCS 14020, pp. 614–624, 2023.
https://doi.org/10.1007/978-3-031-35681-0_40

treatments, the strength of VR relies on its ecological validity by promoting a sense of presence within virtual environments, which can simulate daily-life scenarios [6, 7]. Sense of presence has been defined as the ability of people to respond and act to sensory stimuli within a virtual environment as if it were real [6]. For example, some studies showed that using VR in ASD children with low to moderate symptom severity leads to benefits in the treatment of social skills, non-verbal communication, stereotypes, and sensorial reactivity [8, 9]. The use of VR typically involves head-mounted displays (HMDs), which differ in their widespread use and provide in users a significant sense of presence. Unfortunately, due to the device dimensions, weight, and sensory difficulties, HMDs are not always well accepted by ASD children [10]. As an alternative, semi-immersive VR settings can be implemented wherein HMDs are replaced by large wall projections [10]. The Cave Automatic Virtual Environment (CAVE) is a surround-screen projection-based system. This alternative has been implemented in recent studies with young ASD population, which turns out to accept this type of system [10–12]. For example, a training study using the CAVE reported improvements in emotion recognition, affective expression, and social reciprocity in the ASD population [13]. However, this type of setting involves waiving the system's portability.

Consequently, we raised the critical question of whether a novel portable hybrid reality device setup (PHRED) could be a feasible alternative for ASD treatment based on new technologies. The idea is to test a semi-immersive VR system that does not require the use of a fixed wide space, such as the CAVE, and that can be easily transported and installed in different settings. Concretely, we introduce a usability study primarily aimed at exploring two interaction modes within the VR tasks: with a gaming remote controller and the user's hand. Secondary objectives of the study concerned exploring a) the preferred interaction mode, which action between selection and dragging was more efficient for task action, and b) the sense of presence perceived by users within the novel portable system. This study and the goals set, allow the construction of the basis for a larger study.

2 Method

2.1 Participants

Nine primary school children aged 7–8 were included in the study. Five were TD children (age in months, $M = 96{,}80$; $sd = 8{,}87$; males = 2, females = 3). The remaining four had a diagnosis of level 1 ASD (age in months = $89{,}50 \pm 6{,}403$ males = 2, females = 2). Expert clinicians previously diagnosed ASD through the Autism Diagnostic Observation Schedule 2 (ADOS-2) [15] and assessed comorbidities. Similarly, in the TD group, the experimenter screened for possible comorbidities via an ad hoc questionnaire to the parents.

Prior to the study, caregivers were informed about the experimental procedure and were given a written consent form for the children's participation. All participants were voluntarily recruited via social media.

2.2 Apparatus

The PHRED comprised a screen monitor LG 86" 16/7 SoC TV Signage, a computer Compatible Nvidia GeForce GTX 1070 CPU Intel i7 – 7700 @ 3.60 Ghz, the Azure Kinect DK (Microsoft Corporation, 2019), and a Wii remote controller (Nintendo®, 2006) connected to the computer by a Wireless Sensor DolphinBar (MayFlash, 2014). The Azure Kinect DK and the Wireless Sensor Dolphin-Bar were placed at the bottom of the screen monitor, at 50cm high from the ground (see Fig. 1).

Fig. 1. Kinect DK and Wireless Sensor DolphinBar.

The Azure Kinect DK had a depth camera in resolution mode 640 x 576 at 30 frames per second. The user's mobility area was set as two square meters at a distance of 1.5 m in front of the monitor (see Fig. 2). The mobility area was delineated with marks on the floor.

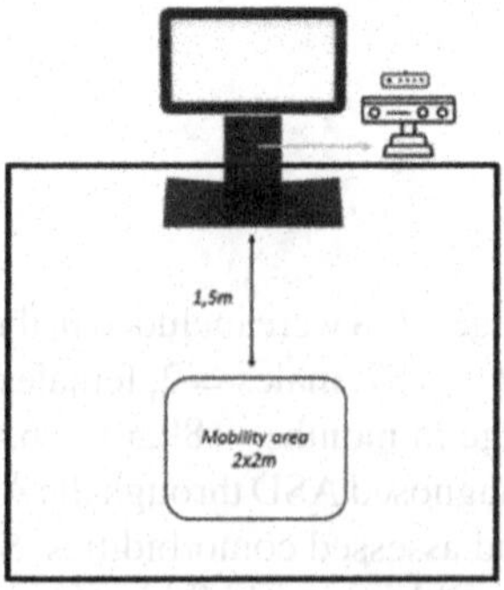

Fig. 2. Experimental setting.

Participants experienced two types of interaction modes with the virtual elements: the virtual hand and the Wii remote controller. The Azure Kinect DK enabled interaction with the virtual hand. It detected the user's body and projected it as a non-filled virtual body shape into the virtual environment (see Fig. 3a and c). Participants were asked to choose between male or female virtual body shapes to foster their meta-self-recognition in the virtual body, which provided the interaction based on the virtual hand. The virtual body shape mirrored the participant's body movements, thus enabling interaction with the application by moving their own hand. The second interaction mode consisted of a Wii remote controller, which worked as a pointer device through the Wireless Sensor DolphinBar. In this scenario, the virtual body shape projected by the Azure Kinect DK was not displayed on the screen. Instead, a hand-like cursor was projected following the movements of the Wii remote controller by the children. Through these two sets of apparatus, the user was able to interact with the system.

2.3 Virtual Tasks

The stimuli consisted of four gamified tasks created through the Unity® software. The tasks differed between them for the type of interaction mode involved (virtual hand and Wii remote controller) and the task action (selection and dragging). Indeed, each type of task (selection and dragging) was performed with the two proposed interaction modes. The virtual hand interaction mode required basic physical movements with the upper limbs to enable the interaction with the system while the Wii remote controller interaction mode required fine movements.

The selection tasks required selecting three pictograms displayed on the monitor (doll, ball, and car) in sequential order. The virtual selection was made by positioning either the virtual hand or the Wii remote controller on the target and holding the position on it for 0.5 s. Each time a pictogram was selected, it would disappear, and the next would appear automatically. In the virtual hand selecting task (HS), participants selected the pictograms moving the hand of the virtual human shape projected by the Azure Kinect DK (see Fig. 3a). In the Wii remote controller selecting task (WS), participants selected the same pictograms using the Wii remote controller (see Fig. 3b).

From the other side, the dragging tasks required dragging three green puzzle pieces and joining them to a red one that remained static in the central portion of the screen. Virtual dragging was implemented by passing the virtual hand (or Wii remote controller) over the green puzzle piece. This piece was automatically released once it reached a near area of the target red piece. Each time a puzzle piece was dragged correctly, it disappeared, and the next appeared automatically. In the virtual hand drag task (HD), participants performed the dragging using the virtual hand of the virtual body shape projected by the Azure Kinect DK (see Fig. 3c). In the Wii remote controller drag task (WD), the virtual actions were made using the Wii remote controller (see Fig. 3d).

In the tasks, the pictograms and puzzle pieces were placed in three different screen areas (right, left, and above) and presented one by one in a randomized order.

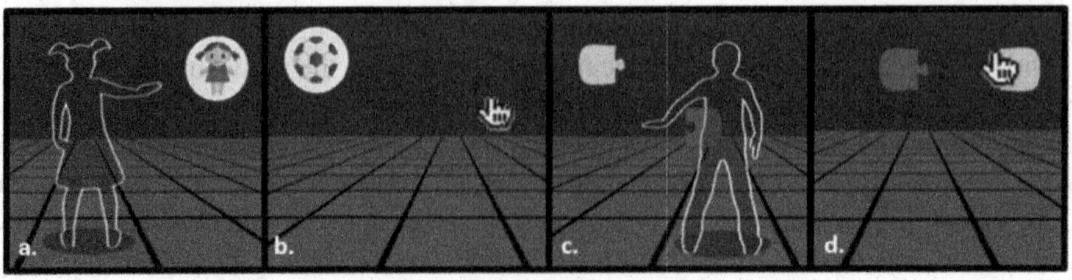

Fig. 3. Screen captions of the four tasks. a. HS; b. WS; c. HD; d. WD.

2.4 Measures

Behavioural Response. Each completed trial of a task corresponded to a certain degree of accuracy. Response time was calculated by subtracting the moment of execution (in selecting and dragging) from the moment of stimulus onset for each trial task. Mean response times were computed merely on the completed trials for each task.

Perceived Task Difficulty. After each task, the Single Easy Question (SEQ) [15] adapted for children was administered to investigate how difficult was perceived the interaction mode during the task. Participants were asked, "How difficult was it for you to use the virtual hand/Wii remote controller during this game?" The answer options were visually presented by a 5-point Likert scale in form of five emoticons that ranged from a happy face to a sad face, as extreme poles. Labels reflecting the meaning of emoticons were given under each of them. The labels ranged from "not at all" under the happy face to "very much" under the sad face. Children chose the option by reading it out.

Perceived Sense of Presence. After completing all tasks, children answered three questions on a 5-point Likert scale examining the sense of presence [see 16, 17]. These questions were slightly adapted to make them more understandable to children. The resulting sense of presence questionnaire (SPQ) asked: 1) "did it seem to you that what you saw on the screen was real?" 2) "did you feel like you could touch the objects on the screen?" 3) "did you feel yourself inside the screen while you were playing?" For each question, a Likert scale as for the SEQ was, and the child was expected to indicate a response. The answer scores were reversed, and a global index of the sense of presence was computed for each participant by adding up the three responses. The greatest achievable score representing the optimal sense of presence is 15.

Interaction Type Preference. Finally, at the end of the study, an ad hoc qualitative question was visually administered to assess children's preferences for using the virtual hand or the Wii remote controller as an interaction mode. Participants were asked whether they liked more playing with the virtual hand or the Wii remote controller. They were expected to respond by pointing to the image of their preferred interaction mode.

2.5 Procedure

The testing was completed in one single session per participant. All participants received basic and standardized information on the experimental setting and how to interact with the system (e.g., they were shown the mobility area in which they could interact). When participants were ready to start the experiment, they chose between the male and female virtual human shapes. Afterward, participants underwent an initial familiarization phase to familiarize themselves with the system and this type of interaction. The familiarization task consisted of a game used in previous studies but adapted to the above-described setting [12]. Specifically, they had to kick a virtual ball. This task was chosen to foster the meta-self-recognition in the virtual human shape without involving the upper limbs, which were the main body parts involved in the experimental tasks based on this type of interaction mode. At the end of the adaptation phase, the virtual tasks in the study were presented in a randomized order. During each task, a maximum execution time of 90 s was given after which the exercise was aborted. This maximum execution time was established to avoid frustration in children in case they were struggling with task execution. After each task, the corresponding SEQ was asked. At the end of all the tasks, SPQ was administered, and finally, the virtual hand-Wii remote controller comparison question was asked.

2.6 Data Analysis

Data analyses were performed using SPSS Statistics 22 (IBM, 2018). Differences between participants' age in the two groups were analyzed by independent samples t-test assuming equal variances.

To test the main objective, whether there was a preference between virtual hand and Wii remote controller interaction, three different analyses were carried out. First, it was performed a repeated measures ANOVA on the SEQ responses with interaction mode as a within-subject factor and groups as a between-subject factor. Second, the response time associated with the interaction mode was computed per each subject within each task. A repeated measures ANOVA with interaction mode as within-subject factor and group as a between-subject factor was run on the response times as dependent variable. The accuracy regarding the virtual hand task was 100% in the TD group and 85,71% in the ASD group. On the other hand, the accuracy regarding the Wii remote controller task was 96,66% and 41,60%, respectively Third, the question addressing preference was analyzed through a chi-square test of independence to evaluate the relationship between the groups and the interaction mode.

Regarding the task action objective, only the two tasks regarding the preferred interaction mode were considered for this analysis. A repeated measures ANOVA with the task action as within-subject factor and group as between-subject factor was performed on response time.

Finally, the Cronbach alpha and the global index mean of the SPQ were reported. An independent samples t-test test assuming equal variances on the SPQ global indexes was also run to compare the sense of presence in the two groups.

3 Results

The age difference between the groups was not statistically significant, $t(7) = 1.376$, $p = .211$.

Regarding the main objective, the SEQ analysis reported a main effect of the interaction mode, $F(1,16) = 19.871$; $p = .0004$ (see Fig. 4). Participants reported that playing with the virtual hand ($M = 1.39$; $sd = .61$) was less difficult than playing with the Wii remote controller ($M = 3.17$; $sd = 1.29$), regardless of the group they belonged to. No statistically significant difference was found either at the group level, $F(1,16) = .364$; $p = .554$, or in the interaction between groups and interaction mode, $F(1,16) = .004$; $p = .951$. The mean response times in the two interaction modes evidenced a significant difference regardless of the group participants belonged to, $F(1,16) = 20.05$; $p = .0004$ (see Fig. 5). The time interaction with the Wii remote controller ($M = 36.76$ s; $sd = 28.89$ s) required on average significantly more time than the execution with the virtual hand ($M = 16.11$ s; $sd = 21.96$ s). In addition, a between the main effect of group was found as statistically significant, $F(1,16) = 7.390$; $p = .015$ (see Fig. 6). Regardless of the type of interaction mode, TD children needed on average less time ($M = 15.02$ s; $sd = 6.29$ s) to perform a task than ASD children ($M = 40.70$ s; $sd = 7.04$ s). No statistically significant difference was found in the interaction effect between the groups and the interaction mode, $F(1,16) = 2.695$; $p = .120$. Finally, in the preference question, the relationship between the groups and the preferred interaction mode was not significant, χ^2 (1, N = 9) = .090, $p = .764$.

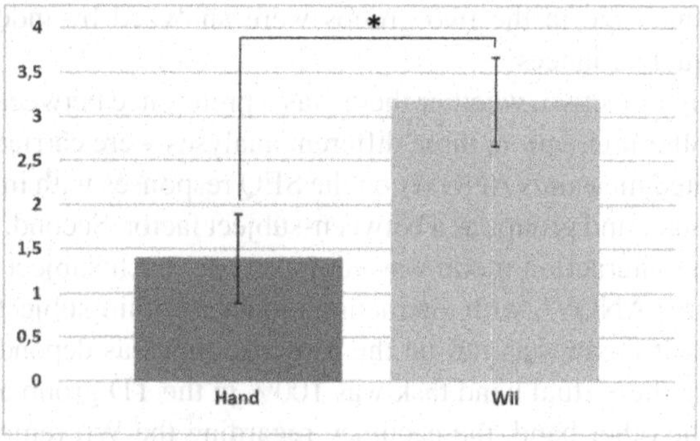

Fig. 4. Reported mean SEQ in the two interaction modes regardless of the group. $*p < 0.05$.

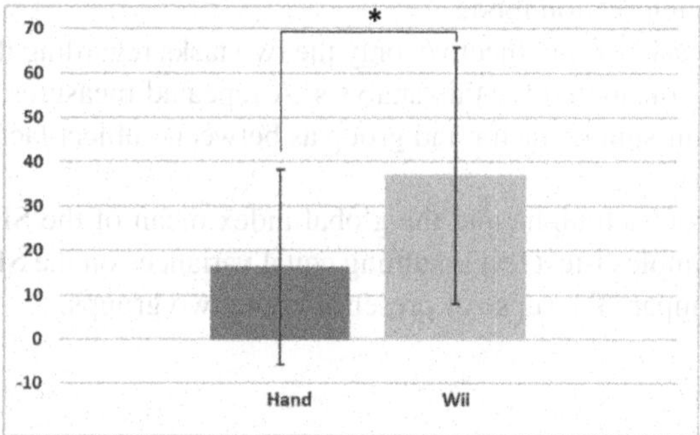

Fig. 5. Reported mean times in the two interaction modes regardless of the group. $*p < 0.05$.

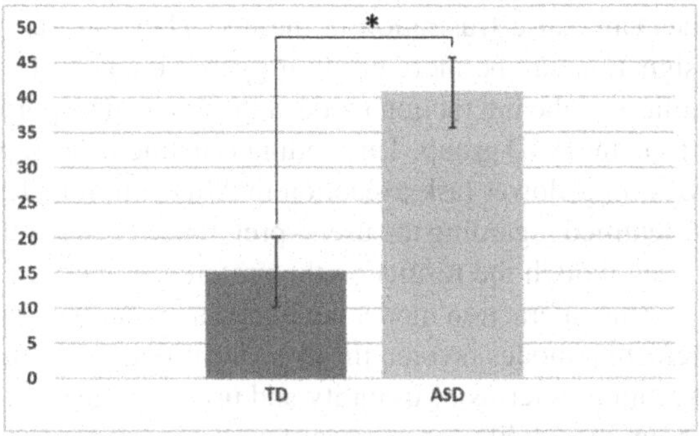

Fig. 6. Reported mean times in the two groups regardless of the interaction mode. *$p < 0.05$.

Regarding the secondary objective on the efficiency in task action with the preferred interaction mode, no statistically significant difference has been found either at task level, $F(1,7) = 4.814$; $p = .064$, or between groups, $F(1,7) = 1.633$; $p = .242$ or in the interaction effect between the groups and the task action, $F(1,7) = 1.714$; $p = .232$. Participants did not differ in the mean response time in the HS and HD.

Finally, in the SPQ the Cronbach α of .905 was reported, and the global index of the sample was $M = 13.00$; $sd = 3.04$. Regarding the sense of presence in the TD group ($M = 11.80$; $sd = 3.76$) and ASD group ($M = 14.50$; $sd = .58$), the difference was not statistically significant, $t(7) = 1.401, p = .204$.

4 Discussion

The purpose of this study was to test the usability of two interaction modes within the developed PRHED system. In doing so, the task difficulty and the preference of the interaction mode were investigated. The secondary objectives concerned the efficiency in executing the task actions in the preferred interaction mode, and the verification of the perceived sense of presence by users.

First, it is worth mentioning that results must be interpreted with caution, given the small sample size involved in the study. The present findings helped to deepen the knowledge regarding user interactions within the novel proposed PHRED, but further research will need to be repeated with a larger sample nonetheless.

The data obtained from the SEQ showed that participants perceived less difficulty in using the virtual hand than the Wii remote controller. This was also supported by the results on mean response time in each interaction mode. Indeed, the virtual hand mode needed less time, on average, for execution than the Wii remote controller interaction mode. This may be explained by the fact that the interaction based on the virtual hand was more direct and immediate (not mediated by a device), involving the users' hands. On the contrary, the Wii remote controller required users to be more skillful in the sense of controlling an interaction device in order to perform actions in the virtual environment. The slow and fine movements required to move the Wii remote controller on the virtual elements might have led to the need for higher response time to perform the tasks, as well as a greater user's perceived effort in terms of usability. It has been shown that, usability issues can cause frustration in the user [18] and that in ASD children, frustration and resignation can be more easily triggered than in TD children [12, 19]. Furthermore, regardless of the interaction mode, a lower mean response time was found in the TD group than in the ASD group. This finding is in line with empirical evidence of previous studies regarding slower task execution in ASD children [12, 20, 21]. Finally, no difference was identified regarding the users' preference between the two interaction modes. However, even though the results on the preference question did not unravel a certain preference for the interaction mode, the findings on the SEQ and mean response time in the two interaction modes favored the hypothesis that the virtual hand was more efficient in task execution in terms of usability and user experience. It should be noted that the absence of significant differences regarding the interaction mode preference in the two groups might also be due to the reduced sample size.

Regarding the task action, no significant effect was found in the mean times either at the task or group level. This could indicate that selecting and dragging required similar effort in execution. This finding suggested that the interaction mode was sensitive for users in terms of performance, while the action required to be performed in the most efficient interaction mode did not affect the task action. It seemed that both actions could be performed efficiently with the virtual hand.

Finally, the PHRED seemed to convey a great sense of presence, as indicated by the SPQ global index of $M = 13.00$, $sd = 3.04$. In addition, the perceived sense of presence did not differ between groups since they reported similar values. Although the interface was basic, participants stated that interacting in the virtual environment was very engaging. Likely, the greater sense of presence had a role in providing a better user experience in the virtual environment.

In summary, the findings suggested advantages for usability and performance regarding the virtual hand interaction in contrast to the Wii remote controller. No difference has been found between selecting and dragging as task actions, suggesting that both of them can be implemented in the PHRED for task accomplishment. Finally, the PHRED provided a significant sense of presence in the two groups.

These findings serve as an exploratory foundation for a broader project: ADAPTEA. They may be useful to deepen the feasibility of different modes of interaction, task action, and the capability to convey a sense of presence within a novel semi-immersive portable VR setup, such as the PHRED. With this information, it will be possible to design a viable virtual treatment for ASD by following the usability findings on the virtual hand. The study might be helpful for research on ASD and VR by exploring novel modes of interaction. Furthermore, in future studies, it would be of scientific interest to control further clinical variables, including for instance, motor coordination measure and IQ.

Acknowledgments. This work was supported by the project funded by the Ministry of Science and Innovation of Spain ADAPTEA (PID2020-116422RB-C21). It was also co-founded by the European Union through the Operational Program of the European Regional development Fund (FEDER) of the Valencian Community 2014–2020 (IDIFEDER/2018/029 and IDIFEDER/2021/038).

The authors acknowledge the valuable contribution of José Roda Belles, a virtual reality and information technology programmer. He developed the virtual interactive tasks and integrated the body tracking recording and the Wii remote controller into the virtual system.

References

1. Jyoti, V., Lahiri, U.: Virtual reality-based joint attention task platform for children with autism. IEEE Trans. Learn. Technol. **13**(1), 198–210 (2019). https://doi.org/10.1109/TLT.2019.2912371
2. Ke, F., Moon, J., Sokolikj, Z.: Virtual reality–based social skills training for children with autism spectrum disorder. J. Spec. Educ. Technol. **37**(1), 49–62 (2022). https://doi.org/10.1177/0162643420945603
3. Ravindran, V., Osgood, M., Sazawal, V., Solorzano, R., Turnacioglu, S.: Virtual reality support for joint attention using the floreo joint attention module: usability and feasibility pilot study. JMIR Pediatr. Parenting **2**(2), e14429 (2019)
4. Ramachandiran, C.R., Jomhari, N., Thiyagaraja, S., Maria, M.: Virtual reality based behavioral learning for autistic children. Electron. J. E-Learn. **13**(5), 357–365 (2015)
5. Yuan, S.N.V., Ip, H.H.S.: Using virtual reality to train emotional and social skills in children with autism spectrum disorder. London J. Primary Care **10**(4), 110–112 (2018). https://doi.org/10.1080/17571472.2018.1483000
6. Slater, M., Lotto, B., Arnold, M.M., Sánchez-Vives, M.V.: How we experience immersive virtual environments: the concept of presence and its measurement. Anuario de Psicología **40**, 193–210 (2009)
7. Malihi, M., Nguyen, J., Cardy, R.E., Eldon, S., Petta, C., Kushki, A.: Data-driven discovery of predictors of virtual reality safety and sense of presence for children with autism spectrum disorder: a pilot study. Front. Psych. **11**, 669 (2020). https://doi.org/10.3389/fpsyt.2020.00669
8. Frolli, A., et al.: Children on the autism spectrum and the use of virtual reality for supporting social skills. Children **9**(2), 181 (2022). https://doi.org/10.3390/children9020181
9. Herrero, J.F., Lorenzo, G.: An immersive virtual reality educational intervention on people with autism spectrum disorders (ASD) for the development of communication skills and problem solving. Educ. Inf. Technol. **25**(3), 1689–1722 (2019). https://doi.org/10.1007/s10639-019-10050-0
10. Alcaniz Raya, M., Marín-Morales, J., Minissi, M.E., Teruel Garcia, G., Abad, L., Chicchi Giglioli, I.A.: Machine learning and virtual reality on body movements' behaviors to classify children with autism spectrum disorder. J. Clin. Med. **9**(5), 1260 (2020). https://doi.org/10.3390/jcm9051260
11. Alcañiz Raya., et al.: Application of supervised machine learning for behavioral biomarkers of autism spectrum disorder based on electrodermal activity and virtual reality. Front. Hum. Neurosci. **14**, 90 (2020). https://doi.org/10.3389/fnhum.2020.00090
12. Minissi, M.E., Giglioli, I.A.C., Mantovani, F., Sirera, M., Abad, L., Alcañiz, M.: A qualitative and quantitative virtual reality usability study for the early assessment of ASD children. In: Annual Review of Cybertherapy and Telemedicine 2021, p. 47 (2021)
13. Horace. et al: Virtual reality enable training for social adaptation in inclusive education settings for school-aged children with autism Spectrum disorders (ASD). Blended learning: Aligning theory with practices, pp. 94–102 (2016)
14. Lord, C., Rutter, M., DiLavore, P.C., Risi, S.: Autism diagnostic observation scale-WPS (ADOS-WPS). Los Angeles: Western Psychological Services (1999)
15. Laubheimer, P.: Beyond the NPS: Measuring Perceived Usability with the SUS, NASA-TLX, and the Single Ease Question After Tasks and Usability Tests. Nielsen Norman Group (2018). https://www.nngroup.com/articles/measuring-perceived-usability/. Accessed 15 Sept 2022
16. Chung, D.H., Yang, H.C.: Reliability and validity assessment in 3D video measurement. J. Broadcast Eng. **17**(1), 49–59 (2012). https://doi.org/10.5909/JEB.2012.17.1.49
17. Yu, M., Yang, M.R.: Effectiveness and utility of virtual reality infection control simulation for children with COVID-19: quasi-experimental study. JMIR Ser. Games **10**(2), e36707 (2022)

18. Mendoza, V., Novick, D.G.: Usability over time. In: Proceedings of the 23rd Annual International Conference on Design of Communication: Documenting & Designing for Pervasive Information, pp. 151–158 (2005)
19. Jahromi, L.B., Meek, S.E., Ober-Reynolds, S.: Emotion regulation in the context of frustration in children with high functioning autism and their typical peers. J. Child Psychol. Psychiatry **53**(12), 1250–1258 (2012). https://doi.org/10.1111/j.1469-7610.2012.02560.x
20. Rodgers, R.A., Travers, B.G., Mason, A.H.: Bimanual reach to grasp movements in youth with and without autism spectrum disorder. Front. Psychol. **9**, 2720 (2019). https://doi.org/10.3389/fpsyg.2018.02720
21. Zapparrata, N.M., Brooks, P.J., Ober, T.M.: Slower processing speed in autism spectrum disorder: a meta-analytic investigation of time-based tasks. J. Autism Develop. Disord. 1–23 (2022). https://doi.org/10.1007/s10803-022-05736-3

OBA: An Inclusive Botanical Garden for Children with ASD

Susanna Pelagatti(✉) and Camilla Poggianti

Dipartimento di Informatica, Università di Pisa, Pisa, Italy
susanna.pelagatti@unipi.it

Abstract. In recent years, the mission of museums has expanded, adding to the preservation of cultural heritage the need to reach ever new users, including those with special needs. Accessibility has become a central issue in enabling people with physical, sensory, or cognitive disabilities to access culture. In our work, we focus on visit to the Pisa Botanical Garden and Museum by children with Autism Spectrum Disorder (ASD) and cognitive impairments. Contact with nature has important therapeutic functions for children with ASD. However, new environments and unfamiliar sensory stimuli can unsettle them. The goal of our work was to use the appeal of technology to create an interactive website that allows them to learn about the garden before visiting it. The website is accessible to children with ASD and includes multimedia materials and educational games. The main purpose is to help teachers find a way of inclusion for educational visits, since in Italy children with ASD are included in traditional school lessons. The site was developed in a participatory way together with garden operators, teachers, caregivers and by observing children with ASD. The site was initially tested in 2019 during three school visits with four male youth with ASD, whose observations triggered an iterative improvement process. Usability testing followed from 2021, involving four classes from an elementary school. The results of the SUS questionnaire showed great potential; children with ASD were enthusiastic about the activities carried out and expressed interest in repeating the virtual experience long after the museum visit.

Keywords: Accessibility · autism spectrum disorder · museum experience · website efficacy

1 Introduction

Autism Spectrum Disorder (ASD) is an early onset neurodevelopmental disorder that primarily affects three domains: social interaction, language and communication, and behavior (the symptomatic triad of ASD). The overall prevalence of ASD measured by the Centers for Disease Control and Prevention network in the United States was 23.0 per 1000 (one of 44) in the most recent report published in December 2021 [1]. Based on current knowledge, the only possible intervention for ASD is early diagnosis followed by personalized and multidirectional intervention [2]. However, even if many skills can be learned and people with ASD can gain some autonomy, many critical issues remain.

M. Antona and C. Stephanidis (Eds.): HCII 2023, LNCS 14020, pp. 625–644, 2023.
https://doi.org/10.1007/978-3-031-35681-0_41

In particular, most people with ASD find it difficult to orient themselves in new environments rich in multisensory stimuli, to accept sudden changes of plans, to decode a sophisticated and figurative language.

On the other hand, people with ASD are generally attracted to technology, which, thanks to its predictability, allows them to overcome the fear of face-to-face interaction, especially with people they do not know well. Therefore, in recent years, increasing attention has been paid to the use of digital tools for ASD in school, at home, during therapy, etc., proposing the incorporation of different types of technology (from the simplest to the most sophisticated) in every aspect of daily life to improve functional abilities [3]. More recently, the appeal of technology has also been used to improve the accessibility of cultural activities such as museum and exhibition visits [4–7].

In this paper, we describe OBA (Orto Botanico Accessibile), a website that uses technology to make the Pisa Botanical Garden and Museum more accessible. Organized largely in outdoor spaces, the museum provides information and captivating details about many plant species. OBA is actually part of a larger accessibility intervention that began with training some museum staff on methods of interacting with and involving people with ASD as well as organizing environments and activities. Appropriate visit itineraries were then established and digital materials for organizing the visit were made available on the museum's website, OBA, which offers a series of serious games to familiarize people with ASD with the environment prior to the visit, while encouraging generalization of knowledge gained through the experience. The activities were developed in a participatory manner in collaboration with garden staff, teachers, caregivers, and by observing children with ASD during garden visits.

The main contributions of this paper are: (1) the description of OBA and the participatory process of its design, and (2) the discussion of the SUS test we conducted with a group of teachers who used the material to organize inclusive garden visits.

The paper is organized as follows. Section 2 discusses the right to museum education for people with disabilities, focusing on the needs of people with ASD and the use of technology in inclusive programs. Section 3 reviews the relevant literature. OBA is detailed in Sect. 4, while Sect. 5 discusses SUS testing and the results obtained. Section 6 concludes.

2 Background

Museums are the flagship of culture. According to the statutes of ICOM (International Council of Museums), adopted on August 24, 2007, the best definition is the following:

> "[…] is a non-profit, permanent institution in the service of society and its development, open to the public, which acquires, conserves, researches, communicates and exhibits the tangible and intangible heritage of humanity and its environment for the purposes of education, study and enjoyment [8]."

It follows that it is important for a museum to know its audience. But what exactly is meant by audience? Much of the programming is aimed at families and tour groups, but modern museums aim to be more than that [9].

Over time, museums have evolved in line with societal trends and paid more attention to their visitors. Looking at the measures taken and the increasing focus on accessibility, one concludes that museums should include everyone who wants to visit them, including people with disabilities.

Provisions for the general public have long included consideration of physical barriers and universal design of a space. Examples include: captioning for the hearing impaired, ramps and elevators for people with mobility impairments, signs in Braille, and audio and video descriptions for the blind and visually impaired [10].

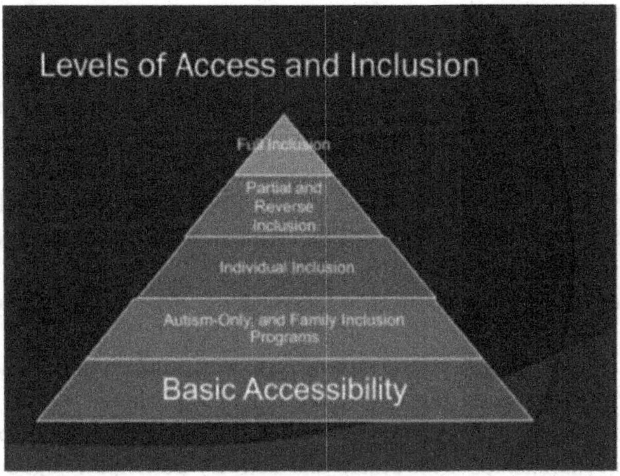

Fig. 1. Levels of Access and Inclusion in museums. Picture from [11].

Figure 1 describes the pyramid of accessibility levels in the context of accessibility and inclusion for people with ASD [11]. When discussing accessibility and inclusion in the context of ASD, we refer to a series of measures that are interrelated and must all be considered when implementing museum programs that can be used by people with this type of sensory impairment. *Basic accessibility* is about simple signals and anticipations to prepare for engagement in the museum, such as videos, photos, and the like, which do not necessarily make programs, events or exhibitions fully accessible.

Autism only and family inclusion programs provide programs and events only for people with ASD and their families, such as early openings or setting up locations with low sensory stimulation, usually with support from trained staff. However, these are not inclusive services because they provide separate experiences. In *Individual inclusion*, the museum provides special materials for the person with ASD to approach the visit alone or with the support of a caregiver. For example, we may provide welcome packets with books that use PECS or AAC, photo books, or sensory boxes with various objects.

In *Partial inclusion*, people with ASD have the opportunity to participate in a regular visit for a limited time with people without disabilities. For school visits, this gives children with ASD the opportunity to participate with their peers in a regular setting while receiving support and assistance as needed. This may mean that the child has to leave the place for a while or that periods of "decompression" are prepared by administering special digital material. On the other hand, *Reverse inclusion* refers to the inclusion process that is activated during the museum visit of children without disabilities in programs that are entirely focused on ASD.

Finally, we speak of *Full inclusion* when all the measures described so far are implemented and combined with digital resources that help create a fully inclusive experience by promoting sensory engagement, cognitive understanding, and emotional well-being for people with ASD and related disorders. In particular, accessibility tools appear to be extremely helpful for a large portion of audiences with ASD [11].

2.1 ASD and Assistive Technologies

In recent years, research has focused on the important role of technology in the lives of people with disabilities, with the goal of ensuring both personal autonomy and that of the family system in which the person with a disability is embedded. Despite the environmental interventions and assistive devices already mentioned, today we can no longer do without the use of technological aids. Renzo Andrich, a freelance engineer and expert in assistive technologies for people with disabilities, summarizes this concept with the equation of the "*4 As*" [12]:

Assistive technologies + Assistance (personal) + Adaptations of the environment (individual) = Autonomy.

A simplification of reality that shows how accessibility, tools and support are complementary concepts and allies in supporting the outcome.

However, according to Andrich, it is about developing the ability to plan one's own life, enter into relationships with others and actively participate together in building society, thus:

$$\text{Autonomy} = \text{Relationship}.$$

It was against this backdrop that the concept of Assistive Technologies was born:

> "The tools and technical solutions, hardware and software, that enable the disabled person, overcoming or reducing the conditions of disadvantage, to access the information and services provided by computer system [13]."

Assistive is intended to underscore the commitment this technology has to helping people with disabilities reach their full potential, compensating for their difficulties and allowing them a greater degree of autonomy. The goal is to convert information that is inaccessible to the person into another accessible format or provide a way to use input devices that meet the person's need [10].

The choice of assistive technology depends on several factors, especially personal factors. Different disabilities equate to different assistive technologies. In relation to Autism Spectrum Disorder, studies confirm that different types of technologies help compensate for verbal and social challenges while providing alternative ways to communicate, learn, and socialize [14]. Another important factor is the curiosity these people have about technology. Based on the different abilities that people with ASD bring to the table, we can offer different ways to support them:

- Simple supports (low technology). There is no need to use electronic media, and we use low-technology, tangible items such as maps, photos, and so on.
- Medium supports. Recording devices, projectors, calculators, etc.
- Sophisticated supports. Computers, tablets, alternative keyboards, speech synthesizers, etc.

If we focus on high-tech assistive device, the tool par excellence that seems to catch the attention of people with ASD the most is the computer. Research on children with ASD who use computers has found that attention is increased, appropriate behavior increases, generalization of skills increases, agitation decreases, and stereotypies decrease [15].

The potential of computers stems from the predominant visual stimulation of the screen (which promotes attention) and the predictability that reduces anxiety and uncertainty of face-to-face interactions [16].

2.2 Autism-Friendly Museums

While debates about disability access to museums have traditionally revolved around physical barriers, technological, digital, and informational barriers have become more important with the increasing use of technology. Cultural institutions now recognize that the same attention given to physical barriers must also be given to non-physical barriers and access to information [10]. However, designing accessible museum visits for people with ASD is not trivial. Indeed, each person on the spectrum is unique and unrepeatable. To suggest a stimulating program, the following list includes the most common and effective actions taken by what we can now call *autism-friendly museums* [17]:

- Encourage preparation for the visit: provide informational materials in advance.
- Early access: provide early or late opening of the museum and give staff the opportunity to create a distraction-free environment.
- Establish isolated spaces: reserve quiet spaces to prevent stimulus overload.
- No restrictions on entering or leaving: allow the person to leave and return to the meeting place as needed without forcing them to do anything.
- Availability of trained staff to respond appropriately to needs.

By incorporating apps, tablets, and smartphones into careful activity planning, we can further transform the museum experience. Technology has the potential to make museums even more ASD-friendly. In this regard, it is fair to say that there is growing interest in developing museum applications for these disruptions, just as there is evidence of the value of touchscreen devices in helping to enhance a range of opportunities and capabilities of these devices, museums are creating opportunities for active participation and entertainment. In fact, museum apps for people with ASD often provide social guides, games, hints, maps to highlight quiet areas or tactile spaces, etc. Trying to interact with staff can be a source of anxiety for a person with ASD. Therefore, it is useful to develop apps that allow them to find answers to certain questions on their own.

2.3 Related Work

The rapid growth of apps has attracted museums because of their ability to reach a variety of audiences and encourage new forms of exploration and interaction [18].

Several museums now offer programs for people with ASD. However, most of them require that the person with ASD be supported by a caregiver to facilitate the visit. Below, we review the proposals that come closest to our approach.

Since 2017, the Canada Science and Technology Museum (CSTM) in Ottawa has been committed to providing universal accessibility to visitors with motor, visual, and auditory impairments, as well as varying cognitive abilities. Their experiences in improving the museum experience for people with ASD are described in [4]. They began with a series of in-depth interviews involving four students and a male adult with ASD accompanied by caregivers. The interviews with the target audience and tutors, accompanied by on-site observations, yielded interesting results that were used to formulate improvements related to the museum experience for people with this disorder. The result showed the need for (1) trained staff to assist the visitor; (2) support materials that are also useful for tutors; (3) different ways to plan the visit in advance, such as documents and videos accessible on the website, to reduce the decisions to be made on site. Thus, the museum was provided with a "sensory guide" to be made available in advance in preparation for the visit, organized early openings and events for people with low sensitivity, and then began reflecting on useful tools to make the visit engaging for people with ASD. A key issue was the need to improve navigational aids, as participants were often confused by the layout of the CSTM. The website was redesigned according to identified needs to improve navigation and comprehensiveness and to include more pre-programmed information.

Another interesting experience was in Bristol (UK) at the M Shed Museum [19]. In this case, a group of children with ASD were involved in the design of the *What's Bristol* application. The aim of the project is to provide an enriching experience within the museum walls, improve social skills, and promote learning in the museum context. The design process (from which we drew inspiration for OBA) involved four major phases: (1) context discovery and understanding the needs of the target audience, (2) conceptualization through prototype development, (3) user testing to evaluate the embryonic version of the application, (4) redesign. The purpose of the within-project testing phase was twofold: to motivate participants to express their ideas and to determine their preferences regarding the specific features of the application. The sample studied was divided into two groups (green class and blue class), all belonging to the autistic spectrum but with different cognitive abilities and language difficulties. By mutual agreement, the two groups expressed a preference for sounds and pictures as types of rewards, appreciated the ability to customize colors, and the ability to access instructions for activities to be performed through both text and voice readers. Instead, the preferred digital tools appear to be animations and images. Different cognitive levels led to different preferences regarding layout design (who prefers list, who prefers grids) and navigation (position of buttons on top or bottom). Based on the results, it was decided to base the application on a treasure hunt game that allows users to discover different points of the city, introducing role-playing such as impersonating a group of detectives or journalists. The app focuses entirely on the game during the visit, without dealing with pre-visit preparation or later post-visit follow-up. The results were encouraging even with a limited number of children.

One source of inspiration for our work was the apps from *Infiniteach* [7], a Chicago-based startup dedicated to developing inclusive technologies. The app welcome, engage, and support visitors with disabilities and their families at museums, zoos, aquariums, and other cultural institutions. Each museum app includes:

- Visual and annotated exploration guides: way to prepare for the visit by reading and viewing multimedia materials.
- Creation of a personal museum plan: you can structure your visit by checking the boxes next to the attractions you want to visit.
- Communication tools: tap-to-talk icons help with communication and reminders, avoiding contact with staff that can cause anxiety for individuals.
- Games: you can take breaks by interacting with digital games during the visit.
- Maps: allow visitors to find quiet places or areas reserved for special experiences [7].

One of the strengths of their products is that they do not only focus on the on-site visit, but properly emphasize the preparation phase by providing the child with ASD with appropriate materials to gently introduce them to the future experience. This further emphasizes the extreme importance of the moment before the visit, including the importance of anticipating the activities in which the person will be involved.

3 Methods

In general, the main goal of technology design is to maximize the intended user group to create universal designs. However, the concept of universal design loses its effectiveness when it comes to designing for people with disabilities who have special needs. These benefit from highly customized systems that are the result of participatory design [20].

Our work begins with considerations for co-designing a website to provide access to the Pisa Botanical Garden and Museum for children with cognitive disabilities. Since the needs of all stakeholders and the definition of guidelines are at the heart of participatory design, it was necessary to involve a group of stakeholders and an interdisciplinary group consisting of:

- Psychology and psychotherapy experts from Synopsis Pisa.
- ASD therapists of the Autismo Pisa Onlus Association.
- Museum operators and accessibility project managers of the museum system of the University of Pisa.
- IT experts from the CNR of Pisa.

3.1 Design Process

The first phase of the design process was exploratory in nature to identify the needs, strengths, and interests of the children with ASD who were involved in the experience. Therefore, it was considered useful to attend afternoon meetings organized on site for small group of children with ASD and observe them participating in the activities designed by the museum accessibility project leaders. These boys were considered as co-designers. The children's contribution to the design was included by observing their interactions with people, their favorite on-site activities, and sensory stimuli.

This laid the foundation for an active discussion among the members of the aforementioned interdisciplinary group, which resulted in a list of potentially interesting multimedia products to be implemented. Initial development followed, ending with the creation of the prototype products that were later made available to the children.

The first test of the material took place on site in 2019 and included four male adolescents with ASD. After an initial and traditional welcome phase, the experience alternated between hands-on and multimedia activities supported by the digital material created to date. Some issues emerged during direct observation, which are summarized below:

- Varying activity times: an activity that lasted only a few minutes for one of the participants required more time for the other, who need constant stimulation.
- Adaptability of activities: when one of the participants needed reinforcement and help to perform certain types of exercise, the other often did them on their own, resulting in downtime that could create feelings of boredom.
- Balanced consideration: when working with people with different disabilities, there is often a tendency to focus efforts on the one who is most lacking. This is a mistake in the area of cognitive disabilities: it is necessary to consider people equally, encourage them and to praise them in case of success.

The information gathered in this way allowed for timely adaptation of the material developed. Above all, it became clear how important it is to create several versions of the tools and adapt them by creating different levels of difficulty.

The children participated in the co-design process by interacting with the prototypes and concrete material and expressing their interest. The meetings helped ensure that all the material went through an iterative improvement process before being incorporated into the final website.

4 Project Presentation

A museum visit, adapted to the specific programs for sensory disorders, is undoubtedly an important learning experience, but also an opportunity for recreation and escape from routine. However, to benefit from these experiences, three things should be ensured for people with ASD:

- An approach to initiative.
- An ad hoc organization of activities in the field and the provision of appropriate tools.
- Encouraging the generalization of what is learned during the experience to directly affect the overall well-being with which the person copes in his or her daily life.

Our project is aimed at children with ASD, aged 8 to 15, who are approaching the Pisa Botanical Garden and Museum for the first time by participating in inclusive programs developed by the museum accessibility route managers. Following the symptomatic triad of ASD analyzed in the introduction, children's immersion in a new environment can cause stress and behavioral problems.

When designing an inclusive visit, it is important to get the person with ASD and their caregivers to approach the museum and be able to handle atypical situations. To facilitate this, we considered creating materials that go beyond simple social stories and photographic images of places.

Finally, when we thought about the support such a product could provide for people with sensory impairments, we found that there was a lack of interest in promoting generalization of what was learned during the museum visit. Remembering past experiences can positively influence a child's behavior and make everyday life easier. Therefore, we believe that museum application developed for people with ASD should also focus on a third moment, that after the visit. Based on this need, the interdisciplinary project OBA is taking shape.

4.1 Goals

The project aims to develop multimedia materials to create an innovative relationship between children's museum visits and the museum experience of children with ASD.

Key objectives of OBA include:

- To explore new means of making the approach of the child with ASD to the museum experience more serene, moving from short playful visits to more complex, educational, and structured encounters.
- Provide families and caregivers with a tool that includes guidelines they can follow first in preparing for the event, second in conducting the activity itself, and third in consolidating and remembering the experience.
- An innovative tool that facilitates the organization and handling of materials for both the museum operator and the parents.

4.2 Developed Material

The website created provides a technology toolbox that, in a context such as the botanical garden, must take advantage of the sensory aspects of the visitor to ensure maximum engagement.

The following is the list of digital tools developed:

- Cognitive games: purely playful and informative purpose. Four games were developed:
  - Memory game with pictures of botanical garden and labels (Fig. 2, left).
  - Sequence game to counteract the deficit in temporal processing. We help the child traces the life cycle of a flower by asking him to drag the different stages to the correct place (Fig. 2, right).
  - Collocation game. The child must place each element in the appropriate area. The elements are of three types: flowers, trees and low plants that must be placed on the law, topsoil, and gravel, respectively (Fig. 3, left).
  - Emotion quiz to promote understanding and management of emotions. The child displays animated gifs that simulate typical botanical garden behaviors (e.g., smelling a plant or poking oneself with a plant). The person must determine

a response that matches the action by choosing between two different moods represented by two emoji (Fig. 3, right).

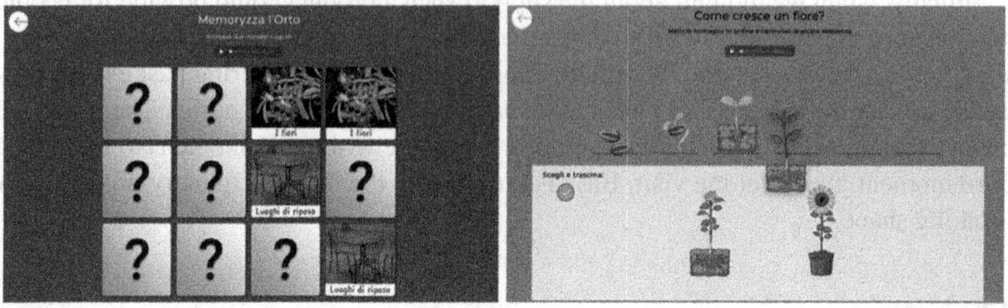

Fig. 2. On the left, the memory game "Remember the botanical garden" with the instructions that suggest connecting two identical images, such as the purple flower card (with the descriptive heading "the flowers") and the table with chairs (with the descriptive heading "resting places"). On the right the sequence game "How does a flower grow?" with the instructions that suggest arranging the pictures to create the correct sequence. The box in the lower half of the interface suggests the user to select the suggested elements and drag them to the correct area. (Color figure online)

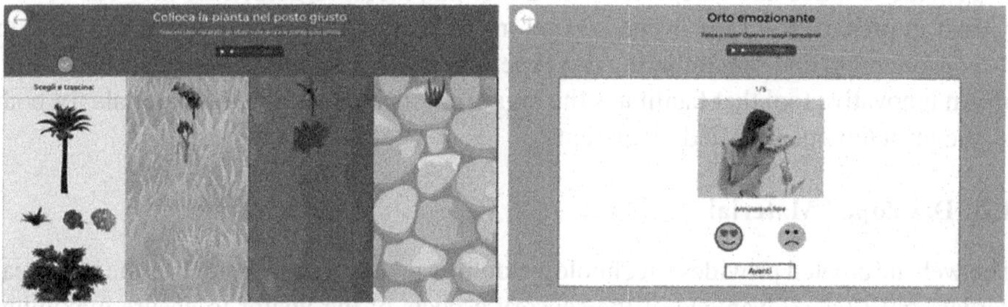

Fig. 3. On the left, the collocation game "Place the plant in the right place" with the instructions that suggest placing flowers on the lawn, trees on topsoil, and low plants on gravel. The box on the left side of the interface suggests the user to select the suggested elements and drag them to the right place. On the right the emotion quiz "Exciting botanical garden" with the instructions that suggest looking at the animated gif and associate it with a consistent mood, whether sad or happy. Below the animated gif is a text description of the action (like "smell a flower" in the example) and a button that says "next" to continue with the test. (Color figure online)

These games are not necessarily intended for a specific time but can be useful in different contexts. On site, to combine manual and digital activities and set up decompression phases. In the pre-visit phase, to prepare the visitor for the museum experience. In the post-visit phase, to promote consolidation of what has been learned.

- Digital preparation activities: digital materials designed to prepare the child with ASD for the museum visit by completing brief computer-based activities. These include:
  - A cognitive game called "Let us prepare the backpack": useful for understanding what items to bring to best enjoy the experience.
  - Photo gallery of the botanical garden with descriptive captions about the places being visited.
  - Video modeling: a technique in which desired behaviors are demonstrated through a video representation of the behavior [21]. The videos were made to show the child in advance how to perform the activities at the site in hopes that the child would learn through imitation.
- Printable materials: as needed, it may be useful to print some of the digital materials created, such as a map of the botanical garden, a social story in AAC to establish a routine, and a certificate of participation to serve as a final reinforcement of the activities.

At the end of the design, all these digital elements will be transformed into a responsive website that can be easily used by children, caregivers, and the parents themselves.

4.3 Architecture and Graphic Design of the Website

Knowing the scope and being well informed about the use cases and the target user, we decided to provide the website with a three-part structure.

From the home page, the user accesses the three main areas:

1. Preparation area: consisting of the digital preparation activities.
2. Games area: consisting of the four cognitive games.
3. Downloadable and printable materials area.

The implementation of the participatory design helped to increase the usability of the website by ensuring navigability, reduction of waiting time, completeness of content, comprehensibility of information, and communicative effectiveness.

In the design of each page, special attention was paid to the characteristics of the target audience. The structure, design, and interaction modes were created to maximize the level of accessibility and facilitate the implementation of the content. Accessibility requirements for people with cognitive impairments have recently been summarized by the W3C [22].

In the following point, we summarize the requirements that we have found to be most critical in a museum setting:

- Distributed web architecture, usable with mobile devices. The child can choose to use a PC or a tablet, depending on his needs.

- Simplicity of the interface, which must be perceptible, operable, and understandable. The presence of few elements, the use of AAS and labels, attention to the use of colors and sounds to avoid distraction and feelings of anxiety and/or confusion.
- Adaptivity to present the test according to the child's abilities. Providing three different levels of difficulty to meet the different abilities of the person.
- Error-free system. The games are designed to avoid any possibility of errors that could lead to unexpected responses from the child.
- Reinforcement and feedback. Animated gifs and congratulations are displayed at the end of each activity, and after completing all activities, the child can download a certificate to fill in with their details to reward themselves for participating in all multimedia activities. Providing reinforces is useful because the stimulus following a behavior increases the likelihood that the behavior will occur again.
- Listener preference for reading: each proposed digital activity is explained by a written command that is always supplemented by speech support. The inclusion of audio elements that read instructions aloud in a robotic voice meets the needs of a person with ASD who listens rather than reads.

The choice of the difficulty level is made by the user immediately after entering the home page, before accessing the specific activities. Depending on the severity of the disorder and the specific abilities of the child with ASD, he/she can choose between:

- Easy level of difficulty.
- Intermediate level of difficulty.
- Advanced level.

Once the difficulty level is selected, the proposed activities, especially the cognitive games, are automatically adapted ad hoc. The main differences that distinguish one difficulty level from another are the inclusion of distracting elements, which are zero at the basic level and then increase more and more at the advanced level.

Figure 4 shows what was just explained in terms of the cognitive game of backpack preparation. At the basic level, there are as many items to drag and drop as there are boxes to pick up items, so there are no distracting items. In the advanced level, there are more elements than can be placed in the spaces provided, so the user is forced to select those that suit the final purpose.

4.4 Discussion

Looking at some of the products and projects that are circulating today, you can see the commitment to developing tools that aim to set up decompression phases on site: games to distract while having fun, and maps that show high-interest locations for people with ASD as out-of-the-way, less noisy places [7, 23]. Although the game aspect should not be left on the sidelines, our multidisciplinary team decided to go beyond the pure entertainment aspect. We therefore devoted ourselves to the development of serious game, that is, games whose main application areas include education. Indeed, games of this type have great potential: they can meet the need for better education [24]. Our cognitive games go beyond what has already been tested in the scientific literature in terms of museum accessibility, because they are designed to be both attractive and

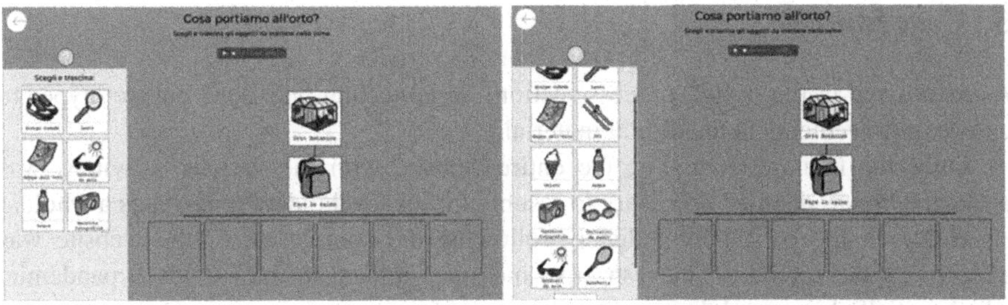

Fig. 4. On the left, the basic level of the backpack preparation game and on the right, the advanced level. The user interface shows at the top the title of the cognitive game ("What should we take to the botanical garden?") and the instructions suggest selecting and dragging objects (card with explanatory labels) to the target area that might be useful during the museum experience. In the box on the left side of the interface, a text command suggests the type of interaction: "Select and drag".

educational. Moreover, studies confirm that children with ASD prefer repetitive sensory games with cause and effect [25]. Given this goal and the desire to educate and promote autonomy, the cognitive games we propose to be played on site exploit the typical deficits of this disorder: understanding and managing emotions, temporal processing, preference for the favored channel (vision), limited interests, and adherence to a routine without flexibility.

Some digital projects point out the importance of preparing children with ASD for the new museum experience, limiting themselves to providing standard materials such as social stories in AAS and photo galleries. OBA improves and adds weight to the preparation time by providing additional suggestions:

- A cognitive game that instructs the child in an activity he or she performs daily (preparing the backpack), but in relation to the museum visit. The goal is to prepare while having fun.
- Videos of activities in which the visitor participates, filmed with the video modeling technique, to ensure learning based on imitation and avoid moments of discomfort on the spot caused by the novelty of the situation.

In contrast, no digital project designer for people with ASD museum visits seems to give due importance to the moment after the visit. OBA is also designed to be consulted some time after the museum experience, to keep alive in the child's memory the whole journey in which the child participated. Always having a website that collects cognitive games, photos, and videos of the experience itself promotes one of the most important goals of those who advocate for the autonomy of people with these disorders: generalization. The tools available to children through OBA promote generalization of skills and learning in environments and contexts other than those in which experience took place. As has been mentioned in previous sections, generalization can have a direct impact on the overall well-being with which the person copes in his or her daily life and improve autonomy and behavior management.

5 Case Studies

As mentioned in the design process section, initial testing was done on prototypes to ensure improvements to the digital material.

Once the final product, i.e., the entire website with the various activities, was packaged, it was deemed necessary to resubmit it to stakeholders to test it as a whole.

However, the period immediately following the completion of the website was affected by the spread of the restrictive measures related to the Covid 19 pandemic, which initially hampered the post-development phase.

After the end of the pandemic, it was not until 2021, coinciding with the resumption of museum accessibility projects at the Botanical Garden and the Museum of Pisa, that effectiveness of OBA could be verified by conducting usability tests.

It should be remembered that in Italy children with ASD are placed in classes with non-disabled people and are usually supported by a specialized teacher who prepares accessible material and acts as a tutor. In the school environment, the botanical garden is a popular destination for outdoor activities.

OBA was tested in four elementary school classes. At least one child with ASD was present in each class.

As soon as museum managers learned of the presence of children with ASD in the classes that were to participate in the trial, they contacted the teachers and introduced them to our project. After providing initial guidance on the proper use of the website, they recommended its use at the three key moments already mentioned: before the visit, during the museum visit, and after the visit. In the end, OBA was used by entire class, not just children with ASD, and proved to be an appropriate tool for promoting inclusion.

When the museum experience was over and enough time had passed to ensure generalization of what had been learned, we gave a questionnaire to the teachers of the classes involved to collect feedback and conduct a usability assessment.

5.1 Questionnaire Structure and System Usability Scale

After an introductory section dedicated to the collection of general data to properly identify the target audience, the questionnaire includes a series of questions about the use of the website. It was considered appropriate to ask immediately in which of the three phases the website was mainly used, which activities most attracted the attention of the class (with special reference to children with ASD), and to collect open-ended comments related to teachers' observation of students using the material.

The most important section is devoted to the System Usability Scale questionnaire (SUS), one of the most robust and well-tested psychometric instruments for perceived usability. It consists of ten statements that participants must agree with on a scale of 1 to 5, where 1 represents "strongly disagree" and 5 represents "strongly agree". Since odd and even statements have reverse polarity, to calculate the final score:

- Subtract 1 from the participant's assigned score for odd numbered items.
- Subtract from 5 the score assigned by participant for the even numbered items.

If you add the recalculated scores and multiply the value obtained by 2.5, you will get a score that ranges from a minimum of 0 to a maximum of 100. Sources confirm that an average final score of 68 or higher indicates a system that meets usability requirements [26].

In our case, the questionnaire statements were adapted to appropriately assess usability for the target population (children with ASD). Table 1 shows the list of ten adapted questions.

Table 1. The customized statements in our SUS questionnaire for children with ASD

Statement ID	Text of the statement
S1	I think this website could be used frequently by children with ASD
S2	I found the website unnecessarily complex for children with ASD
S3	I found the website very easy to use for children with ASD
S4	I think the child with ASD needs the support of a person who is already able to use the website
S5	I think the child with ASD finds the various features of the website well integrated
S6	The child with ASD found inconsistencies among the various features of the website
S7	I think most children with ASD could learn to use the website easily
S8	The child with ASD found the website very cumbersome to use
S9	The child with ASD was very familiar with the website during use
S10	The child with ASD needed to learn many processes before being able to make full use of the website

5.2 Results

The questionnaire SUS was completed by the respective teachers of four elementary school classes in Pisa who participated in garden accessibility programs through the website OBA.

Table 2 provides general information to identify the target audience that participated in the usability test.

Table 2. General information about the target group that participated in the usability test of OBA

Class ID	Average age	Total number of students	Students with ASD	Severity of the disorder
C1	8	18	1	Level 1: mild autism
C2	8	22	1	Level 2: moderate autism
C3	10	21	1	Level 1: mild autism
C4	11	17	1	Level 3: severe autism

Having collected the scores of the four classes, it is interesting to observe their distribution. Table 3 shows the mean and the standard deviation of the points awarded for each statement.

Table 3. Mean and standard deviation of the scores awarded for each statement

Statement ID	S1	S2	S3	S4	S5	S6	S7	S8	S9	S10
Mean	4	3.5	3.75	2	3.25	3.8	2	2.75	3	3.25
Standard deviation	0	1	0.5	0.82	0.96	0.5	0.82	0.96	1.41	0.96

Finally, Table 4 shows the final score given by each teacher according to the questionnaire of SUS on our website. Recall that the final score should be between a minimum of 0 and a maximum of 100.

Table 4. Final SUS score for each class awarded to OBA

Class ID	Final score SUS
C1	82.5
C2	80
C3	92.5
C4	57.5

5.3 Observations

Consistent with the data, OBA can generally be considered a tool with promising potential for use with children with ASD. Indeed, the average SUS score of C1, C2, C3, and C4 (Table 4) is 78.125, a good result considering that the threshold is usually 68.

Consider the final scores individually:

- Only C4 did not meet the minimum score, scoring 57.5 out of 100. This deficiency raises the question of the actual OBA target score. The child in this class had severe deficits in verbal and nonverbal social communication and showed a strong sense of frustration and distress during the visit, being hypersensitive to many sensory inputs. It follows that a tool such as OBA, useful as it may be, does not provide important benefits in conjunction with a severe degree of autism that requires very extensive support.
- C1 and C2 scored high, which were similar to each other.
- C3 scored the best, which is interesting considering the average age of the class, which is higher than C1 and C2. From this it can be deduced that with increasing age and support through inclusive teaching, an increase in autonomy can be observed.

In general, study participants felt that they could easily use the website with children with ASD (S3) and that they could use it regularly (S1) to support activities to provide a change of pace from lessons designed for them.

However, two statements negatively impacted the overall ratings. In general, teachers denied the possibility that a child with ASD could easily learn to use the website because of its complexity in some parts (S7, S8). Considering the good results on the other statements of the test, it is possible to reflect on how the teachers interpreted these last two statements from the point of view of "using the website alone". Since it is common for people with ASD to rely on the support of a tutor, these data do not have a particular impact on the usability rating, although they suggest the indispensability of support during use (S4).

From the data, it appears that OBA is an instructive and enjoyable tool that increases the frequency of positive behaviors, in part due to the reinforcement policy used.

In addition to the SUS part, teachers were asked to answer some open-ended questions from which useful information for possible future development was derived. In particular, it was found that:

- In preparation section, the most appreciated activity was the photo gallery with explanatory captions. This highlights the ongoing commitment of the multidisciplinary team to use the sensory channel preferred by people with ASD (vision) to create infographics and not just textual content.
- Further evidence of is that the most popular game in the serious games section was the memory game, which was based entirely on photographic content.
- The certificate that had to be completed at the end of all the activities was described as an excellent reinforcement, prompting the children to request similar activities for other museum visits.

In summary, the questionnaire indicated a tendency to select a medium level of difficulty not only for moderate autism, but also for mild autism. Hence the skepticism (confirmed by the C4 class results) about the actual possibility of realization in cases of Advanced autism. These children would most likely not be able to perform all activities.

Teachers remain convinced that children with mild to moderate autism can benefit from such a tool, preferably when supported by competent tutor. The latter admitted that they felt facilitated in preparing the visit and generalizing the knowledge learned through this technological toolbox.

Considering the feedback collected, the desire to look for new resources to make the approach to the museum experience more serene and to provide families and tutors with a tool guide (OBA's central objectives) seems to have been fulfilled.

6 Conclusions

Technology can help make museums and botanical gardens accessible to people with ASD. We described OBA, a website that helps children with ASD become familiar with the Pisa Botanical Garden before visiting. The goal is to reduce anxiety and stress due to multisensory stimuli in an unfamiliar environment, and to arouse and enhance curiosity. We tested OBA to prepare children with ASD for school field trips, as children with ASD in our country are placed in a traditional school setting. Teachers were asked to respond to a SUS questionnaire about the experience. The results are extremely encouraging and show great potential, especially for children with mild and moderate ASD. Of interest was the clear preference for activities that included photographic images and the extreme usefulness of the suggested reinforcers. This is supported by several teachers' statements about children's willingness to repeat the digital activities even after the experience ended. Thus, the goal of OBA, which is not only related to the preparatory phase of the visit but represents a collection of material that can be used later, has been achieved and underlines the great importance of the playful moment in the learning phase.

In our future work, we plan to enrich the proposed activities using Augmented Reality. In recent years, a positive impact of AR in the world of people with ASD has been demonstrated in several areas: improving social skills, improving autonomy, and increasing cognitive and motor skills [27]. The use of this technology is increasing exponentially in botanical gardens and museums. Therefore, OBA 2.0 aims to use AR as a vehicle and support to further facilitate access to museums and ensure greater interaction and easier immersion of the person in the environment. We are currently developing three-dimensional models of plants, taking advantage of three-dimensional audio, implementing serious games with the ability to interact with other players as well, and, most importantly, making great use of Augmentative Alternative Communication to make greater use of the sense of sight, which in part ensured the success of the first version of OBA and the one described in this article.

Acknowledgements. We thank the staff of the Pisa Botanical Garden and Museum and the staff of the University of Pisa involved in museum accessibility projects for their helpfulness.

We thank the experts in psychology and psychotherapy from Synopsis Pisa and the ASD specialists from the Autism Association Pisa Onlus for their support in understanding this neurodevelopmental disorder.

Thank you to the experts of IT of CNR Pisa for their support in the concrete implementation of the technological material.

Finally, special thanks to the children with ASD, their families and caregivers who participated in the pre-tests and to the schools that participated in the final tests.

References

1. Maenner, M., et al.: Prevalence and Characteristics of Autism Spectrum Disorder Among Children Aged 8 Years – Autism and Developmental Disabilities Monitoring Networks, 11 Sites, United States, 2018. Morbidity and mortality weekly report. Surveillance summaries 70(11), pp. 1–16 (2021). https://pubmed.ncbi.nlm.nih.gov/34855725/
2. Rogers, S., Wallace, K.: Intervention for infants and toddlers with autism spectrum disorders. In: Amaral, D., Geschwind, D., Dawson, G. (eds.) Autism Spectrum Disorders 2011, pp. 1081–1094. Oxford Academic, New York (2012). https://oxfordmedicine.com/view/https://doi.org/10.1093/med/9780195371826.001.0001/med-9780195371826-chapter-061
3. Stokes, S.: Tecnologia assistiva per bambini con autismo. Technical report, Genitori Contro Autismo Blog (2009). http://www.genitoricontroautismo.org/files/Doc1TecnologiaAssistiva.pdf
4. Hoskin, E., et al.: Assessing the experience of people with autism at the Canada science and technology museum. In: ACM CHI Conference on Human Factors in Computing Systems, pp. 1–7. Remote (2020). https://dl.acm.org/doi/10.1145/3334480.3382834
5. Solima, L, Tani, M., Sasso, P.: Social innovation and accessibility in museum: some evidence from the SoStare al MANN Project. Il capitale culturale (23), pp. 23–56 (2021). https://riviste.unimc.it/index.php/cap-cult/article/view/2518
6. Garzotto, F., et al.: Improving museum accessibility through storytelling in wearable immersive virtual reality. In: 3rd Digital Heritage International Congress (Digital Heritage), pp. 1–8. San Francisco (2018). https://www.researchgate.net/publication/335429280_Improving_Museum_Accessibility_through_Storytelling_in_Wearable_Immersive_Virtual_Reality
7. Infiniteach Our Work. https://www.infiniteach.com/our-work/. Accessed 2023/01/16
8. ICOM Museum Definition. https://icom.museum/en/resources/standards-guidelines/museum-definition/. Accessed 2023/01/16
9. Vrsalović, S.: Programmes by the Ethnographic Museum for Persons Suffering from Autism Spectrum Disorder. Etnološka Istraživanja (22), pp. 121–133 (2017). https://hrcak.srce.hr/198106
10. McMillen, R.: Museum disability access: social inclusion opportunities through innovative new media practices. Pacific J. (10), pp. 95–107 (2015). http://hdl.handle.net/11418/554
11. Rudy, L.: Autism in the Museum. Technical report, Autism in the Museum Blog (2013). http://www.autisminthemuseum.org/p/blog-page_20.html
12. Andrich, R.: Concetti di base su ausili e accessibilità. Technical report, Corso di Alta Formazione sulle Tecnologie Assistive per le persone con disabilità (2019). http://portale.siva.it/files/doc/library/corso_nf_andrich_01_printout.pdf
13. Parlamento italiano: Disposizioni per favorire l'accesso dei soggetti disabili agli strumenti informatici. Legge 4 (2004). https://web.camera.it/parlam/leggi/04004l.html
14. Debora, M., Kagohara, D., et al.: Using iPods® and iPads® in teaching programs for individuals with developmental disabilities: a systematic review. Res. Dev. Disabilities **34**(1), 147–156 (2013). https://www.sciencedirect.com/science/article/abs/pii/S0891422212001941?via%3Dihub
15. Valencia, K., et al.: The impact of technology on people with autism spectrum disorder: a systematic literature review. Sensors **19**(20), 1–22 (2019). https://pubmed.ncbi.nlm.nih.gov/31623200/
16. Murray, D.: Autism and information technology: therapy with computers. In: Powell, S., Jordan, R. (eds.) Autism and learning: a guide to good practice, pp. 100–117. David Fulton, London (1997)
17. Coates, C.: Making the Museum Autism Friendly – Best Practice from Around the World. Museum Next (2019). https://www.museumnext.com/article/making-the-museum-autism-friendly/

18. Fisher, M., Moses, J.: Rousing the mobile herd: apps that encourage real space engagement. In: Proctor, N., Cherry, R. (eds.) MW2013: Museum and the Web 2013. (2013). https://mw2013.museumsandtheweb.com/paper/rousing-the-mobile-herd-apps-that-encourage-real-space-engagement/
19. Magkafa, D., Newbutt, N.: The process of involving children with autism in the design of a museum-based application. MW2013: Museum and the Web 2013, pp. 1–15. Vancouver (2018). https://www.researchgate.net/publication/327535003_The_process_of_involving_children_with_autism_in_the_design_of_a_museum-based_application
20. Manesha, A., et al.: Expanding designing for one to invite others through reverse inclusion. In: 23rd International ACM SIGACCESS Conference on Computers and Accessibility, pp. 1–4. Association for Computing Machinery, New York (2021)
21. Bellini, S., Akullian, J.: A meta-analysis of video modeling and video self-modeling interventions for children and adolescents with autism spectrum disorders. Exceptional Children **73**(3), 264–287 (2007). https://journals.sagepub.com/doi/10.1177/001440290707300301
22. W3C. Cognitive Accessibility at W3C. https://www.w3.org/WAI/cognitive/. Accessed 2023/01/16
23. Young V&A Info. https://www.vam.ac.uk/info/young. Accessed 2023/01/16
24. Bellotti, F., et al.: Assessment in and of Serious Games: An Overview. Advances in Human-Computer Interaction, vol. 2013, pp. 1–11 (2013). https://www.hindawi.com/journals/ahci/2013/136864/
25. Buschi, A.: Il gioco nel bambino con autismo. Technical report, Occhi di Bimbo Blog (2018). https://occhidibimbo.com/gioco-nel-bambino-autismo/
26. Boscarol, M.: I questionari del Protocollo eGLU per valutare i servizi web. Technical report, Progetto Performance PA (2015). http://egov.formez.it/sites/all/files/i_questionari_del_protocollo_eglu_per_valutare_i_servizi_web.pdf
27. Vita, S., et al.: ARtis: How AR supports the guided experience in museums for people with Autism. Paper. In: Proccedings of the First Workshop on Technology Enhanced Learning Environments for Blended Education (teleXbe2021), pp. 1–6. University of Foggia, Foggia (2021). http://ceur-ws.org/Vol-2817/paper38.pdf

Comparison of Different Interaction Formats for Automatized Analysis of Symptoms in Children with Autism Spectrum Disorder

Larisa Pliska[1](✉), Isabel Neitzel[1], Michael Buschermöhle[2], and Ute Ritterfeld[1]

[1] TU Dortmund University, Emil-Figge-Straße 50, 44227 Dortmund, Germany
larissa.pliska@tu-dortmund.de

[2] KIZMO GmbH, Steinweg 13-17, 26122 Oldenburg, Germany

Abstract. Observation and assessment of interactional difficulties in children with suspected Autism Spectrum Disorder (ASD) are part of the gold standard in the ASD diagnostic process. The risk for a diagnosis of ASD can be assessed involving the three typical symptom categories speech/language, facial expression, and interaction. However, identifying ASD turns out to be staff-intensive and time consuming and hereby often delaying the start of therapy and support for the child and the family. Automatized analyses, for example of eye contact or mimic response, could facilitate early screening and hereby contribute to more efficient diagnostic routines. Such automatized screening can build on advanced language and mimic processing technology already available. However, the validity of automated screening depends on the elicitability of behavior that signifies ASD. Therefore, a proof of principle is required to demonstrate that a mediated approach does indeed elicit ASD symptoms that are usually observed during natural face-to-face interaction. **Research aim:** The goal of this paper is to show preliminary results on the validation of diagnostic comparability of real and simulated interactions between a child with ASD and an examiner. Specifically, the simulated interactions would be most useful for an automated screening if they could be based on pre-recorded stimuli and not only be mediated in real time. **Method:** For such a proof of principle approach we apply a within-design with five conditions in which the emerging symptoms in children diagnosed with ASD are contrasted with regard to speech, facial expressions, and communication behavior. Both, the authenticity of the communication situation (face-to-face vs. video call vs. pre-recorded video) as well as the child's interlocutor (real person vs. video recording vs. digital avatar) are varied and conditions fully counterbalanced. After each condition, the child is prompted to reflect about the perceived authenticity of the test situation and their interactional involvement. Inclusion criteria include boys with an established diagnosis of ASD at elementary school age who are verbally fluent. **Results and implications:** Although data collection is still ongoing we present preliminary results based on two children. The observations suggest that digitally delivered content is highly appealing and perceived as appropriate for children with ASD. Further data collection and analyses will inform whether typical and relevant ASD symptoms in the participants will be observable in mediated and even fully automatized conditions. However, our first impressions already demonstrate a great potential for automated measurements with low personnel effort.

M. Antona and C. Stephanidis (Eds.): HCII 2023, LNCS 14020, pp. 645–656, 2023.
https://doi.org/10.1007/978-3-031-35681-0_42

Keywords: Autism Spectrum Disorder · Human-computer-interaction · Automatized analysis

1 Automatized Analysis of Symptoms in Children with Autism Spectrum Disorder

Autism spectrum disorder (ASD) is classified as a neurodevelopmental disorder and is characterized by persistent deficits in mutual social interaction as well as communication and by restricted, repetitive and stereotyped behavior, interests or activities [2]. The clinical appearance of ASD is heterogeneous and the symptoms are multifaceted, thus varying widely from person to person [2, 28]. A child with a potential diagnosis of ASD can be assessed involving the three typical symptom categories speech/language, facial expression, and interaction. In the ASD diagnostic process, observation and assessment of interactional difficulties in children with suspected ASD are part of the gold standard [17]. Standard procedures for diagnosing ASD take several hours [26], which results in the diagnostic process to be staff-intensive and time consuming [25]. The required effort contributes to long waiting times for a diagnosis and often delays the start of therapy and support [26]. For example, a study by Wiggins and colleagues (2006) shows significant delays of over a year between the parents' initial suspicion and the child's diagnosis of ASD, resulting in uncertainty for the whole family [29]. In addition, child therapy can only start when a diagnosis has been established [18] with waiting times causing to miss out on support opportunities. Studies demonstrate that the early start of intervention leads to better developmental outcomes [16, 29]. In this context, early screening of children with suspected ASD is extremely important so that those with indication of a diagnosis can be diagnosed more profoundly and be included earlier in intervention programs [16, 29] while others may be taken off the waiting list.

Digital applications and new technologies are promising tools for diagnostics in general [14] and possibly also for identification of ASD. Specifically, automated analyses of eye contact or mimic response may facilitate early screening, contributing to more efficient diagnostic routines. Especially eye movement has been recognized as biomarker for ASD diagnosis [16] that has the potential to detect signs of ASD even before other behavioral symptoms become apparent [31]. Other studies show that increased visual preference for dynamic geometric images, rather than social images, can be used as an early biomarker of severe ASD [19, 22]. In addition, automated speech analytics offer some potential for diagnostic application [11, 20]. Moreover, digital analysis tools and simulations already provide promising results for the diagnostic of social interaction, facial expression or gaze direction detection [9, 24]. The latest mobile technology can be used to capture facial expressions and gestures in three dimensions by combining cameras with depth sensors. Thus, automated screening that captures symptoms based on gaze, speech, and interaction can build on the advanced speech and facial expression processing technologies that are already available.

Yet, it needs to be demonstrated that such mediated approach allows to elicit relevant ASD symptoms usually observed during natural face-to-face interaction. In this regard, previous studies report that social interaction with virtual characters (avatars)

can be very similar to face-to-face interaction in relation to the perception of emotional expressions [8]. In the context of virtual reality use, for example, the findings of Forbes and colleagues (2016) suggest that imitation respectively mimicry in ASD can also appear when interacting with avatars [10]. In general, individuals with ASD seem to respond very well to virtual representation and computer-mediated interactions [1, 5, 7]. For example, a study by Berger and colleagues (2022) was able to show that first, younger children (1- to 3-year olds) responded positively to virtual environments and presentations [6]. Second, ASD relevant symptoms actually occurred in media use [6]. In other words, the ASD-relevant symptoms could be observed in the spontaneous and elicited behavior during synchronous virtual assessments [6]. Since virtual environments in particular promote interaction with avatars [4], an automated digital screening system with the use of virtually elicited interactions may be even particularly attractive to children with ASD [12]. However, the validation of diagnostic comparability of real and simulated interactions is still needed. In our project[1], we aim to evaluate mediated formats for simulated interactions with respect to their comparability with real interactions and hereby identify their respective diagnostic value. This paper presents the applied methodological approach and exemplary data from two children.

2 Method

2.1 Participants

Participants are children with diagnosed ASD. In order to approximate this with respect to symptoms highly heterogeneous target group, the current phase of research includes only boys aged six to eleven years who communicate verbally fluently and do not show cognitive impairment. Recruitment of 25 participants with ASD is still ongoing. In addition, a control group with typical development with comparable number of persons will be eventually added in which sex and age are matched to the ASD-group.

The findings presented in this paper are preliminary results from two participating boys (both aged six years) with diagnosed ASD. Both participants are monolingual German-speakers and communicate verbally with fluent speech flow. Despite the ASD diagnosis, no additional physical diagnosis nor cognitive impairment was reported for these children. However, both children had a psychiatric diagnosis of impulse control disorder. Visus and hearing abilities were unimpaired. All diagnostic information was provided by the parents and is based on medical examinations and parent questionnaires.

2.2 Research Design and Testing Materials

To investigate the potential of mediated formats on eliciting ASD relevant symptoms in the areas of gaze, speech, and interaction, a within-subject-design was realized involving five conditions representing a hierarchy of successive mediation (see Fig. 1).

[1] The research project IDEAS (Identification of autism spectrum disorder using speech and facial expression recognition) is funded by German Federal Ministry of Education and Research (BMBF), funding code: 13GW0584D.

A face-to-face condition is to be understood as a baseline condition, since it comes closest to an everyday conversation situation. Systematically, from condition to condition thereafter, both the time course (real-time vs. pre-recorded) and the authenticity of the interlocutor (real person 'live' vs. pre-recorded, digital avatar 'live' vs. pre-recorded) are varied. The digital avatar was created using Apple's Memoji software [3] and visually mimics the experimenter, who conducts all testing. Each participating child completes all five conditions in two sessions. In order to control for systematic effects, the conditions are fully counterbalanced.

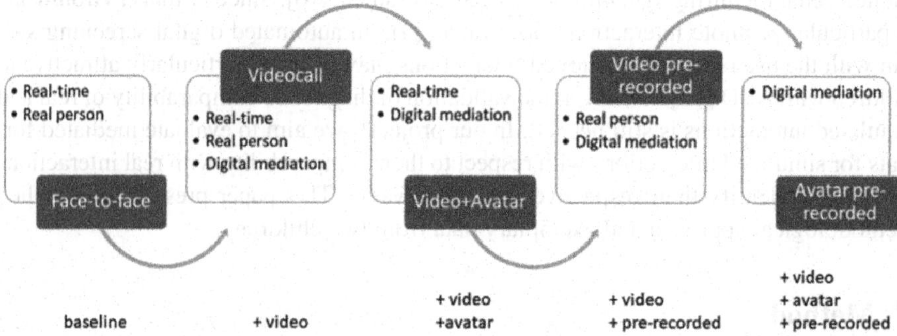

Fig. 1. Conditions in the current investigation, counterbalanced in characteristics concerning authenticity of communication and the child's interlocutor. Conditions are presented in blue boxes, characteristics are visualized on the x-axis.

In each condition a number of tasks were presented to elicit behavior in the areas of gaze, speech, and interaction. All tasks were conceptualized to potentially elicit ASD symptoms, for example an impairment in recognition of basic emotion [13]. For this purpose, findings from other studies were evaluated and prioritized [15, 30]. For example, video material was used by Polzer et al. (2022) [23] and pictures of emotions were used by Negrão et al. (2021) [21]. Overall, each condition comprises the same order of seven task types: (1) warm-up/conversational situation, (2) imitation of gestures, (3) imitation of mimic expressions, (4) assessment and explanation of emotions (image-based), (5) contrasting social and non-social images, (6) contrasting social and non-social videos, (7) farewell, partly interrupted by a first-time or re-calibration to record eye movements.

Variation of conditions of mediation in a within-subject-design has to ensure comparable content in each condition. However, in order to avoid repetitive behavior, it is essential that content is not merely replicated from one condition to another. Therefore, content used in each condition was parallelized. For example, in an interview sequence, which is conducted at the beginning of each condition (based on Drimalla et al., 2020 [9]), the same sequence of questions is offered in each condition (e.g., open question, decision question, yes/no question, open question), but a different topic of conversation is chosen (e.g., seasons, animals,...).

2.3 Testing Procedure

The tests were carried out with extensive and high-quality technical equipment. Eye movements (i.e., eye position and gaze direction) as well as 52 facial expression features (e.g., movement of the left corner of the mouth, raising of the right eyebrow, or opening of the jaw) are captured and recorded with up to 60 frames per second using a custom-made app (KIZMO Face-Analyzer[2]) running on an iPad. The data of each recording are stored as numerical values for later analysis with MATLAB [27]. Facial expressions of emotions can often be identified using just a small subset of the facial expression features and are thus be evaluated over time. The presentation of the visual stimuli as well as the experimenter in the digitally mediated conditions makes use of several iPads (including iPad Pro 11", 3rd gen.; iPad OS 16.3) and FaceTime-technology by Apple (iPad OS-Version 16.3; [3]). Speech is recorded using a TASCAM DR-40X recorder and a Sennheiser MEB table microphone with the aim of automated evaluation.

Figure 2 illustrates the test setting with a pilot participant. The child sits with an unobstructed view of the external screen, which is used to transmit the digitally mediated conditions, and of the test administrator in the face-to-face condition. Placed behind the child's back a technical assistant controls and monitors the stimuli and recordings with the KIZMO app during the test.

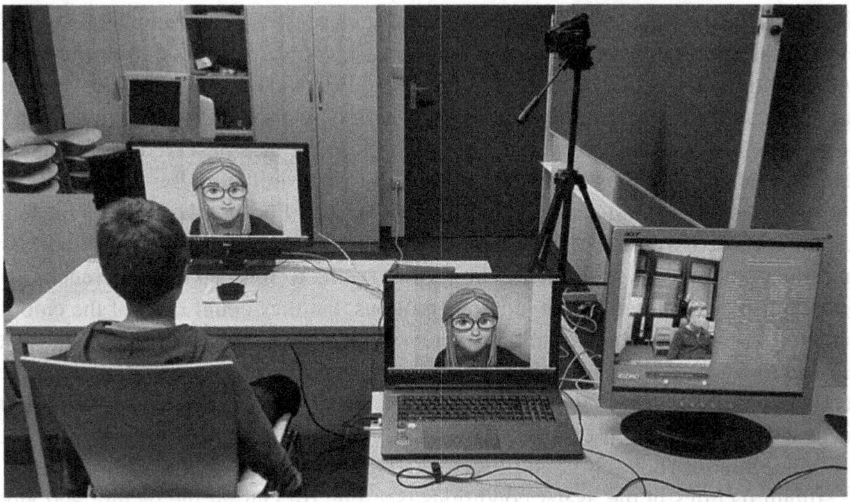

Fig. 2. Test setting in the avatar-video-condition.

[2] For the research purposes of the IDEAS project, KIZMO GmbH has developed a native iOS app (KIZMO Face-Analyzer) for use on iPads to capture facial and gaze data on demand. The app is not available to the public.

2.4 Data Analysis

To assess gaze, language and interaction, the videos from the survey were analyzed and the raw data from the KIZMO app was evaluated using MATLAB[3]. The analysis of the viewing direction in MATLAB is always based on the previous calibration. For development of facial expression analyzer, the relevant mimic features of an experimenter and a typically developed, healthy child were utilized.

3 Preliminary Results

Each condition comprises the same order of seven task types, where eye tracking calibration for later analysis via MATLAB is central. In the calibration process, the raw gaze points recorded by the app are correlated with the corner points of the screen in order to allow an interpretation of the raw data in terms of where the test subject looked at a certain point of time. Figure 3 shows an example of eye tracking calibration results with MATLAB. This calibration allowed us to see when the children weren't looking at the screen. For example, in the face-to-face condition, the experimenter sits to the left of the screen. In the interact situation, the child should look at the left side of the screen (see Fig. 4).

In the warm-up/conversational situation and farewell, both children interacted only with direct questions and mostly with one-word sentences. The interaction did not differ between the conditions. In addition, imitation gestures were successfully prompted in each condition. Task three (imitation of facial expressions) on the other side, was obviously difficult for both children to solve. They merely focused on the mouth (see Fig. 5) and slightly hinted at the other occurring changes in the face observed. Consequently, their own mouth positions changed only slightly when imitating the presented facial expressions and the emotions were hardly recognizable. For the two children the facial features recorded with the KIZMO app show no specific features that are indicative for certain emotions. Again, the media format seems to not make a difference. Both children displayed difficulties in judging emotions, but they could label of the emotion presented on screen. When the children were specifically asked what they look like when they feel this way, they did not show any mimic expressions of any emotion under neither condition. With regard to the task of contrasting social and non-social pictures and videos, both children focused almost exclusively on the social presentations. However, it is noticeable that both children often looked at the experimenter´s avatar and not at the stimuli pictures in the avatar conditions (see Fig. 6). During the picture and video task the avatar is presented in the bottom right corner. The focus of gaze is also in the bottom right corner.

[3] KIZMO GmbH has written code in MATLAB to analyze the raw data from the KIZMO Face-Analyzer application. The code is not available to the public.

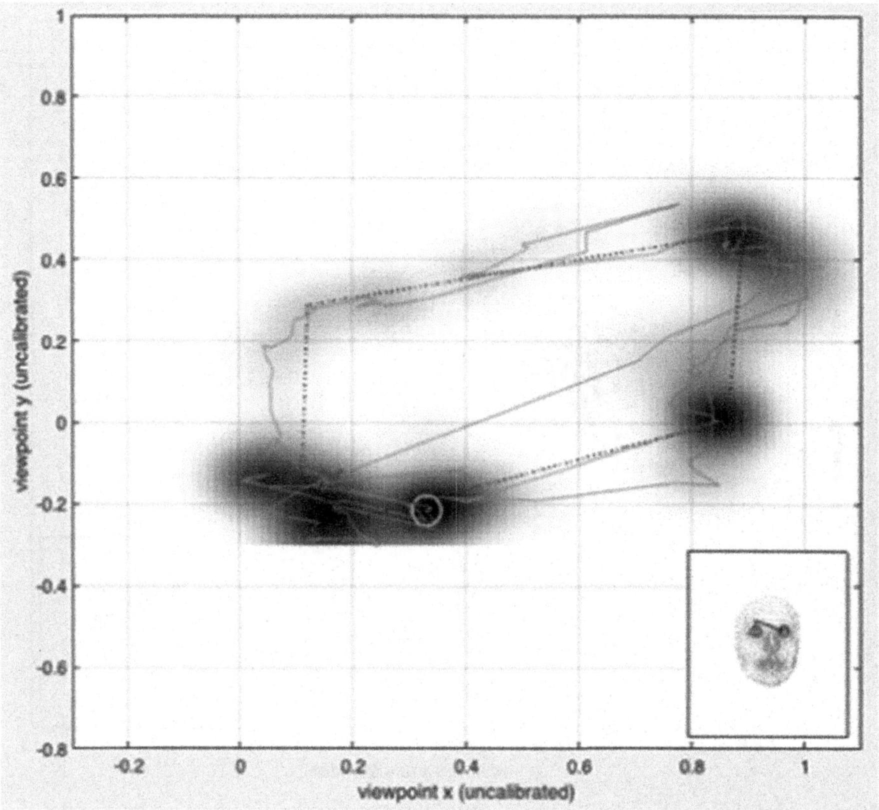

Fig. 3. Calibration results in MATLAB: the blue dotted line indicates the estimated frame of the computer screen that the child looked at. The screen appears to be warped due to distortions in the gaze tracking technology. The red line indicates the raw viewpoints of the child over a certain period of time. A gray-shaded color code indicates the calculated density of viewpoints: darker areas mean that the view has lingered there longer than in brighter areas. The green circle indicates the current maximum of the probability estimate of the most recent viewpoints. The red cross indicates the current viewpoint.

4 Implications and Outlook

The present analyses report the first insights into our study on the possibilities of measuring digitally mediated screening content in children with ASD. So far, some limitations in the areas of emotion imitation became visible in the two children as they hardly moved their mouths. Thus, it seems very challenging to detect emotions. However, previous research indicates that especially eye contact and recognition or imitation of facial expressions are most important diagnostic markers [15, 30]. Evaluation of eye movements in our two children also revealed a preference for the social images, which seems to contradict the expectation that social situations might be less attractive than geometric images for individuals with ASD [22]. However, both children commented that the images and videos were boring, so the rather low complexity of the stimuli (i.e., pictures

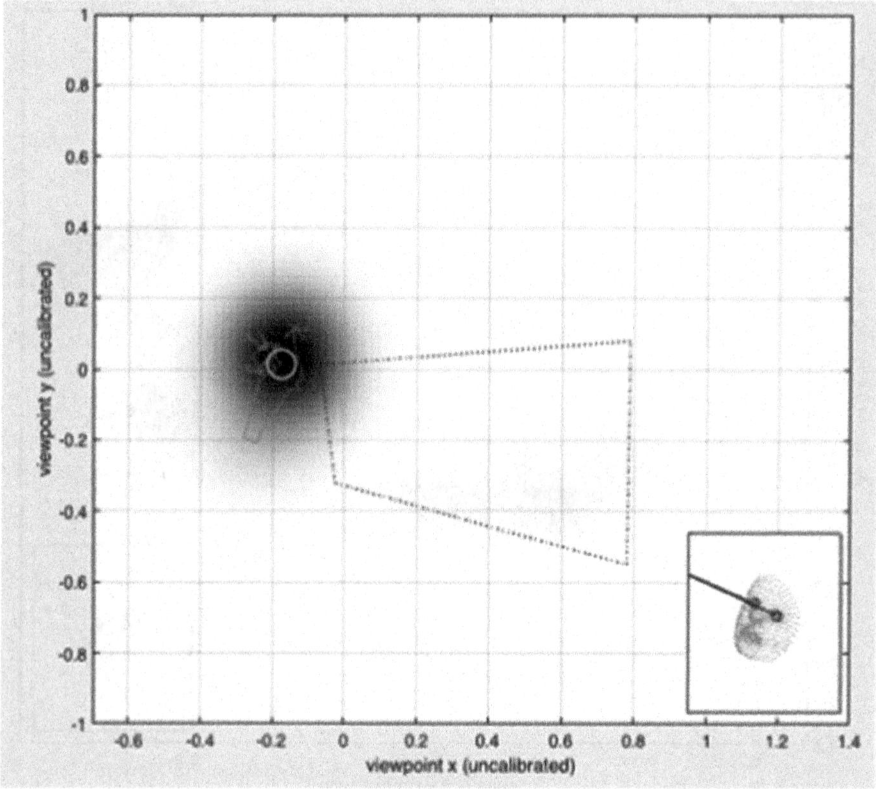

Fig. 4. Direction of gaze during the interaction in face-to-face condition. The green circle indicates the current maximum of the probability estimate of the most recent viewpoints. The red cross indicates the current viewpoint. A gray-shaded color code indicates the calculated density of viewpoints: darker areas mean that the view has lingered there longer than in brighter areas.

of universe) could have resulted in a bias in being less comparable to the images with social content. Since at this point only preliminary observations of two children can be reported, results do not yet allow any conclusions to be drawn about the meaningfulness and diagnostic discriminatory power of individual tasks. However, the findings underline how strongly the sensitivity of automated evaluation depends on the selection of task and stimulus material.

With regard to the different conditions (media format), participants seemed comfortable on the interaction level, but less with the tasks. First, they found the frequent calibration too boring as there was no variation. Consequently, calibration had been adjusted so that the process is different during each calibrating task. In addition, both children expressed boredom with the videos. In the picture task in particular, the children focused more on the avatar than on the stimuli pictures, possibly indicating a potential marker for ASD. In general, participants' preference for conditions three and five (the avatar conditions), suggests that digitally delivered content is highly appealing and perceived as appropriate for children with ASD. This is congruent with findings

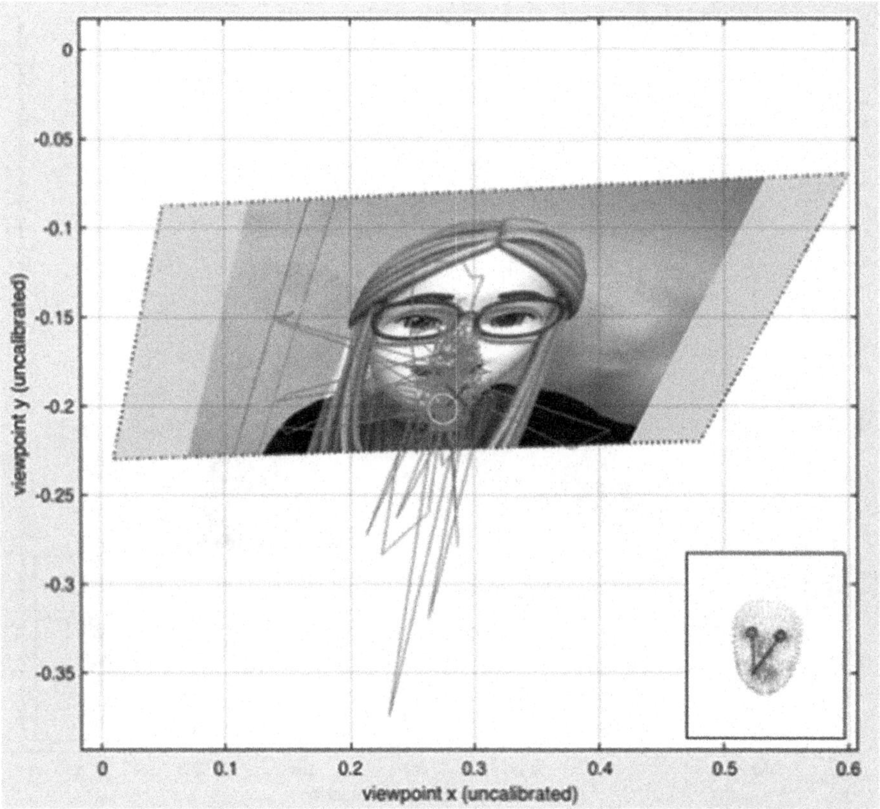

Fig. 5. The focus of the mouth during the facial expression imitation task in the avatar condition. The green circle indicates the current maximum of the probability estimate of the most recent viewpoints. The red cross indicates the current viewpoint. The red line indicates the raw viewpoints of the child over a certain period of time.

of Berger et al. (2022) [6], who reported a positive response of participants with ASD to media-mediated diagnostic content. Whether in our investigation - as in that study, which, however, did not systematically vary the digitally mediated content - resilient ASD symptoms will occur in the participants over all mediated conditions remains to be seen in further data collection and analyses. However, the methodological feasibility of a systematic variation of the characteristics of analog vs. digital communication could be demonstrated and encourages continuation with the study design. This not only forms the basis for possible further use in the diagnosis of ASD, but also implies a great potential for automated and thus fully reproducible measurements with low (hopefully in the long term minimal) personnel effort.

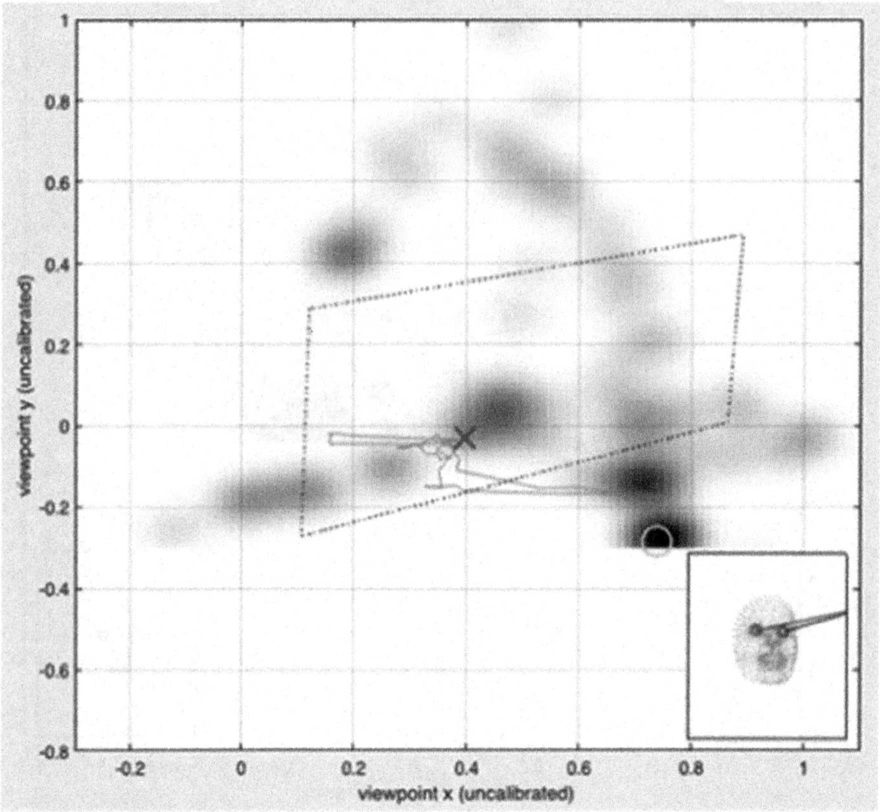

Fig. 6. Focus of the avatar during the image task. The green circle indicates the current maximum of the probability estimate of the most recent viewpoints. The red cross indicates the current viewpoint. The red line indicates the raw viewpoints of the child over a certain period of time. A gray-shaded color code indicates the calculated density of viewpoints: darker areas mean that the view has lingered there longer than in brighter areas.

References

1. Akhtar, Z., Guha, T.: Computational analysis of glaze behavior in autism during interaction with virtual agents. [Conference paper]. In: IEEE International Conference on Acoustics, Speech and Signal Processing (ICASSP), Brighton, UK (2019, May 12–14)
2. American Psychiatric Association: Diagnostic and statistical manual of mental disorders. Arlington: American Psychiatric Publishing (2013)
3. Apple Inc.: *iPad OS-Version* (16.3) [Software] (2023). https://www.apple.com/de/ipados/ipados-16/
4. Bekele, E., Zheng, Z., Swanson, A., Crittendon, J., Warren, Z., Sarkar, N.: Understanding how adolescents with Autism respond to facial expressions in virtual reality environments. IEEE Trans. Visual Comput. Graph. **19**(4), 711–720 (2013). https://doi.org/10.1109/TVCG.2013.42

5. Bellani, M., Fornasari, L., Chittaro, L., Brambilla, P.: Virtual reality in autism: state of the art. Epidemiology Psychiatric Sci. **20**, 235–238 (2011). https://doi.org/10.1017/S2045796011000448
6. Berger, N.I., et al.: Characterizing available tools for synchronous virtual assessment of toddlers with suspected autism spectrum disorder: a brief report. J. Autism Dev. Disord. **52**(1), 423–434 (2021). https://doi.org/10.1007/s10803-021-04911-2
7. Charlton, C.T., et al.: Effectiveness of avatar-delivered instruction on social initiations by children with Autism Spectrum Disorder. Research in Autism Spectrum Disorders **71**(101494) (2020). https://doi.org/10.1016/j.rasd.2019.101494
8. de Borst A.W., de Gelder, B.: Is it the real deal? Perception of virtual characters versus humans: an affective cognitive neuroscience perspective. Front. Psychol. **6**(576) (2015). https://doi.org/10.3389/fpsyg.2015.00576
9. Drimalla, H., et al.: Towards the automatic detection of social biomarkers in autism spectrum disorder: introducing the simulated interaction task (SIT). Npj Digital Medicine **3**(25) (2020). https://doi.org/10.1038/s41746-020-0227-5
10. Forbes, P.A.G., Pan, X., de C. Hamilton, A.F.: Reduced mimicry to virtual reality avatars in autism spectrum disorder. J. Autism Dev. Disord. **46**(12), 3788–3797 (2016). https://doi.org/10.1007/s10803-016-2930-2
11. Gale, R., Chen, L., Dolata, J., van Santen, J., Asgari, M.: Improving ASR systems for children with autism and language impairment using domain-focused DNN transfer techniques. Interspeech **2019**, 11–15 (2019). https://doi.org/10.21437/Interspeech.2019-3161
12. Georgescu, A.-L., Kuzmanovic, B., Roth, D., Bente, G., Vogeley, K.: The use of virtual characters to assess and train non-verbal communication in high-functioning autism. Front. Hum. Neurosci. **8**, 1–17 (2014). https://doi.org/10.3389/fnhum.2014.00807
13. Griffiths, S., Jarrold, C., Penton-Voak, I.S., Woods, A.T., Skinner, A.L., Munafò, M.R.: Impaired recognition of basic emotions from facial expressions in young people with autism spectrum disorder: assessing the importance of expression intensity. J. Autism Dev. Disord. **49**, 2768–2778 (2019). Doi:https://doi.org/10.1007/s10803-017-3091-7
14. Jonas, K., Jaecks, P.: Digitale Diagnostik: Innovative Wege für die Sprachtherapie [Digital Diagnostics: Innovative Ways for Speech Therapy]. In: Fritzsche, T., Breitenstein, S., Wunderlich, H., Ferchland, L. (eds.), Spektrum Patholinguistik (Band 14), pp. 1–29. Potsdam: Universitätsverlag Potsdam (2021)
15. Kamp-Becker, I., Tauscher, J., Wolff, N., Küpper, C., Stroth, S.: Is the combination of ADOS and ADI-R necessary to classify ASD? Rethinking the "Gold Standard" in diagnosing ASD. Front. Psychol. **12**, 727308 (2021). https://doi.org/10.3389/fpsyt.2021.727308
16. Lin, Y., Gu, Y., Xu, Y., Hou, S., Ding, R., Ni, S.: Autistic spectrum traits detection and early screening: a machine learning based eye movement study. J. Child Adolesc. Psychiatr. Nurs. **35**(1), 83–92 (2022). https://doi.org/10.1111/jcap.12346
17. Lord, C.E.: Autism: From research to practice. Am. Psychol. **65**(8), 815–826 (2010). https://doi.org/10.1037/0003-066X.65.8.815
18. McCarty, P., Frye, R.E.: Early detection and diagnosis of autism spectrum disorder: why is it so difficult? Seminars Pediatric Neurol. **35**(100831) (2020). https://doi.org/10.1016/j.spen.2020.100831
19. Moore, A., et al.: The geometric preference subtype in ASD: Identifying a consistent, early-emerging phenomenon through eye tracking. Molecular Autism **9**(19) (2018). https://doi.org/10.1186/s13229-018-0202-z
20. Neitzel, I., Tuschen, L., Ritterfeld, U.: Automatisierte Sprachentwicklungsanalysen in Forschung und Diagnostik: Potentiale und Barrieren [Automated language development analyses in research and diagnostics: potentials and barriers]. Sprache Stimme Gehör **47**(2), 84–88

21. Negrão, J.G., et al.: The child emotion facial expression set: a database for emotion recognition in children. Front. Psychol. **12**(666245) (2021). https://doi.org/10.3389/fpsyg.2021.666245
22. Pierce, K., Marinero, S., Hazin, R., McKenna, B., Barnes, C.C., Malige, A.: Eye tracking reveals abnormal visual preference for geometric images as an early biomarker of an Autism spectrum disorder subtype associated with increased symptom severity. Biol. Psychiat. **79**(8), 657–666 (2016). https://doi.org/10.1016/j.biopsych.2015.03.032
23. Polzer, L., Freitag, C.M., Bast, N.: Pupillometric measures of altered stimulus-evoked locus coeruleus-norepinephrine activity explain attenuated social attention in preschoolers with autism spectrum disorder. Autism Res. **15**(11), 2167–2180 (2022). https://doi.org/10.1002/aur.2818
24. Robles, M., et al.: A virtual reality based system for the screening and classification of Autism. IEEE Trans. Visual Comput. Graphics **28**(5), 2168–2178 (2022). https://doi.org/10.1109/TVCG.2022.3150489
25. Sachse, S., Spreer, M.: Grundlagen zu Auffälligkeiten und Diagnostik im Kontext der Sprachentwicklung [Basics of abnormalities and diagnosis in the context of language development]. In: Sachse, S., Bockmann, A.-K., Buschmann, A. (eds.) Sprachentwicklung. Entwicklung – Diagnostik – Förderung im Kleinkind- und Vorschulalter, pp. 165–175. Springer, Berlin (2020)
26. Tariq, Q., Daniels, J., Schwartz, J.N., Washington, P., Kalantarian, H., Wall, D.P.: Mobile detection of autism through machine learning on home video: a development and prospective validation study. PLoS Med. **15**(11), e1002705 (2018). https://doi.org/10.1371/journal.pmed.1002705
27. The MathWorks Inc.: MATLAB (2021b) [Software] (2023). https://de.mathworks.com/products/matlab.html?s_tid=hp_ff_p_matlab
28. Wawer, A., Chojnicka, I.: Detecting autism from picture book narratives using deep neural utterance embeddings. Int. J. Lang. Commun. Disorders, 1–14 (2022). https://doi.org/10.1111/1460-6984.12731
29. Wiggins, L.D., Baio, J.O.N., Rice, C.: Examination of the time between first evaluation and first autism spectrum diagnosis in a population-based sample. J. Dev. Behav. Pediatr. **27**(2), 79–87 (2006). https://doi.org/10.1097/00004703-200604002-00005
30. Wolff, N., et al.: Abilities and disabilities – applying machine intelligence in diagnosing Autism spectrum disorders. Front. Psychol. **13**, 826043 (2022). DOI: https://doi.org/10.3389/fpsyt.2022.826043
31. Zwaigenbaum, L., Penner, M.: Autism spectrum disorder: advances in diagnosis and evaluation. BMJ **361**(k1674) (2018). https://doi.org/10.1136/bmj.k1674

Introducing CALMED: Multimodal Annotated Dataset for Emotion Detection in Children with Autism

Annanda Sousa[1](✉), Karen Young[1], Mathieu d'Aquin[2], Manel Zarrouk[3], and Jennifer Holloway[4]

[1] University of Galway, Galway, Ireland
{a.defreitassousa1,karen.young}@nuigalway.ie
[2] K Team, LORIA CNRS/INRIA/Université de Lorraine, Nancy, France
mathieu.daquin@loria.fr
[3] LIPN, Université Sorbonne Paris Nord, Villetaneuse, France
azarrouk@sorbonne-paris-nord.fr
[4] ASK - All Special Kids, Geneva, Switzerland
jennifer.holloway@allspecialkids.org

Abstract. Automatic Emotion Detection (ED) aims to build systems to identify users' emotions automatically. This field has the potential to enhance HCI, creating an individualised experience for the user. However, ED systems tend to perform poorly on people with Autism Spectrum Disorder (ASD). Hence, the need to create ED systems tailored to how people with autism express emotions. Previous works have created ED systems tailored for children with ASD but did not share the resulting dataset. Sharing annotated datasets is essential to enable the development of more advanced computer models for ED within the research community. In this paper, we describe our experience establishing a process to create a multimodal annotated dataset featuring children with a level 1 diagnosis of autism. In addition, we introduce CALMED (Children, Autism, Multimodal, Emotion, Detection), the resulting multimodal emotion detection dataset featuring children with autism aged 8–12. CALMED includes audio and video features extracted from recording files of study sessions with participants, together with annotations provided by their parents into four target classes. The generated dataset includes a total of 57,012 examples, with each example representing a time window of 200 ms (0.2 s). Our experience and methods described here, together with the dataset shared, aim to contribute to future research applications of affective computing in ASD, which has the potential to create systems to improve the lives of people with ASD.

Keywords: Affective Computing · Multimodal Emotion Detection · Multimodal Dataset · Autism

---

Supported by Science Foundation Ireland under Grant number SFI/12/RC/2289_P2.

M. Antona and C. Stephanidis (Eds.): HCII 2023, LNCS 14020, pp. 657–677, 2023.
https://doi.org/10.1007/978-3-031-35681-0_43

1 Introduction

Affective Computing is a relatively new area in Computer Science that aims to create computer systems able to identify, process, respond to and generate emotions in human users [3,24]. One of the most commonly investigated areas of Affective Computing is automatic Emotion Detection (ED) [3], also referred to as affect recognition, affect detection, and emotion recognition. ED aims to automatically identify people's cognitive states or emotions, e.g. happiness, anger, and fear [14]. ED systems, utilising different media inputs such as texts, video, audio and sensor signals, extract implicit cues from facial expression, eye gaze, and tone of voice. When combining more than one type of data, they are called *Multimodal* Emotion Detection systems, which tend to outperform unimodal systems [6,23].

Most of the advancement in ED has been focused on the general population, i.e. users with typical neurological development, usually referred to as neurotypicals. When applying those systems to a specific population, e.g. children with autism, the systems usually do not perform well, mainly because of this particular population's way of expressing emotions [15]. Autism Spectrum Disorder (ASD) is a developmental disorder with a spectrum manifestation of traits characterised by impairments in social interaction, communication and repetitive patterns of behaviour and interests [1]. Among the results of a recent meta-analysis [25] that compared the facial expression production between a typical development (TD) population and people with autism, they found evidence that people with autism display facial expressions less often and less frequently than people with TD. Also, people with ASD expressions are lower in quality and less accurate. In the work of [10], the results showed that a Random Forest model needs more facial landmarks to classify facial expressions from children with autism than it needs from children with typical development. Those works together provide additional evidence that ED systems developed for children with typical development do not perform well when applied to children with autism, motivating the need to develop ED systems specifically tailored to children with autism. "Level 1 diagnosis of autism" is a terminology defined by DSM-5R [1] referring to ASD without significant cognitive and language impairments. Also sometimes referred to as high-functioning autism, previously known as Asperger Syndrome [9]. Throughout this paper, we will use the terms ASD and autism interchangeably.

Annotated datasets are a fundamental part of the creation of emotion detection systems. The emergence of more advanced computer models is heavily impacted by sharing these datasets within the research community. However, the creation and sharing of those datasets lead to a series of ethical challenges, requiring the research team to establish specific measures for protecting participants' rights, privacy, and well-being while maintaining the value of the created dataset to the research and the research community. Those issues appear from the first step of data collection, which often involves eliciting, capturing and tagging people's emotional expressions, to disseminating a sharable version of the data. When the emotion detection dataset features children with autism, representing a case of a vulnerable population with a medical condition, additional concerns must be considered. Examples of ethical matters in this scenario include:

- selecting tasks to evoke the target emotions without causing emotional harm to the children,
- addressing the participant's right to privacy as opposed to the important task of sharing resources in the research community, and
- designing a data protection plan to comply with the participants' rights as defined by the General Data Protection Regulation (GDPR).

Previous research works have investigated the challenges of developing an emotion detection system tailored for children with autism. [4,5,12,15,20]. These studies created ED systems for children with ASD, demonstrating that it is viable to model how this population expresses emotions and automatically predicts their emotions. As part of their work, they created their own annotated datasets. In addition, the works of [11,19] specifically created annotated datasets featuring individuals with ASD. Samad's dataset [19] includes facial action units instead of emotions. Meanwhile, ElKaliouby's dataset [11] contains data on adults with ASD instead of children. All these works reported having had to go through the phases of creating an emotion detection annotated dataset. However, the authors of those works did not share their resulting dataset nor the resources they generated during the dataset creation.

In this paper, we describe our experience establishing a process and measures to design a data collection framework with the ultimate goal of creating a multimodal emotion detection annotated dataset featuring children with a level 1 diagnosis of autism.

We then introduce CALMED (Children, Autism, Multimodal, Emotion, Detection), the resulting multimodal (video-audio) emotion detection dataset. Children from 8–12 years old with a level 1 diagnosis of autism were invited to perform computer-based emotion elicitation tasks to evoke each of the target emotion zones. The dataset is annotated with four emotion zones (green, yellow, red and blue) based on the "emotion zones for regulation" framework [13]. The annotation task was performed by the participants' parents, who watched and selected which emotion zone their child was expressing at each moment.

The top four modalities of data input used in the emotion detection field are: 1. video, 2. physiological signals, 3. audio, and 4. text [21]. Initially, CALMED was planned to include three modalities, video, audio and physiological signals. However, due to COVID-19 restrictions, the experiment setup required to be adapted and physiological signals input had to be excluded from the multimodal dataset since it would require close contact with participants to collect this data. Thus, our multimodal dataset includes two modalities of data input: video and audio. This bimodality is the most explored in multimodal emotion detection [3].

CALMED, the annotated dataset for emotion detection described in this paper, has the following features:

- Compliant with Ethics guidelines and recommendations, with a main focus on the participants' emotional well-being;

- Compliant with Data Protection legislation for handling personal data;
- Multimodal dataset (video and audio data inputs);
- Features children (8–12 years old) with a diagnosis of level 1 autism;
- Annotated by the participants' parents into four classes representing emotion zones;
- Data collected in a naturalistic setup, not posed emotions;
- Data collected using computer-based task environment, as opposed to dialect eliciting tasks, i.e., from a conversation with the participant.

We also share the resources we created during the process, with the hope that they will benefit future research in creating and sharing their own emotion detection dataset featuring particular population, especially ASD population. Thus, future researchers can reuse the resources here presented, or customise them to adapt to their specific research goals. The additional resources shared in this work are three artefacts, namely:

- a computer-based task environment web system, for emotions' elicitation sessions;
- an annotation web system, to support the dataset annotation process;
- a working dataset generation system, to create an annotated dataset from the annotation process.

By sharing the dataset, this paper's contribution is unique since none of the previous research that created emotion detection datasets involving children with autism shared a dataset artefact with the research community, primarily due to privacy issues. While ED for the general population has plenty of available resources, e.g. annotated datasets, ED for ASD suffers from scarce available resources, with not even one annotated dataset available. Thus, the research team believes that making more resources available to support the creation and sharing of annotated datasets featuring populations with ASD can lead to advancing this specific application of the ED field.

The rest of the paper is organised as follows, Sect. 2 describes the process and methods used to elicit and capture the original data from the participants. Then, Sect. 3 describes the methodology to create and process the multimodal annotated dataset. This is followed in Sect. 4, with a description of the dataset characteristics and a discussion about its applicability, limitations and perspectives. Finally, the paper concludes with a discussion of future work directions.

2 Data Collection

As introduced before, previous works [4,5,11,12,15,19,20] have created affective computing systems focussing on people with ASD; each of these was required to create their own dataset since none was available. In general, they followed the steps enumerated below.

1. Modelling emotions definition,

2. define and design the eliciting tasks,
3. design the study session and task environment,
4. define data to be collected and create a data protection plan,
5. apply for ethics approval,
6. define inclusion and exclusion criteria of participation in the study,
7. recruit participants,
8. run study sessions,
9. define annotators, and running annotation sessions,
10. generate the final working annotated dataset from the original data collected.

This section describes the methods used while creating CALMED for steps 1–8, while Sect. 3 describes the methodology for steps 9–10.

2.1 Modelling Emotions

Modelling and representing emotions is one of the inherent challenges in affective computing. Emotion definitions come from psychology and might be imprecise or fuzzy, making them difficult to apply to computer models [3]. Usually, in affective computing, emotions are represented by the seven basic emotions, i.e. surprise, happiness, anger, disgust, contempt, sadness and fear, making them a set of categories. We can also find emotions represented according to the two dimensions of arousal (strong or weak) and valence (positive or negative), which usually take continuous value between -1 and 1 [17].

However, for emotion detection applied for ASD, researchers tend not to work with the basic emotions from the general ED field. They argue that basic emotions are not the best target emotional states for applications of ED for autism from a pragmatic perspective. They, instead, work with different emotion states, e.g. anxiety (a prevalent co-occurring condition to ASD) or engagement level for instance [15].

Following the previous related works, which did not focus on the seven basic emotions, we selected other emotional states as labelling targets for CALMED dataset. We labelled the data using a framework called "*the zones of regulation*" [13]. This framework is extensively used in psychology to help children with ASD, and other neurological conditions learn emotion regulation since it is common for children with ASD to present impairments in emotion regulation [22].

The zones of regulation framework has four different zones represented by colours (See Fig. 1). One of the emotion zones is the calming zone, represented by the **green** zone. This ideal state is where the child is calm, relaxed, and ready to work, listen, and interact. The warning zone (**yellow** zone) indicates that the child is presenting signals of agitation or excitement. This state can originate from both positive and negative emotions. It can start from intense happiness or excitement and also from frustration. The high-agitation zone (**red** zone) indicates that the child is upset or angry, presenting severe difficulties in keeping control of their emotions. The last zone is the slowing zone, the **blue** zone, in which the child is on low energy and showing emotional signals of being sad, tired, sick or bored. In this state, the child might move slower than usual, stop speaking or show delays in interactive responses.

Green Zone
Calm
Happy
Relaxed
Focused
Feeling Okay
Yellow Zone
Excited
Worried
Frustrated
Silly/Wiggly
Loss of Some Control
Red Zone
Terrified
Mad/Angry
Devastated
Out of Control
Elated/Ecstatic
Blue Zone
Sad
Sick
Tired
Bored
Moving Slowly

Fig. 1. The Four Emotion Zones, based on "The Zones of Regulation", a Social Emotional Learning Framework [13]. The CALMED dataset is annotated with these four labels. (Color figure online)

We obtain several benefits by using this emotions zones' framework as a target for labelling emotions. Firstly, the framework includes guidelines on activities to lead children back to the calming zone, and since the ultimate goal of creating a multimodal dataset is to develop affective computing systems to support children with ASD, using the "zones of regulation framework" makes it easy to incorporate the framework's activities to calm the child within an affect-sensitive interface. Second, parents of children with ASD are more likely to be familiarised with this framework because it is commonly used in the context of autism, hence making the labelling task by the parents more comfortable. Thirdly, considering the children's well-being, it is less harmful to the emotional comfort of children with ASD during the emotion elicitation experiment to elicit the four emotion zones than other strong negative emotions, e.g. fear and anxiety. This way we could elicit and observe all the four zones without causing a strong emotional discomfort on the participants.

2.2 Ethics

This research is based in Ireland; thus, it must comply with Irish legislation and GDPR. The data collection involves children, which generates an additional challenge to address. Ireland has specific regulations for research involving children as participants. For instance, assent from the child is mandatory in addition to the parent's consent. Thus, if the parent allows the child to participate, but the child does not want to, the researcher can not go further with the data experiment. Such cases were encountered during this research's data collection. To obtain the assent from the child, we need to use age-appropriate language while being transparent and explaining what will be asked of them. Furthermore, we created age-appropriate materials to seek assent from children and to explain to them what the research participation would entail. We only talked to the children after obtaining permission from their parents.

The most critical ethical concern is not to cause harm during the data collection sessions. The data collection objective was to capture naturalistic manifestations of emotions from children with autism. So we needed to elicit these emotions to record them and later annotate them. There are positive and negative emotions, so we decided early on not to elicit strong negative emotions which could cause emotional discomfort for the children, e.g. fear and phobia.

We also put in place additional measures to protect the participants' emotional well-being. All sessions happened in the presence of a postgraduate psychology student who had experience working with children with ASD. This measure provided specialised support in case the participants got overwhelmed by emotions during the session and could not regulate themselves. As additional measures for emotional well-being, calming activities were included between each eliciting task to support the participants' emotion regulation, helping them calm themselves during the study session.

The University of Galway's research ethics committee reviewed and approved the proposed ethics measures.

2.3 Data Protection

Another important aspect of this data collection framework is the data protection plan. We needed to ensure that the personal data collected was secure and kept private from unauthorised access. Personal data is defined as any data that can be used to identify an individual, either by direct identification or through some sort of data engineering. To define the action and measures to put in place to protect the personal data and the participants' rights, we conducted a Data Protection Impact Assessment (DPIA), generating a plan with specific action points to follow on how to deal with the personal data resulting from this project. The university's data protection officer approved the DPIA. Some examples of actions we followed to ensure the participant's rights include:

- Provide comprehensive information on all aspects of the research for participants' parents, with a project's website, information sheets and other materials.
- Provide information on the participants' right to withdraw from the research.
- Provide information on the participants' right to have their data deleted.
- Protect the right to privacy, ensuring only the research team can access the participant's data.

To make the information more available to participants and the general public, we created a website with all the documents and relevant information about the project.[1].

[1] http://emotion-asd.datascienceinstitute.ie.

2.4 Privacy and Sharing Resources

None of the previous works which created annotated emotion detection datasets featuring children with autism shared their resulting dataset mainly due to privacy reasons. Since the raw recording files contain personal data, we needed to eliminate the identifiable aspect of the data to make it possible to share an annotated dataset. The approach we selected is, instead of creating a dataset featuring the raw video and audio files, to create a dataset with numerical and categorical features extracted from the original files. More detail on the feature generation can be found in the Sects. 3.3 and 3.4.

Making only available the extracted features instead of the original files is not an ideal approach to sharing resources in the research community because the researchers will not be able to extract their features. However, that is a necessary step, and the benefits of having a dataset with extracted features outweigh the previous limitation of not having a dataset at all. Not having an available dataset resulted in each new research work ought to start from scratch, creating a new dataset with all the steps and procedures involving its creation, consuming much time, material and people resources, which might be a limiting factor when defining a research project, leading to less research being conducted in this specific application.

2.5 Study Session Setup

Our goal for the study session was to collect video and audio data from children with autism while they were engaged in the four emotion zones. Thus, we needed to elicit each emotion zone during a study session with participants. The elicitation is usually done by asking participants to perform evoking tasks. In order to create a more valuable dataset, it is essential to collect data following a setup as close as possible to the intended use-case scenario [18]. For our case, we visioned a multimodal dataset as a resource to create affect-sensitive computer systems for children with ASD. Therefore, the closest scenario to elicit emotions is a computer-based task environment, i.e. where the participants interact with a computer system during the elicitation study session.

The study sessions happened entirely online, over a Zoom video call, which was recorded. Initially, the study session was planned to happen in a lab room prepared with a computer, a high-resolution camera and a semi-professional microphone. However, due to pandemic restrictions, we could not conduct face-to-face meetings, making it necessary to adapt the study session to an online remote setup. The session was then a Zoom video call in which the researcher first talked to the participant, using age-appropriate language, seeking their assent and explaining the session and tasks. The participant then accessed an URL[2] to the task environment software and clicked the "Start button" to start the session. The system is programmed to automatically follow each task in sequence without requiring manual human commands. While the child is engaged with the task

[2] http://task-environment.datascienceinstitute.ie/.

environment software, the Zoom video call is still on, recording the participant's camera and audio.

The resulting video/audio file from the participant session is the raw file for the dataset creation. Using the participant's camera and microphone, on one side, does not guarantee the quality of the input, creating an additional challenge of noise and low-quality media. However, on the other side, it generates more realistic videos in a setup that an eventual affective computing system is more likely to encounter.

We invited children and their parents to participate in the data collection study. The inclusion criteria were that the child had to have a level 1 diagnosis of ASD and to be within the age range (8–12 years old). We limited the age range to before the teenage phase, where other co-occurring conditions usually manifest and influence how the person expresses emotions. In addition, we needed to have written consent from the parent or guardian and verbal assent from the child. An exclusion criterion was having a history of cognitive or language impairment that does not fall under the level 1 diagnosis of autism and not attaining assent from the child. The study session was designed to last for no more than 30 min, and we asked each participant to attend two different sessions.

As reported by all previous works, finding participants was challenging, especially because we were amidst a global pandemic. We had study sessions with four participants, one girl and three boys, with an average age of 10.25 (+-1.7). Table 1 summarises the participants' details and the number of sessions they attended. All the sessions generated close to four hours of recorded video/audio files.

Table 1. Summary of participants information

	Gender	# Sessions	Age
Participant 1	Male	1	8
Participant 2	Female	2	12
Participant 3	Male	2	10
Participant 4	Male	2	11

All study sessions followed the following agenda:

1. Initial greetings with discussion on the child's interests (4 min).
2. Explanation of the session using age-appropriate language (3 min).
3. The session - the child accesses and follows the tasks on a web system (20 min).
4. Ending conversation (2 min).
5. Gifting the child with a certificate - with visual art involving the child's special interests (1 min).

2.6 Emotion Elicitation Tasks

During the study session, the participant accessed a web-based software we created that encompasses four different eliciting tasks and calming activities. Each of the four eliciting tasks aims to evoke one of the emotion zones. Figure 2 shows screenshots of some parts of the Task Environment System.

The eliciting tasks follow the sequence: green, yellow, red and blue zone. The order of the eliciting tasks focused on the participant's emotional well-being. It is expected that a participant already experiences some level of anxiety from participating in the study. They are talking to someone they do not know and doing something outside their routine, two things that tend to cause anxiety for individuals with ASD. We, therefore, did not want to aggravate it by starting the session by eliciting negative emotions. Hence, the first task is to calm the participant, eliciting the green zone, starting with a relaxed, happy and calm tone. Following the green zone, we elicit the yellow zone, which involves some uneasiness and agitation, and next, we elicit the red zone. The last emotion zone is the blue zone since we expected that by this point, the child would start to get tired, so we would naturally observe the blue zone. We defined this order to foster a more gentle progression towards the more challenging emotions so that the change to the red zone would not happen too abruptly, which could cause increased emotional discomfort.

The eliciting tasks are as follows: watching a video with funny and cute animals for the green zone (3 min), playing a game for the yellow zone (3 min), completing a challenging maths worksheet with a visible timer for the red zone (3 min, see Fig. 2a), and watching a boring video for the blue zone (3 min). Right after each eliciting task, the system includes a prompt for a simplified emotion state self-report with three options, happy face, neutral face and unhappy face (see Fig. 2b). The self-report does not include the four emotional zones because it could be too complex for the children, especially considering that alexithymia, difficulty in naming one's emotions, is common in individuals with autism.

Between each of the tasks, the system also includes a calming activity (1.5 min) which serves a twofold purpose: First, to help the child to calm and regulate their emotions, decreasing the possibility of emotional discomfort, and second, to return the participant's emotions to a baseline before moving forward to the next emotion zone elicitation (see Fig. 2d).

In addition, the system includes a visual schedule with the four tasks crossed throughout the session to help the participants have a sense of the time passing and what to expect during the session and when the session is close to the end. This technique is widely used in psychology to support children with ASD so they feel less anxious (see Fig. 2c).

The system at http://task-environment.datascienceinstitute.ie/ is configurable depending on the session number, i.e. one or two, the child's age for the maths worksheet, i.e., younger, default and older, and the time allocated for each task and activity. The system is currently configured for the first session, with "older" as a maths worksheet configuration and the default activity time (3 min per task). The source code for the system is available for the research

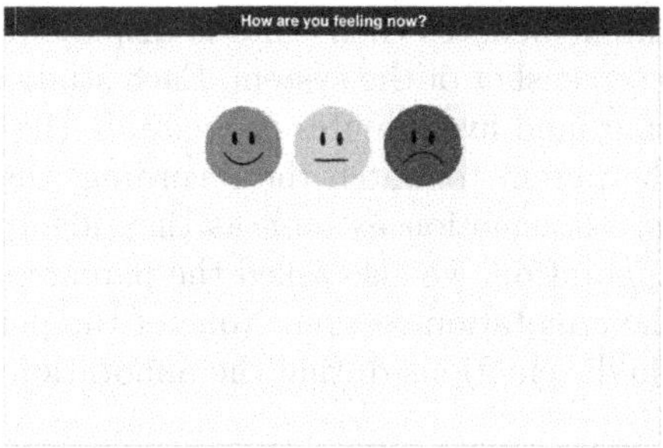

(a) Screenshot of the eliciting task for the red zone, a maths quiz with a timer.

(b) Screenshot of the emotion self-report to be selected by the participant after each eliciting task.

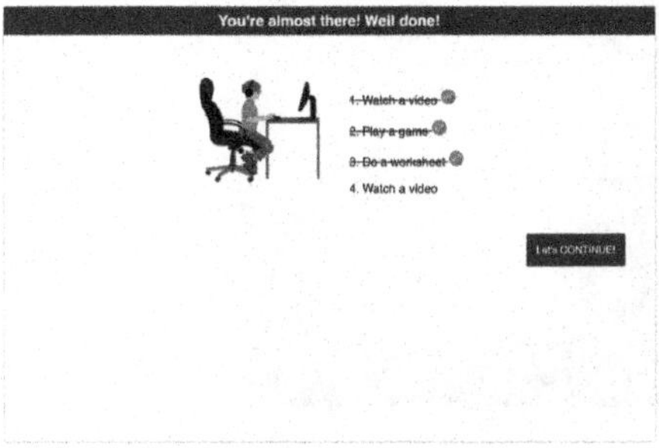

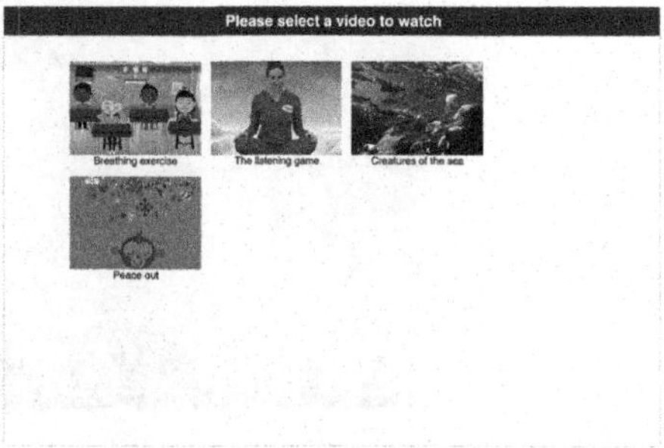

(c) Screenshot of the visual agenda to support participants regarding the passing time.

(d) Screenshot of the calming activities to be selected by the participant between each eliciting task.

Fig. 2. Screenshots of the Task Environment System, a web system created to support the study session with participants. Participants accessed the system through a web browser and completed the eliciting tasks. The system can be accessed at *http://task-environment.datascienceinstitute.ie/*.

community by request. Hence other researchers can reproduce the same study session or configure it to meet their research goals.

3 Dataset Creation

3.1 Data Annotation by Parents

Since children with autism can individually display emotions in a particular way, we asked each participant's parent to annotate their child's emotions throughout the study session, acknowledging that they know their child's emotions best. We created a system to support the annotation process. The parent's interface to the system is composed of the video recording of their child's study session with four buttons below it; each button represents an emotion zone to be clicked when the parent believes their child is displaying the given emotion zone. Figure 3 shows a screenshot of the system. Each study session recording was divided into videos of around five minutes to facilitate the annotation by the parent. We instructed the parent to watch the recording; they should click on the button representing the emotion as soon as they identified an emotion zone. At the end of the annotation, we also asked the parents to answer a brief questionnaire regarding the annotation session. None of the parents reported difficulty identifying their child's emotions during the annotation session.

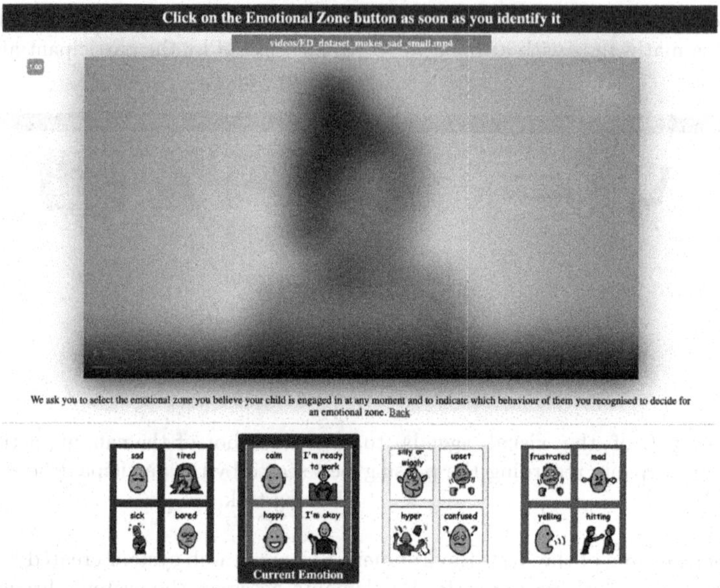

Fig. 3. Screenshot of the Annotation System, a web system created to support the annotation process by the participants' parents. The parent watched their child's study session recording and selected the appropriate emotion zones by clicking on the buttons below the video.

3.2 Dataset Creation Overview

The study sessions with the participants and the annotation sessions with the parents generated the raw data to be processed as a working annotated dataset. The raw files are converted into a working dataset via a pipeline process depicted in Fig. 4. First, following the diagram in Fig. 4, we conducted study sessions (1.1) with the participants and annotation sessions (1.2) with the parents, obtaining the data for the dataset creation (1.3–1.5). We then used OpenFace [2] and OpenSMILE [8] to extract video and audio features, respectively (2.1 and 2.2). We then process the result of the parent's annotation sessions (2.5) into a dataset,

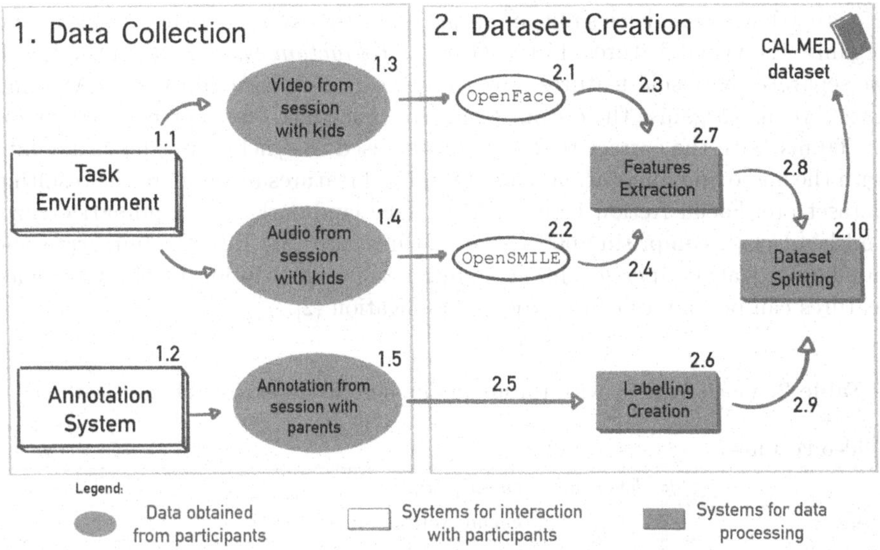

Fig. 4. Pipeline with an overview of the CALMED dataset creation process, from data collection to dataset creation, including all the systems developed.

i.e., a .CSV file with annotation from each session (2.6). In sequence, we clean, organise and synchronise the features datasets to the annotation datasets (2.7). At this point, we have a set of .CSV files with video, audio and annotation features for each session, all containing a column with the video timestamp that we use for synchronisation (2.8 and 2.9). These .CSV files represent the whole dataset without any split into different sets. Lastly, we created a split of the train, validation and test sets, with 80/10/10 proportions (2.10), resulting in the CALMED dataset.

The following sections present a detailed description of each of those steps.

3.3 Video Features Extraction

Each study session produces audio and video files of around 30 min in length. To decrease the file size and facilitate the processing step, we split audio/video files into smaller files, each of around five minutes.

We used OpenFace [2] to generate the visual features for the CALMED dataset. OpenFace is a toolkit composed of computer vision algorithms capable of executing essential tasks for visual affective computing, such as facial landmark, facial action unit detection, head pose, and eye gaze estimation. OpenFace has been widely used in the literature to generate visual features for analysing facial behaviour.

We passed the five-minute video files to the OpenFace tool for video feature extraction. The tool extracts visual features for each frame, returning a massive .CSV file with all the numerical visual features and timestamps (the output 2.3 in

Fig. 4). We use OpenFace's output as the input to a system created to clean and organise the visual features. In the *Features Extraction* system, 2.7 in the Fig. 4, we separate the visual features into groups, e.g., Facial Action Units (AU) and gaze. We also organise the output from OpenFace into our desired time window of 200 ms, with the correct timestamp to be used to synchronise the visual data with the audio and annotation data. The visual features included in the resulting dataset are: Facial Action Units (FAUs), face landmarks, eye landmarks, gaze, and head pose, comprising 669 visual features in total. Table 2 summarises the number of features per group. A comprehensive description of the OpenFace features can be found in the project's publication [2].

Table 2. Video features with feature group, description and number of features.

Video Features

	# of Features	Description
AUs	35	Facial Action Units
Gaze	8	Eye gaze direction vector
2d_eye_landmark	112	Location of 2D eye region landmarks in pixels
3d_eye_landmark	168	Location of 3D eye region landmarks in millimetres
face_2d_landmarks	136	Location of 2D landmarks in pixels
face_3d_landmarks	204	location of 3D landmarks in millimetres
head_pose	6	Location of the head with respect to camera
Total	669	

3.4 Audio Features Extraction

We similarly repeated the steps described in the last section for audio features extraction using OpenSMILE [8] for acoustic features creation. OpenSMILE is a robust system capable of extracting a vast set of audio features. We defined a selection of audio features to be included in the dataset based on the Extended Geneva Minimalistic Acoustic Parameter Set (eGeMAPS). The eGeMAPS is a set of features curated as a recommendation of audio parameters for voice research and affective computing. The parameters were selected based on: 1) how extensively and successfully these parameters were used in the literature, 2) the theoretical significance of the parameter, and 3) the potential of an acoustic parameter to represent physiological changes that occur in the voice during affective processes [7]. From eGeMAPS, we selected 75 parameters resulting from Low-Level Descriptors (LLDs) extracted from audio files and sorted them into four groups: frequency, energy/amplitude, spectral (balance) parameters, and additional temporal features. Table 3 summarises the number of features per type.

Table 3. Audio Features with feature group, description and number of features.

Audio Features	# of Features	Description
Frequency	24	Frequency related parameters, e.g., pitch, jitter
Energy Amplitude	15	Energy/Amplitude related parameters, e.g., shimmer, loudness
Spectral Balance	30	Spectral (balance) parameters, e.g., alpha ration, Hammarberg Index
Temporal Features	6	Temporal features related, e.g., rate of loudness peaks.
Total	75	

The methodology described above to create and synchronise the dataset's visual and audio features is based on the methodology used by AVEC-2018 [16] when using the RECOLA [17] multimodal dataset, which shares some similarities with the CALMED dataset, including the video and audio data inputs.

3.5 Dataset Labelling

From the annotation sessions, we get a .sqlite file with each emotion zone selected by the annotator and the video's timestamp indicating when the emotion was chosen. From this file, we produce a .csv file where each row represents a time window of 200 ms and the assigned label for the given time window. Each row corresponds to one example within the labels dataset.

The steps to create the labels dataset are as follows, they are executed in the *Labelling creation* system (marked as 2.6 in Fig. 4):

1. Create a .CSV file with a row representing each time window of 200 ms of a given video file of a session with a participant;
2. Read the emotion zones selected by the annotations in the .sqlite file and;
3. Assign the corresponding annotation for each row in the dataset.

One challenge during this step was identifying how close the annotation time was to the real emotion utterance. During the annotation, we collect the time of the video when the annotator pressed the emotion button, which occurs with an inherent delay after the parent identifies the emotion. In other words, the emotion expression started some point before the time the parent marks it. For this study, we empirically defined the delay time as equal to one second. In practice, we marked in the dataset that the emotion started one second before the timestamp selected by the annotator.

3.6 Dataset Splitting

After creating a features dataset of audio, video and annotation labels, we then split it into three different sets: train, validation and test sets, with a proportion of 80/10/10, respectively, each of them containing the same four emotion zones distribution. To accomplish the same distribution of emotion within train, validation and test sets, we followed the steps described below. We utilised the sample method of Pandas Python library with a random state value of 25. Each participant's data appear in the train, validation and test sets, i.e., there are no participant data only present in one of the splitting sets.

Within a given session's data:

1. We selected all the examples of a given emotion and split them randomly into train, validation and test with the proportion of 80/10/10, respectively,
2. We repeated the previous step with the other emotions,
3. We then concatenate all the same dataset types together, i.e., the train data from green, yellow, blue and red emotion zones, and so on, generating then train, validation and test set following the same distribution of labels.

The splitting method described above considers each time window of 200 ms as an independent example in the dataset, not following the time sequence of the video. However, CALMED dataset includes all video/audio/labels timestamps, allowing researchers to create alternative splits according to their research needs. Any additional split type created by the research team will be available under request.

4 Analysis and Discussion

4.1 Dataset in Numbers

The CALMED dataset comprises a total of 57,012 annotated examples, each representing a time window of 200 ms, created from data collected across all the participant sessions. The number of examples per class is as follows: 30,882 examples of green, 9,858 examples of yellow, 3,179 of red, and 13,093 of blue. When looking at the splitting numbers, we have 45,608 examples in train, 5,702 in validation and 5,702 in test sets. Table 4 summarises the number of examples per class in the different sets of the data.

The number of examples in the green emotion zone is significantly larger than in the red emotion zone, i.e. around ten times more. This unbalanced dataset characteristic was expected due to our decision to prioritise the participant's well-being. Since the red class models some negative and demanding emotions, during the sessions, we wanted to elicit the red zone in the least amount of time so as not to cause emotional harm to the participants. Thus, the resulting dataset presents a significantly lower number of examples of the red class than the green class.

Table 4. Number of examples per class across the different sets of the data.

	Green	Yellow	Red	Blue	Total
Whole Dataset	30,882	9,858	3,179	13,093	**57,012**
Train Set	24,704	7,886	2,543	10,475	45,608
Dev Set	3,089	985	319	1,309	5,702
Test Set	3,089	987	317	1,309	5,702
Participant 1	5,158	788	390	3,156	9,492
Session 1.1	5,158	788	390	3,156	9,492
Participant 2	8,139	3,788	1482	3,020	16,429
Session 2.1	3,664	2,444	829	1,386	8,323
Session 2.2	4,475	1,344	653	1,634	8,106
Participant 3	8,534	3,193	595	4,456	16,778
Session 3.1	4,939	1,072	516	2,265	8,792
Session 3.2	3,595	2,121	79	2,191	7,986
Participant 4	9,051	2,089	714	2,461	14,315
Session 4.1	4,483	800	278	1,474	7,035
Session 4.2	4,568	1,289	436	987	7,280

4.2 Applicability, Limitations and Perspectives

The CALMED dataset was created as part of a research project aiming to create a multimodal emotion detection system for children with ASD. Thus, we foresee that the main scenario in which CALMED can be applied is to train and test machine learning systems for affective computing tailored to children with ASD. Insights and knowledge are expected to emerge from creating a classifier model, such as, the most viable features, modalities and fusion layer techniques to be applied for emotion detection in the context of people with ASD. Moreover, this has the potential to generate knowledge for both the affective computing and psychology fields.

There are other subsets of the general population that are known to also express emotions differently from a typical population, e.g. people with schizophrenia, brain damage, and some mental health condition such as depression. All those populations could also benefit from the advancement of affective computing systems. However, to accomplish that, it would also be necessary to create annotated datasets featuring these populations. The methods described, and the systems shared in this paper could be extended, adapted and applied to designing and creating these annotated datasets.

The CALMED dataset could also be applied to evaluate the viability of creating a person-independent model, i.e. an emotion detection model applied to individuals whose data was not present in the training dataset. For this purpose, the dataset would need to split so that some participants' data do not appear in the training dataset, which is not the case now, as mentioned in Sect. 3.6.

Sharing only the extracted features as opposed to the original files can be considered a limitation since other researchers will not be able to extract their features. However, that was a middle-ground solution to both protect the participants' privacy and have a first-of-its-kind valuable resource shared within the research community.

As reported by previous works, the research team faced the same challenges in recruiting children as participants for creating a dataset. Thus, one of the main limitations of the dataset is the limited number of subjects, which implies that it does not encompass a wide diversity in the extracted data. However, we were able to extract meaningful knowledge from the data collected and expect to have more participants in the future to generate more data.

Another aspect to note concerns the annotation performed by participants' parents. Some of the previous works decided to use annotation by parents, while others selected annotation by specialists instead. We do not yet know if the parents' annotation carries any biases or noise or to what extent they are reliable, so it would be helpful to have an additional annotation from a specialist in ASD who does not know the participants and compare these two sets of annotation-checking for agreement rate, differences in the distribution of emotions, among others.

5 Conclusion and Future Work

This paper introduced CALMED (Children, Autism, Multimodal, Emotion, Detection), a multimodal (video-audio) emotion detection dataset featuring children aged 8–12 years old with a level 1 diagnosis of autism. The multimodal dataset includes audio and video features extracted from recording files of study sessions with participants, together with annotation provided by their parents into four target classes (green, yellow, red and blue) based on the "the zones of regulation" framework [13]. The generated dataset includes a total of 57,012 examples. Each example represents a time window of 200 ms (0.2 s) of audio and video extracted features and an emotion annotation. The resulting dataset is available for the research community upon request.

This paper's contribution is unique since it shares an audio/video features dataset with the research community. By sharing the features dataset with the research community, we maintain the privacy of the subjects while still making available resources to facilitate further research in this emotion detection application, which has the potential to improve systems of automatic ED applied to children with ASD. We hope that our experience and methods described here contribute to future research applications of affective computing in this scenario, for instance, educational platforms, and self-identify emotions assistance tools, among others.

The small sample size of participants did not allow us to create a more diverse dataset regarding gender, culture, and language. Thus, further participant recruitment and data collection would benefit the dataset, including children from other cultures, countries and backgrounds. Using the task environment and annotation systems shared here, the data collected would be consistent, and other research groups could further expand the dataset.

A further study will investigate how a specialist annotation compares with the parents' annotation of the participants' emotions. Our research group has already completed the annotation of emotion zones by such a specialist. It is now working on generating a new dataset which will be compared with the original annotation by the parents.

A natural progression of this work is to create a multimodal ED machine learning system, an ongoing work in our research group. Initial results have been obtained, and further steps are being taken to improve the classification accuracy. The resulting system will feature in a future publication.

Acknowledgements. The research team would like to thank Dr Ciara Gunning who provided specialised advice, training on how to interact with children with ASD, and revision of the data collection experiment design and materials, together with support on the recruitment of participants. We also thank Aindrias Cullen for his comprehensive advice on data protection legislation, so we could design a project that is compliant with GDPR. We thank still Adhara Correa Soto, Alisha Garvey, Hannah Callanan, and Liam Finnerty for their participation and support during study sessions with participants. And lastly, we thank all the lovely participants and their parents who made this project possible. We hope you harvest the results of this research. It was a pleasure to meet and work with each of you.

This publication has emanated from research conducted with the financial support of Science Foundation Ireland under Grant number SFI/12/RC/2289_P2

References

1. Association, A.P.: Diagnostic and statistical manual of mental disorders (DSM-5®). American Psychiatric Pub (2013)
2. Baltrusaitis, T., Zadeh, A., Lim, Y.C., Morency, L.P.: Openface 2.0: Facial behavior analysis toolkit. In: 2018 13th IEEE International Conference on Automatic Face & Gesture Recognition (FG 2018), pp. 59–66. IEEE (2018)
3. Calvo, R.A., D'Mello, S., Gratch, J.M., Kappas, A.: The Oxford handbook of affective computing. Oxford Library of Psychology (2015)
4. Chu, H.-C., Tsai, W.W.-J., Liao, M.-J., Chen, Y.-M.: Facial emotion recognition with transition detection for students with high-functioning autism in adaptive e-learning. Soft. Comput. **22**(9), 2973–2999 (2017). https://doi.org/10.1007/s00500-017-2549-z
5. Dawood, A., Turner, S., Perepa, P.: Affective computational model to extract natural affective states of students with Asperger Syndrome (AS) in computer-based learning environment. IEEE Access **6**, 67026–67034 (2018). https://doi.org/10.1109/ACCESS.2018.2879619
6. D'mello, S.K., Kory, J.: A review and meta-analysis of multimodal affect detection systems. ACM Comput. Surv. (CSUR) **47**(3), 43 (2015). https://doi.org/10.1145/2682899
7. Eyben, F., Scherer, K.R., Schuller, B.W., Sundberg, J., André, E., Busso, C., Devillers, L.Y., Epps, J., Laukka, P., Narayanan, S.S., et al.: The geneva minimalistic acoustic parameter set (gemaps) for voice research and affective computing. IEEE Trans. Affect. Comput. **7**(2), 190–202 (2015)

8. Eyben, F., Wöllmer, M., Schuller, B.: Opensmile: the Munich versatile and fast open-source audio feature extractor. In: Proceedings of the 18th ACM International Conference on Multimedia, pp. 1459–1462 (2010)
9. Gaus, V.L.: Cognitive behavioural therapy for adults with autism spectrum disorder. Adv. Ment. Health Intellect. Disabil. **5**(5), 15–25 (2011). https://doi.org/10.1108/20441281111180628
10. Grossard, C., et al.: Children with autism spectrum disorder produce more ambiguous and less socially meaningful facial expressions: an experimental study using random forest classifiers. Molecular Autism **11**(1), 1–14 (2020). https://doi.org/10.1186/s13229-020-0312-2
11. el Kaliouby, R., Teeters, A.: Eliciting, capturing and tagging spontaneous facialaffect in autism spectrum disorder. In: Proceedings of the Ninth International Conference on Multimodal Interfaces - ICMI '07 p. 46 (2007). https://doi.org/10.1145/1322192.1322203, http://portal.acm.org/citation.cfm?doid=1322192.1322203
12. Kushki, A., Khan, A., Brian, J., Anagnostou, E.: A Kalman filtering framework for physiological detection of anxiety-related arousal in children with autism spectrum disorder. IEEE Trans. Biomed. Eng. **62**(3), 990–1000 (2015). https://doi.org/10.1109/tbme.2014.2377555
13. Kuypers, L.: The zones of regulation: a framework to foster self-regulation. Sensory Integration Special Interest Section Quarterly **36**(4), 1–4 (2013)
14. Liu, B.: Sentiment analysis: Mining opinions, sentiments, and emotions. Cambridge University Press (2015)
15. Liu, C., Conn, K., Sarkar, N., Stone, W.: Physiology-based affect recognition for computer-assisted intervention of children with Autism Spectrum Disorder. Int. J. Hum. Comput. Stud. (2008). https://doi.org/10.1016/j.ijhsc.2008.04.003
16. Ringeval, F., et al.: Avec 2018 workshop and challenge: Bipolar disorder and cross-cultural affect recognition. In: Proceedings of the 2018 on Audio/Visual Emotion Challenge and Workshop, pp. 3–13 (2018)
17. Ringeval, F., Sonderegger, A., Sauer, J., Lalanne, D.: Introducing the recola multimodal corpus of remote collaborative and affective interactions. In: 2013 10th IEEE International Conference and Workshops on Automatic Face and Gesture Recognition (FG), pp. 1–8. IEEE (2013)
18. Ritter, F.E., Kim, J.W., Morgan, J.H., Carlson, R.A.: Running behavioral studies with human participants: A practical guide. Sage Publications (2012)
19. Samad, M.D., DIawara, N., Bobzien, J.L., Harrington, J.W., Witherow, M.A., Iftekharuddin, K.M.: A Feasibility study of autism behavioral markers in spontaneous facial, visual, and hand movement response data. IEEE Trans. Neural Syst. Rehabilitation Eng. **26**(2), 353–361 (2018). https://doi.org/10.1109/TNSRE.2017.2768482
20. Sarabadani, S., Schudlo, L.C., Samadani, A.A., Kushki, A.: Physiological detection of affective states in children with autism spectrum disorder. IEEE Trans. Affect. Comput. (2018). https://doi.org/10.1109/taffc.2018.2820049
21. Saxena, A., Khanna, A., Gupta, D.: Emotion recognition and detection methods: a comprehensive survey. J. Artif. Intell. Syst. **2**(1), 53–79 (2020)
22. Scarpa, A., Reyes, N.M.: Improving emotion regulation with CBT in young children with high functioning autism spectrum disorders: a pilot study. Behav. Cogn. Psychother. **39**(4), 495–500 (2011). https://doi.org/10.1017/s1352465811000063
23. Soleymani, M., Garcia, D., Jou, B., Schuller, B., Chang, S.F., Pantic, M.: A survey of multimodal sentiment analysis. Image Vis. Comput. **65**, 3–14 (2017). https://doi.org/10.1016/j.imavis.2017.08.003

24. Tao, J., Tan, T.: Affective computing: a review. In: Tao, J., Tan, T., Picard, R.W. (eds.) ACII 2005. LNCS, vol. 3784, pp. 981–995. Springer, Heidelberg (2005). https://doi.org/10.1007/11573548_125
25. Trevisan, D.A., Hoskyn, M., Birmingham, E.: Facial expression production in autism: a meta-analysis. Autism Res. **11**(12), 1586–1601 (2018)

Personalized Music Therapy Information System Based on Algorithmic Composition in the Treatment of Autism Spectrum Disorder

Chaoguang Wang[1,3] and Lusha Huang[2](✉)

[1] Guangdong University of Finance and Economics, Guangzhou, China
[2] Guangzhou Academy of Fine Arts, Guangzhou, China
lusha.huang@connect.polyu.hk
[3] Bournemouth University, Poole, UK

Abstract. We utilize information technology, especially artificial intelligence algorithms and computer music techniques, to enhance the emotional understanding abilities of children with autism. The proposed information system includes a machine composition engine, a music therapy app, and a music database for coping with autism. First, we will develop a machine composition engine to provide the effective, economic, and personalized music therapy for autistic children. Music therapy has been validated as helpful for autism, and it is very suitable for children with limitations in physical activity and functional fitness. The music generated explicitly for recognizing and understanding certain emotions will have a much better curative effect by considering the preference and the situation of individuals. In addition, the usage of artificial intelligence will largely reduce the cost and time of music composition. Second, we plan to develop a musical therapy app that is child friendly. We will consider the special needs of the children, such as the size of the font, in mobile application design. It will provide a joyful and engaging way for children to relieve autism and benefit their psychological well-being and quality of life. Finally, we will build a large-scale music database for the free usage of the public and promote our service to the world. The research will provide an effective, low-cost, and personalized music therapy information system that directly benefits children with autism and their families by improving their emotional understanding, and informing the development of upcoming products and services, especially artificial intelligence technology.

Keywords: Algorithmic Composition · Autism Spectrum Disorder · Emotional Understanding

1 Introduction

Autism Spectrum Disorder (ASD) is a disorder that is increasingly prevalent in children, with an estimated 1% suffering from the condition globally. With the advancement of technology and the increased use of video games and the internet, ASD symptoms are increasing and leading to an increase in cases (Krishnan et al. 2021). By using music

M. Antona and C. Stephanidis (Eds.): HCII 2023, LNCS 14020, pp. 678–686, 2023.
https://doi.org/10.1007/978-3-031-35681-0_44

therapy, algorithmic composition, and the internet as a tool for distribution, it is possible to utilize these new technologies in a positive way in the treatment of ASD and other disorders.

1.1 Autism Spectrum Disorder

It is reported that ASD currently affects approximately one out of 160 children across all ethnic and socioeconomic groups in the world (World Health Organization 2017). As estimated, there were over 10 million people diagnosed with autism in China in 2018. However, it was pointed out that this number was extremely underestimated, and China already has the largest group of autistic individuals in the world. For instance, it is estimated there are around two million children under 14 persons with an autism spectrum disorder in China in 2018 (Wucailu Center for Children with Autism 2018), and if we include their families, ASD is a part of daily life for a considerable population.

The main classes of treatment for ASD currently available are behavioral treatment, medication, and experimental treatment. Behavioral treatment usually consists of psychological therapy such as behavior therapy, family therapy, interpersonal therapy, and psychoeducational input (Ladd 2008). Medication is usually in the form of stimulants such as methylphenidate or other chain-substituted amphetamines. Alternatively, non-stimulant medication in the form of antipsychotic drugs is also used for treatment. While stimulants increase the levels or effect of neurotransmitters such as dopamine, non-stimulants work counteractively by blocking dopamine receptors. Both forms of medication can prove effective, but adverse effects can come from both due to the addictive nature of stimulants and dopamine deficiency caused by non-stimulants (Ladd 2008). Medication for ASD in either form may also be dangerous in the long term, although studies in this area are limited.

It is estimated that the medical costs of behavioral interventions for children with ASD are US$40,000–60,000 per year per child (Centers for Disease Control and Prevention (CDC) 2015). Applying these estimates to two million autistic children under 14 in China, only the behavioral intervention costs of caring for this population are between US$80 billion-US$120 billion per year. As aforementioned, the actual number of autistic people in China should be much higher. One report released by the Centers for Disease Control and Prevention (CDC) of the USA in 2020 stated that the rate of ASD rose again by ten per cent, with 1 in every 54 children in the USA diagnosed with autism. There will be an increased need for care staff, facilities and additional funding to support children with ASD, especially new innovative technologies (Mangafa, Moody, Woodcock, & Woolner 2016).

While ASD has been extensively studied, there is no singular cure for it, and it is considered a chronic disease, with up to 50% of children who are sufferers going on to express symptoms when they are adults. Because all autistic children have specific cognitive defects, methods of visual or spoken instruction that are used with normal children may not be suitable to the autistic child. It has been observed that what autistic children see is not as good as the apprehension of what they hear (Alvin & Warwick 1991). The early study indicated that individuals with ASD showed a preference for auditory stimuli presented in music over other stimuli. Studies revealed that adults with ASD have intact processing of musical emotions (Gebauer et al. 2014), and many individuals with ASD can perceive emotion in music (Brown 2016). Heaton discovered that individual with ASD have a unique attraction to music and may even have enhanced musical abilities (Heaton 2009). It was demonstrated that there was no significant difference between the children with ASD and neurotypical groups in the identification of musical emotions (Whipple et al. 2015). What's more, music therapy can factor in motivation, a key tool for helping ASD sufferers (especially children) concentrate on a specific task. Hence, it is pertinent to the use of music as a specific means towards the treatment of the autistic child, especially in inducing their emotional understanding.

1.2 Music Therapy for Autistic Child

Music therapy has been defined as the "clinical and evidence-based use of music interventions to accomplish individualized goals within a therapeutic relationship" (American Music Therapy Association 2005). The World Federation of Music Therapy (WFMT) defines music therapy as "Music therapy is the professional use of music and its elements as an intervention in medical, educational, and everyday environments with individuals, groups, families, or communities who seek to optimize their quality of life and improve their physical, social, communicative, emotional, intellectual, and spiritual health and well-being. Research, practice, education, and clinical training in music therapy are based on professional standards according to cultural, social, and political contexts" (WFMT, 2011).

It is reported that more than forty percent of the population that music therapists serve today are individuals with ASD (Kern and Tague 2017). Three main goal areas targeted by music therapy worldwide are Communication skills (79.2%), emotional skills (76.1%), and social skills (64.8%). Deficits in social skills lead to problems with friendships, romantic relationships, daily living, and vocational success (Barnhill 2007). By contrast, communication deficits of autistic individuals are characterized by impairments regarding joint attention and social reciprocity, challenges with verbal language cues, and poor nonverbal communication skills.

The mechanism of musical stimuli is thought to be a unique accommodation for ASD, as rhythmic and structural components provide an external cue or anchor to help children with ASD to recognize, predict, and respond (LaGasse 2017). Musical cues that facilitate emotional responses are embedded in music's tempo, sound level, timing, intonation, articulation, timbre, vibrato, tone attacks, tone decays, and pauses (Juslin 2000). Music therapy interventions are highly effective in improving communication, social skills, and personal responsibility in children with ASD (Whipple 2012). The unique stimulus provided by music can help engage children with ASD in meaningful social interaction and socio emotional reciprocity (LaGasse 2017). Music therapy is believed to be a promising intervention for individuals with ASD, and most studies reported positive outcomes (Simpson and Keen 2011; Kern and Tague 2017; LaGasse 2017).

A number of studies have explored music therapy as an intervention to develop emotional understanding in children with ASD. 43.1% of music therapy for individuals with ASD selected emotional skills or emotional regulation as the goal area (Kern et al. 2013). Katagiri (2009) reported that music therapy increased the decoding skills of emotions for children with ASD, in which pre-recorded improvised music was designed to reflect target emotions. They pointed out that music can be one highly effective intervention to enhance emotional understanding in children with autism. Brown demonstrated that facial emotion recognition in children with ASD is affected by emotionally congruent background music (Brown 2016). Music therapy uses engaging musical experience to enhance emotional understanding, thus addressing one of the core problems of children with ASD.

As the music therapy market keeps growing, it also suffers high manpower input and high monetary costs. Music therapy today suffers high manpower input and high monetary costs. One individual session of music therapy mostly lasts 45 min, and a group session appropriately lasts 60 min, with an hourly charge from US$30–59 to over US$100 for individual and group sessions (Kern and Tague 2017). And furthermore, the average treatment duration of music therapy may last 1–3 years or even 4–6 years. For example, there were only 54 registered music therapist in Hong Kong in 2018. The use of composing music was one predominant form of music intervention reported (Simpson and Keen 2011), in which the music is composed prior to the intervention and implemented using a recording. However, the price of original composed music is very high. For instance, the industry standard (IS) rate for minutes of original music is US$1,000-$1,200 per minute. The high cost of music therapy is interpreted as leading to one primary concern of music therapists today for lack of funding (Kern and Tague 2017). As pointed out by some researchers, computer-based music activities (e.g., making music videos or use of apps) have emerged as a new music therapy technique (Kern et al. 2013), and may improve the efficiency of music therapy and render its' cost competitively, especially in music composing.

2 Methodology

2.1 Algorithmic Composition

Algorithmic composition enables the computer to generate music like human composers via intelligent algorithms (Cope 1992; Van Der Merwe and Schulze 2011), which can provide a large number with low-cost and personalized music as a solution for children with autism. Algorithmic composition fascinates researchers in different fields because it intends to approximate artistic creation, the most charming and mysterious part of human intelligence (Holland et al. 2016, Jaques et al. 2017). Additionally, the machine-composed music has shown significant commercial potential in entertainment, game, health, and education (Chen et al. 2018). Algorithmic composition is believed to be a promising technology to provide effective, low-cost, and personalized music therapy urgently needed by the autistic children community.

The new technology of algorithmic composition promotes and benefits all-round music therapy progress, mainly in three aspects. First, the App can provide easy-access, low-cost music therapy with a wide variety of music generated by algorithmic composition. The algorithmic composition can improve the effectiveness of music therapy by generating the music automatically. Second, the music can be specially designed for both good musicality and the purpose of therapy. Autistic children are rarely treated with music they enjoy, but most music therapists choose existing music for their patients. The key to music therapy is that the music should be selected according to the target listener's preferences. This will make it easier for them to listen to the music they need rather than caregivers putting music they do not like on the stereo. The algorithmic composition can generate numerously individualized and preferred music for the persons (Hu et al. 2020). The music generated explicitly for recognizing and understanding specific emotions will have a much better curative effect by considering the preference and the situation of individuals. Third, the cost of music composition can be largely reduced, which now is over US$ 1000 per minute for the original human-composed music. The usage of artificial intelligence will largely reduce the cost and time of music composition.

2.2 Music Therapy App and Implication

It aims to investigate the use of algorithmic composition music therapy to treat children with autism and to develop related software tools. The goal of our music therapy intervention is to help children with ASD gain a deeper understanding of four basic emotions (happiness, sadness, anger, and fear). Our objectives include: 1) Develop a musical therapy App based on algorithmic composition; 2) Pilot the music therapy software among a sample of children with autism; 3) Promote and train health professionals or parents to use the software and related material.

Our plan of action consists of 3 separate parts: the development of music therapy App, the pilot study among children with ASD, and training and promotion for using of the App (Fig. 1).

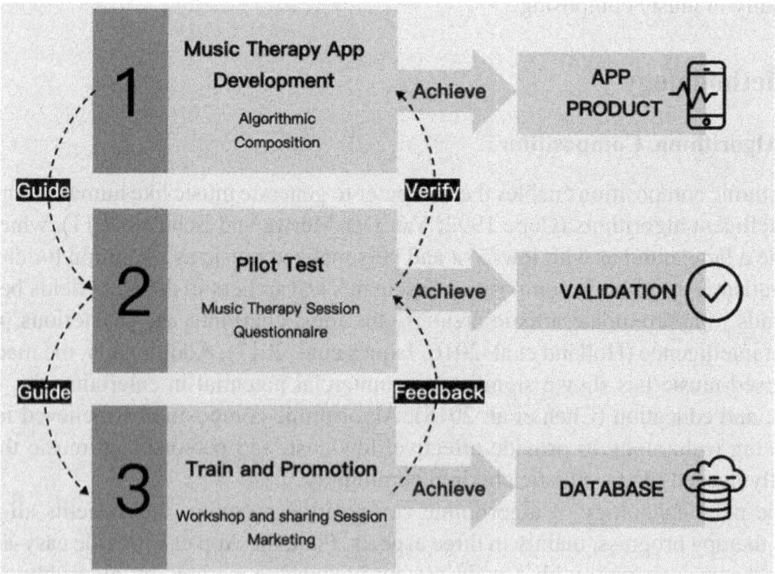

Fig. 1. Research roadmap

Music Therapy App Development. An App for music therapy will be developed based on algorithmic composition and aims to induce four emotions of happiness, sadness, anger, and fear. These emotions are thought to be four basic human emotions described by psychology research (Ekman & Friesen, 1971), and cover both the negative emotions (i.e. sadness, anger and fear) as well as positive emotion (happiness) as classified by the dimensional mode of emotion (Watson & Tellegen, 1985).

These four emotions have been used as target emotions by music therapists to be elicited in music and communicated to listeners (Juslin 2000; Katagiri 2009). Especially, it was reported that autistic children have more difficulties in the recognition of negative emotions than positive emotions (Ashwin et al. 2006; Katagiri 2009, Brown 2016). For instance, their understanding of the emotions of sadness, fear, and auger improved significantly more than their understanding of happiness.

Pilot Test of the App. This part will investigate the influence of music therapy Apps on children with ASD's ability to recognize four basic emotions (happiness, sadness, anger, and fear) depicted in facial photographs and their response time. The researchers from psychology, music therapy and computer science will co-design a set of experiments to assess the effectiveness of App and investigate its long-term impact on the children with autism.

Participants aged 0–18 years with a type of ASD will be recruited for the pilot of the APP. Individual Music therapy can be conducted in schools, homes, music therapy clinics, or hospitals. Participants will listen to musical excerpts conveying emotions and be required to rate expressions of happiness, sad, joy and anger in pictures under four music listening conditions (happy music, sad music, anger music, and fear music). We will measure participants' abilities to recognize facial expressions and corresponding emotions themselves pre and post music therapy.

Several standardized scales or published observational scales will be used as the secondary outcome measures to determine the efficiency of the music therapy App. Parent questionnaires, such as the Autism Treatment Evaluation Checklist, the Functional Emotional Assessment Scale, and the Vineland Social–Emotional Early Childhood Scales, will be distributed to determine the impact of music therapy treatment on children with ASD. Parental questionnaires are commonly used in music therapy research because the participants in the studies are often children who may not have verbal or cognitive skills to report on their own perceptions of their abilities.

Training and Promotion. Parents and health professionals working with children affected by ASD will be trained to use the App as an aid to therapies. We plan to develop an online course for parents and health professionals that is designed to prepare them to use the music therapy App for children with ASD. This course will contain 3–7 topic-specific e-learning modules, covering essential topics, including the theory and background of music therapy, emotional understanding skills, guideline of App, and monitoring progressing. These modules will be designed such that they can be taken independently or as a structured sequence. We then employ new media, such as Facebook, Twitter, WhatsApp, WeChat, to distribute and promote this online course to audiences.

We also propose a set of workshops, seminars, and sharing sessions on training and promotion of using the App as an aid to therapies. Some workshops/seminars will be given by our colleagues, and we will invite external guests, including school teachers and music therapists, for others. Interested parents and professionals can enroll in workshops/seminars based on their needs, and can then propose their intended music therapy sessions. It will directly benefit the autistic children and their families, especially by enhancing emotional understanding.

As ASD occurs primarily in children, the target group is the patients' parents/guardians. Also targeted will be endorsements, as well as societies and treatment groups. By targeting existing treatment groups and societies, we can offer them an alternate mode of therapy in an already established community with many of the target audience already present. Marketing may also be applicable to schools, where ASD is prevalent and usually the first establishment of detection.

3 Conclusion

Music therapy has been demonstrated to be highly effective in improving social interaction and socio-emotional reciprocity. The mechanism of musical stimuli is thought to be a unique accommodation for ASD, as rhythmic and structural components provide an external cue or anchor to help children with ASD to recognize, predict, and respond. It is reported that more than 40% of the population that music therapists serve today are individuals with ASD. As far as we know, this is the first project that aims to study and develop algorithmic composition therapy for the treatment of children with ASD.This research will provide effective, easy-access, and low-cost intervention for ASD suffering using algorithmic composition technology.

This project will allow us to produce a music therapy App and related database, which will enable the practitioners to provide both individual and group music therapy for autistic people. The App will be available to all to download free of charge for non-commercial use, and the results, in turn, will expand our database with more participants' data. The database will document music therapy practices from participants for reference, e.g., participants' background, duration and intensity, quality elements, and best practices. It is anticipated that this database will support parents and professionals in conducting their own music therapy sessions for autistic children.

Autistic children, parents and health professionals will form a community that provides support for treatment, where they can share examples and discuss related topics, such as problems and challenges encountered, engaging and assessing children in music therapy, the impact of the App on autistic children. Users will also be able to join a music therapy club, whereby rewards and prizes will be used as an incentive for joining. An online community and support for ASD and music therapy will then be set up in order for guardians and patients to share feedback and communicate with other ASD sufferers. Feedback can be gained following their practice which may help other patients overcome their symptoms, and the prospect of building an online community for ASD to share their experiences through the music therapy will help create a network of support which patients or guardians can use to manage the disorder more effectively. Acting on the side effects of the traditional treatment of ASD the method helps to drastically reduce the costs of health services.

The proposed App will facilitate the well-being of autistic children and their families by improving their emotional understanding, communication, and social skills. We are confident that this research will be a beneficial success for children with ASD, their parents, and health providers in China and worldwide.

Acknowledgments. This study was supported by the grant of "Research on the Designing the Mobile Phone Interaction Experience for People with Visually Impairments in 5G era" (Ref No.: 2021WQNCX034) from the Guangdong Province Colleges and Universities Young Innovative Talent Project, the grant of "Game Mechanic and Element for Predicting Game Addiction of Adolescents in Guangdong Province" (Ref No.: 2021GXJK480) from the 2021 Education Science Planned Project (Special Project for Higher Education) in Guangdong Province, and has received funding from the European Union's Horizon 2020 research and innovation programme under the Marie Skłodowska-Curie grant agreement No 900025 (CfACTs).

References

Alvin, J., Warwick, A.: Music Therapy for the Autistic Child, 2nd edn. Oxford University Press, London (1991)

American Music Therapy Association. What Is Music Therapy? (2005). http://www.musictherapy.org/about/quotes/. Accessed September 11, 2018

Ashwin, C., Chapman, E., Colle, L., Baron-Cohen, S.: Impaired recognition of negative basic emotions in autism: a test of the amygdala theory. Soc. Neurosci. **1**, 349–363 (2006)

Barnhill, G.P.: Outcomes in adults with Asperger syndrome. Focus Autism Other Developmental Disabilities **22**(2), 116–126 (2007)

Brown, L.S.: The influence of music on facial emotion recognition in children with autism spectrum disorder and neurotypical children. J. Music Therapy **54**(1), 55–79 (2016)

Centers for Disease Control and Prevention (CDC): Data & Statistics (2015). https://www.cdc.gov/ncbddd/autism/data.html. Accessed September 16, 2018

Chen, G., Liu, Y., Zhong, S., Zhang, X.: Musicality-novelty generative adversarial nets for algorithmic composition. In: ACM International Conference on Multimedia (1607–1615) (October 2018)

Cope, D.: Computer modeling of musical intelligence in EMI. Comput. Music. J. **16**(2), 69–83 (1992)

Gebauer, L., Skewes, J., Westphael, G., Heaton, P., Vuust, P.: Intact brain processing of musical emotions in autism spectrum disorder, but more cognitive load and arousal in happy vs. sad music. Front. Neurosci. **8**, 192 (2014)

Heaton, P.: Assessing musical skills in autistic children who are not savants. Philosophical Trans. Royal Soc. London B: Biological Sci. **364**(1522), 1443–1447 (2009)

Holland, S., et al.: Music and HCI. In: Proceedings of the 2016 CHI Conference Extended Abstracts on Human Factors in Computing Systems (2016)

Hu, Z., Liu, Y., Chen, G., Liu, Y.: Can machines generate personalized music? a hybrid favorite-aware method for user preference music transfer. IEEE Trans. Multimed., 1–13

Jaques, N., Gu, S., Bahdanau, D., Hernández-Lobato, J.M., Turner, R.E., Eck, D.: Sequence tutor: conservative fine-tuning of sequence generation models with KL-control. In: International Conference on Machine Learning, pp. 1645–1654 (July 2017)

James, R., et al.: Music therapy for individuals with autism spectrum disorder: a systematic review. Rev. J. Autism Dev. Disorders **2**(1), 39–54 (2015)

Juslin, P.N.: Cue utilization in communication of emotion in music performance: Relating performance to perception. J. Exp. Psychol. Hum. Percept. Perform. **26**(6), 1797 (2000)

Katagiri, J.: The effect of background music and song texts on the emotional understanding of children with autism. J. Music Ther. **46**(1), 15–31 (2009)
Kern, P., Rivera, N.R., Chandler, A., Humpal, M.: Music therapy services for individuals with autism spectrum disorder: a survey of clinical practices and training needs. J. Music Ther. **50**(4), 274–303 (2013)
Kern, P., Tague, D.B.: Music therapy practice status and trends worldwide: an international survey study. J. Music Therapy **54**(3), 255–286 (2017)
Krishnan, V., Krishnakumar, P., Gireeshan, V.K., George, B., Basheer, S.: Early social experience and digital-media exposure in children with Autism spectrum disorder. Indian J. Pediatr. **88**(8), 793–799 (2021). https://doi.org/10.1007/s12098-021-03666-z
Ladd, G.: NHMRC guidelines for clinical practice for ASD and PTSD. J. South Pacific Underwater Medicine Soc. **38**(1), 54 (2008)
LaGasse, A.B.: Social outcomes in children with autism spectrum disorder: a review of music therapy outcomes. Patient Related Outcome Measures **8**, 23 (2017)
Marcus, A. (ed.): DUXU 2016. LNCS, vol. 9747. Springer, Cham (2016). https://doi.org/10.1007/978-3-319-40355-7
Simpson, K., Keen, D.: Music interventions for children with autism: narrative review of the literature. J. Autism Dev. Disord. **41**(11), 1507–1514 (2011)
Whipple, J.: Music therapy as an effective treatment with Autism Spectrum Disorders in early childhood: a meta-analysis. In: Kern, P., Humpal, M. (eds.) Early Childhood Music Therapy and Autism Spectrum Disorders: Developing Potential in Young Children and Their Families, pp. 59–76. Jessica Kingsley Publisher, London and Philadelphia (2012)
Whipple, C.M., Gfeller, K., Driscoll, V., Oleson, J., McGregor, K.: Do communication disorders extend to musical messages? an answer from children with hearing loss or autism spectrum disorders. J. Music Ther. **52**(1), 78–116 (2015)
World Federation of Music Therapy (2011). What is music therapy? http://www.wfmt.info/WFMT/Info_Cards_files/ENGLISH%20-%20NEW%20What%20is%20music%20therapy.pdf. Accessed September 11, 2018
World Health Organization (WHO). Autism spectrum disorders: Fact sheet (2017). http://www.who.int/mediacentre/factsheets/autism-spectrum-disorders/en/. Accessed September 11, 2018
Wucailu Center for Children with Autism: Report on the development of autism education and rehabilitation industry in China. Beijing: Beijing Normal University Press (2018)
Van Der Merwe, A., Schulze, W.: Music generation with Markov models. IEEE MultiMedia **18**(3), 78-85 (2011)

Author Index

M. Antona and C. Stephanidis (Eds.): HCII 2023, LNCS 14020, pp. 687–690, 2023.
https://doi.org/10.1007/978-3-031-35681-0

Printed in the United States
by Baker & Taylor Publisher Services